To
the memory of
Prof. George H. Sabine

A History of Political Thought
Plato to Marx

SECOND EDITION

SUBRATA MUKHERJEE
Former Professor and Head
Department of Political Science
University of Delhi

and

SUSHILA RAMASWAMY
Associate Professor
Department of Political Science
Jesus and Mary College, New Delhi

PHI Learning Private Limited
Delhi-110092
2026

In fond memory of ***Shri Asoke K. Ghosh*** *(October 1942 – February 2024), Founder Chairman and Managing Director of PHI Learning, whose vision endlessly inspires.*

The Legacy Continues. . . .

Published by Pushpita Ghosh, PHI Learning Private Limited, Rimjhim House, 111, Patparganj Industrial Estate, Delhi-110092 and Printed by Gopsons Printers Pvt. Ltd., A-14, Sector-60, Noida, Gautambudh Nagar, Noida, Uttar Pradesh-201301.

₹ 1095.00

A HISTORY OF POLITICAL THOUGHT: PLATO TO MARX, Second Edition
Subrata Mukherjee and Sushila Ramaswamy

ISBN-978-81-203-4389-4 (Print Book)
ISBN-978-93-906-6955-4 (e-Book)

Contents

Preface

This book now in its second edition was first published in 1999, and since then has seen several reprints. We thought that it is appropriate to revise the book incorporating the topics added in the revised course curriculum. The new edition contains two new chapters on Mary Wollstonecraft and Immanuel Kant and an Appendix on John Rawls, who is credited for reviving the normative classical tradition in political theory in the post-Second World War in the twentieth century. The views of some of recent commentators like Carole Pateman have also been incorporated.

Our students have been greatly helpful in bringing to our notice the portions that need greater clarity and elaboration and we would like to thank them all.

Subrata Mukherjee
Sushila Ramaswamy

Preface to the First Edition

Political theory is one of the core areas of Political Science. Many argue that the entire edifice of the discipline is based on it as no comprehension of any other area in any meaningful manner is possible without an understanding of political theory. In recent years, along with the traditional emphasis on Western political theory, there has been growing interest in non-European sources of political theory. Confucianism and ancient Indian political tradition with special reference to *Kautilya* are increasingly getting more recognition. Added to this is a renaissance in political theory in the West as there are more participants in the debate today than at any other time in history. Today nobody talks of the death or decline of political theory though there is a realization, as observed by Walzer, that political theory is some kind of alienated politics since participants in the debate have marginal or perhaps no impact on policy makers or the process of policy making except for the Neo-Conservatives in the United States.

This, however, does not diminish the utility of political theory as an academic discipline, for, it is not confined to dealing with contemporary problems of localized nature, but with a wider canvas since it debates and deliberates the definition of a good social order. As Sabine wrote long ago, political theory develops as part of politics, and just as there is no concluding chapter to politics, so there is no concluding chapter to political theory. With the collapse of totalitarian communism and authoritarianism, both right wing and left wing, the debate regarding good social order is conducted within the paradigms of liberalism and social democracy. The increasing consensus on fundamental issues has made it possible for greater universal recognition of concepts like the rule of law, constitutionalism and civil society.

For comprehending the intricacies of contemporary political theory, the starting point is the Classical tradition. In understanding the hoary tradition of political theory, a dissection and continual reinterpretation of the classics in political theory is an important exercise. Ever since Plato raised the question of "What is justice" in the *Republic*, the debate about the nature and meaning of good and just order continues. The classical tradition that began with Plato ended with Hegel who was the starting point of the last classical thinker Marx. After Hegel, began a period of refinement and clarification, as indicated by MacIntyre, a trend that continues till today. Nowhere is this more evident than the fact both Rawls and Nozick acknowledge that they were refining and updating Kant and Locke, respectively. Even in the writings of Habermas the imprint of Kant is noticeable.

This book examines in detail the fascinating evolution of the history of political thought—rich and diverse—through the works of eleven seminal political thinkers who form the classical tradition (Plato, Aristotle, Machiavelli, Hobbes, Locke, Rousseau, Burke, Bentham, Hegel, J.S. Mill and Marx). It has also an introductory chapter on political theory. In understanding the works of these thinkers, it should be noted that each thinker was responding to the specific questions of his time while at the same time addressing the perennial issues of political discourse like power, distribution of advantages in situations of scarcity and conflicting claims, the art and science of leadership, the factors of stability, change and conservation, the relationship between ethics, politics and economics, and the role of women in society. We should also take note of the clear manifestations of localism and Eurocentrism in some of the later classical thinkers.

The book also critically dissects recent interpretations by Arendt, Ashcraft, Berlin, Macpherson, Miliband, Oakeshott, Pateman, Pitkin, Pocock, Popper and Skinner.

While the conclusions of this book and any errors or discrepancies that may have crept into it can be attributed to us, this endeavour, which is the outcome of considerable research, has benefited from the notable contributions of many people. The greatest indebtedness is to George H. Sabine, to whose memory this book is dedicated, for being the most important inspiration and guide. In addition, we have learnt a lot from other important theorists like Sir Isaiah Berlin, Sir Karl R. Popper, Hannah F. Pitkin, Giovanni Sartori and Sheldon Wolin.

We would never have ventured, into this exciting arena of political theory but for the constant encouragement and support we received from (late) Prof. Frank Thakurdas who taught us the most important ingredient to political theorizing, namely, to have one's own view and the capacity to defend it intelligently and with conviction. We are indebted to Prof. Milton Fisk, Prof. Barbara Goodwin, Prof. David McLellan and Prof. Jon Quah for their continual help and appreciation. We would also like to thank our students and colleagues, Mr. H.C. Jain, Librarian, University of Delhi, South Campus, Ms. Madhu Maini, Librarian, Jesus and Mary College, the librarian and the staff of the American Center, the British Council, Indian Council of World Affairs at Sapru House, Indian Institute of Public Administration, Max Mueller Bhavan, and the Central library at the University of Delhi.

Finally, we would like to express our gratitude to the editorial and production team of PHI Learning, the Publishers, for doing a splendid and painstaking job in bringing out this book.

Subrata Mukherjee
Sushila Ramaswamy

1

What is Political Theory?

> The ideas of economists and political philosophers, both when they are right and when they are wrong, are more powerful than is commonly understood. Indeed the world is ruled by little else .... The power of vested interests is vastly exaggerated compared with the gradual encroachment of ideas .... It is ideas, not vested interests, which are dangerous (Keynes 1936: 383–384).

> So long as rational curiosity exists—a desire for justification and explanation in terms of motives and reasons, and not only of causes or functional correlations or statistical probabilities—political theory will not wholly perish from the earth, however many of its rivals, such as sociology, philosophical analysis, social psychology, political science, economics, jurisprudence, semantics, may claim to have dispelled its imaginary realm (Berlin 1980: 172).

> The object of science is to show things happen, and why, in the nexus of cause and effect, they do happen .... what I mean is simply that it is not the function of science to pass ethical judgment.... The political theorist, on the other hand, is essentially concerned with the discussion of what ought to be. His judgments are at bottom value judgments (Cobban 1953: 335).

Political theory is a personal endeavour to understand and experience the present political reality and also to evolve a mechanism in order to transcend the present imperfect society leading to perfection and a more just order. This includes a study of the evolution, nature, composition, need and purpose of the governmental apparatus, and also an understanding of human perception and nature, and its relationship with the larger community. The golden age of political theory is from Plato (428/27–347 BC) to George Wilhelm Friedrich Hegel (AD 1770–1831).

Political theory is one of the core areas in political science. It is only recently that political theory has emerged as an academic discipline. Prior to this, those engaged in the enterprise styled themselves as philosophers or scientists. A distinction is made between political theory and political philosophy, political theory and political science. This differentiation arose because of the rise of modern science, which brought about a general shift in intellectual perceptions.

Political science tries to provide plausible generalizations and laws about politics and political behaviour. Political theory reflects upon political phenomenon and actual political behaviour by subjecting them to philosophical or ethical criteria. It considers the question of the best political order, which is part of a larger and a more fundamental question, namely the ideal form of life that an individual should lead within a larger community. No political theory eulogizes a Robinson Crusoe. In the process of answering immediate and local questions, it addresses perennial issues, which is why a study of the great books is imperative. These books contain the quintessence of eternal knowledge, and are an inheritance not of any one culture, place, people or time, but of entire humankind.

> Political theory is the most appropriate term to employ in designating that intellectual tradition which affirms the possibility of transcending the sphere of immediate practical concerns and "viewing" man's societal existence from a critical perspective (Germino 1967: 7).

There is no tension between political theory and political science, for, they differ in terms of their boundaries and jurisdiction, but not in their aim. Political theory supplies ideas, concepts and theories for purpose of analysis, description, explanation and criticism, which in turn are incorporated in political science.

> Political theory was political science in the full sense, and there could be no science without theory. Just as we may speak of theory as either the activity of theorizing or the recorded results of the theorizing, so political theory may legitimately and accurately be used as synonymous with political science (Germino ibid: 7).

Some commentators distinguish between the terms political theory, political thought, political philosophy and political ideology though many treat these terms interchangeably. *Political philosophy* provides general answers to general questions to concepts and theories such as: *justice, right,* the distinction between *is* and *ought,* and the larger issues of politics. Political philosophy is part of normative political theory, for it attempts to establish the interrelationships between concepts. It would not be wrong to say that every political philosopher is a theorist, though not every political theorist is a political philosopher. Political philosophy is

> a complex activity which is best understood by analyzing the many ways that the acknowledged masters have practised it. No single philosopher and no one historical age can be said to have defined it conclusively, any more than any one painter or school of painting has practised all that we mean by painting (Wolin 1960: 2).

There is an intimate and ongoing relationship between political philosophy and philosophy. The credit for it goes to Plato for whom the good of the individual was inextricably linked with that of the community. Subsequent well-known philosophers have "contributed generously to the main stock of our political ideas, but they have given the political theorist many of his methods of analysis and criteria of judgment" (Wolin ibid: 2). The difference between philosophy and political philosophy is not with regard to method or mood: it relates to the subject matter. While philosophy attempts to understand, as Wolin says, "truths publicly arrived at and publicly demonstrable" (Wolin ibid: 4), political theorists try to explain the meaning of 'political' and its relationship with the public sphere. Political theorists since Aristotle (384–322 BC) have tried to find answer to what constitutes the political, rather than being interested in political practices or their applications. When Aristotle argued that an individual needs, and can find fulfilment only through, a political community, he was emphasizing on the commonness of the political space, that political rule is

> ... concerned with those general interests shared by all the members of the community; that political authority is distinguished from other forms of authority in that it speaks in the name of a society considered in its common quality; that membership in a political society is a token of a life of common involvements; and that the order that political authority presides over is one that should extend throughout the length and breadth of society as a whole (Wolin ibid: 10).

This view has been reiterated in recent times by Hannah Arendt (1906–1975) and Michael Joseph Oakeshott (1901–1990). They saw political life as a distinctive form of human organization with special value, a place for freedom, honour and full human development. They were concerned with the autonomy of the political, safeguarding it particularly from the onslaughts of social and economic issues. Remarkably similar to this view was that of Easton, for whom politics meant an authoritative allocation of values. The subject matter of political theory was linked to a quest for a proper and legitimate form and scope of politics as a practical activity. Equally important is the demarcation between the public sphere and personal space. While it has been traditionally contended that political theory is about the public domain, recent writings by feminists have questioned this focus. The issue was on the agenda ever since Mary Wollstonecraft (1759–1797), followed by John Stuart Mill (1806–1873), spoke of subjugation in the private domain, insular to the ideals of freedom, equality and justice that dominate the public sphere.

> But it has not been until recently that debates about this form of 'slavery', and its entwinement with the public and the private have touched the centre of political theory. Indeed, recent debates have been broadened to include questions about the patriarchal construction of the central categories of political thought; the political meaning of sexual difference; the relation between the intimate, familial and domestic, and the economy and state; and the interconnections among nature, reason, politics and the sexes (Held 1991: 7–8).

Traditionally, a political theorist understood and analyzed the political as implying the limits of state action. The idea of the modern state, sovereign internally and externally, with supreme jurisdiction over its territorial space, was the subject matter of normative political theory and of political analysis in social sciences. However, with globalization brought about by a global economy, transportation and communication, development of intergovernmental and quasi-supranational institutions, regional and international organizations, and growth of complex intricate interrelationships between states and societies, the fate and future of the nation-state is increasingly becoming a focus of enquiry. The fact is that:

> Issues like religion, or prices, or race are not by nature *a priori* either political or non-political. They are made or become political in certain times and places. And that means, in those times and places they are lifted out of unplanned drift and placed on the political agenda as conscious collective concerns (Pitkin 1973: 523–24).

Political thought is the thought of the whole community. This includes the writings and speeches of the articulate sections, like professional politicians, political commentators, social reformers and ordinary persons of a community. Thought can be in the form of political treatises, scholarly articles, speeches, government policies and decisions, and poems and prose that express the anguish of people. Thought is time bound. In short, political thought includes theories that attempt to explain political behaviour, values to evaluate it and methods to control it. One notable example of inclusion of the normative perspective in a political document is the American Declaration of Independence (1776), which spoke of 'life, liberty and the pursuit of happiness'. Similarly, the Preamble to the Constitution of India has been considered by Barker as the best possible articulation of a collective desire of an entire nation.

Political *theory,* unlike *thought,* refers to the speculation by a single individual usually articulated in treatise(s) as models of explanation. It consists of the theories of institutions, including those of the state, of law, of representation and of election. The mode of enquiry is comparative and explanatory.

> Political theory attempts to explain the attitudes and actions arising from ordinary political life and to generalize about them in a particular context: thus political theory is concerned about/with the relationships between concepts and circumstances. Political Philosophy attempts to resolve or to understand conflicts between political theories which might appear equally acceptable in given circumstances (Crick 1973: 5).

Political ideology is a systematic and all-embracing doctrine which attempts to give a complete and universally applicable theory of human nature and society, with a detailed programme of attaining it. John Locke (1632–1704) has often been described as the father of modern ideologies. Marxism is a classic example of an ideology summed up in the statement that the purpose of philosophy is to change and not merely interpret the world. All political ideology is political philosophy though the reverse is not true. The twentieth century has seen many ideologies like Fascism, Nazism, Communism and Liberalism. A distinctive trait of political ideology is its dogmatism which, unlike political philosophy, precludes and discourages critical appraisal because of its aim of realizing the perfect society. Political ideology, according to Germino and Sabine, is a negation of political theory. An ideology is of recent origin, and under the influence of positivism, is based on subjective, unverifiable value preferences.

Germino distinguishes between a political theorist and a publicist in that while the former has a profound understanding of issues, the latter is concerned with the immediate questions. By this distinction, Germino considers Aristotle, St. Thomas Aquinas (1224–1274), Niccolò Machiavelli (1469–1527), Thomas Hobbes (1588–1679), Jean Jacques Rousseau (1712–1778) and Hegel as theorists, but their contemporaries Phaleas, Giles, Botero, Filmer, Condorcet and de Maistre as publicists. The gap between a theorist and a publicist is wide and divergent, differing "fundamentally in orientation, scope, emphasis, tone and terminological sophistication" (Germino 1967: 14). In this context, Germino rejects Mannheim's thesis of sociology of knowledge, which contended that belief structures have a social origin, and that social science knowledge is dependent on the class origin of a theorist, thereby precluding objectivity.

> While the data offered by the "sociology of knowledge" are of obvious relevance in explaining the thinking of some propagandists for mass movements they are of scant significance in helping us understand a Plato or Hegel (Germino ibid: 13–14).

Furthermore, Germino, like Plato, also distinguishes between mere opinion, and knowledge, the latter being the starting point of a political theorist.

Every political theorist plays a dual role, that of a scientist and a philosopher. The way he would delineate the roles would depend on one's temperament and interests. Only by combining the two roles can he make worthwhile contributions to human knowledge. The scientific component of a theory can appear coherent and significant if the author has a preconceived notion of the aims of political life. The philosophical basis is revealed in the manner in which reality is depicted (Hacker 1961: 2–3). Political theory is

> dispassionate and disinterested. As science it will describe political reality without trying to pass judgement on what is being depicted either implicitly or explicitly. As philosophy, it will prescribe rules of conduct which will secure the good life for all of society and not simply for certain individuals or classes. The theorist, in theory, will not himself have a personal interest in the political arrangements of any one country or class or party. Devoid of such an interest, his vision of reality and his image of the good life will not be clouded, nor will his theory be special pleading ... . The intention of ideology is to justify a particular system of power in society. The ideologue is an

> interested party: his interest may be to defend things as they are, or to criticize the status quo in the hope that a new distribution of power will come into being ... Rather than disinterested prescription we have rationalization .... Rather than dispassionate description we have a distorted picture of reality (Hacker ibid: 4–5).

Political Theory as the History of Political Thought

Courses in political theory normally offer detailed and elaborate study of books or particular political philosophies from Plato to contemporary times, from a historical perspective. These books are studied for their normative statements about the desirability of certain types of institutions, governments and laws, which are generally accompanied by rational arguments. The classics are portrayed as timeless in quality, permanent in relevance and universal in their significance. The Classical tradition demonstrates a great deal of unity in style and manner of argument, which is why it constitutes a common school of enquiry. However, in spite of this intrinsic unity, the classics offer divergent interpretations of politics, and this makes their study useful for understanding contemporary politics.

Political Theory as Technique of Analysis

When Aristotle remarked that the individual is a political animal, he indicated the primacy of politics and the fact that political thinking takes place at various levels and in a variety of ways. The 'political', in such a view, became not only all-pervasive, but also the highest kind of activity. Politics symbolizes a collective public life, wherein people create institutions that regulate their common life. It also denotes the importance of political activity, which was described by the famous Italian Marxist, Antonio Gramsci (1891–1937) as an activity par excellence.

Common-sense questions and political opinions merit an answer, for instance: Are individuals equal? Should the state be more important than the individual? How does one justify violence employed by the state? Is there an inherent tension between freedom and equality? Is the minority justified in dictating terms to the majority and vice versa? Our responses to these statements often reflect *what ought to be the case,* rather than *what is the case.* At stake here is a choice between values and ideals. By exercising one's preferences, one also (unknowingly) subscribes to a political ideology which means that answers to questions will vary not only according to individual opinion, but also depending on one's value preferences. It is because of this basic reason that political theory has to be a part of an open society for, amongst us there would always be liberals and conservatives. Training in political theory helps us to answer the aforesaid questions logically, speculatively and critically.

> Political theory is, quite simply, man's attempts to consciously understand and solve the problems of his group life and organization ... . [It] is the disciplined investigation of political problems ... not only to show what a political practice is, but also to show what it means. In showing what a practice means, or what it ought to mean, political theory can alter what it is (Sabine 1973: 3–5).

Political theory had been used to either defend or question the status quo. Taking into cognizance the facts and details, it explains and describes politics in abstract and general terms that allow space for critical imagination. As a discipline, political theory aims to describe, explain, justify or criticize the existing institutional arrangements and power equations in society. Some commentators like Goodwin (1993: 265–266) emphasize the centrality of the power paradigm whereas others like Talcott Parsons (1902–1979) downgrade it, comparing it to money in modern societies. Recent important works by John Rawls (1921–2002) and Robert Nozick (1924–2002) do not emphasize 'power' at all. It is interesting that Rawls emphasizes a well-ordered society, identifying justice, stability and efficiency as its main ingredients, without any attempt to speak about the distribution of power.

Political Theory as Conceptual Clarification

Political theory helps to understand the concepts and terms used in a political argument and analysis. For instance, the meaning of freedom, equality, democracy, justice, rights, etc. These terms are frequently used not only in daily conversation, but also in discourse of political theory. An understanding of these terms is important for it helps us to know the way they have been employed, distinguish between their definitions and their usage in a structure of argument. Many, like Weldon (1953), stress the need to scrutinize concepts in ordinary pre-theoretical language.

An analysis of concepts also reveals the ideological commitment of a speaker or/and writer. A liberal defines freedom as implying choice and absence of restraints, while a socialist links freedom with equality. A liberal defines a state as an instrument of human welfare, while for a socialist a state is an instrument of oppression, domination and class privileges. Conceptual clarification is definitely possible but cannot be neutral. Those engaged in it overtly or covertly subscribe to value preference, and in this sense their task is not different from the authors of classics in political theory.

Political Theory as Formal Model Building

This perception, particularly popular in the United States, looks to political theory as an exercise in devising formal models of political processes, similar to the ones in theoretical economics. These models serve two purposes. First, they are explanatory, offering systematically the factors on which political processes are based. Second, they are normative, for they try to show the consequences that would accrue from following a certain rule. A good example of such an exercise is Antony Downs' (1957) theory of electoral competition which viewed the voters as trying to gain maximum utility from an election result, and parties as teams trying to maximize their probability of winning. Downs then showed how parties, in order to win, devise ideological stances. Another important model is Kenneth Arrow's (1963) impossibility theorem, which stated that, among other things, where a democratic choice had to be made between more than two alternatives, the outcome would very likely be arbitrary, influenced by the procedure employed to exercise the choice. Josef Schumpeter's (1976) elitist theory of democracy was based on the assumption that a human being takes his economic life more seriously than the political one.

Political Theory as Theoretical Political Science

The emergence of political science in the twentieth century has led some political scientists to look upon political theory as a mere theoretical branch of the discipline. An attempt is made to integrate empirical observations with a systematic explanation of one's everyday experiences in the world. This view dispenses with the normative content of traditional political theory. Though mere explanation of political phenomena is possible, grounding it in empiricism would not be adequate. Any attempt to formulate a political theory free of normative elements would inherently fail. This is because any explanation of political events would mean an interpretation of the intentions and motives of the participants, and such an interpretation would bring forth normative issues.

CHANGING CONTEXT OF WORDS AND ITS IMPLICATION FOR POLITICAL THEORY

Like ideas even words are to be contextualized. This proposition, Raymond Williams (1958) defends by contextualizing five words in the English language, i.e. industry, democracy, class, art and culture. In the context of these words the last few decades of the eighteenth century and the first fifty years of the nineteenth century is of crucial significance. All these words which were a part of the English vocabulary were used for a long time but acquired a new and significant meaning at this aforesaid period. Williams argues that this change in words can be described some kind of a map which reflects a larger change in life and thought and the subsequent changes in language itself. With drastic changes in the life itself in all its significant manifestations—social, political and economic—and the altered relationships of institutions and activities led to this sea change in the meaning and contextualization of words.

In the context of the industrial revolution, the word *industry* which was associated with particular human character meaning individual attributes became a description of a collective word for manufacturing and productive process. The earlier use continues even today but ever since Smith changed the context of the word industry the latter use is more common. *Democracy* which had a Greek origin, meaning government by the people, came into the English language at the time of the American and French Revolutions as 'it was not until the French Revolution that democracy ceased to be a mere literary word and became part of the political vocabulary' (ibid: 14). The present use of the term *democracy* till the eighteenth and the beginning of the nineteenth century, was equated with mob-rule and was supposed to be both dangerous and subversive. But the connotation totally changes with the struggle, as expressed by Williams, as 'democratic representation'. The word *class* in the modern sense begins around 1740. Before this time, class had a connotation of describing division of a group in school and college taken from logic and philosophy. But towards the end of the eighteenth century, class in the modern social sense came into use with expressions like higher class, middle class and a middling class. The phrase working class comes into use around 1815 and upper class in 1820s. The important phrases like class prejudices, class legislation, class consciousness, class conflict and class war followed this early trend and the phrase upper middle class was first used in the 1890s and the lower middle class only in the twentieth century. *Art* also reflected this process of change. Originally it meant an individual skill but subsequently it came to refer to an institution meaning 'activities of a certain kind' (ibid: 15). Earlier art was any kind of human skill but in the new context it meant a specialized category of imaginative or creative arts. Similarly culture which was understood as "tending of natural growth" changed to something which is "doing in itself" i.e. "a general state or habit of the mind linked to human perfection, intellectual development within the entirety of society within a larger framework of general category of arts" (ibid: 15). Later it encompassed the entirety of all arts and culture came to mean the whole society including the material, the intellectual and the spiritual. Williams considers this changing connotation of *culture* is of striking importance as the change reflects the change in the other key words of industry, democracy and class. The importance for political theory in this changed contextualization is two-fold: (a) the changes in society connotes total alteration in the meaning of some key words and (b) the change reflects the new personal and social relationships that inevitability came out of the significant changes in this period of quick change. This means that the new idea of culture not only came as a response to the new industrial society but also to a new social and political phenomenon called democracy. Apart from this total transformation of older words a lot of new words emerged to describe the new situation like ideology, intellectual, rationalism, scientist, humanitarian, utilitarian, romanticism, atomistic, bureaucracy, capitalism, collectivism, commercialism, communism, doctrinaire, equalitarian, liberalism, masses, medieval, medievalism, primitivism, proletariat, socialism, unemployment, cranks, highbrow, isms and pretensions.

KEY THEORETICAL CONCEPTS IN POLITICAL THEORY

A reader getting introduced to political theory for the first time may think it sufficient to study the institutions rather than abstract concepts, in order to understand the character and nature of society. While a study of institutions is possible, one realizes that institutional arrangements vary from society to society because they are based on divergent sets of ideas. This realization takes us to the heart of the matter as to what is more important—reality or ideas, fact or concept. Do ideas reflect reality, or is reality based on ideas?

It may be difficult to find satisfactory answers to these perennial questions that would satisfy everybody. However, in trying to define them, one comes across categorizations and labels that become useful tools in analysis. For instance, an *idealist* like Plato would contend that there exist some permanent immutable ideas to which reality should approximate. On the contrary, there are those like Locke, who believe that concepts are derived from our observation of the material reality, and are called *materialist* or *realist*. Usually, though not always, a materialist approach is *empirical* and *inductive* in nature. An inductive method of reasoning means that general statements are derived from observing particular facts. It is the opposite of the *deductive* form of reasoning, in which the conclusion of an argument is validly inferred from some premises.

A *descriptive* theory is one that describes reality and constructs explanations on the facts collected. In contrast, an *evaluative* theory analyzes ideas with reference to other concepts and values. The opposition between descriptive and evaluative theory is reflected in a distinction made between *facts* and *values*. Facts are empirically verifiable, while values are not as they cannot be substantiated. *Deontology* is ethical theory which considers certain moral duties as self-evident and absolutely binding, irrespective of the consequences. As opposed to this is *teleology* or *consequemialism*, which believes that the rightness or wrongness of actions is determined by their good or bad consequences. It also holds that events can be explained, and evaluation is possible only by considering the ends towards which they are directed. The Kantian, and in recent times, Rawlsian theory, is deontological. Classical utilitarianism is teleological. An important distinction is made between *normative* and *empirical* theory. A normative political theory is prescriptive, for it sets standards or forms of conduct and does not describe facts or events. Normative statements include words like *ought, should* and *must.* An empirical social scientist would observe reality and experience, and then construct a general theory based on a plethora of facts and data. It does not accept *a priori* knowledge.

Closely related to empiricism is *pragmatism,* a philosophical theory associated with the American philosophers C.S. Peirce (1839–1914), William James (1842–1910) and John Dewey (1859–1952), which holds that beliefs have a meaning and justification because of their practical results. It also accepts the fact that the subject of knowledge is not merely a recipient of sensation, but also an active inquirer. Some see experience as intelligible in isolation, without any reference to the nature of its object, or to the circumstances of its subject. This implies that there is no need to explain the social condition of an experience. Such a view was implied in David Hume's (1711–1776) theory of the relation between *idea* and *impression,* and Bertrand Arthur William Russell's (1872–1970) *Logical Atomism.* Experience and fulfilment of desires as the basis of human nature is articulated by *utilitarianism,* which judges human actions in terms of the pleasures promoted/increased and the pain caused/decreased.

As opposed to empiricism, *rationalism* contends that the world can be known through the power of reason, and reason can correct experiences delivered by the senses. Rationalism had its origins in Plato, but it is popularly associated with modem theorists beginning with Rene Descartes (1596–1650), culminating in the German academic philosophy of the Enlightenment. The exponents of rationalism were Baruch (or Benedict) Spinoza (1632–1677) and Gottfried Wilhelm Leibniz (1646–1716). Rationalism was criticized by Immanuel Kant (1724–1804) but re-emerged in the writings of Hegel. Max Weber (1864–1920) understood rationalism in the sense of preferred legal-rational authority over others—traditional and charismatic. Rationalism used by J.S. Mill meant search for rational solutions other than prejudices, and scientific explanations other than mysticism. It also means favouring clear and explicit solutions based on principles. Rationalism has been regarded as a political vice by theorists like Oakeshott, who pointed out that a rationalist mind is skeptical of any authority other than reason, dismissing tradition, custom, habit and group experience as irrelevant.

A distinction is also made between *subjective* or personal/individual and *objective* or impersonal/impartial. Rousseau spoke of the general will promoting objective good of the community. Another term, *relativism,* connotes that values and principles do not have universal or timeless validity and that, there is no absolute criterion of truth. Values are valid within a social group or an individual person or an age. It is commonly associated with *historicism,* which has two meanings. In the late nineteenth century it meant uniqueness of all historical phenomena, and that each age should be interpreted in terms of its own ideas and principles. The second meaning, associated with Sir Karl Popper (1902–1994) means belief in large-scale laws of historical development, on the basis of which predictions could be made.

INTELLECTUAL INFLUENCES RESPONSIBLE FOR THE DECLINE OF POLITICAL THEORY

Since the time of Hegel, political theory faced its challenge of ideology and positivism. When Karl Heinrich Marx (1818–1883) proclaimed that his intention was not to interpret to the world but to change it, he obliterated the distinction between theory and practice. He produced an anti-theory, offering to humankind the most radical form of messianic and ideological thinking (Germino 1967: 57). For Marx, reality had to be comprehended in practical productive activity. Theory lost its critical dimension, for it was described as the tool of the privileged class. This makes Marx an ideologist, and not a political theorist.

Ideology, as defined by Antonio Louis Claude Graf Destutt de Tracy (1754–1836), meant the science of deciphering the origin of ideas. He held that all thoughts were reflected and determined by sense-experience, as the world of sensation is the only reality. He also pointed out that a truly scientific study of human beings would help in exposing illusions and abstractions which had no roots in reality. All forms of abstract thought, including religion and philosophy, had to be discarded. He rejected all kinds of critical enquiry.

Positivism

The positivization of the social sciences mainly came out of the tremendous influences of Isidore Auguste Marie Francois Comte (1798–1857), who has been regarded as the father of positivism. Determined to formulate a new master-science of human beings which he described as 'sociology', he asserted that only sense-experience was real. Metaphysical, ethical and theological theories had no use. Positivism emphasized precision, constructive power and relativism. In this context, political theory did not convey any meaning.

Positivism contends that analytical statements about the physical or social world fall into three categories. First, such statements can be useful tautologies, meaning repeating the same things through different words, and purely definitional statements that give specific meaning to a particular concept or phenomenon. Second, statements are to be empirically tested by observation to assess their truth or falsity. Third, statements that did not fall into the aforesaid categories and lacked analytic content had to be dropped. In short, the positivists understood meaningful analysis as possible only through useful tautologies and empirical statements. This precluded metaphysics, theology, aesthetics and ethics, for they merely introduced obscurity into the process of enquiry. Positivism aimed to be "value free" or "ethically neutral", patterning itself on the natural sciences in deciding about the right and wrong of issues.

Empiricism believed that observation and experience as sources of knowledge were central to the many shades of positivism. Comte integrated this assumption with two more ideas. First, he reviewed the development of the sciences with a view to ascertaining the thesis of unity among the sciences, natural and social, whereby they could be integrated into a single system of knowledge. Second, with the idea of a unified science, he founded sociology in the belief that scientific knowledge offered the requisite clues for control over both nature and society. With the help of these three tools of analysis—empiricism, unity of science and control—positivism in the nineteenth century focused itself on society in general, in the hope of overcoming the existing malaise and realizing a better future.

Logical Positivism

A revitalized form of positivism appeared in the form of *logical positivism*, espoused by the Vienna Circle consisting of mathematicians, philosophers and scientists in the 1920s and 1930s. Members of this group included Moritz Sclick (1882–1936), Rudolf Carnap (1891–1970), Otto von Neurath (1882–1945), Victor Kraf and Herbert Feigl (1902–1988). Those who were associated with it were Ludwig Wittgenstein (1889–1951), Hans Kelsen (1881–1973) and Popper. Wittgenstein provided an intellectual link between the circle and the school of linguistic philosophy that thrived in Oxford and other English universities in the twenties and thirties of this century.

Logical positivists reject traditional metaphysics' cognitive status. For them, scientific propositions are of two kinds: analytic or synthetic. An analytic statement is logical or mathematical in nature. It is synthetic when a "proposition adds something to the meaning of a given term". Verifiability is the criterion for synthetic or substantive and factual statements suggesting that a synthetic statement had meaning only if it was capable of empirical verification. Lack of empirical verification means that a statement cannot be proved to be true or false, and so is meaningless. From this standpoint, traditional political theory is rejected as unverifiable and meaningless. Logical positivists espouse a more radical form of empiricism—phenomenalism—restricting experience of sensations as the basis of science. They insist on logical analysis and aim to unify the sciences on the premise that experience supplied the subject of all science, and logic the formal language to link descriptions of experiences and formulate laws and theories.

The impact of logical positivism on political thought was twofold. First, by its principle of verification, it viewed politics as metaphysical, beyond science, essentially non-rational and arbitrary. Science, on the contrary, would instruct us as to what *would* happen rather than what *should* happen. This distinguished them from the positivists who attempted to make politics scientific. Second, to be scientific meant adopting those aspects of science that logical positivism identified as science. It considered physics as a paradigm of a unified science and that science proceeds inductively from observations to laws.

Popper's Method

An amendment to the principle of verification was suggested by Popper with his principle of falsification, which he used to solve the problem of induction, popular ever since Francis Bacon (1561–1626) invented it, known as "Hume's problem". Popper's seminal achievement was to work out a reasonable solution to the problem of induction (Magee 1984).

Hume was the first to raise doubts about the inductive method. He convincingly argued that no number of singular observations, however large and foolproof could really lead to a scientifically satisfactory general statement. For instance, if one particular *A* was exactly the same as another *B*, it was not logically defensible that all *A*s would be *B*s. Even if a very large sample was taken to arrive at a definite conclusion, it would merely remain a psychological fact and not a logical one. This was true of predictions as well, as past experience did not imply that the same would continue to happen in future. It was an inherent limitation of observation, as it was not possible to observe future events. The propensity to accept the validity of the inductive method emerged more from our psychological conditioning rather than from logic. Hume concluded that non-scientific law really had a rationally secure foundation.

Following Hume, Popper rejected the traditional view of science and replaced it with another, by pointing out the logical asymmetry between verification and falsification. This meant that no number of cases of *A* that brought *B* could really establish that all *A*s were *B*s. Such universal notions were unprovable and disprovable. By the principle of falsification, a theory continued to hold until it was falsified, and therefore falsification, and not verification, was the more suitable method for scientific enquiry. All knowledge was provisional, based on hypotheses. Such formulations had to be continuously scrutinized by negative instances of falsification. Knowledge, developed in a process of conjectures and refutations, open to searching and uncompromising tests. Arguments were always tentative and could be criticized for their validity. The basis of falsification was "common-sense realism" and indeterminism, essential for proper functioning of a critical method.

Theory formulation was rigorous in Popper's method, as it had to withstand refutation. Refutation of existing knowledge led to the emergence of new problems, and possibly a subsequent solution which advanced knowledge. The challenge was to go beyond the existing evidence that enabled one to face a new situation. The implication for this was that a theory, whether true or false, would lead to more accumulation of knowledge by new discoveries and inventions, and thus result in better theories.

Scientific discoveries were mostly accidental. All knowledge was incomplete and provisional. What is considered to be the truth today may be falsified tomorrow? But the new paradigm could also be provisional and might be refuted again, and because of this no theory could claim finality. At best, it could claim that it was better than the preceding theory. Science as a body of well-established facts was incorrect, as in scientific enquiry nothing was permanently established, and as such nothing was unalterable. Accuracy was also provisional, as all measurements, both of time and space, could be within a certain level. Quest for knowledge was a consequence of the problems faced and attempts made to solve them. Exactness is an illusion, and there is no point in trying to get it. However, this does not mean that since we cannot get a final answer to anything, humankind cannot make progress as the quest for a greater degree of accuracy expands the horizon of our knowledge. Advancement is always possible, but whether we have reached the goal or not would always be open to question. Popper put this argument with reference to two of the greatest scientists, Newton and Einstein. The latter's theory of relativity superseded Newtonian laws of gravitation.

Popper established the conjectural nature of scientific knowledge. He contended that no theory could be relied upon as the final truth. At best, one could say that it was supported by every observation so far, and was more precise in terms of prediction than the available alternative, but it was still possible to replace it with a better theory. He denied the traditional assertion that scientists were looking for the maximum degree of probability, given the evidence. On the contrary, statements that carried with them the maximum possible information, which in all probability might be false, were required. Since they were highly falsifiable, they were also highly testable. For Popper, falsification in whole or in part, was the anticipated fate of all hypotheses. Therefore, one had to seek criticism, for the bigger the fault, the greater was the prospect for improvement. On the basis of this paradigm, he attacked the theories of Plato, Hegel and Marx.

Popper's arguments were very similar to those of the theory of relative truth of Mohandas Karamchand Gandhi (1869-1948). Gandhi, like Popper, conceded that it was practically impossible to know the truth, though all of us were its seekers. At best, one knew one's version of it. Gandhi, like Popper, was opposed to any form of dogmatism and determinism.

Linguistic Philosophy

Linguistic philosophy was also critical of traditional political theory. Most of the linguistic philosophers agreed with the logical positivists that metaphysical statements are value judgments, which have emotive and not cognitive value. Philosophy was described as "second-order study" devoted to conceptual enquiry. Though linguistic philosophy resembled that of the Vienna Circle, it was more open towards metaphysical experiences due to the influence of Wittgenstein. The latter's *Tractatus Logico-Philosophicus* (1921) contended that there might be truths that could not be expressed through the language of sense-experience. Weldon pointed out that the function of political philosophy was not to provide new information about politics and its conclusions, as they had no bearing on the decisions of practical politicians. Moreover, philosophers must refrain from suggesting reforms. Linguistic philosophy dismissed political/philosophical thought as a misconceived enquiry, for it took up the wrong questions. Weldon's thesis about the lack of influence of political thinkers on politicians can be challenged by pointing to the enormous influence Locke exerted on the makers of the American constitution, President Clinton's reference to Thomas Jefferson (1743–1826), the inspiration Gandhi derived from John Ruskin (1819–1900), Henry David Thoreau (1817–1862) and Count Leo Nikolayevish Tolstoy (1828–1910) and late Prime Minister Nehru's indebtedness to Fabian collectivism.

Weber played a crucial role in exposing the limitations within positivism. He conceded the "value related" nature of social science enquiry. The human mind does not randomly observe reality. It makes a conscious choice depending on one's interest. He repeatedly stressed that although science was related to values, it could not validate them.

> An empirical science can teach no one what he *ought* to do, but only what he *can* do, and under certain circumstances, what he *wants* to do. The validation of values is an affair of faith, and besides this *perhaps* a task of speculative thinking about life, the world, and its meaning, but certainly never an object of a science that is based on experience (Weber 1958: 54–55).

The later decades of the nineteenth century till the end of the Second World War were a bleak period for political theory (Germino 1967). However, this observation ignored the contributions of Bernard Bosanquet (1848–1923), Antonio Gramsci (1871–1937), Thomas Hill Green (1836–1882) and Leonard Trelawny Hobhouse (1864–1929). The challenges posed by positivism and ideology were largely countered by Soren Kierkagaard (1813–1855), Vilfredo Pareto (1848–1923), Gaetano Mosca (1858–1941), Henri Bergson (1859–1941), Alfred North Whitehead (1861–1947), Benedetto Croce (1870–1940), Max Scheler (1874–1928), Robert Michels (1876–1936), Karl Theodore Jaspers (1883–1969), and the theorists of the Frankfurt School.

With the emergence of political science as a professional discipline, since 1903 political theory was one of the sub-fields. In the 1920s, Merriam and the University of Chicago School played a key role in attempting to make political science more scientific. Methods and concepts from other fields such as psychology and sociology were incorporated in order to make political science quantitative, an approach stressed by Merriam and Wallas. In the 1920s, despite the increasing use of scientism, there was not much schism between empirical scientific theory and study of the history of ideas. The two were seen as complementary. Science was used for practical reform and further rational public policy.

BEHAVIOURALISM

Though the full import of the behavioural revolution became clear in the 1950s, the roots of the movement emerged in the early years of this century. It reaffirmed many of the basic ideas of American political science, though it brought about a significant change in the research programmes within the discipline. In the process, it represented a conservative revolution (Gunnell 1987: 388). Behaviouralism, as articulated by Easton, tries to organize research in political science on the model of the natural sciences. It emphasizes the need to develop a pure science of politics, giving a new orientation to research and theory-building exercises within the discipline. In the process, it rejects political theory as a merely chronological and intellectual history of ideas, with no practical relevance in comprehending contemporary political reality. Throughout the fifties, those who were committed to evaluative an prescriptive analysis and study of the classical tradition, perceived scientism of behaviouralism as a threat to political theory. The behaviouralists, on the contrary, claimed that normative political theory was a serious hindrance to scientific research.

> It was from these debates that many of the subsequent images of political theory—whether as a world-historical activity concerned with criticism and restructuring of political life or as a mode of cognitive science—would emerge (Gunnell ibid: 388).

Behaviouralism remained the dominant theme even in the sixties in the United States. It focused on the simple question: Why do people behave the way they do? It differed from other social sciences by its insistence that: (a) observable behaviour both at the level of an individual and a group was the basic unit for analysis, and (b) that it was possible to empirically test any explanation of that behaviour. It rejected *a priori* reasoning about human beings and society, and preferred factual and statistical enquiries. It believed that experience alone could be the basis of knowledge. Within this framework, behaviouralists analyzed the reasons for mass political participation in democratic countries, elite behaviour in the contexts of leadership and decision making processes, and activities of non-state actors in the international arena, like the multinational corporations, terrorist groups and supranational organizations.

The Behavioural movement, which came into prominence in the 1950s and 1960s, had its philosophical origins in the writings of Comte in the nineteenth century, and in the logical positivism of the Vienna Circle in the 1920s. Behaviouralism did not accept all the philosophical arguments of the positivists. At a time when behaviouralism was gaining wide currency, many social scientists subjected positivism to a critical scrutiny, though behaviouralism was strongly influenced by positivism.

A behaviouralist, like a positivist, will ascertain the correctness of an explanatory theory. He will evaluate explanatory theories in three ways: internal consistency, consistency with respect to other theories that seek to explain related phenomena, and capacity to generate empirical predictions that can be tested against observation. Only empirical testing can decide between competing theories. It is the stress on empirical observation and testing that characterize the behavioural approach. A behaviouralist systematically compiles all the relevant facts, quantitative and qualitative, for an evaluation of a theoretical statement. Furthermore, behavioural analysis asserts that all scientific theories and/or explanations must in principle be capable of being falsified. This reflects behaviouralism's commitment to Popper's revision of traditional positivism, whereby he (a) substituted the principle of falsification for that of verification, and (b) simultaneously identified falsification as the criterion for deciding a scientific from a non-scientific theory. A scientific theory will generate empirical predictions which are capable of being falsified. If they do not do so, they are sophisticated tautologies, elegant and detailed, but unable to explain anything meaningfully. Behaviouralists emphasize that a theory should explain something and should be capable of being tested against observation. In the strict sense, positivists and behaviouralists would rule out normative theories, as they do not contain empirical and definitional statements, for there can be no room for moral arguments which form the core of normative theory. For instance, Lasswell and Kaplan, writing on the classics in political theory, concluded:

> A rough classification of a sample of 300 sentences from each of the following yielded these proportions of political philosophy (demand statements and valuation) to political science (statements of facts and empirical hypotheses): Aristotle's Politics, 25 to 75; Rousseau's Social Contract, 45 to 55 .... Machiavelli's Prince, by contrast, consisted entirely (in the sample) of statements of political science in the present sense (Lasswell and Kaplan 1952: 118).

However, this assumption has been severely criticized by Germino by contending that:

> Political theory is neither reductionist, behavioural science nor opinionated ideology. It is the critical study of the principles of right order in human social existence (Germino 1967: 6).

Brecht observes:

> Research upon research can be done, and statement can be piled upon statement, on what Plato, Aristotle, St. Thomas, Locke, Rousseau, Kant, Hegel and a hundred others of the great philosophers have thought about values and about what science can do regarding them. There is no end of delight for the scholar, and no end of discovery or rediscovery of deep observations, penetrating arguments, appealing speculations. No relativity need tune down our statements about what others said and what their theories were. Yet what we are dealing with is *history*—

> history of ideas, and history of science; it is not science unless we accept their ideas as still scientifically valid today; and if we do so, it is our responsibility to say how through the old ideas, and through which of them the present crisis in theory can be overcome. Otherwise we merely ignore the problem in a particularly sophisticated manner (Brecht 1965: 11–12).

Furthermore, Germino argues that this exercise also has a scientific basis, with roots in internal human experience. It can also be tested and verified. It is based on the Heraclitan doctrine of deep knowing in contrast to much knowing. Sabine also echoed this view. Germino's emphasis, like M.N. Roy's (1887–1954) position in radical humanism, is on the centrality of human experience, which includes the ethical, metaphysical and theological dimensions. Any other method for such an enquiry is inadequate, as the basis of political theory-building is experiential, and not strictly experimental. Gandhi's use of the inner voice to defend an action would meet the approval of this kind of argument.

The major tenets of the behavioural credo include the following:

1. *Regularities,* or uniformities in political behaviour, which can be expressed in generalizations or theory.
2. *Verification,* or the testing of the validity of such generalizations or theories.
3. *Techniques* for seeking and interpreting data.
4. *Quantification* and measurement in the recording of data.
5. *Values,* as distinguished between propositions, relating to ethical evaluation and those relating to empirical explanation.
6. *Systematization* of research.
7. *Pure science,* or the seeking of understanding and explanation of behaviour, before utilization of the knowledge for solution of societal problems.
8. *Integration* of political research with that of other social sciences (Easton 1965: 7).

CRITICISM OF BEHAVIOURALISM

Behaviouralism, like positivism, has been criticized for its mindless empiricism. Both Hempel and Popper reject the 'narrow inductivist view' of scientific enquiry, whereby they argued that a proper enquiry was possible only if relevant facts were supported by clear minimum theoretical expectations. They dismiss enquiries based on the idea of 'all the facts up to now' as irrelevant, for mere fact-gathering could never accomplish much, ... "for a collection of *all* the facts would have to await the end of the world, so to speak; and even *all the facts up to now* cannot be collected since there are an infinite number and variety of them" (Hempel 1966: 11).

Though positivism tried to move away from a narrow, inductivist approach in the 1950s, the scholars working within the behavioural tradition during the same time still remained committed to the inductive method in research. Their emphasis on data, and consequently downgrading of theory, led to two undesirable tendencies within the behavioural persuasion. The first was a tendency to stress on what could be easily measured, rather than what might be theoretically important. The second was a tendency to concentrate on phenomena that were readily observable, rather than study the covert and profound structural factors that contribute to change and stability within the political system. Behaviouralism proclaimed to offer a "value free" and "scientific" theory steering clear of ethical and political bias. They considered a theory good if it was consistent with observation.

The shortcomings of behaviouralism, as enumerated by Easton (1997: 15), include the following:

1. A tendency where behaviouralism pursued fundamental rather than applied knowledge, to distance itself from immediate political reality, and neglect the special responsibilities of an intellectual.
2. A conception of scientific method that seemed to direct attention away from human actors and their choices, and towards the conditions that influence and constrain action, resulting, it was claimed, in a subjectless, non-humane discipline, one in which human intentions and purposes played little creative part.
3. The naive assumption that behavioural political science alone was free of ideological presuppositions that might shape its substantive concerns, and its conception of its own methods of inquiry.
4. The uncritical acceptance of a pristine, positivist interpretation of the nature of science, despite much criticism that had already gained credibility even among many of those favourable to the continued use of the scientific method in the pursuit of social understanding.
5. The entrapment in a degree of professionalization that increasingly hampered communication not only with the general public, but even with other disciplines that were no less specialized.
6. An apparent indifference to the resulting fragmentation of knowledge, even in the face of the need for the use of this knowledge to solve whole social problems that, by their nature, are undifferentiated as to discipline.
7. An acknowledged inability to deal with value concerns, to describe the nature of the good society, with the denigration of values to a non-scientific, and therefore, non-confirmable status.

Much of this criticism of behaviouralism were made by critics who felt that the movement was ill-conceived and flawed in its conception. They contended that it was not possible to establish regularities in human behaviour, which made it difficult to explain it through the methods of science.

According to Germino the meaning of behaviouralism had become elusive. There were many differences within behaviouralism; it was not a monolithic group. Many who were self-styled behaviouralists did not agree with Lasswell for the need to establish a closed society that could be scientifically controlled. They were reticient about the scientific method and began to regard classical political theory appreciatively. Conformity with behaviouralism in the strictest sense would only lead to a closed society, unless there were two changes: One a rejection of rigid reductionism and scientism which may lead to the second, namely a rescue of political theory and restoring it to its former glory. Germino charged behaviouralists like Cobban, Easton and Waldo for their inability to separate normative political theory from political and ideological doctrines and Utopian constructions. He clarified that in criticizing behaviouralism, he was not against empirical research, for the great masters like Aristotle, Machiavelli and Mosca undertook such an approach.

> What I object to is the tendency among the advocates of a so-called scientific as opposed to a philosophical political science to decapitate political science and to argue that only propositions purporting to refer to or describe 'empirical'—sensorially observable—facts may be considered part of political science. The neglect of critical standards in terms of which we order and evaluate our data is the principal defect of the new or behavourialist political science. This neglect often leads to the adoption of uncritical standards which do not hold up at all well to theoretical reflection. The rebirth of political theory would not lead to the neglect of empirical research ... but to the correction of claims that such studies constitute the whole of political science. Such a rebirth would focus again on the need for elaborating criteria in order to evaluate political behaviour, the importance of paradigm, the crucial question of the highest good and best society for man as man, the dilution of the paradigm for concrete historical conditions, etc. (Germino 1967: 192–93).

IS POLITICAL THEORY DEAD?

In the middle of the twentieth century, many observers were ready to write an obituary on political theory. Some spoke of its decline (Cobban 1953 and 1960a; Easton 1953). Others proclaimed its death (Laslett 1957; Dahl 1958). One referred to political theory being in the doghouse (Riemer 1962: 1). The major reason for such a dismal view was that the classical tradition in political theory was by and large loaded with value judgements beyond the control of empirical testing. The criticism of normative theory came from the logical positivists in the 1930s, and subsequently from behaviouralists.

Easton contends that since political theory is concerned with some kind of historical form, it had lost its constructive role. Political theory as practised by William Dunning, Charles H. McIlwain and George Holland Sabine had declined into "historicism", for it dissuaded students from a serious study of value theory.

> In the past, theory was a vehicle whereby articulate and intelligent individuals conveyed their thoughts on actual direction of affairs and offered for serious consideration some ideas about the desirable course of events. In this way they revealed to us the full meaning of their moral frame of reference. Today, however, the kind of historical interpretation with which we are familiar in the study of political theory has driven from the latter its only unique function, that of constructively approaching a valuational frame of reference, ... In the past, theory was approached as an intellectual activity whereby the student could learn how he was to go about exploring the knowable consequences and, through them, the ultimate premises of his own moral outlook ... . Scrutiny of the works by American political theorists reveals that their authors have been motivated less by an interest in communicating such knowledge than in retailing information about the meaning, internal consistency, and historical development of past political values (Easton 1953: 234–35).

Dunning, in his three volumes entitled *A History of Political Theories* (1902) set the tone for research in political theory. His training as a historian enabled him to approach political theory primarily as offering problems of historical change, and sought to unfold the role of political ideas in this process.

> As a result political theory, for Dunning, becomes a historical account of the conditions and consequences of political ideas. He seeks to uncover the cultural and political conceptions of an age and to isolate the influences of these ideas, in turn, on the social conditions (Easton ibid: 238).

Easton calls Dunning a historicist, for he deflected political theory from moral consideration and consciously avoided dealing with moral issues in a purely historical context. Dunning perceived political theory as essentially historical as it involved research into issues that arose from observation of political facts and practices. He confined his study to the legal rather than the ethical dimensions of political life, though subsequently his students broadened it to encompass empirical theories of political activity. He regarded moral views as products of caprice, dogmas without justification, hence not worthy of analysis or interpretation. He also neglected the meaning and logical consistency of ideas.

McIlwain's *The Growth of Political Thought in the West* (1932) used historical research, for he considered political ideas as an

> effect rather than an influential interacting part of social activity. Being virtual ciphers in the changing patterns of actual life, ideas can have meaning only as a part of a history of theories in which ideas may condition subsequent ideas, but in which they leave no impact upon action (Easton ibid: 241).

The title of McIlwain's work revealed the historical nature of his study. It tried to show the evolution of ideas in the West on the premise that ideas had a history. It considered ideas as justifying behaviour, though they might influence political activity, in the sense that ideas motivated individuals to act. The influence of ideas was exclusively confined to the domain of ideas. McIlwain felt that the history of ideas had a sense of continuity, which was why it made sense to trace its evolution. Unlike Dunning, who regarded ideas as contributing causally to the process of history, McIlwain focused on the historical contexts from which an idea emerged.

> ... political theory is here construed as a branch of the sociology of knowledge, which deals primarily with the circumstances shaping knowledge as it has varied over time. The task of the political theorist is to show the way in which a social milieu molds and shapes political thought. It is concerned with the exclusively empirical task of uncovering the determinants of ideology (Easton ibid: 244).

Unlike Dunning, McIlwain's work showed respect for moral issues, since a theory was more than mere propositions rooted in observation. He preferred an inclusive history of theory that paid attention to a political idea which justified political practices and institutions. The moral defence was important, for he was particularly concerned with the way human beings defined good political life. The impression that McIlwain's work gave was that moral issues were worth discussing and endorsing. In spite of the special role he assigned to ideas, he was a historicist, as he was not strongly influenced by moral judgements, the reason being, that he regarded moral standards as unprovable. He contended that in the past, some of the most important assertions remained unproved, because by nature they were unprovable. This made values a matter of personal opinion, representing an emotional response to experience. He believed that moral judgements were subjective and relative, for it was important to affirm one's moral premises. However, that did not deter him from grappling with one of the issues of moral relativism, namely that if all moral beliefs were results of individual life experiences, then could one claim his belief to be better than that of others? Such an argument would only render discussion of values meaningless, for each could set forth his values, which were as good as those of others. In that case only a historical approach was useful to understanding moral problems. McIlwain would not agree to this reasoning, for he believed in the superiority of his own moral outlook. But the fact that he did not go beyond the historical analysis proved that his

> historicism, in practice, indicates the firm grip that this interpretation of the consequences of moral relativism has upon his study of political theory.... The fact that McIlwain confines himself to historicism, however, indicates that he has not availed himself of this alternative conception of the meaning of moral relativism (Easton ibid: 248).

Sabine's *A History of Political Theory* (1937) singularly influenced studies in political theory more than any other book. Like Dunning and McIlwain, Sabine considered the historical study of theory as an appropriate approach to the subject matter. The impression that one got from the book and from a description of his method was "that a historical study of theory provides its own self-evident justification" (Easton ibid: 249). Sabine combined the approaches of both Dunning and McIlwain. Like the former, he believed that political thought was a part of the political process which interacted and influenced social action. With the latter, he thought it was necessary to describe and analyze moral judgements in each theory. Sabine considered moral judgements as determining factors in history and not merely rationalizations of an activity. Moral judgements were not inferior to factual propositions, as Dunning contended. Though Sabine reiterated Dunning in his interpretation of the relation between ideas and action, he differed from the latter in his conception of the nature of the history of political theory, by his emphasis on the role of ethical judgements.

For Sabine, every political theory could be scrutinized from two points of view: as social philosophy, and as ideology. As ideology, theories were psychological phenomena, precluding truth or falsity. Theories were beliefs, 'events in people's minds and factors in their conduct' (Sabine 1939: 6–7), irrespective of their validity or verifiability. Theories played an influential role in history, and therefore the task of a historian was to ascertain the extent to which these theories helped in shaping the course of history.

A theory had to be examined for its meaning, rather than for its impact on human actions. Viewed in this perspective, a theory comprised two kinds of propositions: factual and moral. Sabine focused on factual rather than moral statements, for the latter precluded descriptions of truth or falsity. He regarded values as reflecting human preferences for 'some social and physical fact'. They were not deducible from facts, nor could they be reduced to facts. They were not rationally discovered, as they were expressions of emotions. Since political theory advanced some statements of preference, value judgements formed the core of its theory and explained the reason for its existence. The moral element characterized political theory, which was why it was primarily a moral enterprise. In spite of factual propositions within a theory, a political theory on the whole can hardly be true in depicting a particular episode or period.

Easton then examines the reasons for the decline of political theory into historicism. First and foremost is the tendency among political scientists to conform to the moral propositions of their age, leading to a loss of the constructive approach. The emphasis is to uncover and reveal one's values, which implies that there is no longer the need to enquire into the merit of these moral values but merely understand their 'origins, development and social impact' (Easton 1953: 257). History is used to endorse existing values. Second, moral relativism is responsible for the attention this theory receives with history.

> The vital fact about this meaning of relativism is that the description of the conditions surrounding the emergence of moral preference does not by itself necessarily imply any opinion about the merit or demerit of these preferences. It does not demonstrate values to be either equal or unequal in worth. It merely indicates that they are equal in their origins, in the sense that they are each a product of historical

> circumstances. If we wished, we could of course compare them with regard to other qualities such as their moral worth. This would however be a separate and independent task. To do so we would need first to establish an acceptable moral standard in terms of which varying preferences could be compared. But barring agreement on such a standard, two differing value judgments can be said to be neither better nor worse when each stands by the side of the other. They just differ and are incommensurable until some third standard of comparison is adopted (Easton ibid: 261–62).

Third, beginning from the latter half of the nineteenth century and till the early part of the twentieth century, there was beyond doubt considerable agreement on values in Western Europe. Sharp differences on ethical questions got diffused. With greater unity in moral perceptions, value theorists focussed more on the history of moral ideas.

REVIVAL OF POLITICAL THEORY

In the 1930s, political theory remained a study of the history of ideas, particularly with the purpose of defending liberal democratic theory in opposition to totalitarian Communism, Fascism and Nazism. The aims and direction given by Merriam were furthered by Lasswell, who tried to establish a scientific political theory with the eventual purpose of controlling human behaviour. Unlike the classical tradition, scientific political theory would describe rather than prescribe.

Political theory in the traditional sense was alive in the works of Arendt, Theodore Adorno (1903–1969), Herbert Marcuse (1898–1979), Leo Strauss (1899–1973), Oakeshott, Bertrand de Jouvenal and Eric Vogelin (1901–1985). Their views were diametrically opposite to the broad ideas within American political science, namely its commitment to liberal democracy, faith in science and a faith in historical progress. They also rejected political messianism and utopianism in politics.

Arendt's main focus was on the uniqueness and responsibility of the individual human being with which she initiated her criticism of behaviouralism. She contended that the behavioural search for uniformities in human nature would only contribute towards stereotyping the human being. In *The Human Condition* (1958), she observed:

> The unfortunate truth about behaviorism and the validity of its "laws" is that the more people there are, the more likely they are to behave and the less likely to tolerate nonbehaviour. Statistically, this will be shown in the leveling out of fluctuation. In reality, deeds will have less and less chance to stem the tide of behavior, and events will more and more lose their significance, that is, their capacity to illuminate historical time. Statistical uniformity is by no means a harmless scientific idea; it is no longer the secret political ideal of a society which, entirely submerged in the routine of everyday living, is at peace with the scientific outlook inherent in its very existence (Arendt 1959: 40).

Arendt rejected the idea of hidden and anonymous forces in history. Like other leading figures in the revival of political theory, she also pointed to the essential incompatibility between ideology and political theory. She was aware of the loss of human experience in the modern world and desired a need to recover a sense of dignity and responsible freedom in human action, seeing it as a basis for the revival of political theory. Through the example of Eichmann, the transportation expert manning the trains to the Nazi concentration camp at Auschwitz, a "perfectly normal man", she illustrated the difference between responsible action and efficient automatic behaviour.

Oakeshott's main theoretical achievement was his philosophical analysis of experience, which attempted to resurrect the multidimensionality that was denied to experience by positivism and ideology. Oakeshott understood experience to be a concrete whole with different kinds of "modes". The modes constituted "arrests" in experience, and only from the perspective of philosophy whose purpose was to identify each mode and define its relationship with other aspects of experience. In *Experience and its Modes* (1933), he identified four principal modes of, or arrests in, experience: history, science, practice and poetry. Science concerned itself with measurement and quantification, history with the past, practice with an act of desiring and obtaining, and poetry with imagination and contemplation.

Oakeshott did not define philosophy, other than indicating it to be an activity undertaken in discoursing upon experience and its modes. When philosophizing, one left the tight model islands of incomplete experience and charted the "open sea of experience". He conceded that philosophy could not serve as a guide for practical life for it was not "clear-sighted, not for those who are fashioned for thought and the arduous of thought, who can lead the world. Great achievements are accomplished in the mental fog of practical experience. What is farthest from our needs is that kings should be philosophers" (Oakeshott 1933: 320-21). Philosophy served truth. It was not determined by its historical setting. Though its place and time was important, the key question remained: could it maintain what it asserted?

Oakeshott did not distinguish between subject and object, fact and value. He distrusted any accepted route or pattern which explained his skepticism of rationalism, with its efforts at systematization and categorization. The process of politics and the very basis of rationalist enquiry were incompatible and mutually exclusive. He rejected the contention that philosophy could learn from the methods of science.

> The understanding of politics as an empirical activity is, then, inadequate because it fails to reveal a concrete manner of activity at all. And it has the incidental defect of seeming to encourage the thoughtless to pursue a style of attending to the arrangements of their society which is likely to have unfortunate results; to try to do something which is inherently impossible is always a corrupting enterprise (Oakeshott 1956: 5).

Philosophy, for Oakeshott, was not practice, and had to be sought for its own sake. It had to "maintain its independence from all extraneous interests, and in particular, from the practical interest" (Oakeshott 1933: 3). Philosophy was not about preaching a doctrine, though every philosopher had a preacher within him. It was involved "not in persuading others, but in making our own minds clear" (Oakeshott ibid: 3). It could not be popular, and any attempt to popularize it would only debase it. Nor was it a search for a universal system which consisted of knowledge about every aspect of reality. A philosopher sought "valid" and not "universal" knowledge (Oakeshott ibid: 1). Political philosophy for Oakeshott, like Arendt, was philosophizing about politics which did not promise salvation. In this context he rejected ideology, for political philosophy did not promise "bogus eternity".

> ... political ideology purports to be an abstract principle, or set of related abstract principles, which has been independently premeditated. It supplies in advance of the activity of attending to the arrangements of a society a formulated end to be pursued, and in so doing it provides a means of distinguishing between those desires which ought to be encouraged and those which ought to be suppressed or redirected (Oakeshott 1956: 5).

Oakeshott ruled out political ideology and empiricism in an understanding of politics.

> Wherever else politics may begin, they cannot begin in ideological activity ... . Just as scientific hypothesis cannot appear, and is impossible to operate, except within an already existing tradition of scientific investiga-tion, so a scheme of ends for political activity appears within, and is valuable only when it is related to, an already existing tradition of how to attend to our arrangements (Oakeshott ibid: 12).

Like Arendt, Oakeshott described politics "as an activity of attending to the general arrangements of a collection of people, who in respect of their common recognition of a manner of attending to its arrangements, compose a single community" (Oakeshott ibid: 12). He looked to political relationship as one between peers whose views were mutually important, implying that politics was about persuasion rather than coercion. He rejected the idea of final solutions or ultimate goals in politics, for like human life, politics was continuous, involving endless adjustments. Like Aristotle, Arendt and Burke, he stressed on the limits in politics. Echoing Albert Camus (1913–1960), he emphasized that the present suffering could never be justified in the name of some abstract vision of the future. Politics did not arise from instant desires nor from general principles, but from existing traditions of behaviour. Both political crises and their solutions stem from within a tradition of political activity.

> In political activity, then, men sail a boundless and bottomless sea; there is neither harbour for shelter nor floor for anchorage, neither starting-place nor appointed destination. The enterprise is to keep afloat

> on an even keel; the sea is both friend and enemy; and the seamanship consists in using the resources of a traditional manner of behaviour in order to make a friend of every hostile occasion (Oakeshott ibid: 15).

As far as political philosophy was concerned, it cannot be called a 'progressive' science. The important thing was history. In fact

> ... it has nothing but a history, which is a history of the problems philosophers have detected and the manner of solution they have proposed, rather than a history of doctrines and systems ... . Political philosophy cannot be expected to increase our ability to be successful in political activity. It will not help us to distinguish between good and bad political projects; it has no power to guide or to direct us in the enterprise of pursuing the intimations of our tradition. But the patient analysis of the general ideas which have come to be connected with political activity—ideas such as nature, artifice, reason, will, law, authority, obligation, etc.—in so far as it succeeds in removing some of the crookedness from our thinking and leads to a more economic use of concepts, is an activity neither to be overrated nor despised (Oakeshott ibid: 20).

Jouvenal, like Arendt, opposed the modern trend of converting politics into administration, depriving it of the potentiality for creativity in the public sphere. Both conceived politics as a competitive process and were concerned about totalitarianism. They opposed ideological sloganeering and utopianism. Politics essentially involved moral choice, with the purpose of building and consolidating individuals.

Strauss, a historian of political thought and an eminent theorist, reaffirmed the importance of classical political theory to remedy the crises of modern times. He doubted the contention that all political theory was ideological in nature, mirroring a given socio-economic interest. All political thinkers were motivated by the possibility of discerning the principles of the right order in social existence. A political philosopher was primarily interested in truth (Strauss 1959: 12). Past philosophies had to be studied with an eye on coherence and consistency, which had to be gathered diligently and ingeniously. The authors of the classics in political theory were superior not only because they were geniuses, but also because they wrote with utmost care, with each word and sentence in its right place and meaning.

Strauss scrutinized the methods and purposes of the "new" political science and concluded that it was defective when compared with classical political theory, particularly that of Aristotle. For Aristotle, a political philosopher or a political scientist had to be impartial, for he possessed a more comprehensive and clear understanding of human ends than those who were partisan. Political science and political philosophy were identical, because science consisting of theoretical and practical aspects was identical with philosophy. Other characteristics of Aristotelian political science were that it evaluated political things, defended autonomy of prudence in practical matters, and viewed political action to be essentially ethical. Behaviouralism denied all these premises. It separated political philosophy from political science, substituted the distinction between theoretical and practical sciences with that between the theoretical and applied sciences, perceiving the latter to be derived from the former, but not in the same manner as was visualized in the classical tradition. Behaviouralism was disastrous, for it denied knowledge regarding ultimate principles. The rise of totalitarianism proved the bankruptcy of positivism for it seemed helpless, unable to distinguish right from wrong, just from unjust. Strauss countered Easton's charge of historicism by alleging that it was the new science that was responsible for the decline in political theory, for it pointed to and abetted the general political crisis of the West because of its overall neglect of normative issues.

> The habit of looking at social or human phenomena without making value judgments has a corroding influence on any preferences. The more serious we are as social scientists, the more completely we develop within ourselves a state of indifference to any goal, or of aimlessness and drifting, a state which may be called nihilism. The social scientist is not immune to preferences; his activity is a constant fight against the preferences he has as a human being and a citizen and which threaten to overcome his scientific detachment. He derives the power to counteract these dangerous influences by his dedication to one and only one value—to truth... . (1) It is impossible to study social phenomena, i.e., all important social phenomena, without making value judgments ... a society cannot be defined without reference to its purpose. (2) The rejection of value judgments is based on the assumption that the conflicts between different values or value systems are essentially insoluble for human reason ... . The belief that value judgments are not subject, in the last analysis, to rational control, encourages the inclination to make irresponsible assertions regarding right and wrong or good and bad. One even creates the impression that all important human conflicts are value conflicts, whereas, to say the least, many of these conflicts arise out of men's very agreement regarding values. (3) The belief that scientific knowledge, i.e., the kind of knowledge possessed or aspired to by modern science, is the highest form of human knowledge, implies a depreciation of pre-scientific knowledge (Strauss ibid: 19, 21–23).

Strauss equated behaviouralism's value-free approach with "dogmatic atheism" and "permissive egalitarianism". It was based on dogmatic atheism, for it sported an attitude of "unreasoned unbelief. It was rooted in permissive egalitarianism because the distinction between facts and values meant to its proponents that

> ... men can live without ideology: they can adopt, posit, or proclaim values without making the illegitimate attempt to derive their values from facts, or without relying on false or at least inevident assertions regarding what is. One thus arrives at the notion of the rational society or of the non-ideological regime: a society that is based on the understanding of the character of values. Since this understanding implies that before the tribunal of reason all values are equal, the rational society

> will be egalitarian, or democratic, permissive and liberal; the rational doctrine regarding the difference between facts and values rationally justifies the preference for liberal democracy—contrary to what is intended by that distinction itself (Strauss 1962: 324).

Vogelin thought of the inseparableness of political science and political theory, as without the latter the former was not possible. Political theory was not ideology, Utopian or scientific methodology, but an experiential science of the right order in both the individual and society. It dissected critically and empirically the problem of order.

> Theory is not just any opining about human existence in society; it rather is an attempt at formulating the meaning of existence by explicating the content of a definite class of experiences. Its argument is not arbitrary but derives its validity from the aggregate of experiences to which it must permanently refer for empirical control (Vogelin 1952: 64).

The Frankfurt School, to which Adorno and Marcuse belonged, emerged in Germany in the 1920s and attracted some of the best minds of contemporary German social sciences. Its origin could be traced back to a debate about the nature of Marxism that followed the defeat of the left wing workers' movement in West Europe after the First World War, the collapse of the mass left wing political parties in Germany, the rise of Stalinism, and with its institutionalization, the total degeneration of the Soviet Revolution and the meteoric rise of Fascism and Nazism in Europe, eclipsing Marxism. This bitter experience shattered the school's faith in the inevitability of the historical march towards socialism. Reactions to these events came in the writings of Gramsci within Italy, and from the Frankfurt School within Germany.

The school was directly associated with "an anti-Bolshevik radicalism and an open-ended or critical Marxism" (Held 1983: 182). It was a "para-Marxist movement" (Kolakowski 1981: Vol. III: 341). The school rejected both capitalism and Soviet socialism, and like the Eurocommunists, tried to project a third alternative. But a great deal of pessimism and anti-utopianism prevented them from projecting a bright future, as was done by Marx himself. With an emphasis on totality and rejection of crude determinism, the members of the school produced a large number of scholarly works in humanistic science, philosophy, empirical sociology, psychoanalysis, theory of literature, law and political theory.

Though the works of the members of the school were recognized as a distinct category under the term *critical theory,* there was no attempt to form a core unity, and the adherents differed widely in their approaches and emphasis. Their commitment ended with a general agreement for a necessity to provide a critical theory of Marxism. They were opposed to all forms of positivism and were critical of any possibility of a value-free social science. They rejected Marxist interpretations based on crude materialism or dogma. The most well-known political theorist, Jurgen Habermas, (1929–) belongs to this school. His famous theory of *legitimization crisis* assesses advanced capitalism and communicative action. He is committed to the enlightenment philosophy of faith in the power of reason and progress, and thus becomes a critic of postmodernism.

Kolakowski (ibid: 341–342) lists six basic characteristics of the Frankfurt School: (a) It does not treat Marxism as sacrosanct, but as a helpful tool in analyzing and criticizing culture, (b) Its programme is strictly non-party in orientation, for it never identified with any political movement, either with Communism or social democracy. In fact, it is hostile towards both of them, (c) It is profoundly influenced by the interpretation of Marxism developed by George Lukacs (1885–1971) and Karl Korsch (1886–1961) in the 1920s, (d) It is opposed to the concept of praxis and emphasizes autonomy and independence of theory, (e) Differing with Lukacs, it accepts the Marxian position on exploitation and alienation of the proletariat, though it did not identify with the Communist Party. The school doubted the proletariat's revolutionary role of liberation and dropped this part of Marx's teaching altogether subsequently, (f) In spite of its revisionist outlook, it considered itself a revolutionary intellectual movement rejecting the reformist plank, though it advocated a complete break with the past.

BERLIN'S VIEWS ON POLITICAL THEORY

Sir Isaiah Berlin (1909–1997) started off as a logical positivist but the First World War led him to develop a critical response towards it. He was uncon-vinced about the anti-metaphysical claims of the logical positivists. At the same time he also doubted the contention that problems of philosophy were problems arising from linguistic confusion. His criticism of logical positivism was compiled and published as *Concepts and Categories* (1978), in which he contended that "our understanding of reality already includes the conception of it as existing independently of us and our understanding, so that our reflection of what we mean when we characterize that reality cannot accommodate the positivist idea that truths about reality should be equivalent to truths about us" (Williams 1980: xii).

Berlin rejected Oakeshott's proposal that dilemmas insoluble by reason could be resolved by going back to tradition. He considered philosophy to be important, for it highlighted the incoherence of practices though it could not resolve them. He opposed philosophy, proposing radical social reforms, for its role had to be humble to straighten the crookedness in our thoughts. "The goal of philosophy is always the same, to assist men to understand themselves and thus operate in the open, and not wildly, in the dark" (Berlin 1992: 49).

Berlin's conception of the role and function of philosophy was linked to his idea of freedom and pluralism, namely the existence of an indefinite number of competing and irreconciliable ultimate values from which a choice had to be made, and that this choice could not be forced on others. He denied that a structure of liberties within a liberal society could be derived from any theory, or formulated in any system of principles, since the choice among conflicting liberties was often a choice among incommensurables. He zealously defended the idea of individuality and human diversity, and distrusted all general schemes of human improvement that did not take into account local history, culture and social conditions. He believed that any effort to harmonize the divergences that exist among human beings would only lead to violence and suffering.

Berlin accepted that it was the absence of a commanding work in the twentieth century that led to the declaration that political theory was dead or dying. The reason for this was the absence of critical dimension, and had nothing to do with the nature of political theory. Political philosophy could survive in a society in which ends collided, for:

> In a society dominated by a single goal there could, in principle only, be arguments about the best means to attain this end—and arguments about means are technical, that is, scientific and empirical in character: they can be settled by experience and observation or whatever other methods are used to discover causes and correlations; they can, at least in principle, be reduced to positive sciences. In such a society no serious questions about political ends or values could arise, only empirical ones about the effective paths to the goal ... . It follows that the only society in which political philosophy in its traditional sense, that is, an inquiry concerned not solely with the elucidation of concepts, but with the critical examination of presuppositions and assumptions, and the questioning of the order of priorities and ultimate ends, is possible, is a society in which there is no total acceptance of any single end (Berlin 1980: 149–150).

Berlin was convinced that political philosophy in the traditional sense could be pursued only in a pluralist society, for any kind of analysis involved a critical inquiry, and that was not possible under rigid monism. Monists were Platonists, Aristotelians, Stoics, Thomists, Positivists and Marxists, who understood political problems in scientific terms and saw solutions to human problems as being technical, for human ends were objective in accordance with some discoverable laws. The pluralists did not see the possibility of human perfection and distrusted empirically the possibility of attaining the final solution to the deepest human problems. Skeptics and relativists were pluralists.

Berlin pointed out that philosophical analysis brought out the sharp differences that existed between concepts and value preferences. Political thinkers searched for validity and truth in an attempt to understand whether a model distorted reality. Disputes and doubts could arise regarding values and the relationship between values.

> These questions are not purely technical and empirical, not merely problems about the best means to a given end, nor are they mere questions of logical consistency, that is formal and deductive; but properly philosophical (Berlin 1980: 151).

WOLIN'S DEFENCE OF THE CLASSICAL POLITICAL TRADITION

Traditional political theory did not get marginalized under the dominance of behaviouralism. In the premier American universities, important works in political theory emerged in the 1950s and 1960s. An important critic of behaviouralism, Sheldon Wolin accuses behavioural political scientists of abdicating their true "vocation" in their concern for method. He not only addresses the attack mounted on traditional political theory by behavioural social scientists, but also explains the beauty and usefulness in the tradition of political theory from Plato to contemporary times. He offers comments on the substance and significance of political theory, along with suggestions on how to revitalize political theory or political philosophy.

Wolin's masterpiece, *Politics and Vision: Continuity and Innovation in Western Political Thought* (1960), conveys his view that political theory represents "seeing" political phenomena in two senses. The first (and more obvious) is that political theory provides a description of the political. The second (and more significant) is that political theory constitutes a form of aesthetic or religious vision (Wolin 1960: 18). In the second sense, political theory relates to the imaginative capacity of the theorist, "an esemplastic" power that "forms all into one graceful intelligent whole" (Wolin ibid: 18). Through fanciful statements, a theorist exaggerates aspects of political phenomena in an abstract manner, the interconnection of which is invisible, with the purpose of illuminating it. Imagination is necessary since no political theorist has the capacity to observe all political things directly.

This imaginative element of "seeing" is described as an architectonic vision, for political phenomena are portrayed and shaped in the light of a vision of Good which lies external to the political order. This ordering element has differed throughout tradition. It was religious, historical and in recent times economic, but all of them possess one common trait—a "futuristic quality, a projection of the political order into a time that is yet to be" (Wolin ibid: 20). Besides, through an exaggerated portrayal of the political order, one can get an idea of the possibilities of political life that serves as "a necessary complement to action" (Wolin ibid: 20).

In his subsequent writings, Wolin classifies political visionaries as "epic theorists". An "epic" theory differs from other kinds of theories and methods by its structure of formal features and its "structure of intentions" (Wolin 1969: 1078). Comparing it to Kuhnian paradigms, an epic theory ushers in a new way of looking at the world by reassembling existing political institutions and relationships. All epic theories are governed by a public concern, a quality which is important for anyone engaged in the enterprise of political theory. By public concern, Wolin means two things. First, the object examined is common to the whole community, and in this context he mentioned Cicero's description of the commonwealth as a *res publica,* a public thing. Second, philosophy, as pointed out at the outset, is intrinsically public for it gives knowledge that enables individuals to become wiser in their conduct of life. Epic theories surface mainly during times of crisis.

> The range of possibilities appears infinite, for now the political philosopher is not confined to criticism and interpretation; he must reconstruct a shattered world of meanings and their accompanying institutional expressions; he must in short, fashion a political cosmos out of political chaos (Wolin 1960: 8).

However, Wolin did not say that epic theory emerges only in times of crisis. Though crisis brings forth an epic theory, even during periods of tranquillity the possibility of political chaos leads to a search for order and stability. Epic tradition is also inspired by the fact of immortality, the hope to achieve a "memorable deed through the medium of thought" (Wolin 1970: 4). The purpose of great minds is not to merely state the "logical or factual merits of the words but an attempt to compel admiration and awe for the magnitude of the achievement" (Wolin ibid: 5).

Wolin pointed out that a political theorist tried to understand and alter the whole of politics, but the "whole" he knows was with reference to a particular context. Theorizing about politics contained a paradox. A theorist aimed to provide an understanding about the whole of politics but, compelled by necessity, he reduced the whole to manageable proportions, emphasizing some aspects at the expense of others (Wolin 1968: 319). Every political philosophy... represented a necessarily limited perspective from which it viewed the phenomena of political nature (Wolin 1960: 21).

Wolin also pointed to another aspect of the relationship between the existing political order and political theory, namely that "institutions establish a previous coherence among political phenomena; hence, when the political philosophy reflected upon society, the political theorist was not confronted by a whirl of disconnected events or activities hurtling through a Democritean void but by phenomena already endowed with coherence and interrelationships" (Wolin ibid: 7). The existing coherence was given by a continuous tradition of political thought, and it was this tradition that posed as the biggest inhibitor for the theorist. Previous theorists bequeath a legacy, namely the function of "preserving the insights, experience, and refinements of the past, and compelling those who would participate in the Western political dialogue to abide by certain rules and usages" (Wolin ibid: 22). Though the philosophical inheritance might circumscribe the terms of the discourse, it also facilitated it by providing familiar vocabulary, concepts and terminology allowing fresh insights and new interpretations. Each theorist confronted the fundamental issues of his time and place, but in the process the issues were scrutinized by the insights of the past for the purpose of their applicability to the present. As a result

> ... a political philosopher unavoidably infects his own thought with past ideas and situations. In this sense the past is never wholly superseded; it is constantly being recaptured at the very moment that

> human thought is seemingly preoccupied with the unique problems of its own time. The result is, to borrow Guthrie's phrase, a "co-existence of diverse elements", partly new, partly inherited, with the old being distilled into the new, and the new being influenced by the old. Thus the Western tradition of political thought has exhibited two somewhat contradictory tendencies: a tendency towards an infinite regress to the past and a tendency towards cumulation ... or a tendency towards acquiring new dimensions of insight (Wolin ibid: 26).

The combination between the insights from the past with those of the present gave to the Western political tradition not a "fund of absolute political wisdom, but rather a continuously evolving grammar and vocabulary to facilitate communication and to orient the understanding" (Wolin ibid: 26–27). Viewed in this perspective, individual theorists and the Western political tradition have to be studied best in the light of historical development.

> ... since the history of political philosophy is, as we shall see, an intellectual development wherein successive thinkers have added new dimensions to the analysis and understanding of politics, an inquiry into that development is not so much a venture into antiquarianism as a form of political education (Wolin ibid: 27).

Through the example of Arendt's writings, Wolin showed how the great theories of the past "might be used to illuminate the predicaments of the age" (Wolin 1977: 92–93). He described Arendt's theorizing as "an act of recovery, or reacquiring lost meanings of remembering" (Wolin ibid: 96). Theories of the past should be used for a better understanding of politics, but they need not be judged in light of contemporary standards alone. Wolin echoed Germino when he observed that in its concern for method, contemporary political theory had abandoned the critical dimension, which was always been one of its major characteristics. It no longer furnished a radical critique of the basic principles of politics, as:

> There has been an effort to imbue political scientists with what is understood to be the ethic of science: objectivity, detachment, fidelity to fact, and deference to intersubjective verification by a community of practitioners (Wolin 1969: 1064).

Wolin distinguished between a scientist and a theorist, for both tried to clarify an individual's view of the world, but "only the former attempts to change the world itself (Wolin ibid: 1064).

KUHN'S SEMINAL CONTRIBUTION

Thomas Kuhn (1922–1996) observed that in every age a discipline solved some of its problems but in the process generated new ones. His observation was made with reference to the natural sciences, but it was equally valid in the social sciences, and could be seen as a critique of the behavioural quest for a standardized scientific theory and explanation. His notion of paradigm as "research firmly based upon one or more past scientific achievements, achievements that some particular scientific community acknowledges for a time as supplying the foundation for its further practice" interested social scientists (Kuhn 1970: 10). A paradigm was a perspective, a set of beliefs and ideals—conceptual, theoretical and methodological—of a scientific community helping the latter in the selection of problems, evaluation of data and formulation of theory.

In perceiving the nature of a paradigm, Kuhn conceded the difficulty of discovering rules that would help scientific traditions. The concepts, laws and theories of science were found historically in prior experience, not in abstract, and they became the basis of scientific learning and research. A paradigm established limits of what was possible, and stated the boundary with regard to enquiry. A successful paradigm helped the scientific community in the selection of problems and finding solutions. A scientist working with the help of a successful paradigm normally did not see beyond his assumptions. First, the *preparadigmatic phase,* in which no single theoretical approach or school predominated within a scientific community, although there might be a number of competing approaches. Second, the *paradigmatic phase,* in which the scientific community followed a dominant paradigm. Third, the *crisis phase,* where the dominant paradigm faced challenges and revisions, allowing a new paradigm to evolve, with a possibility of reviving an old one with appropriate modifications. Fourth, the *scientific revolution* phase, which occurred when the scientific community shifted to different paradigms. The traditional, behavioural and post-behavioural approaches did not fit into the Kuhnian definition and analysis of paradigm (Chilcote 1981: 58-59).

Wolin (1968) observes that no scientific revolution has occurred, and as such there exists no such dominant and new theory among political scientists along the lines suggested by Kuhn. There is no significant theory like that of Newton, except a framework of guiding assumptions, "the ideological paradigm reflective of the same political community" that applies to political science (Wolin 1969: 1064). Kuhn's work

> along with new challenges in the philosophy of social science (such as those advanced by Peter Winch and Alfred Schutz) to the idea of positivistic social science, began to spill over into political theory. Much of the discussion in the 1970s was devoted to metatheoretical debates about the nature of social scientific theory and explanation. While the earlier critique of behaviouralism had raised questions about the value of science as such and had largely accepted the same positivist conception of science as behaviouralism, the new critique questioned not only the idea of the methodological unity of science but the adequacy of the prevailing conception of natural science (Gunnell 1987: 389).

These debates weakened the claims of positivism. Political scientists began to devote more to policy and substantive issues than to just having a scientific image. Policy sciences and theories like rational choice and the Prisoner's Dilemma started to receive much attention.

POST-BEHAVIOURALISM AND NEOBEHAVIOURALISM

In 1969, Easton announced a new revolution in political science: post-behaviouralism. It placed less emphasis on the scientific method and empirical theory, and laid more stress on the public responsibilities of the discipline.

The tenets of post-behaviouralism included the following. First, substance preceded technique, which meant the pressing problems of society became tools of investigation. Second, behaviouralism itself was seen as ideologically conservative and limited to abstraction, rather than to the reality of the times in crisis. Third, science could be evaluatively neutral, for facts were inseparable from values, and value premises had to be related to knowledge. Fourth, intellectuals had to shoulder the responsibilities of their society, defend human values of civilization, and not become mere technicians insular to social problems. Fifth, the intellectual had to put knowledge to work and engage in reshaping society, and sixth, the intellectual must actively participate in the politicization of the professions and academic institutions (Easton 1969).

The behaviouralists accepted that theoretical analysis had to remain the starting point of any serious empirical research. In fact, theory not only played a pivotal role in post-behavioural analysis, but also accepted the possibility of different theories yielding different observations. This possibility made the task of subjecting rival theories to empirical testing far more complex. For the post-behaviouralists, a theory, in order to be treated as an explanatory theory, in the first place has to be evaluated, i.e. tested empirically.

Easton (1997: 16–17) also pointed out that dissatisfaction with behaviouralism led to revisions in the method and content, favouring a revival of interpretive understanding and historical analysis, and a complete rejection of systematic methodology, at the same time emphasizing the need to introduce formal modelling and rational actor deductivism. Moreover, new concerns such as feminism, environmentalism, ethnicity, racial identity and equality and nuclear war have emerged. There is a general loss of central focus regarding the subject matter and consensus about methodologies. He announced the beginning of neobehaviouralism in order to bring about a new unity in the theoretical focus of the discipline.

WHY IS THE CLASSICAL TRADITION IMPORTANT?

A distinctive aspect of the history of political theory is the large number of classics known for their comprehensiveness, logical consistency and clarity. These works, rightly described as "classics", address both local issues and contain principles of universal significance. They offer rival conceptual frameworks which enable us to choose and state our preference.

In spite of the bewildering variety among the classics, it is possible to list the major subjects that they address. These are the characteristics of human nature and the basis of rational motivation, the reasons for society, the nature, functions and organization of political authority, and political change and stability.

The classics in political theory normally arise during periods of acute crisis or great transition and not during settled times. They usually flourish in an age of transition from one era to another, when a great churning occurs and issues are debated and discussed. The crisis by itself does not produce; instead it acts as a catalyst. There are exceptions. For instance, Indian society in the seventeenth and eighteenth centuries witnessed tumultous changes marked by crises and stresses but did not yield any political theory. Therefore a crisis has to be understood in the context of a framework of political values and institutional arrangements. The quest for a good life and good society, optimism and hope are the major inputs in a worthwhile project in political theory. A situation of hopelessness usually deters political theorizing.

The text of a political theory has also to be understood with reference to a specific situation in order to comprehend the contents of the political philosophy of that period.

> ... theories of politics are themselves a part of politics. In other words they do not refer to an external reality but are produced as a normal part of the social *milieu* in which politics itself has its being. Reflection upon the ends of political action, upon the means of achieving them, upon the possibilities and necessities of political situations, and upon the obligations that political purposes impose is an intrinsic element of the whole political process ... . Thus conceived, the theory of politics no more reaches an end than politics itself, and its history has no concluding chapter (Sabine 1973: preface to the 1st edition).

This, as Sabine cautions us, should not be overemphasized. In spite of the fact that political theory reflects particular incidents, it cannot be dismissed as being relevant to that particular event alone. The important thing that Sabine seeks to emphasize is that even in localized events, the perennial issues of politics find a place. A political theorist turns to the past with a view to analyzing the present and foreseeing the future. It is this defining element that makes a political tract of a particular period a masterpiece. Though there may be different reactions to a particular situation, one could also find similarities in the responses patterns. Among the varied responses, some authors may have perceptive insights and effectiveness, which is why their work(s) occupy a position of pre-eminence. The greatest political theories are those that have dealt with the immediate situation and issues effectively, while suggesting lessons which are valid for other times as well. It is like the themes of Shakespearean plays enjoying timelessness, being valid for all times and places. The classics in political theory are no different.

Sabine also tells us that in its attempt to deal with the totality, a political theory text has to take into account small details. It has to be careful while deliberating for posterity. A text has to be logically constructed, descriptive and convincing enough to be able to persuade its readers about its point of view. Though a theorist is not a disinterested observer, his account cannot be partisan. Political theory is not sloganeering either. It is neither a tactical manoeuvre in class struggle nor a participant in the national aspiration for power. A political theory must contain three elements: (a) factual statements, (b) what is likely to happen, and (c) what ought to happen, i.e. the desirable thing to happen. Therefore it is not one-dimensional. In analyzing particular situations, it must attempt the ideal. It must not contain properties that could be contradicted by rational criticism.

The great classics were composed by political exiles or by failed politicians like Plato, Machiavelli, Hugo Grotius· (1583–1645), Sir John Fortescue (1394?–1476?), Hobbes and Locke. At times, political theory, as Sir Leslie Stephen remarked, is the child of a revolution or an indication of an impending one. Plato and Aristotle sought to recreate the magic and pre-eminence of the Greek city states or the *polis* which were fast fading into the past. Besides Italian unification, Machiavelli focused on the various dimensions of the newly emerging commercial society. Hobbes and Locke addressed questions relating to crisis of political authority in times of English *civil war*.

The classics in political theory give us explanations about politics, its meaning and value. In that sense, a historical understanding of the classics becomes imperative, for the texts are in response to actual political reality. The relationship between theory and reality remains important. A theorist supplies a critical faculty with the purpose of explaining, defending or questioning that reality. In the process, a theorist also imagines a framework of political organization different from present practices. Though a theorist theorizes within the existing political practices, he may depart from it when framing their ideal.

Besides being influential, a classic in political theory (as in other fields) contains a wealth of information, ideas and values that cumulatively enriches human thought and action. A great theorist is one who articulates logically with rigour, insight and subtle nuances the dilemmas of his age, and dissects the problems that confront the generation to which he belongs. He stands out among his contemporaries not so much for originality of ideas—rather rare in human thought—but for the incisiveness, clarity, and power of the doctrine(s). Scientific invention or discovery is .practically out of reach for a political theorist. What he can aspire for, at best, is comprehension and articulation of the spirit and temper of his age, linking them with new ideas and events within a framework of refinement and advancement.

Political theory, like any intellectual enquiry, is partly a communication with the past, establishing an empathy with the great minds and having a continuous discourse with history. This in itself could be a disenchanting exercise, as Stephen Spender compared it to an obstacle race where philosophers race, manoeuvring and navigating logical obstructions, with some getting ahead of others. Moreover every age is characterized by its own problems and dilemmas, so it is important to identify and understand the trends in a particular time period. But such localism need not be a hindrance to the essential richness of a classic as demonstrated by Aristotle's *Politics,* which justified the prejudices of its time (like slavery), but was able to offer brilliant insights into the basic issues of politics, like stability, revolutionary change, the importance of family and property in sustaining the state.

Sabine considers it remarkable that in the course of 2500 years, two periods of approximately 50 years each, and at both times, confined to highly restricted sections, political theory flourished. These two periods are the fifth century BC during the time of Plato and Aristotle, and the seventeenth century, the phase of the English Civil War of 1641 till the Glorious Revolution of 1688, with Hobbes and Locke as the principal theorists. Both these periods witnessed changes of momentous significance in the course of European social and intellectual history: the first period saw the collapse of the city states and their replacement from their position of cultural leadership, surely indicative of the moral and political upheaval of the ancient world. The second period saw the formation of the first constitutional state on national lines, creating the basis of scientific and intellectual changes that governed the Western world at least till 1914. Sabine links fundamental developments in political theory to the shifts that take place from one set of formation to another. In other words, innovation in political theory occurs when the older institutions become inoperative and newer ones emerge. Crises and tumultuous changes have a catalytic effect on political theory.

Germino (1967: 37–44) identifies the characteristics of an authentic political theory, common to all classics from Plato to Hegel. These are openness, theoretical intention, focus on universal, perennial problems, realism, acknowledging the limits to knowledge, and intellectual honesty and integrity. In elaborating these characteristics, Germino points out that a theorist exhibits an ability to transcend his narrow concerns by maintaining a critical distance, and addresses issues of larger importance. A theorist interprets reality to be able to focus on questions of perennial concern.

Hacker (1954), in his reply to Easton, points out that the great books in political theory should be saved, for they offer insights not only into the time period in which they were written, but also into contemporary times. He points out that a theory has two functions. It should not only explain behaviour (causal theory), but also tell how individuals ought to behave (ethical theory). He classifies the great books into ten categories, advising how they have to be studied. *Capital and Carbuncles,* essentially biographical in nature, tells us how a particular book came to be written in a particular way. *Hero Worshippers* takes into account all the writings of a single author. *Intellectual Plagiarism* tells us of the indebtedness of a theorist to his predecessors and contemporaries. *Who said it first* tells us, for instance, that Aristotle was the father of political science, Machiavelli the father of modern political thought, Comte the father of sociology, and so on. *The Mind Readers* gives us an idea of what the theorist really desired to convey. *The Camera Eye* offers us the thoughts some had during certain historical periods. For instance, the contrasting analysis of Edmund Burke (1729–1797) and Thomas Paine (1737–1809) during the French Revolution familiarize us with the responses of different groups to a particular event. *Influencing the Intelligentsia* is similar to *Intellectual Plagiarism,* with the difference that some theorists like Bosanquet become important because of Hegel and Green's influence on his writings. *Influencing the Masses* includes books that are directly linked to political events. For instance, Locke's *Two treatise* is intimately connected with the events leading to the Glorious Revolution. *The Logic-Book* makes a text important for its logical nature. Finally, *Timelessness* explains the continuing relevance of the classics, for they offer insights and solutions that remain valid till date. For instance, Aristotle's comparative method, analysis of revolutions, role of the middle class; Machiavelli's advice to political rulers; Hobbes' emphasis on commodious living; Rousseau's notion of popular sovereignty, are cited in the political discourse of today. It is for these reasons that Hacker contends the need to preserve the great books, for they remain valuable both as explanations and prescriptions. If approached in the aforesaid manner, they form the central theme of political theory.

HOW TO STUDY THE CLASSICS

There is considerable disagreement as to whether emphasis should be given to historical contexts in which political theorists write or analyze these ideas, divorced from the time and context from which they arise. The textualist approach, dominant since 1945, holds that classics in political thought can be studied without reference to their historical context, as exemplified in the writings of Hacker (1961) and Plamentaz (1963). Political theory is considered as a sub-category of philosophy and its central concerns are to clarify concepts used in political discourse and debate and second, to critically examine and evaluate political beliefs and principles (Raphael 1990; Heywood, 1999). The textualists allege that while historical understanding of the milieu in which these texts have originate may give us some insights but they do not play a central role in interpreting them.

Skinner (1966), Pocock (1971), Dunn (1979) and Collini (1983), are the leading exponents of contextualism. They contend that a mere textual approach is inherently weak, for it overlooks the historical background, namely the purpose and the motivation and the intention behind a text. Every text is the result of a conscious effort of the author(s). To ignore the historical context could lead to an error in interpreting and understanding the texts. Macpherson (1973) pays attention to the concerns of the author by situating him in the historical society in which the text was composed. This approach emphasizes that political theory itself has a history (Ashcraft 1986; Dunn 1979; Tully 1988).

The contextualists are skeptical about the claims of the textualists who assert that there are universal and timeless questions and problems that the great political texts of the past raise. Skinner maintains that to suggest that these writings provide answers to fundamental political questions that confront contemporary society is far fetched. The political and moral assumptions and beliefs that underlie the great works of political theory are historically specific creation. The great works raise questions and provide answers that should be viewed as relative to the particular societies and cultures from which they emerged.

The contextualists point out that to understand the formulations and theoretical statements about politics it is necessary to stress the interrelationship between political theory and practice. The texts are in response to specific events, controversies, debates and crises reinforcing Berki's observation that "political thought issues out of practical experience and not the other way around" (1977: 32). The historians of political thought also point out that the writers of the past intended to communicate with particular audiences. Only when we comprehend the writers' intentions, their use of language and the words that prevailed at that point of time can one understand the meaning of these texts. Merely reading it without any reference to time and social, economic and cultural milieu would be to approach the texts in the 'biblical' sense as if their meaning can be ascertained simply by reading it and reflecting on its universal message' (Berki ibid 31).

In interpreting classics, one must keep the time period of the text in mind. This enables us to see the way a word has been defined, the different meanings that it gives rise to and the intentions of the author, and relate it to the immediate social and political environment, the aims and purpose of writing the text, how well the author has tackled the problems vis-a-vis his contemporaries, and finally the meaning of the text today. It is through the consideration of these aspects that we can perhaps understand why, among a host of innumerable tracts, only some have been elevated to the status of classics. It also helps to see and appreciate the plurality of ideas that exists within a particular time-frame.

For example, Rousseau's attempt to distinguish between government, democracy, state and sovereignty is a case in point. The word *sovereignty* was used to describe the power of the people acting as lawmakers themselves and not through their representatives. Neither was sovereignty a characteristic of the state. It differed from the government, which administered and enforced the law but could not make the law. Sovereignty meant the exercise of power by the people directly. The diverse contributions of Rousseau make him a genius, in the opinion of Catlin.

Since political theory is by and large descriptive, a historical approach is important, for that would help us to see how political theory varies according to time and circumstances. It helps, as Dunning says, to know the "successive transformation" of a particular idea or concept, or as Sabine says, the "re-interpretation and re-adaptation" of received beliefs and theories. Furthermore, as Sabine argues, ah examination of the history of political theories reveals that its literature is not a product of a laboratory. The authors have an eye fixed on the public forum, and if political theories are produced in quantities, then it is a symptom that society itself is undergoing a period of stress and strain.

Another way of approaching texts is by placing them in the tradition of Western political theory or philosophy. Such an approach has been used by Strauss (1952) and Wolin (1960). They understand the tradition, not as a chronological sequence of books and writers, but as a narrative discourse in which the writer consciously articulates and elaborates a theme.

Strauss argued that political philosophers from Plato to Hegel grappled with the problem of natural right, namely stating and justifying transhistorical standards of right or justice. The Greeks defended this proposition, whereas modern theorists reject it. For both philosophical and political reasons, Strauss favoured the Greek position and characterized modern political theory as degenerative, for it gave rise to ethical relativism and the death of political theory as it was practised. The moderns looked to comfort, affluence, and avoidance of death to mean good life, which could be secured not through rational understanding, but by gaining power over nature. The premoderns rejected this view, for they considered human desires as insatiable, making it difficult to realize happiness. Moreover, mere scientific power without a knowledge of ends would only lead to crude hedonism. As a result, modern thought rejected Divine revelation, eternal Nature or inevitable History as contributing a yardstick for measurement, leading to uncritical acceptance of liberal democracy without exploring alternatives.

Strauss did not regard political philosophy as a historical discipline. Though knowledge of history was important for political philosophy, "it is only preliminary and auxiliary to political philosophy; it does not form an integral part of it" (Strauss 1949: 30). Furthermore, refuting the claim that a text was historically conditioned, Strauss observed that every political situation consisted of elements that could be found in other political situations as well, and that explained why a classic was evergreen.

Wolin contends that traditional political theory attempted to define the dignity, distinctiveness and the importance of the political, which disintegrated since the seventeenth century, leading eventually to the decline and sublimation of the political. Within this framework, he selected thinkers for whom the political was primary, general and integrative. It is imperative to discern the philosophical teachings of thinkers who try to clarify the meaning of the political, rather than focus on their historical backgrounds. The philosophical content should not be confused for historical understanding. Many, like Pocock (1962, 1971, 1980), Dunn (1968a), Skinner (1969) and Gunnell (1978) reject the idea that it is possible to identify a unity in tradition, and that the great masters were engaged in a common activity, or addressed some common issues.

Many see the classics as addressing questions and elucidating themes that are of perennial interest. Such a perspective is offered by Hacker (1961), Plamentaz (1963) and Bluhm (1965). Viewed in this manner, political theory is perceived as a complex and comprehensive activity that deals with universal and eternal issues to convince readers that the classics are relevant to contemporary times.

However, mere historical study is not sufficient. Care must be taken to see that the texts do not get submerged within the pages of history. As Iain Hampsher Monk (1992, x–xi) points out that such an approach would stifle their capacity "to formulate statements with any reference beyond the historically parochial" thus denying them any significance for contemporary times. Emphasis on the historical context of the text might result in the possibility of the writer and text getting fragemented and disappearning into context.

It is important to look for consistency, coherence, clarity, truth, reliability and certainty in the text, for that would enable us to see how best a text is in terms of providing a conceptual paradigm. Each text advances, defends and justifies a set of values or preferences, and it is important to see how best it does it. For this, one must look at the internal consistency of a text, and then compare it with that of others written in and during that time, for such a relative assessment will tell us why, out of a plethora of books, only some become great or immortal. Sabine feels that it is possible to enumerate the properties that political theories have actually had, and examine a variety of questions relating to the truth and validity of political theories.

There is moreover a need to recognize that there exists a broad Western political tradition to which diverse political thinkers, from different circumstances and concerns adhere to. Nothwithstanding the wide variations there exists a history of political thought "one broadly defined, yet coherent tradition of political discourse. We are not faced with a chaotic whirl of disembodied ideas and texts, but with a concrete world of interlacing and interweaving visions" (Berki 1977: 36–37). Some thinkers have treated "the past as a treasure trove from which they can draw for their own purposes" (Morrow 1998: 5). Rawls says he is reviving and updating Kant and Nozick of Locke thus continuing "with the ancient practice of pillaging the classics in search of ideas and styles to be revived for their own time" (Tuck 1993: 72). Aristotle in *Politics* refutes many of the formulations of Plato's *Republic*. Paine provides a liberal defence of the French Revolution in response to Burke's conservative critique. Wollstonecraft is critical of Burke and Rousseau in her formulations of the first principles of feminism.

A classic can be interpreted from a philosophical perspective that is by its efforts at developing a set of moral principles for the purpose of evaluating political events and guiding political choice. The important fact is that, "moral concepts are embodied in and are partly constitutive of forms of social life. One key way in which we may identify one form of social life as distinct from another is by identifying differences in moral concepts" (MacIntyre 1971: 1). The philosophical approach bestows upon the reader/scholar the role of a judge, for the idea is to evaluate the differing conceptions of moral principles and political theories.

A noticeable fact that emerges while interpreting the classics is that the history of political theory is marked by both continuity and change. Concepts undergo a change in the course of their evolution, yet one can see a remarkable continuity. Originality lies in the course of their interpretation and redefinition. This explains the complexities and intricacies within the tradition.

Classics are also reinterpreted following new frameworks of analysis. For example, feminism has enabled us to take a fresh look at the texts with certain questions in mind like the position accorded to women, perceptions regarding sexual relations, the home as a place of equality and justice. The republican view of politics has led to reinterpretation of thinkers like Machiavelli, the authors of the *Federalist Papers* and Locke from the standpoint of their analysis of the public space, civic virtues and the obligations of private citizens towards their states.

Classics are an indispensable part of liberal arts education, because their authors engage themselves and their readers in a discourse of the problems and issues of their time and place. Such an understanding heightens the appreciation of the possibilities and limits of political action and theorizing. The importance of the classical tradition has been succinctly captured by Strauss.

> The return to classical political philosophy is both necessary and tentative or experimental... . We cannot reasonably expect that a fresh understanding of classical political philosophy will supply us with recipes for today's use. For the relative success of modern political philosophy has brought into being a kind of society to which the classical principles as stated and elaborated by the classics are not immediately applicable. Only, we living today can possibly find a solution to the problems of today. But an adequate understanding of the principles as elaborated by the classics may be the indispensable starting point for an adequate analysis, to be achieved by us, of present day society in its peculiar character, and for the wise application, to be achieved by us, of these principles to our tasks (Strauss 1964: 11).

LIMITATIONS OF THE CLASSICAL TRADITION

It is important to keep in mind that the classics, in spite of their timelessness, exhibit limitations and shortcomings. As Hegel rightly stated, every thinker is a child of his time, and this is reflected in their perceptions and theories too. Plato and Aristotle wrote to an audience whose social base was narrow. Their ideal was the city state or the *polis* with limited citizenship, excluding the majority. They were forgotten in the immediate context of the post-Aristotelian philosophies of Stoicism, Epicureanism and Cynicism. This narrow perception led to what Sabine calls a politics of withdrawal. Machiavelli's prescriptions could not anticipate the Reformation within the Christian Church. Hobbes considered his portrayal of human nature to be universal. Hegel's glorification of the state led to its exaltation at the cost of civil society. Marx virtually misrepresented capitalism. J.S. Mill was confident that representative democracy would not succeed in backward and/or heterogeneous societies only. One can find a similar bias even in commentaries on the classics, as evident from a change in interpretation with regard to most of the great masters.

Gender Bias

Most mainstream philosophers have either ignored or dismissed cursorily the position and status of women. They have reiterated, justified and defended women's subordination on the alleged natural and biological differences between the sexes, and have also pointed to the inherent physical and mental superiority of the male. In doing so, they have reinforced the stereotyped image of the woman as an emotional, irrational and sensual person in need of male guidance and domination. In many cases this has been without a critical examination of their personal biases and prejudices.

Most of them—which includes Aristotle, Rousseau and Hegel—contend that a woman's rightful place is her home, and that being burdened with household chores she did not have sufficient time for politics, philosophy, art or science. While they articulate the need for men to have leisure time to devote to public causes and universal issues, they presume that women did not feel similarly. Rousseau and Hegel regarded women as subversive to the unity and order of the polity, and were willing to deny them citizenship rights. Even Kant, who spoke of moral equality and the importance of moral law, precluded women.

Plato, in *The Republic* (380–370 BC), was one of the earliest exponents of total political and sexual equality. He observed that women could perform functions that men did. But he too abandoned this idea and defended the patriarchal family system in the second-best state developed in the *Laws* (350 BC).

The ideas of freedom, equality, individuality, personal autonomy, contractualism and voluntarism which ushered in the modern period also brought about a significant transformation in the lives of both men and women. The early liberals were the first to accept the idea of sexual equality. They attacked patriarchy. They considered women as human beings with minds of their own, regarding them as free, equal and rational.

The intellectual and social ferment in the eighteenth century produced feminism. It arose as a middle-class movement demanding a re-examination of the theories of citizenship and natural rights. The French Revolution promised a free and equal society, but left women out. The Revolution, though libertarian in most respects, was conservative on the gender issue. Most men continued to see the home as the rightful place for women. Just as the failure of early liberalism to fulfil its own promise led to the rise of Marxism, similarly it was silence on the part of natural rights theorists on the status, role and position of women that gave rise to feminism. This neglect prompted Olympe de Gouges (1748–1793) in France to proclaim a manifesto of her own entitled the *Proclamation of the Rights of Women and Female Citizens*. In England, Wollstonecraft brought out her *A Vindication of the Rights of Woman* (1792). The early feminists were inspired by Locke's writings.

The only mainstream male philosopher to espouse the cause of women, pleading for the need to reorder the private sphere on the same lines as freedom, equality, justice, self-worth and dignity that govern the public sphere, was J.S. Mill. He not only rejected patriarchy, but also insisted that liberal principles apply to women, family and the home. He combined his academic concern with political activism when he campaigned for women's suffrage in 1865, regarding it as the most important public service. Many socialists like Claude-Henri Comte de Rouvroy Saint Simon (1760–1825), Francois-Marie Charles Fourier (1772–1837), Friedrich Engels (1820–1895) and August Bebel (1840–1913) also wrote on the gender question, linking women's emancipation with the overall liberation of society.

The feminists during the first wave pleaded for equal rights and opportunities for women, while the second wave, beginning in the last quarter of the twentieth century, desired restructuring of society. There was a realization that the earlier demand for redistribution of resources and rights did not bring about substantive equality. Feminists brought out the limitations of mainstream Western political tradition, namely its male centredness. In spite of their confessions and attempts to offer universalistic prescriptions, most of the classics exhibit a gender bias and prejudice. The initial focus was to enquire the reasons for the exclusion of women from the political process. Subsequently, they resurrected texts, articles and writings to formulate a feminist political theory.

Eurocentricism

Furthermore, some of the great masters were also eurocentric, dismissing non-Western civilizations as unchanging and unhistorical. Along with Greece, the first philosophical world-views emerged simultaneously in two other centres—India and China both in the sixth century BC. Both of them developed their own distinct and individualistic styles of philosophy.

We have evidence that the art of writing was invented in Egypt in 4000 BC, and subsequently in Mesopotamia. Writing here took the form of pictures. Soon these pictures were conventionalized, and words were represented in the form of ideograms, as they still are in China. It took thousands of years for the development of alphabetical writing. The earliest civilizations were along the fertile regions of the Nile, Tigris and Euphrates. Here agriculture was the mainstay of the people.

Egypt had a highly evolved system of tax administration, with a standardized system of revenue collection and drastic penalties for extortion and bribery on the part of tax collectors. The legal code admonished its officials to be patient, impartial and just. The Mesopotamian empires, in spite of the theocratic pretensions of the royalty, had governments that had earthly concerns. The code of Hammurabi (1792–1750 BC) was a social product containing generations of political experience, thought and usage, with strict penalties for giving false witness, committing theft, and being unjust in marital relationships. The code embodied a conception of civil justice.

For the Hebrews, the monarch was both an agent of God and a symbol of the people, implying that besides divine sanction the monarch needed the support of his people. Hebrew thinkers repudiated the idea that priestly and kingly functions could be exercised by the same person. The reason for this separation was that the priest could check and criticize the king, if necessary. The Hebrews did not have a systematic and well-formulated theory of politics. Their thought mostly centred on religion. They were also convinced that divinity permeated all aspects of social and political life. This impeded the development of particular sciences. On the other hand, the interrelationship between religion and divinity prevented the Hebrews from developing an "other-worldly" approach to politics that characterized some interpretations of Plato and many versions of "Christianity" (Sibley 1981: 29).

Chinese political thought was rich and diverse. The first tracts were associated with the Chou dynasty, and these consisted of poems, historical and court records, cryptic and elusive sayings, with lengthy commentaries. Of particular significance was "the Mandate of Heaven", which stated that the ruling house could govern the empire, provided its rule was virtuous and beneficent, which it would lose if it became corrupt or inflicted disasters on its people. The other equally significant concern was the impeccable moral behaviour of some early sage rulers, one of whom bypassed his own son and selected a commoner, for the latter's virtue was better than his son's.

Confucius (Kung Fu Tzu, 551–479 BC) can be regarded as the first political thinker, whose views were contained in the *Analects*. He held a minor office in his native state and led a modest life. He was a scholar and teacher, though later accounts described him as a great official and one who possessed supernatural powers. His ideal was a rule by moral example rather than military superiority or hereditary succession. The ruler and his officials and advisers were to be virtuous and meritorious. He did not distinguish between political and familial authority, regarding society as an extension of the ruler's household and a well-ordered family as the foundation of the state. He advocated self-control and duty towards others. He accepted social hierarchy and the division between the peasant and the literate, though he held that learning made human improvement possible. He taught that human beings should be in harmony with nature, through nature and government. Government was not a divine institution but a product of human reason and sound virtue. Here his ideas were similar to those of Plato and Aristotle.

Another Confucian philosopher, Mencius (Meng Tzu, 372–289 BC) advanced the doctrine of nature, reason and virtue as the basic requirements of a state. He looked upon the original human heart as reflecting the cosmic order. The Chinese did not look upon political authority as supernatural and the emperor as divine. They justified and defended revolution. Mencius even declared that a ruler who departed from reason and virtue could be executed. A ruler was responsible for the quality of governance and was accountable to his subordinates. Throughout Chinese thought runs an ideal that a ruler must ensure the safety and prosperity of his people.

A rival school of Confucianism was legalism, consisting of diverse elements but given a philosophical touch by Han Fei Tzu (280–233 BC). The earliest legalists were Shang Yang (d. 338 BC) and Shen Pu-hai (400–337 BC). Shang Yang desired to organize the state along military lines as an efficient instrument of war. Hereditary officers would be replaced and encouragement would be given to agriculture and handicrafts to counter idle consumption and merchant activity. In a Taoist sense, he instructed the ruler to be non-attached and strive to attain sagehood. Han Fei Tzu preferred the state to be ruled by law rather than the will of a prince.

Taoist political theory is the most difficult to elaborate. Its earliest exponent was Chuang Tzu, stressing simplicity in human existence. Lao Tzu (middle of the third century BC) agreed with Confucius about the principles of a government. He also insisted that calmness of the mind came from a lack of attachment to transient things in the world. In fact, he anticipated Rousseau when he held that human beings became corrupt with the passage of civilization. He glorified rural simplicity, whereby the old practices were followed and the clever, prevented from having a definite say. He also instructed the sage ruler to adopt a principle of non-interference, similar to the physiocrats and Adam Smith (1723–1790), as the best way to secure happiness and prosperity. He held that more laws and regulations would only encourage thieves, for corruption increased with governmental control. Mo Tzu (479–390 BC), a rival and a critic of Confucius, held that every policy of the state should promote the needs of the common people and not waste resources on elaborate ceremonies and rites.

Confucianism and its variants remained the dominant philosophical tradition in China. Many elements of Confucianism were retained in Mao

Zedong's (1893–1976) Marxism. In recent years the Confucian value system has been regarded as being responsible for the stupendous success of the East and South-East Asian countries. A leading exponent of the Asian value system is the former prime minister presently a senior minister in Singapore, Lee Kuan Yew, who attributed rapid industrialization, economic growth and high levels of productivity without dislocating the family and traditional values to Confucianism. In fact, Confucianism has been seen as communitarian, in contrast to the individualism of the Western tradition. The Asian way is projected as a distinct alternative route to modernity. Huntington (1993) concedes that Confucianism is the most profound challenge to the hegemony of Western ideology, and that cultural differences not only exist but could also ignite clashes between civilizations. Huntington ignores the fact that the growth of human ideas and institutions is a result of cooperation of all civilizations, a point lucidly narrated by Durant. Doctrines like clash of civilizations or eurocentricism, and in recent times a refined version of Said's orientalism, are particularistic challenges to mainstream political theory which is based on Grotius' principle of universality and a minimum everywhere. The contention of the Asian values school that the Western tradition is wholly individualistic is not right. No tradition is wholly individualistic or wholly communitarian. Most of them contain a happy mix of libertarian individualism, with concern for social commitment and common good. While cultural plurality is to be respected, it should not be particularistic so as to become divisive. In fact: "We have a universal responsibility to use a single standard in judging human misfortune and injustice wherever they may occur" (Sakharov 1989: Preface).

A typical example of the Western assessment of Indian political thought is provided by Dunning (1902), who concluded that India did not have any political thought because of the dominance of religion and theology. Dunning, quoting Spender, mentions Egyptian and Chinese political thought, but omits India. This is a very prejudiced view. In fact, the tradition of Indian political speculation is very old, dating back to the Vedic period (1500–1000 BC). In the twelfth century, Kalhan's *Rajtarangini* provided some very interesting insights into politics. Furthermore, the *Upanishads,* the *Dharmasutras,* the Buddhist texts, the *Arthasastra, Manusmriti* and the *Santiparva* of the *Mahabharata* provide a rich cluster of political ideas.

Unlike the wide variety of political ideas that ancient Greece provided, ancient Indian political theory follows the pattern beginning with the Vedas, except for the Buddhist tradition. The primary reason for this was the fact that though some states were oligarchical and republican, by and large most of them were monarchies. Two other crucial factors impeded the development of political theory. One was the sway of religion, and the second was the *Brahmin* domination, with strict division of society into four distinct castes, each performing distinct functions. Even with Kautilya (321–296 BC), with his elaborate and skilful dissection of public administration and statecraft, there was an overall acceptance of the social order. This explains that the *Saptanga* theory, though more elaborate than a similar theory in the Western tradition, needed divine sanction to buttress political authority. This led to a basic imperfection in theorizing, as divine laws were unchangeable and society was strictly divided into four groups with separate functions and duties. Added to this was the factor of domination by *Brahmins* (the most privileged group), with exemption from taxation and punishment, constituting a state within the state. Like the Chinese, ancient Indians also believed that a ruler's first duty was to protect his people and their social needs. The ruler was subject to constitutional checks and could be questioned by his advisers and people. A just state was one that was based on *dharma,* an all-embracing term covering justice, duty and virtue.

From the eighth century onwards, the period of Islamic thought begins. With the predominance of an Islamic religious code, civil law was a part of religious law. Non-Muslims were not considered full members of society. In the fifteenth century, new ideas started emerging under the enlightened reign of Akbar, who tried to reform and bring about equality irrespective of individual religious beliefs. Jahangir and Shah Jahan followed the tradition of Akbar, which was totally reversed by Aurangzeb, who reverted to religious orthodoxy.

In the eighteenth century, the impact of European civilization was felt. This was of great significance, because after a century of anarchy and stagnation it created awareness in the minds of educated Indians. This was because not only Aurangzeb but even the Marathas, who arose in protest against Aurangzeb, were not receptive to new ideas. The failure of the Marathas was due to their inability to innovate (Sarkar 1973). Modern Indian political thought begins with Raja Rammohun Roy (1774–1833). A distinctive aspect of political theorizing in the non-Western world has been that this exercise has been carried on by activist theoreticians like Gandhi, Mao and Roy.

CONCLUSION

Since the seventies, there has been resurgence in political theory, largely due to the efforts of Habermas, Nozick and Rawls. The themes that figure prominently since its revival are broadly social justice and welfare rights theory within a deontological perspective, utilitarianism, democratic theory and pluralism, feminism, postmodernism, new social movements and civil society, and the liberalism-communitarian debate (Marion-Young 1996: 481–500; Glaser 1995: 23). In fact, communitarianism fills the void left by the declining popularity of Marxism (Barry 1995: 24–29). This unprecedented lease of life that political theory has received is restricted to the universities and the academia and as a result it is "a kind of alienated politics, an enterprise carried on at some distance from the activities to which it refers"

(Walzer 1989: 337). This resurgence also suggests that earlier pronouncements about its decline and/or demise were premature and academically shortsighted.

This new-found enthusiasm has been confined to liberal political discourse mainly due to the seminal work of Rawls, which fulfilled Germino's wish for a need to strengthen the open society. Recent liberal theory in its revived sense focuses on the idea of impartiality and fairness, in the belief that "discrimination must be grounded on relevant differences" (Benn and Peters 1959: 133). It is no coincidence that a well-formulated and detailed analysis of the concept of justice, long overdue since the time of Plato, emerges in Rawls, for whom justice meant fairness. Rawls attempts to furnish an answer to how a just society should distribute liberties, opportunities, income, wealth and bases of self-respect.

Among the competing ideologies which ushered in the twentieth century, only liberal democracy, unlike Fascism and Communism, permitted free exchange of ideas, synchronized (and adapted, if necessary), theory in the light of practice and identified the elements that constituted a just political and social order, without being doctrinaire and dogmatic. However, much of this new, liberal political theory is in the nature of refining and clarifying the earlier theoretical postures. Moreover, the loss of challenge by both Fascism and Communism, the first because of its defeat in the Second World War, and the second, which collapsed due to its own internal contradictions, also prove that Utopian and radical schemes are no longer theoretically and practically desirable and feasible alternatives.

This is true even of postmodernism and deconstructionism, which are suspicious of the dominant discourse and build their formulations with references to differences. But the essential formulations of Jacques Derrida (1930–2004) and Michael Focault (1926–1984) provide new interpretations and meanings to old readings. They question the universalism and generalizations of Western theory and the Platonic-Kantian idea of good. They reject the possibility of the realization of the perfect set of laws, which would always lead to domination and unfreedom of some who constitute "the other". However, postmodernism is also only a critique without much prospect of providing a viable alternative. Its impact has been more pronounced in literature than in the social sciences and political theory. Another contemporary concern is multiculturalism. Charles Taylor (1931–) justifies cultural recognition beyond rights of association, speech and tolerance, for culture is a way of life. He pleads for the preservation of indigenous culture mainly in the context of the French in Quebec. But commentators like Richard Rorty (1931–2007) point out the dangers of cultural essentialism, as even when individual rights are preserved, emphasis on culture can be both coercive and oppressive. "The implicit cultural essentialism of a good deal of celebratory multiculturalism disguises the powerful intracultural politics of determining the right of authoritative description" (Rorty 1994: 158).

Political theory since the time of Plato has responded to its time and place. Our own time and that of the future are no different. A variety of political theories would flourish, depending on the political agenda of a particular time and place. But our age differs from the ones that preceded it. It is an age of technology, manifest in the microchip revolution and satellite networks. With nation states becoming more porous and receptive to outside influences, political theory too must respond to the increasing globalization and role of technology. The nature of this change has been summarized by a Swiss economist, William Rappard (1955), who some years ago listed the four reasons for America's unparalleled prosperity, something that applies to others as well: mass production; a passion for productivity; the spirit of competition; and the application of science to everyday economic needs. This exercise by Rappard, both in method and assessment, is similar to that of Polybius (203–120 BC), a Greek prisoner in Rome, who could discern and state the reasons for the dominance and superiority of Rome against Greece.

Lord John Maynard Keynes (1883–1946) graphically underlined the importance that ideas exert, and if they have to continue to be influential and remembered by posterity, this is only possible if they deal with the complexities of our time within the parameters set by the great masters of political theory. Any serious and worthwhile political theory would have to shed its intellectual complacency and maintain the rigour of the discipline that one finds in the classics. As aptly remarked by Sartori:

> Knowledge grows, *inter alia*, by acknowledging error. But Political Science hardly adheres to this rule. Over the decades the profession has shown little taste for self-criticism. Our self-perception tends to be that we are always progressing, if only sluggishly and non linearly. But are we (Sartori 1993: 15)?

2

Plato

> The book *(Republic)* may be regarded not only as a philosophical work, but as a treatise on social and political reform. It is written in the spirit of a man not merely reflecting on human life but intensely anxious to reform and revolutionize it (Nettleship 1967: 6).

> Plato's estimate of the human race is at once incredibly low and incredibly high... . Between the wisdom of the low and the docility of the rest the human race has never been so exalted or so abused (Sinclair 1951: 166).

> I believe that Plato's political programme far from being morally superior to totalitarianism, is fundamentally identical with it. I believe that the objections against this view are based upon an ancient and deep-rooted prejudice in favour of idealizing Plato (Popper 1945: Vol. I: 87).

In the entire history of political thought no thinker evoked the admiration, reverence and criticism that Plato (428/27–347 BC) did. This outstanding Greek philosopher has left behind many important works, out of which three, the *Republic,* (380–370 BC), the *Statesman* (360 BC) and the *Laws* (350 BC), are of perennial interest to all those interested in the history of political ideas. Plato has been generally regarded as the founder of philosophical idealism by virtue of his conviction that there is a universal idea in the world of eternal reality beyond the world of the senses. He was the first to formulate and define political ideas within a larger framework of a philosophical idea of Good. He was concerned about

> ... human life and human soul or human nature, and the real question in it is as Plato says, how to live best... what is the best life?... is to him inseparable from the question, what is [the] best order or organization of human society (Nettleship 1967: 5).

Plato perceived political philosophy as an architectonic science of society, and like Socrates (469–399 BC) and the Sophists, distinguished the political from the other dimensions of life. Within the European intellectual tradition he conceptualized the disorders and crises of the actual world and presented to his readers a vision of a desirable political order, which till today fascinates his admirers and detractors. He has been described as a poet of ideas, a philosopher of beauty and the true founder of the cult of harmonious living. He has been praised for his denunciation of crass materialism and brutish selfishness. Both Francois-Marie Arouet Voltaire (1694–1778) and Friedrich Wilhelm Nietzsche (1844–1900) characterized Platonism as the intellectual side of Christianity (1955). Many like John Ruskin (1819–1900) and William Morris (1834–1896) were attracted by Plato's concern for human perfection and excellence. Ralph Waldo Emerson (1803–1882) exclaimed ecstatically

> Plato is philosophy and philosophy is Plato for out of Plato comes all things that are still written and debated among men of thought .... Burn the libraries for their value in this book (Emerson 1965: 120).

Plato has been credited for laying the foundations of Greek political theory, as he explored, analyzed and covered a wide range of philosophical perspectives and issues, on which the Western political tradition rests. Aristotle, a critic of Platonic ideas in the Republic, rejected many of them, but extends Plato's formulation in the *Laws*. It is for this reason that Whitehead, paying the most fitting tribute to Plato stated that the entire European philosophical tradition is nothing but a set of footnotes to Plato.

While Plato's admirers have been numerous, he has had his share of critics too, beginning with Aristotle. Most of his recent critics have been in the twentieth century within the liberal tradition (Thorson 1963: 2). They assailed Plato for his hostility towards progressive, humanitarian and democratic ideals, and regarded him as the philosophical forerunner of modern day totalitarianism, which itself is a twentieth century phenomenon. Paradoxically, the liberals in the nineteenth century were more appreciative of Plato, claiming him to be a liberal of that period (Nettleship: 1967).

LIFE SKETCH

Plato was born in May-June 428/27 BC in Athens in a distinguished, aristocratic, though not affluent, family. His father, Ariston, traced his ancestry to the early kings of Athens, even to Poseidon, the God of the Sea. His mother, Perictione, was a descendant of Solon (640–559 BC), the famous lawgiver of Athens. Perictione's brother Charmides and uncle Critias were among the 30 tyrants who ruled Athens after its defeat in the Peloponnesian War (431–404 BC). Plato had one sister (Potone), two brothers (Adeimantus and Glaucon), and one half-brother (Antiphon).

Plato's real name was Aristocles, which meant the "best and renowned". He was given the nickname "Plato", derived from *platys,* because of his broad and strong shoulders. He was known for his good looks and charming disposition. He excelled in the study of music, mathematics, poetry and rhetoric. He fought in three wars and won an award for bravery. He never married.

Plato met Socrates in 407 BC at the age of 20 and since then was under his "hypnotic spell" (Durant 1939: Vol. II: 510). So decisive and persuasive was the influence that he abandoned the idea of becoming a poet. It was natural that the trial and execution of Socrates in 399 BC proved to be a turning point in Plato's life. The last discussion that Socrates held was immortalized in *Crito.* Plato could not attend the discussion on account of illness. It should be noted that Socrates was not the only one to be executed. There were others too. Both Anaxagoras (500–432 BC) and Protagoras (481–411 BC) were banished from Athens, and subsequently Aristotle too would have met a similar fate had he not gone into exile.

In 404 BC Athens witnessed an oligarchic revolution led by Plato's relatives. At this time Plato took an active part in politics, from which he withdrew later following the restoration of democracy, the death of Critias and Charmides, and the execution of Socrates. He left Athens and fled to Megara, where he took refuge with Euclid (300–260 BC), the renowned geometrician. From Megara he went to Egypt to study mathematics and the historical traditions of the priests. He returned to Athens in 395 BC and for the next few years fought for the city of Corinth. In 387 BC he visited the Pythagorean philosopher, mathematician and political leader Archytas at Taras in the south of Italy.

In 386 BC, on returning to Athens, Plato's friends gifted him a recreation spot named after its local hero Academus, or Hecademus. It was here that Plato established his Academy, which became a seat of higher learning and intellectual pursuits in Greece for the next one hundred years. The academy was not the first of its kind, for there were others, like the Pythagorean school of Crotona established in 520 BC and the School of Isocrates in 392 BC, but it was perhaps the most well-known.

The Academy was initially a religious group dedicated to the worship of Muses and its leader Apollo. The academy, like the Pythagorean School admitted women. Mathematics which included arithmetic and advanced geometry, astronomy, music, law, and philosophy were the main subjects for study. The importance of mathematics was clear from the inscription at the portals of the academy, "medeis ageometrtos eisito", or "let no one without geometry enter here". "It is noteworthy that modern Platonists, with few exceptions are ignorant of mathematics, in spite of the immense importance Plato attached to arithmetic and geometry, and the immense influence they had on his philosophy" (Russell 1961: 146). The close link between mathematics and philosophy that Plato began was followed by others, like Hobbes and Jeremy Bentham (1748–1832).

The Academy concretized the possibility of a science of knowledge with which one could reform the world. Plato saw in the academy a training school for future philosophic rulers. The *Republic,* composed at this time, served as its prospectus (Foster 1975: 34). Teaching in the Academy was imparted through lectures, Socratic dialectics and problem-solving situations. For Plato, the search for truth was not through mere instruction and theoretical knowledge, but with the guidance of an advanced mind. Through the academy, Plato kept alive the Socratic legacy. In course of time the Academy also became the prototype for subsequent universities and institutions of higher learning.

> The founding of the Academy is a turning point in Plato's life and in some ways the most memorable event in the history of European science. It was the culmination of his efforts. It was a permanent institution for the pursuit of science by original research (Taylor 1926: 5).

Plato devoted the bulk of his time and energies in organizing and managing the Academy. In 367 BC he visited Sicily on the invitation of Dion in order to make the late king Dionysius' nephew and heir, Dionysius II, a philosopher king. However, Dionysius resented Plato's assertion that geometry held the key to statecraft, forcing Plato to return home. In 361 BC Plato made another visit, with a view to securing the recall of Dion, now in exile, and to bring about reconciliation between Dion and Dionysius II. Plato was sold as a slave and was released only after the payment of a ransom.

Plato spent the last years of his life at the Academy, teaching and instructing. He died in 347 BC while attending the wedding feast of one of his students. As merry making continued past midnight, Plato decided to catch up with some sleep, retiring to a corner in the house, never to wake up. In the morning the revellers realized that he had died. On hearing the news of his death, the whole of Athens came to pay respects to one of its most distinguished and erudite citizens.

PLATO'S CORPUS

Plato's works include the *Apology of Socrates*, 23 genuine and 11 disputed dialogues, and 13 letters. Though the exact dates could not be fixed for the various writings, they have been roughly divided into four periods: (a) the period Plato came into contact with Socrates till his trip to Sicily. During this time he wrote *Apology, Crito, Enthypro, Laches, Lysis, Charmides, Protagoras* and the first book of the *Republic*. These were generally described as Socratic dialogues; (b) the transitional period in which Plato's theory of ideas emerged were in the dialogues like *Meno, Gorgias, Enthydemus, Cratylus, Lesser Hippias, Greater Hippias, Ion and Menexenus;* (c) the period of maturity in which the dialogues *Phaedo, Symposium, Phaedrus* and books two to 10 of the *Republic* were written; and (d) the last one included the *Statesman* and the *Laws*, dialogues totally devoid of Socrates' influence.

Apology was an imaginative and satirical version of Socrates' defence trial. It was noteworthy that Gandhi translated this tract into Gujarati. The basic premise of *Apology* was that Socrates had a divine mission to philosophize and elevate his soul, and encourage others to do the same. *Crito* explained the question and extent of political obligation and disobedience. *Enthypro* stated that service to the divine holiness was a noble activity which would elevate the soul. *Phaedo* presented a rational case for the immortality of the soul. *Charmides* explained the idea of self-knowledge or the Socratic dictum of "know thyself" and considered temperance or self-control as the key to maintaining one's equilibrium. *Laches* explored the meaning and definition of courage. *Protagoras* contained the views of the Sophist Protagoras, contrasting them with those of Socrates, a theme continued in *Lesser Hippias* and *Greater Hippias*. The latter explained that good had nothing to do with values that were pleasant and useful, an idea propagated by the Sophists. *Meno* continued with the idea of teaching virtue, as stated in *Protagoras. Menexenus* was a critique of the Periclean "Golden Age".

In *Gorgias,* Plato passionately pleaded for the need to adhere to one's Conscience. He dismissed the idea that art was a matter of expediency. *Symposium* explained the concept of Love or Eros, the possibility of transcending a desire for material objects and developing a passion for Beauty in its super-sensuous form. It also explored the nature of Forms as objects of mystic contemplation by the immortal soul. *Timaeus* examined the origin of life in the imaginary continent of Atlantis. Here, God was seen as an intelligent and effective force providing order in the world. *Philebus* focused on ethics and good life.

The *Republic,* the *Statesman (Politicus)* and the *Laws* were Plato's major works in political philosophy. The *Republic* was an amalgam of Plato's ideas in the field of ethics, metaphysics, philosophy and politics. Its basic theme was justice and the benefits that accrued from being just. The *Statesman* defended the superiority of the rule of law as opposed to personal dictatorship. Where a sovereign law existed, limited monarchy was better than democracy, but in its absence sovereign democracy was better than an irresponsible autocratic rule of one or a few. Plato defined a statesman as one who was entitled to rule without laws and the consent of his subjects, for he knew what was best for them, similar to the idea in the *Republic.* The *Laws* was the longest of Plato's dialogues. It regarded a mixed constitution as the best, for it moderated between the two extremes—despotism and freedom. This phase of Plato was similar to that of Aristotle. Though Aristotle rejected Plato's *Republic,* he accepted most of the arguments of the *Laws.* It is for this reason that Aristotle's "ideal state is always Plato's second best" (Sabine 1973: 99). However, the tone of both the *Republic* and the *Laws* was authoritarian and hierarchical.

CONTEXT OF THE *REPUBLIC*

The *Republic,* concerning justice, the greatest and most well-known work of Plato, was written in the form of a dialogue, a method of great importance in clarifying questions and establishing truth. It was one of the finest examples of the dialectical method as stated and first developed by Socrates. Though Socrates did not provide a theoretical exposition of the method, he established a clear-cut pattern of dialectical reasoning for others to follow. He placed dialectics in the service of ethics, defining virtue as a basis for rational and moral transformation. He used the method to secure answers about human beings and society, and not nature. "Political philosophy emerged by way of an ethical question which nature could never answer; the problems of men were not strictly coterminous with the problems of nature" (Wolin 1960: 30).

The discussions in the *Republic* were conducted in a single room among Socrates, Cephalus and his son Polemarchus, Thrasymachus, Glaucon and Adeimantus. Cephalus, Polemarchus and Thrasymachus appeared in Book I, while the discussion in the later books was carried on by Socrates and Plato's two brothers. In fact, Socrates was the main spokesman.

The *Republic* in Greek meant "justice", and should not be understood in its Latin sense meaning "the state or the polity" (Barker 1964: 168). It began with the quest of understanding the Idea of Good, and explained how a perfect soul could be developed. Its core has been succinctly summarized as follows.

> Philosophy meant to him what it meant to his master. The Socratic philosophy, analyzed and formulated in the early dialogues, was not the study of nature or logic or metaphysics; it was the pursuit of wisdom, and to achieve wisdom would be to achieve human perfection, well being and happiness. This again meant not merely "caring for one's own soul" as an isolated individual, saving himself and leaving society to its fate. Human excellence, as Plato and Aristotle after him always maintained, is the excellence of an essentially social creature, a citizen. To produce this experience and consequent well being is the true end of the "Royal Art" of statesmanship. Hence the life of philosophy and the life of the active statesman ought not to be, as they appeared to Callicles, alternative careers, but a single life in which all the highest powers of man would find full expression. Society could be saved only by reuniting the two elements which had been drifting apart (Cornford 1945: xxiv).

The book explored the notion of justice and its realization within the individual and the state. It sketched a detailed picture of the polity and social institutions, with a view to attaining human excellence and perfection. It had an elaborate scheme of education, which led Rousseau to comment that it was hardly a political work, but the finest treatise on education ever written. It contained a detailed examination of the meaning of good life and outlined the means to achieve it.

> The *Republic* is a book which defies classification. It fits into none of the categories either of modern social studies or of modern social science. In it practically every side of Plato's philosophy is touched upon or developed, and its range of subject matter is such that it may

> be said to deal with the whole of human life. It has to do with the good man and the good life, which for Plato connoted life in a good state, and with the means for knowing what they are and for attaining them. And to a problem so general no side of individual or social activity is alien. Hence the *Republic* is not a treatise of any sort, nor does it belong to politics, or ethics, or economics, or psychology, though it includes all these, and more, for art and education and philosophy are not excluded (Sabine 1973: 52).

Anti-Democrat

A common perspective could be discerned in the political belief structures of Socrates, Plato and Aristotle. They were essentially aristocratic conservatives who spoke and defended the values, ways of life and attitudes of an aristocracy (noble families, the landed property owners and the warriors) that was on a decline. Though aware of the degeneration, they were keen on revitalizing and reforming the aristocracy so that it could once again become the basis of civic life. This was seen as the best way to counter the sweep of the democratic revolution led by traders, artisans and merchants, and the crass materialism and individualism that was slowly engulfing Athenian society. Plato equated democratization with moral corruption and degradation, and endeavoured to reform and revolutionize the general quality of human life. Athens of the fifth century BC was similar to England of the nineteenth century. Both had an aristocracy that enjoyed social status and wealth, but did not exercise a monopoly of political power. In both, the aristocracy had to demonstrate, had to acquire power by means of impeccable behaviour (Russell 1961: 126).

The *Republic* was an indictment of the Athenian way of life and its vibrant participatory democratic institutions. Plato dismissed the Athenian practice of happy versatility, whereby every Greek male adult could participate in the political process and offer a political opinion, as amateurism. He attacked democracy for another reason—the incompetence and ignorance of politicians, for that gave rise to factionalism, extreme violence, and partisan politics, which were the causes of political instability. Moreover, democracy did not tolerate highly gifted persons, a view that was reinforced by the execution of Socrates. Plato blamed the restored democracy in Athens for the death of Socrates. However, he neglected the fact that Socrates was close to Critias and Alcibiades, two of the 30 tyrants who passed the death sentence, and was also given an option to go into exile, which he refused to avail. It was Socrates who chose to face trial and accept the foregone death sentence.

> Nothing can be more sublime than the bearing of Socrates during and after his trial, and this sublimity must not be sentimentalized by the representing of Socrates as the victim of an ignorant mob. His death was almost a Hegelian tragedy, a conflict in which both sides were right (Kitto 1951: 153–154).

Plato deliberately ignored these facts in order to build his case for a rule by a small group of privileged and extraordinary persons endowed with esoteric wisdom. Plato's aversion to the democratic experiment, which reached its zenith during the time of Pericles (493–429 BC), was partly intellectual and partly personal. Though he was introduced to democratic ideas by his stepfather Pyrilampas, a close friend of Pericles, he remained an aristocrat both by birth and conviction. These were reinforced by Critias and Charmides.

Plato wrote at a time when Athens was at the crossroads after defeat in the Peloponnesian War. The age of Pericles with all its glory and achievements had paled into insignificance due to the defeat of Athens in the Peloponnesian War (431–404 BC). Athens under Pericles has becomes the political, cultural and intellectual centre of Greece. However, the defeat of Athens in the War was due to an error in military strategy. Victorious Sparta did not fare any better as an imperial power, for it lacked the training and expertise to handle foreign affairs, leading to the rise of Persia within a short period of time. Plato mistakenly castigated Athenian democracy for the defeat. It should be noted that Athenian democracy was limited, for it debarred aliens, slaves and women from participating in the political process. In spite of the narrowness, it was the "fullest in the directness and equality with which all the citizens control legislation and administer public affairs" (Durant 1939: Vol. II: 266). It remains till today an example of a vibrant, participatory democracy. Rousseau resurrected its ideals when he criticized the English representative democracy as freedom of the English people once in five years.

The clash between Athens and Sparta, the two power centres at that time, was depicted by Plato as representing two opposing ideologies, competing political systems and different lifestyles. In many ways Athenian-Spartan rivalry resembled the cold war between the United States and the former Soviet Union after the Second World War. Athens was individualistic, excelling in literary pursuits, highly creative, democratic and open. Sparta on the other hand was statist, regimented, oligarchic and militaristic. Plato concluded that Sparta's military victory was due to its political and social system. He tried to infuse the communitarian spirit of Sparta into the individualistic Athenian society, and temper democracy with aristocratic values. However, the model that he sketched in the *Republic*, far from integrating the two models, was highly holistic, elitist, regimented and authoritarian. Instead of being objective,

> Plato is always concerned to advocate views that will make people accept what he thinks virtuous; he is hardly ever intellectually honest, because he allows himself to judge doctrines by their social consequences. Even about this, he is not honest; he pretends to follow the argument and to be judging by purely theoretical standards, when in fact he is twisting the discussion so as to lead to a virtuous result. He introduced this vice into philosophy where it has persisted ever since. It was probably largely hostility to the Sophists that gave this character to

> his dialogues. One of the defects of all philosophers since Plato is that their inquiries into ethics proceed on the assumption that they already know the conclusion to be reached (Russell 1961: 95).

Critic of Sophism

Plato belittled the Sophists in general, though he treated Protogoras and Gorgias (490/85–398? BC) with great respect. Sophism was a rival school of the Socratic tradition. Philosophically it stood for relativism, skepticism, individualism, and humanism, and was generally acknowledged as the founding school of democracy and social change. Following the proposition of Protogoras that "man is the measure of all things", the Sophists opposed aristocratic and conservative values, and in this sense were democratic.

Plato dubbed the Sophists as "teachers of spiritual wares", criticized their utter disregard for absolute truth and imparting knowledge for a fee. The last charge was totally unjustified. The Sophists, unlike Plato, did not enjoy personal wealth, nor did they have students who made substantial donations. Interestingly, modern scholars and professors who never refuse a generous honorarium and salary have been more sympathetic to Plato than the Sophists (Russell ibid: 94)!

Plato denounced the Sophists for their oratorical and intellectual acrobatics, and teaching students to win arguments not through the power of reason, but with the help of the spoken word (explaining the origin of the word *sophistry*). Even Aristotle condemned them for their lack of first-hand political experience, making them inadept and incompetent teachers of politics.

The Sophists laid the foundations of systematic education for the young, and analyzed ethical questions with the help of reason. Ironically, both these aspects influenced Socrates/Plato, much as the latter denigrated the Sophists.

Philosophical Influences

Besides his admiration for the Spartan model, Plato was philosophically influenced by some of its predecessors and contemporaries. One definite inspiration was Pythagoras (582–500 BC), from whom Plato borrowed many ideas like the importance of mathematics, belief in other-worldliness and in the immortality of the human soul, sexual equality, and the idea of the philosopher ruler. Pythagoras believed that renunciation of earthly goods and purification from sensuality held the key to salvation. He also believed in the teaching of Orphics, namely the transmigration of souls.

A biographer of Pythagoras, Iamblichus, pointed out that Pythagoras travelled widely, studying the teachings of the Egyptians, Assyrians and

Hindu Brahmins in India. Herodutus informed us that Pythagoras borrowed the doctrine of the transmigration of souls from the Egyptians, although this was quite unlikely since the latter had no belief in it. On the contrary, it was quite possible that he was influenced by India, since his religious, mathematical and philosophical ideas were known in India in the sixth century. Interestingly, Pythagoras, like the Jains and the Buddhists, extended the principle of non-violence to all life forms, and was strictly vegetarian. The Pythagorean Theorem of the hypotenuse was known to the Indians since Vedic times (Rawlinson 1937: 5). In Pythagoras and Plato, "we find a decisive break with the Greek tradition of rationalism and humanism. The mystic tradition is definitely un-Greek in its character"(Radhakrishnan 1974: 135). Pythagoras also founded a society whose members were bound by definite religious and ethical rules of conduct. In fact, Plato's ideal state in the *Republic* was patterned after this society.

From Heraclitus (544–484 BC), Plato realized that nothing was permanent in this sensory world. Things constantly changed, modifying themselves into new shapes and forms, captured graphically in the statement "from everything One is made and from One, everything". Heraclitus believed that the essential harmony hidden in nature eventually manifested itself through harmony in the opposites. Heraclitus was the most profound of the pre-Socratic thinkers. He taught three things: eternal change, unity, and the inviolability of the laws of the world order (Zeller 1955: 64). While Heraclitus taught the notion of perpetual flux, the search for permanence and belonging began with Parmenides (540–470 BC), who said nothing changed.

Parmenides dismissed sense objects as illusions, and regarded the "One" as the only real thing which was infinite and indivisible. Unlike Heraclitus, he did not think of the "One" as the unity of opposites, since there were no opposites. It was not God. He thought of it as material and extended and spoke of it as a sphere. Since the whole of it was present everywhere, it could not be divided. Through reason one could comprehend this Being, while the senses were the source of all errors.

Interestingly, both Heraclitus and Parmenides distrusted the senses as sources of evidence and relied more on thought, but they did it in opposite ways. For the former, the senses gave an illusion of a permanent being and that fire was the basic substance behind it. For the latter, sensation was deceptive. It came and passed away. What lay behind it was the unchangeable being. In Plato's theory of Ideas, the influence of both Heraclitus and Parmenides was apparent, for he assigned supremacy to the world of Being that could be discerned and comprehended by intellect and reason, relegating the world of becoming that was perceived by the senses to a secondary position.

The most persuasive influence was that of Socrates, from whom Plato accepted the teleological rather than a mechanical explanation of the world and of perceiving political phenomena within an ethical framework. It has to be noted that the Greeks did not perceive society in a compartmentalized way. Politically, they did not draw a distinction between state and society, and within society, its different spheres. Holism permeated not only the social and political organizations, but also the way knowledge was comprehended. Philosophy, to begin with, included all branches of human knowledge, the natural and the social sciences. It was not merely an academic exercise, but also a way of life, which was why they advocated a lifelong pursuit of knowledge. It was the broadness of knowledge that the Greeks emphasized, rather than the in-depth specialization which we see in the modern world. Philosophy meant not only the study of man in society, but also the study of the universe and nature. Most of the philosophers of the ancient world would be envied in modern times for the range and breadth that they covered. They were truly encyclopedic minds. Their achievements were astounding at a time when there were no printing presses, universities or computers.

Plato and Aristotle inherited from Socrates the belief in the existence of absolute standards and the need to differentiate right from wrong. They

> ... advocated correct forms of human conduct; and that this seems plainly incompatible with ... the principal task of philosophers is to assess the reasons for and against, and clarify the implications of possible lines of choice, not to indicate what is right ... philosophy has a double task to perform: to examine and, in particular, to criticize the presupposi-tions of value judgements made or implied by men and their acts (Berlin 1978: 19).

Accepting the Socratic dicta "virtue is knowledge" and "a life unexamined is not worth living", Plato argued that wrong deeds had their origin in ignorance, whereas knowledge led to right actions and happiness. Knowledge for Plato represented a vision, transcendence from the world of appearance to the world of Reality. This process was described as the "conversion of the soul", to ensure that the power that existed in a soul was turned in the right direction. However, attainment of knowledge did not mean leading a life of contemplation, for it had to be combined with service to the community. Thus, for Plato, there was a societal dimension to individual excellence.

> The fundamental idea of the *Republic* came to Plato in the form of his master's doctrine that virtue is knowledge. His own unhappy political experience reinforced the idea and crystallized it in the founding of the Academy to inculcate the spirit of true knowledge as the foundation for a philosophical statecraft (Sabine 1973: 53).

Knowledge and Opinion

Plato differentiated between the intelligible world and the world of the senses. The former was the world of Being or Beauty or Forms, and the latter the world of becoming or beautiful or opinion. The world that we see, touch and experience through our senses was not real, but a copy, for things constantly changed and were fluid. Though its existence could be experienced in daily life, it was not real. The Real world of true things was the world of "Ideas", which was perfect, eternal, immutable and fixed. It was never created and had always existed from the beginning in a perfect way. It was independent of all things and immune to the changes that occurred in the sensory world. All that one experienced was because of the influence of the world of Idea upon matter, the other principle in the universe. Matter was not the "real" world but an impression, a raw material to receive the Idea. Therefore all changes and distortions in the sensory world were due to matter and not because of the Idea. In *Timaeus*, Plato explained that the world of senses was created by "an architect", the Demiurge, who brought the ideal world and matter together—without, however, explaining how the three came together.

Plato described the working of the human mind and the way it acquired knowledge with the help of: (a) the allegory of the Cave; (b) the metaphor of the Divided Line; and (c) the doctrine of Forms. He believed that individuals have different capacities for learning and attaining knowledge. He also asserted that most of us live in the darkness of the Cave, which represented the realm of beliefs. At the mouth of the cave was daylight, symbolizing knowledge. This was akin to the Hindu belief. The teacher or the guru meant one who helped a person to attain enlightenment from darkness. Martin Heideggar (1889-1976) pointed out that Plato, through the allegory of the Cave, intended to state the essence of education and the meaning of Being. Moreover, Plato was also the first to emphasize the problem of universals, when he stated that there was a Form or Idea for everything that exists in the real world.

PHILOSOPHER RULER

The theory of the philosopher ruler was the linchpin of Plato's Ideal State. It was derived from the conviction that the philosopher had the knowledge, intellect and training to govern. The innumerable references to the immortality of the soul implied that philosophy was the only key to heaven (Berki 1977: 55). Ruling, like any other task, required skills and qualifications, and its aim was the general well-being of all. A good ruler was one who not only preserved the lives of his subjects, but also transformed them as human beings.

> When the supreme power in man coincides with the greatest wisdom and temperance, then the best laws and the best constitution comes into being; but in no other way ... . Until Philosophers become kings in this world, or till that we now call kings and rulers really and truly become philosophers, and political power and philosophy thus come into the same hands ... there is no other road to real happiness, either for society or the individual (Plato 1955: 282).

No one, before or after Plato, gave governance the importance and worth it rightly commanded, nor did anyone convincingly argue a case for philosophers acquiring political power in the best interests of human society as Plato did. The philosopher ruler was the right person to govern, for he would be least enthused about acquiring power for self-aggrandizement. Good governance precluded mediocrity, chance, accident and nepotism and focus on who ruled. Existing states were imperfect because philosophers were not rulers. The Ideal State was a yardstick to judge political practices. Thus, "the ideas of Plato provide the first full mirroring of the dramatic encounter between the ordering vision of political philosophy and the phenomenon of politics" (Wolin 1960: 34).

Who is a Philosopher?

On Glaucon's insistence, Socrates defined a philosopher as one who loved wisdom, had a passion for knowledge,and was always curious and eager to learn. On seeking clarification as to whether theatre fans and music lovers qualified, Socrates underlined that a philosopher was one who loved Truth. Furthermore, he distinguished between *Beauty* and *beautiful things*. Beauty was a single thing which manifested itself in the form of a beautiful face, a beautiful colour, or a beautiful voice. These represented different things but shared a common quality that of beauty itself. Theatre fans and music lovers could appreciate beautiful things, but were incapable of seeing and understanding the nature of Beauty itself. A person who understood Beauty itself had *knowledge*, and a person who saw only beautiful things had mere *beliefs* or *opinions*.

Socrates then pointed out that knowledge ought to have an "object". If one claimed to know something, then that something, one knew must exist. If one knew it perfectly, then the thing ought to exist in the fullest possible sense. If it did not *really* exist, then one could not *really* know it. This was true of belief, except there was an important difference that the object of belief did not exist in the full sense; it was less than real than the object of knowledge. What might be beautiful in a given situation need not be so in another. The objects of knowledge could never have a dualistic consequence. Beauty itself could never be ugly, whereas beautiful things could be, depending on the situation. Following Socrates, Plato believed that the 'Ideal was Real'. "Throughout Plato's philosophy there is the same fusion of intellect and mysticism as in Pythagoras, but in the final culmination mysticism clearly has the upper hand" (Russell 1961: 141).

Why should Philosophers Rule?

A philosopher by his grasp of the Idea of Good was best qualified to rule, implying that knowledge could be obtained only by a select few who had the leisure and the material comforts. Plato shared the general Greek perception that leisure was essential for the pursuit of wisdom. A philosopher would be able to administer justice and act for the good of the community. He would have a good character, a calm disposition and a sound mind. He would have the qualities of a ruler, namely truthfulness, high-mindedness, discipline and courage. Undaunted by death, and being a lover of truth, he would be honest and forthright. He would not be petty or mean, being above physical and material pleasures. Devoid of emotional ties and economic considerations, he would be public-spirited and wise. Since the state was directed towards the highest and noblest ends:

> Good men will not consent to govern for cash or honours. They do want to be called mercenary for exacting a cash payment for the work of government, or thieves for making money on the side; and they will not work for honours, for they aren't ambitious...the worse penalty for refusal is to be governed by someone worse than themselves. That is what I believe, frightens honest men into accepting power, and they approach it not as if it were something desirable out of which they were going to do well, but as if it were something unavoidable which they cannot find anyone better or equally qualified to undertake. For in a city of good men there might well be as much competition to avoid power as there now is to get it, and it would be quite clear that the true ruler pursues his subjects' interest and not his own, constantly all wise men would prefer the benefit of this service at the hands of others rather than the labour of affording it to others themselves (Plato 1955: 89–90).

Adeimantus entered the discussion between Glaucon and Socrates. He disagreed with Socrates' conclusions, and claimed that philosophers could not possibly rule well, for the good philosophers that one saw around were useless to society, and the bad ones downright villains. Socrates agreed with this contention, but blamed society for being disrespectful of knowledge and wisdom by giving more weightage to success and wealth. Fearing debasement, a philosopher preferred to become a social outcast and live in an ivory tower. Politicians in societies were admired and respected not for their wisdom and goodness, but for their ability to flatter people and satisfy their basest desires and instincts. Just as a sick person sought the help of a doctor for cure, similarly a diseased polity must take the assistance of wise and noble rulers. A diseased polity was one where naked ambition, acquisitiveness and appetite subordinated wisdom, reason and temperance.

> Plato's political philosophy is a blend of rigorous social nihilism and political affirmation. The nihilism springs from his desire to cleanse the political state of all the influences he saw as erosive and destructive of political unity. The mission of the political community is the means whereby all the native powers and excellences of the individual are brought to fruition (Nisbet 1973: 25).

Plato insisted that politics and philosophy ought to be safe for one another. A philosopher ruler would make a wise legislator and frame laws in accordance with the Idea of Good. Statecraft was ultimately soulcraft, linking the political with the ethical (Taylor 1926: 131). For Plato, an Ideal State ruled by the philosopher ruler was a divine institution perfectly worthy of emulation and imitation. Political philosophy became a practical enterprise, in which various possibilities of establishing a good society in light of the philosopher's vision of Good was the aim. The Idea of Good was the highest form of knowledge. It could be compared with the Sun, for it illuminated all intelligible and knowable things.

Plato described an Ideal State as one based on timeless and unchanging principles, suggesting that an ideal pattern existed which could be discerned and employed to reform a diseased polity, and transform it into a thing of beauty and health. He was convinced that the totality of political phenomena could be comprehensible to the human mind and malleable to human art (Wolin 1960: 35). He implied that political order was highly malleable and could be moulded in order to receive the right imprint or motif. Thus, political philosophy became architectonic in nature, establishing a duality

> ... between the form-giving role of political thought and the form-receiving function of political "matter". Political knowledge, like all true knowledge, was essentially a science of order, one that traced the proper relationship between men, indicated the sources of evil in the community, and prescribed the overarching pattern for the whole. It aimed not at describing political phenomena, but at transfiguring them in light of a vision of the Good ... . The effect of this was to impart to political philosophy *qua* projective quality. The political philosopher, by an act of thought strove to project a more perfect order into future time ... . Thus at the centre of the enterprise of political theory was what an imaginative system ought to be and what it might become ... no one has ever surpassed Plato in insisting upon the moral urgency and centrality of political vision (Wolin ibid: 35).

Philosophic Absolutism

Socrates assigned supremacy of reason untrammelled by laws through the idea of philosophic rule. He was confident that philosophic rule would eschew tyranny or force, for that would be anathema to reason. A good ruler, like a good doctor, could change prescriptions in view of the disease. Any attempt to bind the rulers to laws and procedures could stifle creative innovations. The only recognizable limits to philosophic rule were the following: (a) To maintain the size of the state, (b) To watch over the distribution of wealth to ensure that there would be no extreme poverty or excess wealth. Plato warned that if every city became a city of two, one of the rich and the other of the poor, it would be unstable, (c) To retain the prescribed system of education, for it is geared to creating and sustaining the Ideal State. Any change would undermine the principles of the state and, (d) To frame laws that would conform as closely as possible to the philosophic ideal. Plato's attitude to change was peculiar and contradictory. On the one hand, he desired freedom to enquire and think about the nature of the universe and religion. On the other hand, he was extremely suspicious of change. On the one hand, he was desirous of pursuing scientific investigations and contemplation that would revolutionize men's perceptions, outlooks and even their political systems. On the other hand, he was in constant search for principles that could guarantee social and political stability. He never fully resolved this contradiction (Sibley 1981: 78). Significantly, Plato's dilemma could be found in the determinism of Marx.

Plato's rationale for conferring absolute power to the enlightened philosopher ruler was essentially to achieve two unrelated aims. The first was to avoid tyranny and caprice, the second being the welfare of the community. Strict control over education, family life, property and living arrangements ensured that the ruler did not become self-serving, imperious and dictatorial. Plato was confident that austerity and self-denial would lead to the cultivation of temperance and endurance, making the ruler selfless. He saw philosophic rule as being beneficial to both the ruler and the subject. He was confident that it would promote the happiness of the entire community. By happiness he meant harmony, efficiency and moral goodness.

> It was Plato's belief that a selfless ruling group dedicated not to politics but to philosophy, would solve the problem of absolute power. In existing societies, where the rulers were selected by irrational methods, absolute power was bound not only to corrupt the rulers, but to degrade the citizenry as well. The citizen of the Platonic community, however, would be benefited by the exercise of absolute power, because, in the last analysis, he would be compelled and controlled not by a personal power but by the impersonal agents of timeless truth. The subject was to be under "the same principle as his superior, who is himself governed by the divine element within him". The truth superior over ruler and ruled alike was by definition in the true interests of both ... political power becomes etheralized into principle (Wolin 1960: 56–57).

Criticism of the Philosopher Ruler

Plato denied the participation of the average person in politics and decision making processes. He defined citizenship not as participation, but in terms of the shared "benefits flowing from that principle" (Wolin ibid: 47). To allow participation would be "to pave the way for government by opinion" (Wolin ibid: 58). By discounting the opinion of the average person, Plato tried to play safe and prevent any opposition, criticism, dissent or even disobedience. He justified it on the grounds that these lead to factionalism and particularism, whereas a good society should promote the common good. However, this argument in itself was erroneous, for reasonable and moderate levels of dissent and criticism were essential for growth and development. This was as much true for individuals as it was for a state. Plato's arguments were similar to those who advocate army rule in contemporary times.

Plato rejected majoritarianism and popular participation on the rounds that the ordinary person did not have the capacity to comprehend absolute truth and the Idea of Good. This proposition could be questioned on the grounds whether anyone comprehended the whole of the absolute truth. Truth is, at best, relative or as "I see it", which could be at variance with other versions. What happens if claims of absolute truth were falsified (Popper: 1963)? What were the ways of ensuring that the collectivity actually benefited from the knowledge that the philosopher ruler claimed to be in possession of? In a similar fashion, Kuhn's seminal work convincingly argued that what was perceived as truth was always determined by the dominant view at a particular time and place. This he called a paradigm, as scientific enquiry was impossible without it, but he also acknowledged the transient nature of any such paradigm when the old science was replaced by a new one, with a transitional period of disequilibrium.

However elevating and ennobling a vision Plato offered in terms of ruling, the fact remained that any state (including the one governed by the best and the wisest) would be diverse, which ought to be represented and respected. A state that was intolerant to divergence of opinion would not only be unjust, but also be inherently unstable. To ignore the political view of the humblest of citizens and deny avenues for participation was not only patronizing and authoritarian, but also unhealthy. The strength of a political system was derived from the participation of its citizen members, for it ensured the accommodation of diverse interests and opinions through consensus. A political society that strived to achieve a greater degree of unity by being insensitive to diversities would be inherently weak. "A political judgement... is 'true' when it is public, not public when it accords to some standard external to politics" (Wolin 1960: 63).

The Platonic ideal was criticized by Aristotle for confusing unity with harmony; if a political community was tightly organized and unified, it would cease to be a political association. The essence of a state was its diversity, making it different from other organizations. The state and the family represented two different kinds of organization, and both ought to remain that way without either imitating the other. In view of the nature of the state and governance, it would be better for a ruler to be worldly wise than to be wise in the world of ideas. Even a philosopher ruler would be better off by being receptive to the views and perceptions of others, instead of merely acting upon his vision of Truth (Beatty 1976: 575).

It was unimportant who governed. The key issue was to minimize misrule and prevent misuse and abuse of power (Popper 1945: Vol. I). Plato's unflinching opinion that absolute power was safe in the hands of the philosopher was misplaced. Concentration of power would have to be prevented, for it generated vice. Unchecked power, even wielded by the best and the wisest, would be intoxicating, for power corrupts, and absolute power corrupts absolutely. The need for institutional and impersonal checks against untrammelled power was absolutely imperative for the well-being and welfare of the community.

In the *Laws,* Plato made a theoretical shift. The end of the political society remained total unity as espoused in the *Republic,* but this was to be attained through an elaborate system of legal regulations and the rule of law. However, a Nocturnal Council consisting of the wisest would make laws regulating every aspect of life, from ante-natal exercises to funerals, making the state as regimented as the one projected in the *Republic.* The idea that a vision of good must be the basis of ruling remained, but the means to secure the objective changed. Plato was also more receptive to the idea of the wisdom of the collective will and the sovereign law. However, statecraft as soulcraft, which for Plato could be realized only in a community, one in sentiment and feeling, remained the underlying idea in both the tracts (Wolin 1960: 63).

Feasibility of the Ideal State

In recent years, there have been doubts about Plato's seriousness in implementing the Ideal State. Strauss (1964) considered the *Republic* as the greatest critique of idealism ever written. It was a satire written with the purpose of demonstrating the limits of what was politically feasible. This was because the ideal state was unrealistic and unrealizable, for the philosopher was not a natural ruler and governing was thrust upon him in the larger interest of the community. Therefore "... the *Republic* conveys the broadest and deepest analysis of political idealism ever made" (Strauss ibid: 127).

Randall (1970: 116–165) pointed out that the *Republic* was a comic irony written with the purpose of demonstrating that the Spartan model was absurd and unworkable. Bloom (1968), agreeing with Strauss, contended that:

> Political idealism is the most destructive of human passions and the *Republic* is the greatest critique of political idealism ever written .... The *Republic* serves to moderate the extreme passion for justice by showing the limits of what can be demanded and expected of the city (Bloom ibid: 408–410).

Strauss and Bloom asserted that Plato did not show a relationship between the two aspects of justice, namely psychic harmony and happiness *(eudaemonia),* at least in the case of the philosopher ruler. There was no proof that ruling would promote the happiness of the philosopher ruler, nor were there compelling and convincing reasons for the philosopher to renounce a life of contemplation and take to ruling. They challenged the traditional viewpoint of Barker (1964: 277–284), Cassirer (1946: 70–73), Cornford (1945: xxxv), Nettleship (1967: 211–215), Sabine (1973: 51–56) and Sinclair (1951: 57–59) which contended that the philosopher ruled out of a sense of duty to do good to others, and regarding the good of others as extended self-interest.

Sabine, explaining further, pointed out that Plato made two fundamental assumptions which were interrelated. These were: (a) that government ought to be an art depending on exact knowledge; and (b) that society existed for the mutual satisfaction of needs by persons whose capacities supplement one another. While the first was intrinsic to human personality, the second referred to education and experience. In view of these two assumptions, Plato was convinced that if ruling was entrusted to experts who could be trained, then governance would be above mediocrity and expediency. Political leadership was both an art and a science. Good governance would confer a dynasty of political rulers who could meet every contingency, rather than have occasional premiers of the people. It would eliminate factionalism and petty groupism in politics. Ruling, for Plato, had to be in accordance with the true dictates of moulding and transforming the state and individuals in light of an absolute standard. Political philosophy had to prevent incompetence and knavery in public life. The philosophers' vision of the Forms and Good was a moralizing experience, and that explained their commitment to the Ideal State of which they were the architects (Vlastos 1968). It supplied the state with an active probing critical intelligence (Klosko 1986: 165). For Plato every individual had a social side. Besides ensuring his own good, a philosopher must also be useful to society, for it was only within a society that an individual realized his true self. The philosophers ruled in order to prevent victimization at the hands of inferior rulers (Barker 1964: 234–240; Cassirer 1946: 73; and Sabine 1973: 59–61).

JUSTICE

An ideal state for Plato possessed the four cardinal virtues of wisdom, courage, temperance or self-control and justice. It would have wisdom because its rulers were persons of knowledge, courage because its warriors were brave, self-control because of the harmony that pervaded the societal matrix due to a common agreement as to who ought to rule, and finally, justice of doing one's job for which one was naturally fitted without interfering with other people. For Plato, the state was the Ideal, of which justice was the reality. Justice was the principle on which the state had to be founded and a contribution made towards the excellence of the city.

The central question of the *Republic* was the meaning of justice or right conduct or morality. It did not refer to legality (Berki 1977; Cross and Woozley 1951). Plato critically examined contemporary views on justice and then defined the concept. Subsequently, he elaborated the application of the concept and its realization within an individual and the state. Justice in the individual was defined analogously to justice in the state.

Different Definitions of Justice

The text opens with a discussion between Socrates and Cephalus on the subject of old age and wealth. Cephalus, old and prosperous, pointed out that wealth by itself did not make one happy, but provided comforts that made life easy. It enabled one to lead a good life and to do what was morally right. Cephalus defined justice as telling the truth, being honest in word and deed and paying one's debts.

Socrates dismissed the argument effortlessly by pointing out that in some cases it might be harmful to speak the truth or return one's belongings, through examples like returning weapons to a mad person, or telling the truth when it was better to conceal it. He did not show that honesty in word and deed was not justice, but rather that such honesty could be harmful. Since all his listeners tacitly accepted the (unstated) argument that justice had to be beneficial, or at least not harmful, he was able to persuade them that Cephalus' view would not be acceptable.

At this point, Cephalus gave up, but the argument was continued by his son Polemarchus. By altering the definition provided by Cephalus, Polemarchus pointed out that justice meant "giving each man his due" or "what was fitting". In short, justice was "doing the right thing", which he qualified to mean doing "good to friends and harm to enemies". Polemarchus reiterated an acceptable part of Greek morality as evident from Solon's prayer, "May I be pleasant to my friends, hateful to my enemies", though this certainly contradicted the teaching in the *Sermon on the Mount*.

With the help of three arguments, Socrates demolished the views of Polemarchus. First, helping friends might also involve ignoble acts like stealing and telling a lie. Second, the idea of being good to friends and bad to enemies was difficult to apply, because a person could make mistakes about one's friends and enemies. A supposed friend might not actually be a friend in reality. Moreover, a person who could do the maximum help could also do the maximum harm. Third, a just person should not harm anyone because those who get injured become even more unjust. Justice was human excellence, and a just person could not harm anybody, including the self. Once again, Socrates did not disprove the concept, but only its application. He merely persuaded Polemarchus to accept what he was saying. Polemarchus could have retorted that spanking a child or a pet dog might not be harmful (from which he refrained, perhaps out of civility). In fact, nowhere did Socrates provide a proper and clear description of Good (Bluhm 1965: 77).

The discussions continued with an interjection from Thrasymachus, a Sophist. After making sure that he would be paid a fee, he agreed and defined justice or right as the interests of the stronger party, namely the ruler. While the strong made all the rules, the weak—the subjects—merely obeyed them. Thrasymachus explained his notion as follows.

> Each type of government enacts laws that are in its own interest, a democracy democratic laws, a tyranny tyrannical ones and so on; and in enacting these laws they make it quite plain that what is "right" for their subjects is what is in the interest of themselves, the rulers, and if anyone deviates from this he is punished as a lawbreaker and "wrongdoer". That is what I mean when I say that "right" is the same thing in all states, namely the interest of the established government; and government is the strongest element in each state, and so if we argue correctly we see that "right" is always the same, the interest of the stronger party (Thrasymachus: cited in Plato 1955: 78).

Socrates responded by pointing out that rulers might make mistakes by not being able to identify their interests and frame laws contrary to their advantage, thus putting Thrasymachus in a tough spot. Instead of following Clitophon's advice to redefine justice as "whatever the strong believe to be in their interest", Thrasymachus made things difficult by charging off in the wrong direction. He replied that rulers by definition could not make mistakes, and if they did so they could no longer remain rulers. He asserted that an unjust life was stronger and better than a just one. Thrasymachus conceded that justice ought not to be in the interest of the stronger, but that was the normal practice and there were plenty of examples to substantiate it.

Through a series of analogies, Socrates showed that justice was *not* the advantage of the stronger, for the ruler's duty was to serve the interests of the people. A ruler's position was similar to that of a doctor, teacher or shepherd. Any art, which included ruling, should be for the welfare of the object, and *not* the subject.

By defining justice as the interest of the stronger, Thrasymachus earned a place in the history of political theory. The fact that Socrates was unable to refute the argument was perhaps an acknowledgement of the fact that it was the strongest who set the standards in society.

Glaucon and Adeimantus were still unconvinced with the arguments furnished by Socrates on the causes of injustice. They argued that individuals were not willingly just, but only out of necessity, in which case injustice was better than justice. Glaucon pointed out that all customary rules relating to religion and morality were imposed on individuals by social sanction, which originated in human intelligence and will. They were based on a tacit consent of the parties. These were conventions which could be altered, changed or repealed by legislative bodies. A law emerged whereby the strong and the weak contract with each other; the strong agreed not to inflict wrong, and the weak accepted not to suffer injustice.

Adeimantus, extending Glaucon's argument, pointed out that existing religious values and education taught the young that injustice was good because of the rewards it brought, thus convincing them that the ideal would be injustice clothed in good reputation. Thus, while "Thrasymachus concentrated on the role of power in defining values, Glaucon was concerned to emphasize the importance of law in any consideration of justice" (Hacker 1961: 28). Both Glaucon and Adeimantus challenged Socrates to show that justice was intrinsically good and reflected an inward quality of the soul, rather than the rewards and good reputation it brought.

At this point Socrates became more constructive, and replied with the help of examples. Using the method of large letters, he said that anything written in big and bold, in contrast to something written in a small size, would receive more attention. Similarly, in order to understand the meaning of justice, one could see its application at the level of the state and then in the individual. Both Glaucon and Adeimantus agreed with this suggestion.

Justice in the State and Individual

Socrates examined the origin of states and cities, and pointed out that they arose out of two reasons. The first was mutual need, and the second, the differences in aptitudes of individuals. Mutual need led to reciprocal services, since the individual was not self-sufficient and depended on others for subsistence. Exchange of services necessitated division of labour and functional specialization, which was possible since individuals differed in their nature and aptitudes. Individuals could be trained to specialize and perform one particular task. Specialization was encouraged to bring about excellence and perfection. It was not to assign any kind of superiority or snobbery to one particular function. It was essentially to recognize and bring to fruition the uniqueness in every individual. Acceptance and organization of diverse human aptitudes would result in social benefit, cooperation and harmony.

Plato made two important points here. The first was that every individual was a functional unit, assigned a particular task with clear-cut obligations and privileges, which one was expected to perform diligently and meticulously. It also underlined the fact that none were born to render a specific function. Certain levels of training and skills were required. Moreover, since everybody would be involved in the performance of a socially required function, it would minimize, if not altogether eliminate, the probability of being a free rider or a shirker. Second, society was visualized as a harmonized, orderly whole, based on the recognition of individual talents and contributions. The functions of a society were broadly three—ruling, defence and production. The last one included all kinds of trades and crafts.

> Plato was the first to picture political society as a system of distinctive or differentiated roles ... each represented a necessary function; each was defined in terms of its contribution to sustaining the whole society: each bore rights, duties, expectations which provided definite guides and signposts for human behaviour and defined the place of the individual within the system. The harmonization and integration of these roles made a political society a functioning interdependent whole. To maintain it required a sharp demarcation among the three classes of the community ... no confusion of roles, no blurred identities. From Plato onwards, one of the distinctive marks of political philosophy was its approach to political society as a functioning system (Wolin 1960: 33).

Theory of Three Classes and Three Souls

Plato explained his arguments for differing individual capacities with the help of the theory of three classes and three souls, an idea borrowed from Pythagoras. He pointed out that every human soul had three qualities: rational, spirit and appetite, with justice as the fourth virtue, architectonic in nature, balancing and harmonizing the other three qualities. He took psychological disharmony among the constituent parts into consideration.

In each soul, one of these qualities would be the predominant faculty. Individuals in whom the rational faculty was predominant would constitute the ruling class, and the virtue of such a soul was wisdom. This soul, a lover of learning, had the power to comprehend the Idea of Good. Those in whom spirit was the predominant quality were the auxiliaries or warriors, and the virtue of such souls was courage, implying the ability to hold on to one's convictions and beliefs in adverse times. Together, the rulers and soldiers would constitute the guardian class. Socrates compared a spirited or *thymotic* individual to a watchdog, capable of great bravery, public spirit and anger while fighting strangers in defence of one's city. It indicated the willingness to sacrifice one's material desires for the sake of the common good. Such a soul was a lover of honour and victory. It was basically a political virtue necessary for the survival of a community and ought to be kept under control. *Thymos*, an ally of reason, was a distinct quality representing self-worth and dignity.

> Plato's *thymos* is therefore nothing other than the psychological seat of Hegel's desire for recognition ... . *Thymos* appears to be related to a good political order in some way, because it is the source of courage, public spiritedness, and a certain unwillingness to make moral compromises ... . A good political order ... must satisfy man's just desires for recognition of his dignity and worth (Fukuyama 1992: 165, 169–170).

Individuals whose souls were appetitive exhibited a fondness for material things. They were lovers of gain and money. These were the artisans, the producing class. The quality of such an appetitive soul was temperance, though Plato did not see temperance as an exclusive quality of the artisan class. He considered it as being necessary for all individuals. Using a Pythagorean analogy between a tuned string, a healthy body and an alert mind, Socrates considered a balanced individual as a just one. He reasoned that in the application of intelligence to activity of any kind, supreme wisdom was to know just when and where to stop. A fool or a quack lacked this knowledge. The underlying idea was that in everything it was important to ensure the "just right" in order to achieve happiness.

Though Plato took into account the role of spirit and appetite in human behaviour, he was convinced that reason must ultimately control and direct emotions and passions. This explained why the rational soul embodied in the philosopher ruler would govern. Unlike Socrates, Plato took into account the irrational aspects of the soul, for the individual was not exclusively rational.

> Thus Plato's conception of virtue centres on psychological harmony. In the just soul each element stays in its own place and performs the task to which it is naturally suited. The result is a condition analogous to the health of the body. The chief benefit of justice is that it allows this condition of psychological harmony to come into existence and to be maintained in his soul (Klosko 1986: 69).

The parallel between the state and the individual led to a problem which Plato did not solve. While in an individual, desires and passions were restrained by reason, Plato was ambivalent when describing the state. He insisted that the artisans and producers would be willing to subordinate themselves to the guardians. He was uncertain about how long this subordination would last. He even recommended the use of force and rhetorical persuasion. With so much control and monitoring, it was doubtful whether the Ideal State could be a happy one.

Justice in the individual meant that every individual was assigned a place in society according to one's natural aptitudes and skills. In other words, justice meant departmental excellence. Furthermore, justice was psychic harmony, balancing and ordering the three elements in accordance with the dominant one. For Plato, restraint was the key to proper development and societal harmony. It also represented a bond that cemented ties between the individual and society. In this sense, justice was social. A just individual was also a good person. His purpose was to show 'how ought we to live' and tried to establish the relationship between virtue and happiness (Irwin 1995). Plato developed the answer to how ought to live 'based on unusually rich account of our nature and the nature of reality' (Reeve 2004: ix). Plato gave three arguments in favour of why a just life was a happy one. First, a just individual limited his desires, for non-satisfaction of desires led to unhappiness. Second, only a philosopher could differentiate between the pleasures derived from the pursuit of reason, and those obtained from appetite and sensuality. Third, pleasures derived from the intellect were more genuine and comforting than those derived from the senses (MacIntyre 1971: 46).

Justice in the state meant that the three social classes (rulers, warriors and producers) performed the deliberative and governing, defence, and production, without interfering with the functions of the others. Justice was "one class, one duty; one man, one work". Plato drew a parallel between the three social classes and the three elements of the human soul. Each soul had a corresponding social class. A just society recognized and educated every individual talent according to the dominant element in one's soul, and ordered these elements into coherent classes. The rulers and soldiers constituted the guardian class. Plato visualized society

> ... as a system of services in which each member both gives and receives. What the state takes cognizance of is this mutual exchange and what it tries to arrange is the most adequate satisfaction of needs and the most harmonious interchange of services. Men figure in such a system as the performers of a needed task and their social importance depends upon the value of the work they do. What the individual possesses, therefore, is first and foremost a status in which he is privileged to act, and the freedom which the state secures him is not so much for the exercise of his free will as for the practice of his calling (Sabine 1973: 60).

Plato understood injustice to mean interference and meddlesomeness. Any interchange in jobs between the three social classes would bring harm to the state and was the worst evil. On the contrary, if the rulers, auxiliaries and artisans performed their respective tasks, then such a state would be just. Plato's conception of justice was distributive, giving what was due to an individual, namely good training and skills, in return for proper discharge of one's responsibilities. A Plato's conception could be represented as follows:

Virtue	*Soul*	*Class*
Wisdom	Rational	Rulers
Courage	Spirited	Soldiers
Temperance	Appetitive	Artisans

Myth of Metals and of Earth-born

Plato sustained his arguments that individuals differed in their capacities and nature with the help of a "noble or a royal lie" which would be uttered by the lovers of truth, the philosopher ruler. The Myth of Metals and of the Earth-born rationalized the fact that all human beings were born of earth, and their bodies were mixed with different metals; the philosophic-rational ones were made of gold, the spirited-courageous ones of silver, and the appetitive ones of bronze. The myth explained and justified individual and class distinctions in a manner that was comprehensible to a lay person. The myth was necessary to sustain the Ideal State, by convincing everyone of their rightful place in society, and the obligations their stations in life entailed. It also suggested that in spite of their differences, all individuals were born of the earth.

Plato recommended that the philosopher ruler, who was entrusted with the task of assigning the different roles to the individuals, propagate the myth in the best interest of the community as a whole. Nietzsche criticized Plato for founding a just and a rightly ordered society with the help of a necessary lie. In Plato's arguments, the usefulness of the social ordering never became clear. The myth, according to Nietzsche, was fabricated by Plato not merely to protect philosophy from political persecution, but also to give philosophy its political influence.

> What Plato does not seem to realise is that the compulsory acceptance of such myths is incompatible with philosophy, and involves a kind of education which stunts intelligence (Russell 1961: 129).

The abuses of the myth far outweighed its uses. It led to rigid class divisions where the ruler was made to look superior to the ruled. This was justified on the basis of race, education and scale of values (Popper 1945: Vol. I: 49). Since Plato deliberately ignored the conception of justice as equality before law (a widely prevalent view at that time), this was done with the purpose of convincing his readers that the Ideal State was indeed "just". Equalitarianism and humanitarianism, accepted as ideals by Athenian democracy, undermined his belief in natural privileges, his anti-individualism, and above all the fact that the state was to exist for the welfare and freedom of its individual citizens (Popper ibid: 92–95).

For Plato, human faculties were not hereditary. An individual's functional role in society was determined by his own natural aptitude, and not by parental lineage. To ensure that the parents did not manipulate to get the best for their child, they were made to give up their child to the state, which in turn would categorize and educate him in the appropriate faculty that he was endowed with. Social mobility between the classes was assured. This in itself was a revolutionary step, considering that all ancient societies were stratified, and Athens was no exception. But Plato, in his eagerness to radically restructure the existing arrangements, proposed a more "fair" scheme, where the hereditary became important to discern individual endowments, but not beyond that. Once the identification was made, every individual could hope to find a rightful place in tune with his talents.

The apparently just arrangement was controlled by the guardians. They would decide and place individuals in accordance with their nature. However, no remedial steps to prevent manipulation by the guardians themselves were suggested. Very likely, the means would defeat the end. While Plato's critics castigated him for subordinating the interests of individuals to the requirements of the social whole, for his admirers the "polis and individual soul was subject to a common Form of righteousness;

and the individual is no more subordinate to the polis than the polis is to the individual" (Sibley 1981: 66). On balance, his critics were right, for the individual's development retained meaning only if it was socially useful. For achieving social ends, individuals were denied their freedom and privacy, and subjected to excessive regulation of their lives. Plato's society was inherently elitist and meritocratic. He tacitly assumed that it would be possible to find the right person for every available job, and one could anticipate the economic requirements of society and plan accordingly.

EDUCATION

The Ideal State ruled by the philosopher was made possible through an elaborate and rigorous scheme of education. The state was wholly constructed around the scheme of education, in the belief that if the state performed its task of conducting and supervising education properly, then it would succeed. Plato looked to education as an instrument of moral reform, for it would mould and transform human souls. Education inculcated the right values of selfless duty towards all, and was therefore positive. It helped in the performance of one's functions in society and in attaining fulfilment. Thus, education was the key to the realization of the new social order. The seriousness with which Plato regarded education could be gauged by the attention and meticulous care he paid to it. Large portions of Books II, III and X were devoted to it. The community of wives and property was confined to a few paragraphs at the end of Book III. Community of wives and property was suggested only to remove the distortions which the education was not able to prevent.

> The one sufficient thing is the guardians' education: if they are well educated, they will see to everything. Education was more important than community of wives and property because it tries to cure the ills at the source while communism tries to prevent distractions that may corrupt the soul (Plato 1955: 190–191).

Commentators took note of the importance Plato assigned to education in the Ideal State. As already stated, Rousseau described the *Republic* as the finest treatise on education to be ever written. His *Emile* (1762) was in response to the suggestions made by Plato with regard to education of men and women. Education offered a cure for all problems, including those that were insoluble (Jaeger 1945: III: 236). It usurped the whole subject matter of legislation (Friedlander 1969: III: 92). It offered a formula for dividing work and achieving harmonious cooperation (Nettleship 1967: 78).

Plato considered the state as an educational institution, and called it the "one great thing". The stress on education was derived from the Socratic belief that "virtue is knowledge", namely to know good was to do good, and like his master, emphasized the need to cultivate one's soul. Impressed by the results of state-controlled education in Sparta, Plato duplicated the same for Athens. An important deficiency in the Athenian curriculum was the lack of training in martial arts that would prepare the individual from childhood to the service of the interests of the state. Besides, education in Athens, unlike Sparta, was left to the family and private schools and for this neglect, Athens paid a price as she allowed rule by the ignorant and inefficient statesmen. Plato attempted to balance the two contrasting models. The education system drew from Athens values of creativity, excellence and individual achievement, which it tried to integrate with that of Sparta, namely civic training.

From Athens came the individual aspect which Plato hoped to integrate with the social side that he borrowed from Sparta. This is because Plato believed that human beings must be inculcated not only with knowledge but also civic sense.

> Plato's plan of training represents therefore an Athenian, not a Spartan, conception of what constitutes an educated man. Any other conclusion would have been unthinkable for a philosopher who believed that the only salvation for states lay in the exercise of trained intelligence (Sabine 1973: 70).

For Plato, the human soul was capable of learning as long as it lived, hence education would be a lifelong process. Knowledge was to be acquired for the sake of perfection and excellence. Its goal was to turn the "inward eye" with the help of "right objects towards light". For Plato, the mind was active, capable of directing itself towards objects of study, and if nurtured properly, it was capable of becoming totally receptive to objects from the environment. Plato moulded and established the right environment to ensure that the soul got attracted to things that were beautiful, and then moved towards beauty itself. Thus, while he was a craftsman of individual souls, he was equally attentive to crafting the environment in which the soul grew and developed.

> Platonic education is primarily a moulding of souls ... . Plato holds that the virtue of anything, including the soul, "is a matter of regular and orderly arrangement". It is the function of education to produce such order, which is a necessary condition for the virtue based on correct opinion and a necessary precondition for the virtue based on knowledge. Whereas Socrates, who views the soul as basically rational, sees education as a wakening of thought, Plato believes education to be concerned as much with the non-rational elements as with the rational (Klosko 1986: 118).

Right and proper education could be achieved under the tutelage of an able teacher who stimulated and encouraged thought to bring out the best in the pupil. In his scheme of education, Plato integrated the Pythagorean idea of the immortality and transmigration of souls with a lifelong plan of education. He believed that the human soul was a repository of human knowledge acquired through previous births, with the capacity to remember.

These reminiscences were like flashes that occurred in a mind stirred by the objects that were placed before it.

Plato's elaborate system of education brought forth the crucial importance and interdependence of nature and nurture in shaping human character. He accepted that individuals differed in intelligence and capacities, which were determined at the time of birth. They were permanent, but within their limits, individuals could be moulded. The way an individual led a life, whether happily or unhappily, was determined by upbringing. Talent and training were both required to bring out the best in an individual. For centuries, scholars remained divided on the issue whether nature or nurture played the determining role in shaping human beings. Many stressed that individuals were born with a basic nature which remained unchanged throughout life. On the other hand, many held that given the right training and environment, individuals transcended the disadvantages of their birth. In recent years, scholars have reiterated Plato's belief that nature and nurture exerted equal influences on the development of a human being.

> Neither will do without the other; you cannot create the required nature, but you can by nurture do everything. Short of that, and without the proper nurture the best nature is likely to turn out ill as to turn out well (Nettleship 1967: 77).

Plato was also confident that young minds could be shaped, if directed properly. He stressed the tremendous receptive potential of the human mind, which was why early education played a crucial role in the overall development of the individual. At this point, the educator might try and train the individual to restrain desires, for control and harnessing of non-rational aspects of the soul was an important prerequisite for the full development of the rational. Elementary education helped to attain the first goal, while higher education ensured the development of a rational soul.

Elementary Education

Plato recommended a state-controlled, compulsory and comprehensive scheme of education in two phases: In the first phase, elementary education that would be confined to the young till the age of 18, followed by two years of compulsory military training and then higher education the second phase for the selected persons of both the sexes who would be members of the ruling class, from the age twenty to thirty five. In doing so he promoted two aims: first to ensure universal literacy and second adequate and proper training for the members of the ruling class in the state. While elementary education made the soul responsive to the environment, higher education helped the soul to search for truth which illuminated it. It trained the human eye to respond slowly to the glow of pure light through strict discipline and hard work. Elementary education enabled the individual soul to develop fullness of experience, both theoretical and practical. It trained the human mind in moral and aesthetic judgement. It developed the physical body to be healthy and athletic.

Both boys and girls received the same kind of education, far beyond the physical distinctions. Plato did not find any difference between the sexes in talents and skills, thus making a subtle criticism of the secondary status accorded to women in ancient Greece. The theme of women's participation in politics was the main subject of one of the comedies of Aristophanes (447–385 BC) *Women in Parliament* (*Ecclesiazusae*) which discussed the status of women as early as 393 BC. Plato followed Aristophanes.

Elementary education consisted of music and gymnastics, designed to train and blends the gentle and fierce qualities in the individual and creates a "harmonious person". Gymnastics provided poise to feelings, and tempered spirits. It involved the training of the body for the sake of the mind. Music tried to soften the spirit by developing the nascent power of reason. It inculcated the power of right opinion. The rhythm and diction of poetry, the sound of musical instruments, the shades, colours and shapes of art not only gave an artistic sense, but also carried with it a moral suggestion, a love for doing the right thing. It would uphold the social practice of each individual doing one work, without being a busybody. It was to instill values of simplicity, justice, conformity to a single principle and acceptance of austere life.

> And so we may venture to assert that anyone who can produce the perfect blend of the physical and intellectual sides of education and apply them to the training of character is producing music and harmony of far more importance than any mere musician's tuning of strings (Plato 1955: 176).

Plato recommended censorship of literature and music to encourage the virtues necessary in the guardian class, for denuding the spirit and making reason supreme. Censorship of poetry, stories and tales was undertaken to ensure that the impressionable young minds were not exposed to harmful ideas. Plato forbade Lydian and Ionian harmonies, for they expressed sorrow and lethargy respectively. Only Dorian and Phrygian ones were permitted, for they inculcated courage and temperance respectively. He prohibited the reading of Homer and Hesoid, for they showed gods behaving badly on certain occasions. Their poems made readers fear death, did not reflect the importance of decorum, and discouraged temperance by praising the rich feasting and other lusts of gods. Plato was particularly insistent that children not fear or hate death; otherwise they would not develop courage needed on the battlefield. He recommended that children be made to sit on horseback and taken to the sight of actual war, so that they develop a fearless attitude towards death. Children were to be told stories about gods and great persons to ensure their good moral upbringing. Plato's idea was to shut off all vice and ugliness from the life of a young person.

Plato permitted the playing of simple musical instruments: the lyre, the cithara and shepherd pipes. The principles that governed the selection of poetry, literature and musical instruments, also dictated the selection of other forms of art: painting, weaving, embroidery and the making of furniture. He prescribed strict diet control, with the purpose of imbibing what Pericles considered "love of beauty without extravaganza, of culture without softness". None would eat fish or cooked meat, sauces or confectionery. Roast meat was allowed. The diet would be such that none would fall sick. These measures aimed to bring about poise of feelings, control of emotions and a harmonized social being. The environment had to be made beautiful and harmonious, because of the indelible impression it left on the soul.

> We shall thus prevent our guardians being brought up among representations of what is evil, and so day by day and little by little, by grazing widely as it were in an unhealthy pasture, insensibly doing themselves a cumulative psychological damage that is very serious. We must look for artists and craftsmen capable of perceiving the real nature of what is beautiful, and then our young men, living as it were in a healthy climate, will benefit because all the works of art they see and hear influence them for good, like the breezes from some healthy country, insensibly leading them from earliest childhood into close sympathy and conformity with beauty and reason (Plato ibid: 162–163).

Training in the right virtues through stories and the like would create the perfect members of the guardian class. With such a beginning, advancement towards right conduct became more pronounced as one grew older.

Education in arts would be followed by two years of compulsory military training. The guardians were perfected as professional warriors. Luxury and self-indulgence were prohibited with the purpose of strengthening the spirit, without making it rigid or harsh. Plato reiterated the Athenian practice which provided for compulsory military service between the ages of 17 or 18 and 20. Elementary education perfected those souls who were receptive to habit and conditioning. These souls would become auxiliaries.

Higher Education

At the age of 20, a selection was made. The best ones would take an advanced course in mathematics, which would include arithmetic, plane and solid geometry, astronomy and harmonics. Arithmetic was necessary, for it used "pure intelligence in the attainment of pure" truth" (Plato ibid: 324). Truth, for Plato, resided in Thought and not in sense particulars. Besides this philosophical value, arithmetic had a practical value too, namely the use of numbers. Warriors were to learn the use of numbers in order to arrange the troops (Plato ibid: 331). Arithmetic, because of its philosophical and practical use, was studied by the best. Geometry helped in the choice of positions and methods of tactics. It helped in easily acquiring the vision of the Idea of Good. Astronomy and harmonics had the same value as arithmetic and geometry. Astronomy was not merely restricted to observation of heavenly bodies, nor was harmonics a learning to discriminate notes by ear, but both tried to elevate the mind from sense perceptions and cultivate the power of reason. Higher education was to cultivate the spirit of free intellectual enquiry.

Those who did not qualify to join this exclusive category of esoteric minds would become soldiers, and form the second tier of the ruling elite. The first course in the scheme of higher education would last for 10 years. It would be for those who had a flair for science. At the age of 30 there would be another selection. Those who qualified would study dialectics or metaphysics, logic and philosophy for the next five years. They would study the Idea of Good and the first principles of Being. They would receive partial experience for ruling. They would accept junior positions in military and political life till the age of 35. This period would last for the next 15 years. By the age of 50, the philosopher ruler was fully equipped. He would devote the greater part of his time to contemplation and philosophy, along with political obligations. Since he would have grasped the idea of Good, he would be in a position to do good to the community. Since Plato subjected ruling to scientific training, he was categorical that only those perfect in true knowledge could make good rulers, for they would ensure the good of others.

> Behind training lies the need of knowing what to teach and what to train men to do. It cannot be assumed that somebody already has the knowledge which shall be taught; what is more urgently needed is more knowledge. The really distinctive thing in Plato is the coupling of training with investigation, or of professional standards of skill with scientific standards of knowledge. Herein lies the originality of his theory of higher education in the *Republic* (Sabine 1973: 55–56).

The true goal of education for both Plato and Aristotle was to inculcate the values of civic virtues. They framed an educational curriculum that would impart "a moral liberal education rather than a study of political science. What they sought was rather a frame of mind which will respond in a just, responsible and self manner to public issues" (Heater 1990: 6). Both believed that education would be an effective remedy for corruption and instability that affected the states of their time, by injecting into the citizens a sense of rights and obligations. They were convinced that a system of education controlled and regulated by the state would teach the citizenry the traditions and laws of the state. For Plato,

> ... the educational system serves both to undergrid and sustain the idea of political order and to provide a ladder, so to speak, up which those who have the capacity can climb to escape the contingencies and

> limitations of political life. These two purposes, according to Plato, are not contradictory. Rather they do support and sustain each other. Without political order, the life of contemplation would be impossible, for conflicts and near chaos would be forever interfering with the calm required for study and mystic experience. Without study and mystic experience, the wisdom necessary to sustain the political order would be lacking (Sibley 1981: 74).

COMMUNITY OF WIVES AND PROPERTY

While education, for Plato, was designed to create the proper environment for the nurturing and development of the human soul, the community of wives and property tried to eliminate all the negativities that obstructed the proper growth of the individual. Since the stress was on creating a meritocratic society in which every individual would perform tasks appropriate to one's nature, the community of wives and property ensured that nepotism, accident, family ties and pedigree or wealth would not be the criteria of selection for social stations and their assigned tasks. It ensured that since governance was a selective and specialized function, only the best and deserving would make it. The rulers of this kind would pass off the benefits of good ruling to the rest of society that stood disenfranchised.

Plato abolished private family and property for the guardian class, for they encouraged nepotism, favouritism, particularism, factionalism and other corrupt practices among rulers. Politics did not mean promoting one's personal interests. Instead it was to promote the common good. Plato thereby established a high standard for governing and governors.

Plato proposed that the members of the guardian class live together in common, like soldiers in a barrack. They would not possess any gold or silver. They would only have the small amount of property that was necessary. None would own a house or storeroom, namely an exclusive private space. They would receive a fixed quota from the producing class, depending on what was required for subsistence. The life of the guardians would be in accordance with the rule followed among the Greeks that "friends have all things in common".

In the *Republic*, Plato devoted greater space and consideration to community of wives than to property. This was because he was perturbed by the negative emotions of hatred, selfishness, avarice and envy that the family encouraged. He disliked the exclusivity that the private family fostered in its members. In addition, he was dismayed by the secondary position women held within the family, confined to perform household chores.

The Platonic scheme was based on the premise that women and men were identical in natural endowments and faculties. Like Pythagoras, he accepted that men and women did not differ much and that they should be treated equally. Following Aristophanes' proposal in *Ecclesiazusae*, Plato accepted women as legislators and rulers. There were two distinct ideas that were embedded in Plato's community of wives: reform of conventional marriage, and emancipation of women. To achieve these, he proposed abolition of permanent monogamous marriages and private families. These were restricted to guardian women alone.

Conventional marriage led to women's subordination, subjugation and seclusion. He rejected the idea of marriage as a spiritual union or sacrament or bond based on love and mutual respect. However, marriage was necessary to ensure the reproduction and continuation of the human race. He, therefore, advocated temporary sexual unions for the purpose of bearing children. He relieved women of child rearing and child care responsibilities.

Plato proposed strict regulation of sexual intercourse, which was to be performed in the interest of the state by ensuring that the best and the fittest of human stock were made available. The philosopher ruler would decide on sexual unions.

> There would be as many unions of the best of both sexes, and as few of the inferior as possible ... . No one but the Rulers must know how all this is being effected; otherwise our herd of Guardians may become rebellious ... we must then institute certain festivals at which we shall bring together the brides and bridegrooms ... the number of marriages we shall leave to the Rulers' discretion ... . I think they will have to invent some ingenious system of drawing lots, so that, at each pairing off, the inferior candidate may blame his luck rather than the rulers (Plato 1955: 240).

Plato viewed the ideal age for marriage to be between 25 and 55 for men and 20 and 40 for women. He forbade relationships between mothers and sons, and between fathers and daughters. Men and women were freed from permanent marital ties, not with the purpose of encouraging sexual promiscuity, but rather for securing the greatest good of the community (Barker 1964: 257–258; Sibley 1981: 71). Abortion was recommended for illegitimate children, those that were not sanctioned by the state or were the result of mating by persons beyond the prescribed age limits.

Once children were born, they would be taken care of by the state-maintained nurseries, which would be equipped with well-trained nurses. Except for the philosopher ruler, none would know the parentage of these children. Even the biological parents and their children would be oblivious of their relationship, the idea being that all children would be respectful towards their elders in the same way as they would, had they been their parents. Conversely, all elders would shower equal love and affection on all the children, as if they were theirs.

> Each generation of children will be taken by officers appointed for the purpose, who may be men or women or both—for men and women will of course be equally eligible for office ... . These officers will take the children of the better Guardians to a nursery and put them in

> charge of nurses living in a separate part of the city: the children of the inferior Guardians, and any defective offspring of the others, will be quietly and secretly disposed of (Plato 1955: 241).

Plato's meritocratic society gave very little importance to birth. He did not believe that skills and talents were hereditary which passed from one generation to another. Through mock marriages, rigged lottery and eugenics, individual aptitudes would be sifted and classified, ensuring high standards of excellence. Eugenics has been popular with many diverse schools like the Fabians, Nazis and the idea of superman influenced thinkers like Nietzsche. True, as Plato suggested, disposing of invalids and deformed babies was common in the animal world, but it seemed insensitive to apply the same in the human world, which prides itself as being compassionate and benevolent. It was also heartless of Plato to propose that medicines were to be abolished to prevent prolongation of the lives of extreme and chronic invalids.

Plato did not mention the institution of slavery. Far from abolishing it, he merely regarded it as unimportant (Sabine 1973: 66). Being a universal institution on which the Athenian/Greek economies were based, he could not conceive, like Aristotle, that it would be temporary and would change with new modes of technology.

Critical Evaluation

While Plato's scheme may apparently seem liberating, it implied excessive regimentation with very little privacy and individuality. In trying to ensure that family life was not corrupted with narrow sectarianism and selfishness, Plato went to the other extreme and eliminated the emotional bonding that the family provided.

Plato certainly challenged some of the cherished conventions within human society. Many of his critics were disturbed by these proposals. Aristotle was the earliest of those who disagreed, giving a detailed reason as to why the family and private property were important for the happiness of the individual and the welfare of the state. Both Grube (1935) and Taylor (1926) dismissed Plato's proposals as abhorrent for they did not take into cognizance the deepest human emotions that marital and family life involved. Strauss (1964) reiterating Aristotle looked to the family as a natural institution and questioned Plato's wisdom in abolishing it. However, Plato's defence of the abolition of private households and monogamous marriages found strong adherents among the early socialists like Saint Simon, Owen and Fourier.

Plato insisted that a temperate attitude towards property was necessary for the security and well-being of the state. Too much acquisitiveness and love for one's possessions ruined unity, harmony and moral goodness of the state. Plato clearly perceived the disastrous consequences of combining economic and political power on purity and efficiency, for that would bring about corruption and split the state in two. Thus, Plato was the first to understand the implications of the role that economic factors play in politics, for excessive wealth and poverty would be ruinous to the health of the state. He was aware of the constant civil strife in Greek cities. He blamed inequality as a cause of political instability and social upheaval.

Plato permitted the third social class to enjoy private families and property, but that would be under the strict control and supervision of the guardians. He subordinated both the guardians and the artisans to a moral ideal: the welfare of the state and the collectivity. While the guardians were entrusted with the task of ruling and governance, they would lead strict, austere lives. The artisans did not have the right to participate in the political process, but enjoyed emotional ties and had possessions. Plato played fair with both the sections of the society in terms of rewards and denial. The characteristics of the Platonic Ideal State were class, communism, civility, control, contentment and consensus (Hacker 1961: 30).

Plato's communism was ascetic, similar to the life found in a monastery, though many see this as a forerunner of modern-day socialism. Communism was more than common ownership of property: it symbolized different types of economic management. It conceived of society free of exploitation and oppression, based on social justice, equity, freedom and democracy.

REGENERATION OF THE IDEAL

Having outlined the details of an Ideal State, Plato examined other types of regimes, accounting for their decline and decay. He listed four: timocracy, oligarchy, democracy and tyranny. Each of these regimes had a corresponding type of human being. The eventual fate of all regimes was tyranny. Though he described how regimes declined into tyranny, he did not explain how they could recover from tyranny.

Plato's account of historical change was pessimistic. He held that anything that came into being would degenerate. He was aware that a chain of creation, decay and dissolution gripped the world firmly, and it was only at rare intervals that individuals could snatch a brief moment of seeming immortality.

> The concluding note of Plato's political science is not of an unlimited arrogance that man can fashion a polity untouched by time, but of a heroism chastened by the foreknowledge of eventual defeat. It is, in Shelley's words, "Eternity warning Time" (Wolin 1960: 68).

The failure to regulate reproduction signalled the first departure from the Ideal State. Succeeding generations lacked the talents of their parents, and coupled with neglect of the process of education, there was a decline in the quality of the ruling class. The new rulers would value wealth and money-making activities, marginalizing the wise and the intelligent.

Timocracy was characterized by the love of victory and honours, ambition and passion to excel in war and money-making.

The next regime was an oligarchy, a state ruled by the wealthy few. It came into being when individuals gave more attention to wealth and money-making and less to virtue. Society got divided into the super-rich and the very poor. The lust for wealth undermined the rule of law and principle of moderation. The poor revolted against such decadence, and the result was a democracy. Democracy was characterized by licence, wastefulness, insolence, anarchy and the democratic man gave more importance to his desires and appetites. There was no order or restraint. Quantity rather than quality was the main criterion honouring all values on an equal basis. Pleasures were measured more for their intensity and duration, rather than their intrinsic and differentiated merit. Democracy deteriorated into tyranny. The tyrant made his people creatures of his will, confiscating their labour. Too much licence led to servitude, and people were willing to make themselves virtual slaves in return for security.

In the *Statesman*, Plato divided the states into lawful and unlawful states, a classification that Aristotle adopted when he spoke of good and perverted forms of government in his *Politics*. For Plato, there were three law-abiding states, and their corresponding corrupt and lawless states. The rule of one yielded monarchy and tyranny; the rule of a few, aristocracy and oligarchy; and the rule of many included moderate and extreme democracy. For the first time, Plato conceded two kinds of democracy, and made it the best of the lawless states, though the worst of law-abiding states. Both forms of democracy were better than oligarchy, and even monarchy, tacitly admitting the importance of popular participation and consent in the polity.

PLATO'S SECOND-BEST STATE

While the ideal or perfect state remained the one ruled by the philosopher ruler as the epitome of reason and untrammelled by general rules, in the *Laws* Plato described what he regarded as his second-best state. It was perhaps hindsight that the philosophical ideal was unattainable, for it made excessive demands on the state as an educational institution, and neglected laws which were products of experience. This led Plato to examine the place of law in a state.

In the *Laws*, government by law was supreme, applying equally on both the ruler and the subject. The law-bound state would be a polity that combined the wisdom of monarchy with liberty for the purpose of stability, harmonizing and balancing opposite political principles and practices. The task of the lawgiver was to blend the two. Laws must be prolific, dealing with the specific details of possible and potential conflicts between public and private interests. Since private property was permitted, laws were to involve minute regulation.

The city would consist of 5040 households, with each family having an equal plot of land as their inalienable right. The most worthy child would inherit the land, and excess children would be turned over to those families where the number was few. If the city got populated, it could think of schemes of colonization. Meanwhile, it would try out birth control methods to control undue increase in population. In general, every man was expected to marry by 35; otherwise he would have to pay an annual fine or tax. It was ironic that such a suggestion came from a person who never married.

Both the *Republic* and the *Laws* spoke of the need to curtail the ugly consequences of inequality and economic power. Wealth was accorded an inferior position. The disparity between the possessions of the richest and the poorest was to be in the ratio of four to one. Through ancestral acquisition the limit on poverty was to be decided, and no man was allowed more than four times this value. If by trade or other means an individual acquired more, the excess reverted to the public treasury. All citizens were to register their possessions with a public agency, and records were to be kept open for public inspection. There were to be strict regulations on gold and silver. Metals only in the form of money were permitted, expressing Plato's distaste for usury.

The economy of the *polis* was to be subordinated to the requirements of both body and soul. Plato looked to division of labour as the ordering principle, with slaves performing agriculture, free men who were not citizens looking after trade and industry, and the citizens exclusively doing political functions. Both the economy and the polity would reflect the principles of a mixed or blended constitution. All those eligible and fit for military service would vote for the selection of the guardians of the law. The first 300 candidates would be selected through an election. Through a second ballot, this number would be reduced to 100. From these 100, approximately one-third (37) would be chosen in a third election. There would be a nocturnal council consisting of the 10 eldest members. Of the 37 guardians, the director of education and certain priests were chosen for their virtue. This council was above the law, with powers to control and direct all legal institutions of the state. The nocturnal council was similar to the philosopher ruler of the *Republic*. Through an elaborate process, the council of 360 persons would be chosen. Candidates would be chosen by the entire citizen body from each of the four classes into which the city had been divided on the basis of wealth. Here Plato reiterated the divisions made by Solon and Cleithenes (515–495 BC). In the second election, all citizens would reduce the candidates from each class to 180. Finally, 90 would be selected through a system of draw of lots from each of the four categories. Plato believed that the political system should reflect the economic divisions of the city. With regard to public appointments, Plato recommended the blending of aristocratic nomination and popular elections.

Plato also looked to the topography of a city. The ideal was a self-sufficient agricultural community capable of sustaining a rugged and temperate populace. He believed that a common race, language, law and religion were desirable, but did not place undue emphasis on them. He reiterated his inherent distrust and dislike for commercialism and industrialism.

Like the *Republic,* even in the *Laws* Plato looked to education as holding a decisive position, both with regard to the maintenance of the *polis* and the improvement of laws. The guardians of the law were to appoint a committee of women, who, through persuasion and gentle pressure, would see to the strict adherence of marriage laws, so that reproduction was kept under control. In the case of a couple having no children, divorce was recommended after 10 years of marriage. Certain members of the committee would act as matrons, supervising the very young and the nurses. The child began formal education at the age of three, and till six would receive flexible training. The emphasis again was to develop the "natural" talent as far as possible. At the age of six, the two sexes would be separated, but both boys and girls would receive a long public education under teachers paid by the *polis.*

Plato reiterated the need for training in music and gymnastics, similar to the recommendations in the *Republic.* He also recommended rigorous censorship of literature and art, equal educational opportunities for women, and compulsory education for all. However, he gave greater attention to religion which would be regulated and supervised by the state. He forbade any kind of private religious exercises that undermined the unity of the state, and advocated performance of public rites by authorized priests. In the process, he undermined the influence of disorderly religion that held sway over women and hysterical persons. For Plato, religion provided a set of rules of conduct and was closely linked to one's moral behaviour. He recommended harsh penalties, including death for atheists. Laws would be both educational and coercive. As tools of education, they would teach the individual how to live best, and as instruments of coercion, they would compel those who refused to obey.

IS PLATO A FORERUNNER OF MODERN TOTALITARIANISM, OR THE FIRST FASCIST?

It was in the first quarter of the twentieth century that the Platonic system was subjected to critical enquiry. Most of the critics were from the liberal democratic tradition, with a strong commitment to democracy and individual rights. This was also the period when scholars began to dissect totalitarianism, and in tracing its intellectual ancestry, some saw an affinity between Plato's scheme with those that existed in Fascist Italy and Germany and Communist states in Eastern Europe and the former USSR.

Fite (1934) denied that the aim of Plato was to search for the notion of maximum happiness and self-development of individual citizens.

Instead, the focus was to protect a small group of erudite rulers, numbering just one per cent within a larger group of the privileged leisure class, who constituted only 10 per cent of the population. The rest of the population was neglected, despised and made to sacrifice for the benefit of the few. Fite accused Plato of ignoring the uniqueness of each individual, and disregarding mutual respect in relationships. Plato's perception of marriage, he felt, was more a view of a "stock breeder". He defined social good in a manner that resembles the "ironclad" system of Communist Russia.

Crossman (1939) contended that Plato was wrong for his time and ours. Plato's endeavour was to construct a perfect society, free of three evils that confronted Athens: class war, bad government and bad education. Sparta became the alternative ideal, for it was relatively free from social and political instability. Crossman found Plato making erroneous assumptions, and these were: (a) the poor faith he had in the ability and intelligence of the common man, (b) his mistaken belief that a just government could be established by a revolution, and (c) that final truth could be discovered by suppressing freedom of thought. Crossman concluded that Plato made the profoundest attack on the basic premises of liberal democracy, namely equality, freedom and self-government, because he had very little faith in the capacity of each individual for self-development, freedom and individuality. Plato offered security, prosperity and the noble lie through the Myth of Metals and the Earth-born. Crossman wrote:

> The perfect state is not a democracy of rational equals but an aristocracy in which a hereditary caste of cultured gentlemen care with paternal solitude for the toiling masses (Crossman 1939: 40).

Winspear (1940: 272) characterized Plato's scheme as a blueprint by an authoritarian reactionary with a plan to employ force, but sufficiently subtle to conceal his intentions under fine phrases. He, however, admired Plato for advocating self-abnegation and dedication to the cause of general human welfare.

Toynbee (1934: 89) looked at Plato as being cynical, reactionary and inhumane, though immensely intelligent, highly imaginative and deeply concerned with the welfare of his fellowmen. Plato was praised for his altruism and his recommendations derived from an analysis of Athenian society, which was lacking in moral convictions. Joad (1966: 66–68) saw many similarities between Fascism and Plato's tyrant state, but conceded that there were fundamental differences too. The key difference was that in Plato's Ideal State, the ordinary person achieved happiness, and the state was built on the ideas of absolute good and justice.

Russell (1961) questioned the feasibility of finding a set of "wise" persons who could be entrusted with governing. He contended that since it was an insoluble one, democracy was the best bet. Plato suggested that the wise be given suitable training, but did not clarify what constituted suitable training. Russell also compared the guardian rulers to the small elite that captured power after the Bolshevik revolution in Russia in 1917. The Platonic Ideal State ruled out creativity and innovation, and would only be successful in achieving

> ... wars against rough equal populations, and it [would] secure a liveli-hood for a certain small number of people. It [would] almost certainly produce no art or science because of its rigidity; in this respect, as in others, it [would] be like Sparta. In spite of all the fine talk, skill in war and enough to eat [was] all that [would] be achieved. Plato had lived through famine and defeat in Athens; perhaps subconsciously, he thought the avoidance of these evils the best that statesmanship could accomplish (Russell ibid: 131).

Berlin (1969) pointed out that Plato did not grant the individual the freedom of choice, which was an inalienable human right. Along with it, Plato also rejected pluralism or acceptance of different values and lifestyles, for he believed that there was a solution to all human problems, and the universe was directed towards a single goal. Like Popper, Berlin attacked the historicism of Plato in *Historical Inevitability* (1954), along with that of Hegel and Marx, but dropped Plato, out of reverence for the Oxford establishment (Carr 1965: 92).

The most scathing attack came from Popper (1945), who accused Plato, along with Hegel and Marx, as enemies of the open society. An open society was one which allowed its members to openly criticize the institutions and the structures of power without fear of reprisal, with education as distinct from indoctrination, allowing freedom of thought, action and belief, on the grounds that none would have the monopoly of the truth. It would allow members to develop naturally, without any outward supervision by persons alleged to be superior in intelligence or moral virtues, nor would they be subjected to rigid discipline in the name of social cohesion, public order and public good.

Popper's distrust of dogmatism and ideological blueprinting formed the backdrop of *The Open Society and its Enemies* (1945). Having experienced the brutality, inhumanity and insensitivity of Fascism and Communism, Popper questioned any theory that claimed to be a science. The distinction between science and non-science, according to Popper, was that the former could be proved and tested, while the latter shunned falsification by constantly embracing qualifications to accommodate every possible fact.

In *The Open Society*, Popper attacked the historicism of Plato, Hegel and Marx, to point out that their attempts to provide total and scientific explanations of society with the help of laws of history (which they claimed they had discovered), were essentially totalitarian in aim, principles and purpose (1945: Vol. I: 5–13; 37-40; 486–488). A scientific theory, according to Popper, was one which did not try to explain everything. It ruled out most of what could possibly happen, and would be considered as falsified, if what it projected did not happen. This was the essential problem with both Marxism and psychoanalysis. If a theory could explain all sorts of possibilities, without any attention to the actual state of affairs substantiated by observation and experimental results as evidence, then it contained no scientific information.

For Popper, any totalitarian system was a denial of the open society, for it did not recognize individual merit, advocated indoctrination instead of education, and predicted the course of development of human society on the basis of general and vague laws of history. Utopianism proceeded on the premise that it was possible to have first-hand knowledge based on some set of laws that governed human society and individuals (1945: Vol. I: 12, 97–105). Since for Popper change was inevitable, and

> ... the fact that change is never going to stop renders the very notion of a blueprint for the good society nonsensical, for even if society became like the blueprint it would instantly begin to depart from it. So not only are ideal societies unattainable because they are ideal, they are unattainable also because, to correspond to any sort of blueprint at all, they would have to be static, fixed, unchanging, and no foreseeable society is going to be those things. Indeed, the pace of social change seems to get faster, not slower, with every year that passes. And the process is going to have, so far as we can see, no end. So to have any hope at all of corresponding to the realities a political approach must be concerned not with states of affairs but with change. Our task is not the impossible one of establishing and preserving a particular form of society: it is to maximize our control over the actual changes that occur in a process of change which is never-ending—and to use that control wisely (Magee 1984: 106).

In *The Open Society*, Popper offered a general guiding principle for public policy: minimize avoidable suffering. Specific social evils could be alleviated by a practical approach on the basis of identifying the causes of unhappiness. An open society would maximize the freedom of the individuals in accordance with their wishes, if it just decided to mitigate unhappiness. Such an approach entailed an extension and a guarantee of a wide range of freedom of choice which would be available to individuals through public provision of education, arts, housing, health and other aspects of social life. The open society would be one where there was a balance between state intervention and market freedom, within a framework of constitutionalism and the rule of law.

As opposed to holistic revolutionary changes, Popper advocated piecemeal social engineering with stress on gradualism and evolutionary changes, for that ensured the possibility of rectifying mistakes and wrongs, since it was not possible to conceive of all the consequences that a policy or a decision would entail. Such reforms would be modest and democratic, for they would try and accommodate differing points of view, publicly discuss and reveal the conclusions and consequences of the proposals.

Popper dismissed the question of an ideal society as a purely academic one, irrelevant to science. In politics, as in science, it was not the analysis of concepts, but a critical examination of theories and subjecting them to the test of experience that was important. Within this framework, Popper characterized Plato's Ideal State as being inimical to the principles and beliefs of the open society.

Popper (ibid: 48–49, 52, 564–567) characterized Plato as anti-individualist, anti-humanist and anti-democratic, having the aim of "arresting all social change". This was achieved by establishing a society that was regimented, hierarchical and unequal, where the individual counted as long as he contributed to the social whole. In the Platonic state, it was the interest of the ruling elite that mattered exclusively, with strict supervision and collectivization of interests of the other classes. These were reinforced with the help of censorship, ban on innovation in education, legislation and religion, and continual propaganda. Politically, such a state exercised total control. Economically, such a state was an economic autarchy (Popper: 1945: Vol. I: 47–55, 86–87, 132–133, 166–167, 177–178, 468, 537).

Popper's critique differed from that of other critics, not because he castigated Plato for his reactionary illiberalism and anti-humanitarianism, for his attack was even more fundamental. It questioned the efficacy of scientific knowledge, and along with it the optimism and claim to design a perfect society. Russell, writing on Popper's critique, pointed out that though his views were unorthodox, they were thoroughly justified. Levinson (1953), who defended Plato on the grounds that he belonged to a different social space-time, had to concede that Plato, far from opening, was in fact closing society by obliterating the distinction between the private and public spheres, and by regimenting the lives of the ordinary citizens. Levinson admitted that the greatest of all revolutions has been the transition from a closed to an open society. One could only conclude by reiterating Gilbert Ryle, a Platonic scholar, that Popper's critique ensured that Platonic exegesis would never be the same again.

CONCLUSION

> Western thought, one might say, has been either Platonic or anti-Platonic, but hardly ever non-Platonic (Popper 1968: 163).

Plato was the first systematic political theorist, and a study of the Western philosophical tradition begins with his masterpiece, the *Republic*. He was the first to create a body of writing that spanned many areas—art, epistemology, ethics, language, love, mathematics, political theory, religion and science. He was credited for establishing philosophy as a unified and complex discipline, proposing radical solutions to the political community and human life. Utopian thought in the West also begins with Plato. While the *Republic* would always remain a timeless classic, Plato influenced successive generations of followers with his the *Statesman* and the *Laws*, for Aristotle made the latter two the starting point of his inquiry.

The *Republic* dealt with the question of achieving justice in society. In answering this question, it focused on other interrelated themes, like the right kind of life, the nature of human beings, the purpose and goals of political association, the ideal type of political system, the classification of constitutions, the need for good, upright rulers, and the nature and meaning of knowledge.

Plato emphasized that a good political community was one that promoted the general well-being of all its citizens. An important feature of such a society was the strong sense of community that its members shared. No one was favoured at the expense of the other. All were granted a fair share in the benefits. The philosopher ruler was the right kind of person to rule, for he was least interested in capturing power or making money. With a number of allegories like master-slave, shepherd-sheep, Plato tried to replicate automatic command and obedience as a model of the ruler-subject relationship, which, however was rejected by Aristotle on the ground that a political relationship, unlike others, was based on equality. Interestingly, this argument of Aristotle was reiterated by Locke in his critique of Robert Filmer (1588-1653) and patriarchalism.

The rulers, being enlightened despots, were given absolute powers but were put under strict regimentation through collective households and property to ensure that they did not use their privileged positions to exploit the rest. The artisans were denied political participation, but were allowed to retain their families and property. Since the average person failed to understand the meaning of what constituted the good, it became necessary for the political leader to educate him. Moreover, Plato insisted that rulership, like any other skill, required specialized training and apprenticeship. Society benefited if the right person performed the right job to avoid the maladies of a round peg in a square hole. Plato defended this argument deftly with the theory of three classes and three souls, emphasizing the bottom line that a good state, like a good individual, should exemplify moderation in character, thereby possessing the qualities of wisdom, courage, temperance and justice. Plato maintained that justice was good in itself and not only for its consequences. It was valuable as it leads to the happiness of its possessor.

One of the casualties of the argument for specialization of skills was political participation by the average individual. Plato was critical of the Athenian democratic practice that distinguished between government based on law and one subjected to human will, preferring the former, for it guaranteed moral equality of individuals and consent by the governed.

> At all events the ideal state ... was simply a denial of the political faith of the city state, with its ideal of free citizenship and its hope that every man, within the limits of his powers might be made a sharer in the duties and privileges of government ... . Plato's omission of law from his ideal state cannot be interpreted otherwise than as a failure to perceive a striking moral aspect of the very society which he desired to perfect (Sabine 1973: 73).

Plato's society was highly structured, ordered, hierarchical, regimented and meritocratic, where everyone was expected to perform the duties that were allotted. Unlike Smith, Plato did not view division of labour as a economic matter. Specialization was a fundamental moral and social principle which would govern the Ideal State. He ruled out wealth, gender and birth as criteria for distributing privileges and favours. Theoretically, children born in one class could reach the top but that was more an exception than the rule. Plato's classification was similar to the rigid caste distinctions practised in ancient India. However, his classes were not castes, for membership in them was not hereditary (Sabine ibid: 63). Society was sustained by a rigorous educational system and the science of eugenics. A glaring shortcoming is the silence on the institution of slavery in the *Republic.* This does not mean that Plato abolished the institution. Slavery was the basis of Greek economies. It is interesting that until Campanella, all utopias presupposed slavery.

Education would craft out every individual according to his potential, thus emphasizing the importance of nurture and training. The science of eugenics, conducted with utmost secrecy and careful selection of the mates, would ensure that genetic endowments were carefully transmitted to the children, thereby underlining that nature and nurture together shaped and formed an individual. Heredity was important to the extent that it supplied the raw material, but it was training and discipline that made possible the complete development of an individual. It conveyed the optimism of human excellence and perfection, though it expressed very little faith in the qualities of the average person. While education in arts was more a reform of the Athenian curriculum, the scheme of higher education was the most innovative. Plato overlooked the positive side of Athenian education, namely its creativity, all round excellence and human versatility. The fact that Plato recommended state-controlled compulsory education implied that he rejected its privatization and commercialization. Plato was convinced that good education would result in the overall improvement of society and that "if education is neglected, it matters little what else the state does" (Sabine 1973: 69).

Interestingly, since Plato, this idea has remained a cornerstone of Western societies. Even the guru of laissez faire and the minimal state, Smith, insisted that education, along with defence, and law and order, should be under the control of the state. The success of East Asia is largely due to a widespread, compulsory, state-controlled education system. Eugenics was prescribed with a view to preserving purity and quality, emphasizing that few were better than the many, thus suggesting racial overtones (Popper 1945: Vol. I). Society was strictly controlled with the help of censorship in art and literature and diet restrictions.

Plato was the first to allow women to become rulers and legislators. His scheme of collective households, temporary marriages and common childcare were accepted as necessary conditions for the emancipation of women by the socialists of the eighteenth and nineteenth centuries. But he was not a feminist in the modern sense in which the term has been used, namely giving women an equal and independent status with rights.

He understood individuality within a social context, and equality within a social stratum. He advocated sexual equality with the purpose of utilizing women's resources for the benefit and development of the community as a whole. However, it was to his credit that he was the first to point out that any sexual discrimination had to be justified.

The whole bent of Plato's thought was the welfare and development of the community. Adeimantus, provoked by the startling proposals relating to family and property for the guardian class, stated that the guardians would not be happy by these strict ascetic measures but Plato pointed out that the happiness of the whole community and not of a particular class was the aim. Furthermore, Plato pointed out that the happiness of the guardians were not being sacrificed for the happiness of the society. Despite being an anti-individualist, he made a strong defence for the individual—"his justice, his security and his freedom from want, uncertainty and ignorance" (Nisbet 1990: 103). One could discern a devotion to the individual as well as a devotion to the state in his political writings. The state was not repressive, but the source of virtue and individuality. It was the foundation of moral life. According to Plato, self-interest was morally dangerous and harmful as it corrupted individuals and perverted social life. The Ideal State however precluded plurality, for diverse allegiances led to inevitable and intolerable conflicts. The Ideal State, with unity as its goal, was projected as an essential precondition for both order and genuine freedom.

> The problem for Plato, as it was to be the problem for Rousseau two thousand years later, was that of discovering the conditions within which the absolute freedom of the individual could be combined with absolute justice of the state (Nisbet ibid: 103).

Plato's political theory affirmed absolutes and permanent truths, against the ethical relativism of Heraclitus and the democratic upsurge in Periclean Athens. His dialogues "are the earliest and the most fertile source of discussion of ultimate values, efforts to question conventional morality" (Berlin 1978: 3). This quest to find the ideal and perfect manifested itself in the form of rule by an aristocracy of intellect, suggesting that any deviation from the ideal represented degeneration, imperfection and therefore was evil. He desired to arrest all change, for he conceived a perfect state to be static and unchanging (Popper 1945). Philosophically, he combated Heraclitan logic by invoking a mystical distinction between the intellect and sense; politically, he countered the democratic temper by defending an aristocracy of philosopher rulers. His state, apparently radical, actually embodied the values of a conservative aristocracy, like order, stability, meritocracy and rule by the few.

Plato's Ideal State has been both an inspiration and a warning for subsequent efforts in Utopian projects. Thomas More's (1478–1535) *Utopia* (1516), Fra Tomaso Campanella's (1568–1639) *The City of Sun* (1602), and Francis Bacon's (1561–1626) *The New Atlantis* (1627), were patterned on the lines of the *Republic*. Plato's attempt cautions us against utopianism, for utopianism has led to totalitarianism. At the heart of a Utopian project is the chimerical idea of finality, which is inherently incompatible in a world that is essentially pluralistic and not amenable to complete solutions. Any effort to depict a perfect blueprint is not only methodologically unsound, but also politically dangerous. It is not possible to foresee everything and plan accordingly. Assuming that total planning is possible (like Plato and other Utopian theorists suggest), who is to plan the planners (Popper 1945)? Utopianism is politically dangerous, for it ignores and abuses individuality, liberty, plurality, tolerance, freedom of choice and democracy (Berlin 1969).

In a world of rapid change with history compressed, any radical programme of social action and utopianism is ill-equipped and inadept to cope with stresses and shocks, thus becoming a dinosaur. It is with the help of realistically conceived and practically feasible theories emphasizing moderation, gradualism and majoritarianism, that change which is permanent and swift, can be addressed. In realizing this essential fact, Aristotle scored over Plato, as his realism proved to be much more enduring and valuable than Platonic idealism, which remained unrealizable and impracticable.

3

Aristotle

> Aristotle bestrode antiquity like an intellectual colossus. No man before him had contributed as much to learning. No man after him could hope to rival his achievement (Barnes 1982: 1).

> Aristotle was primarily an encyclopaedist and with the partial exception of Democritos he was the first one. Earlier philosophers had tried to explain the universe, but Aristotle, who shared their ambition, was the first to realize that such an explanation should be preceded by as complete an inventory and description if it is possible. He did not simply understand that need but, what is more remarkable, he satisfied it. The totality of his work represents an encyclopaedia of the' available knowledge, much of what was obtained by himself or because of his leadership. It is easy to find holes or errors in that encyclopaedia, but the amazing thing is that it was as good, as comprehensive and durable, as it was (Sarton 1969: 93).

> For us, nowadays, Aristotle is a philosopher, and still perhaps the greatest name in the history of philosophy, but until three centuries ago he was more even than that; his work covered the whole range of the natural sciences, and he was considered a grave authority there as well. His systematic scientific conceptions have been superseded, although he is still reckoned to have been an accurate observer. For us his philosophical fame alone remains, but we shall not appreciate his significance for the medieval thinkers unless we recapture the idea of him as the master of those who know in every field of human speculation. The recovery of Aristotle was for the middle ages the acquisition not only of a philosophical system but of a whole encyclopaedia of scientific knowledge. To the men of that time he appeared almost as a personification of the human reason which they sought to integrate with the divine revelation acknowledged by them in Christian tradition ... (Hawkins 1969: 366).

By any reckoning Aristotle (384–322 BC) was a genius well-versed in a number of disciplines: aesthetics, biology, ethics, logic, physics, politics and psychology. He combined research with teaching, dominating the entire spectrum of human thought for centuries. Even today he remains the starting point for any scholarly enquiry in political science. Though Aristotle was a disciple of Plato, his masterpiece the *Politics* differed both in temper and content from that of his mentor. His primary interest lay in subjects like human behaviour, political institutions, constitutions and factors of political stability.

In the history of Western intellectual tradition, both Plato and Aristotle enjoy a pre-eminent position as the great masters. While Plato was an idealist and a radical, Aristotle is a realist and a moderate.

Aristotle has been regarded as the father of political science as he was the first to analyze, critically and systematically, the then existing constitutions and classify them. His classification of constitutions is still used in understanding constitutions comparatively. He was one of the earliest to use the compa-rative method, a method that has continued to be relevant even today.

Aristotle regarded political science as the master science, for it studied human beings in a political society, implying that a human being can lead a meaningful life only as a member of a state. Like Plato, Aristotle regarded aristocratic rule of a few, exercising power on behalf of and for the benefit of the people as the ideal, but realized the difficulty in achieving the ideal. Therefore, on grounds of feasibility, accountability and efficiency, Aristotle advocated a mixed form of government in which all citizens would rule and were ruled by rotation, ensuring that none had a monopoly over political power. Aristotle understood the importance of power sharing and elite accommodation, on which all the successful democracies of today are based.

The desire for knowledge was the single motivating factor in Aristotle's life. "His whole career and his every activity testify to the fact that he was concerned before all else to promote the discovery of truth and add to increase the sum of human knowledge" (Barnes 1982: 1). Aristotle believed that the quest for knowledge was universal among humans, for they were endowed with a mind to think. Happiness consisted in a life devoted to intellectual activity and contemplation. He refused to believe that the reality of everyday experience was either senseless, or a pale reflection of some more basic, higher reality. He saw logic in reality, a logic that required careful observation and reasoning to discover and understand.

LIFE SKETCH

Aristotle was born in 384 BC at Stagira, which is located on the north-eastern coast of the Aegean Sea. His father, Nicomachus, was a court physician to King Amyntas III of Macedon. The family was affluent. Aristotle developed a long-lasting interest in medicine and biology.

"He had every opportunity and encouragement to develop a scientific bent of mind; he was prepared from the beginning to become the founder of science" (Durant 1953: 49).

Not much was known about Aristotle's character and personality, except that he had a sense of humour, was a good speaker and extremely persuasive in conversation. There were many stories about him. One account portrayed him as having squandered his wealth due to self-indulgence, compelling him to join the army to avoid starvation.

In 367 BC Aristotle, 17 years of age, joined Plato's Academy. He remained in the Academy for the next 20 years, first as a student and then as a member of the faculty till 348 BC, and left the Academy for Asia Minor after Plato's death. Very likely, his departure had to do with the issue of succession within the Academy. Besides Aristotle, Speusippus, Plato's nephew, and Xenocrates aspired for the position. Speusippus got it. If loyalty was the matter, then of the three, Xenocrates should have succeeded Plato, for he remained a faithful adherent to Plato's theory. Speusippus too rejected Plato's theory of ideas in its original form. Very likely, the reason was to keep the property within the family and avoid the legal hassles of its transference to a non-Athenian. However, this reason fell flat, for Xenocrates succeeded on the death of Speusippus in 335 BC. Aristotle's decision to leave Athens after Plato's death could be partly because of his strained relations with Speusippus, and partly due to the anti-Macedonian feelings in Athens. Aristotle had close links with Macedon.

Aristotle's trips to Asia Minor got him interested in natural sciences. He met an old friend and an active politician, Hippias, whose niece he married. In 343 BC, Aristotle accepted the offer of Philip of Macedon to tutor the 14-year-old young prince Alexander. In 336 BC, Alexander succeeded to the throne after the assassination of his father, which meant having no time for studies. Aristotle left for Athens. Macedonia emerged as a dominant power in the region. It began to establish an empire, when many Greek cities including Athens came under its shadow, following the battle of Chaeronea in 338 BC.

Aristotle established his school, Lyceum, when he was denied an opportunity to head the academy for the second time. From 335 BC till his death, he devoted himself to research, teaching and administrative duties in Lyceum. Lyceum was more than a school or university. It was a public leisure centre, where Aristotle lectured to his chosen students in the mornings and to the general public in the evenings. Being an informal school, it had no examinations, degrees, syllabi, official enrolment and fees.

Aristotle pursued his studies in biology and history in Lyceum. By then, he had collected a large number of biological specimens. Many of them were sent by his students, including Alexander. His students also helped him to collect and compile research material, based on which Aristotle studied 158 constitutions. It has to be noted that amongst his contemporaries, Aristotle had the largest collection of personal books and manuscripts. After Euripides, (480-406 BC) he was the first to put together a library and lay down the principles of library classification. Plato referred to Aristotle's home as "the house of the reader".

Meanwhile, Aristotle's relations with Alexander got strained, reaching a breaking point in 326 BC, when one of his close friends, a philosopher, Callisthenes, accused Alexander of becoming an oriental monarch. Callisthenes was imprisoned and subsequently killed. Perhaps Aristotle would have suffered a similar fate, but for the fact that Alexander got busy with his plans to invade India. Within Athens, Aristotle's position became precarious, for he was seen as belonging to the pro-Macedonian faction.

Macedonia as an empire under Alexander began to threaten the liberty and independence of small city states that the Greeks had traditionally cherished. Alexander's sudden death in 323 BC was followed by a general revolt against Macedonian rule. When Athens declared war on Macedonia, Aristotle thought it was wise to leave the city, not only fearing for his life, but also denying Athens a second chance to commit a crime against philosophy, the first being the trial and execution of Socrates.

Ironically, in spite of his close links with Alexander, and the latter's world conquests, Aristotle remained oblivious of the fundamental changes in the political complexion of the city states. He continued to see the self-sufficient and self-governing city state or the *polis* as his ideal, at a time when the *polis* was in its twilight period, being relegated to history. All this happened over a 16-year period, when Macedonia incorporated the city states into an empire, and Alexander began to forge links between the Greeks and non-Greeks. Curiously, Aristotle's political outlook and belief "did not reflect these changes, nor did he make any effort to combat these. In that sense, "the *Politics* is a retrospective anachronism" (Kenny 1994: 284).

Aristotle spent the last year of his life in Chalcis in Euboea. He died in 322 BC at the age of 62, on account of "chronic indigestion rendered acute by overwork", as certified by his physician.

ARISTOTLE'S CORPUS

In the entire history of political theory, there is no thinker comparable with Aristotle. One of his ancient biographers remarked that he wrote a large number of books—close to 150—in every field, and most of them were excellent. Many of these have been lost, and only 20 per cent survive, which were lecture notes belonging to the Lyceum period. A catalogue of Aristotle's titles spoke of the breadth of subjects and his mastery over them. Some of the titles were: *On Justice, On the Poets, On Wealth, On the Soul, On Pleasure, On the Sciences, On Species and Genus, Deductions, Definitions,*

Lectures on Political Theory (in eight books), *The Art of Rhetoric, On the Pythagoreans, On Animals, Dissections* (in seven books), *On Plants, On Motion, On Astronomy, Homeric Problems* (in six books), *On Magnets, Olympic Victors, Proverbs* and *On the River Nile.*

These were works on arts, astronomy, biology, botany, chemistry, constitutional history, epistemology, ethics, intellectual history, language, law, logic, mathematics, mechanics, metaphysics, natural history, physiology, politics, psychology, and zoology. He had done extensive research on the nature of motion, space and time. "Choose a field of research, and Aristotle discoursed upon it. His range is astonishing" (Barnes 1982: 3). He established the foundations of many disciplines. Unlike Plato, Aristotle wrote on a much wider range. While Plato was restricted to branches of philosophy (epistemology, metaphysics and moral philosophy), Aristotle's included several subjects of natural sciences.

> If Plato can lay claim to being the first political philosopher, then there is little doubt that Aristotle stands as the first political scientist. Aristotle's conception of a science of politics, when contrasted with later approaches, is a straightforward one: it is based on the observation and classification of political institutions and behaviour (Hacker 1961: 71).

The most well-known of Aristotle's works were the *Politics,* the *Nicomachean Ethics* and the *Eudemian Ethics* or *On the Soul. The Constitution of Athens* dealt with the Athenian constitution. Very likely, there were written notes on the other 157 constitutions as well, but all of them seem to have got lost. Aristotle's style was simple and scientific. Unlike Plato's literary and poetic style, Aristotle's was terse, with concise arguments. His lecture notes were more an exposition of his research interests. He pursued research not in isolation, but in the company of his colleagues and friends.

The central theme of the *Politics* was the *polls,* an institution that was unique to fifth century BC. There was a detailed examination of the nature of the state and its origins, an analysis of the ideal state and the different constitutions of actual states, the concepts of citizenship, law and constitution. "It presupposes a small Mediterranean world which was a world of 'urbanity' or civic republics (the largest with an area of 1000 square miles, but many with 100 or less), and which stood, as such, in contrast with the world of 'rurality' in which the nations or *ethne* lived. There was some notion among the Greeks of a community called 'Hellas', but it was in no sense a political community" (Barker 1979: xlvii). The various books of the *Politics* do not form an integrated thesis. While Barker believed that three distinct sets of lecture notes combined together to form the *Politics,* Ross saw it as a compilation of five separate treatises (Ross 1924: 236). Jaegar (1923: 300) saw it as a unified, well-written treatise, though it was composed over a period of 15 years. "*The Politics* is analytical, descriptive and (in intent at least) practical" (Miller 1987: 26).

In the *Nicomachean Ethics,* Aristotle instructed the student to study the human soul. The immortality of the soul was the focus in the *Eudemian Ethics.* He attributed to the soul an existence that was natural and separate from that of the body, and believed that the dead had a superior existence to the living. In the two books on ethics, he discussed the nature of individual happiness or well-being, while in the *Politics* he regarded the state as the chief source and avenue for the realization of individual happiness. The object of the *Politics* was both speculative and practical, for it explained the nature of the ideal city in which the happiness of the individual would be realized, and also suggested ways and means of making existing states serve individual citizens, more than they did in Aristotle's time or had been so in the past.

One could distinguish three main phases in Aristotle's philosophical evolution. The first was the Athenian period, the second, the period of his travels, and the third, the second phase of his stay in Athens. As an entrant to the Academy, Aristotle adhered to many of Plato's ideas evident in his works the *Eitdemus* and the *Protrepticus* (Jaegar 1923). Jaegar described Aristotle's departure from Athens after Plato's death as "an expression of a crisis in his inner life". During his travels, Aristotle was convinced that Speusippus had only inherited the office but not the spirit of Plato, thus breaking away from Platonic philosophy and developing his own. The second major change came when Aristotle returned to Athens and began teaching at Lyceum.

While in the first two phases, Aristotle was concerned with metaphysical and epistemological problems, in the third phase he devoted himself to the "organization of research". It was during this time that such works as the biological treatises and collection of constitutional histories were embarked upon. They represented a "scientific type of exact research into the real world that was something absolutely new and pioneering in the Greek world of the time" (Jaegar ibid: 178).

These two phases of Aristotle were discernible in the *Politics.* Book II dealt with the Ideal State, a historical study of earlier theories, and criticism of Plato; Book III with the nature of the state and citizenship, and Books VII and VIII on the construction of the Ideal State, written shortly after Aristotle's departure from Athens, following the death of Plato. Books IV, V, and VI belonged to the period of Lyceum, for they dealt with the study of actual states, mainly democracy and oligarchy, along with the reasons for their decay and factors that could ensure their stability. Book I was the last to be written. It was during the second phase that Aristotle

> ... conceived a science or art of politics on a much larger scale. The new science was to be general; that is, it should deal with actual as well as ideal forms of government and it should teach the art of governing and organizing states of any sort in any desired manner. This new general science of politics, therefore was not only empirical and descriptive, but even in some respects independent of any ethical

> purpose, since a statesman might need to be an expert in governing even a bad state. The whole science of politics, according to the new idea, included the knowledge both of the political good, relative as well as absolute, and also of political mechanics employed perhaps for an inferior or even a bad end. This enlargement of the definition of political philosophy is Aristotle's most characteristic conception (Sabine 1973: 97).

While Aristotle's efforts in historical and constitutional researches were impressive, his accomplishments in natural sciences were equally commendable. He collected and observed specimens in astronomy, biology, chemistry, meteorology, physics, psychology and zoology. In fact, just as he is revered as the father of political science, he enjoys a similar position in biology and zoology. His *History of Animals,* which, if translated, would read as *Zoological Researches,* discussed in detail the parts of animals, their diet, habitat and behaviour. It was noteworthy that he observed and wrote about every animal and insect that was known to the Greeks. His other work on the same subject, *Dissections,* did not survive.

CRITIQUE OF PLATO

The influence of Plato on Aristotle was profound and pervasive. Aristotle shared with Plato many of the basic perspectives enunciated in the *Republic,* namely the hierarchy of human nature, justice as a relation or order among parts, and the inevitability of social classes. But he also diverged from his master in several significant ways, namely on the ideal regime, the dimensions of ethics, and the causes of revolution.

On the death of Plato, Aristotle paid tribute to him as a man whom evil men should abstain from praising, and who was the first to demonstrate both in terms of his own life and his writings that it was possible to be, simul-taneously, good and happy. Aristotle was equally appreciative and critical of Plato. Much of his criticism was made when Plato was alive. Though he was the most well-known and the best among the Platonists, he was not a thorough-going Platonist. The fact that Aristotle could differ from his master speaks highly of Plato, who encouraged his disciples to develop a critical perspective, regarding nothing as a sacred cow, including that taught by one's teacher. Aristotle remarked that 'Plato was a friend; Truth was a greater friend'.

Aristotle, like Plato, believed in the unified theory of sciences, but disagreed on how this unity was to be achieved. Like Plato, he was concerned with knowledge as a search for the causes and explanations of things. However, Aristotle, true to his scientific temperament, tried to *explain,* more than merely *observe and record,* data. Plato and Aristotle as logicians were concerned with problems of ontology, providing answers or clarifications to philosophical problems and puzzles. Aristotle learnt in the academy that "knowledge must be systematic and unified. Its structure is given by logic, and its unity rests at bottom on ontology. It is essentially explanatory. It poses deep philosophical problems" (Barnes 1982: 22).

Aristotle did not believe in Plato's optimistic claim that all knowledge could be founded upon a single set of axioms. He recognized the independence of the sciences, but stressed the need for a system. He divided knowledge into three major categories: productive, practical and theoretical. Productive knowledge was concerned with the making of things, for instance rhetoric and poetics. Practical science focused on action, namely how one ought to act in different circumstances with the knowledge that one possessed. Both politics and ethics belonged to this category. Theoretical sciences aimed to explore Truth as their ultimate goal, deduced with the help of logic from self-evident principles. Aristotle divided theoretical knowledge into First Philosophy (theology), mathematics and physics. First Philosophy dealt with "being qua being", and examined the nature of first cause. In the Middle Ages, it came to be referred to as metaphysics. Mathematics included arithmetic and geometry. Physics included botany, biology and chemistry. "In spite of its insufficiency, Aristotle's classification exerted a very strong influence upon the whole development of philosophy and science down to our own day" (Sarton 1969: 93).

Aristotle described politics as the master science and art, for it determined the ordering of the sciences to be studied in a state by every class of citizen. Within the ambit of politics came subjects like military science, economics and medicine, which assumed meaning by focusing on the primary or general good of humans. Aristotle equated 'Good' with happiness or *eudaimonia,* and was confident that it could be attained through education, a branch of politics.

Aristotle criticized Plato's theory of Forms on three grounds. First, he denied that the "general" could be "substantial". Second, he criticized Plato for making "properties" of things *outside* the things of which they are properties. Third, he questioned Plato for supporting Forms or Ideas as causes of phenomena, when in reality they lacked a moving force. In doing so, he proceeded to distinguish between Matter and Form. Matter was the raw stuff out of which specific things emerged. It was shapeless and undefined. However, within Matter there existed some latent form that differentiated one thing from the other. Form, according to Aristotle, was in Matter and not outside it. Matter was "potentiality", and Form "actuality". The Form within Matter provided definite shape, making it less indefinite and undifferentiated. It should be noted that Aristotle arrived at the conception of relation between Matter and Form as potentiality and actuality by his studies in biology. Having examined and observed the embryos of pigs and cattle, he could state that they did not differ, yet one embryo in normal circumstances became a hog and the other a cow. He explained that this was possible because of the presence of Form within each, which was impressed itself on what appears to be undifferentiated Matter. For Aristotle, while Form gave matter its shape, matter itself was undifferentiated and shapeless. But neither could achieve its actuality without being attached to what he termed as an "efficient" cause. Each Form was itself a reflection of a final cause. The latter provided the form which worked within the matter that was launched by the efficient cause. Extending the Socratic idea, Aristotle contended that a complete account of a thing was possible only if the parts were examined with reference to their implicit purpose or end.

Aristotle's political philosophy was both a critique and a corrective of Plato's ideas. As opposed to Plato's radical reforms in the *Republic*, Aristotle sought to conserve and preserve existing traditions and institutions. This made Aristotle a liberal conservative, proposing realism and gradualism as the best options in politics, subsequently reiterated by Burke and the English Fabians. His principles of the golden mean, advocacy of mixed constitutions, faith in middle-class rule as being best for ensuring a stable and enduring government, conviction of the family being the bedrock of the state, and the necessity of property to ensure self-sufficiency and fulfil the instinct of possessiveness in the individual, indicated his philosophy of moderation and belief in continuity. He "valued individual quality, privacy and liberty above social efficiency and power" (Durant 1953: 80). Aristotle emphasized conservation and moderation, and these remained guiding principles in his political philosophy.

Aristotle was critical of the scheme of the Ideal State that Plato outlined in the *Republic*. He contended that Plato's emphasis on unity, instead of harmony within a state, would only lead to excessive regimentation and the cessation of the state as a political association. A state was essentially a plural and diverse institution encouraging and cultivating a rich social life. Social differentiation was the key ordering principle of a good, stable state. Aristotle pointed out that the absence of plurality of aims and viewpoints did not purify politics. On the contrary it destroyed it. He did not reject the Platonic belief that every political community should be guided by the highest good, but he disagreed with Plato by insisting that a community should recognize and promote other goods as well.

Aristotle proceeded to examine the social institutions that Plato advocated in his scheme of the Ideal State, namely the community of wives and property. The unity that Plato desired, according to Aristotle, was more appropriate for a household rather than for a state. Within a family there were three kinds of relationships, while a state had just one kind of relationship: between the governed and the governors. Unlike the family, the state was an aggregation of different kinds of individuals. Aristotle contended that the role of the statesman could not be confused with that of a slave owner or the head of the family, for the statesman's role, unlike that of the husband and master, was a political one. Aristotle separated the political from the non-political, a distinction which Locke and the liberals subsequently incorporated and made it the cornerstone of liberalism.

As far as the community of wives was concerned, Aristotle felt that the Platonic scheme did not improve traditional family ties, for none would feel responsible for others in the absence of personal care and affection. Altruism was only possible if it was an extension of self-love. The good of the many had to be based on the good of the self. In Plato's scheme, the whole notion of personal love got diluted in the absence of real feeling and due to general indifference and neglect.

> What is common to the greatest number gets the least amount of care. Men pay most attention to what is their own; they care less for what is common; or at any rate, they care for it only to the extent to which each is individually concerned (Aristotle 1979: 44).

Instead of being cared for by one's father, it was quite possible to be ignored by so many "fathers". Furthermore, kinship became merely fractional. If a thousand were fathers to a child, then each father would be merely one-thousandth of a father. Therefore, "it is better to be own cousin to a man than to be his son after the Platonic fashion" (Aristotle ibid: 45).

Fraternity, for Aristotle, was important for it would be the best bulwark not only against civil dissensions, but also against deviant tendencies like incest, parricide and fratricide. In order to care and feel affection for a person, it was necessary that a person belonged to one, a feeling that one liked. Under the Platonic scheme, both were totally ruled out. Furthermore, the transposition of ranks that Plato advocated could not be carried through anonymously. For Aristotle, the scheme of community of wives and property would lead to a one-person state, obliterating social differentiation. In the absence of divergent elements making different contributions, even self-sufficiency would be lost.

> A household is an institution which attains a greater degree of self-sufficiency than an individual can; and a *polis,* in turn, is an institution which attains self sufficiency to a greater degree than a household. But it only attains that goal, and becomes fully a *polis,* when the association which forms it is large enough (and diversified enough) to be self-sufficing. On the assumption, therefore that the higher degree of self sufficiency is the more desirable thing, the lesser degree of unity is more desirable than the greater (Aristotle ibid: 42).

Aristotle regarded the family as a natural institution, to abolish which would be detrimental to both the individual and society. The fact that the family, along with the institution of property, had stood the test of time was a proof of their usefulness. Even for the wisest, family and material possessions were cherished for their intrinsic worth and the happiness they gave. A family helped the individual to develop his very best, by inculcating civic duties and personal love, contributing to stability of the state. Aristotle did not elevate the public sphere above the private, nor was he keen to eliminate the private. On the contrary, the private and public were complementary, each requiring the other for diversity and stability. In this formulation, his thought was a precursor of the modern innovation of civil society which advocated a balance between the private and the public (political) sphere.

For Aristotle, property was necessary not only to fulfil the possessive instincts of owning something, but also to encourage goodness and philanthropy. Common ownership, as opposed to private property, was problematic, since individuals

> ... do not share equally in work and recompense, those who do more work and get less recompense will be bound to raise complaints against those who get a large recompense and do little work. Indeed it is generally true that it is a difficult business for men to live together and be partners in any form of human activity, but it is specifically difficult to do so when property is involved (Aristotle ibid: 49).

Aristotle exhibited rare wisdom, rightly pointing out, that it was easier to equalize men's desires than to ensure an equal distribution of property. He raised the pertinent point of how to reward those who work harder and showed greater initiative. Some would always produce more, and therefore would expect and demand greater rewards commensurate with their efforts. The failure of communism with regard to property, work and reward in the modern period vindicated Aristotle. He was the first political philosopher to realize the need for recognizing merit, and the need to institutionalize just reward.

Aristotle contended that it would be wrong to attribute all the troubles in the world to the institution of property. In fact, most of these stemmed from the evils of human nature, which even communism could not correct. Instead, what was required was a moral change through education and training under good laws. While communism might liberate individuals from the ugly consequences of private ownership of property, it denied them the benefits that accrued from possessing something. It strived to promote a false sense of unity which undermined the very notion of a *polis* as an aggregation of different members. The other possible way of stemming the evils of private ownership was through the principle of the Golden Mean, or moderation. This ensured a middle path steering clear of wealth and poverty, opulence and squalor, and would help in the maintenance of property within limits as prescribed by nature. A reasonable amount of property, along with education, would inculcate the right attitudes of using property as instruments of public welfare. Aristotle also mentioned the virtues of benevolence and generosity that private possessions endowed, reducing selfishness and envy. He was convinced that a well-regulated institution of property would be socially beneficial. Even with regard to this argument, Aristotle's moderation found many adherents, and triumphed over the radicalism of Plato on the grounds of feasibility.

Furthermore, Aristotle pointed out that under a system of common wives, the third social class was ignored. If farmers were to be put under a common regime of wives and property, then how would their position be different from that of the guardians? On the other hand if they were allowed private property and family then it would result in the creation of two states within one, each opposing the other. Not only was the farmer denied the education that was provided for the guardians, but

> ... it ... fails to throw any light on other questions—such as the position of the farmers in the political systein, the nature of their education, and the character of the laws they are to observe. We thus find it difficult to discover—and yet this is a matter of the highest importance—how the farming class is to be constituted if the common life of the guardians is to be preserved (Aristotle ibid: 53–54).

Aristotle was equally critical of Plato's theory of the philosopher ruler. Permanent rule by a philosopher would lead to discontent and dissension not only among the ordinary citizens, but also among the high-spirited and the soldiers. This was dangerous, for it prevented circulation among elites and denied an opportunity to the ambitious to rule.

Aristotle pointed out that politics was not merely about the rule of the capable. A stable polity would have to accommodate the aspirations of different claimants. In Plato's Ideal State, not only were workers prevented from assuming office, but even among the guardians not everyone was in a position to aspire for one. As opposed to rule by perfect persons, Aristotle preferred constitutional rule, for it not only checked arbitrary power, but also ensured a periodic rotation of office-bearers. Though he feared the levelling tendencies within democracies, he was more concerned about the detrimental effects, both moral and practical, of an aristocratic monopoly on social and political honours. Furthermore, he was skeptical of Plato's contention that the knowledge of the wisest ruler(s) was better than the customary law.

> There is another matter which must not be ignored—the teaching of actual experience. We are bound to pay some regard to the long past and the passage of the years, in which these things (advocated by Plato as new discoveries) would not have gone unnoticed if they had been really good. Almost everything has been discovered already, though some of the things discovered have not been co-ordinated, and some though known are not put into practice (Aristotle ibid: 52).

For Aristotle, a good ruler ought to be worldly-wise rather than wise in the world of ideas. Moreover, from his own experience he could realize clearly and strongly the difficulty in attaining truth (scientific truth), though one could pursue it indefinitely.

> He does not reject (Plato's) discovery of the nature of scientific knowledge, nor his belief that the pursuit of such knowledge is the proper task of the philosopher; but he introduces a distinction which had been unknown to Plato, between the theoretical and the practical exercise of reason. Scientific knowledge is possible only of what is necessary and universal... but they are not found in the realm of human affairs which is the field of practical activity (Foster 1975: 122–133).

Like many of Plato's later-day critics, Aristotle argued that Plato deprived his guardian class the material and psychological reasons to be happy on the grounds that the object of legislation was the happiness of the whole state.

> It is impossible for the whole of a state to be happy unless most of its parts, or all, or at any rate some, are happy. The quality of being happy is not of the same order as the quality of being even. The quality of being even may exist in a whole without existing in either of its parts: the quality of being happy cannot ... . If the guardians are not happy, what are the other elements of the state which are? (Aristotle 1979: 54–55).

If the guardians were not happy, then it was possible that they would replicate the same kind of life for others, defeating the purpose of justice as defined by Plato as making a soul happy. Aristotle was critical of denying the lower classes the right to political opinions and participation. Such a denial would make them hostile. Unlike Plato, Aristotle did not dismiss their opinions as irrelevant. Moreover, Aristotle could perceive that participation achieved consensus on political issues or "opinions", and

> ... among the most important and exacting tasks of government in a civilized society is the distribution of various goods, such as public office and power, social recognition and prestige, wealth and privilege. The question posed by the distributive role of government is: from what elements ought a judgement about distribution be fashioned? In maintaining that community "opinions" ought to be a vital element, the central issue does not revolve around the truth or falsity of these opinions, but around the special kind of rationality demanded of a judgement that is to apply to the whole community (Wolin 1960: 61).

Aristotle shared with Plato his dislike for democracy, but, unlike Plato, was willing to accept democracy as unavoidable. This reluctant acceptance of democracy as inevitable in Aristotle was shared by Alexis de Tocqueville (1805–1859). He conceded to the greater populace participation and did not, like Plato, make it restrictive. He accepted constitutional rule "not as a concession to human frailty but as an intrinsic part of good government and therefore a characteristic of an ideal state" (Sabine 1973: 99). A stable government for Aristotle was one which recognized the individual's right to property and human freedom. In the *Ethics,* he was respectful of the opinions and views of the old and wise, and even asserted that consensus constituted ethical truth. In the *Politics,* he placed great merit on the judgement of the many, their collective virtue and collective capacity, their entitlement to rule and respect for popular opinion.

> Thus in politics the statesman cannot do anything he chooses, but he can wisely choose those courses which tend at least to a better and more desirable development of social institutions and of human life.

> In order to do this he needs to understand both what is possible and what is actual ... . His investigations always combine two purposes. They must be empirical and descriptive, because without the knowledge of the actual he cannot tell what means are at his disposal or how the means will turn out if used. But they must consider also the ideal dimension of the facts, for otherwise the statesman will not know how his means should be used to bring out the best that his material affords (Sabine ibid: 123).

Aristotle agreed that Plato's prescriptions in the *Laws* did not differ considerably from the ones proposed in the *Republic*. The major theme of the *Laws* was legislation, with very little of constitution. Plato's attempt was to institute a government that resembled existing reality, but ultimately it became a duplication of the ideal described in the *Republic*. Except for the community of wives and property, all other features were mentioned. Education had the same purpose. Common meals were provided to both men and women. Freedom from menial chores and leisure received the same importance. Citizens could bear arms (the number of whom was increased from 1000 specified in the *Republic* to 5000). The *Laws* stipulated a large territory and did not pay attention to foreign relations between states. Nor did Plato state the amount of property or the number of children that citizens could have. Landed property would be distributed by equal lots, ignoring the balance that ought to be preserved between population and property. Plato's system of government resembled Aristotle's polity, but the accent was more on the oligarchic rather than the democratic element.

Despite Aristotle's criticism of Plato, there were many similarities which could not be overlooked. Like Plato, Aristotle ensured the sovereignty of law with the rulers as its guardian, "its servant". Aristotle's description of the state as evolving from the family, the patriarchal nature of early states, the need for a state by everyone except an angel or a beast, war as a means for peace and not as an end in itself, the role of education, mixed constitutions, the roles of agriculture and retail trade, were some of the common points. Thus,

> ... while Aristotle, in the beginning of Book II of the *Politics*, criticizes both the *Republic* and the *Laws* (the former in greater, the latter in less detail), he was really much more interested in the *Laws;* and while he was largely indebted to the *Laws* for his general theory of politics, he was under the greatest debt to the *Laws* for his picture of an ideal state. If Aristotle wrote the *Politics* and arranged the content under the categories and in the scheme of his own philosophy, Plato supplied a great part of the content. There is as little absolutely new in the *Politics* as there is in (let us say) the Magna Carta. Neither is meant to be new: both are meant to codify previous development (Barker 1979: 444).

Aristotle retained and redefined many of Plato's ideas, but his contribution was in building a philosophical system based on empiricism.

> He may not have been so original or provocative like his master but he had a tremendous knack to organize from a complex set of details and facts patterns or tendency making him a giant in the history of science. He used this skill in social sciences deftly turning away from delineating an ideal state much on the lines of Plato and investigating first constitutional history and subsequently the structure and functioning of states based upon observation and history. Aristotle was the founder of this method, which has been on the whole the soundest and most fruitful that the study of politics has evolved (Sabine 1973: 123).

CONCEPTION OF HUMAN NATURE AND STATE

The state, according to Aristotle, was the highest form of political union, for it represented the pinnacle of social evolution. It was necessary, for it provided a framework for the satisfaction of basic wants and also ensured a means to secure and realize good life in a uniquely human sense. An individual found fulfilment from the advantages made possible by a state through its common endeavours, and one who did not feel its need was either an "angel" or a "beast". The state was prior to the individual, in the sense that it provided opportunities for the achievement of full humanity. Social affiliation gave to individuals their species identity.

> All associations are in the nature of parts of the political association. Men journey together with a view to some particular advantage, and by way of providing some particular thing needed for the purposes of life; and similarly the political association seems to have come together originally and to continue in existence, for the sake of the general advantage which it brings (Aristotle 1979: 2).

The state was an instrument for an individual's self-perfection. Far from being artificially or contractually created, it evolved naturally. Aristotle contended that man by nature was a political animal, making the state necessary and desirable. The significant point to note is that Aristotle's reference to nature confirmed the debate between *nomos* (convention) and *phusis* (nature) that dominated Greek political theory in the fifth century BC. As advocates of the *phusis* argument, both Plato and Aristotle asserted that the state and its laws were more than a product of convention. It was a natural institution reflecting individuals' needs and purposes, given human gregariousness and sociability.

Like Plato, Aristotle asserted that education was an effective way to produce political unity, though he criticized his mentor for not recognizing its economic significance. If the farmer and the guardian were to receive the same education, then how could one expect them to perform different functions? Conversely, if they did not receive similar education, then it would be a mistake to assume that education could unify the city. For Aristotle, education was more than merely acquiring skills and common beliefs, a point reitctated by Smith in his plea for the division of labour, and the specialization of skills. Education, to Aristotle, symbolized a way of life, for individuals learned largely by doing. Its goal was not unity, but to foster and protect a way of life that encouraged and sustained diverse social and political activities.

Aristotle was convinced of the individual's innate sociability and the natural desire to congregate and remain in society, by virtue of the fact that a human being enjoyed a unique capacity for moral choice and reasoned speech. Not only did reason distinguish humans from other social species, but they alone had a perception of good and evil, right and wrong, just and unjust, implying that these faculties could be developed only in company with others, and not in isolation. Not only was social cooperation necessary, but also desirable.

For Aristotle, the good of a community was clearly the greater, the perfect thing to attain and preserve, than the good of a single individual. This did not mean that an individual could be made to sacrifice the private for the public. Rather, being poor judges of their own interests, individuals could be educated in virtue to achieve their own happiness and excellence, in congruence with common good. Once this was attained, citizens could be habituated through laws and political life to follow the virtuous path, resulting in a well-ordered public arena. The individual's social nature and the implied "political" content resulted in virtuous public behaviour necessary for the pursuit of private happiness. For Aristotle, private life was a necessary, though not a sufficient, condition for enjoying a full human existence.

Aristotle pointed out that individuals could cultivate reasoned speech and moral choice with a view to achieving their full potential. The absence of these qualities would mean that human beings were worse off than animals.

> Virtues are implanted in us neither by nature nor contrary to nature; we are by nature equipped with the ability to receive them, and habit brings this ability to completion and fulfillment... we are provided with the capacity (dynamic, [or] potential) first, and display the activity (energia, [or] actuality) afterwards (Aristotle 1979: 15).

When Aristotle characterized human beings as essentially social, he had in mind those animals which live and work together as a community, like ants, bees, cranes, elephants and wasps. According to Aristotle, animals are social or individualistic; individualistic animals like the big cats live together, but that is confined only to their pride consisting of the male, the female and their cubs. Social animals, though not applicable to all gregarious ones, have a single common activity that unites them and that is the reason why human beings orbit towards the state. Rights of citizenship enable the use of one's unique human faculties through participation in the common life of the community. The desire for human company, a basic and universal human need, is so deeply entrenched that even saints and monks who otherwise renounce normal society and human relationships, form their own communities.

> What effectively distinguishes the citizen from all others is his participation in Judgement and Authority, that is, holding office, legal, political, administrative ... . There are different kinds of citizens, but... a citizen in the fullest sense is one who has a share in the privileges of rule ... a share both in ruling and in being ruled with a view to a life that is in accordance with goodness (Aristotle ibid: 94).

In the opening passages of Book III, Aristotle examined three topics: the nature of a state; citizenship; and the virtues of a good person and a good citizen. The state was an association of persons for the sake of securing the best moral life. The quality of life within a state would depend on those who constitute it and the end they wished to pursue. Accordingly, the end of the state depended on who could be its members, and how they wished to lead a life that was individually satisfying. In order to answer these questions satisfactorily, Aristotle defined a constitution not just as a form of government or a set of norms, but as a way of life, for *that* determined the moral character of a state. A state existed as long as its form of government endured, and any change in its constitution signified a change in its way of life too. Only within an Ideal State was a good person and a good citizen identical. In Aristotle's thought, "law, constitution, state, form of government all tend to coalesce, since from a moral point of view they are all equally relative to the purpose which causes the association to exist" (Sabine 1973: 105).

Arendt looked upon Plato and Aristotle as espousing a distinct sense of public life within the *polis*. Political activity for them assumed importance only after the satisfaction of human needs, both procreative and economic. Division of labour arose not so much out of need as from a desire to live well. It was for this reason that they regarded the *polis* as the highest and the most comprehensive form of human association. It aimed at the highest good, for the driving force behind every community was a notion of good. It represented a partnership based on justice and friendship or general solidarity. It is interesting that similar sentiments on the state were expressed by Burke. The *polis* was natural, and hence prior to the individual, not in the chronological, but in the teleological sense. It represented the whole with the individuals as its parts, for the individuals were not self-sufficient. The state tamed the savagery in human beings and made them just.

> Man is thus intended by nature to be part of a political whole, and there is therefore an immanent impulse in all men towards an association of this order ... . Man, when perfected, is the best of animals; but if he be isolated from law and justice he is the worst of all. Injustice is all the graver when it is armed injustice; and man is furnished from birth with arms (such as, for instance, language) which are intended to serve the purpose of moral prudence and virtue, but which may be used in preference for opposite ends. That is why, if he be without virtue, he is an almost unholy savage being, and worse than all others is the indulgence of lust and gluttony. Justice (which is his salvation)

> belongs to the *polis;* for justice, which is the determination of what is just, is an ordering of the political association (Aristotle 1979: 7).

Aristotle pointed out that the state evolved from lower associations. The first association was a household or the family, which arose to satisfy an individual's biological urges and everyday wants. A cluster of households became a village, and a group of villages constituted a political community or the *polis.* Each of these—household, village and the state—indicated different levels of self-sufficiency or autarchy.

> ... the final and perfect association, formed from a number of villages ... (is) the *polis*—an association which may be said to have reached the height of full self-sufficiency, or rather we may say that while it *grows* for the sake of mere life (insofar, and at that stage, still short of full self-sufficiency), it exists (when once it is fully grown) for the sake of a good life (and is therefore fully self-sufficient) (Aristotle ibid: 4–5).

The nature of an association was in its end, namely self-sufficiency, which meant not only the satisfaction of economic needs, but also the realization of the full human potential. This was possible only within the *polis.* The *polis* was the most sovereign and inclusive association offering a framework for a full and true life.

> ... the *polis* belongs to the class of things that exist by nature, and that man is by nature an animal intended to live in a *polis.* He who is without a *polis,* by reason of his own nature and not of some accident is either a poor sort of being, or a being higher than man: he is like the man of whom Homer wrote in a denunciation: clanless and lawless and heartless is he (Aristotle ibid: 5).

Both Plato and Aristotle regarded the *polis* as a complete form of reality. They zealously stressed its self-sufficiency and self-governing characteristics, projecting it as their political ideal too. Aristotle specifically stated that a *polis* should be large enough to guarantee self-sufficiency, and small enough to ensure good government. He defined a state as "a union of families and villages in a perfect and self sufficing life by which we mean a happy and a honourable life" (Aristotle ibid: 35).

NATURE OF HAPPINESS OR *EUDAIMONIA*

Having stated that good was the purpose of every community, Aristotle identified good as happiness. In the *Ethics* and the *Politics,* he was "concerned with the practical science of human happiness ... . The *Ethics* shows us what form and style of life are necessary for happiness; the *Politics* what particular form of constitution, what set of institutions are necessary to make this form of life possible and to safeguard it" (MacIntyre 1971: 57). The pursuit of happiness was clearly a human function, and referred to a soul's activity. Like Socrates and Plato, Aristotle was concerned about tending one's soul with a view to attaining happiness.

Happiness represented activity, the quest for excellence. In order to do things and do them well, to prosper and to flourish, certain skills were needed. Excellence led to success. Whether in pursuit of moral virtue or in the exercise of reason, happiness was in a life of activity or activities that were undertaken for their own sake. Happiness, for Aristotle, was not a state of mind or feeling, but referred to the quality of life in the organized and active expression of one's powers and capacities. In other words, it was defined in terms of a function in accordance with a person's virtue or excellence. Happiness was identified with Good, identified as the object of human endeavour. Good varied according to different categories: in quality, it referred to justice; in quantity, to moderation; and in time, to opportunity. He therefore rejected the notion of unified Good in its transcendental sense.

In the *Rhetoric,* Aristotle regarded a life of sufficiency and self-reliance as being a happy one. A pleasant life would be one with abundant possessions, security of property, good family and social status. In the *Nicomachean Ethics,* he clarified it as ethical virtue and pursuit of reason. In the *Eudemian Ethics,* he contended that to live meant to know, to think collectively, implying that individual and social consciousness were intertwined.

For Aristotle, rational and irrational were two qualities of a soul. The irrational aspect was further subdivided into vegetative and appetitive. The vegetative part was common to plants, animals and humans, for it contributed to the growth of the organism by controlling nutrition, excretion and other bodily functions. It related to the unconscious aspect, for it functioned best when the body was asleep. The appetitive aspect was the emotional side of a human person.

The rational aspect, on the contrary, was limited to the human person only. It referred to the deliberate and conscious aspects, and could be developed to its full potential through discipline and purposeful direction. It was natural for an individual to contemplate and act rationally, for that led to happiness. Aristotle then concerned himself with the means and conditions under which an individual could be happy. Happiness was attained by the exercise of two types of virtues, the ethical and the intellectual.

Intellectual virtue was the knowledge of final causes, and that included "practical wisdom" (*phronesis*) or a virtuous ethical behaviour, and "wisdom" (*sophia*) or the knowledge of eternal and unchanging objects. Aristotle personally favoured a life devoted to contemplation, viewing it as the best and highest form of human activity, and stating in the *Ethics* the reasons for his preference. Reason (*nous*) was the best guide, and contemplation meant a continuous and a pleasant activity which could be exercised for its own sake. It was a divine activity. But Aristotle realized that a life devoted to pure contemplation was ennobling for the individual who was partly and not wholly divine. Only a philosopher could realize a life of contemplation, for he alone was the one who needed the least of external goods. However, a philosopher should live among people and act in a manner that exemplified ethical virtues.

Ethical virtues involved bravery in battle (courage), honesty in business dealings (justice) and generosity towards one's city and friends, magnificence and liberality. An ethically virtuous individual had self-esteem, enabling one to assess one's worth to the community (magnanimity, proper ambition) in a proper perspective. It implied that such a person would be temperamentally balanced, reliable, amiable and moderate. It was possible to acquire these qualities within the *polis* through active participation in its institutions. Moral virtue, according to Aristotle, could not be taught, for it was a product of right actions instilled through habit, training and discipline. The emphasis was to acquire excellence by *doing* rather than *knowing* the right thing. In the context of defining ethical virtues, Aristotle formulated his notion of the "Golden Mean" or "Nothing in excess", which in simple words meant moderation. It is interesting to note that the idea of moderation was so deeply entrenched in the Greek psyche, that by the end of the classical era it had become one of the grand dicta of the Hellenic world.

In the *Ethics*, Aristotle explained in great detail the working logic of the mean. For instance, courage was a mean between cowardice and recklessness. Similarly, temperance was a mean between abstinence and self-indulgence, generosity between meanness and extravaganza, modesty between bashfulness and shamelessness, ready wit between buffoonery and boorishness, liberality between prodigality and meanness, and proper pride between vanity and humility. Some virtues, like truthfulness, did not fit into this scheme. Too much or too little exercise impaired bodily functions. Likewise, too much or too little food or drink destroyed health. The middle path, or the via media, was the one to be established as the general rule of right conduct and moral virtue. Aristotle then listed the virtues that characterized a gentle person—courage, self-control, generosity, magnificence, great- or high-mindedness, a nameless virtue between ambition and its lack, gentleness, friendliness, truthfulness, wittiness and shame. These virtues constituted the golden mean.

Aristotle applied the principle of the golden mean to his analysis of the political and social structures of the state, as evident from his extensive analysis of the "mixed constitutions" in the *Politics*. He attributed the decline, or even the demise of a state, to disproportion. Structurally, this problem was manifest in "pure" constitutions, for it excluded some classes and interests by disenfranchisement, leading to factionalism, so rampant in Greece. Aristotle's solution was to balance the forces of exclusiveness with those of equality, quality with those of quantity, democratic with oligarchic tendencies.

In addition to an ethically virtuous nature, a happy man required "external goods" like health, wealth and friends. These were instruments for the exercise of one's virtues. For instance, friendliness could not be demonstrated unless one had friends. Friendship was the noblest of all these external goods. It was more important than justice, for between friends justice was not needed. Moreover, when individuals are just, friendship would still be beneficial. Perfect and fine friendship was possible only among few, who were equal in status and stable in character. It required time and effort to cultivate good friendships, in the same way as one could not be generous unless one had wealth. For Aristotle, certain things, like birth in a good family, well-behaved children, beauty and intelligence, add to happiness. Conversely, their lack dampened happiness. While happiness implied contemplation plus virtue, it also meant external goods. He was equally assertive that the pursuit of human excellence could not be in isolation, for humans were social animals. Happiness increased when shared.

Aristotle placed great premium on education, as it trained emotions and impulses in persons, and worked for good as defined by the legislator or the ruler. The task of education was to inculcate moral, social and civic qualities in an individual, develop habits of good citizenship, and in a good *polis*, good persons. Humans had to be taught to do the right thing. "The final aim of education in goodness is to make our immediate judgement as to what is right to coincide with the spirit of wise legislation" (Joad 1966: 91).

Aristotle described the ideal man as one who

> ... does not expose himself needlessly to danger, since there are few things for which he cares sufficiently; but he is willing in great crises, to give even his life, knowing that under certain conditions it is not worthwhile to live ... to confer kindness is a mark of superiority. He does not take part in public displays... . He is open in his dislikes and preferences, he talks and acts frankly .... He is never fired with admiration .... He cannot live in complaisance with others, except it be a friend ... he is not fond of talking .... It is no concern of his that he should be praised, or that others should be blamed. He does not speak evil of others, even of his enemies, unless it be to themselves. His carriage is sedate, his voice deep, his speech measured, he is not given to hurry, for he is concerned about only a few things; he is not prone to vehemence, for he thinks nothing is very important. He bears the accidents of life with dignity and grace, making the best of his circumstances like a skillful general who marshals his limited forces with all the strategy of war. He is his own best friend and takes delight in privacy, whereas a man of no virtue or ability is his own worst enemy and is afraid of solitude (Aristotle 1962: iv [3]).

The aim of the state for Aristotle was

> ... to produce cultured gentlemen—men who combine the aristocratic mentality with the love of learning and arts. This combination existed in the highest perfection in the Athens of Pericles, not in the population at large but among the well-to-do. It began to break down in the last years of Pericles (Russell 1961: 204).

HOUSEHOLD (SLAVES, WOMEN AND PROPERTY)

The household was important in Aristotle's political philosophy, for it fulfilled the basic and important functions of an individual, namely the instinct of self-preservation and procreative functions, and for the satisfaction of economic needs. It trained the young ones to be good citizens by inculcating civic and moral virtues. Hence "of the two lesser communities, the household and the village, which are parts of the *polls* and precede it in time, the household is much more important in Aristotle's ethical and political theory" (Mulgan 1977: 38).

Aristotle, like Plato, realized that private interests of the members of a household might clash with those of the *polis* as a whole. It was for this reason that he attached considerable importance to the training of the inmates of the household and to the organization of the household.

> Every household is a part of a *polis.* The society of husband and wife, and that of parents and children, are parts of the household. The goodness of every part must be considered with reference to the goodness of the whole. We must therefore consider the government (of the whole *polis)* before we proceed to deal with the training of children and women—at any rate if we hold that the goodness of children and women makes any difference to the goodness of the *polis.* And it must make a difference. Women are half of the free population: children grow up to be partners in the government of the state (Aristotle 1979: 37–38).

The key figure was the head of the household, the father, who acted as a link between the political community and his household. Being a citizen and a full member of the *polis,* he was also the master of his house, his family and property. He exercised control over the household in three ways: as a husband over his wife, as a parent over his children, and as a master over his slaves. The fourth component of a household was "acquisition". Each of the other three relationships, involving the head, required a different kind of ruling.

Slavery

Aristotle discussed at length the relationship between the master and the slave. He tried to explain the relevance and use of slavery, an institution that was universal. Greece was no exception. Unlike Plato, who ignored the institution, Aristotle defended slavery both from the point of view of the slave and the master, the householder. Many feel that Aristotle endorsed and systematized Plato's views on slavery. Plato protested against the enslavement of Greeks by Greeks in the fifth book of the *Republic.* In the *Laws,* he recognized the need for legislation for slaves. He clubbed them with children, for having imperfectly developed minds. Personally, Aristotle recommended less harshness towards slaves. He also rejected the enslavement of the Greeks, but thought it proper for barbarians who were by "nature" slaves (Barker 1979: 1vii).

> Greeks regard themselves as noble not only in their own country, but absolutely and in all places; but they regard barbarians as noble only in their own country—thus assuming that there is one sort of nobility and freedom which is absolute and another which is only relative... just as man is born of man and animal of animal, so a good man is born of good men (Aristotle: 1979: 16).

Aristotle distinguished between animate and inanimate instruments in a household. The slave was an animate instrument intended for action and not for production; unlike artisans, a slave did not create a product, but only helped in the business of living within the household. Since, as an instrument, he served his master, he had no interests other than those of the master. The slave not only was a slave of his master, but also belonged entirely to him in the same way as a possession was spoken of not only as a part of something else, but also as belonging wholly to it. The master, on the contrary, was a master to the slave, and did not belong to him. He distinguished between conventional and natural slaves. The former were not slaves by nature. They had reason and were qualified to be citizens in their own state. However, they became slaves if taken as prisoners of war, a common practice during Aristotle's time. Natural slaves lacked reason, hence had to be under the permanent subordination of the master.

Aristotle believed that some persons were by nature free and others slaves. A natural slave's chief use was of his body. Though he possessed enough mind to control himself, he could understand and profit by the control of a superior mind. A family slave, by serving the interests of "his" family, got elevated. Since he served a moral purpose, he enjoyed benefits which were moral.

> ... anybody who by his nature is not his own man, but another's, is by his nature a slave; secondly, that anybody who, being a man, is an article of property, is another man's; and thirdly, that an article of property is an instrument intended for the purpose of action and separable from its possessor (Aristotle ibid: 11).

Aristotle justified slavery from the point of view of the householder and the slave. A householder gained for he was relieved of menial chores, giving him the leisure time for moral and intellectual pursuits that would enable him to contribute to the affairs of the state and fulfil his duties as a citizen. A slave imbibed moral and intellectual excellence from his master, which if left to himself would have been difficult. Aristotle justified slavery on the grounds of triumph of reason and virtue, the master representing reason and virtue, and the slave absence of reason, and non-virtue or less virtue. For a slave, the choice was between inferior and no virtue, differing from his master for whom it was a choice between inferior and perfect virtue. Thus, slavery was seen as being mutually beneficial and just. Moreover, it was in conformity with the principle of ruling and subordination that one saw in nature at large. Aristotle was categorical that the subordination of the slave must be towards endowing the slave with virtue and not to augment wealth, otherwise a slave would lose the one advantage that slavery brought forth, namely the guidance of his life by one of superior virtue.

Aristotle believed that men differed from one another in their abilities and mental faculties, and justified slavery for those lacking in these qualities. A slave could not govern himself, for he lacked the reason to do so. Aristotle was against making the defeated foe a slave. Prisoners of war could be made slaves only if success in war indicated superior intelligence of the victors. He also rejected the idea of making a person a slave to one who was merely superior in power and not in excellence. If the causes of a war were basically just, then prisoners of war could be made slaves.

The theory of slavery was based on two assumptions: first,men were divided in respect of their capacities for virtue; and second, that it was possible to determine the category to which an individual belonged. He recommended humane treatment for slaves, and conceded to them freedom if they so desired. Ross (1924: 241ff.) defended Aristotle's attitude towards slavery by arguing that "while to us he seems reactionary, he may have seemed revolutionary to them". Popper rejected this observation.

> Aristotle's views were indeed reactionary as can be best seen from the fact that he repeatedly finds it necessary to defend them against the doctrine that no man is a slave by nature, and further from his own testimony to the anti-slavery tendencies of the Athenian democracy (Popper 1945: Vol. I: 282).

Furthermore, Aristotle pointed out that a master-slave relationship differed from the one between a political ruler and the subjects. A slave, unlike a subject, was a tool of the master. Here, Aristotle invoked a distinction between a natural and unnatural slave. A natural slave had reason only to the point of recognizing a command and obeying it, for he lacked the capacity to direct himself. "The master must simply know how to command what the slave must know how to do" (Aristotle 1979: 18). He did not say what would be done with conventional slaves. Interestingly, he expressed in his will that his own slaves would be freed and not sold. In the *Ethics,* he suggested that a slave could become his master's friend. In Book VII of the *Politics,* he recommended their emancipation as a reward for good service. He also realized that the institution of slavery was not permanent. It would go with advancement in technology.

> If every instrument would accomplish its own work, obeying or antici-pating the will of others ... if the shuttle would weave, or the plectrum touch the lyre, without a hand to guide them, the chief workmen would not need assistants, nor masters slaves (Aristotle ibid: 10).

Women and Family

Aristotle provided a common-sense defence of the family. He did not abolish private households, for the family was a source of pleasure for both men and women, since it created and established a bond that united members, allowing them the space for the exercise and development of their individual talents. Writing on the family, the relationship between the husband and wife, parents and children he observed:

> "There seems to be a friendship between man and woman by nature. For the human being by nature is more disposed to live in pairs than in *polis,* inasmuch as the household is prior in time and more necessary than the *polis,* and the creation of children is more common with other animals. Among other animals, the community extends only this far (to the creation of children), [not only] for the sake of reproduction, but also for various aspects of their lives. Immediately, the work is divided, and there is one task for men and another for women. So they assist one another, putting their individual talents into the common good. On account of these things, there seems to be both usefulness and pleasure in this sort of friendship. This friendship also exists in accordance with virtue, if they are both good. For there is a virtue of each, and they are pleased by this .... It seems that children are a bond, wherefore marriages without children dissolve more quickly. For children are a common good for both and what is common holds them together (Aristotle ibid: 214).

Aristotle was critical of the Socratic-Platonic conception of communism, on the premise that to abolish the family would mean its destruction as a school of moral and civic virtues for the young. The family fostered love and friendship, and established a bond between its members in an orderly way. Its natural hierarchy ensured stability, and offered the preconditions for the pursuit of virtue. His defence of the family was similar to the arguments developed by Hegel. He was appreciative of the attention that Socrates and Plato gave to women's education, but he was critical of their proposal for sexual equality as it ignored the diversity that existed in the private sphere. For Aristotle, the private sphere was the foundation on which the public was organized. To ignore this link would result in an unstable and unnatural enterprise (Saxonhouse 1985: 83–86).

Aristotle was equally critical of the Spartan model, which granted unrestricted freedom to its women, resulting in divisiveness and disunity. By emphasizing virile power, men were made martial and ascetic, while women were left uncontrolled by both traditions and the laws of the state making them self-indulgent and luxurious. As a result, women could not be trained in the art of courage, nor did they learn to submit to authority, thus leaving them to pursue their private interests rather than common good. He concluded that to ignore women was to overlook one-half of the happiness of a society, making the latter unstable and vulnerable.

Aristotle was emphatic that women should be made a part of the city and its educational process, but could be left out of the political process.

For Aristotle, women and the family belonged to the private realm, which was really the world of the particular rather than the universal. Like Plato, he regarded the world as hierarchically structured, where the better ruled over the inferior, the strong over the weak, and the soul over the body. The male being superior, stronger and better, ruled over the female—a defective, incomplete male. He described a "woman as an infertile male", "a male is male in virtue of a particular ability and a female in virtue of a particular inability". The male was the active partner and the female passive, required primarily for sexual reproduction. Had it not been for this, remarked Aristotle, this particular deformity in nature would not have existed. In marriage, the husband by his superior virtue was the more useful, and hence the dominant partner. Though the husband-wife was interdependent, they were not equal.

The family, for Aristotle, was a natural aristocracy where the man had a say on things that were worthy of his consideration, leaving the rest to the woman. Violation of this norm within the family would pervert an aristocratic relationship into an oligarchic one, for self-interest rather than the interest of the community would then become the overriding concern. A well-ordered family was one that took into account differences between its individual members, and ensured that each worked in a manner so as to contribute to the common good. Accepting this differentiation made it easy to distribute tasks and authority that were naturally ordained and readily accepted.

A husband-wife relationship differed from the one between a governor and the governed, which kept changing. In a political community, the position of the ruler and the ruled interchanged depending on circumstances and the dictates of justice. But in a husband-wife relationship, the former was endowed with a natural gift for command, and the latter for obedience. It was constitutional, with adequate space for constant negotiation, debate and arbitration, as in the case of normal politics. It was not despotic, like the one between a master and his slave. The husband-wife relationship was exercised in the interests of the members of the household to enable the husband to emerge a winner, reinforcing his dominance as the "head" within the household, while the master-slave relationship was conducted solely for the benefit of the master. A slave had no rational capacity and acquired some intelligence by serving his master. He was not like a child who had potentiality of a deliberative faculty, but would remain dependent on his father as long as his faculty was immature, undeveloped and incomplete. A girl's deliberative faculty, however, remained undeveloped even after she became a woman, which explained her subordination to a man. A son had to be trained to become a free man, a citizen. A daughter's training would be appropriate enough to make her subordinate to her father and then to her husband. The relationship between the father and child was similar to that of a king and his subjects.

Aristotle pointed out that a ruler must possess full and perfect moral virtues. Though moral goodness may be found in all persons, temperance, fortitude and justice were not to the same degree in women as they were in men. He agreed with Sophocles (496–406 BC), reiterating his statement that "a modest silence is a woman's crown" and regarded quietness and modesty as a special form of their goodness. Aristotle was critical of Euripides for assuming that women could be clever and manly, dismissing these as inappropriate. While a man's goodness was goodness in the absolute sense, a woman's goodness remained relative. However, the woman was not a slave. She was a free being, a complement to the man. Though women constituted half of the free population, they were confined to the private sphere of the household since personal family ties were natural.

A woman's rightful place was her house because of her special abilities as a wife, mother and householder. While a man acquired, a woman's function was to "keep and store". In that sense, her role was similar to that of a statesman within the city—preserving what had been acquired and ensuring stability. The family was a sphere of inequality, with differentiation in power and authority arising from sex, age and ability (Saxonhouse ibid: 87). Interestingly, Aristotle considered the family to be the seat of inequality, and hierarchy gave rise to the more majestic and important *polis,* the sphere of equality.

A woman as a mother spent a great part of her youth and time in bearing and rearing children, unable to enjoy leisure that a man had, and therefore was decisively disadvantaged. Women were to be excluded from the public realm because their deliberative faculties were inconclusive and lacked authority. Political life, for Aristotle, required participation by those who were equal both with regard to leisure time and possessions, for they had to engage themselves in reasoned discourse about (un)just issues. Women did not have these so they could not play a direct political role. Using this criterion, he also ruled out slaves and workers. "His concern that the public realm serves as the arena for the highest human activities (after philosophy) led to his demand for such an intellectual engagement" (Saxonhouse ibid: 88).

Interestingly, many of these themes were reiterated by Rousseau in his *Emile.* Rousseau too entertained a stereotypical image of women. Since men and women differed sexually their education would also differ. It was astonishing that even extremely gifted individuals like Aristotle and Rousseau could not rise above the prevailing prejudices and localism on the gender question.

Aristotle devoted considerable attention to issues of reproduction when he discussed the city of his dreams. For ensuring the health of the population, he recommended a 20-year gap in marriage, for a man's sexual ability began declining at 70, while a woman's at 50. This gap ensured that one was not reproductively active when the other had been incapacitated. The ideal age for marriage in case of women was 18, and for men 37. Aristotle, like Plato, saw marriage as an arrangement for "the provision of a stock of the healthiest possible bodies for the nurseries of our state" (Aristotle 1979: 325–326). A mother provided *materials* to the child, while a father *the rational soul,* so it was necessary to take into account the father's mental health. He advised women to undertake more physical exercise, for the child in their wombs would draw from their strength totally ignoring their idle minds, thereby implying that the growing child in no way benefited from his mother's mind. Aristotle confused between women's reproductive capacity and their sexual urges.

Aristotle did not, like Plato, advocate equality of the sexes. But this did not mean that he did not accord any role for women. He granted a woman distinct role in society, a position within her family and the home. It was here that she could demonstrate her unique abilities as a wife, mother and a homemaker, preserving and stabilizing the family and home, and giving birth to and educating the young. The woman, though free, was like a slave, for she lacked reason, which was why she should submit to the superior wisdom of men. While a slave helped in the orderly functioning of a household, a woman managed her family and home.

Unlike Plato, Aristotle retained the private realm to which the family belonged, as it was crucial for the pursuit of excellence within the community and provided the foundation of the *polis.* He warned of conflict, dissolution and chaos when the family and women were ignored, as in the instance of the city conceived by Socrates and Plato, or the one that existed in Sparta. It was for this reason that he rejected the Socratic-Platonic conception as being unnatural and detrimental to the health of the *polis.* In fact, he pointed out that the *polis* by its diverse and plural nature differed from the household. Unity was achieved when its differentiated parts worked in harmony according to an overriding principle. However, the unity that Plato aspired for and proposed by eliminating the private sphere would eventually, according to Aristotle, only stifle the city and lead to its extinction.

> But a state which becomes progressively more and more of a unity will cease to be a state at all. Plurality of numbers is natural in a state; and the further it moves away from plurality towards unity, the less a state it becomes and the more a household, and the household in turn an individual... so, even if it were possible to make such a unification, it ought not to be done, it will destroy the state (Aristotle ibid: 15–22).

From the point of view of feminists, both Plato and Aristotle raised a crucial issue. Was the family an instrument or an obstacle to sexual equality? Could the family be the arena in which women could attain freedom and fulfilment? Plato assumed that women could be free only if the institutions of monogamous marriages and private families were abolished. Aristotle, on the contrary, defended the private family vigorously, on the grounds that it made possible for the moral development and the position of women within the household, for which they were best suited, and for the training of children as future citizens. Both viewpoints had their strong adherents and antagonists in the ensuing years, in fact centuries. Interestingly, Aristotle's arguments with regard to the importance of a private sphere and family have been reiterated by the liberals. The liberals, however, disagreed with Aristotle on the position and status of women. Early liberals like Wollstonecraft and J.S. Mill viewed women primarily as homemakers and wives, but argued for equal legal and civil rights and demanded equal opportunities in education, employment and suffrage.

Property

Both Plato and Aristotle regarded economic activity as highly significant for the purpose of political analysis. Economic activity had to be subordinated to political, since the former was concerned with a single good, while political was concerned with good life as a whole in its multidimensional sense. In discussing acquisition of wealth, Aristotle distinguished two modes: natural and unnatural. The natural included hunting (brigandage, fishing, pursuit of birds and bees), grazing and husbandry. It was natural, because nature not only gave them to all individuals for fulfilment of their needs, but also fixed a limit on its consumption in accordance with subsistence.

The intermediate stage was barter, which was natural to the extent of allowing one to acquire whatever was needed for the purposes of life. The use of money, however, led to other forms of acquisition. Retail trade was one form with no limits on acquisition, and hence was an illiberal occupation. Aristotle, following the Greek prejudice, rejected retail trade on moral grounds, for the end of wealth, whether household income or that of a state, should be good life. He was critical of small businessmen, shopkeepers and petty usurers, for they were corrupted by a desire for financial gain. He preferred landed property to trade and commerce. The important thing was not the greater or unlimited, but the *right* amount of wealth. Aristotle remained sufficiently ambiguous about what could be regarded as the right amount of wealth. Good life was his main focus. He saw an intimate link between the pursuit of bodily pleasures and a man's ethical character. He stressed that material goods were necessary for leading a good and happy life, though they were not an end in themselves. In his scale of values, happiness of the soul was infinitely superior and higher than any other pleasure in the world.

The most basic form of good economic activity was directed towards the use of the product. In this context, Aristotle cited activities like fishing, shoemaking and farming. In activities where the producer and his family directly benefit, in the sense that their needs are fulfilled, it would have use-value. However, as society became more complex, trade increased and specialization of labour became the organizing principle, products were made for purpose of exchange. Thus, products assumed an exchange value in addition to a use-value.

Aristotle was the first to pay attention to the economic basis of political institutions by focusing on the character and distribution of wealth and its influence on the form of government. He considered extreme inequality of wealth as an important cause for revolutions. He defended private property, but was a great believer in well-distributed wealth.

> With the partial exception of the Levellers from Aristotle to the late eighteenth century it was generally agreed that it is the greatest blessing for a state that its members should possess a moderate and adequate property (Heater 1990: 168–169).

Distributive Justice

Justice, for Aristotle, was a complete virtue, though not absolute. It was in relation to one's neighbour. The social character of virtue was "universal" justice or lawfulness. Both Plato and Aristotle believed that the primary task of a state was to ensure justice. Aristotle distinguished between distributive, and corrective or rectificatory or remedial justice.

Distributive justice meant that offices and wealth, rewards and dues were distributed among different social classes according to their contributions based on merit, defined in accordance with the spirit of the constitution. In an oligarchy, merit meant wealth, while in an aristocracy, it was related to virtue. In an ideal state, merit meant virtue. Since in Aristotle's perception the objective end of the state was to ensure and promote good life, the group that contributed most to this end could legitimately claim most of society's honours. On this premise, he believed that a virtuous minority or an aristocracy supplied the most direct and significant benefits to society. In the last resort, it would also mean the enthronement of one person with supreme virtue, or an absolute divine monarchy. Besides virtue and wealth, Aristotle recognized freedom as an important criterion with regard to the end of the state. Freedom meant free birth, and also being independent of others.

Aristotle agreed with Plato's assertion that only virtue and wisdom ought to be criteria of who would rule and exercise political power, but wondered how to approximate it in practice. Although Aristotle identified virtue as the ultimate qualification for office, he allowed for the enfranchisement of popular and oligarchic elements as well. He tried to assimilate the two doctrines of distributive justice that prevailed during his time. One was the democrats' assertion that equality derived from free birth, or that each would count for one, and no one for more than one. The other was the oligarchs' view that superiority in one represented superiority in others as well. The two principles of equality and superiority could be made compatible, if both were subordinated to justice.

Distributive justice set forth in the *Politics* clearly recognized the contribution of each major unit to society and its unique claim to political participation—while numbers mattered in popular claims, wealth was an important component in an oligarchic claim, and virtue in an aristocratic claim— thus giving a share to everyone in the political process. The allotment of honours was based on the relative assets of each group. The principle of mean balanced the political opportunity of the few, many and the rich, and was infinitely superior to the partisan principle offered in an unmixed or pure constitution.

Distributive justice meant proportionate equality, and was linked to a theory of just rewards or equal shares according to the merit of its recipients. Each person would be awarded responsibilities as well as financial benefits in proportion to one's just deserts.

> The advantage of Aristotle's doctrine is that it satisfied the demands of social justice in both aspects: the point of proportionate equality is more equitable than the democrats' conception of mere numerical equality. Similarly the idea of special privilege which his doctrine introduces is more justifiable than the oligarch's claim that either wealth or noble birth by itself deserves the highest rewards ... . Proportionate equality is grounded in the principle of fair and reasonable inequality of treatment (von Leyden 1985: 4, 6).

Rectificatory or remedial justice was meted out by a judge in matters like contracts or criminal law, where the merit of a person was not the consideration. The important fact was that all persons would be treated in a manner of equal merit. Aristotle regarded equality as crucial to social justice, and justice as central to equality.

Inequality, for Aristotle, arose when equals were treated unequally, and unequals equally. It accepted the belief that individuals differed in capacities, interests and achievements. Moreover, the varied dimensions of human life—social, cultural and economic—differed in importance. It was necessary to distinguish between the deserving and the undeserving. He tried to counter the principle of equality by justifying inequalities. The reason was twofold. One, the desire for equality was more in the nature of a wish rather than being grounded in reality. Second, even if one accepted the demand of equality as a moral one, it still failed to be convincing for it contradicted "the spirit of morality with its presupposition of men's different stations and functions, especially their obligations and duties of obedience on the one hand and their rights and positions of authority on the other" (von Leyden ibid: 6).

RULE OF LAW AND CONSTITUTION

Aristotle was categorical that a rightly constituted law was the final authority, and that personal authority was only desirable if for some reason it was not easy to codify laws to meet all general contingencies. Aristotle's ideal was constitutionally-based order. Laws were less arbitrary and fairer, since these were impersonal as compared to rule by a person. "[t]he rule of law is preferable to that of a single citizen: even if it be the better course to have individuals ruling, they should be made law-guardians or ministers of the laws" (Aristotle 1979: 146).

Aristotle contended that a free political relationship was one where the subject did not totally surrender his judgement and responsibility, for both the ruler and the ruled had a defined legal status. The "passionless authority of law" gave to the magistrate and the subject a moral quality and dignity respectively. A constitutional ruler, unlike a dictator, ruled over his willing subjects by consent.

> The relation of the constitutional ruler to his subjects is different in kind from any sort of subjection because it is consistent with both parties remaining free men, and for this reason it requires a degree of moral equality or likeness of kind between them, despite the undoubted differences which must exist (Sabine 1973: 99).

The authority that was wielded by a constitutional ruler over one's subject was different from the one that the master wielded over his slave, since the latter lacked reason to rule himself. Political authority also differed from the authority that a husband exercised over his wife and children. Aristotle contended that a serious flaw in Plato's reasoning was his failure to distinguish political authority from that of household, as evident from Plato's comment in the *Statesman* that the state was like a family writ large. A child, not yet an adult, would not be entitled to being treated as an equal. Women, being inferior, were unequal to men. A political relationship was one of equality. On the contrary, an ideal state would not be constitutional or political if the differences between its members were so great that they did not have the same virtue. An ideal state is "an association of equals, and only of equals, and its object is the best and highest life possible (in which the slave cannot share). The highest good is felicity; and that consists in the energy and perfect practice of goodness" (Aristotle 1979: 298–299).

Constitutional rule had three main elements. First, it was a rule in the general or common interest of the populace, as compared to a rule by a faction or a tyrant which was in the interest of a ruler, one or few. Since it was lawful, a government was carried on in accordance with general regulations and not by arbitrary decrees. Moreover, a government could not act contrary to the constitution. Third, constitutional government meant willing subjects ruled by consent, rather than by force.

Aristotle took a cue from Plato's suggestion in the *Laws* that laws were necessary for a moral and civilized life. Civility of law was possible if one perceived law as wisdom accumulated over the ages and generations resulting from customs, both written and unwritten. For Aristotle, "experience must represent a genuine growth in knowledge, though this growth registers itself in custom rather than in science and is produced by common-sense rather than by learning. Public opinion must be admitted to be not only an unavoidable force but also, up to a point, a justifiable standard in politics" (Sabine 1973: 101). Aristotle, unlike Plato, contended that the collective wisdom of the people was superior to that of the wisest ruler or legislator, for "the reason of the statesman in a good state cannot be detached from the reason embodied in the law and custom of the community he rules" (Sabine ibid: 102).

A constitution for Aristotle was not only a basic law determining the structure of its government and allocation of powers between the different branches within a government, but it also reflected a way of life. A constitution gave an identity to the *polis*, which meant that a change in the constitution brought about a change in the *polis*.

> For, since the *polis* is a community of citizens in a constitution, when the constitution of the citizens changes and becomes different in kind the *polis* also does. We may compare this with a chorus, which may at one time perform in a tragedy and at another in a comedy and so be different in kind, yet all the while be composed of the same person (Aristotle 1979: 99).

A political community, like all other communities, involved concerted actions and joint activity working towards a common purpose. It could be distinguished from other associations by the fact that it had a supreme authority, which was defined along with the common purpose by its constitution. A constitution could be described as "an organization of offices in a state, by which the method of their distribution is fixed, the sovereign authority is determined, and the nature of the end to be pursued by the association and all its members is prescribed" (Aristotle ibid: 156).

From the foregoing paragraphs, it would be evident that a constitution had two aspects: the ethical or the aims and goals to be pursued by a community; and the institutional or the structure of political institutions and offices, and the distribution of power. In its ethical sense, a constitution, for Aristotle, provided the identity of a state, for it examined the relationship between a good citizen and a good man. As a result, different constitutions required different kinds of good citizens, whereas a good man was always the same. Only under an ideal constitution was there an identity between a good man and a good citizen. A good citizen was one who possessed the moral wisdom to become a good ruler and a good subject. A state was a moral institution contributing to the realization of the moral qualities in its citizens.

The institutional aspect involved the determination of the sovereign power and the allocation of powers among the offices. The most important institution was a civic body, which was sovereign. Every constitution had to contain three elements, namely deliberative, the official or magisterial, and the judicial. The deliberative had four functions.

1. It was responsible for the most important decisions in foreign policy, matters of war and peace, and the making and breaking of alliances.

2. Making and interpreting laws.
3. Administration of severe penalties, such as death, exile and confiscation of property.
4. Election of magistrates and their examination on completion of their term.

Aristotle assigned a comprehensive array of powers to the deliberative branch of government, since it was supreme. It controlled the magistrates and the courts by controlling the laws that regulated their functions, and by retaining the power to decide judicial and executive issues.

Aristotle analyzed and compared 158 constitutions, thereby uniting the empirical and speculative modes of enquiry. He built on Plato's classification of constitutions in the *Statesman* by taking into account the ends of a constitution and the number who wielded political power. Constitutions promoting general well-being of the governed were true or good, whereas those that fettered the interests of the ruled were bad or perverted. A government ruled by one, few or many in the general interest of the community was monarchy, aristocracy and polity respectively. Conversely, a government ruled by one, few or many in the self-interest of the ruler was tyranny, oligarchy and democracy res-pectively. In each of these true and perverted constitutions, merit within the system of distributive justice was defined in a particular way befitting the constitution.

Aristotle regarded monarchy as a true form of government, for it was possible to have a virtuous person as a ruler who would be able to stand outside the law and be its single guardian. However, he pointed out, historically, public interest even in a monarchy was best secured through a system of rules framed by a legislator who would also be the founder of the city. He was generally skeptical of finding a virtuous person who could be a monarch. He distinguished five types of kingship. The first was the Spartan model where the kings were responsible for military and religious matters. The second was a mixture of kingship and tyranny, to be found among the barbarians. The third was dictatorship, which existed in the early part of Greek history. The fourth kind, associated with the heroic age, was kingship which was hereditary and ruled by law. Initially, they wielded unlimited powers, with the king being a judge with powers to control religion, but eventually their powers got circumscribed. The fifth one was absolute kingship, or rule by one person who controlled everything.

For Aristotle, a monarchy developed into an aristocracy, which was a true form of rule by a few. There were three kinds of aristocracy, all of which were mixed constitutions employing, besides virtue, other principles. The first kind, as seen in Carthage, combined virtue with wealth and number. The second, as in Sparta, combined virtue with the democratic principle of freedom. The third combined wealth with freedom, and was more oligarchic. The third form of true government was polity, a kind of mixed rule in which the claims of the many and the propertied were held in check by law.

As far as perverted forms of government were concerned, tyranny—defined as the arbitrary power of an individual responsible to none, governing all alike, whether equals or better, for its own advantage, not that of its subjects, and therefore against their will—was a perfect counterpart of monarchy. Tyranny degenerated into an oligarchy with the interest of the few, the rich being the sole concern. Aristotle described four types of oligarchy. The first was a moderate one, close to a polity, where the rulers ruled in accordance with law. Access to office was based on property, which was not restrictive. For higher offices, Aristotle recommended a large share, and a smaller one, for low but essential offices. The second one was more exclusive. It was the rich and the few who enjoyed few benefits. The third one was still more restrictive and narrow, with the hereditary governing elite. The fourth one was a small rich coterie which ruled without laws.

The third and the "least bad" of perverted forms of government was democracy, the rule by the poor and the majority. This was because the many, "when they meet together may very likely be better than the few good, if regarded not individually but collectively, just as a feast to do which many contribute is better than a dinner provided out of a single purse" (Aristotle ibid: 123).

The many contrary to one, or the expert, was a better judge of policies including music and poetry. Tyranny was the worst of the perverted forms.

Aristotle contended that there was a difference between democracy and polity, between rule by the best (aristocracy) and rule by the richest (oligarchy). The difference between a monarchy and a tyranny was an ethical one. Monarchy was better than an aristocracy, which in turn was better than a polity. Tyranny was worse than an oligarchy, which in turn was worse than a democracy. Aristotle thereby provided qualified support for democracy.

While actual governments were bad, democratic government tended to be the best. Here again he described four kinds of democracy, which follow a progression from a moderate to an extreme one. Moderate democracy had some sort of property qualifications for officials, with the majority of people being agricultural and unmindful of political offices. The second type was similar to the first one, but without property qualifications for officials and granting everyone the right to hold office as long as they were not disqualified by birth. There would be no payment for performance of public duties, and government was governed in accordance with law. In the third kind, citizenship qualifications were relaxed to include all freemen, including aliens and children of emancipated slaves, who were excluded from the first two types. In an extreme democracy, all restraints were removed, being totally lawless with full rights to demagogues.

In Aristotle, there was hardly a discussion of the ideal type except sketchy details, but a concern with the best practicable state, pointing out that a monarchy and aristocracy were best suited for ideal forms of state, since goodness was their aim. Moreover, monarchy of the ideal type was suited to domestic rather than political rule. Aristotle believed that politics, like all arts and sciences, had to not only consider the ideal constitution, but also know what was practicable and enduring under the given circumstances. In considering the feasibility of a constitution, Aristotle took into account the virtue and intelligence that an average individual possessed.

> The whole bent and bias of his thought must be toward the view that the ideal while conceded to be an effective force, must still be a force within the actual current of affairs and not dead against it... . The ideal state represented a conception of political philosophy which he inherited from Plato and which was in fact little congenial to his genius. The more he struck out an independent line of thought and investigation, the more he turned towards the analysis and description of actual constitutions. The great collection of one hundred and fifty eight constitutional histories made by him and his students marks the turning point in his thought and suggested a broader conception of political theory. This did not mean that Aristotle turned to description alone. The essence of the new conception was the uniting of empirical investigation with the more speculative consideration of political ideals. Moral ideals—the sovereignty of law, the freedom and equality of citizens, constitutional government, the perfecting of men in a civilized life—are always for Aristotle the ends for which the state ought to exist, what he discovered was that these ideals were infinitely complicated in the realization and required infinite adjustments to the conditions of actual government. Ideals must exist not like Plato's pattern in the Heavens but as forces working in and through agencies by no means ideal (Sabine 1973: 104, 109).

Plato classified governments on the basis of their law-abidingness, while Aristotle used the criterion of general welfare and the number who wielded political power. For Aristotle, "there are two distinct claims to power, one based upon the rights of property and the other upon the welfare of the greater number of human beings" (Sabine ibid: 106). The correction to Plato's formal classification enabled Aristotle to consider the justifiable claims to power in a state by adjusting and accommodating all claimants. He did not question Plato's proposition that wisdom and virtue had an absolute claim to power, and tried to make it operative in practice. For Aristotle, a state ought to realize justice in its fullest and largest sense, for justice meant equality.

Aristotle granted an absolute moral claim to power to those who possessed wealth, for the state was not a trading company or a contract. He rejected Plato's solution of community of property as disastrous, and pointed out that there was not much of a difference between a plundering democracy and an exploitative oligarchy. However, he thought it unrealistic and unwise not to protect property, since property guaranteed good birth, sound education, reasonable associations and leisure. While the proprietied had an important claim to political power, equally convincing was the argument of democrats that numbers did matter. Aristotle concluded that no class had an absolute claim to power, for the law was sovereign. But law was relative to its constitution. A good state would have good laws, and conversely a bad state would have bad laws.

> Legality itself then is only a relative guarantee of goodness, better than force or personal power, but quite possibly bad. A good state must be ruled according to law but this is not the same as saying that a state ruled according to law is good (Sabine ibid: 107).

Among the ideal types, Aristotle concentrated on monarchy rather than aristocracy. Monarchy would be the best form if a wise and a virtuous king could be found. Being a god among humans, the monarch ought to be allowed to make laws. To ostracize and check the monarch would be unjust. It would be best to allow the monarch to rule, but Aristotle was not sure whether to grant anybody the *absolute* right to rule. So much was his belief in equality between citizens in a given state, that he made no exception even when it came to perfect virtue. The principle of equality would have to be the ordering principle of both good and perverted governments.

In Book IV, Aristotle identified social class as another criterion while defining constitutions. By social classes he meant the rich, poor and occupational groups, such as farmers, artisans and merchants. He took into account economic factors, seeing them as decisively influencing the political system. "He long ago pointed out that the constitution of a state had its roots in what the moderns term as its social system" (Neuman 1900: 223).

In considering actual states, Aristotle clearly distinguished the ethical from the political and placed great importance on the constitution as an arrangement of offices. Subsequently, he distinguished law from the political structure of an organized government. He separated the political from the economic and social structure, thereby explicitly stating the separation of state from society.

> He was able to use the distinction in a highly realistic fashion when he shrewdly remarked that a political constitution is one thing and the way the constitution actually works is another. A government democratic in form may govern oligarchically, while an oligarchy may govern democratically (Sabine 1973: 112).

Polity

An analysis of the political factors in a democracy and an oligarchy enabled Aristotle to consider the form of government that would be suitable to a large number of states, assuming that for its realization no more virtue or political skill was needed than what the states could gather. Though not an ideal, it was the best practicable state in accordance with his principle of the golden mean, obviating the extreme tendencies within oligarchic and democratic systems. This was called polity or constitutional government, a name given to moderate democracy in Book III.

Aristotle distinguished between a democracy and an oligarchy by referring to them as majority and minority rule. Democracy was a constitution with a majority government which the free-born and poor controlled. In an oligarchy, government was controlled by a minority, namely the rich and the better-born. Democracy did not exclude the rich or well-born from holding office or participating in politics. Oligarchy usually imposed qualifications for voting and holding offices.

Aristotle accepted the presence of a wealthy class and relatively poor citizens as inevitable. But from the viewpoint of political stability, it was necessary to enlarge a group that was neither rich nor poor, namely the middle class. The rich enjoyed great benefits and privileges, but were unwilling to accept discipline. The poor, because of their deprivation, lacked spirit and enthusiasm. Therefore, the middle class constituted the mean in the social structure, not only balancing the oligarchic and democratic elements, but also mixing them in the right proportion so as to ensure stability. The middle class was a countervailing force, neutralizing the centrifugal tendencies generated by contending forces which, if unchecked, would lead to the demise of the city. The larger the middle class, the greater the possibility of tranquillity and stability in the state, for it steered a middle path between the insolence of the rich and the unruly behaviour of the bitterly poor. Aristotle agreed with Euripides' description of the middle class states as "save states", and observed:

> In all states there may be distinguished three parts, or classes, of the citizen body—the very rich, the very poor and the middle class which forms the mean ... as a general principle the moderation and the mean are always the best ... in ownership of all gifts of fortune a middle position will be the best. Men who are in this condition are the most ready to listen to reason. Those who belong to either extreme ... find it hard to follow reason ... those who enjoy too many advantages ... are unwilling to obey and ignorant how to obey. This is a defect which appears in them from the first, during childhood and in home life; nurtured in luxury, they never acquire a habit of discipline, even in the matter of lessons. But there are also defects in those who suffer from the opposite extreme of a lack of advantages: they are far too mean and too poor spirited. We have this, on the one hand, people who are ignorant how to rule and only know to obey, as if they were so many slaves, and, on the other hand, people who are ignorant how to obey any sort of authority and only know how to rule as if they were masters of slaves. The result is a state of envy on the one side and on the other contempt. Nothing could be further removed from the spirit of friendship or the temper of a political community (Aristotle 1979: 181).

Aristotle's solution of putting the middle class in power flowed from his observations that in an oligarchy, the rich were fined if they did not serve as judges and the poor were given no pay, whereas in a democracy the poor were paid and the rich were not fined. Both these were extreme practices. It was important to find a mean where the poor were given a moderate pay, while the rich were fined at the same time. It was the middle class which provided the common ground and was crucial to the societal mix. A stable society had to balance forces of quality and quantity. Quality referred to an exclusive category of birth, wealth, property, social position or education, while quantity meant numbers, the claims of the mass of people to political participation. Through a combination of the lot (elections, property qualifications and relative merit), he hoped that a balance could be attained and maintained in the realm of policy formulations and execution. The historical model that Aristotle had in mind for the polity was the one drafted in 411 BC at a time when democracy was temporarily eclipsed in Athens (Ross 1924: 259).

Aristotle saw in rule by the middle class fulfilment of two important political ideals: equality, and consensus. Its civility would smoothen the rough edges in society, for it would know how to simultaneously command and obey as free people. It would be a bulwark against selfishness, tyranny, unlawfulness and instability. For Aristotle, since any state was better than an anarchy, he preferred a mixed state to a pure one more, for that was more enduring.

> The polity reflects a kind of condensation of his practical political wisdom. Much of its basis is to be found in Plato's Statesman and Laws; ... . In its balance caution, and absence of any adventurous spirit, the polity is almost a perfect epitome of Aristotle's ethical-political position (Sibley 1981: 100–101).

A polity took into account freedom, wealth, culture, noble birth, and numerical superiority. It also gave scope for the attainment of goodness. It symbolized the principle of Mean or moderation or the middle-way principles of practical politics (Sinclair 1951: 23). Popper viewed Aristotle's best state as a compromise between three things: a romantic Platonic aristocracy, a "sound and balanced" feudalism, and some democratic ideas; but feudalism has the best of it (Popper 1945: Vol. II: 3). The reason for Popper's assessment was because Aristotle excluded slaves and producers from the citizen body, though he conceded the right of participation to all citizens. Like Plato, he argued that the working class could not rule, and that the ruling class should not work nor earn any money. They could own land but not work on it. He defended the right of the leisured class to rule.

Citizenship

Aristotle placed the theme of citizenship at the centre of his political analysis because of his belief in a law-based government. This was contrary to Plato, who ignored the issue and placed greater faith on philosophic rule. Aristotle characterized political authority as constitutional between equals, and since an individual was a political animal who found fulfilment only within a *polis,* it was natural for people to aspire for political positions. Constitutional government with respect to citizenship rights allowed people to compete for political office without civil chaos.

Aristotle defined a state as a collective body of citizens. Citizenship was not to be determined by residence, since the resident aliens and slaves also shared a common residence with citizens, but were not citizens. Nor could citizenship be defined by the share one had in civic rights, to the extent of being entitled to sue and be sued in courts of law, for this right belonged to aliens as well. A citizen was one who enjoyed the *right to share in the deliberative or judicial offices,* and was able to exercise his political rights effectively. A citizen also enjoyed constitutional rights under the system of public law.

For Aristotle, a citizen was one who shared power in the *polis,* and unlike Plato, did not distinguish between "an active ruling group and a politically passive community" (Wolin 1960: 57). Aristotle stipulated that the young and the old could not be citizens, for one was immature and the other infirm. He did not regard women as citizens, for they lacked the deliberative faculty and the leisure to understand the working of politics. As far as the working class was concerned, though some states made them citizens, they clearly did not have the aptitude nor the leisure to display the true excellence to shoulder civic responsibilities. A good citizen would have the intelligence and the ability to rule and be ruled. He, however, shared with Plato the perception that citizenship was a privilege and a status to be inherited.

Aristotle pointed out that in order to discharge functions effectively, citizens would inhabit a *polis* that was compact and close-knit. He was critical of Plato's prescription that a citizen body of 5000 would be the ideal, for that was too large and would require unlimited space, such as the sprawling lands of Babylon, rendering impossible functions like military command, public communications and judicial pronouncements. A cohesive citizen body, where everybody would know one another intimately, would be able to settle disputes effectively and satisfactorily, and distribute political offices according to the merit of the candidates. The quality of citizenship would suffer in a larger political community due to lack of intimacy.

Aristotle described a good citizen as someone who could live in harmony with the constitution, and had sufficient leisure time to devote himself to the tasks and responsibilities of citizenship. He regarded the existence of diversity of interests within a citizen body as essential to the practice of citizenship, for it was through a balance of these interests that good government was attained. A good citizen would possess virtue or moral goodness that would help in realizing a selfless and cooperative civic life. He regarded citizenship as a

> ... bond forged by the intimacy of participation in public affairs. The bond was moreover a relationship which was guarded with some jealousy by those privileged to enjoy it. It was neither a right to be claimed nor a status to be conferred on anybody outside the established ranks of the class, no matter how worthy such an outsider might be. Indeed, Greek citizenship depended not so much on rights which could be claimed as on responsibilities which had with pride to be shouldered (Heater 1990: 4).

Both Plato and Aristotle pleaded for responsible and effective forms of education for citizenship. This, they considered, was a cure for the corruption and political instability of their times. They were equally critical of the casual manner in which the Athenian state regarded the tasks of citizenship. As a corrective measure, both prescribed state-managed and state-controlled education. In the *Laws*, Plato made it clear that the guardian of laws controlled the educational system by selecting teachers only from among those who were willing to teach the laws and traditions of the state in a manner determined by the guardians. Both Plato and Aristotle were committed to the idea of state-controlled education. They "believed that different styles of civic education should be used for different purposes. Plato emphasized training in self-sacrifice for rulers and obedience for the ruled; Aristotle emphasized the need to match the educational objectives to the form of government" (Heater ibid: 7).

Revolution: Causes and Remedies

The search for stability through polity made Aristotle examine the causes for instability, change and revolution, and prescribe remedies against unnecessary and incessant change. Unlike Plato, who did not accept change and equated it with decay and corruption, Aristotle on the contrary regarded change as inevitable. Change represented movement towards an ideal. Unlike Plato, Aristotle accepted the possibility of progress. Things changed because they had the potential to inch towards perfection. Aristotle derived his conception of change from his understanding of science and nature.

> The Idea or Form is *in* the thing (like the adult in the embryo), not outside. The destiny of a thing is foretold by its hidden unrealized essence. Evolution proceeds as it does, not because of material causes producing natural consequences, pushing them on ... but by final causes pulling them ahead... . All the things that exist are directed toward an end (which is potentially inside of them); their development is shaped by a purpose. The world is gradually realized because of a transcendental Design, or call it Divine Providence.
>
> Aristotle realized that mechanism and purpose are complementary and inseparable aspects; in the study of nature one must seek for a mechanical explanation or for the leading reason; sometimes the mechanism is clearer, sometimes the reason. In his time practically no

mechanism (for example, a physiologic mechanism) was conceivable; hence, there remained only the teleological explanation (Sarton 1969: 92).

Stability and revolution were important in Aristotle's agenda of political ideals, having perceived a constitution as containing the essence of a state. Aristotle discussed general causes of revolution and then looked into the reasons why individual constitutions changed. Unlike Plato, Aristotle perceived multiple reasons for revolutions, rather than simply a regime's prominent deficiency. He placed greater responsibility on the rulers to ensure stability and justice. The criterion of stability was not majority support for a constitution, but the fact that no class or faction favoured violent change.

Revolution could take the form of change in the constitution of a state, or the revolutionaries may leave the constitution unchanged, and remain content with just accruing more power for themselves. Revolution could make an oligarchy more or less oligarchic and a democracy more or less democratic. It could be directed against a particular institution or a set of persons in a state keeping the form of government intact. The general causes of revolutions were broadly categorized into three.

1. Psychological motives or the state of mind.
2. The objectives in mind.
3. The occasions that gave rise to political upheaval and mutual strife.

The *psychological factors* were the desire for equality in an oligarchy, and inequality in a democracy. The *objectives* in mind included profit, honour, insolence, fear, superiority in some form, contempt, disproportionate increase in some part of the state, election intrigues, wilful negligence, neglect of apparently insignificant changes, fear of opposites and dissimilarity of component parts of the state. The *occasions* that gave rise to revolutionary changes were insolence, desire for profit and honour, superiority, fear, contempt, and disproportionate increase in one part or element of the state.

The particular causes were analyzed in each individual constitution. In a democracy, the unchecked licence given to demagogues, who attack the rich and instigate the masses, was the cause. It could be remedied by granting the right to vote to the poor and the disadvantaged, giving them a stake in the government. In an oligarchy, the oppression of the masses and the dissensions within the ruling elite led to instability. In an aristocracy, the policy of narrowing the circle of government was a cause of instability. Sedition arose when: (a) the rank and file of people were exalted by the idea that they were just as worthy as their rulers; (b) when great men were dishonoured by those in office; (c) when high-spirited individuals were excluded from honours; and (d) when some within the governing class were poor and the others rich. Aristocracies were prone to change when they deviated from the notion of justice, namely a balance between oligarchic and democratic forces as delineated by the constitution.

An aristocracy might change into a democracy when the poor got the impression that they were treated unfairly, compelling them to revolt. In a monarchy, sedition was usually due to fear, contempt, and desire for fame, insults, hatred and desire by neighbouring states to extend their boundaries.

The remedy for preventing a revolution in a monarchy was by inculcating a spirit of obedience to law, especially in small matters, and to distrust charlatans and demagogues. In case of oligarchies and aristocracies, the remedy was in ensuring that rulers were on good terms both with the civic body and those who had constitutional rights. None would be raised too high above the level of his fellow citizens, for inequalities of offices and honours, more than inequities in wealth, drive men to rebellion. Small honours would have to be conferred over a long period of time, ensuring that none became very influential in rapid succession. A magistrate would be appointed to keep vigil over those who did not live in a manner that was in harmony with the spirit of the constitution. In order to neutralize the consequences of a flourishing social group, the management of the state could be given to those who were not doing so well, or by fusing the rich and the poor sections of society, or by strengthening the middle class. A tyrant could prevent instability through a divide-and-rule policy, encouraging class hatred between the rich and the poor, and creating a strong spy system. He would have to appear to be religious, erect public works for the employment of the poor, cut down on lavish expenses and observe conventional rites and practices. In his advice to the tyrant, he anticipated Machiavelli (Barker 1979: 247).

Aristotle pointed out that the source of revolutions and seditions was usually the image of the government. Care would have to be taken to prevent offices from being used for personal gain. In the interest of constitutional stability, three qualities were required for office-bearers in high positions, and these were: (a) loyalty to the established constitution, (b) outstanding adminis-trative capacity, and (c) integrity of character, goodness and justice in forms. Repeatedly, he emphasized on a fusion between oligarchic and democratic forces. He also recommended government propaganda in education, respect for law even in small things, and justice in law and administration, i.e. equality according to one's contributions, as measures to prevent revolutions.

CONCLUSION

Aristotle has rightly been called a political scientist, for he defined the subject matter of politics and identified its core elements, namely sovereignty of law, constitutionalism, faith in moderation, conception of proportionate equality and just rewards, causes and remedies of revolution and polity or the middle class state as the best practicable and stable political system.

All these topics were scrutinized and analyzed in the *Politics*. Rather than being a book, it was a compilation of independent essays and lecture notes. In dealing with these themes:

> Aristotle not only laid the general principles of universal significance but also reflected the prevailing Greek notion which is why it is both interesting and important—interesting in showing the common prejudices of educated Greeks in his time and important as a source of many principles which remained influential until the end of the Middle Ages (Russell 1961: 196).

Aristotle's treatment of the various themes in the *Politics* reflected his empirical and inductive method. With the help of collected observation, common opinion and traditional notions, data was gathered and theory emerged from an analysis of alternative perceptions. While in Plato's metaphysics, the real world, and human understanding and perceptions were devalued, Aristotle dissected reality empirically in the same fashion as a physician diagnosed illness and health.

Aristotle believed that observation was crucial to the study of political phenomena, and the way changes occurred within it helped us to understand its real nature. Change was teleological, meaning movement towards the natural predetermined end. A scientist would look for material, study the structure and its functions, and ask the following questions: Out of what? What was it? From where and for what sake? In other words, these were the material, formal, efficient and final causes respectively. While in a conscious action, the final causes might lie in a purpose beyond the object analyzed in the natural process it was the emerging form that guided development. Aristotle perceived order as being more important than disorder, in view of his acceptance of the idea of an in-dwelling nature. He rejected the argument that change was primary and that all equilibrium analysis was partial and untrue, for there were real structures in things, the world was a plurality of homeostatic systems whose basic plan could be discovered and rationally formulated through an analysis of its structure and functions. As in the case of the world, order was eternal. It was neither imposed from outside, nor did it evolve. Plato understood change as one that had degenerated from his ideal.

For Aristotle, the true end of an individual was happiness, while the end of a state was self-sufficiency, which could be achieved by moderation in its wealth, size, constitution and ruling group. The best individual was one who had realized his nature. The best regime was one which realized or had achieved the quintessence of its nature. There was an intimate link between the human being and the state, for the former by nature was a social person with an instinct of sociability, while the state was a natural institution within which the development and the fulfilment of the individual was possible. It was natural because it offered conditions of good life, the true end of all associations. Green and Bosanquet, the nineteenth-century British Idealists, developed this argument in detail.

For Aristotle, ethics and politics were complementary. Ethics studied the virtues that made up a good individual, whereas politics studied institutions that enabled individuals to find their true potential. Though contemplation for Aristotle was the highest form of activity, he still probed into the practical good of an individual's social relations and existence. Like Plato, the societal dimension was never lost in his theory.

Aristotle's main focus was on the best practicable state or constitution. In the *Laws*, Plato contended that the mixed constitution was the best and most stable regime, a panacea against the cycle of development and degeneration that was implicit in the sixfold scheme. Aristotle adopted the scheme, perfected and elaborated it, and since then it

> ... has served as a basic taxonomy through the ages and into the 19th century ... . It is the first explanatory theory in the history of political science, in which institutions, attitudes, and ideas, are related to process and performance. It is the ancestor of separation of powers theory (Almond 1996: 54).

Of the six regimes, Aristotle saw only four as being important: oligarchy, democracy, polity and tyranny. Aristocracy was the ideal, but difficult to achieve and even harder to sustain. Hence polity, or the mixed constitution, was the best for it reconciled virtue with stability, quantity with quality. Tyranny was the worst. He reinforced his arguments by pointing out that the social structures of cities differed according to their economies, occupations, professions and statuses, but these variations could be reduced in terms of the rich and poor sections of citizens. If the rich dominated it, then it became an oligarchy, and when the poor controlled affairs it became a democracy. When the middle sections held the reigns of authority, extreme forces were ruled out, guaranteeing inbuilt stability. Aristotle's faith in the middle class has been reiterated in the writings of Smith and the English Classical economists. The theme of mixed constitution has been repeated subsequently in the writings of Polybius, Marcus Tullius Cicero (106–143 BC), St. Aquinas, and Machiavelli.

Aristotle was a vigorous critic of democracy but still offered a fair assessment of its advantages. To enumerate some, collective opinions and judgements were more satisfying than individual ones that many rather than few would rule. Its disadvantage was the treatment meted out to the extraordinary. However, he did not, like Plato, fear the mass of people and had more faith in their ability to collectively articulate their judgement on the effects of policies and the ability of the rulers. Here, Aristotle echoed Pericles, who had faith in the ability of the ordinary citizen.

Aristotle defended the rule of law, for it provided stability and reason as opposed to passion. The distinction that he made between numerical and proportionate equality, distributive and corrective justice, the importance of liberal education and leisure, limitations on wealth without undermining the right of property, the distinction between use-value and exchange value, the difference between a good man and a good citizen, the importance of property qualifications with regard to citizenship, have been extremely influential in subsequent political discourse.

Every aspect of justice had a twofold natural foundation: (a) relation to the political community in which each man occupied a position, fulfilled a function and value in proportion to the share of social goods; and (b) private relations with other men whereby every man possessed the same right as others to enjoy a certain number of elementary and inalienable goods. "If the exercise of the rights of the citizen demands respect for proportionality and universal, and this therefore can only belong to all men as such" (cited in Heinaman 1998: 647).

Human nature had twofold variations and was inwardly diversified in its political manifestations, though at the same time it was similar everywhere in the right it conferred on each man to realize, even if in different ways, the capacities inherent in his human essence. This meant that though Aristotle was a believer in the natural inequality of human beings, yet he accepted that there were areas of commonality, as everybody had capacities in different fields. In this sense he pleaded for functional categorization, with the hidden manifestation of equality in ordinary interaction within civil society. This, in modern terminology is referred to as the rule of law. Pointing to the ancient roots of modern constitutionalism as reflected in the US Constitution Shklar traced its origins to ancient Greece and observed that "the very idea of the rule of law depends on Aristotelian logic, that is, syllogistic reasoning" (Shklar 1998: 159).

It was true that Aristotle's political perceptions did not mirror the dramatic and tumultuous changes occurring in the Greek world. His pupil Alexander the Great was building an empire, but Aristotle continued to see the city state as the natural institution for human sociability. He was an admirer of the Athenian model. In fact, his entire political philosophy rejected the cosmopolitan and imperial model of Alexander. It was also a fact that, analyzed in the context of the immediate aftermath, Aristotle was totally forgotten. The reason for this was the narrow base of Greek politics, leading to the exclusion of large segments of society, and the politics of withdrawal as exemplified by the non-political philosophies developed by the Cynics, Epicureans, Skeptics and Stoics.

The Skeptics and Stoics were critical of Aristotle. They thought that his prescriptions ignored the diversity that was found in the world. They were critical of him for projecting the moral values of the Athenian middle class as universal. The criticism of Aristotle gathered momentum in the fifteenth century, but this was more on medieval Aristotelians and not on Aristotle himself. However, in the sixteenth century Aristotle himself was attacked by writers like Justus Lipsus (1547–1606), Pierre Charron (1541–1603) and Michel de Montaigue (1533–1592). Charron went to the extent of criticizing Aristotle for propounding absurd notions. Grotius rejected Aristotle's principles of a minimum core as being inadequate in formulating important concepts like benevolence. By 1640, many Catholic and Protestant theologians developed a skeptical criticism of Aristotle. He was portrayed as a false philosopher, for his prescriptions were based on reason rather than faith. Hobbes rejected the ethical foundations of Aristotelians and the Humanists on the grounds of self-preservation. For Hobbes, Aristotle's theory was an impediment to scientific investigation and "with this complaint Hobbes rejects the whole Aristotelian epistemology of matter and form, essence and existence" (MacIntyre 1971: 130).

The conserving and realistic elements in Aristotle's philosophy were his defence of slavery and confining women within their homes and families. This was because he believed in natural hierarchy among human beings and that individuals differed in their abilities, capacities and intelligence. However, he also realized that slavery was a temporary institution, whose need and utility would be lost with revolution in machinery.

"Aristotle's *Politics* has served as a foundation work for the whole Western tradition" (Edel 1968: 410). The posthumous influence of Aristotle was wider than Plato's. Aquinas, Alighiere Dante (1265–1321) and the entire Christian tradition during the medieval era was inspired by him. Machiavelli used his ideas on mixed constitutions to analyze instability. James Harrington (1611–1677) was influenced by his economic analysis of politics. The sociological dimensions of his thought were taken up by Charles-Louis Secondat Montesquieu (1689–1755). Hegel, Marx, and in recent years the Communitarians like MacIntyre drew their conceptions of an integrated ethical community largely from the vision of Aristotle, seeing society as a whole and prior to the individual. However, the totalitarian implications within Marxism-Leninism had nothing to do with Aristotle's ideal (Barker 1995: xxx–xxxi).

Aristotle "bequeathed a great legacy to political thought, but not to any one school" (Curtis 1961: Vol. I:29). It is for his range, depth and profundity that intellectuals throughout the world continue to pay well-deserved homage to Aristotle as "the master to those who know". He was a great pioneer in political science, and no discussion is ever complete without a reference to his brilliant insights and methods of analysis.

4

Niccolò Machiavelli

> The basic thing about *The Prince* is that it is not a systematic treatment, but a "live" work, in which political ideology and political science are fused in the dramatic form of a "myth". Before Machiavelli, political science had taken the form either of the Utopia or of the scholarly treatise. Machiavelli, combining the two, gave imaginative and artistic form to his conception by embodying the doctrinal, rational element in the person of a *condottiere,* who represents plastically and "anthromorphically" the symbol of the "Collective will" (Gramsci 1971: 125).

> The Renaissance, though it produced no important theoretical philosopher, produces one man of supreme eminence in *political* philosophy: Niccolò Machiavelli. It is the custom to be shocked by him, and he certainly is sometimes shocking. But many other men would be equally so if they were equally free from humbug (Russell 1961: 491).

> Once we restore Machiavelli to the world in which his ideas were initially formed, we can begin to appreciate the extraordinary originality of his attack on the prevailing moral assumptions of his age. And once we grasp the implications of his own moral outlook, we can readily see why his name is still so often invoked whenever the issues of political power and leadership are discussed (Skinner 1981: 2).

Niccolò Machiavelli (1469–1527) commanded a sinister reputation as no other thinker in the annals of political theory. "The murderous Machiavel" as William Shakespeare (1564–1616) called him, was depicted on the Elizabethan stage as a professional inventor of stratagems, a guide to rogues, usurpers and tyrants and the term "Machiavellism" symbolized villainy. The initial reaction to Machiavelli's writings was one of shock, and he himself was denounced as an inventor of the devil. "A damned Machiavel", commented Shakespeare, "holds the candle to the devil himself", referring to the devil as "Old Nick" after Machiavelli's first name. This was because Machiavelli sanctioned the use of deception, cruelty, force, violence and the like for achieving the desired political ends.

Interestingly, Machiavelli had his share of admirers. Spinoza regarded him as a friend of the people for having exposed the Prince. Montesquieu regarded him as a lover of liberty, an image that emerged in the *Discourses* (1514–1519) and not from the *Prince* (1513). He separated Machiavelli from Machiavellanism and described him as a pioneer in political sociology. As a disciple of Montesquieu, Rousseau projected Machiavelli as a Republican, a satirist of tyranny and described him as a good citizen and an honourable man. Voltaire read Machiavelli carefully and appreciatively. Denis Diderot (1713–1784) pleaded for his rehabilitation in the *Encyclopaedia* describing him as an erudite man of genius, a cultivated man of letters who wrote some good dramas, hated the despotism of Medici, endured torture because of personal courage, and died like a philosopher. Alfieri called him "Divine", an ardent enthusiast of individual freedom and an unabashed lover of all political virtue resulting in true glory. Giovanni Gentile (1875–1944) described him as a champion of democratic government rather than a supporter of despotism. This view is reiterated by Viroli (1998) who interpreted Machiavelli not as an apologist of tyranny but a defender of republican values such as justice and the common good. For the Enlightenment philosophers, Machiavelli heralded in a new era. He was a historian who laid the foundations of a new science of politics by integrating contemporary history with ancient past. They accepted Bacon's praise of Machiavelli for his realism and pragmatism and the fact that he wrote about human nature, the nature of political society and its actual operations, with a concern about how things *were*, rather than how they *ought* to be. "The whole drift of his work is towards a political realism, unknown to the formal writings of his time" (Lerner 1950: xxxi). Femia (1998) rejected metaphysics and pioneered a pragmatic approach to politics governed by circumstances rather than abstract principles.

The admiration and hostility that Machiavelli received simultaneously were partly due to a misunderstanding of the context in which he wrote his texts, and partly due to sheer ignorance about their contents and implications (Allen 1967: 447). The *Prince*, responsible for Machiavelli's infamy, would not have been written had it not been for Medici despotism and perhaps the hope that the Medici could unite Italy and make it independent. In fact, if it was read along with his *Discourses on the First Ten Books of Titus Livius*, one got a balanced account of him. In the later tract he showed his concern for the moral and political degradation in Italian public life, and the urgency to recreate a healthier social life by resurrecting nostalgically the glory of their Roman ancestors. In this reordering, Machiavelli underlined the importance of politics as a public responsibility and the need for rules and maxims distinct from those applicable in the private sphere. More than anybody else, he emphasized the need to judge politics by a purely political criterion, rendering moral platitudes obsolete and irrelevant. While the *Prince* advised the ruler the ways and means to seize and keep power, the *Discourses* gave instructions on the methods by which a new revolutionary regime could stay in power with the help of people's participation and a philosopher prince.

For Machiavelli, success was the yardstick to measure and judge political activities, and achievements have to be assessed in light of the initial promise. This enabled him not only to be dispassionate in his study of political power shorn of its religious and moral orientations, but also to enquire into the secular origins of political authority and the state. He did not develop his views systematically, for many of them were in response to particular political exigencies. Though diametrically different in temperament and beliefs, Gandhi's writings were also situational. However, this did not suggest that there was no political theory in Machiavelli. The refreshing aspect of his writings was that they were neither speculative nor abstract. He represented the dawn of a new age which *rejected idealization* and insisted on the need to grasp the *realities of politics*. He was the first to grasp the tone of these changes, initiate a scientific study of politics, and hence was honoured with the title of being the "first modern political theorist and scientist" (Olschki 1976: 286–290).

LIFE SKETCH

Machiavelli was born in Florence, Italy on May 3, 1469. He was the third child in a family that was neither rich nor aristocratic, but well-connected with the city's famed humanistic circles. The year Machiavelli was born was the one when Lorenzo de Medici (1449-1492), referred to as "Lorenzo the Magnificent", the "most Florentine of Florentines", became the uncrowned ruler of the principality. Florence was economically prosperous, but suffered a long period of civil strife and political disorder.

Machiavelli loved Florence, his birthplace. Very little was known of Machiavelli's early life. His father Bernado, a civil lawyer, held several important public appointments. Besides his legal practice, Bernado also received rents from his land, making his family financially comfortable. Bernado took considerable interest in the education of his son. Niccolo was well-versed in Latin, but not Greek and Cicero's humanistic studies, which focused on different moral situations with advice on how to tread a virtuous path. Humanistic studies, which thrived in Florence, valued the willing subordination of one's private interests for public good, the desire to fight against tyranny and corruption, and the need to perform noble acts in order to attain glory. Machiavelli's writings reflected these humanistic concerns.

The Medici rule, which ended in 1494, was followed by that of Girolamo Maria Francois Matteo Savonarola (1452–1498), a monk. In 1498, an effective republic was established in Florence. In the same year,

Machiavelli, after having completed his education at the University of Florence, joined the Florentine diplomatic service. At the age of 29, he became the secretary to the second chancery with responsibilities in foreign affairs—diplomatic, administrative and military in nature—giving him insights into the actual working of politics. His humanistic training made him a hardworking, patriotic and scrupulously honest public functionary.

Machiavelli had tremendous faith in history, out of the conviction that the study of history was of crucial significance for an understanding of the contemporary reality. His interest in books was confined only to those that dealt with life's experiences. He spent his evenings wearing fine clothes and reading good books and the classics in his library after returning from work. He felt that he was holding a dialogue with the best minds of the past, and remarked that as he entered the antique courts of the ancients, he felt welcomed by them. Many Renaissance thinkers had their own private libraries or study rooms which they could afford, since Renaissance Italy was extremely rich. The Renaissance was possible because of wealth, as culture flourished only with affluence.

Machiavelli's stint at the chancery gave him an opportunity to meet the influential statesmen of his day, namely Julius II (1443–1513) one of the most dynamic Renaissance Popes, Emperor Maximilian I (1459–1519) of Germany, King Louis XII of France and Cardinal Cesare Borgia (1476–1507), the illegitimate son of the Rodrigo Borgia Pope Alexander VI (1431–1503). Among them, it was Borgia who left a lasting impression and was quoted in the *Prince* for his ruthless and daring leadership, and as an example for the fascinating account of the role of fortune. Machiavelli's doctrine of fortune conceded that even after planning and playing the game of politics with meticulousness, courage and cunning, one could still be unsuccessful. Machiavelli's judgement on the rulers and statesmen of his time was by and large critical.

In July 1500, Machiavelli visited the court of Louis XII on a diplomatic assignment for six months, only to realize that his home state of Florence was held in low esteem because of the lack of an army, a vacillating republican form of government, and rule by merchants who did not want to spend money on the city's military. Machiavelli himself was referred to as *Ser Nihilo,* meaning Mr Nothing. His experience, which formed the core of the *Prince,* taught him the need for being clever, thrifty, cultured, forceful, decisive and ruthless in politics, if one had to succeed. He also realized the importance of a citizen army and a republican government as important ingredients for the glory and success of a state—themes elaborated in the *Discourses.*

On returning home, Machiavelli.got engrossed with personal matters. During his stay abroad, his sister and father died. He married in 1501. In 1502, he was entrusted with another diplomatic assignment, and the experiences during these four months formed the core of the *Prince* and the *Discourses.* Machiavelli became all the more convinced that a state needed a morality of its own, namely that of success, which he identified as the protection and well-being of the people, and defence and extension of state borders. In 1503, Machiavelli went to Rome to make a report on a crisis in the papal court and assess the new Pope, Julius II.

In 1512, the Republic of Florence collapsed. Machiavelli's career suffered, for he was dismissed from his position on November 7, 1512. Three days later, he was ordered to be confined for one year. In 1513, he was tortured and imprisoned, but subsequently granted amnesty with the ascendancy of the new rulers, the Medici family. As a token of gratitude, he dedicated the *Prince* to the Medici family, Lorenzo II de'Medici (1492–1519), Lorenzo the Magnificient's grandson. After his release, Machiavelli spent his time, one of enforced leisure, reflecting on the lessons from his diplomatic experiences, reading history and understanding statecraft, all of which were incorporated in his writings. Machiavelli read non-philosophical texts extensively: those of Frontininus, Titus Livius Livy (59 BC–17 AD), Plutarch (46–120), Polybius (203–120 BC), Cornelius Tacitus (55–117), Flavius Vegetius (450–383 BC), and Xenophon (430–354 BC).

The *Prince* explored the causes of the rise and fall of states and the factors for political success. The tract was not officially published until 1532. Its success was immediate, running into 25 editions after Machiavelli's death. More creative pursuits followed, and a play, *Mandragola,* regarded as one of the best comedies of its time, explored the ideas of immorality, intrigue, duplicity, stratagems and the relationship between ends and means. In 1520, Machiavelli was commissioned by the University of Florence to write a chronicle and the annals of Florence, which was published as the *History of Florence* in 1525. He got a paid job after being without one for a long time. Machiavelli also authored the *Belfagor* and *The Art of War* (1521).

In the *History of Florence,* Machiavelli analyzed and attributed the endemic social conflict and violence in the city state of Florence to a natural class war between the people and the ruling nobility. The cause for instability was the hatred that the poor harboured towards the rich. Interestingly, this was also the reason for civic republicanism. The workers realized the need to protect themselves from government repression and act decisively to secure a better life. This was possible only with the overthrow of the nobility. Marx praised the tract as a masterpiece for its suggestion of a struggle between the haves and have-nots, and that human happiness lay in aligning with the side of the deprived.

Machiavelli would be remembered in history as a diplomat, scholar and a dramatist. In his personal life he was an affectionate person, disloyal husband, a loving father, an eloquent conversationalist, a generous and trustworthy friend with a great sense of humour. He could laugh at himself as easily as he did at the expense of others. He died on June 22, 1527. The following was the inscription on his tombstone: "No epitaph can match so great a name."

RENAISSANCE AND ITS IMPACT

Laski (1936: 31) rightly observes that "The whole of the Renaissance is in Machiavelli. There is its lust for power, its admiration for success, its carelessness of means, its rejection of medieval bonds, its frank paganism, its conviction of national unity makes for national strength. Neither his cynicism nor his praise of craftiness is sufficient to conceal the idealist in him".

To comprehend the full importance of Machiavelli's writings and their context, it is important to understand the series of cultural, economic, social and political changes that began in the fourteenth century called the Renaissance. Its immediate impact was in Italy, which gradually spread to the rest of Europe by the late fifteenth century. The Renaissance signified a rebirth of the human spirit in the attainment of liberty, self-confidence and optimism. In contradiction to the medieval view, which had envisaged the human being as fallen and depraved in an evil world with the devil at the centre, the Renaissance captured the Greek ideal of the essential goodness of the individual, the beauty and glory of the earth, the joy of existence, the insignificance of the supernatural and the importance of the present, as compared to an irrecoverable past and an uncertain future. This return to a pre-Christian attitude towards humans, God and Nature found expression in all aspects of human endeavour and creativity. Humanism, affirming the dignity and excellence of the human being, became the basis of comprehending the modern world. In contrast to the medieval Christian stress on asceticism, poverty, humility, misery and the worthlessness of the earthly person, Humanism defended the freedom of the human spirit and knowledge. The Renaissance signalled the breakdown of a unified Christian society.

At the centre of the Renaissance was the emergence of the new human, an ambitious restless individual, motivated by his self-interest, seeking glory and fame. Self-realization and joy, rather than renunciation and asceticism, were seen as the true ends of human existence and education. Self-fulfilment was no longer viewed as being achieved by repressing natural faculties and emotions. Jacob Burckhardt (1818–1897) in his classic, *The Civilization of the Renaissance in Italy* (1860) pointed out that it was the conception of the new human, the individual motivated by fame and glory, self-actualization and happiness, rather than self-denial and religious faith that formed the essence of the Renaissance. The spirit of individualism and the cult of privacy led to the growth of self-assertion and ushered in the idea of the highest development of the individual.

Alongside the development of the modern individual was the beginning of the modern state. The idea of the modern state, omnipotent and omni-competent, was worked out. The prince had to take charge of everything—preservation of public buildings and churches, maintenance of the municipal police, drainage of the marshes, ensuring the supply of corn, levying taxes and convincing the people of their necessity, supporting the sick and destitute, lending support to distinguished intellectuals and scholars on whose verdict rested his fame for the years to come. More than anybody else, it was Machiavelli who could understand the dynamics of this modern state and the modern individual.

Equally important were the end of the clerical monopoly and the replacement of papal supremacy by secular, sovereign, independent states, each with its own national culture, identity and language. The nation state came into existence and its success was determined not by religious or chivalric, but by political criteria. Explorations and voyages led to geographical discoveries, altering the perceptions regarding the world. The medievalists had viewed the universe with a flat earth at the centre, hell beneath it and heaven as its canopy. The discoveries of Christopher Columbus (1451–1506) and Vasco da Gama (1469–1524) enlarged the geographical horizons beyond the Mediterranean basin and Europe. A new world map magnified the view of the educated.

New geographical discoveries opened up new vistas of trade and religion. This led to growth in commerce and economic development as the basis of modern capitalism. Cities and urban centres emerged. Rational methods of bookkeeping and accounting and complex banking operations mushroomed, eroding the taboo on moneymaking, entrepreneurship and the profit motive. Education, science and humanism ended clerical monopoly, relegating religion to the private space. The invention of printing, the establishment of libraries and universities increased and spread literacy, and revived an interest in Latin classics.

In Europe, it was Italy that experienced the onslaughts of these new commercial, entrepreneurial and economic forces. All these reflected in the political and societal organization of Italy. Politically, Italy was divided into a number of small principalities and five large states: Milan, Venice, Florence, the Papal Domain and Naples. Of these, Florence was the most cultured city, the seat of the Italian Renaissance, producing some eminent and renowned figures. It was the first modern state in the world (Burckhardt 1921: 8).

Though culturally vibrant and creative, Italy remained politically divided, weak, and a prey to the imperial ambitions of the French, German and Spanish. Most of the Italian states were ruled by an oligarchy or an individual tyrant. All of them were unable or unwilling to unite the entire peninsula. The Florentine Republic reflected severe factional conflicts and institutional breakdown. It was a period of heated constitutional experimentation, accelerated by Savonarola who expelled the Medici and destroyed their wonders and wealth.

Italians could not reconcile to the fact that an age of heightened cultural creativity and scientific discoveries coincided with loss of political liberty, leading to foreign domination. Italian society, "intellectually brilliant and artistically creative, more emancipated than many in Europe ... was a prey to the worst political corruption and moral degradation"

(Sabine 1973: 315). It produced some great minds and intellects of that period, like Alexander Botticelli (1444–1510), Leonardo da Vinci (1452–1519), Buonarroti Michelangelo (1475–1564) and Santi Raphael (1483–1520). Its galaxy of artists made Renaissance Italy comparable to Athens of the fifth century BC. However, while Athens flourished politically, with a vibrant participatory democracy, in Italy there was a political vacuum. The old, feudal order had begun to collapse and disintegrate, but the new age, marked by the emergence of the territorial nation state as a sovereign legal-political entity was still in its embryonic form.

Writing at a time of political chaos and moral confusion, Italian unification became the chief objective for Machiavelli, who could see "clearly the direction that political evolution was taking throughout Europe. No man knew better than he the archaism of the institutions that were being displaced or accepted more readily the part that naked force was playing in the process. Yet no one in that age appreciated more highly the inchoate sense of national unity on which this force was obscurely based" (Sabine ibid: 314). Machiavelli's attachment was to his country Italy, and not to a state as an abstract entity. He desired to redeem Italy from servitude and misery (De Grazia 1989: 193). Like Dante, he dreamt of a united, regenerated and glorious Italy. In order to achieve this, any means were justified, for the purpose was the defence and preservation of the state and its people. Considerations of justice or injustice, humanity or cruelty, glory or shame were immaterial in light of protecting the life and liberty of the country.

Freedom of the country and the common good remained the core themes of Machiavelli's writings. A perfect state was one which promoted the common good, namely the observance of laws, honouring women, keeping public offices open to all citizens on grounds of virtue, maintaining a moderate degree of social equality, and protecting industry, wealth and property. The freedom of a country had to be safeguarded with the help of war and expansion. War was a horror, but not worse than military defeat and subjugation. Machiavelli was the precursor of Hegel in making a realistic appraisal of war in understanding reality.

MACHIAVELLI'S POLITICAL THEORY

Machiavelli saw stable political authority and order as necessary for social cohesion and moral regeneration. It was for this reason that he stressed the need for a unified polity, and a republican and free government committed to the liberty of its people. His new way of looking at political behaviour was significantly influenced by Leonardo, a personal friend with whose writings he was familiar. Incidentally, Leonardo was an architect of Borgia, the hero of the *Prince* (Masters 1996: 5). Machiavelli understood the realities of politics, "its lust for power, its admiration of success, its carefreeness of means, its rejection of medieval bonds, its frank pragmatism, its conviction that national unity makes for national strength. Neither his cynicism nor his praise of craftiness is sufficient to conceal the idealist in him" (Laski 1936: 36). He cherished republican liberty, but was aware of the danger tyranny posed, amidst chaos to free institutions. While in the *Prince* Machiavelli highlighted the importance of the security and unity of the state as the primary concerns of a ruler, in the *Discourses* the theme was liberty and republicanism.

Human Nature

The individual, according to Machiavelli, was wicked, selfish and egoistic. He was fundamentally weak, ungrateful, exhibitionist, artificial, anxious to avoid danger and excessively desirous of gain. Lacking in honesty and justice, he was ready to act in a manner that was detrimental to the community. It was only under compulsion or when there was personal gain that an individual was ready to do good. Being essentially anti-social, anarchical, selfish, greedy and sensual, the individual would readily forgive the murder of his father, but never the seizure of property. He was grateful to the extent of expecting benefits and rewards. The individual was generally timid, averse to new ideas and compliants. He desired power, glory and material well-being. Elsewhere, Machiavelli observed that the desires for novelty, fear and love dictated human actions. Individuals establish a government with the strongest and the most courageous becoming lawgivers and leaders as they desire personal safety and security of possessions. Like Aristotle, he believed that the government made the individual just and fair.

Machiavelli conceived human beings as being basically restless, ambitious, aggressive and acquisitive, in a state of constant strife and anarchy. They were discontented and dissatisfied, for human needs were unlimited, but fortune limited their possessions and capacity for enjoyment. Under such circumstances, politics got "plagued by the dilemma of limited goods and limitless ambition" (Wolin 1960: 201). By making scarcity the focal point of his enquiry and political theorizing, Machiavelli "helped to launch the redefinition of the political association, a redefinition which by starting with the legitimacy of conflict of interests, would end by doubting that such an association could afford to pursue final solutions in the handling of conflicts" (Wolin ibid: 232).

Interestingly, Machiavelli presumed that human nature remained constant, for history moved in a cyclical way, alternating between growth and decay. This enabled one to discern general laws of political behaviour with a view to maximizing one's gain. He observed that there was not much difference between how individuals lived and how they *ought* to live, for the one who sacrificed what had to be done in favour of what ought to be done normally sowed the seeds of destruction rather than preservation.

Furthermore, Machiavelli pointed out that the human mind tended to glorify the past, decry the present and hope for a better future. Like Aristotle, Machiavelli characterized the individual as a political animal. While Aristotle implied the innate sociability of the human being, Machiavelli referred to the individual's love for power, reputation, keenness to establish superiority over others, and the innate desire to control and dominate others. However, Machiavelli confined these traits to the elite. He did not, like Nietzsche, deprecate the abilities of the non-elite, nor did he, like Hobbes, see the desire for power and domination as a universal aspiration.

Machiavelli recognized the importance of order provided by a stable, lawful political community consisting of public-spirited and virtuous citizens. Such an arrangement fulfilled the human need of being admired, respected and remembered. A ruler who preserved the state without undermining or flouting laws or inflicting harm attained fame and respect. On the contrary, the absence of civic *virtu* led to moral degradation and corruption.

Analysis of Corruption and Civic *Virtù*

Anticipating Rousseau that civilization meant corruption, Machiavelli observed that it would be possible to achieve mammoth tasks among people who were simple and pure, rather than those living in cities, for they were bad and conniving. Normally, a republic, established when individuals were good, had a greater chance of surviving than that which was founded when individuals were mean and crafty.

Unlike Rousseau, Machiavelli made moral degradation and civic corruption the starting point of his analysis, and looked into factors that fostered public spirit overriding private interests. He saw a definite link between political psychology and political institutions (Plamentaz 1963: Vol. I: 24–27). In the third *Discourses*, Machiavelli declared wealth without worth as a cause of corruption. He extolled the virtue of poverty over wealth, for simplicity of lifestyle brought honour to cities. He saw a nexus between luxurious habits and moral decline. Lack of martial spirit also led to the downfall of civic liberties. If princes and rulers were to be free from corruption, they would have to enact laws that promoted common political liberties rather than their self-interest.

Corruption, to Machiavelli, meant licence, violence, great inequities in wealth and power, lack of peace and justice, disorderly ambition and growth, lawlessness, dishonesty and contempt for religion. It meant the subordination of public values to the private sphere or/and when the public sphere was used for furthering private aims and interests. Usually, societies that were corrupt excluded the common people from playing an active role in government and political life. Machiavelli buttressed this claim by citing two instances of institutional developments that proved to be fatal to liberty within the Roman republic. The first was extending the period of various magistrates holding office. This eventually made Rome servile, and deprived its citizens of their lawful authority. The second was the prolongation of military command, for an increase in the power of the commanders led to the eventual downfall of the republic.

Corruption could be tackled only with extraordinary measures, like rule by a strong prince with overwhelming powers. Machiavelli was convinced that a corrupt people could not achieve nor maintain free politics, for they would be unable to distinguish between subjective private interests and the public domain. They lacked the inner strength to prevent those in power from advancing their private interests, as they themselves, if given the opportunity, would use the political sphere for the pursuit of their private interests (Shumer 1979: 8–9). They would appropriate the state for them-selves.

Machiavelli believed that a measure of public virtue as a common ideal and goal for the entire polity, faith in the system and in persons whom the people trusted were fundamental prerequisites for not only ending corruption, but also in making a beginning of the real development of the individual. Civic *virtù* in a ruler were martial qualities needed to defend the state against external aggression and internal disunity. In an ordinary individual, it meant public-spiritedness and patriotism necessary for ensuring freedom and deterring tyranny.

Attitude to Religion

The novelty in Machiavelli's writings was his attitude towards religion and morality, which distinguished him from all those who preceded him. He was scathing in his attack on the Church and its clergy for their failure to provide moral inspiration. He wrote:

> We Italians then owe to the Church of Rome and to her priests our having become irreligious and bad; but we owe her a still greater debt and one that will be the cause of our ruin, namely, that the Church has kept and still keeps our country divided (Machiavelli cited in Sabine 1973: 316).

Machiavelli was anti-Church and anti-clergy, but not anti-religion. He considered religion as necessary not only for man's social life, but also for the health and prosperity of the state. It was important within a state because of the influence it wielded over political life in general. Though an indispensable part of civic life, it was never an end in itself. As a political tool, princes and rulers were to use religion in their power struggles effectively, but responsibly and cautiously, otherwise it could be disastrous.

Religion was good only if it produced order, for peace brought forth fortune and success.

Machiavelli's attitude towards religion was strictly utilitarian. It was a social force and did not have any spiritual connotation. As a social force, it played a pivotal role because it appealed to the selfishness of man through its doctrine of rewards and punishment, thereby inducing proper behaviour and good conduct that was necessary for the well-being of a society. Religion determined the social and ethical norms and values that governed human conduct and actions. Machiavelli had no interest in philosophic contemplation as the highest form of human life, nor was he interested in what constituted good life. He was, however, very seriously concerned with the display of high moral standards and qualities in public life. The distinction that Machiavelli made between the private and public conceptions of morality was among his important contributions.

Machiavelli was categorical that public spirit was crucial to the stability of the state. One of the key determinants of public spirit was religion, and the other, liberty. He advised the prince to do anything and everything possible to cultivate belief in religion, even if the ruler in his personal capacity was irreligious or had very little faith in religion. He was the first to look upon religion as a coercive force, thereby anticipating Rousseau, Burke and Marx (Bronowski and Mazlish 1960: 34).

Machiavelli's vision was dominated by classical ideas, especially with regard to his key idea, *virtù*, by which he meant masculine and warlike qualities. He admired qualities like courage, self-assertiveness, fortitude, ambition, vitality, intelligence, fame, and strength, which religion should ideally foster. By his own preference, he criticized Christianity, for it made men effeminate, charitable and weak, glorifying qualities like renunciation, humility, lowliness, other-worldliness, asceticism, charity, and patience under injustice. A civic religion for Machiavelli should instil fear and respect for authority and help in the inculcation of military valour.

Machiavelli distinguished between pagan and Christian morality, and chose paganism. He did not condemn Christian morality, nor did he try to redefine the Christian conception of a good person. He dismissed the Christian view that an individual was endowed with a divine element and a supernatural end. He also rejected the idea of absolute good. He observed:

> Goodness is simply that which subserves on the average or in the long run, the interests of the mass of individuals. The terms good and evil have no transcendental reference; they refer to the community considered as an association of individual and to nothing else. At bottom apparently, they refer only to the universal desire for security (Machiavelli cited in Allen 1967: 453).

Machiavelli contended that original Christianity taught virtues that linked internal good of the soul with the generation and training of civic virtù (Gilbert 1939: 453; Berlin 1969: 125). Gilbert found nothing in Machiavelli that was anti-Christianity. In fact, many sentiments in the *Discourses* were Christian, for example the condemnation of luxury. Berlin linked Machiavelli to the pagan and Christian traditions. He set aside Croce's view of Machiavelli as an early liberal moralist, unhappy at the fact that politics and ethics did not go together and a general condemnation if one acted politically. Berlin noted that Machiavelli chose pagan morality that focused on public life, social existence and institutional requirements, while Christian morality was inward looking, individualistic and concerned with the need to tend one's soul. In spite of preferring paganism, Machiavelli did not despise Christian values. Moreover, Machiavelli, according to Berlin, taught us unintentionally the irreconciliability of ultimate values, the impossibility of rationally proving that one set of values was superior to the other.

Though Machiavelli was critical of Christianity, he retained the basic Christian views on the differences between good and evil (Meinecke 1957: 33). For instance, he regarded murdering one's co-citizens, betraying one's friends, disloyalty and irreligiousness as lack of *virtù* not entitled to glory. Machiavelli was clear that Italy needed a religion similar to one that ancient Rome had, a religion that taught to serve the interests of the state. He was categorical that Florentines needed political and military virtues which Christian faith did not impart. His reason for writing *The Art of War* was to teach his fellow citizens the importance of training in arms.

> Machiavelli's conception of civic virtù marked an important stage in the development of modern political thought and practice, for it symbolized an end to the old alliance between statecraft and soul-craft. Hence it would be increasingly taken for granted that while the cultivation of souls and personalities might be the proper end of man, it did not provide the focus of political action. This can be stated more strongly by saying that the new science was not conceived as the means to human perfectibility (Wolin 1960: 237).

Double Standards of Morality

For Machiavelli, a successful ruler or state was one which would be able to acquire, maintain, consolidate and increase power. The survival and the preservation of the commonwealth was his fundamental concern. He prudently calculated the likely consequences of political actions that would achieve national safety. A state and a ruler had to be judged by an independent criterion, the morality of success, which was protection of citizens guaranteeing their well-being, expansion of territory and a zealous safeguarding of national interests. Politics was ultimately and finally a constant struggle for power and domination, which had to be judged by its own rules and norms so that states survived. Machiavelli pointed out that in writing about the rules of politics he was projecting the real truth and not leaving anything to imagination. Commenting on the gulf between *ought* and *is*, Machiavelli observed that

> ... the fact is that a man who wants to act virtuously in every way necessarily comes to grief among so many who are not virtuous. Therefore if a prince wants to maintain his rule he must learn how not to be virtuous. and to make use of this or that according to need ... . Everyone realises how praiseworthy it is for a prince to honour his word and to be straightforward rather than crafty in his dealing, nonetheless contemporary experience shows that princes who have achieved great things have been those who have given their word lightly, who have known how to trick men with their cunning, and who, in the end, have overcome those abiding by honest principles (Machiavelli 1950: 66).

Machiavelli did not condone the use of immoral or wicked ways. To him, the *end* was important, which could be attained by any means. He arrived at this understanding after observing the political game from close quarters in which ends justified the means. He contended that a ruler need not always *adhere* to conventional morality rather he should be *willing* to do so. He also insisted that a private individual would have to display impeccable moral values of the highest order. For Machiavelli, the home and family nurtured these moral values, teaching the individual the virtues of independence, simplicity, purity, loyalty and trust. He emphasized that an individual adhered to these values, whereas a statesman could be flexible as far as the conduct of state affairs was concerned, but not in private dealings.

Machiavelli separated the private from the public sphere of morality. While the state had a morality of its own—the morality of success—the private individual was at all times to display qualities that were in consonance with the highest moral standards. He spoke of the *raison d'etat* of the state. In politics, fair was foul and foul was fair, depending on circumstances and situations. No general rule was valid, for everything became a matter of political expediency. A prince had to be compassionate, humane, loyal, and honest, while simultaneously willing to use force, fraud, deception and treachery. Machiavelli argued that political actions were to conform to high moral standards, namely compassion, good faith, trustworthiness and honesty in times of stability. However, in times of strife, chaos and disorder, principled politics would spell ruin. He asserted that power was anything but divine, and to think that states came into existence by the will of God was absurd. He also rejected the divine rights theory of kings.

Machiavelli's attitude to religion and morality made him highly controversial. Strauss (1958: 5) characterized him as a teacher of evil. Sabine (1973: 320) saw him as being amoral. Unlike Sabine, Pocock (1971: 160) following Pollock (1911: 43) attributed it to his scientific detachment, enabling him to merely list the rules for political success, without being judgemental. The ruler, for Machiavelli, was a technician. In order to master the art of illusion, he had to be a skilful pretender and dissembler with seemingly good qualities. As to whether morality was coextensive of success, Machiavelli observed:

> I will even venture to say that (the virtues) damage a prince who *possesses them and always observes them,* but if he seems to have them they are useful. I mean that he should seem compassionate, trustworthy, humane, honest and religious, and *actually be so;* but yet he should have his mind so trained that, when it is necessary not to practice these virtues, he can change to the opposite and do it skilfully. It is to be understood that a prince, especially a new prince, cannot observe all the things because of which men are considered good, because he is often obliged, if he wishes to maintain his government, to act contrary to faith, contrary to charity, contrary to humanity, contrary to religion. It is therefore necessary that he have a mind capable of turning in whatever direction the winds of Fortune and the variations of affairs require, and ... that *he should not depart from what is morally right, if he can observe it,* but should know how to adopt what is bad, when he is obliged to (Machiavelli 1950: 85).

Unlike traditional political theory, which contended that ethical conduct was desirable for it would bring about moral elevation, Machiavelli was too realistic to overlook the irony of the political situation. In politics, it was not possible to assess the effect of a virtuous or a wicked act, for it would result in the opposite effect. His rejection of traditional ethics and the quest to find an alternative political ethic that was suitable and appropriate, was derived from a firmly-held conviction that history moved with abrupt jerks in a frenzied way. In a fragmented world, politics had to be linked with *necessita,* meaning those factors that compelled individuals to find ingenious solutions. This was possible only if purely political factors were taken into account, excluding others. Machiavelli's attempt to establish the autonomy of politics was tanta-mount to a denial of ethical absolutes.

> Machiavelli broke with classical theory which had approached the problems of political action with questions of how men could develop their moral potentialities through a life devoted to political office. But for Machiavelli the problem became more acute, for the issue no longer involved the statesman's quest for a moral perfection which, by its very moral quality, would benefit the community; it involved instead the political actor which was driven to break the moral law in order to preserve his society (Wolin 1960: 226).

Machiavelli was aware that civilization and a good society meant high moral standards. But he was realistic enough to accept that a society's moral fabric was made or destroyed by its people. He was not a nihilist or a cynic (Ebenstein 1969: 281). His amorality implied that in specific situations, a ruler would have to resort to tactics that were not considered strictly moral. Therefore, Machiavelli talked not only of the *science,* but also of the *art* of politics. Politics was no longer a means to higher goals like justice or truth, but an end in itself. The criterion of a successful state was efficiency and not legitimacy, so his art of politics applied to both legal and illegal states (Cassirer 1946: 160). He took it for granted that states, like individuals, would differ widely in nature. He also highlighted that in times of relatively stable social order, "all moral questions can be raised from within the context of the norms which the community shares; in periods of instability it is these norms themselves which are questioned and tested against the criteria of human desires and needs" (MacIntyre 1971: 129). According to Femina (2004) Machiavelli founded liberal pluralism, essential to modern governance, that the primary purpose of politics was to resolve the competing claims of diverse interest and values.

Machiavelli separated religion from politics and set the tone for one of the main themes of modern times, namely secularization of thought and life, but the impact was not felt immediately for the next 200 years. Though conscious of the importance of religion as a cementing force in society, he was hostile towards Christianity and looked upon the Roman Catholic Church as the main adversary. He espoused hostility towards religion, considering he was writing in Italy prior to the Reformation. Hence, his

> ... philosophy was both narrowly local and narrowly dated. Had he written in any country except Italy, or had he written in Italy after the beginning of the Reformation, and still more after the beginning of the counter-Reformation in the Roman Church, it is impossible to suppose that he would have treated religion as he did (Sabine 1973: 329).

The Reformation was a religious movement that swept Europe in the sixteenth century challenging the authority, doctrine and the liturgy of the Roman Catholic Church, giving rise to Lutheranism, Calvinism and the Protestant Churches. On October 31, 1517, Martin Luther (1483–1546) posted the Ninety-Five Theses on the church door at Wittenberg, proclaiming that religion was a matter of personal conviction, opposed the splendour that surrounded the papacy and the idea of passive obedience, namely that a Christian should simply obey the constituted authority. John Calvin (1509–1564) reinforced these with a strict regimen, similar to the one proposed in More's *Utopia* (1516). It was Puritan. Calvin's state was a theocratic dictatorship, but as in the case of Luther, Calvinism contributed "intentionally and uninten-tionally, to personal, economic and political individualism" (Bronowski and Mazlish 1960: 121).

Calvin's most important contribution was his acceptance of New Economics, namely the capitalist economic system. He opposed the accumulation of wealth, the self-indulgent and ostentatious display of riches, and usury on the poor, but did not oppose the payment of interest on borrowed capital. Weber attributed the rise of capitalism to the Calvinist Puritan ethic of worldly asceticism, and in particular English Puritanism. Richard Henry Tawney (1880–1962), criticizing Weber's thesis, emphasized more on circumstances and movements—economic and intellectual—for the origins of capitalism. The link between capitalism and the Protestant ethic was not as simple as Weber suggested, although he pointed out that the commercial classes in seventeenth-century England were the possessors of a particular brand of social expediency, which was different from that of the conservative elements. Toynbee pointed out that Calvinism because of its rigorous discipline and individualism, appealed tremendously to the rising bourgeoisie.

The Protestant Reformation led to a counter-Reformation and a cold war between the Catholics and the Protestants. Out of the Renaissance and the Reformation came the scientific revolution that spanned from 1500–1700, and was responsible for the creation of the modern world. It taught people to think differently about the world and the universe. Nicolaus Copernicus (1473–1543), Tycho Brahe (1546–1601), Johann Kepler (1571–1630) and Galileo Galilei (1564–1642) were the principal participants. The humiliation and torture of Galileo put an end to the scientific tradition in Italy. The year Galileo died, Sir Isaac Newton (1642–1727) was born. With that, science moved away from the Mediterranean basin to North Europe (Bronowski and Mazlish ibid).

SCIENCE OF STATECRAFT

Machiavelli's science of statecraft (or maxims to the ruler) developed out of his ministerial correspondence, study of history and its lessons, the wisdom of the ancient and from examples of great and noble deeds (Butterfield 1962: 69). He cautioned unwise princes that they would come to grief if they ignored these maxims, for by adhering to them they would be free from their dependence on fortune. He believed that history taught, and to ignore its lessons would be suicidal. He used Livy's history of the Roman republic as a reference point, and instructed them to imitate the conduct of Rome in every aspect.

Importance of History

Machiavelli's attitude to history was practical. History tended to repeat itself, rather than create or generate new things. Change was essentially kaleidoscopic, with no fundamental transformation. Change was cyclical, alternating between growth and decay. He also stressed on the need to read and imitate the lives and fortunes of great men and use them as guides for understanding the present.

> Whoever considers things present and things past will easily understand how the same appetites and humours are and always have been incident to all states and people, so that by diligently examining the course of

> former ages it is an easy matter for men to foresee what is going to happen in any commonwealth, and not only to provide such remedies against future evils as their predecessors did, but (if there be no precedent) to strike out new ones on the basis of existing analogies. But since considerations of this kind are too often neglected or little understood, or are beyond the knowledge of those men who govern states, it comes to pass that the same evils and inconveniences take place in all ages of history (Machiavelli 1950: 39).

Furthermore, he asserted firmly and categorically that:

> Wise men say (perhaps not unjustly) that in order to form an impression of what is yet to come, we ought to consider what is already passed; for there is nothing in this world at present, or at any other time, but has and will have its counterpart in antiquity; which happens because these things are operated by human beings who, having the same passions in all ages, must necessarily behave uniformly in similar situations (Machiavelli ibid: 43).

Machiavelli, like the other Renaissance thinkers, could not visualize that civilization could continually and constantly evolve with new ideas and perceptions. Believing in the idea of a closed culture, Greece and Rome remained the reference point that humans were to go back to (Butterfieid 1962: 40). They did not have the idea of progress as understood by the thinkers of the French Enlightenment in the eighteenth century.

Republican Politics and Notion of Liberty

Machiavelli distinguished between republics and princedoms, free and unfree states. Free states were those "which are far from all external servitude, and are able to govern themselves according to their own will" (Machiavelli 1950: 129). A republic was superior to a princedom, which however did not suit all people, except those who were highly public-spirited. Machiavelli's admiration for the ancient Romans was essentially because they had a republican form of government under which they "had achieved unexampled greatness and power" (Butterfieid 1962: 44). None of its rulers had inherited the throne. He admired the Romans for their zeal for freedom and devotion, patriotism and love for their country, which was possible only under a republican government.

In the opening passage of the *Discourses,* Machiavelli described the growth of freedom in ancient Rome and argued that those who had displayed prudence in constituting a republic had looked upon the safeguarding of liberty as one of the most essential things for which they had to provide. The primary task of a legislator was to enact laws that would guarantee and safeguard liberty. Rome could achieve greatness because of its continual efforts at introducing new institutions that made liberty possible. Machiavelli's adulation of Rome stood in stark contrast to the criticism of Hegel.

The three books of the *Discourses* were devoted to the exploration of the theme of liberty. The first showed how Rome achieved greatness through republican liberty by getting rid of its kings. The second depicted the progressive expansion of Rome as a military power, and its ability to fulfil the liberty of its people. The third spoke about the efforts of particular men in Rome who had contributed to the continuation of political liberty.

Freedom, to Machiavelli, produced not only powerful states but also strong individuals, whose strength was not in dominating or influencing others but in the independence of spirit, in their ability to think and decide for themselves. By liberty, he meant independence from external aggression and internal tyranny, implying the right of people to be able to govern. Freedom was the effective exercise of political rights that was possible among public-spirited and self-respecting individuals. Only a patriotic people could be truly and genuinely free. Conversely, a corrupt people possibly could not maintain liberty. For Machiavelli,

> the justification of law is nothing to do with the protection of individual rights, a concept that makes no appearance in the *Discorsi* at all. The main justification for its exercise is that, by coercing people into acting in such a way as to uphold the institutions of a free state, the law creates and preserves a degree of individual liberty which, in its absence would promptly collapse into absolute servitude (Skinner 1990: 305).

For Machiavelli, liberty was threatened by human selfishness. It was threatened when one began to entertain a false notion that personal liberty could be maintained by evading one's civic obligations, or redesigning institutions that maximized their personal gain. By doing so, common good, civic institutions and even personal liberty were subverted.

Machiavelli saw devotion to the public cause as a necessary precondition for claiming and enjoying private freedom without fear or interference. He thought that great leaders could inspire qualities in their people. Other measures for inculcating civic *virtù* were through religion and good laws, for these constituted the guarantees of liberty. Since an individual was good only by necessity, the fear of punishment and the coercive power of law would ensure good behaviour, restraining unruly ambitions. Machiavelli also mentioned the role of a lawgiver, who could enact good laws to regulate people in the same way that hunger and poverty made them industrious. He somehow did not think education could play a role in fostering civic virtues.

Machiavelli saw liberty as being possible within the framework of law. Laws ensured the enjoyment of liberty by all, for they prevented interference and curtailed the corrupt use of wealth. Laws not only protected individuals from a corrupt leader, but also liberated them from following their natural self-destructive tendency, namely the pursuit of self-interest. On a comprehensive scale, Machiavelli recommended the creation of a special magistracy as a guardian of liberty to ensure that liberty was not violated.

Machiavelli did not distinguish between different forms of government, nor did he attempt to classify governments. He did not enquire into the nature of political institutions and practices, though he was convinced that the freedom of an individual could be preserved only in a community of free people who could freely participate in public offices. He regarded all governments as defective, for in any case a good government thrived only for a short time, and bad ones by their nature subverted the state. Like Aristotle, he preferred a mixed constitution, for it was stable and was the best available option. He saw the Roman republic as a good example of a mixed government, for the consuls represented the monarchical principle, the senate the aristocratic, and the *comitia* and tribunes democratic ideas. As a result, common good was promoted at all times, preventing factionalism. A mixed constitution preserved the liberty of a virtuous people and provided stability to the state.

The other way of ensuring that self-interested individuals were willing to risk their lives for the liberty of their community was to make them take an oath binding them to defend the state at all costs. This would make them less frightened, and prevent them from shying away from their duties. If they fought, they might lose their lives, but if they refused, they would have to face the wrath of the gods.

Machiavelli desired the emulation of the Roman example, whereby a state was established for the purpose of aggrandizement, but if it had to succeed and be stable, a high level of public spirit was required. However, he believed that nothing was likely to last long, for everything got corrupted and degenerated, except perhaps the radical selfishness of the individual. He adhered to a cyclical view of history where prosperity led to decay and dissolution, resulting in rebirth. States commenced as monarchies developing into oligarchies, followed by popular governments. A popular government might lead to a monarchy, but the cycle was rarely exhausted. At some point a state might fall prey to external aggression.

Machiavelli did not hope for any real or substantial progress for individuals with insatiable appetites and desires, who remained poor creatures, highly restless and discontented. The unlimited nature of human wants led to constant aggrandizement and domination, which could not be avoided partly because of human discontentment, and partly because conflicts and wars ensured the health of the body politic. Peace, according to Machiavelli, was relaxing and disruptive.

Machiavelli, on the one hand, admired a free, virile and resourceful people, and on the other hand a strong, powerful and successful leader. While on the one hand he admired a republican form of government, on the other he prescribed a despotic princedom for reforming a corrupt people and in establishing a state. Therefore, Machiavelli

> patched together, rather precariously, [as] the theories respectively of founding a state and of preserving it after it is founded ... he had one theory for revolutions and another for government (Sabine 1973: 325).

If a state had to endure and be stable, people's participation, respect for rights, and, in particular, property and adherence to law and customs were very important. Machiavelli was convinced that people's participation through the electoral process would yield a steady supply of leaders. He had immense faith in elections, for people were prudent and wise, with a rare capacity to judge issues. People, in comparison to a prince, made fewer mistakes. Their choice of magistrates was better than those made by the prince. People in general were more stable, trustworthy and grateful, capable of looking to common good and promoting it. He equated the voice of the people with the voice of God. For Machiavelli,

> ... people are more governable than aristocrats who vie with another for power and domination. Since people desire security for their wives and property they can be handled properly if these basic human needs are satisfied. By vesting greater faith in the masses as opposed to heroic leaders Machiavelli showed greater insights into the nature of political mass rather than any other thinker before the nineteenth century (Wolin 1960: 229).

Machiavelli emerged as a consistent, passionate and devoted champion of people's participation and republican liberty, for he was convinced that a government by people was far better than government by a prince (Skinner 1990: 159). This created the image of Machiavelli as a scientist or a technician, merely surveying dispassionately the different forms of government and laying down a science of statecraft (Cassirer 1946: 156).

Violence and the Need for Caution

Machiavelli was convinced that the use of violence could be controlled, but could not be altogether eliminated. He recommended the cautious and judicious exercise of despotic violence, for otherwise it would create widespread distrust and hostility towards the government, resulting in instability. He saw violence as a shock therapy to cure corruption and rejuvenate civic *virtù*. Machiavelli

> ... regarded the science of violence as the means for reducing the amount of suffering in the political condition, but that he was clearly aware of the dangers of entrusting its use to the morally obtuse. What he hoped to further by his economy of violence was the "pure" use of power, undefiled by pride, ambition, or motives of petty revenge ... [he] was aware of the limited efficacy of force and who devoted himself to showing how its technique could be used more efficiently, was far more sensitive to the moral dilemmas of politics and far more committed to the preservation of man than those theorists who, saturated with moral indignation and eager for heroic regeneration, preach purification by the holy flame of violence (Wolin 1960: 223–224).

The government ought to use force carefully even in external affairs. While war was inevitable and unavoidable, its consequences could be minimized by discipline, organization and strategy. Machiavelli advised the prince to carefully consider his resources, for a war started for a trivial reason could not be stopped easily. Moreover, if a prince emerged weak after victory, it would mean that he had overestimated his resources. Machiavelli observed that it would be a grave mistake to avoid a war that was necessary, but it would be equally reckless to prolong it or to initiate one that was unnecessary.

Machiavelli exhorted the need to follow the Roman example even with regard to territorial expansion. The aim of imperialism was to preserve the wealth of the subject populations and their native institutions, thus minimizing the costs of devastation to both the conquered and the conqueror. Imperialism would become a mere transfer of power if handled efficiently. Machiavelli focused the attention of his readers on the international arena which was more prone to conflicts of interests and forces of ambition and passion than domestic politics. This was because the international arena lacked arbitrating arrangements such as law and institutional procedures, a point reiterated by Hegel.

In the domestic arena, the presence of political institutions, the rule of law and norms of civilized conduct helped in regulating human behaviour, thereby reducing the instances where force and fear would have to be applied. Once again, he stressed the importance of the republican form of government, for people's participation constituted a form of social power, which if dealt with properly, would reduce the use of violence in a society. A republican government was maintained and sustained by the power of its people, rather than by exerting force over them. People's identification and participation in the system would economize the employment of violence, which was why the prince should cultivate and secure people's support. Machiavelli very rightly asserted that only a weak regime would intensify the use of violence and cruelty. If far-reaching changes were brought about consensually, then the human costs would be very minimal.

Advice to the Prince

Machiavelli cautioned the prince against excessive generosity, strictness or kindness, and stressed the need for moderate behaviour. A prince had to be gentle or severe depending on the situation. His relationship with his subjects was similar to the one between a father and his children. A prince had to be strong, and demonstrate his strength whenever necessary. He had to govern his state responsibly and efficiently, ensuring its stability and survival. He had to retain the upper hand and initiative at all times. He had to be held in awe, if not fear. He had to be careful in selecting the methods and means by which he ruled. He had to uphold conventional standards of morality and notions of right by preserving the foundations of religion.

The prince had to abstain from the property and women of his subjects, for these matters, if violated, affected men's sensibilities, driving them to the point of resistance. A prince had to select his officers and advisers carefully, should not hesitate to purge those who had been disloyal. The ruler had to constantly try and expand the state's territory and play the balance of power game skilfully by appearing to be the defender of weaker states. Machiavelli advised the prince to adopt a policy of coalition rather than remain isolated, for neutrality was impossible both domestically and internationally. It would be better to support one side and wage an honest war; otherwise one became prey to the victor or got isolated in a later crisis. The best thing to do was to join a weak rather than a strong state, for in case of a common victory the gains would be marginal, but the losses would be low in case of a common defeat.

Machiavelli insisted on the need for legal remedies against official abuses in order to prevent illegal violence. A prince, in order to succeed, had to be willing to act ruthlessly, combining the valour and courage of a lion with the cunning and shrewdness of a fox. This was because a lion could ward off wolves and a fox could recognize traps. A ruler had to be courageous to fight his enemies, and cunning enough to detect conspiracies. He could do this only if he could change his colours like a chameleon, for in a corrupt age greatness could be achieved only by immoral means. A prince had to know to fight with the help of laws and force. While laws were for civilized persons, force was for the brutes. Both represented two different styles of fighting and could be combined, if necessary, to achieve effective results. Force was necessary since the individual was wretched and dishonourable.

Furthermore, Machiavelli pointed out that princes ought to exterminate the families of the rulers whose territories they wished to possess securely. Opponents ought to be murdered otherwise they could plan their revenge. True liberality consisted in being stingy with one's own property but generous with that of others, a prudent use of virtue and vice in order to be happy, conferring benefits little by little so that they would be appreciated more strongly, never to leave a defeated foe wounded, for there would be a sure retaliation, and causing sufficient injury so that they would hurt less and last for a short time. Machiavelli also advised the prince to imitate great figures from the past, and cited the examples of Alexander the Great, Achilles, Caesar, and Scipio Cyrus. He repeatedly referred to Moses, Cyrus, Romulus and Thesus as princes who attained their positions through their own arms and ability, and so worthy of imitation.

Role of the Lawgiver

Machiavelli attached great importance to the role of the lawgiver, in the conviction that laws contributed to civic virtues, ensuring the health of the body politic. A lawgiver was needed to reform a corrupt society, establish a successful state and shape the national character of a people by giving them suitable laws and government. Machiavelli described the lawgiver as an architect not only of the state, but also of society, with its economic and religious institutions, and moral norms, for the lawgiver could tear down old states, establish new ones, change governments and laws, and transform people's natures and qualities. The lawgiver had to satisfy the ambition of the elite and that of the lower classes while restraining both at the same time, channelize the intellectual power of the few and the physical power of the many into the service of the power and glory of the state, from which both derived enjoyment. Though the lawgiver was omnipotent, Machiavelli did not develop "a general theory of political absolutism as Hobbes did later" (Sabine 1973: 324).

Unlike Rousseau, who assumed essential goodness in human beings and that it was society which corrupted them, Machiavelli saw human nature as basically evil and wicked and hence instructed the lawgiver to take cognizance of this fact. The lawgiver would have to balance the ambition of one class and group with that of the other in order to establish a society of lasting good. Rousseau's lawgiver, on the other hand, created the conditions for individuals to realize their true potential and become truly human and intelligent.

Nature of the State

Machiavelli's state was a secular entity, with no relation to the church. It was morally isolated, with no obligation to anything outside itself. It was independent and all its relations were accidental. A state was necessary, for it existed to fulfil the desire for security of person and property. Machiavelli defined the state as an organized force for the maintenance and security of possessions. A state had to try and augment territory and power for itself. It either expanded or perished. It had to look upon its neighbours as actual or potential enemies.

A well-ordered and stable state could be successful if it had a strong government at the centre, an integrated public authority recognized by all, and a citizen army. Machiavelli saw good laws, religion and a citizen army as the support structures for a stable and strong state. There could be no good laws without good arms, and if there were good arms, good laws inevitably followed. An army should consist of its own citizens between the ages of 17 and 40, physically well-trained in arms and military skills, and psychologically prepared to fight a battle if necessary. A citizen who was unwilling to defend his state lacked civic *virtù*. It was the duty of a ruler to create and maintain an efficient, well-disciplined, well-equipped and loyal citizen army. A state with a citizen army would be able to ward off potential threats from its neighbours and other ambitious states, and also defend itself against civil strife and internal dissensions. Machiavelli repeatedly stressed the fact that a state had to be in a position to fight for preserving its independence and liberty, and for this a citizen army—and not mercenaries—was a basic requirement.

Machiavelli cautioned the ruler from using troops of other states, for they would not only exhaust the treasury, but also invariably fail at crucial times. He also rejected the use of mercenaries, after seeing Vitelli and his men fail the Florentines in 1499 while trying to capture Pisa as an outlet to the sea for trading purposes. Mercenaries owed no loyalty and would switch their allegiance on a larger offer of money. Moreover, unlike a citizen army, mercenaries did not fight for a cause on behalf of a state.

Machiavelli was equally hostile to hereditary monarchy and feudal nobility (besides mercenaries), and the established Church and its clergy, perceiving these to be enemies of a good and stable social and political order. He was critical of the gangsterism of the aristocracy, for they looted and impoverished ordinary people. They could be restrained with the help of an all powerful non-hereditary monarchy which would restrain individual ambitions and prevent the corruption of powerful private citizens—usually the cause of decay within the body politic. In order to achieve this, Machiavelli even suggested the need to use massive violence and political interventionism.

> Despite the dynastic ambitions of Italian princes, and the continuing strength of the hereditary principle in Renaissance statecraft, Machiavelli's *Discourses* are filled with contempt for hereditary princes and are profoundly anti-aristocracy (Brown 1981: 18).

Machiavelli's ideal was a republic. The nobles were tyrannical and anti-liberty. A well-ordered state had to ensure that the rich did not buy their offices with money. It would have to give opportunities to the best and the deserving. Such a state would attain glory, stability and success. He identified the state with government or with its personal head. In the *Prince*,

> ... all his attention was riveted on the human figure of the man who held the reins of government and so epitomized in his person the whole of public life. Such a conception, determined directly by the historical experience which Machiavelli possessed in such outstanding measure and presupposing a sustained effort on the part of the central government, was essential to the success and pre-eminence of the doctrine. This was a turning point in the history of the Christian world. The minds of political theorists were no longer trammelled by Catholic dogma. The structure of the State was not yet threatened in other directions by any revolt of the individual conscience ... . It was an era in which Unitarian States were being created amid the ruins of the social and political order of the Middle Ages, an era in which it was necessary to place all the weapons of resistance in the hands of those who had still to combat the forces of feudalism and particularism.

> It was, in short, an era in which it was essential that the freedom and grandeur of political action and the strength and authority of central government should be clearly affirmed (Chabod 1958: 120).

Machiavelli, in his analysis of the characteristics and dynamics of the modern nation state, understood the strength that was derived from possessing a common language and customs. In fact, he pointed out that newly acquired territories could be effectively retained provided they shared one language, similar traditions and were not used to liberty for a long period, for otherwise subjugation would be difficult.

Machiavelli was against the use of violence for private reasons other than the *raison d'etat* of the state. He condemned the petty, small-minded and badly executed acts of violence so widely prevalent in Florence. He forbade the violence of a tyrant who captured power for personal reasons and wiped out persons of *virtù* in order to rule alone and notoriously. He praised the great, glorious violence that a republic used in its conquests and expansion.

It was somewhat paradoxical that the realism and cynicism of Machiavelli did not last till the end of the *Prince.* He abruptly departed, and passionately appealed to Medici to raise the standard of Italy against the foreigner. There were no hints of such an appeal till one reached the last chapter, though it might have been there all along, and perhaps that was the reason for writing the book. He had to contend with an Italy which did not respect religion, law and moral obligation. He desired to show to his fellow beings the causes of public misery, of the extreme instability of Italian governments, the destructiveness of factionalism and the general inability to cope with foreign invasion from which Italy suffered. His general purpose was to revive public spirit rather than advocate any particular form of government. He wanted a ruler assisted by an able army to free Italy from the barbarians. There was no indication in the book as to whether this aim would be achieved. But he was convinced that only unification would bring about prosperity and security. He wanted Italy to be like France and Spain. In fact, he admired the French constitution where the king was abound by law and custom and its people were secure and free. The primary thing was independence. Everything else was secondary. In that sense, Machiavelli became a precursor of the nineteenth-century Italian nationalists Cavour, Garibaldi and Mazzini. In spite of his candid realism, he could not resist the temptation of being idealistic, and entertained the possibility of what *ought to be* rather than what *is.* If viewed in this light, then Machiavelli was not completely cynical or nihilistic.

Theory of Change and Fortune as a Woman

Machiavelli's theory of change combined historical and psychological factors. Historical changes occurred due to the role of fortune, which held the key to success. Machiavelli described fortune as a woman to whom *vir* or manliness was attracted. The relationship between *virtu* and dame fortune was addressed in terms of masculine and feminine nature (Pitkin 1984). *Virtù* was to politics what virility was to sex (Ball 1984: 524–525).

According to Machiavelli, fortune favoured and befriended the brave. Fortune was compared to a violent river, which when aroused caused havoc by flooding the plains, tearing down trees and buildings, destroying everything that came in its way. Continuing with the allegory of the river, Machiavelli advised the rulers to build floodgates and embankments to contain the raging river within the barricades. Fortune destroyed those who did not sufficiently safeguard their interests. Fortune, being fickle, could be contained only by those who had the capacity to change. Furthermore, Machiavelli suggested that instead of yielding before fortune, one had to act boldly and decisively. Fortune would ruin those who submitted meekly or those who did not protect or adapt themselves. Men conquered fortune by acknowledging its power in order to prevent a stream from becoming a raging torrent.

> ... fortune varying and men remaining fixed in their ways, they are successful so long as these ways conform to circumstances, but when they are opposed then they are unsuccessful. I certainly think that it is better to be impetuous than cautious, for fortune is a woman, and it is necessary, if you wish to master her, to conquer her by force; and it can be seen that she lets herself be overcome by the bold rather than by those who proceed coldly. And therefore, like a woman, she is always a friend to the young, because they are less cautious, fiercer, and master her with greater audacity (Machiavelli 1950: 94).

Machiavelli's discussion of fortune and *virtù* had to be understood in the context of Italian humanism (Skinner 1981: 48-77). Fortune was no longer the "inexorable force of providence", but a "capricious power" of irrational happenstance. Through his creative power and assertiveness, man would be able to control and shape his destiny against the flux that fortune unleashed. By doing so, Machiavelli reiterated the view of the humanists that the human predicament had to be seen as a struggle between man's will and fortune's wilfulness, setting aside the Christian perception of fortune as a life force, a divine necessity with very little room for human manoeuvre and free action.

Machiavelli repeatedly advised his prince to follow his maxims and precepts if he wanted to avoid the ruin or the sudden revolutions caused by fortune. He believed it was possible to effect change and bring events under human control by systematic and self-conscious statesmanship, for "he protested against the view that man cannot change events; he complained of those people who allow things to be governed by chance" (Butterfield 1962: 17).

To Machiavelli, the right person was needed at a given point in time of history. Elite circulation could either be slow or fast, peaceful or violent, depending on the situation. The psychological factors that supply the motive for change were the ones that Machiavelli considered the qualities of a lion or a fox, an aspect that was refined by Pareto in his analysis of the elite. Machiavelli saw change as never-ending, being a law of history supported by the laws of psychology.

Machiavelli probed into the causes and effects of social disturbances and in particular conspiracies. He identified: (a) rivalries among the great, namely the rich and the socially superior; and (b) the endemic and natural enmity between the great and the people, or the rich and the poor, as the two main causes for disturbances. After Aristotle, it was Machiavelli who discussed social dissensions and their causes. He was particularly concerned with factional strife, and saw equality of treatment as a possible cure. He categorically asserted that the stability of a government would depend on the satisfaction of the dominant interests within it.

CONCLUSION

Machiavelli's importance was in providing an outlook that accepted both secularization and amoralization of politics. He took politics out of the context of theology, and subordinated moral principles to the necessities of political existence and people's welfare. He had very little interest in non-political matters. Even his interest in spiritual and religious matters was strictly political. His philosophy was public and not private. The absence of religious polemics in Machiavelli led the theorists who followed to confront issues like order and power in strictly political terms.

> The *leitmotiv* of Machiavelli's posthumous life was his great assertion as a thinker, representing his true and essential contribution to the history of human thought, namely, the clear recognition of the autonomy and the necessity of politics "which lies outside the realm of what is morally good or evil". Machiavelli thereby rejected the mediaeval concept of "unity" and became one of the pioneers of the modern spirit (Chabod 1958: 116).

Machiavelli was also the first to speak of the *raison d'etat* of the state. He could perceive the forces shaping the modern nation state like nationalism, national security, and territorial integrity, militarism as forces to safeguard and further state interests. His achievement lay in confronting the secular state and scientifically enquiring into its nature and behaviour. His political realism allowed him to remain neutral towards the means that were to be employed for achieving the ends. Political activities were to be analyzed and appreciated keeping in mind whether they would achieve the objectives for which they were intended. Like the Sophists, he "judged actions not as actions, but solely in terms of their consequences" (MacIntyre 1971: 128). He could foresee the rise of science and capitalism (McIntosh 1984: 184). Some recent interpretations even view him as the earliest exponent of liberalism and pluralism (Berlin 1997: 322–325).

Machiavelli was the first to state and systematically espouse the power view of politics, laying down the foundations of a new science in the same way as Galileo's Dynamics became the basis of the modern science of nature (Cassirer 1946: 130). Machiavelli identified politics as the struggle for the acquisition, maintenance and consolidation of political power, an analysis developed by Hobbes and Harrington in the seventeenth century, Alexander Hamilton (1755–1804) and James Madison (1751–1836) in the eighteenth century, Pareto, Mosca, and Michels in the nineteenth century, and Edward Hallett Carr, Robert Dahl, David Easton, Hans Morgenthau, Morton Kaplan and Harold Lasswell in the twentieth century.

By emphasizing the importance of the study of history, Machiavelli established a method that was extremely useful. However, in spite of being a keen observer of history, he presumed that human nature remained permanent and constant, making it possible to deduce principles of political behaviour (Sabine 1973: 320). However, the reason for such a presumption was because of the fact that he lived in an age of flux, where the political order was transient. The "belief in a timeless human nature with permanent needs" became the yardstick to measure and explain the "transience of political and social orders" (MacIntyre 1971: 129). In spite of his depiction of the dark side of human nature, he never lost faith in the importance of good society and its role in shaping human beings. He was the first to study extensively the role of corruption in political-life. His writings brought about the central moral dilemmas of political life, for he spoke of unsavoury and unpalatable truths. He rightly observed that in political life, purity of life and goodness of heart mattered little. Success was important, and to be successful, a good person had to learn to be bad without appearing to be so. Glory, liberty and *virtù* constituted the essential ingredients of political success in Machiavelli's lexicon. He lamented the decline of *virtù* in contemporary Italy, which prevented its unification and independence. He condemned an ostentatious and luxurious life, which precluded acts of glory and *virtù*.

Machiavelli also accepted conflict as permanent and universal, seeing it as natural, unlike his predecessors who viewed social conflict as unnatural and curable by certain kinds of social systems. The basis of social conflict was the permanent struggle between the common man and the powerful and the moneyed, though he did not explain the struggle in economic terms. He understood struggle in terms of war between states for power and domination. Within a state, the cause for domestic instability and strife was the desire among the majority for security of their lives and possessions, while a small number, the oligarchs, sought to dominate and control the masses. From Polybius, Machiavelli realized that conflict was not only widely prevalent, but it could also be transformed into an instrument to promote socially useful ends. The difference in the nature of conflict between a corrupt and a virtuous commonwealth was the degree and quality of conflict, and not the presence or absence of it. In a virtuous commonwealth, conflict was conducted within the confines of the common good, respect for law and authority and with minimum use of violence. Freedom meant tolerating social conflict. Conflict, if well managed and handled by political compromise, became a source of strength and vibrance to the political process.

To illustrate the difference, Machiavelli used the Roman example, contrasting it with that of Florence. In Rome, conflict between the plebians and patricians was institutionalized within the senate and the popular assemblies with their tribunes without sapping the vitality of the republic or the liberties of the citizens. In contrast, in Florence, with atomization of society and each person becoming an island, religiousness, civic *virtù*, honesty and respect of authority declined. Factionalism and conspiracies were rampant and government became an arena for powerful coteries. Economic inequalities increased, indolence and luxury undermined the social fabric, virtue declined, and greed increased. Enforcement of law became weak and was compromised according to contingencies. So, unless there was a renewal of the civic order and a return to the first principles, even prudent statesmanship would not be able to stem the tide towards degeneration and decay. Machiavelli accepted that change was the way of life and everything, even the best-ordered states like Rome and Sparta, would decline.

For Machiavelli, a well-ordered state ensured the well-being and security necessary to combat social conflict and the radical selfishness of human nature. The state had no higher end or any divine purpose. It did not have a personality different or superior to those who constituted it. Successful states depended on the presence of a strong military, protection of the life, property, family and honour of every citizen, economic prosperity without promoting individual economic aggrandizement, strict regulation of luxury, good laws and respect for authority, recognition of meritorious citizens, and opportunities for the ambitious to rise within the state based on ability. A well-ordered state was also one where the citizens knew for certain the legal consequences of their actions. Hence, Machiavelli proposed a rational legal system that eliminated arbitrariness, guaranteed legal equality, regularized procedures for the redressal of grievances, prohibited retroactive laws, and executed laws efficiently and vigorously.

Machiavelli also formulated the "West's first general theory of conspiracy" (Wood 1968: 510). He believed that most political situations were conspiratorial or counter-conspiratorial in nature. In the *Art of War*, he equated conspiracy with military combat, requiring surprise, secrecy, planning, preparedness, flexibility, swiftness, decisiveness in execution, assessment of strengths and weaknesses, and cunning. He also understood political and military leadership as being identical. He founded modern military science, thus influencing those who followed him, from Maurice of Nassau to Clausewitz.

Machiavelli was one of the exponents of civic republicanism, inspiring subsequent theorists from diverse standpoints like Jean Bodin (1529/30–1596), Hobbes, Harrington, Spinoza, Montesquieu, Rousseau, Burke, Hegel and de Tocqueville. Machiavelli and his contemporary Francesco Guicciardini (1483–1540) prescribed institutional and moralistic remedies to secure and protect civic freedoms. A stable republic supported by patriotic citizens, who in turn should place public good over private gain (especially the pursuit of wealth), refrain from factional squabbles, and willingly fight for the defence of their country, guaranteed freedom. Patriotism was sustained by the continual participation of citizens in civic affairs and religion, other than Christianity. The crucial issue for Machiavelli was the possibility of civic *virtù* among a citizenry in a commercial society. He looked upon the Swiss as having honour, but they could not provide the rulers that Europe or Italy needed. The problem that confronted Machiavelli also vexed Ibn Khaldun (1332–1406) who accepted civility and cohesion as mutually incompatible. However, the problem was solved with cities providing the first element and the tribes the second. For Khaldun, the Turks, Arabs and Berbers provided an inexhaustible supply of rulers and warriors who would complement the "uncohesive atomized specialist of the productive urbanized and sedentarized world" (Gellner 1994: 72).

Machiavelli also emphasized the importance of a wise constitutional machinery alongside civic *virtù,* as well as the importance of mixed constitutions as expressed in the writings of Aristotle, Polybius and Aquinas while engaging in a polemic with Guicciardini. The last preferred an Aristotelian, Venetian-Spartan aristocracy. Machiavelli contended that in a mixed government the separate classes would, through the institutions of representation, limit one another's power, thereby ensuring liberty for all. This defence of limited government as a necessary condition for safeguarding liberty started a tradition that continues even today. Machiavelli was also convinced that the rule of law would supersede factional and private interests, and hence he explored a constitution that would uphold anu preserve the rule of law. In his opinion, a constitution with established institutions and procedures would partly prevent usurpation. He also defended distribution of power with accountability which made it possible to impeach any official of the state.

Machiavelli was a keen and perceptive observer of the systems in the East, and according to him these states contained ingredients which he thought to be crucial. The Eastern central state was not an apex body within a complex pyramid of power. Both in law and otherwise, there was sufficient dispersal of effective authority. As a result, society never got disrupted nor rendered helpless. But the Eastern state had a strong centre, which, if destroyed, would mean its end.

Gramsci praised the greatness of Machiavelli for separating politics from ethics. Following Croce's description of "Marx as the Machiavelli of the proletariat", Gramsci tried to analyze the ramification of the political aspect of Machiavelli's theory by writing *The Modern Prince* which remained incomplete. In the *Prison Notebooks* (1925–1936), there were a number of references to Machiavelli, and Gramsci pointed out that the protagonist of the new prince in modern times could not be an individual hero, but a political party whose objective was to establish a new kind of state.

Machiavelli distinguished acts of morality and immorality in the conventional sense. Though critical of the Church and Christianity, Machiavelli was born and died a Christian. His attack on the Church was due to his anti-clericalism, rather than being anti-religion. In comparison, paganism of the ancient world seemed preferable.

> The breakthrough of Renaissance political theory lay in Machiavelli's treatment of the legitimacy of regimes and political leaders. Prior to the *Prince* and the *Discourses*, writers treated political regimes dichotomously as pure and corrupt, normative and non-normative, in the original Platonic and Aristotelian senses. Machiavelli, viewing politics as practiced in Italy in the 15th and 16th centuries, legitimized non-normative politics as unavoidable, as survival-related, as part of reality ... . Machiavelli touched the nerve of political science with this "value-free" orientation and his na,me has become a synonym for moral indifference and political cynicism. The issues raised by this venture into realism are still fluttering the dovecotes of political philosophy (Almond 1996: 58).

Undeservedly, Machiavelli was seen as the devil's agent, confined to permanent infamy for preaching villainy and duplicitous pursuit of political power. It was the price that he paid for making the first attempt to develop a new science of politics and identifying the .essential ingredients of modern political theory. It was his good fortune that the greatest political thinker that Italy produced did not meet the same fate as Galileo did.

5

Thomas Hobbes

The Leviathan is the greatest perhaps the sole masterpiece of political philosophy written in the English language ... and the history of our civilization can provide only a few works of similar scope and achievement to set beside it ... . What makes *Leviathan* a masterpiece of philosophical literature is the profound logic of Hobbes' imagination, his power as an artist. Hobbes recalls us to our mortality with a deliberate conviction, with a subtle and sustained argument (Oakeshott 1975: 3, 154).

Despite the rigorousness of the theory ... despite the powerful animus against autonomous associations and the limitations put upon religion and all other autonomous systems of morality, it is the *individual* whom Hobbes has in his mind as the embodiment of virtue. Hobbes did not seek the extermination of individual rights but their fulfillment. This could be accomplished only by removing social barriers to individual autonomy. In his eyes the greatest claim of the absolute State lay in its power to create an environment for the individual's pursuit of his natural ends (Nisbet 1990: 123).

As a consequence of the extraordinary attention paid to the logic and scientific methodology of Thomas Hobbes' writings by recent scholars, we have all but set aside the importance of the fact that Hobbes was, in the first instance a political theorist (Ashcraft 1978: 27).

Eventful incidents in the life of eminent thinkers often help in dissecting their outlook and philosophical foundations. Thomas Hobbes (1588–1679), who was the greatest political thinker produced by the English-speaking people, vindicated this proposition. In logical construction, clarity of thought and originality of ideas, there were few parallels to the magnificent edifice that he built. His major emphases on peace, order, security and commodious living became important in the political vocabulary of subsequent theorizing. The cover of his masterpiece summed up the gist of his theory by identifying all the important components of a modern society, namely atomistic individuality and all-powerful sovereign (Wolin 1960: 266). It was this clear exposition of the idea of good that led Hobbes to develop a theory that differed totally from Aristotle. Unlike Aristotle, Hobbes insisted that human beings were not naturally social, and that politics and the state were artificially created, a product of convention and deliberate human action.

Hobbes' paramount consideration for order in society emanated largely from two happenings in his life, resulting in his fear of violent death and the need for all the contentment of life. These two unrelated incidents in his life help us to understand Hobbesian political philosophy. The first was the fear of the Spanish Armada that stimulated his mother's labour and Hobbes' premature birth. The second was the outbreak of the English Civil War in 1641, and the fact that Hobbes was the first to flee from England. At the age of 84, when, looking back on his life, he felt it was fear that held the key. His observance, "Fear and I were born twins", was an apt summary of his political philosophy. Fear was the basis of his philosophy which led him to argue a case for despotism.

Hobbes regarded self-preservation as a supreme right. This notion he borrowed from Grotius, who contended in *The Law of War and Peace* (1625) that all individuals had a right to preserve themselves and that, other things being equal, no one could ever be blamed for doing what they did in order to survive. Both Grotius and Hobbes considered the right of self-preservation as a sufficient basis for morality, at least in its minimalist or natural sense. If self-preservation was the most basic right, then an individual would not be aggressive towards others unless provoked or threatened. Both Grotius and Hobbes looked upon benevolence as possible in complex human relationships.

Hobbes differed from Grotius in understanding that even an individual who pursued the right of self-preservation would still remain unpredictable and dangerous towards others. This followed from his thorough-going skepticism about knowledge in general. Since it was difficult to obtain an accurate knowledge of the external world and that of other people's minds, there was no certainty about how *others* would behave towards us. In the absence of such certainty, each individual would have to make that judgement about the intentions and motivations of others encouraging him to make that pre-emptive strike against others. As a result, pre-civil society was one of anarchy. Hobbes departed significantly from others in not regarding conflicting desires as the causes of the human condition. Conflict arose due to independency of human judgement (Tuck 1989: 57). Though this argument was sound and convincing, it must be remembered that Hobbes (like Machiavelli) was confronting the dilemma of limited resources and unlimited desires. The problem of scarcity was writ large in their world-views. Human beings were characterized as hostile and competitive because of this important fact.

Hobbes, like Richard Hooker (1533–1600) was the first to write philosophical tracts in English instead of Latin. While Hooker's main concern was with jurisprudence, Hobbes' range was more diverse, namely ethics, metaphysics and physics. Beginning with Hobbes, political philosophy in England was conducted in English. Hobbes readily discarded antiquity for he had very little respect for anything classical. He firmly adhered to logic and reason as intellectual tools, and was not much interested in reading or observing.

Hobbes' political philosophy in the *Leviathan* (1651) was a reflection of the civil strife in England following the execution of Charles I (1600–1649). Many of his contemporaries like Clarendon (1676) and Whitehall (1679) condemned the book, regarding it as a good doctrine for popish cabal since it contained "lewd principles". Filmer (1659) agreed with its conclusions, but rejected the premises.

LIFE SKETCH

Hobbes was born on April 5, 1588. He was the second son. His birth was premature. His parents were relatively poor. His father was a member of the clergy near Malmesburg, Wiltshire. He was brought up by his uncle. In his younger days, he was a bright student and mastered a number of languages. He could speak and read Latin, Greek, French, Italian and English. While he was still a schoolboy, he translated Euripides' *Medea* from Greek into Latin, and throughout his life this continued. His first publication was a translation in English of Thucydides' *History of the Peloponnesian War* in 1629. Besides, just before he died, at the age of 86, he translated Homer's *Odyssey* and *Iliad* into English. Throughout his life he wrote verses in Latin and English. He was a quick writer of both prose and verse, and the last 10 chapters of the *Leviathan* (approximately 90,000 words) were written in an amazing time-span of less than a year.

Hobbes learnt scholastic logic and physics at Oxford University. He also spent time reading maps. However, he disliked the education imparted at Oxford, dismissing scholasticism as a collection of absurdities. After completing his education, he was recruited in 1618 into an aristocratic household, the family of William Lord Cavendish, who came to be known as the Earl of Devonshire. At first he was a tutor, and later became a secretary. The rest of his life was spent in the employment of this family or its neighbours and cousins. He accompanied Lord Cavendish's son on a grand tour of Europe in 1610–1615. In 1630, he escorted the son of another family on a four of Europe and in 1634–1635 he took the son of his pupil of 1610 on a journey similar to the one he had taken with his father. These tours gave Hobbes a unique opportunity to meet both politicians and intellectuals, enabling him to gain many new insights. He met eminent people like Galileo Galilee, Pierre Gassendi (1592–1655) and Marin Marsenne (1588–1648). He corresponded with Descartes who was in hiding in the Netherlands; finally the two met in 1648. Of all the places that he visited, Venice made the most lasting impression.

For a while during the period of the Civil War in 1641 and the Thirty-Year war (1618–1648), Hobbes had to deal with matters like horses. Interestingly, he also studied details of telescopes, which he felt would give a decisive military advantage to the country that could innovate one. In 1634, he discussed problems of optics and physics and subsequently met various French mathematicians and philosophers. This led to his disassociation with conventional Aristotelian physics.

By the end of 1640, Hobbes had written two drafts of philosophical works, which included *De Cive* (1642). With a fear of persecution by the Long parliament for his *Elements of Law,* which was a brief for his master and supporters in the debates in parliament, he fled to France in November 1640 and stayed there till the winter of 1651–1652. The publication of the *Leviathan* led to his estrangement with Charles II. He returned to England and submitted to the republican government under Oliver Cromwell (1599–1658), and received a pension from Charles II (1630–1685). In 1655, *De Corpore* was published. In 1657, the *Leviathan* was reported to the parliamentary committee as "a most poisonous piece of atheism".

In 1647, Hobbes fell seriously ill, and could never recover fully. From 1648, he started developing symptoms which indicated Parkinson's disease. But in spite of ill health, his famous work, the *Leviathan,* appeared in April 1651. It was an astonishing method of publication, as Hobbes sent instalments each week from Paris to London for setting in type, with proofs being sent back within a week. The experience of Hobbes to the reaction of his work was terrifying, and in the last part of his life he attempted many books to vindicate himself. In 1688, a revised Latin edition of the *Leviathan* was published. In 1670, the *Behemoth* was published. In 1683, the *Leviathan* and the *De Cive* were condemned and burned at Oxford University.

Hobbes served the Cavendish family faithfully for more than four generations, and in his old age was treated by the family as more than a servant, but less than an honoured guest. In October 1679, he fell ill and finally died of paralysis on 3 December. "He seems in fact to have died much as he had lived, a witty and skeptical humanist" (Tuck ibid: 39). It was said of Hobbes that he worked hard for his longevity. John Aubrey, his biographer and friend, tells of the exercises, walking up and down hills very fast, playing tennis and having rub-downs as measures that Hobbes undertook for keeping fit. Moreover, during the night after everyone had gone to sleep, Hobbes would sing a "prick-song". "Here then is a philosopher with a very unphilosophic aversion to death, an aversion that Hobbes eventually posited as fundamental to human nature and a force for wisdom in human affairs" (Minogue 1973: iv). Hobbes spent his time mediating and philosophizing, writing down his "darting thoughts" in a notebook that he always carried with him. He was a voracious reader, and read anything that he came across. He was conscious of being a self-taught philosopher.

DEVELOPMENTS IN SCIENCE AND THEIR INFLUENCE ON HOBBES

Philosophically and methodologically, Hobbes was influenced by new developments in the physical sciences and by the works of Bacon, Kepler and Galileo. This was the period not only of religious strife, but also of scientific temperament, for there was immense curiosity about nature and the desire to eschew the supernatural. Both Bacon and Kepler visualized an order behind the diversity in the universe. Galileo laid down the principles of mechanics, observing that the task of a scientist was to discover primitive notions of complex objects in simple ones. He rejected Aristotle, and looked to Plato's *Timaeus* for an understanding of the universe.

Plato was the earliest among philosophers to understand the implications of the Pythagorean formula of "One behind the Many", by the use of mathematics to study Forms or Idea that were behind the world of senses subject to motion and change. However, with Galileo and others, the question was to construct a mathematical theory of motion, rather than of motionless Form. The general tone of the new science tried to despiritualize nature, by abolishing the distinction between animate and inanimate. It clearly identified and established the difference between the inner from the outer worlds. The new science explained the natural world mechanically with reference to simple motions. The inner world was subjective, and the outer world objective. The relationship between the two was contingent. It assumed that thinking was an activity that took place within one's mind, which could be deciphered by none other than the thinking subject. A subject's thoughts could not be understood by his external actions and behaviour.

Hobbes and Descartes accepted the argument of the Skeptics, and pointed out that it was not possible to have a direct and honest experience of the external world; all that one could comprehend was the internal activity within one's brain. Though Descartes raised this question in his *Discourse on the Method* (1637), it was Hobbes who suggested that for purposes of philosophical enquiry we should presume the existence of a single brain, and then speculate whether such a brain could perceive and experience. Unlike Descartes, he took it for granted that such a mind could be satisfied, that the material world was the only world, and that the universe consisted of nothing but matter in motion or at rest. Its experiences were caused by the motion of these objects, and not because of the presence of God. For Hobbes, spirit was nothing but a movement in certain parts of an organism. Motion was the cause of all things. Thought and physical processes were distinct expressions of the universal category of "motion". He concluded that since matter alone existed, thought must itself be motion. Physical laws could be the basis of human psychology and behaviour.

Following the true spirit of the new science and philosophy, Hobbes adopted the science of geometry to grasp political and moral knowledge. Geometry was useful because of its clear deductive reasoning, for as long as one's premises were correct, one could arrive at the right conclusions. He was captivated by geometry at the age of 40, when he accidentally came across Euclid's *Elements* about which Aubrey wrote:

> He was 40 years old before he looked on Geometry; which happened accidentally. Being in a Gentleman's Library, Euclid's *Elements* lay open, and 'twas the *47. El. libri I.* He read the Proposition. "By G—said he ... this is impossible." So he reads the Demonstration of it, which referred him back to such a Proposition; which proposition he read. That referred him back to another, which he also read. *Et sic deinceps* (and so on) that at least he was demonstratively convinced of that truth. This made him live with Geometry (Aubrey 1962: 150).

Hobbes described geometry as the only science which pleased God and was hence bestowed upon humankind. He was convinced that politics could be as precise as geometry, and referred to the *Leviathan* as a *demonstration.* At the end of Chapter 31, he emphatically proclaimed that he had attempted what no previous philosopher had done, namely to "put in order, and sufficiently, or probably proved all the Theorems of moral doctrine, that men may learn thereby, both how to govern, and how to obey" (Hobbes 1991: 254). For Hobbes, geometry provided the intellectual method to solve the problems of political life. Therefore, he forwarded the *Leviathan* as an extended proof, proceeding from clear definitions and axioms to conclusions that right-thinking Englishmen would simply have to accept. It was a different matter whether he succeeded in his aim or not, but there was no denying the sheer brilliance of his attempt and fascination it aroused. "For it is probable that what was foremost in Hobbes' mind was the vision, not of a new type of philosophy or science but of a universe that is nothing but bodies and their aimless motions" (Strauss: 1950: 409).

Hobbes' second intellectual model was physical science, especially the one practised by Galileo, whom he greatly admired. Galileo's technique of investigation was known as the resolutive composite method. The resolutive part of the method consisted in abstracting all extraneous considerations, and concentrating on the essential facts; for example, in analyzing motion, Galileo focused on the essentials like mass, weight and acceleration. Having identified the basic factors, he recomposed these into a simple and theoretical explanation. The same techniques—resolve, idealize, recompose—were Hobbes' method in political science. He resolved the diseased commonwealth of his day into its constituent parts, individuals and their passions in a "state of nature". Then he recombined these elements into a new body politic, the Leviathan. Hobbes compared his method to taking apart a watch or a small engine in order to know its constituent parts.

Hobbes contended that the aim of all philosophy was to give a mechanical theory of the universe. This was seen as a problem in geometry. Atoms had no properties of their own, except when seen as a part of certain laws of motion. Matter was in a state of perpetual motion. The problem was how it moved from one state of motion to another. The human being was also an automaton, for all his actions could be explained by the laws of motion. All motions originated, and were with reference to, the human body. It would function harmoniously with minimum friction, like a wrist watch, if arranged properly. If not, then the parts would destroy one another.

Hobbes's *mechanical* materialism differed from Marx's *dialectical* materialism. A mechanical materialist perceived matter to be passive, with change stimulated from the external environment. A dialectical materialist regarded matter as being active, changing from within without much help from the environment. The mechanistic conception implied that the whole was no more than a sum total of the parts that comprised it. The whole was not more important or greater than the constituent parts. Applying the analogy to the state, Hobbes viewed the state as an aggregate and not a compound of individuals.

Thus, the ultimate aim of Hobbes, as of Galileo, was to use the mathematical framework to describe a physical and political phenomenon, as mathematics provided unity, certainty and precision. Following Galileo, he opposed the Aristotelian idea of things moving towards some goal, and then coming to rest. On the contrary, things in motion tended to stay that way. Philosophy, for Hobbes, was strictly utilitarian and practical—a knowledge of the effects which could be produced by a given set of causes, or conversely, of causes that resulted in a set of effects. Like Bacon and Hamilton, he regarded power as the end of knowledge and an instrument to harness the forces of nature. All individuals were equal, but differences arose due to their differing capacity for knowledge. All knew that war and civil strife were the worst possible calamities, but few understood their causes and the ways to avoid them. Very few could comprehend the means by which peace could be maintained.

Hobbes insisted that if science had to gain ascendancy, it would have to receive support from certain sections in society. He emphasized that philosophy and science could only flourish in an affluent society, and cited the examples of Athens and Rome. He cautioned against the pursuit of wealth as an overwhelming goal, for if that happened, it would subordinate knowledge, increase corruption, imperil peace and safety in civil society. England of the seventeenth century was similar to Athens. In both societies, philosophy was no longer pursued for the knowledge and the truth it bestowed, but was seen as a means to earning a living. The political message that he conveyed was that it would be fatal to rely on the advice of those who were more dextrous with making money rather than knowledge.

HOBBES' POLITICAL PHILOSOPHY

Hobbes stress was on fear and self-interest as the two fundamental human motivations which needed to be tempered and controlled by an omnipotent sovereign power. The presence of a sovereign separated a state of nature from a political society. Using the device of the social contract, Hobbes explained the nature of sovereignty, its location, the relationship with the individual, the essential functions of a government, and the origins of a state. Hobbes defended a case for absolute legal sovereignty, since sovereign power was the result of a zero-sum game. Absolute power ensured complete order. Conversely, its absence meant chaos.

In view of the fact that the English Parliament succeeded in extracting a Petition of Rights from Charles I, Hobbes warned his readers through his translation of Thucydides (1628) against any disaffection with the established government. He also cautioned against democracy and the illusionary benefits of a republic. He deplored the fact that the English political system was not functioning smoothly, and was worried about the consequences of disorder and civil war.

The troubles that Hobbes perceived finally arrived in 1640, lasting for the next 20-odd years. During this period, England experienced a tussle between royal and parliamentary forces, the execution of Charles I in 1649, and a stringent Puritan rule under Cromwell. The era came to an end with the restoration of the monarchy under Charles II. Basically, three different overlapping struggles were involved.

1. Parliament against the king.
2. The Puritans against the established church.
3. The expanding economic forces of the towns, ports and countryside against the ossified, old, royal monopolists and landowners.

This was the period of contending political, religious and economic principles, a time of diverse production and diffusion of social ideas. The seventeenth century witnessed ferment in political and religious thought, bringing in a fundamental ideological shift. Increasingly, the community was seen as an artifact created voluntarily through a contract based on mutual agreement for the fulfilment of individual aims and aspirations. This meant that political authority could be judged, evaluated and changed, for it was bound by a constitution and laws, and no longer absolutist in nature. The constitutional state was emerging as the new political formation and subject of political theorizing. Hobbes was the first to grapple with this new entity.

Hobbes equated intellectual ferment with the disorder and violence unleashed by the civil wars, attributing it to the mischievous doctrines spread by individuals collectively referred to as "the seducers". These corrupting notions were: (a) that private citizens could judge the right and the wrong, good and evil; (b) it was a sin to act against one's conscience;

(c) one's conscience might be supernaturally inspired; and (d) that the sovereign power must be limited and divided. Hobbes suspected the Puritans and the universities as being the root cause of seditious activity.

The Puritans' offence consisted in letting their consciences be their guide. In Hobbes' day, conscience was termed "inner light", and Hobbes' irritation lay in the fact that "all England seemed to be ablaze with inner lights" (Wolin 1960: 258). He argued that the Protestant stress on the importance of inner conviction made all "outward things" a matter of indifference, for if true belief, as taught by the Protestants, was private, an inward thing, a matter of the quality of one's faith, then it did not matter what the outward forms used for its expression were. However, this sort of individualism would lead to confusion and anarchy. In the *Leviathan*, he made every effort to prove that it was not permissible to follow one's own conscience other than the sovereign commands,

> ... one of the most important factors establishing and maintaining the identity of a political society was a common political language.... the language of politics differed in the crucial respect that the commonness of meanings depended on a ruling power capable of enforcing them; that is, of declaring, for example the precise meaning of a right and punishing those who refused to accept the assertion (Wolin ibid: 259).

Similarly, Hobbes condemned the universities as centres of sedition and the essential cause of the civil war. He hoped that the *Leviathan* would persuade his readers to act sensibly and prize public order. Order was the overriding concern, just as civil war was the greatest evil. He believed that by bringing order into political thinking, he would have taken a long step towards bringing order into society.

Hobbes conceived of the sources of social dissension in two different ways. In the *Behemoth* (which was sociological in nature), he specified *groups* which had seduced citizens from their obligation to the sovereign—groups such as Presbyterian ministers, Roman Catholics, and the merchants of the trading cities. But in *Elements of Law, De Cive* (*The Citizen: Philosophical Rudiments Concerning Government and Society*) (1642) and the *Leviathan*, which were analytical and philosophical in nature, he presented individuals, not groups, as the root of social problems.

HUMAN NATURE

Hobbes, like Machiavelli, was concerned with the secular origins of human conduct, for he did not theorize about proper behaviour from an understanding of the Idea of Good, or from a revelation of divine commands. Contrary to Aristotle and the medieval thinkers, who saw human nature as innately social, Hobbes viewed human beings as isolated, egoistic, self-interested, and seeking society as a means to their ends.

Individuals were creatures of desire, seeking pleasure and avoiding pain. Pleasures were good and pain bad, which was why men sought to pursue and maximize their pleasures and avoid pain. The pleasure-pain theory was developed in a coherent and systematic theory of human behaviour and motivation by the Utilitarians, especially Bentham in the eighteenth century. In addition to being creatures of pleasure and pain, Hobbes saw individuals constantly in motion to satisfy their desires. Continual success in the attainment and fulfilment of their desires was called felicity, a condition of movement and not rest. Appetites were insatiable, for the satisfaction of some gave rise to others. Satisfaction therefore was a temporary feeling, for individuals were aware of the recurrence of desires. Not only did individuals ensure the means for present satisfaction, but they also provided for future ones.

Hobbes asserted that every human action, feeling and thought was ultimately physically determined, yet he allowed ample scope for voluntary, self-designed and administrated changes in human conditions. Though the human being was dependent on his life, on the motion of his body, he was able, to some extent, to control these motions and make his life. This he did by "natural" means, i.e. by relying partly on natural passions and partly on reason. It was reason, according to Hobbes, that distinguished humans from animals. He drew a distinction between "prudence", which was the accumulation of experience, and "reason" seen essentially in mathematical terms. "When a man *Reasoneth,* he does nothing else but conceive a summe totall, from *Addition* of parcels; or conceive a Remainder, from substraction of one summe from another" (Hobbes 1991: 31).

Reason therefore enabled the individual to understand the impressions that sense organs picked up from the external world, and also indicated an awareness of one's natural passions. Hobbes also introduced, interestingly, the need for an "arbitrator" or "judge" who resolved rational disagreements, since no one individual's reason was necessarily "right", so parties to a dispute needed an arbitrator "to whose sentence they will both stand". This remained a major theme in the entire theoretical construct of Hobbes, that order was absolutely necessary and an indispensable precondition for getting anywhere with human reason, of being able to build any sort of culture.

Hobbes did not exclude the possibility of altruism, listing benevolence, goodwill and charity among passions. Good and evil were names that signified an individual's appetite and aversions. The objects of an individual's desires varied in accordance with his personal characteristics, but all—at least ordinarily—desired self-preservation. Peace enhanced the possibilities of preserving ourselves, so it was good.

It was important to note that the need for an arbitrator was not due to lack of sufficient reason. The more compelling factor was the barriers erected between human beings as a result of their natural passions. These passions were directly related to individuals valuing their life above everything else, and sticking to it at all costs. The "appetites" and "aversions" were basically passions. The feeling towards things depended on how conducive they were in ensuring and maintaining life, and was accordingly described as "good" and "bad". The aim of the individual dictated by passion was to obtain desired results.

Human will, in Hobbes' philosophy, did not imply anything spiritual or transcendental but was related to the natural needs of the body. He mentioned a long list of passions, but the special emphasis was on fear, in particular the fear of death, and on the universal and perfectly justified quest for power. In contrast to classical philosophers, Hobbes did not assign any positive or higher aim to life. There "is no Summum Bonum (Greatest Good) as is spoken of in the Books of the Old Morall Philosophers" (Hobbes ibid: 469). Since individuals would like to do their own thing, pursue their own desires, there was no ultimate human good as a criterion of ethical judgement (Minogue 1973: iv). One could expect, in life, at most only "felicity", which was continual prosperity. "For there is no such thing as perpetual tranquillity of mind, while we live here; because Life itselfe is but Motion, and can never be without Desire, nor without Feare, no more than without Sense" (Hobbes 1991: 46).

Hobbes contended that life was nothing but a perpetual and relentless desire and pursuit of power, a prerequisite for felicity. He pointed out that one ought to recognize a "general inclination of all mankind, a perpetual and restless desire for Power after power that ceaseth only in Death" (Hobbes ibid: 70). Consequently, individuals were averse to death, especially accidental death, for it marked the end of attainment of all felicity. Power was sought for it represented a means of acquiring those things that made life worthwhile and contented, called felicity. The fact that all individuals (and not merely the political elite) sought power distinguished Hobbes from Machiavelli.

Another significant facet of Hobbes' perception that set him apart from both ancient and medieval philosophers was his belief in the equality of men, the fact that men were equal in physical power, and faculties of mind (Hobbes ibid: 86). By equality, Hobbes meant equal ability and the equal hope of attaining the ends individuals aspired for (Hobbes ibid: 86–87). The physically weak may achieve by cunning what the strong could accomplish through force. Hobbes accepted differences in physical or natural endowments. Hobbes also saw human beings as active creatures with a "will". Human beings were endowed with both reason and passions (reason being passive while passions active). Differences in passions created differences in wits, with a desire to excel over others. Since individuals were equal and active, those who succeeded would have more enemies and competitors, and face maximum danger. Hobbes observed that human beings stood nothing to gain from the company of others, except pain. A permanent rivalry existed between human beings for honour, riches and authority, with life as nothing but potential warfare, a war of everyone against the others.

State of Nature

Having described the natural person, Hobbes proceeded to portray the state of nature. In the light of bleak and pessimistic human nature, the picturization of the state of nature was gloomy and sordid. Hobbes saw human relationships as those of mutual suspicion and hostility. The only rule that individuals acknowledged was that one would take if one had the power, and retain as long as one could. In this "ill condition", there was no law, no justice, no notion of right and wrong, with only force and fraud as the two cardinal virtues. Justice and injustice "relate to man in society, not in solitude" (Hobbes ibid: 90). Daniel Defoe's (1660-1731) *Robinson Crusoe* (1719) graphically captured the Hobbesian depiction of an atomistic asocial individual. Society was nut natural; in fact, individuals had to be educated in order to live in one. The state of nature prohibited the possibilities of ensuring commodious living or civilized pursuits that made life worthwhile and meaningful, for:

> In such condition, there is no place for Industry, because the fruit thereof is uncertain: and consequently no Culture of the Earth; no Navigation, nor use of the commodities that may be imported by Sea; no commodious Building; no Instruments of moving such things as require much force, no Knowledge of the face of the earth; no account of Time, no Arts; no Letters; no Society; and which is worst of all, continuall feare, and danger of violent death; And the life of man, solitary, poore, nasty, brutish and short (Hobbes ibid: 89).

The principal cause of conflict was within the nature of man. Competition, diffidence and glory were the three reasons that were responsible for quarrel and rivalry among individuals. "The first maketh men invade for Gain; the second, for Safety; and the third, for Reputation. The first use Violence, to make themselves Masters of other men's persons ... the second to defend them; the third, for trifles ..." (Hobbes ibid: 98).

Hobbes did not attribute the predicament of the natural person to either sin or depravity, but to human nature. The individual was the author of his own ruination. The state of nature degenerated into a state of war, "a war of every man against every man". Such a condition might not exist all over the world, other than in America where the savages lived in a nasty and brutish manner (Hobbes ibid: 89). The state of nature was a condition when political authority failed.

> The state of nature dramatizes what Hobbes takes to be the fundamental dilemma of human existence: that men both need each other and "grieve" each other. Most social life, he tells us, is for gain or for glory, and as we have seen, men pay for these pleasures by a host of small pains and humiliation at each other's hands. Such things are but hints of what would happen did we not live under government. They would very rapidly have impelled men into civil society, so that the state of nature cannot have existed for long, though it is approximated whenever authority breaks down (Minogue 1973: xvi).

Hobbes was not referring to an actual historical process of development of human society. The conditions in which men lived were of their own making. Civil society either controlled or suppressed the natural instincts, but never changed them. Interestingly, Hobbes toned the aggressive view of human nature in *De Cive.* He described the natural state as one of war, which was not responsible for the evil in human nature. In a footnote, he accepted the natural gregariousness of human beings as indicating a desire to come together. Logically, civil societies were not mere meetings, but bonds, that made faith and compacts necessary. For Hobbes, it was the absence of "faith" or trust and not the presence of an evil quality in man that caused human misery in the natural state. The absence of faith was partly due to limited natural reason, and partly due to human inability to decipher the thoughts and motives of others.

Natural Laws

In a state of nature, individuals enjoyed complete liberty, including a natural right to everything, even to one another's bodies. The natural laws, 19 in all, and considered as Articles of Peace, were dictates of reason. These were not "laws" or "commands". Subsequently, Hobbes, like Grotius, argued that the laws of nature were also proper laws, since they were "delivered in the word of God". These laws were counsels of prudence. It prescribes types of civil manners that promote peaceful behaviour.

Natural laws in Hobbes' theory did not mean eternal justice, perfect morality or standards to judge existing laws as the Stoics did. They did not imply the existence of common good, for they merely created the common conditions which were necessary to fulfil each individual good. These laws were immutable. Of the 19, there were three important natural laws: (a) seek peace and follow it; (b) abandon the natural right to things; and (c) that individuals must honour their contracts. Hobbes stressed the fact that peace demanded mutual confidence, for society depended on mutual trust. This led him to conclude that supreme power ought to coincide with supreme authority. Governments had to be always backed by force, if not direct, at least, implicit, for "covenants without swords are but words and of no strength to secure a man at all" (Hobbes 1991: 117).

Contract and Sovereign Power

Since the first law of nature enjoined individuals to seek peace, the only way to attain it was through a covenant leading to the establishment of a state. Individuals surrendered all their powers through a contract to a third party who was not a party to the contract, but nevertheless received all the powers that were surrendered. The commonwealth was constituted when the multitude of individuals were united in one person, when every person said to the other, "I Authorise and give up my Right of Governing my selfe, to this Man, or this Assembly of men, on this condition, that thou give up thy Right to him, and Authorise all his Actions in like manner" (Hobbes ibid: 120).

In the seventeenth century, the notion of the contract as a free agreement between self-interested individuals became an answer to the problems of social cohesion. The third party was a consequence of the contract, an artificial person distinct from the natural individual. It was not the common will of all, for such an idea did not exist but was only a substitute for conflicting individual wills, as that would guarantee unity among multitudes within in a commonwealth. The contract created an artifact in the sovereign authority whereby each individual gave up his right of governing himself, on the condition that others did likewise. The only way to erect the common power,

> ... is, to conferre all their power and strength upon one Man, or upon one Assembly of men, that may reduce all their wills, by plurality of voices, unto one Will; which is as much to say, to appoint one Man, or Assembly of men, to beare their Person; and everyone to owne, and acknowledge himselfe to be Author of whatsoever he that so beareth their Person, shall Act or cause to be Acted, in those things which concerne the Common Peace and Safetie ... (Hobbes ibid: 120).

Each individual, by consenting to a set of rules, guaranteed basic equality with every other member. This also meant that no one possessed more rights than another. The sovereign must treat all the individuals equally in matters of justice and levying taxes. Hobbes defined justice as equality in treatment and equality in rights. It also involved keeping one's promises, for non-performance would lead to an unequal status. Hobbes equated justice with fairness, treating others as one would expect to be treated.

Once the sovereign power was created it would be bestowed with all powers. "This is the Generation of that great Leviathan, or rather (to speak more reverently) of that Mortall God, to which we owe under the Immortall God, our peace and defence" (Hobbes ibid: 120).

The contract created civil society and political authority, for it was a social and political contract. It was a contract of each with the other. A commonwealth could be established by two methods: acquisition, and institution. Acquisition was when individuals were threatened into submission. The process of institution was when individuals, of their own impulse, united, agreeing to transfer all their natural powers through a contract to a third party of one, few or many. Both were contractual, though the process of institution exemplified the essence of contractualism. The contract was perpetual and irrevocable. Individuals limited their sovereignty voluntarily by creating a civil society.

Hobbes preferred the beneficiary of the contract, the third person, to be a monarch. Commonwealths differed not due to the nature of the sovereign power, but in the numbers who wielded and exercised this power. Monarchy was preferable to an aristocracy or democracy because of the following reasons:

(a) the self-indulgence of one compared to that of many would be cheaper;
(b) the existence of an identity of interests between the king and his subjects; and
(c) less intrigues and plots, which were normally due to personal ambitions and envy of members of the ruling elite.

Adhering to the Monist view, Hobbes saw the sovereign power as undivided, unlimited, inalienable and permanent. The contract created the state and the government simultaneously. His defence of absolute state power in reality was a justification of absolute government or monarchy, because of a failure to distinguish between the state and the government. However, absolute power was not based on the notion of the divine rights of kings, but derived through a contract that was mutually agreed upon and willingly acquiesced to. He dismissed the divine rights argument, but was unwilling to press the contractarian argument to its logical conclusion, for he did not provide for either a renewal of consent or a periodic assessment of the sovereign by the people.

The sovereign power or the "dominium", a term used in *De Cive,* was authorized to enact laws as it deemed fit and such laws were legitimate. Hobbes was categorical that the powers and authority of the sovereign had to be defined with least ambiguity. The Leviathan was the sole source and interpreter of laws. He was the interpreter of divine and natural laws. Unlike Bodin, Hobbes did not circumscribe the power of the sovereign by placing it under divine and natural laws. In fact, the Leviathan was not even subject to civil laws, being the *sole source* of these laws. The sovereign was bound by these laws as long as they were not repealed. Hobbes defined the law as a command of the sovereign, a viewpoint adopted by Bentham and John Austin (1790–1859) in their descriptions of sovereignty. Since a law was the command of the sovereign, it could be wrong, unjust or immoral. The sovereign not only administered the law, but also enforced it. Voltaire, like Hobbes, favoured an absolute undivided sovereign power, which, however, would not be despotic. Since he, like Locke, was a passionate defender of liberty, he felt that a strong, centralized monarchy, totally modern and unhindered by medievalism, would ensure a good, just and progressive government.

Hobbes' theory of sovereignty was a precursor of Austin's theory. The sovereign enjoyed absolute powers only because the individuals had totally surrendered *their* powers. Hobbes conceptualized an absolute sovereign power only because of his thorough-going individualism. The absolute sovereign represented the individuals, and was constituted by them for providing order and security, and averting the worst of all evils, civil war (Plamentaz 1963: Vol. I: 116–154).

Hobbes, unlike Bodin, was able to create order and stability by subordinating non-political associations, including the Church and universities. He did not recognize any pre-political order of society based on kinship, religion and other associations, which normally contributed to sociability in the individual. He was quite unsympathetic towards customs, traditions and other moralities that existed outside the purview of the sovereign law. On this basis, he proclaimed that law was not derived from the social institutions of a people, but was the command of the sovereign. This was because he ruled out private beliefs, which he considered to be the source of all seditions and dissensions. He also ruled out divisions and multiplicity of authority for that was an anathema to a stable political order. Authority was either unitary or nothing. He also made the sovereign above the law, thereby giving a death-blow to one of the most cherished legal doctrines of the medieval period.

The sovereign had the right and the duty to govern and conduct policy, protect civil society from dissolution, limit or restrict freedom of expression, opinions and doctrines, control subjects' property, resolve all conflicts through the right of judicature (of hearing and deciding all controversies), make war and peace with other nations, choose ministers, counsellors, magistrates, officers both in peace and war, confer honours and privileges, determine artificial religion and the forms of its worship, and prevent access to subversive literature. The subjects had no appeal against the will of the sovereign. Hobbes was against the division of sovereign authority as advocated by the parliamentarians in the England of his time. The subjects would never have the right to change the form of their government, because they were bound to obey a particular sovereign, and acknowledge his public acts as their own. As the individuals entered into a contract with one another and not with the sovereign power, they could never be freed from the subjection of the sovereign. The sovereign's subjects had a duty and an obligation to obey the sovereign, since the sovereign was the result of their social contract.

Justice for Hobbes was whatever free, rational and equal individuals agreed to leave out. He did not say much about what constitutes a just distribution of goods. As long as the distribution was the result of a freely entered agreement, the outcome was just. He asserted 'laws are the rules of just and unjust; nothing being reputed unjust, that is not contrary to some law" (Hobbes 1991: 182). Just and unjust have meaning in relation to law and the law was the command of the sovereign.

Hobbes was the first to comprehend the nature of public power as a permanent, sovereign, rightful, and authorized representative to exercise powers "giving life and motion to society and the body politic" (Hobbes ibid: 81). Sovereignty characterized the position rather than the person who wielded it. The sovereign will united all in one voice, "one will", and in the process ensured unity. The state, in Hobbes' theory, became the dominant institution in political and social life. The state changed the miserable, poor and nasty lives that individuals led prior to its establishment, and enabled them to pursue their interests. It was the ruthlessness of individuals that made the indivisible power of the state an absolute necessity. To Machiavelli's emphasis on interests, Hobbes added the dimension of fear, and provided a comprehensive theory of political absolutism that reconciled legitimate political authority with conflicting yet justified human demands. The sovereign created enough order to ensure that competition between discrete individuals became peaceful and orderly.

> The use of laws, which are but rules themselves is not to bind the people from all voluntary actions; but to direct and keep them in such a motion as not to hurt themselves by their own impetuous desires, rashness, or indiscretion, as hedges are set, not to stop travellers, but to keep them in the way (Hobbes ibid: 239–240).

Hobbes stipulated that for ensuring civil peace, lesser associations could exist only with the permission of the sovereign. Hobbes did not trust the motives of private associations and factions, for he saw them as a seed-bed for subversion. He subordinated the church to the sovereign. The church, being a corporation, would have a head who had to be a secular sovereign. The teachings of the church were lawful only when authorized by the state. Though a materialist, Hobbes professed faith in God and believed in the essential teachings of Christianity.

The cause for disorder, according to Hobbes, was general desirousness among individuals who were equal. The problem got compounded in a situation of scarcity. Social peace was only possible when individuals abandoned or restricted their passions and appetites, or if the available pool of resources was increased. Since the second option was not feasible, he preferred the first. There was no possibility of a metamorphosis of human nature. Instead, the political order was devised to accept human egoism and self-interest. The state was no longer visualized as a moral institution that would transform individuals. It was to restrain individuals through the overwhelming power of the sovereign, without preventing the pursuit of their desires. Since the state existed for individuals to fulfil their aspirations and ensure their well-being, Hobbes was therefore an individualist and a utilitarian (Sabine 1973: 439). The sovereign's position is similar to a referee in a football match as the grand master of the rules. The political system for Hobbes meant a system of rules which was only possible if there was civil peace. A system of rules could become operative only if justice was understood as fairness, equality of rights and equality of treatment. To the question how would egotists be expected to act fairly towards one another and Hobbes' answer to individuals was follow the cardinal principle of 'do not that to others, you would not have done to yourself'. Fairness did not demand that individual forsake their egotism but that they imaginatively substitute others for oneself. Hobbes' equation of justice with fairness and equality has become part of political lexicon of subsequent liberalism. Furthermore Hobbes also made it clear that it was only with the creation of a common political language that political order was possible. To understand political order as being involving power, authority, law and institutions would be simplistic. The commonness of the meanings in politics depended on the ruling power capable of enforcing them, that is, declaring the precise meaning of right and punishing those who refused to accept the assertion. When this authority was prevented from enforcing definitions then the city was reduced to a condition where each member was at liberty to assign to words the meanings he chose. Hobbes rejected private reason as it not led to confusion of meanings but also destroyed the body politic as a communicating whole (Wolin 1960).

Hobbes' sovereign stood outside the society, and it was only fear and interest that supplied the reason for his existence. However, his analysis of power was over-simplistic, for power required not only the elimination of hindrances but also getting the citizens to participate actively. Hobbes separated community and public will, and it was Rousseau who subsequently "revived the older notion of a community as a corporate fellowship and then endowed it with the unity of will associated with the Hobbesian sovereign" (Wolin 1960: 277). Hobbes defined "representation by the way in which an action was performed, or by standards or expectations to which it must conform, rather than by any agreement concerning the right to do it or responsibility for it" (Pitkin 1967: 75). The authorized sovereign had his limits, bound by the laws of nature to ensure peace and safety. The sovereign had duties towards the subject.

The sovereign would protect his subject from rebellion, and for this Hobbes laid down seven injunctions. The first was patriotic commitment to the status quo. The second, to resist demagogues; the third was to respect the established government. Fourth, there was a specific need for civic education. Fifth was the importance of discipline that was inculcated in the home. Sixth, there was a need for people to be taught about law and order, to abstain from violence, private revenge, dishonour to person and violation of property. Seventh, that right attitudes would bring about the right behaviour. Hobbes had faith in the universities to train and educate the citizen-elite with the help of his *Leviathan*.

Individualism and Liberalism

Individualism and absolutism of the state were two sides of the same coin in Hobbes' theory. Absolute sovereignty was the logical complement to riotous anarchy (Wolin 2004: 235). His premises were individualistic and liberal, but his conclusions absolutist and illiberal, which was why his philosophy contained both liberal and illiberal features (Dunn 1979: 42–43, Held 1984: 14). It was liberal because the state and society were constituted by free and equal individuals who were egoistic, self-interested and selfish. It was liberal because it emphasized the element of consent as the basis of legitimate regulation of human affairs, as a yardstick for independence and choice in society. The illiberal aspect of Hobbes' theory was that an all-powerful absolute sovereign was a self-perpetuating one. There was no procedure to periodically renew the individual's consent to the sovereign power. The subject did not actively participate in the political process, nor was there a mechanism to secure his active support. Society itself was a loose composition of discrete individuals lacking cohesiveness.

The sovereign was the artificial person and continued as long as he did not offer grounds for resistance. Nor was there a check against arbitrary or tyrannical exercise of power in the form of a strong civil society. But it was to Hobbes' credit that he identified the source of absolute sovereign power and clearly defined its powers. The powers of the sovereign were neither intangible nor supernatural. The basis of political authority is consent which Locke refined subsequently through his formulation of two staged contract.

Hobbes accepted the discrete, egoistic, self-interested, atomistic individual as the building block of his all-powerful state edifice. The individual had the right to his private space, namely thoughts and economic activities. The individual did not get subsumed or merged in the all-powerful state. If the individual was threatened, then the Leviathan lost its rationale to exercise. Society was a cooperative enterprise as long as the individuals saw it as necessary for their well-being and benefit. Undoubtedly, Hobbes was the greatest and the most consistent individualist. He portrayed rugged individualism in politics, economics and religion.

> It is one of the oddities of Western political thought that the critics' image of the Hobbesian theory of sovereignty should have been anticipated in the famous frontispiece adorning the 1651 edition of the *Leviathan* ... the picture seems a perfect summary of Hobbes' thought: the blessings of peace are assured only when society is in total subjection to an absolute authority (Wolin 1960: 266).

The Leviathan towered over the surroundings with a sword of war in one hand and the scales of justice in the other, overlooking an orderly and prosperous city, thriving under the peace he made possible. Hobbes reinforced this description by characterizing the Leviathan as the "mortal god", the "greatest of human powers" and "the greatest dominion that can be granted ... limited only by the strength and forces of the city itself, and by nothing else in the world". But as one looked more closely at the frontispiece, one saw that the sovereign's body was composed of a multitude of tiny individual figures—his subjects. The sovereign owed his existence to *them*, and derived his power from *them*. The individuals did not disappear into an anonymous mass or into a cohesive community, but retained their individuality and identity, implying that the awesome power was "less impressive than the rhetoric surrounding it" (Wolin ibid: 266).

Two themes interlaced one another to form the story of the *Leviathan.* One was the concern for order, and the other individualism. Absolutism and individualism complemented one another. The war of all against all resulted in an orderly society, but the race of life continued. Individuals as mechanical apparatuses, and as discrete, were still in competition with each other, striving for power and economic goods, though the conflict was no longer deadly but peaceful and intense. His individuals were post-medieval men of the early capitalist society, independent and essentially masterless (Sabine 1973: 317). Absolutism did not end or marginalize individualism; it fused the separate elements of the political order into an organic community to provide enough order to eliminate the state of war.

Hobbes portrayed the idea of commonality in a society of particulars, and tried to complete the story begun by Machiavelli, namely the impact that the pursuit of interest left on political and social arrangements. Politics was about dealing with conflicting yet legitimate claims in a situation of scarcity.

> One result of Machiavelli's reformulation of political theory was to draw attention to the dynamic element of the uninhibited pursuit of interest and to establish interest as the departure point for most subsequent theorizing … . Machiavelli's prescriptions were woefully lacking in one vital element: some comprehensive principle, some notion of a unifying consensus for coping with the interest-ridden nature of the new politics (Wolin 1960: 239–240).

Hobbes took the atomistic individuals, their instincts and reason, and the contractual agreement between them to be the model, excluding even the family as a source of morality and sociability. There was no place "for relationships of ascribed, historically given, status" (Nisbet 1990: 121).

Liberty and the Right of Self-preservation

Hobbes defined freedom as the private pursuit of the individual, which implied that each individual could create his own conception of freedom within a framework of state authority. Liberty was defined as whatever the law permitted, and on whatever the law was silent. Liberty signified absence of restraints and coercion. Hobbes accepted the right to private beliefs, for conscience was beyond the reach of the Leviathan, who could not oblige men to believe, since thought was free. However, the Leviathan could command the individual to perform ceremonies that were necessary for public worship.

Hobbes made a beginning to identify and safeguard what was essentially a private sphere of the individual, where none, including the state, could exercise control. The private-public divide became more forceful in Locke's philosophy, with his statement on inalienable individual rights and a conception of a limited state.

The limits of the state could be seen from Hobbes defence of property. Although in principle the sovereign was absolute, with rights over private property, there would be no undue interference in the individual's private affairs, including economic activity. The individuals would have the liberty to buy and sell, and otherwise contract with one another. The state could provide public charity for the destitute, but beyond that it was not its task to actively promote the "felicity" of the subjects.

To the vast array of absolute powers that Hobbes assigned to the sovereign, there was only one limitation, namely the right of self-preservation, seen as an absolute right of the individual. The sovereign could not command a man to kill himself, for life was a gift by nature to man; no one could order the killing of an individual. The right remained an inalienable right of individuals, since the basic motive for total surrender of their powers was self-preservation. If the sovereign failed to protect the individual, the individual had the right to resist the sovereign. If resistance was successful, the sovereign ceased to be a sovereign, and individuals would return to a state of nature where there would be no sovereign power to acknowledge. They would be free to obey a de facto new monarch.

The right of resistance could be invoked only when the right of self-preservation got threatened. Hobbes was categorical that human actions were influenced by considerations of safety and not narrow gains, thus ruling out the modern interpretation of some (like Gauthier and Hampton) that Hobbes was interested in calculating utilities (Tuck 1989: 106–108).

The minority could not resist the sovereign on the grounds that it was the *majority* who had chosen the sovereign. Nor could there be resistance to tyrannical rule of the sovereign, for punishment of unjust rulers was to be left to God. Resistance was justified only when the sovereign sought to destroy the individual directly, and not when he tried to destroy others. The right of personality or self-preservation, according to Cassirer (1946), was a universal right in Hobbes' philosophy. As long as the sovereign existed, he enjoyed absolute, undivided, inalienable powers with just one limitation, namely the right to preserve individuals. For Hobbes, a sovereign was one who could remain and act as a sovereign.

Political Obligation

Hobbes offered a number of reasons as to why the sovereign was to be obeyed. First, there was a purely prudential consideration that if individuals disobeyed the sovereign they would be punished. Second, there was a moral consideration that they must honour their contracts, provided others did so as instructed by the first three laws of nature. The *Leviathan* ensured that all parties adhered to the terms of the covenant. Third, there was a political consideration that the sovereign was their duly authorized representative, created consensually by the citizens authorizing him to act on their behalf. Last, Hobbes offered a religious argument when he asserted that the civil law and the law of nature was one, and that both were to be obeyed, since they implied God's commands. Strauss (1936) saw Hobbes' obligation as physical, for the sovereign by virtue of his overwhelming power and authority could ultimately command his subjects to obey him. The subjects on their part obeyed the sovereign out of fear of punishment. Taylor (1938) argued that the Hobbesian theory of political obligation was not logically linked to the psychological nature of man that he presented, but instead arose from the laws of nature that he offered. Taylor insisted that the laws of nature were not mere "pieces of advice about the prudent pursuit of self interest" but were moral laws which dictated duties, and were obligatory because they were commanded by God. Taylor contended that Hobbes' civil philosophy had to be understood in the sense of two contrasting and disconnected subsystems: theistic deontology, and an egoistic psychology.

Oakeshott (1975) thought it would be a mistake to interpret Hobbes' obligation as primarily based on individual self-interest. On the contrary, he viewed it as a mixed obligation consisting of physical, rational and moral obligations. Since civil society was a complex system of authority and power, each element had its own appropriate obligation. There was a *moral obligation* to obey the authorized will of the sovereign, which was not based on self-interest. Moral obligation arose from obedience to the sovereign authority, whose basis was the consent of the governed. There was a *physical obligation* that was derived from the fact that the sovereign represented power, compelling the individual to eventually obey or face the consequences of disobedience. Last, there was a *rational obligation* based on self-interest, as the individual desired peace and order. "Each of these obligations provides a separate motive for observing the order of the commonwealth and each is necessary for the preservation of that order" (Oakeshott ibid: 66–67).

Warrender (1957) believed that Hobbes' political obligation could not be derived from the postulates of human psychology, but from the body of natural laws with an independent authority which Hobbes understood as the will or command of God. The laws of nature played a crucial and pivotal role, for in the lawless state of nature they prompted individuals to contract and establish a sovereign. These laws persisted through the state of nature into civil society, and were essentially moral in nature, prescribing duties. They were morally obligatory, for the sovereign interpreted and rendered them fully operative.

Warrender pointed out that there were two systems in Hobbes' theory: a system of motives, and a system of obligation. The system of motives ended with the supreme principle of self-preservation, while the system of obligation closed with an obligation to obey natural law.

The fundamental law of nature was not self-preservation, but to seek peace, giving

> a more social and less self-regarding appearance that is often associated with Hobbes' theory. These peace enjoining laws are not maxims of personal success nor even personal rules for keeping alive, they are concerned with the conservation of society; and they are, to quote Hobbes, contrary to our natural passions (Warrender 1957: 249).

Hobbes understood political obligation as essentially based on a theory of duty within the natural law tradition. There was a nexus between salvation and obedience, and political obligation was essentially moral.

Macpherson (1973) contended that Hobbes' theory of human nature was deduced from his analysis of man's materialistic behaviour within a bourgeois society governed by the market, and that the theory was not universally valid. Such a view was necessary and possible only in a possessive market society. The materialistic assumption enabled Hobbes to assume that individuals had an equal need to be in continuous motion, and this equal need established an equal right and a moral obligation. The market assumption enabled Hobbes to presume that men were equal in their insecurity. "Hobbes was able to treat his political obligation as a moral obligation because it was derived from a transfer of rights which he treated as moral rights" (Macpherson ibid: 76). Pitkin (1967) pointed out that Hobbes tried to explain and defend political obligation so as to preclude acts of rebellion, revolt, anarchy or civil war. Obligation followed from the law of nature, which dictated self-preservation, and everything logically flowed from it.

WOMEN AND THE GENDER QUESTION

Hobbes as an exponent of human equality argued that nature provided no rationale for inequality of rights and privileges, nor were human relationships natural, for all authority was based on consent. Consent meant submission willingly and voluntarily in exchange for protection of one's life. Since women were as capable as men, they did not require any protection from men. Protection was required by both the subject and the child, who were dependent on the sovereign and parents respectively. In the case of a child, it was the mother as a parent who constituted authority and guaranteed protection by virtue of giving birth to the child. The child in the process granted her its consent.

In the state of nature, every woman who had children became both a *mother* and a *lord*. A mother lost the right of authority over her child if taken prisoner, in which case she selected the person who would exert authority over her child in her absence. Hobbes described the idea of female subordination as a human creation. Male heirs were preferred to females, for they were naturally fitter for labour and danger. In a state of nature, the natural domination of the mother was accepted, because it was *she* who could declare the father of her child.

For Hobbes, the family, like the state, was an artificial or a conventional institution and had to be seen in strictly rational terms. It was a "civil person" by virtue of jurisdiction, not by virtue of marriage or biological parenthood. It was not based on natural ties of sentiments between generations, but, like the state, arose from the consent of its individual members. With regard to who would govern within the family, one would assume that given Hobbes' position on the equality of sexes; he would grant joint rights and authority to both men and women. But this was not the case. He gave to the father exclusive jurisdiction within the family, thereby defending patriarchy. The wife/mother as a free and an equal individual disappeared with the constitution of civil society. The woman became subservient, losing her ability to consent and the right to participate in the political process. Though Hobbes accepted the idea of sexual and gender equality, revolutionary in itself by seventeenth-century standards, he did not reject nor attack patriarchy in the full sense.

Hobbes saw his commonwealth as a creation by the father(s). When discussing the problem of succession to the sovereign in the state, he acknowledged that it would pass from one male child to another, since males had greater wisdom and courage, and were naturally fit to rule. All these certainly contradicted his earlier attack on patriarchal claims. The reason for the shift could be that he did not want a conflict between the male and female once civil society was created. "Hobbes' thought reflects and perpetuates a distinctively masculinist orientation to the realm of politics that continues to be male dominated and governed by masculinist presumptions in our time" (Stefano 1994: 31).

The significance of Hobbes' political thought was the departure he made from patriarchalism of the mid-seventeenth century. He insisted that paternal power in the state of nature was not derived from fatherhood as such. Since the family's importance was only because of its procreative functions, and if sovereignty was a product of procreation, then the mother was also an equal and full partner in the act of generation with claims over the child. By denying the patriarchal claims he dismissed the idea that all authority, including that of the parents, was natural. Subordination among human beings was a product of convention subject to consent.

CONCLUSION

The *Leviathan* of Hobbes has been recognized as one of the masterpieces of political theory, known for its style, clarity and lucid exposition. He laid down a systematic theory of sovereignty, law, human nature and political obligation. He accepted the views of the radical writers of the sixteenth century like Montaigne, and attacked Aristotelianism and

Ciceronian Humanism. He discarded the notion that there was anything as "simply good", for every individual would regard what pleased him as good, and dismiss that which displeased him as evil. The way to overcome this ethical disagreement was by acknowledging that each was justified in defending one's self, and that others could be harmed on grounds of self-defence. Self-preservation was a fundamental right of nature, and equally a basic law.

Hobbes argued that the state was established for human convenience, and obeyed on grounds of expediency. It was obeyed in most cases, since obedience was more agreeable than disobedience. It was a product of human reason, and hence reason and not authority had to be the arbiter in politics. He emphasized that the sovereign would define divine, natural or fundamental law, since it was difficult to obtain agreement among individuals, and thus made power, not right, the focal issue in politics (Hill 1972: 37). Hobbes saw the state as a conciliator of interests, a point of view that the Utilitarians developed in great detail. Hobbes created an all-powerful state, but it was no totalitarian monster. It had to guarantee peace, order and security, and was not interested in self-glorification. The state did not control or regiment areas that were politically irrelevant. Hobbes accepted the fact that there were many types of human activities that had to be left to the realm of the non-political.

Many of Hobbes' critics felt the need to control government by the superior authority of society. Lawson (1657) and Whitehall, contemporary critics of Hobbes, demanded the need to bind the rulers by law, else they would usurp little by little. All of them feared the consequences of arbitrary power. Clarendon and Whitehall asserted that Hobbes had no idea of practical politics, and that his theorem of government was artificial. All his critics insisted on the need to provide for a limited and constitutional authority. Locke himself scorned Hobbes' prescription of providing absolute authority without adequate safeguards to prevent the abuse and misuse of power.

Many of Hobbes' critics denied the reality of the state of nature, both as a statement of fact or as a hypothesis. If individuals were so asocial, they would never have been able to come together to establish a civil society and government. If they could do so, then they would have never gone without it. His critics insisted that Hobbes' depiction of the state of nature was unreal, grossly exaggerated and even misleading. Bramhall (1658: 503) commented that the Hobbesian conception of human nature was a libel on individuals, for he characterized them worse than bears and wolves. Eachard (1672: 14) felt that humankind, contrary to Hobbes' analysis, was tolerably tame and that society did not reflect the wickedness that Hobbes wanted us to believe. Clarendon was confident that God did not make human beings lower than animals. According to his modern interpreters, Hobbes showed human beings to be morally neutral by nature, for it was possible to achieve happiness by one's own efforts, without God's grace. Happiness and goodness were entirely matters of an individual's ability to form society and control it rationally.

Furthermore, Hobbes' notion of absolute state sovereignty was developed at length by Austin and Bentham. He pointed out that Aristotle failed to identify a tenable conception of sovereignty, and mistakenly supposed that laws could be sovereign, for it was not individuals, words or promises but arms that made the force and power of laws. The unsociability of human nature—a facet of human personality—had be taken into cognizance while delineating a theory of sovereignty. Therefore, a human being backed by swords and arms was the true sovereign in a commonwealth. Unlike Aristotle, Hobbes did not see the existence of the state in terms of its guarantee of a good life, but in terms of the security and safety it provided. Relationships between humans were not those of friendship, but rivalry. The significance of Hobbes lies in the fact that he set aside, rebuked and rejected the dominant Aristotelian tradition which looked upon social and political relations as natural, and peace and accommodation as part and parcel of normal functioning. "For two centuries after him self-interest seemed to most thinkers a more obvious motive than disinterestedness, and enlightened self-interest a more applicable remedy for social ills than any form of collective action" (Sabine 1973: 437). Hobbes did not establish the link between social and political factors and the fact that political practices were shaped by social relationships. As a result he was able to clearly identify and establish the ambit of the political (Wolin 1960: 257) "For Hobbes, the political in a society comprised three elements: the authority whose unique office it was to superintend the whole and to exert directive control over other forms of activity; the obligations which rested on those who accepted membership; and the system of common rules governing publicly significant behaviour" (Wolin ibid: 259).

Hobbes' greatest contribution was his philosophy of individualism, making him not only a thorough-going modern thinker, but also a person in line with the times to come. Furthermore, he emphasized that human beings without a government would be in a permanent state of insecurity, viewing war and conflict as permanent and normal conditions. In the process, "Hobbes treats the problems of politics as an aspect of a universal human dilemma involving freedom and security" (Minogue 1973: xvii).

At an international conference held in Helsinki in 1987, an important consensus emerged among scholars that the proposition of a world state might be absurd and premature, for nation states would continue as long as humanity remained concerned with the right of self-preservation and the need to secure commodious living. These observations vindicated the essential postulates of Hobbes' paradigm, and reiterated its relevance for times to come (Airakaninen and Bertman 1989).

In summation, the twentieth century with its complexities and problems has made it possible to appreciate the concerns that Hobbes exhibited namely power, peace and science. There was an interest in trying to understand the "power relations, necessary, possible and desirable between men", for Hobbes was the first to lay down the science of power politics (Macpherson 1968). We share Hobbes' concern in trying to devise ways and means for ensuring order and commodious living. Above all, we share and appreciate his method of science. However, the modern world values the rule of law, rather than the person who really wields it, and in this sense Hobbes' prescriptions were pre-modern. The modern view of power is also different, as Parsons remarked, power in modern society is more like money. It is a functional category like others thus differing considerably from Hobbes' notion. Moreover, with the democratic revolution of the nineteenth and twentieth centuries, struggle for power has been replaced with struggle for recognition, thereby drastically modifying the role of the singular, personalized sovereign. But for understanding this historic transformation of humankind, an understanding of Hobbes is an essential prerequisite.

6

John Locke

What distinguishes Locke from the majority of philosophers is not the cogency today of his arguments as a whole. Rather it is the profundity with which he understood the bearing of philosophy on how men have good reasons to live their lives (Dunn 1984: 87).

Locke's psychological insight may be imperfect, his logic often odd, his general standpoint ungrateful to our generation and not easily understood even within his own personal historical context. His rationalist sociology may seem fantastic, even in comparison with the uncritical traditionalism of a man like Filmer. But after he had written and what he had written had had its enormous impact on the European mind, it was no longer possible to believe that politics went forward in a moral sphere in which the good man was the good citizen. Citizenship was now a specific duty, a personal challenge in a world where every individual either recognized his responsibility for every other, or disobeyed his conscience. Political duties have not changed since then (Laslett 1960: 134–135).

In a more expanded sense, the *Two Treatises* must be seen as emerging from a political atmosphere characterized by the plots and conspiracies of radicals and the use of political repression, government spies, and agent provocateurs to combat the subversive activities of these individuals. An understanding of this political climate is important, I shall argue, to appreciate the way radical political theorist—including Locke—expressed their ideas. It provides, so to speak, the angle of vision for viewing the political content of the *Second Treatise.* In this regard, I will show that the invention and use of a specific language was, on the one hand, an important part of the organizational structure of this revolutionary political movement, and, on the other hand, this language is a pervasive feature of the political writings of the radicals, including the *Two Treatises of Government* (Ashcraft 1980: 431).

Liberalism as a political creed began with John Locke (1632–1704). This was a unique achievement, as there were no liberals before Locke, though there were many socialists before Marx. The origins and detailed delineation of the liberal order, both in the political and societal dimensions, was the singular achievement of Locke. The breadth of vision that Locke espoused by offering a theory which combined constitutionalism, stability, freedom, consent, property and tolerance has played a crucial and pivotal role in an orderly development of Western democracies. The seminal importance of Locke in the evolution of political institutions and theory is accepted by all commentators, but there are wide areas of disagreement about their meaning and implications.

Locke has been interpreted very differently by Laslett (1960), Macpherson (1973) and Ashcraft (1980, 1986 and 1987). Laslett convincingly demonstrated that Locke was neither a spokesman of Whig orthodoxy nor a defender of the Glorious Revolution of 1688. Macpherson (1973), in contrast, analyzed Locke as an apologist and a theorist of bourgeois society. Ashcraft drew attention to Locke's radicalism by his active involvement in the revolutionary process. Ashcraft interprets Locke as revolutionary and that has created problems for both the left and right. All along, the left and the Marxists interpreted Locke as an apologist of bourgeois society. The right found it equally discomfiting to accept that the Glorious Revolution had a revolutionary side to it. All along, they projected it as a symbol of the incremental and evolutionary process of change.

Locke's concepts of constitutionalism, toleration, natural rights, limited consensual and law-based authority; pluralism and property had a significant impact beyond the English settlement of 1688 in establishing and nurturing a liberal society in England, and in inspiring similar traditions in America, France and Holland. The American and the French Revolutions and the constitutional edifice in the United States were Lockeian in spirit and letter. Locke's ideas, especially his doctrine of tolerance, government by consent and realization of human freedom in its economic and political contexts, found concrete expression with the discovery of the American continent, as exemplified by his statement right at the outset of the book that the world in the beginning was like America. It is also interesting to note that the libertarian philosophy characterized by optimism and abundance was made possible as a result of the discovery of America. Prior to Locke, political theorists from Plato and Hobbes were confronted with the problem of scarcity. The discovery of America symbolized human emancipation, making it possible to conceive of a society of plenty, freedom and order.

No political thinker had influenced political theorizing on two different countries in two different continents as Locke did. He was the guiding and spiritual father of the eighteenth-century Enlightenment period, particularly for philosophers like Rousseau and Voltaire. He was acknowledged as the founder of modern empiricism with Hume, Berkeley, J.S. Mill, Russell and Ayer as its exponents. He was also the inspiration for early feminists like Mary Astell (1666–1708), Lady Cudworth Masham (1658–1708), Catherine Totter Cockburn (1769–1849), Lady Mary Wortley

Montagu (1689–1762), Catherine Macaulay Sawbridge Graham (1731–1791) and Mary Wollstonecraft (1759–1797). These feminists accepted Locke's belief in the supremacy of reason, rejection of patriarchy and political absolutism, and in the importance of nurture as opposed to nature. Locke's view of labour as a source of value and entitlement was the framework within which the Classical economists present their case for capitalist appropriation. Paradoxically, the same theory was used by Marx to argue against capitalism and propose a socialist alternative. Thus Locke's "thought provided for the eighteenth century a metaphysics and a theory of education, theology, morals and politics that meshed well with the rising tide of individualism, utilitarianism and capitalism" (Rogers 1990: 11).

Locke was soundly convinced that a society which practised toleration in intellectual and religious matters was the most desirable order that humankind aspired to achieve. His visit to Holland in 1683 reaffirmed this belief. He desired for England a society where citizens could enjoy the liberty and opportunity of free enquiry. He liberated modern thought from the tutelage of Scholasticism, earning him credit as the father of the Enlightenment.

Locke was evasive about his authorship of the *Two Treatises* and, he published these texts anonymously. The only time that he acknowledged it (and that too indirectly), was in 1704 when he wrote a codicil to his will naming the *Two Treatises* among his several other anonymous works for the benefit of the Bodleian library. On another occasion (in 1703), he recommended the books along with Aristotle's *Politics* and Hooker's *Ecclesiastical Polity* to a distant cousin.

There is considerable controversy regarding the time period and the intent of the two texts. The book was published two years after the successful completion of the Glorious Revolution of 1688, the deposition of the Catholic King James II and the accession of Protestant King William and Queen Mary to the English throne. The Revolution marked the beginnings of limited constitutional monarchy and parliamentary supremacy, preparing the way for the emergence of a representative democratic system. Though the realization of mass democracy, with the principle of one man one vote, came about in the first quarter of twentieth century in Great Britain, the significance of the Glorious Revolution and Locke's *Second Treatise* was because it stated clearly the importance of constitutionalism, limited state power and individual rights.

Locke was interpreted as a collectivist (Kendall 1941: 133–135), because of his insistence that the community would be ruled by the will of the majority. He was seen as a champion of individuality (Parry 1964: 163–164, Vaughan 1925: 183, 198). He was the spokesperson of the liberal constitutional order, criticizing Wolin's portrayal of the philosopher for providing an intellectual defence of the sublimation of the political to the social dimension of life (Pateman 1975: 443, 458–462). He was depicted as an enemy of patriarchism, preparing the grounds for women's equal rights (Butler 1978: 148–150).

LIFE SKETCH

Locke was born in a Somerset village in England in the summer of 1632. His parents came from Puritan trading and landowning families, and were sympathetic to the parliamentarians and the Whigs during the Civil War. His father was a notary, while his grandfather was a tanner and clothier. The family was not well-off. However, in later life Locke enjoyed sufficient income from family estates, and was able to lead the life of a gentleman scholar. Locke's father owned some land and lived as an attorney and clerk to the justices of the peace in Somerset. Locke went to Westminster School in 1647, and then enrolled himself in Christchurch College as a student in 1652 for 15 years till 1667. He continued to retain his links with Christchurch, until 1684. After graduation, Locke developed an interest in medicine. He completed MA in 1658, became a lecturer in Greek in 1661, and a lecturer in rhetoric in 1663. In 1664, he became a censor of moral philosophy.

Locke also participated in chemical and medical researches of eminent people like Robert Boyle, Hooker, David Thomas, Richard Lower, Thomas Willis and Thomas Sydenham. The only other political theorist who combined so many interests was Aristotle. From them, Locke learnt a lot, including the important fact that for discovering the secrets of nature, sustained and disciplined observation coupled with humility, patience and hard work were required. The important Continental philosophers of the early scientific revolution, Descartes and Gassendi, influenced him considerably. He was elected a fellow of the Royal Society in 1688. Locke's first works were written at Oxford, namely the *Two Tracts on Government* in 1660—1662, and the *Essays on the Law of Nature* in Latin in 1664. In both these writings, he argued against religious toleration, and denied consent as the basis of legitimate government. Both these early writings were published only in this century. His *Essay Concerning Human Understanding* (1679) was forbidden as a text for tutorial discussions in Oxford and its colleges (Cranston 1957: 468).

In 1665–1666, Locke undertook a diplomatic mission to Cleves. In 1666, he met—for the first time—Lord Anthony Ashley Cooper, later the first Earl of Shaftesbury, an important political figure in the court of Charles II. Within a year of the meeting, Locke joined Ashley's household in London. This proved to be a turning point in Locke's life. In 1668, Ashley underwent a major and difficult liver operation under Locke's supervision, which was successful against all odds. By 1679, Locke became a patron, political associate and friend of the earl. For the next 14 years, till Shaftesbury's death, Locke remained closely associated with the earl, with his own fortunes rising and falling along with those of the earl. Locke was suspected of being the author of *A Letter from Person of Quality to his Friend in the Country*. The pamphlet angered the government, compelling Locke to make a hasty departure for France in 1675. During this time he met French doctors, scientists, and theologians and befriended many of them. He also translated some of Pierre Nicole's moral essays. At the end of April 1679, he returned to London. Philosophers travelled abroad to grasp the wonders of the world, and this was the case with Locke too (Hazard 1952: 7).

From Shaftesbury, Locke learnt the intricacies and responsibilities of the state in the domestic market and external commerce. He also realized that the primary responsibility of the state was to bring economic prosperity. Shaftesbury's commitment to toleration for dissenters made him campaign vigorously for toleration and the freedom of the press. This became evident from *An Essay Concerning Toleration* (1667). Shaftesbury's position during the Exclusion crisis of 1680 impressed upon Locke the need for consent as the basis of a legitimate political system. The earl was the rallying figure during the Exclusion crisis. Shaftesbury was Locke's mentor, friend, philosopher and guide. He played a profound role in shaping Locke's political perceptions and establishing his reputation as an eminent theorist.

In 1683, Locke went into exile in Holland, fearing implication in the Rye House Plot. The British government tried to get him extradited but was unsuccessful. His studentship of Christchurch College was withdrawn in 1684 on a royal command from Charles II. All these punitive measures were taken because Locke had participated actively in the movement for curtailing royal power and supporting the Monmouth's rebellion. Meanwhile, Lord Shaftesbury died in 1683. This explained the anonymity of the *Two Treatises* and the complete secrecy that Locke maintained with regard to his work and activities. This was partly political and partly psychological. He was known to be excessively secretive, and this trait got attenuated due to the volatile and turbulent political phase of the 1680s. He took considerable efforts to conceal his real intentions and activities, and the execution of Alegernon Sidney cautioned all radicals including Locke who was in exile (Ashcraft 1980: 483–485).

During his exile in Holland, Locke completed his *Essay Concerning Human Understanding* (which he had begun writing in 1671), and *The Letter on Toleration,* published anonymously in 1689. After the success of the Glorious Revolution, Locke came to prominence. He returned to England. Three of his works were published, making him famous and distinguished. He spent the remaining part of his life in the household of Sir Francis and Lady Masham in the countryside far north of London. Locke shared a close relationship with Lady Masham before her marriage. She was Damaris Cudworth, daughter of the Cambridge Platonist Ralph Cudworth.

Locke, in the later part of his life, was the Commissioner for Appeals and Trade, who dealt with the problems of the English colonies. He opposed the colonial policy from 1668 to 1675. He looked upon the colonization of America as a solution to the economic crisis in England following the Great Plague of 1665. He opposed colonization for it depleted England of good people. He also feared that colonies would become independent of the mother country and compete with it.

Locke played an influential role in the repeal of the Act for the Regulation of Printing in 1695 and in the re-coinage of the debased English currency in the 1690s. Before his death, he attained fame, both nationally and internationally. Some of his minor works, like *Raising the Value of Money* and *Some Considerations on the Lowering of Interests* appeared in print in 1691, though these were written in 1668. This was followed by the *Second Letter on Toleration* (1691) and the *Third Letter on Toleration* (1692), written in response to the criticism made by Jonas Proast. In 1693, *Some Thoughts on Education* and in 1695, *The Reasonableness of Christianity* were published. Locke died on October 29, 1704.

LOCKE AND THE GLORIOUS REVOLUTION

The historical background of the *Second Treatise* was the years of rebellion and revolution against the English throne, which, however, was not revealed in its preface. Locke stated his objective in writing the text, namely to establish the throne of King William and "... to justify to the World, the People of England, whose love of their Just and Natural Rights, with their Resolution to preserve them, saved the nation when it was on the very brink of slavery and Ruins" (Locke 1960: 171).

The preface had convinced many that the tract articulated and defended the philosophical concepts and the political solution of the Glorious Revolution. (Cranston 1957; Laski 1920: 29; Lamprecht 1918: 141–143; Plamentaz 1963: Vol. I: 212ff; Sabine 1973: 518ff; Stephen 1902: 135; Tawney 1954: 214). Locke was seen as the apostle of the Revolution, and the *Second Treatise* as a justification of the Revolution.

Laslett was among the earliest to digress from this accepted version. He contended that the *Two Treatises* might have been written during the Exclusion crisis of 1679–1681. Though the books were published in 1690, their purpose was not to justify the Revolution. He built his argument on a hint by Fox-Bourne that the *Second Treatise* could have been written before, instead of after, the accession of King William to the throne. The substantial part of the text might have been written in 1682–1683 when Locke was in exile in Holland. The *First Treatise* could have been written during 1681–1682. However, Fox-Bourne, unlike Laslett, thought that the two texts might have been prepared fully after the Revolution. Though they were not written for the purpose of defending the Revolution, they could be seen as the basis of Whig orthodoxy. "The *Two Treatises* turns not to be a demand for a revolution to be brought about, nor a rationalization of a revolution in need of a defence" (Laslett 1960: 60).

Cranston argued out that the texts were written 10 years before the Revolution, in order to justify and create the arguments for the revolution that was being planned. He agreed with Laslett that Locke was a philosopher writing about politics, as evident from the first sentence of the preface.

> Thou hast here the beginning and the end of a discourse concerning government; what fate has otherwise disposed of the papers that should have filled up the middle and were more than all the rest, it is not worthwhile to tell thee [for it shows that] it belonged not to settled years of the reign of William and Mary but to the perilous years of the Protestant Plot against Charles II. The *Two Treatises* when it was first written was a seditious and inflammatory document (Cranston 1957: 202).

In the entire sequence of events leading up to the Glorious Revolution was the crucial figure of the Earl of Shaftesbury. "Without Shaftesbury, Locke would not have been Locke" (Laslett 1960: 40). Very likely, Locke articulated the ideas of Shaftesbury, considering they shared a "community of ideas" (Ashcraft 1980: 431). One could discern a shift and subsequently a change in Locke's political outlook. Till 1659, he was a right-wing monarchist welcoming the Restoration. Till 1664, he was an authoritarian endorsing the Hobbesian position in the *Leviathan*. It was only after 1666, when he met the Earl, that the ideas which were characterized as Lockeian took shape. Prior to this, Locke willingly granted the civil magistrate absolute and arbitrary power over the individual, was opposed to toleration of religious dissent, did not believe in parliamentary supremacy—a theory of inalienable natural rights—nor did he defend the right of the people to resist their rulers. At this time he accepted the distinction between secular and spiritual power, political and religious authority. "The *Second Treatise* was not a text in philosophy but a party book, a work of propaganda designed to promote the political objectives of Shaftesbury and the Whigs" (Cranston 1952: 620).

Ashcraft asserted that the *Second Treatise* was written in 1681-1682. This was followed by the *First Treatise*. Franklin (1978) pointed out that contrary to the compromise formula that emerged during the Glorious Revolution the Lockeian position was not even the majoritarian perspective within the Whig Party. The Whigs in 1688, more than in 1680, were willing to accept parliamentary supremacy and limited constitutional monarchy. Locke accepted the argument of the Whigs that political power was in the nature of a trust, but he understood people to mean the general community, and not when constituted as a parliament. This was a Whig position which became a part of the settlement after the Revolution. Thus, Locke was more radical than the Whigs. The *Two Treatises* contained radical and moderate ideas. Its radicalism was clothed in a language of moderation (Ashcraft 1980: 430). Moreover, the Whigs built their case of parliamentary supremacy and constitutional monarchy by invoking an argument of ancient constitution based on tradition history and customs, whereas Locke espoused liberal constitutionalism by appealing to reason (Resnick 1984: 113–114).

Marshall (1994: 205–291) and Wootton (1993: 49–89) agreed with Ashcraft, but made some clarifications. Wootton contended that the *Second Treatise* was written in late 1681. Marshall, on the other hand, pointed out that the *First Treatise* was written in 1681 and the *Second Treatise* in late

1682 or early 1683, after Charles II began *quo warranto* proceedings against the charter of the London corporation, giving the crown control of the franchise in the city and supervision of the sheriffs who appointed London juries. Both these actions undermined the Whig position.

The seventeenth century was an important period, a watershed in English political and constitutional history. Broadly, four distinct phases could be identified: (a) from the accession of James I to the Civil War in 1641; (b) from 1642 to 1660, a commonwealth under Cromwell; (c) restoration of the monarchy under Charles II in 1660 to the Exclusion crisis of 1679–1681; and (d) the Glorious Revolution of 1688. In all these four phases, the main question centred around the relevance of absolute monarchy, and the need to limit the power of the monarch against the growing assertiveness of the parliament.

The Civil War failed to resolve the problem. The execution of Charles I brought about a breach in the monarchial tradition. While resistance against the king as a person was justified, the title and authority of the king remained intact. On the one hand, the idea that the king could do no wrong gave the king a sense of independence from the parliament. On the other hand, the parliament desired to legislate without the king. In the political tug of war, the idea of absolute, divine, hereditary powers of the king came in handy for the royalists. The parliamentarians, and in particular the Whigs, chose to articulate the idea of political power as a trust, with the parliament or legislature defining the purposes of the trust. In this sense, the character of the English revolution was limited (Laski 1920: 70). Its most distinctive aspect according to Franklin (1978) was (unlike elsewhere in Europe), the House of Commons—the arena where opposing factions advanced their rival theories of sovereignty.

Charles II being childless decided that James II, his younger brother, a devout Catholic, would succeed him to the throne. This meant a reign by unending Catholic monarchs in a Protestant country. The English Parliament would have had to change or ignore the rule of hereditary succession. The problem, unlike in the Civil War, was not the breakdown of sovereignty, but one of its presence and limits. The immediate question was the right of resistance to the sovereign, and if so, when Charles II dissolved the parliament so as to prevent it from excluding James a group of Whigs faced treason. Following the Rye House plot, Lord Russell and Sidney were arrested and executed.

Had James II died without a son, the next in succession would have been his daughter Mary, who along with her husband William of Orange indicated their willingness to accept the English throne. On hearing this news, James II fled unofficially, abdicating and thus avoiding the issue of whether Parliament had indeed appointed William and Mary as joint monarchs.

In this debate between divine, hereditary sovereigns and republican democracy, a need was felt for a theory that could preserve individualism, stability, and consent of the governed, while acknowledging the right of resistance. Hobbes' *Leviathan* was not fully acceptable because of its atheism, harsh egoism and defence of absolute monarchy with a consensual basis. With the Restoration of 1660, the debate between the Royalists and Republicans died down, but resurfaced when the succession of James II became imminent. In the renewed controversy, Filmer's long-forgotten *Patriarcha or the Natural Power of the King* became politically and ideologically important to defend the claims of Charles II. *Patriarcha* was written in 1653–1654 but was published for the first time in 1680 to counter the pressure of the exclusionists and the Whigs. Filmer's theory was refuted by Locke, Tyrrell (*Patriarcha non Monarcha* in 1681) and Sidney (who denounced Filmer from the scaffold).

Filmer's Theory

Filmer contended that patriarchal authority was absolute, and that political authority was analogous to paternal authority. Having created Adam, God gave him authority over his family, the earth and its products. Adam was the first king, and present kings derived their rightful authority from this grant. Adam was both the first father and the first king. Subsequent generations of men were not born free, but were subject to Adam and his successors with the power of fathers derived from God. Since God's original grant to Adam was unconditional, monarchical rule was unlimited. Any attempt to restrain absolutism would result in a limited or mixed monarchy. Divided sovereignty would weaken authority. Filmer did not support tyranny, for he made the monarch obey God's laws.

Filmer was critical of contractualism, contending that if contractual arguments were true, then it would result in two unacceptable consequences which its advocates would find hard to explain. First, it would not be possible to provide for a continuing valid political authority. If all authority rested on consent, then an individual who had not consented was not bound by the laws, implying that minorities, dissenters, non-voters (women and children) need not obey the law and a new ruler if one had not consented to them. This would make society unstable. If on the contrary one contended that succeeding generations would have to obey because their fathers and forefathers had expressed their consent, then such an argument did not differ from the one championed by the patriarchists. Filmer contended, contrary to the contractualists, that men were not born free but into families, and hence subject to the authority of their fathers. Moreover, relationships of subordination were natural. Individuals were not equal, for a son was subject to the authority of his father.

The second argument revolved around property rights. Filmer pointed out that the contractualists like Grotius and Joha Selden 1584–1654 escaped the absolutist implications of Adam's dominion over the world, only by construing God's grant as a general one given to all mankind in common, not a private grant to an individual. Filmer thought it was problematic, for one who tried to defend private property would raise the spectre of communism in economics, just as contractualism aroused the spectre of anarchy in politics. How could a communal grant give rise to private property? Why would God have originally ordained community of possession if it were not to last, and how could the abandonment of this primitive communism be morally binding unless every single individual had consented to it—of which consent there was no record? How could such consent be binding on posterity which would surely be born—according to the contractualists—with its original common right to all?

Filmer thought that those who could explain the origin of government with reference to consent of free individuals would find it difficult to establish either feasible or morally acceptable political authority or rightful private possession of goods. Not only did Locke refute Filmer's patriarchal theory, but he also had to prove that his criticism of contractualism was absurd. In particular, Locke had to explain origins of political power and private property, the two central arguments of Filmer's anti-contractualism.

In the *First Treatise,* Locke rejected the central points of Filmer. These were reiterated in the opening passage of the *Second Treatise.* Locke's arguments were broadly four:

1. God did not give the relevant power to Adam.
2. Assuming Adam had been granted this power did not mean that his heirs had a right to it.
3. Even if Adam's heirs *did* have such a right, there were no clear rules of succession according to which rightful heirs could be named.
4. Even if there were such rules, it would be impossible to identify Adam's actual heirs, considering the time span since God's original grant of power to him (Locke 1960: 307).

LOCKE'S POLITICAL THEORY

The *First Treatise* was a critique of Filmer's theory, while the *Second Treatise* explained the "true original extent and end of civil government". Filmer and not Hobbes was the main antagonist of Locke (Laslett 1960: 60). Nor was Locke presenting a disguised and moderate version of Hobbes, as alleged by some of the late seventeenth-century audiences (Laslett ibid: 82-87; Strauss 1952: 226–230).

Locke adopted the technique of social contract to explain that legitimate political authority was derived from the consent of its people, which could be withdrawn when the freedom of the individual was violated or curtailed. The *Two Treatises* espoused and defended freedom, consent and property as cardinal principles of legitimate political power, which was defined as

> ... the Right of making laws with penalties of Death and consequently all less Penalties, for Regulating and Preserving of Property, and of employing the force of the Community, in the Execution of such Laws and in the defence of the Commonwealth from Foreign Inquiry and all this only for the Public Good (Locke 1960: 308).

Locke saw political power as a trust, with the general community specifying its purposes and aims. He rejected Filmer's claims of absolutism and patriarchism.

Freedom and Rights

The origins of the notion of rights can be traced to late medieval thought and the natural rights tradition to the natural law doctrine in Greek philosophy. In the twelfth century, the concept of rights emerged in European thought and was fully developed by the end of the fourteenth century into a coherent theoretical construct. The Italian philosopher and theologian, Aquinas for whom there existed God-given natural law as an underlying force in the universe stressed on moral duties than rights of individual citizens. Nonetheless, this formed the theoretical background for the emergence of the theories of natural law after fourteenth century, associated with the gradual development of modern secular territorial state.

Individual rights had no meaning in the feudal system which had a complex power structure with the different parts—the vassal, lord and king balancing one another. This delicate but enduring social balance was challenged by the assertion of an absolute divine right of the kings by James I in England in 1610. The promulgation of the doctrine of divine right led to the rise of the contract theory that paved the way for the emergence of a limited constitutional state followed by declaration of rights, the *Bill of Rights* of 1688, thus drawing out a new relationship between the state and the individual. By the end of the seventeenth century, the resistance to the capitalist developments had ceased to exist thus setting into motion, a process that witnessed economic and technical progress, rise of private enterprise and commercialization of agriculture culminating in the Industrial Revolution. It was in England that the concepts of individual rights, constitutional government, political democracy and the Industrial Revolution crystallized and developed.

Locke rejected the idea of divine right of kings and natural arrangement of political authority and advanced the notion of human equality. His theory rested on a firm and explicit moral relationship between the individual and God. Since life was a gift that God had given as a basic moral law of nature no one had the right to kill himself or destroy, rob or enslave others, as all were equal before God. The natural condition was one of freedom and equality regulated by the laws of nature.

The state of nature was not one of licence, for though the individual was free from any superior power, he was subject to the laws of nature. From the laws of nature, individuals derived the natural rights to life, liberty and estate (collectively called property). The laws of nature were known to human beings through the power of reason, which directed them towards their "proper interests". Liberty, for Locke, was not the freedom to do what one chose, but to act within the bounds of the laws of nature. Freedom presupposed order and was possible only within a framework of law. In the absence of law there was no freedom. Law granted freedom as it kept individuals from being subject to the arbitrary will of another person. Liberty was personal independence and thus ruled out slavery as it meant subjugation to the arbitrary will of another person: liberty was to be free from restrain and violence by others, which cannot be, where there was no law. In an explicit statement, Locke stated that freedom as the 'liberty to follow my own will in all things, where the rule prescribes not; and not to be subject to the inconstant, uncertain, unknown, arbitrary will of another man'. In a concise manner Locke offered his views of freedom: 'the freedom, then, of man and liberty of acting according to his own will is grounded on his having reason, which is able to instruct him in that law he is to govern himself by, and make him know how far he is left to the freedom of his own will' (Locke 1960: 325).

Locke defended personal independence and freedom as fundamental human rights. None had a right to coerce or dominate another in the state of nature. Everyone had an equal right to one's natural freedom, without being subjected to the will or authority of any other man. Locke clarified that the laws of nature were those that reason dictated. Since rights and the duty of self-preservation were derived from the laws of nature, the most important of these was the right to hold others responsible for a breach of the law and to punish them accordingly. Though Locke categorically rejected the right of a person to kill one's self, he granted the right to inflict penalties, including the death penalty, on others who had violated the laws in general, or if another person's life was threatened. Locke explicitly rejected the right of the individual to commit suicide and murder.

Locke provided the theoretical basis to the concept of natural rights. His theory had three political implications: (1) since human beings derived and enjoyed equal rights under the law of nature none were under the political authority of another without their consent; (2) the maintenance and protection of these rights was the primary function of the government; and (3) rights set and defined the limits of governmental authority. Locke's arguments were reiterated by Paine and Jefferson in the eighteenth century; the significance being the establishment of link between universality of rights and idea of constitutional liberal government. The *Declaration of the American Independence* (1776) stating that the Creator had endowed the individuals 'with certain inalienable rights' among which the most sacred is liberty and the subsequently first ten amendments to the US constitution in 1789 squashed the revival of the ancient conception of liberty made during the French Revolution of 1789, in which the individual would be subordinated to the collective whole. This resonated subsequently in all the charters on rights including the *Universal Declaration of Human Rights* (1948).

Nature of Political Authority

In order to explain the origin of political power, Locke began with a description of the state of nature, which for him was one of perfect equality and freedom regulated by the laws of nature. The individual was naturally free and became a political subject out of free choice. Even after the establishment of a political society, the individual retained a private sphere where he pursued his activities and aspirations. This dichotomy between the state and society, between the private and public, was fundamental to Locke's theorizing. Since then it has become an integral part of the Western intellectual tradition (Wolin 1960: 305–309).

Locke rejected Filmer's biblical account of the origins of political power, without abandoning religious foundations. His theory rested on a firm and explicit moral relationship between the human being and God.

> For Men being all the workmanship of one Omnipotent, and infinitely wise Maker; All the servants of one Sovereign Master, sent into the World by his order and about his business, they are his Property, whose Workmanship they are, made to last during his, not one another's Pleasure. And being furnished with like Faculties, sharing all in one Community of Nature, there cannot be supposed any such *subordination* among us, that may Authorize us to destroy one another, as if we were made for one another's uses, as the inferior ranks of creatures are for Ours. Every one as he is *bound to preserve himself,* and not to quit his station wilfully, so by the like reason when his own preservation comes not in competition ought be, as much as he can, *to preserve the rest of mankind* and may not unless it be to do Justice on an offender, take away, or impair the life or what tends to the Preservation of the Life, the Liberty, Health, Limb or Goods of another (Locke 1960: 311).

Locke saw this shared duty to God to preserve one's self as part of God's creation as the basic moral law of nature, which existed in the pre-political order or the state of nature. He tried to show that political power could be understood only if it was derived from a state in which all individuals were perfectly free to do, both with regard to their person and possessions, what they thought fit within the bounds of the laws of nature. Locke was emphatic that God had made everything for subsistence and not for waste. Even an individual's life was not his own, but was given by God as a trust, meaning we had no right to destroy or kill ourselves nor could we destroy, kill, rob or enslave other beings who were equal to us before God.

Political authority, like all moral claims, for Locke, was ultimately based on religious obligations, which were the source of all morality. His arguments were politically radical, but far from being secular (Hampsher-Monk 1992: 82). Unlike Hobbes, who argued for an unlimited right of nature that each individual could claim, Locke stressed on a natural duty of self-preservation owed to God for having created us. This duty ruled out strife, for not only did we need to preserve ourselves, but we also needed to perceive the fact that we were all equal before God. The state of nature was therefore moral. Political authority for Locke was not mere power, but *power with right*. A right could only originate from an already existing right, and because individuals had no right to give away their duty to preserve themselves they could not therefore morally or logically grant rightful power to an absolute authority. Locke viewed absolute political power as illegitimate, dismissing Filmer's arguments as wrong and wicked, for it was tantamount to giving up to another a right which one did not *have* in the first place. There was just the relationship between God and human beings. All human authority and relationships were based on trust.

The compulsion to constitute a civil society was to protect and preserve freedom and to enlarge it. The state of nature was one of liberty and equality, but it was also one where peace was not secure, being constantly upset by the "corruption and viciousness of degenerate men". It lacked three important wants: the want of an established, settled, known law; the want of a known and indifferent judge; and the want of an executive power to enforce just decisions. Through the state of nature, Locke tried to tell us the meaning and importance of authority, namely that human beings came together to ensure the observance of the laws of nature, to guarantee the greater possibility of impartiality in the implementation and execution of rules that governed common life, and thereby increase the chance of peace that impartiality entailed. Locke's observation 'In the beginning all the World was America' was about the formation of government in the background of people living together according to reason, without common superior on earth, in mutual assistance, peace, goodwill and preservation. It tells us what government is and what it does by showing what it is not and what it does not do (Laslett 1960: 113).

Locke brought out the perils of human partiality, and how absolute power made partiality potentially dangerous. Flattery and servility would only make it worse. He recognized the tremendous potentiality of power for making human life better, but feared that it had to be entrusted only to those who were responsible towards those on whom it was exercised. Most societies were based on force rather than right. Locke was not an anarchist, distrusting political authority, but he was conscious of the dangers that it posed. Political authority was a trust, and if the terms of the trust were violated, the community had the right to take remedial measures in order to preserve itself. It was on these grounds that he objected to Hobbes' argument that only total order could provide for commodious living. It did not seem credible that people who did not trust one another would entrust an all-powerful sovereign to safeguard their interests. He found it objectionable that there were no safety measures against potential violence and oppression of this absolute ruler. "This is to think that Men are so foolish that they take care to avoid what Mischiefs may be done them by *Pole-cats,* or *Foxes,* but are content, nay think it Safety, to be devoured by Lions" (Locke 1960: 372).

Through a contract, individuals consented to submit to majority rule and organize themselves as a community or civil society. They surrendered their powers partially, namely the three specific rights that constituted the natural right to enforce the laws of nature. Once a civil society was established, the individuals established a government to act as a judge in the nature of a "fiduciary power" for promoting certain ends. Locke described the stages as follows.

> Whosoever therefore out of a state of Nature unite into a Community must be understood to give up all the power necessary to the ends for which they unite into Society ... . And this is done by barely agreeing to unite into one Political Society, which is all the Compact that is, or needs be, between the Individuals that enter into or make up a commonwealth. And thus that which begins and actually constitutes any Political Society is nothing but the consent of any number of Freemen capable of a majority to unite and incorporate into such a society. And this is that, and that only, which did or could give beginning to any lawful Government in the world (Locke ibid: 367).

The community's decisions were by majority rule, unless they specifically agreed to a number greater than the majority, which Locke realized would be more difficult to muster. Though the community appointed a legislative power, it continued to retain supreme power, meaning that the people had the right to assess and evaluate the performance of the legislature. The legislature was the supreme power with a sacred duty to preserve the society. If people found the performance unsatisfactory, they could take steps to change or alter the existing body. "The Legislative being only a Fiduciary power to act for certain ends, there remains still in the People a Supreme Power to remove or alter the Legislative, when they find the Legislative act contrary to the trust reposed in them" (Locke ibid: 402).

Within the government, the legislative power was supreme since it was the representative of the people, having the power to make laws. Besides the legislature there was an executive, usually one person, with the power to enforce the law. The executive, which included the judicial power, had to be always in session. It enjoyed prerogatives and was subordinate and accountable to the legislature. The legislative and executive power had to be separate, thus pre-empting Montesquieu's theory of separation of powers. The third wing of the government was the federative power, the power to make treatises and conduct external relations. With Locke came the eclipse of the political and the identification of the political in a narrow sense with the government. Society became distinct from political arrangements and came to symbolize the whole gamut of human activities. This Lockean position is visible in the writings of the classical economists, the French Liberals and the English Utilitarians (Wolin 1960: 261).

Locke thus advocated a limited sovereign state, for reason and experience established political absolutism as untenable. Describing the characteristics of a good state, Locke said it existed for the people who formed it, and not the vice versa. It had to be based on the consent of the people subject to the constitution and the rule of law. It would be limited, since its powers were derived from the people and were held in trust. It was also limited by natural laws and individual rights.

Locke argued that the state dealt with matters strictly political in nature, and had no warrant to interfere in domains strictly outside the political. Nor could it demand more powers on the pretext of public safety and welfare. Locke categorically asserted that supreme power resided in the people, and the people as a community had the inalienable right to institute and dismiss a government. If a government was dismissed, this did not signify a return to the state of nature, as it was in the case of Hobbes' theory. Moreover, the people chose to specify the powers of the government. Locke astutely observed that people at any given time would not surrender all their powers to an outside body, including their own government. Once the government was instituted, it would be assessed periodically and its actions scrutinized meticulously.

Locke also realized the impossibility of unanimity in every action, for that would imply a return to the state of nature.

> And thus every Man, by consenting with others to make one Body Politick under one Government, puts himself under an obligation to every one of that Society, to submit to the determination of the majority, and to be concluded by it; or else this original Compact, whereby he with others incorporates into one Society, would signify nothing, and be no Compact, if he be left free, and under no other ties, than he was in before in the state of Nature (Locke ibid: 376).

People accepted (and were bound by majority rule) decisions, even if they personally disagreed. Though people granted the legislative power to make law, they always retained a residual right to judge whether its performance was satisfactory and in accordance with the natural laws and take remedial steps if necessary. Hence, Locke was able to justify resistance to unjust political power.

Consent and Political Obligation

The *Second Treatise* tried to explain the basis of legitimate government and the reason why free individuals acquiesced to be subject to an external authority. The answer was simple: namely, free individuals expressed their consent willingly and voluntarily through a contract agreed freely to. As to why they agreed to enter into a civil society and establish a government, Locke explained it with reference to the state of nature.

The state of nature was not only a state of perfect freedom, but also one of perfect equality. Individuals had an equal right to natural freedom. As a true Christian, Locke believed that God created human beings and Earth. Every one had the equal right to share the earth and its fruits, since they were God's creations. Moreover, individuals were subject to the laws of nature. Each had the right to enforce the law and punish the transgressors. In the absence of common legislative, executive and judicial powers in the state of nature, there were disputes on the interpretation of law. In the absence of a common and acceptable arbitrary power, there were disturbances for it became a case of one's word against that of others. Locke, unlike Hobbes, characterized human beings as naturally social and pacific, but did not rule out the possibility of disputes among them. Hobbes used the state of nature to describe the lives of persons without political authority, whereas for Locke the state of nature

> ... is the condition in which God himself places all men in the world, prior to the lives which they live and the societies which are fashioned by the living of these lives. What is designed to show is not what men are like but rather what rights and duties they have as the creatures of God. Their most fundamental right and duty is to judge how the God who has created them requires them to live in the world which he has also created. His requirement for all men in the state of nature is that they live according to the law of nature. Through the exercise of his reason every man has the ability to grasp the content of this law (Dunn 1984: 47).

Like Descartes, Locke optimistically saw each individual as capable of seeking the truth for one's self. For Locke, these most basic truths began from the claim that individuals were essentially conscious beings in a world of physical matter, with which they were constantly interacting. It was through these interactions, of which the most important were our perceptions of the world, that we acquired knowledge or probable beliefs about it. An individual's conscious experience was at the root of having ideas. Locke rejected innate ideas as sources of knowledge. This implied a rejection of moral and religious truths. He never doubted the possibility of everyone reaching it. He questioned the existence of universal moral precepts, considering these differed throughout the world. He thought it was difficult to find any one moral rule that was universally subscribed to. Here, Locke's views were similar to the ones advanced by the Sophists. However, Locke did not pursue his moral views, though he used these arguments to underwrite his political views.

For Locke, men were by nature free, politically equal, creatures of God subject to the laws of nature, and possessors of an executive power of the laws of nature; they became subjects of political authority only by their consent. Without consent there was no political community. Locke spoke of two kinds of consent: express or direct, and tacit consent. Express consent was an explicit commitment given at the time when the commonwealth was instituted. It was interesting that the fundamental Constitution of Carolina which Locke helped to draft, provided for a declaration of one's allegiance to the commonwealth when an individual came of age. In case there was no provision for explicit consent, people's obligation could be gauged by their tacit consent. There were two problems with regard to tacit consent. One was to define tacit consent, and the other was to determine how far it was binding. Locke provided tacit consent in response to Filmer's critique of the contract doctrine. Filmer pointed out that the idea of one contract that was irrevocable meant that subsequent generations were bound by the act of their ancestors making it indistinguishable from the argument of the royalists that God had granted Adam the right to rule which was bequeathed to Adam's heirs. Tacit consent, according to Locke, was demonstrated when,

> ... everyman, that has any possession or enjoyment of any part of the dominions of any government, does thereby give his tacit consent, and is as far forth obliged to obedience to the laws of that government, during such enjoyment, as any one under it; whether this his possession be of land, to him and his heirs forever, or a lodging only for a week; or whether it be barely travelling freely on the highway; and in effect, it reaches as far as the very being of any one within the territories of that government (Locke 1960: 391–392).

The obligation to obey the government would depend on the fact that public power was used for "peace, safety and public good of the people". Moreover, individuals would not yield to the government more power than what they actually possess in the state of nature, which meant that "there cannot be an absolute arbitrary power over their lives and fortunes which are as much possible to be preserved". Lockeian individuals were not committed to unconditional obligation. There was a rational and limited agreement which assured obedience for the preservation and enhancement of life, liberty and property. The validity of the contract would depend on the continuation of these benefits.

Locke also asserted categorically that governments could be altered, amended, changed or dissolved legitimately, and listed five occasions when this was possible. These were as follows.

1. Whenever such a prince or single person established his own arbitrary will in the place of laws.
2. When the prince hindered the legislature from assembling in its due time or from acting freely, pursuant to those ends for which it was constituted.
3. When by the arbitrary power of the prince, the elections and the ways of elections were altered without the consent, and contrary to the common interests of the people.

4. The delivery of the people into the subjection of foreign power, either by the prince or by the legislature.
5. The person who had the supreme executive power neglected laws already enacted, and could not be executed (Locke ibid: 454–459).

Locke insisted that all true states were established by consent. He assumed that a minority would consent in all things to rule by the majority. Through initial and continuing consent, Locke met the critique of Filmer by insisting that legitimate power combined power with right. A government could not be arbitrary: it was bound by the general laws which were public and not subject to individual decrees. All individuals would be governed by the same rules as everyone else otherwise it would violate the natural moral equality of individuals. He clarified that people could use force only against unjust and unlawful authority. The right of disobedience could be exercised by the majority, and not by one person or a small group.

Locke's insistence that there was a higher law above the law of the state became a part of modern democratic theory. It made authority transparent, accountable and subject to change for misdeeds and abuse. He was also sanguine that people would use the right of resistance and revolution wisely as their bitter medicine, and not as a daily bread. It was only when they realized that revolution would result in a better social order, that they would resort to it and not for "every little mismanagement in public affairs" or for trivial causes. Locke emphatically asserted that governments based on consent, coupled with the right of people to rebel, were the "best fence against rebellion". People had the right to judge and assess authority, which was no longer sacred or supernatural. Locke emerged as a thorough-going contractualist, unlike Hobbes whose premises were contractual but whose conclusions supported political absolutism, even though both rejected the divine right of kings and the divine origins of the state. Locke was confident that with more free communication and greater transparency there would be less need for revolution. He ruled out anarchy, and insisted on the need for a just civil authority for upholding a decent and civilized life.

> Unlike the Protestant resistance-theorists of the sixteenth century, Locke did not base his revolutionary theory upon sanctions of conscience or religion; unlike the English parliamentarians of the 1640s, he did not base it on precedents in English law; unlike Algernon Sidney, he did not base it on a metaphysical and metapsychological natural right to liberty; rather he advocated a restrained and considered revolution for the restoration of proper balance in the body politic (Colie 1965: 46).

Locke defended religious toleration and pluralism. In the *Letter,* he assigned the civil magistrate the duty to protect the "life, liberty and indolence of body" of the members of the commonwealth. He held the civil magistrate responsible for regulating religious practice for the peace, safety and security of his people. Though the magistrate was the ultimate judge of how to promote these ends, his judgement could not be more trustworthy, in practice, than that of any other believer. The idea was that truth could look after itself. The magistrate would ensure that other than the necessity of the state and the welfare of the people, no law was made nor were any restraints established. Any attempt to interfere with religious beliefs would be unjust, for each person was responsible for his own salvation. Locke was categorical that no one could give to another person a power that he did not have. He also ruled out religious persecution on the grounds that it could not touch the innermost thoughts, and there was no practical merit in persecuting someone who would confess under stress.

Locke excluded atheists and those religious groups that debarred others from professing and practising their beliefs from the privileges of toleration. Here he was taking a leaf from his experiences in France, where the Huguenots were severely persecuted between 1679 and 1685. The civil magistrate could legally interfere when religious assemblies endangered civil peace, but ruled out interference with a view to questioning their beliefs. Though Locke did not directly justify resistance on grounds of religion, he made it clear that oppression of any kind was intolerable and a sufficient reason for sedition.

Locke defended Christian revelation on the grounds of uncertainties of human perceptions and knowledge. Therefore, any kind of faith, even drawn from scriptural revelation and complemented by human reason, was justified. He repeatedly stressed that each individual was fully responsible for his beliefs and would have to answer God on the day of Judgement. He emphasized that civil magistrates had to be concerned with peace and preservation of society.

Locke's work primarily justified the right of resistance, and in the last resort of revolution, against unjust authority. He repeatedly stressed that authority was legitimate if it was based on the consent of the governed. He emphasized that all authority—political and parental—was a trust, given by God. Therefore, no human being had a right over his own life, since the Christian perception categorically saw life as gifted by God, and that all human rulers could take the lives of their subjects or foreign enemies only if they had acted detrimentally towards public good. It followed that rulers had this right given by God directly and not by the subjects.

Unlike Filmer, who interpreted the rights of rulers as a personal gift from God as giving them ownership over human beings and material goods, Locke made a dear distinction between the duties of subjects to obey and the rights of rulers to command. In most societies, most of the time, the subjects had a duty to obey because civil order and peace were necessary prerequisites for a decent and civilized human existence, but the rulers had a right to command only when they deserved obedience. If they threatened civil peace and order, then the subjects had every right to judge the degree and immediacy of that threat, and could resist it if they thought it to be serious. Political authority became legitimate, and rulers had the legitimate right to command if they had provided practical services to their subjects. For Locke, the ruler became therefore a trustee, far from being an owner of the subject, thereby turning Filmer on his own head.

Parental and Patriarchal Authority

Locke distinguished political from paternal power. Individuals had the right to resist a government that was tyrannical, thus requiring him to show that subjects did not have an unconditional obligation to obey (as contended by the patriarchists), simply by virtue of their birth. He demonstrated the limits of a natural father's authority by separating parental from political authority. Parental authority was natural, not in the sense contended by patriarchists. Political power, on the contrary, was conventional.

Accepting the Christian dictum that children had to obey their parents, Locke pointed out that he was establishing parental rather than paternal authority. Since parental authority was shared, it could not be a model for the rule of an individual, as insisted by the patriarchal monarchists. Obedience towards parents was temporary till one became morally responsible. The rights of the parents were natural not because they had given birth to their children as contended by the patriarchists, but because it was their duty to take care of them and educate them till they were capable of being independent, which could be revoked if they neglected their duties. What was due to the parents was honour and not obedience. Moreover, this honour was due to both fathers and mothers and not *only* to fathers. While children honoured their parents, subjects obeyed the rulers. Inheritance was a virtual right which children had because it was the duty of the parents to not only provide for their survival, but also give them conveniences and comforts of life to the best of their ability.

Locke granted mothers an equal title with fathers to authority over their children. He specified a political role for women, enabling them to enjoy rights and powers within their homes. Mothers had a right to parental respect independent of the will of the fathers, for they had their own responsibilities towards their children. Locke granted freedom to wives from their husbands. For instance, in an unhappy marriage the wife had the liberty to leave her husband. While discussing conquests, he granted the wife property for which she had laboured. He regarded a husband's authority over his wife as derived from a contract and not from nature. He saw women as contributing to civic culture, though he did not expand nor suggest ways and means of their political activity.

Although Locke contended that natural differences between men and women were irrelevant since women were politically equal, he agreed with Filmer that the natural differences between the sexes entailed the subordination of women. He took it for granted that a husband's rule over his wife was a non-political form of power. He conferred on the husband the power of decision making within the family, since he was by nature physically abler and stronger. Through the marriage contract a wife accepted and consented to her domination.

> ... but a Punishment laid upon *Eve:* and if we will take them as they were directed in particular to her, as their representative to all other Women, they will at most concern the Female Sex only, and import no more but that Subjection they should ordinarily be in to their Husbands: But there is here no more Law to oblige a Woman to such a Subjection, if the Circumstances either of her Condition or Contract with her Husband should exempt her from it, then there is, that she should bring forth her Children in Sorrow and Pain, if there could be found a Remedy for it ... for the whole Verse runs thus, *unto the Woman he said, I will greatly multiply thy sorrow and thy conception; In sorrow thou shalt bring forth Children, and thy desire shall be to thy Husband, and he shall rule over thee.* 'Twould, I think, have been a hard matter for any Body, but our A. to have found a Grant of *Monarchical Government to Adam* in these Words ... God, in this Text, gives not, that I see, any Authority to *Adam* over *Eve,* or to Men over their Wives, but only foretels what should the Woman's Lot, how by this Providence he would order it so, that she should be subject her husband, as we see that generally the Laws of Mankind and customs of Nations have ordered it so; and there is, I grant, a Foundation in Nature for it (Locke 1960: 209–210).

Thus, for Locke,

> although a grant of dominion to the patriarch is denied as having any basis in nature, woman's subordination to man is explained as a result of the curse laid upon Eve, the laws and traditions of mankind, and the foundation of nature. Locke in this instance is trying to have his cake and eat it. He ridicules naturalistic arguments for political society which ground patriarchalism in history, scripture, and tradition, and slips in via the Garden of Eden the notion that women's subordination within the conjugal not political, society of marriage may be understood and defended on the basis of nature (Elshtain 1981: 125).

However, in accordance with his stress on self-preservation and natural moral equality, Locke placed limits on the husband's authority, confining it to property and matters of common interest and explicitly denied a right over his wife's life or fortune. As in politics, even family life was based on the premise that individuals were free and equal under the laws of nature. The members of a family had to preserve themselves and fulfil their obligations.

Pateman (1988) pointed out that the social contract theory as developed by Hobbes and Locke did not consider women as persons or citizens with rights in the public sphere, because a tacit sexual contract preceded the social contract by which the consent of the people was elicited to decide on the terms and conditions of their governments. "The sexual contract is the vehicle through which men transform their natural right over women into the security of civil patriarchal right' (1988: 6).

Pateman pointed out that the idea of a free and equal individual which the liberal democratic theory espoused hardly existed, as it was hindered by the inequalities of class, sex and race.

In spite of giving women a political role, Locke continued to see women as mothers and as wives. He was therefore regarded as an early feminist for his considerate views and attitude towards women (Butler 1978: 148–150).

Locke replaced Filmer's absolutist patriarchal model with a liberal redefinition of patriarchal rule. For Filmer, parental authority was divine, natural and unlimited, while Locke separated family life from political authority. While a husband-wife relationship was contractual and therefore voluntary, a parent-child relationship was natural but limited and conditional. The family was needed for procreation of the human race and education of the young.

Property

The theory of property was an important theme in Locke's political philosophy. Like Grotius and Samuel Pufendorf (1632–1694), he pointed out that by human reason and by revelation it was apparent that the earth and its fruits belonged to God, and that God had given them to the human inhabitants in common to enjoy. He tried to answer Filmer's critique of Grotius regarding how individuals could have a private right to any part of a common heritage. He dismissed Filmer's argument that God had given the earth and its fruits "to Adam and his heirs exclusively. More than this, he also argued that it was human labour which distinguished what was privately owned from what was commonly held. Labour was the unquestioned property of the labourer, and by mixing his labour with a piece of land, an individual acquired the right to whatever he had made of that material. The stress was on what human beings made of the earth, how and what they left for posterity. He insisted God had given human beings the earth to make it a better place, full of conveniences of life by entrepreneurship, hard work and reason. It was for "fancy, covetousness of the quarrelsome and contentious". Here also, Locke emphasized that human beings were trustees, stewards who could appropriate and consume by being industrious and creative without wasting, squandering, spoiling or destroying. The philosophy of Puritan ethics pervaded the entire thought of Locke.

In the state of nature, individuals had initially a right to appropriation which was limited to three things. An individual could appropriate only that much for which one had a need, and provided enough and good was left for others. An individual had a right only to that much for which he had mixed the labour of his body and the work of his hand. Labour not only created property but also determined its value. It was labour that made the world different by creating conveniences and increasing productivity. For instance, America, a land of plenty, did not have the conveniences that the seventeenth-century England enjoyed. Locke assumed that scarcity was not a problem, for there was enough for all to find satisfaction, thereby, setting aside the problem of limited means and unlimited human desires.

Locke spoke of individuals in the state of nature having perfect freedom to dispose of their possessions, and persons, as they thought fit. He emphatically clarified that since property was a natural right derived from natural law, it was therefore prior to the government. He emphasized that individuals had rights to do as they pleased within the bounds of the laws of nature. Rights were limited to the extent that they did not harm themselves or others.

The limited right of appropriation and equality of possessions in the state of nature was distorted with the introduction of money. This was because one could possess more regardless of the use of the product, and hoard without injuring anyone. Money also divorced right from convenience. Locke's attitude to the emerging commercial society was ambivalent. He did not reconcile the injunctions within natural law which emphasized equality of property with the inequality of unlimited accumulation which was made possible because of the introduction of money.

Locke assumed the existence of a vibrant economy and civil society prior to the creation of any government. This was to emphasize, which later became the cornerstone of the liberal argument, that civil society was independent of political authority, that economic activity as opposed to politics was more important and that there was a need to separate the private from the public sphere.

> ... Locke initiated a way of thinking in which society, rather than the political order, was the predominant influence. Instead of asking the traditional question: what type of political order is required if society is to be maintained? Locke turned the question around to read, what social arrangements will insure the continuity of government? Locke launched his attack against the traditional model of society, wherein ordered social relationships and institutions were sustained by the direction imparted from a political centre, by substituting a conception of society as a self-activating unity capable of generating a common will (Wolin 1960: 308).

Through the discussions on property, Locke stated that it represented human entitlements and in fact "the great and chief end of men's uniting into commonwealth and putting themselves under government is the preservation" and protection of their property. The purpose of government was to secure human entitlements and ensure lives, liberties and the material possessions of all human beings. Even if the commonwealth was based on freely elected representatives, it could not dispose of the property of its subjects arbitrarily. "The connection between property and the supportive role of society lies in Locke's identification of property with society rather than with the political order" (Wolin ibid: 309).

It was the social character of property that enabled Locke to defend a minimal state with limited government and individual rights, and reject outright the hereditary principle of government. He was willing to defend entitlements that were directly acquired through one's labour, and avoided the issue of inheritance or transactions as gifts.

Locke also wanted to emphasize that no government could deprive an individual of his material possessions without the latter's consent. It was the duty of political power to protect entitlements that individuals enjoyed by virtue of the fact that these had been given by God. It was for the protection of liberties and property that they entered into an agreement instructing the government to recognize these rights and embody them in a statutory form. Since the state was created for the sole protection of property, consequently no part or the whole of the individual's property could be taken without the individual's consent. Besides, no taxes could be levied without the consent of the individual, otherwise it invaded the fundamental right to property and subverted the ends of the government. The American slogan "No taxes without representation" during the Boston Tea Party was typically Lockeian in spirit and content.

Macpherson argued that Locke's views on property made him a bourgeois apologist, a defender of the privileges of the possessing classes. "With the removal of the two initial limitations which Locke had explicitly recognized, the whole theory of property is a justification of the natural right not only to unequal property but to unlimited individual justification" (Macpherson 1973: 221).

As a result, there was a divorce between appropriating and labouring. Simultaneously, Locke also justified and defended class differentials in rights and rationality and wage contracts, in the process becoming a spokesman for a market society providing the moral basis for capitalist society (Macpherson ibid). From a society of equal individuals, Locke accepted two classes with different rights, those with and those without property.

Macpherson's arguments were challenged by Dunn (1968b: 54–58), Laslett (1960: 114–119) and Tully (1980: 150–155), who found it difficult to accept Locke as a spokesman of capitalism. Wood (1984: 101–105) saw Macpherson as distorting history, for Locke could at best be seen as a spokesman of agrarian capitalism. The important fact was that agriculture still dominated the economic scene in the late seventeenth century. Landed property was the main source of wealth, power and social position. Mercantile and manufacturing capitalism on the other hand were still in their embryonic stages. A semblance of market relations had begun to appear but was restricted. Locke's stress on the importance of labour and industry for higher productivity became apparent during the Enclosure movement. The Enclosure movement protested against confiscation of land without the consent of the individual owner. Land was the chief source of wealth and its enclosure increased its yield. Moreover the capitalist landlord could sequestrate the benefits. Not only did Locke have the example of the American colonists in mind but also the "superior productivity of private agricultural economy as compared with the communal tillage of a more primitive system" (Sabine 1973: 486). The claim to land as property without harming anyone else was became an established fact during the Enclosure movement. Moreover, the contention by Macpherson that Locke presumed wage slavery in his conception of property was rejected by Ebenstein, who pointed out that Locke used the term "property" in the broad sense for liberating one's self rather than for enslaving others. For him, as it was with the early liberals, property had a moral dimension. It conveyed independence of the person and possessions.

> By making labour the title to property and the source of value, Locke translated the rise of a new class to power in terms of a new political economy. Although himself a mercantilist, Locke's economic philosophy helped to liberate the ingenious and industrious entrepreneur from paralyzing force and custom (Ebenstein 1969: 390).

Ryan (1965: 220, 228–230) maintained that Macpherson frequently ignored what Locke was saying in the text. Far from creating a political society in which the bourgeois class dominated the working class, as Macpherson claimed, Locke was attempting to prove that everyone shared a common interest in a constitutionally established political society. Dunn (1968b: 68–70) contended that Locke was concerned with questions of social justice. In Locke's under-standing, justice was linked to ownership of property on the one hand and the laws of nature as the will of God on the other hand. The individual's interest in property was constrained by the duty he owed to God. Tully (1980: 150–151) in a similar vein argued that through the concept of property, Locke tried to provide the foundations of economic justice. It raised questions like what a just distribution of the products of labour was, to what extent labour power was to be regulated, and whether labour could be organized without exploitation.

CONCLUSION

Locke was one of the most controversial and influential theorists in the entire history of political thought. He wrote on epistemology, natural law, economics, political theory, education, toleration and theology, making a difference to the intellectual world more than anybody else since Aristotle. His ideas shaped the Enlightenment and the modern world. "The heirs of Locke are, first, Berekely and Hume; second, those of the French *philosophes* who did not belong to the school of Rousseau; third, Bentham and the philosophical Radicals; fourth, with important accretions from Continental philosophy, Marx and his disciples" (Russell 1961: 617).

Locke's notion of property gave rise to some serious criticism, though such criticism normally ignored the libertarian aspect of early liberalism, for property was linked to the idea of equality and self-sufficiency. Locke's emphases on constitutionalism, consent and toleration have been integral components of modern political theory. Locke was also the first exponent of the doctrine of civil society. Benefit and contract were synonymous, leading to his formulation of a conception of government as a trust. Locke also expressed faith in the ordinary man when he conceded a right to rebellion, making people the ultimate and final arbiters of the government's accountability. The radical dimension of this formulation could be gauged from the fact that even a century after Locke, Burke was not even prepared to grant proper democratic representation, and argued for *virtual representation.* If this historic context is kept in mind, then the enormous significance of Locke's libertarianism becomes apparent. To be a champion of individual freedom and extension of democracy before the inauguration of the age of democracy was no small achievement, and in achieving this, Locke immortalized himself.

Locke's political theory addressed four problems: (a) the nature of political power at a time when the nation states were consolidating their status; (b) a proper relationship between religion and politics, and between the Church and the state; (c) actual practice of governing in the early mercantile period; and (d) types of knowledge appropriate to religious and political theory (Tully 1993: 616–652). Locke's theory represented a fundamental shift in intellectual and political consciousness, deflecting subjects from the notions of duty and obedience vis-a-vis their rulers, towards rights and the idea that a government was entitled to their affection and loyalty only if it could successfully provide defined services. He established the dignity of the individual by making a case for both natural and political equality, for God would never accept absolutism—political and parental—as that would imply abdication of one's duty towards self-preservation and freedom. His views on toleration shaped the liberal theory, emphasizing the need to separate religion from the political, the importance of belief, and the injustice in persecution and intolerance.

One of the most important perceptions of America was that it was a nation of Lockeian individualism. Locke was often described as America's philosopher-king. His influence was so pervasive that it was seen as a self-evident truth. Louis Hartz's influential work *The Liberal Tradition in America* (1955) endorsed this view. However, this predominant view has been questioned by some recent revisionist scholars like Bailyn, Pocock and Gordon Wood, who emphasized a more communitarian origin of American political tradition. One such crucial influence was the civic republican traditions of ancient Greece and Rome and sixteenth-century

Florence, manifested in the preservation of virtue and public involvement in civic affairs. But it is generally agreed that such a view was a distortion of Locke's views. It was also a caricature of Locke, portraying him as a possessive individualist. Locke was not for merely maximizing interest. His emphasis was more on human virtues and excellence. His concerns, significant in themselves, were justice, courage, self-sacrifice, humanity, industry and truthfulness, qualities of human character appropriate for a new liberal order. He

> constructs modem moral virtues, including civility, liberality, justice and humanity, on the basis of his egoistic and hedonistic psychology .... To understand this view of human life as an entirely degraded one, bereft of any dignity, is to do an injustice not only to Locke but to liberalism and ourselves (Tarcov 1984: 210).

Locke was the product at the turning point of English history. The Newtonian revolution in science convinced him of the need for a new philosophy. The intellectual temper of England allowed complete independence in the realm of philosophical speculation. Locke did not make a secret of his debt to Descartes, and with his genius grasped the spirit of this new age. He became the philosopher of this new age.

If we list out the items that constitute the liberal world-view: individualism, freedom, consensual limited government, minimal state, constitutional authority, the rule of law, the majority rule principle, separation of powers, sovereignty of the people, representative democracy, property rights, civil society, pluralism, tolerance and the right to judge authority, then Locke is the founding father of liberal political theory. Subsequent liberal theorists have worked within the framework that Locke provided. The ideological triumph of liberalism in the twentieth century over its rivals, Communism and Fascism, prove that the Lockeian insights developed in the context of late seventeenth-century England proved to be the most enduring and satisfying framework among all the competing political ideologies of the last four hundred years.

7

Jean Jacques Rousseau

> If we are asked what are the most enduringly important of his social and political ideas, we might reply, first, the idea that the people are the ultimate source of all legitimate territorial authority; secondly, that government is merely the agent and delegate of the sovereign people; thirdly, that the common good is the criterion of sound legislation and satisfactory administration; fourthly, that the state is organic in nature and not a mere mechanism; fifthly, that the true basis of political obligation is consent, and hence, finally, that there is in the last resort no antagonism between freedom and authority, law and liberty, man and the State (Hearnshaw 1931: 193).

> ... revolutionary "political" theory, as it developed since Rousseau, is already foreshadowed and contained in *The Social Contract;* or to be more explicit, that so far as "political" theory in the strict sense is concerned, Marx and Lenin have added nothing to Rousseau, except for the analysis (which is of course rather important) of the "economic bases" for the withering away of the state (Colletti 1969: 185).

> Rousseau's sovereign is the externalized general will, and, as has been said before, stands for essentially the same as the natural harmonious order. In marrying this concept with the principle of popular sovereignty, and popular self-expression, Rousseau gave rise to totalitarian democracy (Talmon 1960: 43).

Jean Jacques Rousseau (1712–1778) was the greatest thinker that the French produced. In the entire history of political theory, he was the most exciting and most provocative. By the very magic of his style, no other political thinker could come anywhere near him. He was a genius and a keen moralist who was ruthless in his criticism of eighteenth-century French society. He was one of the most controversial thinkers, as evident from the conflicting, contradictory and often diametrically opposite interpretations that existed of the nature and importance of his ideas.

"His philosophy is highly personal, an expression of his own fierce insistence on independence and liberty, but at the same time, paradoxical and complex" (Curtis 1961: Vol. II: 13). Pointing to the volatile implications of his prescriptions, Madame de Stael commented that his new ideas set everything ablaze.

> ... Rousseau ... who was the first of the modern intellectuals, their archetype and in many ways the most influential of them all. Older men like Voltaire had started the work of demolishing the altars and enthroning reason. But Rousseau was the first to combine all the salient characteristics of the modern Promethean: the assertion of his right to reject the existing order in its entirety; confidence in his capacity to refashion it from the bottom in accordance with principles of his own devising; belief that this could be achieved by the political process; and, not least, recognition of the huge part instinct, intuition and impulse play in human conduct (Johnson 1988: 2).

To some, Rousseau appeared as a great champion of individualism (Chapman 1956: 91–144; Derathe 1950: 348–349, 355–356). Others viewed him as a collectivist (Vaughan 1962: 75–81). Many like Cassirer saw him as an incomparable democrat who recognized autonomy, though some like Cobban, Talmon and Taylor viewed him as a precursor of modern totalitarianism (Chapman 1956: 75–88; Russell 1961: 685; Talmon 1960: 74–88). Crocker and Lindsay viewed him as a believer in guided democracy while Popper described him as a romantic collectivist.

To many, he was an advocate of revolutionary changes while others regarded him as a defendant of the status quo. The early socialists, with the exception of Jean B.C. Louis Blanc (1811–1882) and the Saint Simonians like Saint Armand Bazard (1791–1832) and Barthelemy Prosper Enfantin (1796–1864), were uncomfortable with his individualism. His name had been associated with the German Idealists who regarded him as the originator of their political system. Kant praised Rousseau for stating in clear terms the limits of the intellect and emphasizing the importance of immediate sensation. He credited him for teaching him to honour human beings. This divergence in interpretation was due to the ambiguous nature of his theory, making it possible to interpret him in many different ways. "One could always find one's dogma in Rousseau, whether one belongs to the left or to the 'Left of Left' or to right or to the 'Right of Right' " (Barker 1948: xxxix).

Rousseau made a passionate appeal for human equality. Paradoxically, the greatest mind of the Enlightenment had nothing in common with his contemporaries. As a political moralist and a constitution builder, he made Utopian demands. In the *Discourses on Origins of Inequality* (1755) he described how contemporary society fell short of civilized standards. In the *Social Contract* (1762) he stipulated and portrayed a decent and humane society. While the former diagnosed the disease, the latter gave remedies and cures. He mainly focused on whether human beings could enjoy both civilization and freedom, society and moral integrity. He propounded the notion of General Will as the real basis of legitimate power and authority. He highlighted the importance of realizing freedom in the modern age, and pointed to the problems of reconciling freedom with claims of authority. He attempted to reconcile merit, liberty and equality in a society that would be consensual, participatory and democratic. In fact, one would have to read both these works together to understand the full implication of his ideas. The *Social Contract* was a part of a larger work, *Institutions Politiques,* which he conceived in 1744 but abandoned and began to write the *Emile* (1762). Rousseau wrote on institutional arrangements and educational practice as reflected in his works like *Project of a Constitution for Corsica* (1764), *Considerations on the Government of Poland* (1772) and the *Emile.* The last one was strongly disapproved of by the city leadership of Geneva, making Rousseau renounce his citizenship. He sent a rejoinder in the form of *Letters From the Mountain.*

In 1750, Rousseau became famous by winning an essay competition with his *Discourse on the Science and the Arts,* in which he had stated that "our souls have been corrupted in proportion to the advancement of our sciences and our arts toward perfection". Here, he extended the arguments of Machiavelli and Montesquieu about the relationship between luxury and affluence, growth, moral decline and loss of human liberty. Rousseau's severe criticism of luxury and artificiality, rejection of sophistication, and his endorsement of simplicity, and emphasis on natural behaviour, angered his contemporaries. He believed that the arts and sciences originated in human vices as masks to conceal and rationalize human depravity. Contrary to what the Enlightenment professed, progress in the material sense only increased our dependence on commodities, thereby increasing our wants and undermining our natural independence. The less was the desire, the more the freedom. He defended simplicity, innocence, poverty and virtue as opposed to refinement, wit, wealth and decadence. In many respects, Rousseau's theory had a striking resemblance to the subsequent indictment by Gandhi of modern Westernized, materialistic and technological civilization.

Plato exerted a strong and powerful influence on Rousseau, leading to the revival of the influence of the classical tradition in political philosophy.

> What Rousseau got from Plato was a general outlook. It included, first, the conviction that political subjection is essentially ethical and only secondarily a matter of law and power. Second and more important, he took from Plato the presumption, implicit in all the philosophy of the city state, that the community is itself the chief moralizing agency and therefore represents the highest moral value (Sabine 1973: 534).

LIFE SKETCH

Rousseau was born on June 28, 1712 in the city of Geneva. During his lifetime, he accomplished many things including mastery in and writing on music, politics and education. His fame primarily rested on his writings. His father was a watchmaker. His mother's death within a month of his birth disintegrated the family. His parents were Protestants, but Rousseau got converted to Catholicism under the influence of Madame de Warens. He subsequently became Warens' lover. He led the life of a vagabond, and only after many years did he begin to educate himself. His *Confessions* provide the details of his life.

At the age of 30, Rousseau went to Paris and befriended Diderot. The latter's *Encyclopedia* included some of Rousseau's writings on music. From 1743 to 1744, Rousseau became .the secretary to the French ambassador in Venice. He developed an intimate relationship with Therese le Vasseur in 1745, who subsequently became the mother of his five children. All his children were abandoned in an orphanage. He married Therese much later. His eccentric, egoistic and overbearing personality made him sever his friendships with his former friends Diderot, Hume and Voltaire.

Rousseau attained fame with his prize-winning essay *Discourse on the Science and Arts,* in which he rejected progress based on the arts and sciences, as it did not elevate the moral standards of human beings. In the *Discourses,* he traced the rise of inequality and the consequent fall of the human individual. The *Discourses* was dedicated to the natives of Geneva, a city that had left an indelible influence. In the novel *La Nouvelle Heloise* (1761), the themes of his early essays reappeared, and his preference for nature and the simple pleasures of country life became evident. His *Confessions* published posthumously and his *Reveries d'un Promeneur Solitaire* contained idyllic descriptions of the beauty and serenity of the country's natural surroundings. It also had beautiful portrayals of the lakes of Switzerland and the foothills of the Alps.

Rousseau also composed operas. One of his short operas, *Le Devin du Village* (*The Village Soothsayer*) was performed for the first time in Paris on March 1, 1753. It proved to be an instant hit. Even the king of France, despite being tone-deaf, was overheard trying to hum its melodies. Rousseau's music remained the mainstay of the Paris opera for years to come. He also wrote a dictionary of music and devised a new system of musical notation. He was persecuted for religious reasons. The *Social Contract* and the *Emile* were burned both in Paris and Geneva. Facing the threat of imprisonment, Rousseau went into hiding. He died in 1778.

ENLIGHTENMENT

The Enlightenment was described as the Age of Reason. It was a period when thinkers did not establish any particular mode of philosophical speculation, but agreed on many fundamental issues. These were placing indomitable faith in the idea of progress, the need to apply scientific methods, and perceiving reason to be the best guide available for conducting life. The Enlightenment refers to the series of dramatic revolutions in science, philosophy and politics took place in European thought and culture from the mid-seventeenth century through the eighteenth century. It culminates with the French Revolution which saw the violent destruction of the traditional hierarchical, political and social orders—the French monarchy, the privileges of the French Aristocracy and the political power and authority of the Catholic Church and replaced by a new political and social order based on the principles of human rationality, freedom and equality of all. Its roots lay in the scientific revolution ushered in by Copernicus and Galileo. Peter Gay observed that the Enlightenment broke through the dogma of 'the sacred circle', an interdependent relationship between the hereditary aristocracy, the leaders of the church and the text of the bible that had circumscribed thinking. The church sanctioned the rule of the king with whose help the notion of 'divine right of kings' was invoked and the king, in return, defended the church. The Enlightenment was associated with the French thinkers—Voltaire, Diderot, D'Alembert, Montesquieu, and others called *philosophes*. In addition to the French Enlightenment were the Scottish Enlightenment—Hutcheson, Hume, Smith and Reid and the German Enlightenment that included Christian Wolff, Moses Mendelssohn, G.E. Lessing, Leibniz, Goethe and Kant.

> The basic idea underlying all the tendencies of enlightenment was the conviction that human understanding is capable, by its own power and without any recourse to super-natural assistance, of comprehending the system of the world and that this new way of understanding the world will lead to a new way of mastering it (Cassirer 1937: Vol. 5).

Rousseau, a product of the Enlightenment, was aware of these developments. What differentiated him from his contemporaries was his contempt for knowledge, and his strong conviction of its uselessness in explaining the individual's political conduct. He specifically gave a call for discarding "all those scientific books" by asserting that,

> ... these vain and futile declaimers (the philosophers) go forth on sides, armed with their fatal paradoxes, to sap the foundations of our faith and nullify virtue. They smile contemptuously at such old names as patriotism and religion, and consecrate their talents and philosophy to the destruction and defamation of all that men hold sacred (Rousseau 1958: 131–132).

Rousseau protested against intelligence, science and reason, insofar as they destroyed reverence, faith and moral intuition, the factors on which society was based. His protest was a "revolt against reason", for he regarded the "thinking animal as a depraved animal" (Sabine 1973: 530–531). His conviction was reflected by his unhappiness with Grotius, because "his usual method of reasoning is constantly to establish right by force". Rousseau rejected the progressive effects of the power and clarity of reason. Reason might enable individuals to overcome their ignorance, but made them skeptics. It tempered one's chauvinism to the point of destroying one's patriotic sense. It suppressed and distorted natural responses like sympathy and pity. He doubted whether the human mind could be fashioned through education, cultivation of fine manners and a benevolent disposition. He was not optimistic about social reforms in eighteenth-century France.

For Rousseau, arts, manners and politeness not only destroyed martial virtues, but also denied human nature, forcing individuals to conceal "their real selves". In modern society, he observed that happiness was built on the opinions of others, rather than finding it in one's own hearts. Art highlighted this truth, for it was deceitful. The origin of art and sciences was in idleness and the desire for distinction among human beings.

Rousseau implied the irreversibility of the process of corruption in the same way as the process of civilization, which was irreversible. There were two reasons for this. The first was geopolitical. Like Edward Gibbon (1737–1794), Rousseau accounted for renewal of virtue and the destruction of corrupt imperial societies through their conquests by barbarians on the edges of civilization. The second reason was linked to Rousseau's assessment of history and social development in moral terms. In his unpublished *Essay on Wealth,* he tried to see the effects of a nexus between wealth and poverty on the moral person. He dismissed modern society as false and artificial, for it destroyed natural and true culture. The problem remained about what was perceived as natural, and how to answer the question of what was natural.

ROUSSEAU'S POLITICAL PHILOSOPHY

In Rousseau's view, the most fundamental relationship of the human individual was with the society, though the original person lived in a state of nature which was pre-social and pre-political. In spite of his idealization of the state of nature, there was no going back to it, and because of this an examination of what the human person was like in the state of nature, what had become of him as a result of the pernicious process of civil society and the nature of the ideal society, were important questions. He noted the wide differences that existed between the civilized and the natural person.

In a state of nature, the individual was guided by instinct and not by reason. He differed from animals only because he possessed a will and the desire for perfectibility. The basic interest of Rousseau's natural person was very similar to that of Hobbes, as both were guided by a primary need and compulsion of life, namely self-preservation. The difference lay with regard to the state of nature. In the case of Hobbes, this primary need was constantly under threat, whereas for Rousseau:

> The more we reflect on it, the more we shall find that this state was the least subject to revolutions, and altogether the very best man could experience, so that he can have departed from it only through some fatal accident, which, for the public good, should never have happened. The example of savages, most of whom have been found in this state, seems to prove that men were meant to remain in it, that is the real youth of the world, and that all subsequent advances have been apparently so many steps towards the perfection of the individual, but in reality towards the decrepitude of his species (Rousseau 1958: 198–199).

The youth of the world, as Rousseau described this period of the state of nature, was a time when human beings (noble savage) were equal—or more appropriately, unequal—as he mentioned the distinct possibility of some inequalities in this period. Interestingly, even in Hobbes' writings the word 'savage' found mention. It was the discovery of America and with it its 'savage people' that influenced the writers of seventeenth and eighteenth centuries. The most important thing that he emphasized was that these inequalities did not hinder the independence and self-sufficiency of humans, as they could continue to lead "free, healthy, honest and happy lives" (Rousseau ibid: 199). The rise of civilization was attributed to human beings' discovery of metals and agriculture, bringing in division and specialization of labour. It was linked to the institution of private property.

Rousseau did not see reason as an innate quality in the individual. It was mostly dormant until a situation arose in which it was needed. The natural person was able to fulfil his needs without much assistance from reason. A happy individual was not much of a thinking being. Reason, for Rousseau, was an instrument to attain ends, and if one's ends were satisfied effortlessly, then it played a marginal role. The natural person had limited physical desires, but the moment he reasoned, the range of desires also increased, causing him to think about his desires increasingly. The appetite of a rational person was unlimited. Since happiness was dependent on satisfaction of desires, a rational person remained miserable. Reason created artificial and false needs. It was not merely the satisfaction of needs, but also the desire to be a certain kind of person that entailed problems. The natural person ceased to be happy, peaceful and became dependent and miserable, losing both natural equality and innocence. The natural person did not lose his compassion, but the feeling got subsumed under reason.

> Reason is what engenders egocentrism and reflection strengthens it. Reason is what turns man in upon himself … . Philosophy is what isolates him and what moves him to say in secret at the sight of a suffering man, "Perish if you will; I am safe and sound" (Rousseau ibid: 199).

ANALYSIS OF INEQUALITY

In the *Discourses*, Rousseau provided the moral foundations of his social criticism and explored the basis of natural rights by tracing the source of moral values to natural equality and compassion that could be found among individuals. He described the natural person as some kind of a dumb animal. Rejecting the notion of the original sin, he contended that human beings came into this world as pure and good beings, but in the process got corrupted, tarnished, disfigured and degraded by society. This constituted his main point of enquiry.

Rousseau demonstrated how humans who were naturally healthy, good, dumb and roughly equal to one another became sickly, evil, intelligent and highly unequal when they mixed in society. The greatest horror of modern society was the fact that it was a highly unequal one. Having provided the reasons for the "fall" of the human being, his verdict on behalf of modern society was essentially negative. He concluded that for all their efforts, human beings had only succeeded in making themselves miserable.

Rousseau described the human person as endowed with the ability to choose since he was a free agent and not entirely subject to instinct and natural impulse, as other animals were. Moreover, the human being was capable of being perfect, which enabled him to come out of the state of nature, but in the process created an imbalance between one's needs and the ability to satisfy them. Civilization had multiplied the desire for needs, but the inability to fulfil them made human beings unhappy. Rousseau did not see material progress ushered in by modern technology as constituting civility and happiness. Modern civilization was highly unequal, as it did not reflect merely natural, but also artificial inequalities, and hence was corrupting and wrong. Rousseau's argument that acquisition of property caused inequality was implicitly challenged by Smith in his *The Wealth of Nations* when he pointed out that the self-interested individual unintentionally helped to maximize the wealth of society. In another passage in *The Theory of Moral Sentiments* (1759) Smith pointed out that the self-interested individual unintentionally helped to distribute wealth more widely so as to approach equality. Smith also observed that all occupations, if different degrees of reward were balanced against different degrees of toil and trouble, would yield an equal amount of welfare.

Rousseau was an advocate of approximate social equality but not *total* equality. He was willing to permit two sorts of inequality. The first was the natural inequality between the young and old, the weak and strong, the wise and stupid; the second was the inequality that resulted from rewarding those who rendered special service to the community. Natural inequalities and those who made distinguished contributions to society were the only types of inequalities that he permitted. He maintained that existing social inequality did not belong to these types.

Rousseau rejected the idea that social inequalities reflected natural inequalities of talents. It was ridiculous to think that the rich were vastly wealthier than the rest of the population, because they were infinitely more gifted and talented. The real reason was the unscrupulous business practices that they and their ancestors had employed. The same was the case with the powerful. He repudiated differences in ability as the sole justification for social inequalities. Instead, he pointed out how human beings climbed over one another to get to the top. Social equality implied equality of opportunity. While in a capitalist society wealth was used to secure benefits, in a communist society it was power and prestige that conferred privileges. He rejected both these principles of distribution. He ruled out the principle of egalitarianism as a levelling one, as he did not obliterate distinct individual endowments. He wanted society to take these into account and conform to them (Colletti 1969: 190, 192). The basis of natural right was not human reason, but human sensitivity. It was healthy self-interest and pity or compassion that prevented individuals from harming one another, except in legitimate self-defence.

Rousseau saw a direct link between luxury, ever-expanding needs and the rise of art and science, after which true courage failed and virtues declined. Roman history elucidated this argument fully. As long as Rome was poor and simple, it was able to command respect and establish an empire. But the moment it became wealthy, its decline began. Rousseau similarly thought Sparta to be a better example in the cult of natural simplicity than Athens; the latter had to decline because of its elegance, luxury, wealth, art and science. He castigated philosophers for desecrating all that was sacred, and called them charlatans for creating confusion in the minds of men and undermining their ideas of patriotism and religion.

INSTITUTION OF PRIVATE PROPERTY

This state of affairs, a period of ideal bliss and happiness, disappeared with the emergence of private property. In the cases of both Hobbes and Rousseau, the institution of property was absent in the state of nature. But in spite of this similarity, there were important differences in their writings on the emergence of civil society.

For Hobbes, the primary and original purpose of civil society was to make secure the right of self-preservation, the right to life, whereas for Rousseau, since the human person in the state of nature was instinctively good, life as such was not threatened, and as a consequence civil society emerged not for its preservation, but for the protection of the property of a few. In this way civil society was created for the selfish interests of a few people, whereas for Hobbes the need for a civil society was more universal, since life was dear to all, and everybody without any exception would compose the commonwealth for security.

In the case of Rousseau, property was the only artificial right or privilege that emerged in society, and this right belonged to a few. The institutionalization of property rights put an end to the self-sufficiency that existed in the state of nature, bringing misery to the majority.

> But from the moment one man began to stand in need of the help of another; from the moment it appeared advantageous to any one man to have enough provisions for two, equality too disappeared, property was introduced, for work became indispensable, and vast forests became smiling fields, which man had to water with the sweat of his brow, and where slavery and misery were soon seem to germinate and grow up with crops (Rousseau 1958: 199).

Rousseau was not attempting to paint a picture of the evolution of civil society in stages by chronological events. He explained that these investigations were not "considered as historical truths, but only as mere conditional and hypothetical reasonings, rather calculated to explain the nature of things, than to ascertain their actual origin" (Rousseau ibid: 161).

The change from the state of nature to that of civil society was abrupt. It emerged when,

> the First man, who having enclosed a piece of ground, he thought himself of saying "This is mine" and found people simple enough to believe him, was the real founder of civil society. From how many crimes, wars, and murders, from how many horrors and misfortunes might not any one have saved mankind, by pulling up the stakes, of filling up the ditch, and crying to his fellows: "Beware of listening to this impostor; you are undone if you once forget that the fruits of the earth belong to us all, and the earth itself to nobody" (Rousseau ibid: 192).

In Rousseau's ideal, a golden mean between the primitive state of nature and his own contemporary times would emerge. There would be no division of labour. This was akin to the Marxist Utopia. Each would be able to meet one's own needs by one's own efforts. The moment a person became dependent on the other, he lost his independence and autonomy. Human beings not only compared themselves materially, but also liked *others* to recognize them as superior. Not only did property create social dissensions, but it also brought forth new kinds of mutual dependence between the rich and the poor. The rich needed the services of the poor, and the poor required the help of the rich. The distinctions increased and became sharper. The poor coveted the property of the rich, and the rich feared losing it, leading to a state of war similar to the one described by Hobbes. The *Discourses*

> ... attempted to draw upon the anthropological knowledge ... in order to reconstruct systematically the origins of private property and to show how it caused the evils of society to evolve. His (Rousseau's) anthropology was not sound, but his way of looking at social questions in historical terms was full of possibilities for the future. Babeuf inherited this primitive historical consciousness, which later developed into a fundamental element in the revolutionary outlook during the nineteenth century (Fried and Sanders 1964: 32).

However, Rousseau, unlike the socialists, did not advocate common ownership of property or the means of production. He regarded property as the most sacred of all citizens' rights.

> But he had no serious idea of abolishing property and no very definite idea about its place in the community. What Rousseau contributed to socialism, Utopian or other, was the much more general idea that all rights, including those of property, are rights within the community and not against it (Sabine 1973: 536).

Rousseau's ideal, however, was an economic system based on small farmers owning tracts of land. He opposed the sharp distinctions that property ownership entailed. In this sense he could be regarded as a spiritual forerunner of modern socialism, for his perception that property was the source of misery and inequality. His indictment of property, like that of Plato, was on moral grounds.

CIVIL SOCIETY

Rousseau, like Hobbes, failed to provide a logical answer to explain the transformation of human instinct into reason, except that change was abrupt, brought into existence by the will and effort of a few individuals. There would be no going back to the state of nature. Society was accepted as inevitable, for human life was not possible without it. He spoke of a golden past with virtually no hope of recapturing it. In the *Emile,* he distinguished between the state of nature and civil society and stated his preference for the latter.

> Oh! Emile, where is the man who owes nothing to the land in which he lives? Whatever that land may be, he owes to it the most precious thing possessed by man, the morality of his actions and the love of virtue. Born in the depths of a forest he would have lived in greater happiness and freedom; but being able to follow his inclinations without a struggle there would have been no merit in his goodness, he would not have been virtuous, as may be of his passions. The mere sight of order teaches him to know and love it. The public good, which to others is a mere pretext, is a real motive for him. He learns to fight against himself and to prevail, to sacrifice his own interest to the common weal. It is not true that he gains nothing from the laws; they give him courage to be just, even in the midst of the wicked. It is not true that they have failed to make him free; they have taught him to rule himself (Rousseau 1911: 437).

This statement by Rousseau explained his outline of civil society, which was elaborated and developed in the *Social Contract.* In the state of nature the individual was guided by instincts of self-preservation and compassion. While all living creatures shared these qualities, the difference was in the fact that in others these were instinctive, whereas in individuals it was subject to their will.

> Nature lays her commands on every animal, and the brute obeys her voice. Man receives the same impulsion, but at the same time knows himself at liberty to acquiesce or resist: and it is particularly in his consciousness of this liberty that the spirituality of his soul is displayed (Rousseau 1958: 3).

It was because human beings were endowed with a will that they were different from other animals. However, its presence did not destroy their instinctive goodness. Two things followed from this presumption. First, though civilization had a corrupting influence on the individual, the real self would still remain undisturbed. This led to the second proposition that a higher form of political organization was both desirable and feasible. Such a structure would be in accordance with the needs and nature of the individual.

For Rousseau, vanity among human beings and difference in property and possessions led to inequality. The rich became richer and the poor, poorer. Laws were enacted to protect property rights. Civil society degenerated into a state of war, extreme inequality, ostentation, cunning, ambition and enslavement. Through laws and other political devices, the rich were able to corner power and dominate, while the poor descended into slavery. Civilized man was born a slave and died as one. Smith, while reviewing the *Discourses* criticized Rousseau for sharing Bernard Mandeville's (1670–1733) view that there was no powerful instinct in the human being that made him seek society for its own sake and that society was itself an instrument of the cunning and the powerful to maintain their superiority over the weak.

The natural man lost his ferocity once he began to live in society. He became weak. Desires expanded and comforts in due course became necessities, leading to a loss of natural independence. Increasing dependence created problems in human relationships, for it made people vain and contemptuous. While self-esteem was good for a person, vanity led to an individual's social ills. Vanity could not be satisfied for it made the satisfaction of desires difficult. Once an individual became vain, it was difficult to get rid of his vanity.

Thus Rousseau rejected the Enlightenment's belief in human progress of reason through science and technology. The latter did not bring about moral improvement, since continued decadence measured in terms of human unhappiness would be the fate of most contemporary societies. He summarized this state of affairs in the *Emile* as, though God had made all things good, it was man who meddled with them and made them evil. On receiving a copy of the *Discourses,* Voltaire, the high priest of the Enlightenment, replied scornfully that he had never seen any one use such intelligence to denigrate human progress and civilization. Starobinski (1988) regarded it as a substitute for sacred history, for Rousseau had rewritten the Genesis as a work of philosophy, complete with the Garden of Eden, original sin and the confusion of tongues. Its tone was that of a "mystic revealing great secrets". It influenced important social critics, from Robiespierre to Marx, for it focused on freedom and the deepest ills that flow from evil forms of society to scuttle it.

GENERAL WILL AND INDIVIDUAL FREEDOM

In the *Social Contract,* Rousseau portrayed the nature of the higher organization where he attempted to show that a human being's transformation need not always be for the worse, provided the right kind of polity could be built. Unlike the early contractuahsts, Rousseau was keen to show how the *right* rather than the *first* society could be created, for he was hopeful that the right society would transform the noble savage to a humane person, immortalized by his famous words, *"Man is born free and is everywhere in chains"*. It would be a polity that would aim for the general, rather than the particular, interests of its members. The freedom that the noble savage enjoyed in the state of nature would be possible under the right kind of society governed by the "General Will". According to Riley (1998) the notions of the General Will (volontè générale) and Particular Will (volontè particulière) were elaborately used in the works of eminent scholars such as Pascal, Malebranche, Bayle, Fénélon, Bousset, Fontenelle and Leibniz between 1640 and 1715. However, in the writings of Diderot and Rousseau the notion of General Will was secular rather than theological. Society and the individual, in his theory, were complementary. This became very clear at the very beginning of the book.

> I mean to inquire if, in the civil order, there can be any sure and legitimate rule of administration, men being taken as they are and law as they might be. In this inquiry, I shall endeavour always to unite what right sanctions with what is prescribed by interest, in order that justice and utility may in no case be divided (Rousseau 1958: 3).

The right kind of society would enhance human freedom, for nothing was dearer to a person than liberty.

> To renounce liberty is to renounce being a man, to surrender the rights of humanity and even its duties. For him who renounces everything no indemnity is possible. Such a renunciation is incomparable with man's nature; to remove all liberty from his will is to remove all morality from his acts (Rousseau ibid: 8).

Most of the French thinkers of the eighteenth century regarded liberty as crucial to the individual's development. Rousseau too reiterated this theme and regarded liberty as central to his theoretical construct. For Rousseau, the entire objective of a contract was to reconcile liberty with authority. Liberty was fundamental; so was authority, for one could not exist meaningfully without the other. The priority of freedom was the highest, which was the most instinctive urge in the individual, even in the state of nature. He rejected the idea that the social contract involved the surrender of freedom to a third person. Instead, a legitimate polity had to "defend and protect with the whole common force the person and goods of each associate, and in which each, while uniting himself with all, may still obey himself alone, and remain as free as before" (Rousseau ibid: 23).

Rousseau's conception had many positive points. He took it for granted that human beings could not return to the state of nature. Consequently, whatever had to be achieved was discovered only within civil society. This enabled him to dream of a golden past and visualize a future based on a better order and human perfection. Analogically, the difference could be compared with the distinction between primitive communism and true communism that existed in Marxism. Another important aspect in Rousseau's theory was the realization that every human activity was basically related to politics.

> I had realized that everything was basically related to politics, and that no matter how one approached it, no people would ever be anything but what the nature of its government made it. Therefore, the great question of the best possible government seemed to me to reduce itself to this: which is the form of government fitted to shape the most virtuous, the most enlightened, the wisest, and in short, the "best" people, taking that word in its noblest meaning? (Rousseau ibid: 65).

Rousseau regarded consent as the basis of society, but emphasized the importance of the community along with the need to protect individual freedom. A community was created for the benefit of the individual, and Rousseau attempted to reconcile the two claims: that of the community with that of the individual, the claims of authority with those of liberty. A community that was constituted by all consenting individuals voluntarily submitting to the general will was the solution to his paradox of persons born free, but yet in chains. There was a moral transformation in the individual once a community was created. This was because, having voluntarily created it, the community was seen as furthering the individual's moral autonomy. Since it was through society that individuals realized their full potential, it could be reorganized to ensure the freedom that individuals enjoyed when they were in a state of nature. This was possible once the right society was created, for that would maximize (or at least offer the quintessence of) individual liberty.

> To project the question on a grander scale, one can see in Rousseau's political thought an intuitive attempt to reconcile the greatest traditions of western political philosophy, that of "will and artifice" and that of "reason and nature". For general will is surely rationalized well. And yet it is not self rationalized will in a Kantian sense but will rationalized by the standards and conditions of idealized ancient polity. Whatever Rousseau means, in undertaking a fusion of two great modes of political thinking, and however unsuccessful the attempt to make general will a viable conception, one must always, while analyzing and even

> criticizing the result, grant the grandeur and importance of the effort. For if one could succeed in having the best of both idioms, one would have a political philosophy which would synthesize almost everything of value in the history of western political thought (Riley 1980: 97).

Rousseau amalgamated the cohesiveness and solidarity of the ancient Greek *polis* with modern voluntarism and the notion of individual freedom. His ideal republic would be a community of virtue, for only virtuous individuals could be truly free. A free society presupposed virtue. A whole community rested on moral law. From Plato Rousseau got the idea that political subjection was primarily moral and the community was the supreme ethical entity. The community was a moral and collective person and not merely an aggregation. He kept ancient Sparta and Rome in mind as models of his ideal republic. He described the community vested with a "General Will", a will of all individuals thinking of general and. public interests. It was the "Common Me", meaning that the best spirit of the individual was represented in it. The selfish nature of the human individual was transformed, bringing forth cooperative instincts and essential goodness.

> Both Rousseau and Kant denied that rational self-interest is a reputable moral motive and excluded prudence from the list of moral virtues. The outcome might be a more radical doctrine of equality that could be defended on grounds of reason and individual rights, since Rousseau supposed that the moral virtues exist in the greatest purity among the common people (Sabine 1973: 532).

The General Will would be the source of all laws. The human being would be truly free if he followed the dictates of the law. Civil liberty, for Rousseau, was similar to Locke's notion of freedom under civil law. It meant freedom from the assault of others. Individuals are free only if they have physical security. Freedom also meant eliminating the arbitrary will of another person and that would mean the establishment of the rule of law. None should have greater influence in the making of the law and no one would be above the law. Dependence upon a democratic law was liberating but dependence on the will of another person was most shameful. In the *Emile* Rousseau pointed out two kinds of dependence: "dependence on things which is the work of nature; and dependence on men, which is the work of society. Dependence on things, being non-moral, does no injury to liberty and begets no vices; dependence on men, being out of order, give rise to every kind of vice, and through this master and slave become mutually depraved. If there is any cure for this society evil, it is to be found in the substitution of law for the individual; in arming the General Will with a real strength beyond the power of any individual will". Of course, if one had to be free then one had to obey one's own will which meant that one's will and the laws of a state would have to be in harmony. Each individual would have to be a lawmaker, consenting to obey a law if it maximized freedom. Hence he desired that the state to be free would have to be a consensual and participatory democracy. He was categorical that the General Will could emerge only in an assembly of equal lawmakers. It could not be alienated. The "executive will" could not be the "General Will". Only the legislative will, which was sovereign, could be the General Will. Interestingly, the legislature was supreme for both Locke and Rousseau. While Locke defended *representative majoritarian democracy* within which the legislature was supreme, for Rousseau it was *direct democracy* that embodied the legislative will. The individual participated in the articulation of the General Will; for citizenship was the highest that one could aspire for. The General Will could not be the will of the majority. In fact, it did not represent the will of all. It was the difference between the sum of judgements about the common good and the mere aggregate of personal fancies and individual desires. It would always aim and promote the general interests and will of all its members.

> The body politic, therefore, is also a moral being which possesses a will; and this general will, *which always tends toward the conservation and well-being of the whole and of each part*, and which is the source of the laws, is for the members of the state in their relations both to one another and to the state, the rile of what is just and what is unjust (Rousseau 1958: 146).

Freedom, for Rousseau, was moral self-determination or the ability of the individual to exercise his autonomy. Unlike Hobbes and Locke, he did not define freedom as merely absence of restraint or coercion. Rousseau believed that submission to the General Will attenuated freedom. He had faith in the educative powers of political institutions to mould people's nature so that their "real" selves overwhelmed their narrow selfish concerns. The General Will would work if it was general in two respects: generality of origin, and of object. The former required that all laws be made by all citizens. Moreover, the laws should be such that they were in the general interest of everyone. This would ensure that the good of all was promoted.

> The Sovereign cannot impose on the subjects any fetters that are of no use to the community. It cannot even will to do so, for under the law of reason nothing takes places without a cause.... The commitments that bind us to the body politic are obligatory only because they are mutual, and their nature is such that in fulfilling them one cannot work for someone else without also working for oneself. Why is the general will always, right, and why do all constantly want the happiness of each of them, if not because everyone applies the word *each* to himself and thinks of himself as he votes for all (Rousseau ibid: 168).

Rousseau also distinguished between independence and liberty, separating them as exclusive of each other. Liberty consisted in acting according to one's wishes. It was not being subject to the wills of other people. Anyone who was a master over others was not himself free. He regarded liberty and equality as being interdependent. Unless people were *equal* they could not be *free*.

Rousseau rejected the idea of total surrender of powers, which made the individual submissive to the sovereign. This would ensure social peace without liberty. In response to Hobbes, he stated: "tranquillity is also found in dungeons; but is that enough to make them desirable places to live in?" Liberty was quintessentially human. Rousseau's concept of sovereignty differed from that of Hobbes and Locke. Hobbes spoke of a total surrender of powers by the individuals to a third party distinct from the people, and delineated the legal theory of sovereignty. Rousseau also spoke of total surrender, but not to a third party. Instead, sovereignty was vested in the political community. It was for this reason that Vaughan (1962) characterized Rousseau's sovereign as similar to Hobbes', with its head chopped off. Hobbes' conception of a personalized sovereign power was missing in Rousseau.

Sovereignty, for Rousseau, was inalienable and indivisible, but vested in the body politic, thereby expounding the concept of popular sovereignty. He was original, for he ruled out transfer of sovereignty and accepted the idea that sovereignty originated and stayed with the people (Cranston 1986: 92-97). Unlike Hobbes, for whom the sovereign was the ruler, the legal state, Rousseau distinguished the sovereignty of the people, the political community from that of the government. It provided the foundation of public right. Locke, on the other hand, shunned the idea of sovereignty for it suggested political absolutism. His conception of a limited state and individual rights led him to the idea that people were sovereign, but their sovereignty was held in abeyance when the government was in power, and within the government it was the legislature that was supreme.

Rousseau saw the government as an agent of the General Will, the sovereign entity in the body politic. Like Montesquieu, he believed all forms of government were not suited to all countries. A government had to reflect the character of a country and its people. He also proposed civil religion for cultivating the moral foundations of the state. Civil religion enabled the citizens to fulfil their duties. It promoted public interest.

> The dogmas of the civil religion ought to be simple, few in number, precisely worded, without explanations or commentaries. The existence of a powerful, intelligent, beneficent divinity that foresees and provides; the life to come; the happiness of the just; the punishment of the wicked; the sanctity of the social contract and of the laws. These are the positive dogmas. As for the negative dogmas, I have limited them to just one, namely intolerance. It is part of the cults we have excluded (Rousseau 1958: 179).

The sovereign could not oblige his citizens to believe these precepts, though Rousseau made belief a condition for membership of a community. A person who did not accept could be banished not because of impiety, but for unsociability, "for being incapable of sincerely loving the laws and justice, and of sacrificing his life, if necessary, for his duty" (Rousseau ibid: 226). Once a citizen had decided to abide by these precepts, he was bound to uphold them. The state could execute anyone who acted as if he did not believe them. For Rousseau, acceptance of religion indicated the limitations of reason.

Rousseau saw toleration as essential, but, like Locke, ruled out being tolerant towards the Roman Catholics and the atheists. He was also critical of philosophical anarchists, for whom law was not all that sacred. Like Machiavelli, he considered religion as necessary for providing a code of conduct and for binding the citizens emotionally to the state. It played an important role in the formation of national spirit. Rousseau tried to free the individual from the tyranny of the clergy, and instead subjected him to the religious principles dictated by the nature and necessities of the state itself. He insisted that only patriotic citizens could enjoy and cherish freedom. He spoke of national education which would eradicate superstitions and prejudices, for it was an education of character rather than of the intellect.

The most controversial aspect of the notion of the General Will was Rousseau's assertion that freedom consisted in following its dictates. True freedom could be realized if one followed the moral law that one had agreed to adhere to willingly and voluntarily. Freedom could not be through maximization of self-interest, but by promotion of certain common ends. The General Will held the key to the moral transformation of the individual, since it consisted of all the real wills as opposed to the actual will. The real will was the capacity and intention within the individual to aim for the general welfare of all. The actual will, however, was the selfish individual will. Rousseau tried to obviate human selfishness by designing democratic institutions that would provide the incentive to accept moral laws which advanced common interests. An important precondition was a certain level of economic and social equality. Even with the acceptance of the General Will, it was possible that there could be an erring individual who might be enslaved by his lower self, and therefore be unfree. In that case the individual could be "forced to be free".

Rousseau did not see any possibility of the General Will becoming tyrannical. As such, he did not provide any safeguards. He was an advocate of liberty involving self-mastery. It signified freedom to do something. Berlin (1969) regarded positive liberty as necessary for a decent humane existence, but found it problematic, for though autonomy and self-control were good, they could be perverted into a "freedom" to achieve "self lealization". Freedom, for Rousseau, meant obedience to a rational will, which in turn suggested the existence of one life plan, one way of life for all people. The metaphysical idea behind positive liberty was monism, that everything could be explained with reference to a single homogeneous principle and discoverable laws. Rousseau's shared experience of life became commonality of interests for Burke. A defence of positive liberty led to determinism and totalitarianism. Rousseau's vision was illiberal, for it presumed that all moral, political and social conflict was a symptom of immorality or unreason, if not error. It also presupposed that a harmonious and conflictless community symbolized identity of wills among free individuals.

ROLE OF THE LEGISLATOR

Rousseau believed that one of the reasons for the success of ancient republics was the role of the legislator. A legislator, an exceedingly rare figure in moments of history with superhuman responsibilities, created persons capable of constituting the General Will. The role of the legislator would be to transform individuals and change human nature, alter the constitution with the purpose of strengthening it, and bring about a complete moral existence to an otherwise partial one. The legislator was a charismatic figure with semi-divine qualities. He was independent of the people, but would devote himself to their happiness by protecting their interests. Rousseau had the same adulation for legislators that one found subsequently in Burke.

The legislator played a key role in the establishment of the state, but not in its routine law-making functions. He proposed laws with the support of the people. Rousseau frequently mentioned Lycurgus, the lawgiver of Sparta as an example. Interestingly, he suggested that he was qualified to be an appropriate legislator for Corsica and Poland. The legislator had to be aware of the size of the territory, which had to be small and compact for self-sufficiency and self-government. Like Plato and Aristotle, he felt that moral character and political participation were best possible in a society that was fairly equal and with sufficient material goods. He did not have any conception of a mass society. Rousseau also gave centrality to the role of education in moulding character, shaping opinions and tastes. He was equally concerned with public ceremonies and public education, for these would instil a sense of national patriotism.

CRITIQUE OF LIBERAL REPRESENTATIVE GOVERNMENT

For Rousseau, contrary to a representative parliamentary government, a *participatory democracy* was desirable, for it secured freedom, self-rule, equality and virtue. These were things that justified restraints on the individual, for they would make him truly happy. And since no existing government fulfilled all these criteria, none of them had an absolute claim to an individual's obedience. Salvation of the individual would be through politics and not through religion (Colletti 1969: 146). It was with the destruction of the present coercive society, and with the institution of a free form of political and ethical community that salvation would be attained. Rousseau, like Plato, believed in the primacy of politics.

Rousseau rejected the English parliamentary system of government, for it gave the people the illusion of freedom whereas in reality the English people were free only during the time of elections. Once representatives were elected, people lost their freedom.

> Sovereignty cannot be represented, for the same reason that it cannot be alienated ... the people's deputies are not, and could not be, its representatives; they are merely its agents; and they cannot decide anything faintly. And law which the people has not ratified in person is void; it is not law at all. The English people believes itself to be free; it is gravely mistaken; it is free only during the election of Members of Parliament; as soon as the Members are elected, the people is enslaved; it is nothing (Rousseau 1958: 141).

Rousseau firmly believed that freedom was a reality when people actually governed and took part in the law-making process. It was when people exercised their freedom devoid of appetites that they were truly their own masters. He therefore proposed direct participation in legislation, for human will could not be represented. The contract enabled the citizens to be as free as the individuals, for:

> In giving himself to all, each person gives himself to no one. And since there is no associate over whom he does not acquire the same right that he would grant others over himself, he gains the equivalent of everything he loses, along with a greater amount of force to preserve what he has (Rousseau ibid: 153).

The identification and submersion of the individual with the community was something that went against the liberal argument which strictly defended the protection of an individual's private space, and over which the individual was the sovereign person. The fact that the individual had rights was a kind of a protective shield through which the individual safeguarded his autonomy. This implied that the individual had rights against the state, which could be invoked when the state overstepped the limits of its authority.

Rousseau tried to grapple with the problem of devising public life in a manner that would secure and protect the moral liberty of the individual. Liberty was obedience to self-prescribed laws. He saw the need for democratic institutions to protect the true freedom of the individual. He rejected representative institutions as these were based on the idea of "winners take it all". He ruled out competitiveness not only in economics but also in politics, for competitiveness killed cooperation and fellow feeling. On the other hand, anarchy was unpleasant. Moral liberty could be secured only in an association in which not only was the whole community defended and protected, but also the individual member. He ruled out factions and organized interest groups, for they undermined popular sovereignty and moral liberty. Law had to be made by fully-informed and equal citizens. To a Lockeian liberal, Rousseau's identification of liberty with the public domain would seem illiberal, which was why many of Rousseau's critics saw Rousseau's "General Will" inspiring twentieth-century totalitarian leaders like Hitler and Stalin. Rousseau rejected the Lockeian liberal solution of instituting government for the protection of private property, for even though all were treated equally it would only lead to formal equality. It was to the advantage of the rich, who wished to protect their property from the poor. Rousseau derived a great deal of inspiration from Locke, but differed significantly from his prescriptions of limited government and a minimal state.

Rousseau has been the inspiration to theorists of participatory democracy in recent times. Pateman (1970) drawing insights from Rousseau observed the inconsistency that existed between universal formal rights and class inequality in participation which she felt could be resolved only through institutions that encourage self-management. Democracy at the workplace would have to deal with complex problems like market instabilities, coordination of resources and availability of different types of labour and skills. Democracy also would have to be reconciled with efficiency and leadership. She accepted the core institutions of liberal democracy, competitive parties, political representatives, periodic elections but she favoured direct participation and control over immediate local bodies complemented by party and interest group competition in governmental affairs.

FEDERATION OF NATIONS FOR WORLD PEACE

The ideals of republicanism and democracy ushered in by the two major revolutions in the eighteenth century, in America and France, also saw the rise of a school of pacifist thinking that rejected the medieval moral-legal doctrine of war, including that of just war. The notion of just war posited that there be a just cause, a right authority for initiating the use of force, a right intention on the part of the party/parties employing such force, that the resort to force be proportional (not doing more harm than good), that it be a last resort, that it be undertaken with the end of peace as its goal and there a reasonable hope of success. Three types of just cause were recognized in the Middle Ages: to retake something wrongfully taken, to punish evil and to defend against an attack either planned or in progress. All these ideas existed in the Roman thought and the practice of war in the classical era. In the twentieth century international law self-defence against an armed attack in progress was the major justification for the use of force.

The pacifist writers—Desiderius Erasmus (1466/1469–1536), More (1478–1535), John Amos Comenius (1592–1670), Emeric Crucé (1590–1648), Francois Fénelon (1651–1715), William Penn (1644–1718), Abbé de St. Pierre's (1658–1743), Voltaire, Rousseau, Kant and Bentham derived their inspiration from the Stoics and early Christian radical positions and were reinforced by the then European ideals of cosmopolitanism, humanitarianism and bourgeois internationalism. Common in their perceptions was their profound skepticism to war and the military profession and the great goal of life for European intellectuals was human happiness without any trace of the tragic (Hazard 1963: 18). There was considerable disagreement as to the means—whether it would be through the application of scientific and technical reason or through man's return to nature and rediscovery of his original simplicity—but all of them were convinced that society was on the threshold of breaking away from the shackles of traditional authority and superstition, erase the historic curses of ignorance, disease and war and begin as articulated by Condorcet 'upon the absolutely indefinite perfectibility of man, which knows no other limit than the duration of the globe upon which nature has placed us'. There was complete cynicism about the doctrine of just war seen as smokescreen to hide the aggressive impulses of ambitious monarchs. However, none of them at the turn of the eighteenth century, including Kant, advocated world government, as they resisted the "very idea of concentrating power in the form of world government.... The mood was one of suspicion of all political power and of faith in the beneficence of individual human reason and wisdom" (Heater 1990: 55). Montesquieu pointed out that reason would help human beings discover universally valid rules of reciprocity, which, if enforced by positive law, would maintain peace, security and a certain degree of fairness within civil society. Montesquieu, reiterating Mandeville counted on the transformation of human existence by the 'spirit of commerce' guided by the new science of finance or economics. Commercialization would help human beings get rid of their prejudices that veil their true needs. By recognizing the common need and aspirations, human beings discovered their humanity thus transcending previous religious, ethnic and national sectarianism. Once captivated by the allure of peaceful trade, human beings would look to military exploits and war with increasing disgust. Commerce brought in frugality, economy, moderation, work prudence, tranquility, order and rule. Montesquieu's defence of manufactures, commerce, finance, riches and even luxury enabled him to not only take his stand with the moderns and against the Greeks but also influence Bentham and Kant to regard trade and commerce as the basis of perpetual peace. Voltaire poked fun at the two kings each of whom had *Te Deums* sung in his own camp after the battle and defends a republican government as it allows people to constantly renew the sovereign power, a point central to the Kantian thesis for perpetual peace. Voltaire was ambivalent about people's right to revolt and dismiss an unjust ruler. Despite considering the republican government as the ideal he supported constitutional monarchy ruled by an enlightened despot.

The eighteenth century was full of projects for abolishing war and establishing peace, namely that of Crucé *Le Nouveau Cynée* or *The New Cyneas* (1623), Penn's *Essay toward the Present and Future Peace of Europe* (1693), St. Pierre's *A Project for Making Peace Perpetual in Europe* (1713),

Rousseau's *A Lasting Peace through the Federation of Europe* (1774), Kant's *Perpetual Peace* (1795) and Bentham's *Plan for a Universal and Perpetual Peace* (1789). Crucé suggested that armies should be abolished and called for a world court. Crucé's importance was his foresight that international organizations were crucial to solve international disputes. Among the various peace plans Penn was the pioneer to have envisioned disarmament as the most effective guarantee for international peace. He stressed the importance of peace in view of the suffering and destruction that war entails. War could be prevented within a framework of justice for both individuals and groups if conflicts could be resolved in a fair way. Justice could be ensured if governments enforced laws impartially. For maintaining peace in Europe, he proposed a Sovereign Parliament of European states to decide disputes collectively and enforce decisions though states could still maintain their sovereignty in internal matters, thus anticipating the European Union.

Rousseau like Abbé de St. Pierre's (1658–1743) believed that federation established lasting peace. He summarized Pierre's voluminous plans and pointed out that while private wars have been prevented with the institution of governments, larger wars could be prevented with the formation of a federation that would unite nations just as nations, unite individuals under the authority of law. He observed that such an arrangement was not new as it existed, in an embryonic form, in the Germanic Body, the Helvetic League, and the States General of the Netherlands, and the ancients had the Greek Amphictyons, the Etruscan Lucumonies, Latin *feriae,* and the city leagues of the Gauls. For the success of the federation, Rousseau stipulated four necessary conditions: (1) every important power must be a member; (2) the laws they legislate must be binding; (3) a coercive force must be capable of compelling every state to obey the common resolves; and (4) no member may be allowed to withdraw.

Rousseau's plan consisted of five articles. The first will set up a permanent alliance with a congress to settle and terminate by arbitration or judicial pronouncement all conflicts. The second will decide which nations shall have a vote, how the presidency shall pass from one to another and how the contribution quotas shall be raised to provide for common expenses. The third declared the permanence of existing boundaries. The fourth specified how violators shall be banned and forced to comply by the means of the arms of all the confederates. The fifth recommended majority vote to begin with but three quarters after five years and unanimity to change the articles.

Rousseau explained how his plan would remove the six motives that lead to war and these motives could be (1) to make conquests, (2) to protect themselves from aggression, (3) to weaken further a powerful neighbour, (4) to maintain their rights against attack, (5) to settle a difference which has defied friendly negotiation and (6) to fulfil some treaty obligations. Rousseau was confident that with the exception of conquest the federation will be able to accomplish all the other purposes and even in conquest it will be able to deter by marshalling all the powers against the aggressors. Rousseau listed many of the evils and dangers that prevailed in Europe of his time, such as injustice because of might, insecurity of nations, military expenses due to external attacks or their threats, no guarantee for international agreements, unsafe and expensive means of obtaining justice when a wrong was committed, risk and inconvenience of wars, loss of trade during crises and general impoverishment and lack of security. The benefits of arbitration were certainty of settling disputes peacefully, abolition of the causes of disputes, personal security for rulers, fulfilment of agreements between rulers, freedom of trade, reduced military expenses, increase in population, agriculture and public wealth and happiness. Rousseau also concluded that St. Pierre's plans were not adopted because the princes were short-sighted in their ambition and greed for power. The other related reasons were their refusal to submit themselves to arbitration and their blind pursuit of their self-interest neglecting the wisdom of general good. He considered revolution as the only means to establish the federation but sensing the violence it would unleash, he realized that it would be dreaded and would be difficult to establish under the existing circumstances.

WOMEN AND FAMILY

Rousseau defended the patriarchal family. He saw the family as a natural institution, and the oldest of all societies. It was based on natural ties of love and affection, and originated in the biological process of procreation and in the natural differences between the sexes. The family provided the model for other social institutions that were natural. Within the family, age preceded youth, and males had a natural authority over females. In fact, he regarded women as a permanently subversive force within the political system, a point reiterated subsequently by Hegel. He preferred patriarchal families, partly because they needed a single authority (which could not be exerted by the wife because she periodically got confined by reproductive activities), and partly because the man had to dominate his wife to ensure that she was chaste and virtuous. He repeatedly argued that a good woman would stay within the family circle, avoiding social distractions and political preoccupations. It was interesting to note that Rousseau's concerns with natural goodness and social corruption did not figure in his analysis of the status of women. He assigned a subordinate position to women in society, and an education that would be suitable to an inferior position.

For Rousseau, men and women differed in virtues. While a man's virtue was his rational capacity, a woman's virtue was her sexuality, which meant chastity, gentleness and obedience. Since the functions of men and women differed, their education would also have to be different.

The difference in the biological constitution of women—pregnancy, nursing the young—did not enable them to be at par with men, and thereby engage in activities that were similar to the ones that men pursued. While men could have the maximum freedom, women would be trained in accepting the constraints and dictates of social and public opinion. If women tried to be like men, they would cease to have qualities that were purely womanly. On the contrary, they would acquire qualities of both men and women, which they would be unable to reconcile and assimilate, falling below their own standards. The woman had an identity only in relation to a man, and therefore her education had to be geared to please and be at the mercy of a man.

> Woman is specially made for man's delight. If man in his turn ought to be pleasing in her eyes, the necessity is less urgent, his virtue is in his strength, he pleases because he is strong. I grant you this is not the law of love, but it is the law of nature, which is older than love itself … . If woman is made to please and to be in subjection to man, she ought to make herself pleasing in his eyes and not provoke him to anger (Rousseau 1911: 322).

Rousseau did not think women to be suitable for abstract and speculative truths, and for principles and axioms of scientific study. For Rousseau their studies would be *practical*, for women loved finery, were naturally cunning and more talkative than men. He pointed out that little girls loved to play with dolls and took to sewing rather than reading and writing. He did not believe that traits in children developed out of the socializing process.

Rousseau regarded women as a source of sexual passion. Nature had made women the stimulator of men's passions, hence men had to try and please them if their desires were to be satisfied. Men in this sense were dependent on women, who controlled them through their gentleness, their kindness and their tears to get what they wanted. As long as men were dependent on women for love, women would get what they wanted. The sole protection men had was to repress women's sexuality and their own passionate selves.

> He (Rousseau) was one of the most powerful critics of the notion of original sin, and insisted on the natural goodness of man, especially his sexual desire—if sexism means insistence on essential differentiation of function between men and women both naturally and socially, then Rousseau was indeed a sexist. If on the other hand it means treating women as objects and subordinating them, he certainly was not a sexist. Rather he was concerned with enhancing the power of women over … . It is the related-ness, the harmonious relatedness of men and women, which he takes as the model and foundation of all human relatedness (Bloom 1986: 71).

Rousseau, like Aristotle, regarded the family as the first form of society, though the relationships within a family needed a different kind of regulation from the ones within the state. The relationship between the father and children was based on love and the superior physical strength of the father. Paternal authority was established by nature as long as the children needed protection. The father needed the ultimate and sole control over his wife's sexual independence in order to assert his control over the children. Rousseau reinforced the "renewed eighteenth century emphasis on female chastity and monogamy" (Eisenstein 1986: 60). He recommended the Athenian model where women confined themselves to the private space of the home, enjoying the status of a wife, mother and householder, and wrote:

> When Greek women married, they disappeared from public life; within the four walls of their home they devoted themselves to the care of their household and family. This is the mode of life prescribed for women alike by nature and reason (Rousseau 1911: 330).

Paradoxical as it may seem at first glance, Rousseau did not accept patriarchal households where the husband/father was the absolute person with total authority over his wife and children. He believed in the ideal of a compassionate marriage where the wife was a companion to her husband. It was for this reason that a woman had to be educated up to a point of making her agreeable to her husband and intelligent to her children, *but not beyond that*. A free, equal, rational and independent being with a mind was beyond his conception. Many of these arguments were critically analyzed and rejected by Wollstonecraft in her *A Vindication of the Rights of Woman* (1792).

It was suggested that Rousseau did not consider women as inferior, but accorded them a subordinate position for the sake of the family which he held very dear. However, there was no denying the fact that Rousseau, who had been the first to highlight the effects of inequalities and questioned many of the inherited assumptions, reiterated many of the male prejudices without critically dissecting them. He also failed to articulate an equal status for women in the family and home. However, he glorified women as mothers and wives, roles most women performed.

> There were a few greater enemies of sexual equality than Jean-Jacques Rousseau, yet he was revered and adored by women everywhere .... Rousseau might have told women (gracefully) that they were weak and stupid, but he also told them that they were beautiful, that they were the moral ally of humanity and that they are utterly necessary for men's happiness .... The secret of Rousseau's success was he glorified and aggrandized women in the only career open to them that of wife and mother—and he promised them in return love, respect and happiness. It might have been a more subtle form of belittlement and new justification for exploitation disguised as sentimentalism but it set the tone for much of the nineteenth century (Proctor 1990: 179).

Though Rousseau was inspired by Plato, he did not share Plato's belief in sexual equality and giving women a share in the political process.

CONCLUSION

Rousseau's theory, like Marx's, was international in character. There was a conception of the human family and an international federation as the end of his political ideal. He also projected the body politic as a moral being which would preserve the welfare of the whole as well as its constituent parts. It was the source of all laws, and determined the relationships between its members. It would be an end in itself and also a means to an end. Rousseau was also seen as the spiritual father of the French Revolution of 1789. Burke referred to him as "the insane Socrates of the National Assembly". Many of the ideas of Rousseau were put into practice during the "later and more terrible phases of the Revolution" (Vaughan 1962: 21–22).

Rousseau provided an excellent analysis of human nature in politics. He refused to look at the individual as a supernatural entity. He rejected the idea of natural sociability that the ancients propounded, and also the notion of radical selfishness and egoism that the moderns stressed on. He supported the idea of transformation of human nature from a narrow self-seeking being into a public-spirited person. He took the individual as he was, "partly rational, partly emotional, influenced by considerations of utility, but even more swayed by passions and prejudices, at bottom moral and virtuous, but easily corrupted by bad institutions, and in most cases, dependent for the maintenance of his virtue of good ones. He brought to the fore the importance of ethics in politics as he was not interested merely in happiness or utility" (Cassirer 1946: 70). In the last resort, the value of Rousseau's political thought, "was not completely individualist, while at the same time it was equally not based on any glorification of society as distinct from the individuals of which it was composed" (Cobban 1964: 168). He had the most rigorous and revolutionary theory of sovereignty conceived as omnipotent and omnipresent. The state represented the pinnacle of human existence, the source of all morality, freedom and community. Its purpose was not merely to resolve conflicts, but to be a means to liberate the individual from the uncertainties and hypocrisies of traditional society. The state was a redeemer of the individual, enabling the latter to escape the "torments, insecurities and dissensions of ordinary society" (Nisbet 1990: 125–126, 138). "Sovereignty, for Rousseau, is not a mere legal thing; it is the sum total of all virtues and even freedoms" (Nisbet ibid: 110).

The individual and the state were two themes in Rousseau's theory. Both were simultaneously sovereign. Both were needed to realize a just social and political order. To see Rousseau as an individualist or a champion of state absolutism would be to do injustice to the complex kaleidoscopic nature of his political philosophy. What emerged was a radical individualism on the one hand,and uncompromising authoritarianism on the other (Nisbet ibid: 126). His individualism was not in the sense of an immunity from the state, but one that was coextensive of the state.

Rousseau's political philosophy, by implication, according to Cobban, discussed the subject matter of the politics of the twentieth century, like the reality of nationalism, state sovereignty, the need for economic equality and the state's role in realizing it, the bases of popular politics and the reconciliation of these with the principles of politics based on a rational, self-determining individual (Cobban 1964: 170). Rousseau also pointed out the close relation-ship between liberty and equality, and the fact that without equality, liberty would be non-existent. He abandoned his initial hostility to property, and accepted it as an essential institution of society. Unlike Locke, he recognized how property could become an instrument of private domination, which was why property had to be controlled by the General Will. He considered property as being the root cause of moral corruption and injustice. Since industrial society was not yet an existing reality, he idealized a property-owning society where everyone would be equal and independent. In this he retained the Lockeian spirit.

Liberty, for Rousseau, was the greatest good. Liberty was only possible when dependence between human beings was eliminated, if not at least regulated by law. He understood liberty as participation and popular sovereignty. It was for this reason that many see his philosophy as being compatible with collectivism, Jacobinism, despotism and totalitarianism. It was anti-Lockeian, for there was no effort to preserve the rights of the individual against the state (Vaughan 1962: 48). The *Social Contract* sounded the death-knell of individualism, which had held sway since the days of Locke (Vaughan ibid: 138).

Rousseau's theory was egalitarian, anti-hierarchical, republican and democratic. Like Locke and Montesquieu, he was critical of the nobility and benevolent despots and upheld the rule of law. Nobody (other than Rousseau) stressed the importance of community on the grounds that interdependence and cooperation enhanced the powers of human beings, and that socialization enabled them to acquire consciousness and rationality. However, he was not an unabashed supporter or admirer of modern society and civilization.

> Rousseau's solution for the ills of society was not to beckon men to the woods, nor to advocate the destruction of all social inter-dependencies. He proposed, instead, paradox: let us create a society which causes men to grow close to one another, to become so strongly solidary that each member will be made dependent on the whole society and, by that very fact, be released from personal dependencies (Wolin 1960: 371).

There was no denying the fact that Rousseau's political philosophy was one of the most innovative, striking, remarkable, and brilliantly-argued theories. In the entire history of social and political ideas, there were only a few parallels to his edifice in its force of argument and passion for outlining a structure which was supposed to put an end to, most, if not all, human predicaments.

His most spectacular achievement was that he understood the pivotal problem that faced individuals in society—how to reconcile individual interests with those of the larger interests of society. He tried to resolve this delicate problem in his own way, by depicting human nature in operation under the sway of an all-comprehensive political structure. The attempt by itself was highly laudable, as this was the most important problem that a political theorist faced, and in most cases the resolution was far from satisfactory.

Rousseau's influence has changed over the last three centuries. In the eighteenth century, he was seen as a critic of the status quo, challenging the concept of progress, the core of the Enlightenment belief-structure. In the nineteenth century, he was seen as the apostle of the French Revolution and the founder of the Romantic Movement. In the twentieth century, he has been hailed as the founder of the democratic tradition, while at the same time assailed for being the philosophical inspiration of totalitarianism. These indicate that it has not been possible to interpret Rousseau within a single framework of analysis.

Rousseau was not Eurocentric in the same sense as Hegel, Marx, J.S. Mill and Montesquieu. He certainly transcended the localism that characterized their philosophies. While he scored on this front, he fell abysmally short in extending the conception of human equality to include women. He was a powerful exponent of human equality, which, paradoxically, did not include gender as a category. Had he perhaps overcome the prejudices of his time, he could have become the first spokesperson of a true, universal paradigm of an ideal political order.

8

Immanuel Kant

> Kant is a political philosopher of the very first rank whose evolutionary political goals would, if actually realized, constitute a valuable revolution in history (Riley 1987: 267).

> What Kant aimed to set forth in the *Critique of Pure Reason* was the limits of pure reason. He had to solve this problem by logical means. He spoke as an epistemologist, limiting knowledge to its own domain, to the field of possible experience and to the principles of morality (Cassirer 1945: 78).

> The *Critique of Pure Reason* is the most important work of philosophy to have written in modern times; it is also one of the most difficult. It poses questions so novel and comprehensive that Kant judged it necessary to invent technical terms with which to discuss them. These terms have a strange beauty and compellingness, and it is impossible to acquire a full appreciation of Kant's work without experiencing the order and connectedness that his vocabulary imposes upon the traditional problems of philosophy (Scruton 1982: 10).

Immanuel Kant (1724–1804), along with Gottfried Wilhelm Leibniz (1646–1716), primarily a mathematician, and Johannes Wolfgang von Goethe (1749–1832), a writer, were the leading figures of the German Enlightenment or *Aufklarung* that began around 1650, and ended around 1800. In the absence of religious conflict and hostility between the nobility and the middle class, German Enlightenment was different from the enlightenment movements in other parts of the world. It developed and led to cultural and then national unity, and greater freedom of press and an improved judicial system. On the whole, it helped to develop modern German philosophy. Unlike French philosophy that was empiricist, German philosophy embraced mysticism. The German thinkers were more erudite but also more professorial and more abstract than their British and French counterparts. Unlike Britain, Germany did not offer much to the intellectuals by way of taking part in politics mainly because of a different and an authoritarian political structure. Kant, undoubtedly a striking personality of the period with his faith in human rationality and perfectibility, described the enlightenment as

> the liberation of man from self-imposed tutelage. Tutelage is the incapacity of using one's own understanding except under the direction of another. This tutelage is self-imposed when its cause lies not in the lack of understanding but in a lack of resolution and of courage... . Dare to use your own understanding. That is the motto of Enlightenment. Self thinking was to seek the highest touchstone of truth in one's self, i.e., one's own reason (Kant cited in Hallowell 1960: 118).

In the general background of the period of the enlightenment, the French Revolution of 1789 exerted considerable impact on Germany. It aroused German political thinking from its deep slumber and paved the way for modern political thought (Gooch 1920; Reiss 1970: 8). Many, in Germany, welcomed the revolution at first regarding it as the dawn of the new age. But the disillusionment set in with the onset of reign of terror. Kant and Goethe, the then two leading minds in Germany assessed correctly that while the revolution answered a great political need in France, the situation in Germany was still not ready for revolutionary activity. The bourgeoisie had come into existence in Germany, as in Britain and France, but it had not become emancipated from the dominance of the princes and aristocracy. Germany was relatively poorer as compared to Britain and France and despite the self-confidence of the bourgeoisie, political freedom was restricted. Freedom of speech meant freedom to criticize religion, but not the government. Another impeding factor was the small size of most German principalities as that meant much closer supervision of the subjects by rulers than in larger countries. Bureaucratic control and the lack of economics of scale hindered economic development sapping the self-confidence of the bourgeoisie. But in spite of such formidable local impediments, Kant, transcending such localism could embark on the boldest attempt to grasp the spirit of the enlightenment and think of a higher state in human evolution.

Kant's most seminal contribution was in making politics subordinate to morals, and the need to treat all individuals as means and ends. He spoke of the importance of reason and the need for international peace. His philosophy was essentially individualistic and liberal. Kant's philosophy, because of these reasons, has continued to inspire subsequent political theorists, particularly within liberalism. Kant's theory was individualistic, a philosophy that affirmed the supreme worth of the individual. This belief in the primacy of the individual was first explicitly stated by Hobbes and developed by Locke.

In the eighteenth century, problem of political obligation within a community was also a problem of human relations which could be best resolved by recognizing individual rights and obligations. Kant, who belonged to this school, defined the community as the 'kingdom of ends' which meant treating humanity in one's own person, and in that, of others as an end and as means but never as means alone. Its philosophical foundation were laid down by Rousseau and according to Kant, Rousseau was a restorer of the rights of humanity, a thinker who unmasked the distortions and concealment and discovered the 'real human person'. Kant was concerned with moral law and autonomy of human will which he identified with the realization of freedom.

LIFE SKETCH

Kant was born in a poor and pious family of Scottish descent in 1724. He was the fourth of the nine children in a family of harness-maker. He entered the university at the age of 16, and graduated six years later. Unable to secure an academic position, Kant worked as a private tutor in many homes. He obtained a post at the age of 31 as private docent without a salary with responsibilities of delivering public lectures and securing meagre reward from private tuitions.

Kant led a quiet life as a professor in his native town Konigsberg. His fame rested on three philosophical treatises *Critique of Pure Reason* (1781), *Critique of Practical Reason* (1788) and *Judgment* (1790). His political ideas were developed after the French Revolution of 1789 in *Towards Eternal Peace* (1795), the *Metaphysical Elements of Justice* (1797) and *The Conflict of the Faculties* (1798). He subscribed to the idea the politics ought to be governed by moral principles even though he made a clear distinction between moral motives and legal motives. The *Critique of Pure Reason* was in response to the questions on perception and reality posed by Descartes, Hume, Leibniz and other contemporaries. It proposed that all persons were born with an innate sense of raw experience which Kant termed as transcendental idealism. While the enlightenment philosophy in general proposed that the human mind discovered the law of nature for Kant, it was the mind that gave the laws of nature. The *Critique of Pure Reason* stated that human beings were born with ideas and perceptions of the world and, as such, would not be possible to know what was real and what our perception was and, therefore, empirical evidence could not be tested either. In pointing out that only a select few universal truths in the world were valid, Kant effectively diverged with the premise of the entire French enlightenment. In the *Groundwork for the Metaphysics of Morals* (1785) Kant argued for reason as the basis for moral action and that any action undertaken out of convenience or obedience could be considered moral, even if it was the right action to take. The morality of an action depended on the motivation for the action.

Kant was influenced profoundly by Rousseau, whom he admired and revered and whose portrait hung prominently in his study. Interestingly, Rousseau's portrait was the only one that he possessed. It was well known that Kant, who was known for his punctuality and clock work regular routine forget time when he received Rousseau's *Emile* (1760). He was so absorbed reading the book that he forgot his daily walk. He regarded Rousseau "not as a founder of a new system, but as the thinker who possessed a new conception of the nature and function of philosophy, of its vocation and dignity" (Cassirer 1945: 1). Out of the Kantian philosophy emerged subjective idealism of Johann Gottlieb Fichte (1762–1814), Friedrich Wilhelm Joseph von Schelling (1775–1854) and Hegel. Arthur Schopenhauer (1788–1860) too was influenced by Kant.

Kant led a life filled with routine and discipline. It was said that housewives in Konigsberg would set their clock by his time of passing. His house was simple and Spartan. He had instructed his manservant to wake him up at 5 o'clock every morning. He would work till 7 o'clock wearing his nightcap and robe. After delivering his morning lectures he would return to study till one and then have a single meal and following it with a walk no matter what the weather was like. He liked to walk alone believing that conversation would cause men to breathe in open air which was unhealthy. His love for solitude was balanced by his desire for people. He invited people to join him during his midday meals, ensuring a favourite dish of his guest was prepared, conversing delightfully till 3 o'clock and ending the meal with a hearty laughter. He believed that laughter would lead to better digestion. He was averse to noise, music and visual arts. He twice contemplated marriage, but never got married.

Kant delivered his last lecture in 1796. Towards the end of his life he lost clarity of mind, the ability to recognize his friends and even to complete a simple sentence. He became senile. He finally died on 12th February 1804. His funeral was attended by a large number of people. In spite of his senility, he was regarded as the best mind and the greatest glory of Konigsberg. His grave was restored in 1881 after having crumbled. His remains were removed in 1924 and deposited with a cathedral. In 1950, the sarcophagus was broken and vandalized. By that time, Konigsberg ceased to be a seat of learning, became a part of the former Soviet Union and was renamed after one of Stalin's henchmen. Even during the heyday of communism in the Munich University Kant's immortal phrase, written in the *Critique of Practical Reason* and engraved on the wall of Konigsberg castle, 'Two things fill the heart with ever renewed and increasing awe and reverence, the more often and the more steadily we mediate upon them: *the starry firmament above and the moral law within* was not erased which explained Kant's standing at a time when those in power were totally against his philosophy.

Context of Kant's Political Thought

Most of Kant's political thought was written after the completion of the first treatise, the *Critique of Pure Reason,* in 1781. He considered rationalism and empiricism as inadequate methods of explanation to account for mathematics and science, particularly Newtonian science. The problem with induction was brought out by Hume, thereby arousing Kant from his dogmatic slumber. In order to refute Hume and to vindicate science philosophically he began his enquiry from mind rather than experience. According to him the laws of nature were constructions of the mind and not inherent in nature. The world had to be explained with reference to necessary principles logically prior to and independent of experience, and not merely with reference to experience and only then it was possible to see any order in nature. It was the mind that enforced uniformity, coherence and order. It was noteworthy that Kant had the greatest respect for empirical fact and was a scientist, but observed that the world of appearances or the phenomenal world was not self-sufficient for the purpose of explanation; on the contrary what was required was *a priori* principles and ideas of reason. Therefore, the philosophical problem of epistemology which he took up how was synthetic *a priori* judgements possible? In other words, the question was the need to formulate propositions that were necessary, universal, logically independent of sense experience and capable of being contradicted. He referred to this function of mind in ordering scientific experience as the Copernican revolution in philosophy and his arguments and elaboration in the *Critique of Pure Reason* was innovative in philosophy. Other than areas of human experience, how to understand science through moral experience was the subject of the *Critique*.

To understand moral conduct it was necessary to discover rules or principles which were logically independent of experience and capable of contradiction. These rules, he called practical synthetic *a priori* judgements, and these underline all moral decisions and were inherent in all arguments about moral issues. In order to justify these rules we must suppose that a person was not only a phenomenal being, subject to strict casual laws, but also a noumenal being who was free. Moral decisions were only possible only if the will was assumed to be free to act. Each person had a will which alone made a moral choice and to will was to decide on action. An action, however, was a moral only if it was done for the sake of duty. In a case of conflict of interest this criterion allowed us to distinguish between actions which were right and those which were not. It allowed us to distinguish between duty and desire. Kant called the general moral law the categorical imperative as it categorically instructed us to act in accordance with the objective principle of morality. Not only was a person a means for the arbitrary use of this will or that, but in all his actions he must be regarded at the same time as an end. This assumption led to the second formulation of the categorical imperative which was "Act always so that you treat humanity whether in your person or in that of another always as an end, but never as a means only". Its implication was that man should not merely be subject to another will but he should be his own law-giver. This led to another formulation of the categorical imperative which said, "Act always in such a way as if you through your maxims a law-making member of a universal kingdom of ends". To act for the sake of duty was to act in order to conform to some self-imposed law' suggesting that man's actions did not take place in a vacuum, but always in relation to other men, thus alluding to a system of principles that govern organized human relations. Kant made it clear that the pursuit of happiness, if made the maxim of one's actions, the will was not autonomous; it did not then live under self-imposed laws, but followed heteronomous principles on which, a sound moral theory could not be established. A practical law of reason, on the contrary, was the principle which made certain actions a duty. Kant regarded all propositions of right are *a priori* propositions; as they are law of reason. Politics for him was a part of metaphysics of morality as it dealt with the question of what we ought to do in our social and political context and it was concerned with establishing criteria by which we could settle public conflicts of interests. The principle of universality required that our social and political relations should be governed and our public conflicts settled in a universal manner and that necessitated the existence of law. The principles of morality went beyond purely legal questions as they affected private inner decisions by men which could neither be regulated nor enforced publicly. Law was the outer shell of the moral realm that made inner decisions. Moral actions could be commanded while legal actions were enforced. An action was a moral action only if the maxim on which it was based agreed with the idea of duty; morality was concerned with subjective motives while law was concerned with the actions themselves, i.e. with objective facts.

POLITICAL IDEAS

The principles of right (*Recht*) were the principles of politics based on law. For Kant, it was never right that ought to be adapted to politics; on the contrary, it was politics which ought always to be adapted to right. The philosophical examination into politics must establish political actions that were just or unjust. It must show by what principles demands of justice could be made in a given situation. Justice must be universal and it could be brought about only by law. A coherent political order must then be a legal order. As in ethics, actions ought to be based on maxims capable of being formulated as universal laws, in politics, political arrangements ought to be organized according to universally valid laws. What mattered was the arrangement which established that the free actions of one person can be reconciled with the freedom of the other in accordance with a universal law resulting in the universal principle of right which reads as follows: "Every action which by itself or by its maxim enables the freedom of each individual's will to coexist with the freedom of everyone else in accordance with a universal law is right". This universal principle of right imposed an obligation upon a person, but it did not expect, let alone required him to act in accordance with it. It directed that if freedom had to be restricted in accordance with right, and if justice was to prevail, it must do so in accordance with this universal principle of right. To restrict freedom in this manner did not entail interfering with the freedom of an individual but merely establish the conditions of his external freedom. The universal principle of right was basically an application of the universal principle of morality, as outlined in the categorical imperative, to the domain of law, and thus to the arena of politics. Since it was morally necessary to realize external freedom a person could be compelled by others to carry out his duty of entering civil society. In doing so one needs to become morally better off. Political problem must be capable of solution not only by good men but by a nation of devils. The basis of a constitution and of all laws was allowing the 'greatest possible human freedom in accordance with laws which ensure that the freedom of each can coexist with the freedom of all the others'. This for Kant was the universal principle of political right. From this all other principles of politics follow.

A state was a union of a group of men under laws based on the principle that we ought to be treated as ends and not as means, and since we must be considered our own law-givers, we should be asked to consider as right only those laws to which we could agree or ought to have agreed if we had been asked to do so. An important corollary of this principle is that all laws are public laws. The sovereign had both rights and duties. He had the right and the duty to coerce his subjects by giving of laws. It was his moral duty to treat his subject as ends and not as means. Kant was not clear whether he was the sovereign (legislature) or the ruler (executive). The sovereign could do no wrong, and the laws given by him are to be obeyed. But the positive law which was given had to be still judged by the standard found in the principles of right. The rulers could not be judged by the sovereign since it this were done the legislature would usurp the power of the executive or judiciary which was self-contradictory and thus not right.

Kant was vexed with the problem of sovereignty considering he reverted back to it time and again. Sovereignty resided or originated in the people which ought to possess legislative power. However, a monarch could possess it as a representative of the people in a derivative form and Kant was sure that if the monarch exercised this power together with executive power, his rule would be despotic. It was also the moral duty of the sovereign to give just laws and to introduce constitutional reforms for the establishment of a republican constitution. The subjects could not coerce the ruler or the sovereign to exercise these duties as these are moral and not legal duties. This also implied inalienable rights of men. In a state of nature, the war of all against all may prevail, but in a state where men live under law it would be different. Men are free, equal and self-dependent derived from the idea of freedom. If all persons are free they must be equal and the freedom of all persons was absolute and could only be universally and equally restricted by law. Each free person must also be self-dependent. The idea of freedom entailed individual's autonomy, as an individual he had the power to exercise his will independently, unhindered by improper constraint. The individual thus became the starting point of his enquiry into politics.

Kant rejected utilitarianism in politics as the purpose of politics was not to make people happy. Political arrangement should be organized in a manner not with the aim of promoting happiness but should allow persons to attain happiness in their own way. In the process he rejected benevolent despotism and defending in his writings on politics, by Frederick the Great. The ruler would have to make such laws and act in such a manner so that his subjects would not try to destroy the state and to overthrow the system of laws. For this purpose, men must be treated as ends and not as means. Here lies a paradox of political freedom. Man's freedom could be safeguarded only by his submitting to coercion; as law presupposes coercion and thus infringement of individual freedom. Kant like Rousseau saw man's membership of civil society, of his citizenship of the state the reason for this state of affairs, but he solved the paradox seeing it as a necessary condition of civilization. He tried to explain as follows: persons were free only in so far as, in the case of a conflict of interest, they obey the law to which they have agreed, i.e. submit to coercion which was legally exercised, on the basis of public law given by the sovereign authority. The sovereign too was obliged to respect the laws which he had authored, thus differing from Hobbes, for whom the sovereign was the above the law and the law was the command of the sovereign. Individual, according to Kant, preserved his freedom by remaining his own law-giver. Every subject participated in all legislation as a fellow legislator and the ruler when legislating ought to respect this right of his subject. This solution ensured freedom and security for all. Political freedom, then, was independence from coercion by another will.

If freedom was the first principal right of a citizen in a sate, equality was the second. Individuals must be equal before the law; legislation must not make any exception and the law should not be administered in a manner that allows for exceptions. Kant attacked the system of feudal privilege and rejected in principle, slavery or any inferior political status for a citizen. His focus, however, was on political equality and left out economic equality. He granted the right of person to own property. For effective political participation economic independence was required. The third principal right, independence required that each citizen ought to have a right to participate in the formation of government through the right of vote. Each citizen ought to have one vote, however larger his estate might be. None would have more legislative power than what was agreed to by law regarding the delegation of legislative power. While every one was free and equal and ought to enjoy the protection of law, not everyone had the right to participate in the making of laws. For Kant, active citizens were those who were independent and passive were those who were dependent. Only the former had the right to vote and to legislate. Women were disqualified. But any legislation ought to be enacted as if it had secured the participation of passive citizens, as the latter had inherently the same rights as the active citizens. A person should not be dependent on another economically, like a servant or an employee or else he could not act independently and freely in politics. Every self-dependent citizen, if not tainted by crime or insanity had the duty to participate in legislating. None could be coerced by others except by a public law executed by the sovereign similarly none could deny himself of this right either. These three rights of freedom, equality and self-dependence show that in a properly organized state, men could find security and justice. Unlike Rousseau Kant did not consider the state of nature as a state of perfection and that society had corrupted man; on the contrary, the individual was civilized by society. Like Hobbes Kant saw the state of nature as a state of war of all against all.

A will that could bind everyone equally, i.e. a collectively universal will alone could give security to one and all and that meant everyone had to restrict his freedom so as to make possible the establishment of such supreme power and to avoid conflict with the freedom of others. Using the social contract device Kant explained the existence of state governing people by a system of civil law. The social contract however was not a historical fact as such a conception was fraught with dangers, as it could, very likely, encourage disobedience or even active rebellion against, the existing law. The social contract was a practical idea of reason, a state that ought to be established in accordance with the principles of right.

For Kant human personality was immensely valuable. He conceived of society as composed of autonomous self possessed individuals, each having inalienable rights including the important right to pursue happiness in one's own manner. Championing the cause of individualism he made a distinction between natural law (right) and civil law (also right), both private and public. He distinguished between two basic types of rights—innate right and acquired right. The former referred to a person's claim to respect of others of his personal integrity while the other referred to a person's claim to external possession consistent with the exercise of his capacity for freedom. Unlike Locke, but like Rousseau, Kant regarded the state as developing and extending individual's natural rights. Right to freedom was the only one and true natural and innate right.

> Freedom is independence of the compulsory will of another and in so far as it can co-exist with the freedom of all according to a universal law, it is the one sole original, inborn right, belonging to everyman in virtue of his humanity (Kant 1970: 150).

When the state was formed by the people,

> It is not to be said that the individual in the state has sacrificed a part of his inborn external freedom for a particular purpose, but he has abandoned his wild lawless freedom wholly, in order to find all his proper freedom again, entire and unfinished, but in the form of a

> regulated order of dependence, that is, in a civil state regulated by laws of right. This relation of dependence thus arises out of his own regulative law giving will (Kant ibid: 174).

Furthermore, to protect the natural freedom in the civil society, Kant considered "the members of a civil society thus united for the purpose of legislation and thereby constituting a state, are called its citizens and there are three juridical attributed that inseparably belong to them by right" (Kant ibid: 175). These attributes were constitutional freedom, civil equality and political independence. In the *Essay on Theory and Practice* Kant insisted that these attributes were "fundamental conditions according to which along the institution of the state is possible in conformity with the pure rational principles of external human right generally" (Kant ibid: 176).

Kant held that the principle of liberty demanded that no one had a right to compel to be happy in the peculiar way in which he might think of the well-being of others. The principle of equality recognized that the laws of the state were applicable on all its members. He accepted inequalities of wealth and rank among the members of the state, but justified them on the ground that these inequalities were not a negation but the realization of freedom. Kant restricted the right of voting to adult male property owners because others could not be expected to retain their convictions. He viewed laws as those conditions under which the will of one individual could be united with that of other according to a general law of freedom. In obeying the moral law, man was obeying an internal law, a product of his reason which enabled him to act the way he ought to do so. Self-determination was the principle of all morality. A person ought to act on the basis of categorical imperative or general principles were intuitively recognized, for instance, keeping promises or speaking the truth. Every action ought to be in accordance with right which enabled the freedom of each man's will to exist together with the freedom of all others to act according to the universal law.

Kant believed in the supremacy of reason as reason was a distinctive human trait. Since the conditions for harmonious exercise of practical reason was not present, men must strive towards reason and realize the ideal of a kingdom of ends in which reason alone would be sovereign. In order to realize this ideal, a universal league of natures would be required which meant decrease in the importance of the nation state. Kant's philosophy marked by order, law, coherence and consistency was in sharp contrast with that of Rousseau. In the initial phase, Rousseau was viewed by Germans as a prophet of a new gospel of nature and as the thinker who had rediscovered the primitive power of the emotions and passions and had emancipated them from all restrictions, from the restriction of convention as well as that of reason (Cassirer 1945: 13).

For Kant a republican government was the ideal form of government. He differentiated between the republican form of government where the executive was separated from the legislature, and the despotic, where it was not. But this republican form of government was different than a democratic order as the latter could be despotic as it functions on the basis of majority rule. A power was established where all rule, all take decisions about all and also against any one who differed from the prevailing majority view. It would be in contradiction of the universal will and with freedom. A republican constitution was established in accordance with the principles of right if powers independent from one another were set up. First, there was the sovereign in the person of the legislator who represented the united (or general) will of the people, which in theory, was the will of reason. The ruler, i.e. the government or the executive was not the legislator. Finally, neither the legislator nor the ruler was the judiciary. For interpreting the law and for making individual judgements, an individual justice was required and for this, a court of law or a jury would be appointed. The legislative sovereign power would be vested in the people who would act through their representatives. Kant did not advocate the rule of the majority nor its unfettered power to legislate as that represented another form of arbitrary will in action. He did, however, state explicitly that all should combine to give laws, and that legislation would emanate from the united will of all. But he criticized the British constitutional arrangement of the eighteenth century viewing constitutional monarchy as a cloak to autocratic rule. A monarch could become tyrannical. Yet he also maintained that a government in which the government was in the hands of the smallest number of people and representation at its widest, republican rule would be easily assured. He even preferred monarchy to aristocracy. He used the term republican to convey his anti-monarchic sentiments. As he knew of the dangers of one person abusing his power, he did not, like Rousseau, believe that the united will of all could be represented in one person. He wanted sovereign authority to rest with the people or their representatives. He did not want the sovereign to own any private property so as to prevent the play of private interests in the exercise of public power.

The essence of a republican constitution was the respect for law which would bind the sovereign, the ruler and the subjects. The subject or citizen should neither rebel against the laws made by the sovereign and implemented by the ruler. For Kant the law was supreme and disobedience to it was evil. Interestingly, writing in the background of the French Revolution of 1789 which he admired, he observed that the revolution was not a revolution in the legal sense; as the king had surrendered his sovereign power to the Third Estate. Kant's view on rebellion was ambivalent. The people, he maintained, could not possess a right to rebel and that rebellion would undermine the whole system of laws, create anarchy and violence and destroy the civil constitution as demanded by the idea of social contract. If a constitution contained an article permitting a people to rebel or to depose a sovereign, a second sovereign would thereby be established. Once the revolution had taken place, attempts to undo it and re-establish the old order would be wrong, as being citizens it was men's duty to obey. If a government was newly established, as in England in 1688, it had to be accepted and obeyed. On the other hand, there existed no right to punish the ruler for deeds committed as ruler, for the ruler's deeds, in principle, were not subject to punishment. The sovereign could not be punished for issuing unjust laws or for committing unrightful political actions as these would be tantamount to rebellion. The sovereign had the right to dismiss the ruler, but he had no right to punish the dismissed ruler for actions committed as ruler. Judicial action against, and punishment of, the ruler were worse than the assassination of a tyrant.

Kant instructed the sovereign to promote the spirit of liberty. People had the right of public criticism, not only freedom of the press but also the right of open criticism of the powers. The right to criticize in public along with the principle of limits of tolerance was guaranteed by the republican constitution.

PHILOSOPHY OF HISTORY

Kant believed that the history of the human race could be viewed as progress towards a perfect political constitution as well as in the arena of morals. The various states in the moral development of human beings were anomy, heteronomy and autonomy. In the primitive natural anomic stage, the human impulses were naive and innocent which were similar to Rousseau's belief of human beings in the earlier stages of the state of nature, the pre-civilization stage of human beings. Human civilization began when human beings made a break with this natural state and accepted the obligation of moral law imposed from outside. This, according to Kant was the stage of heteronomy. However, there was still a higher form which Kant called autonomy which was destined to be a state of absolute freedom in which the individual obeyed only a self-imposed law which Kant called the moral imperative.

The process of history, according to Kant, was not mechanical or rigidly deterministic. He argued that we could think of history as progressive and make our efforts, but beyond that nothing was plausible. However, looking at history of human beings, Kant asserted there was reason to believe that the natural process supported the ultimate goal of perpetual peace. He explained this with reference to the idea of human beings' unsocial sociability depicting a split personality for human beings could not live with fellow beings and could not do without them either. In earlier times, human beings spread over the entire surface of the earth to escape others, but the necessities of existence led to the development of trade and commerce which brought people together. In the same process, Kant believed nations would be brought together making the dream of perpetual peace a reality.

> However visionary this idea (perpetual peace) may appear to be, it is nevertheless the inevitable issue of the necessity in which men involve one another. For this necessity must compel the nations to the very resolution—however hard it may appear—to which the savage in his uncivilized state, was so unwillingly compelled, when he had to surrender his brutal liberty and seek rest and security in a constitution regulated by law (Williams 1983: 12).

Kant was not interested in the chronological history of human beings. Instead he gave a logical argument like Aristotle's assertion that man was a social animal and considered human history and civilization to be progressive marching towards the goal of eternal peace. However, Kant was realistic enough to acknowledge the many difficulties that human beings were to surmount in order to reach that goal. Interestingly, he pointed out that human beings were anti-social. The unsocial sociability in human beings was the means by which nature brought about the development of their innate capacities. Kant believed that one could fully comprehend history if one understood the conflict among human beings. He did not ignore the role of strife in human life. Like Hobbes, he saw in the antagonism among men, in the war of all against all, the mainspring for the establishment of civil society. Kant's philosophy of history was the consequence of his political theory. He condemned rebellion as it ran counter to the principle of law and the progress towards rationality, namely the establishment of a republican constitution could not help up for long. Rebelling against the powers would not only delay but even retard the process. It would not be long before that reason asserted itself and the principles of right respected.

Kant sought to discover the natural laws of history in the same manner that Kepler had discovered natural laws of planets. By plans of nature, Kant did not mean the existence of an actual legislator or mind called nature but the need to understand an idea such as the one that nature had a purpose in history. This idea could not be understood with reference to a scientific enquiry, but it was clear that one could not understand history without an understanding of it. However, this idea ought not to be treated as a scientific law. Since Kant's main concern was with human freedom, the development of human freedom provided the clue as facts of history. Therefore, Kant assumed that a plan of nature ought to educate humankind to a state of freedom. In other words, since human beings were endowed with reason by nature, the purpose of nature was to ensure the development of rationality for that constituted the human essence. History was a progress towards rationality, but this did not mean a continuous advancement towards rationality all the time. He explicitly rejected the idea of linking progress to experience and instead tried to understand it with reference to the moral character of human beings. This moral character could be realized in legal arrangements, namely a republican constitution.

> He was in one both a typical and supreme representative of the Enlightenment, typical because of his belief in the power of courageous reasoning and in the effectiveness of the reform of institutions (when all states are republics there will be no more war); supreme because in what he thought he either solved the recurrent problems of the Enlightenment or reformulated them in a much more fruitful way (MacIntyre 1971: 190).

In the *Idea for a Universal History with a Cosmopolitan Aim,* Kant reiterated and recast some of the philosophical ideas of his predecessors and contemporaries. From the Stoics he took the view that nature did nothing in vain or accidentally, but that its regularities reveal a functional organization in which each part played a necessary role. The exercise of rationality constitutes human freedom and found its highest accomplishment in political cosmopolitanism. Like Augustine, Kant too saw providential significance in history. While Augustine differentiated between the City of God from the temporal human city, Kant focused on realization of chiliastic hopes within human history from human determination. Kant reiterated the belief of Grotius about the existence of universal natural laws in conformity with human rationality that govern political and moral rights among nations; that these laws were discovered rationally rather than empirically, but unlike Grotius, did not base the need and legitimacy of rational laws on divine authority. He did not share Grotius' assumption of naturally sociability of human beings; on the contrary believed in the fundamental unsociability of human beings in his argument. Like Hobbes, Kant thought that peace and political organization arose from the rational recognition that competition and conflicts imperil the natural human tendency to self protection. For Hobbes, rationality was the precondition for the possibility of political organization, whereas according to Kant, rational civic organization would emerge gradually from the realization that antagonism would threaten the natural instinct of self-preservation. Kant, like Leibniz and Smith, asserted that there was a hidden pattern, a law that underlies and harmonized the apparently destruction narrowly self interested activities of human beings; the hidden nature of nature manifested to those who could rightly understand history and economics. Unlike Mandeville, Kant did not think that public virtue emerged from private vices; rather it was the product of rationally constructed political institutions. Like Smith, Kant thought that morality required self-legislating reflective activity whose origins Smith located in the development of moral sentiments while Kant located it in the activity of the rational will. Kant, like Rousseau, shared the latter's distrust in the ability of social affections to provide a reliable source of rational morality. He too, like Rousseau and the Stoics, constructed a mystical story of the stages in the emergence of rational self-legislation. Both Rousseau and Kant believed that a just civil society could be achieved through constitutional political organization and that genuine individual and political freedom was autonomy, which for Rousseau was possible only in small isolated polities, whereas for Kant, autonomy was possible only through the peace ensured by cosmopolitan political organization. Kant agreed with Leibniz about the existence of a providential order behind the apparent random natural chaos, but disagreed with Leibniz that cosmic harmony expressed divine will. Leibniz's divinely ordained harmony was temporal while Kant believed that cosmopolitan harmony could be attained by free human activity through a long and antagonistic struggle. Interestingly, Kant's successor Hegel also saw history as a description of the antagonistic but providentially progressive emergence of a rational and self-legislative world order, but did not share Kant's optimism of a cosmopolitan world order. Marx shared Kant's belief that history was driven forward by paradoxes and contradictions, but not his concern of rights and civil society.

NOTION OF PERPETUAL PEACE AND COSMOPOLITANISM

Kant was the first philosopher to make a case in a systematic manner for perpetual peace among nations as Nature's inherent purpose. The invisible hand of Nature was working its way through human history converting individual egoistic, competitive, aggressive human actions into higher state of peace. In the *Science of Right* (1790), he discussed the rights of nations, international law and also the universal right of humankind. Inspired by Rousseau's emphasis on the dignity of the human being Kant insisted that ethically people ought to be treated as ends in themselves and that means, a ruler had no right to treat his people as objects for his ambitions and wars. The people had rights but did not owe any duty to the sovereign. According to Kant it was sovereign who had duties towards the people.

Kant's insistence on human dignity led him to emphasize on some important key concepts like individual rights, equality before law, the need for a correct legal procedure and an educational system that enhanced reason. Moral law and the autonomy of the individual formed the basis of freedom which was possible only under the rule of law. Hence, laws were necessary and it was our duty to respect the law. But law could be administered only in a state without prejudice to rank and privilege, which was a union of human beings. Laws were the conditions by which the will of one particular individual would be harmonized and united with the will of others within the framework of a general law whose basis was freedom. Only in a republican state would all human beings be free, equal, independent and autonomous. "A constitution", according to Kant, was "where the subject is not a citizen, and which is therefore not republican, it is the simplest thing in the world to go to war ... reason as the highest legislative moral power, absolutely condemns war as a test of rights" (Kant 1970: 178).

For Kant, morality and self-determination were the same thing and a person acted on the basis of categorical imperative which implied acceptance of general principles which one recognized within oneself and was not self-contradictory and was universally applicable. This framework allowed Kant to make a synthesis between individual's own moral will and the universal law. Action followed a philosophy of right which allowed the freedom of existence of an individual while allowing all others to exist equally on the basis of a universal law.

According to Kant, since human beings were endowed with reason by nature, the purpose of nature was to ensure the development of rationality for that constituted the human essence. History was a process towards rationality and linked progress with reference to the moral character of human beings. With his firm conviction in human rationality, Kant condemned servility and cherished independence of mind. He regarded paternalism as the worst form of despotism. Members of a civil society were united for the purpose of legislation, and thereby constituted a state. Citizens were endowed with three juridical attributes that inseparably belonged to them by right. These attributes were constitutional freedom, civil equality and political independence. Kant did not dwell into the ways and means of achieving a republican constitution, but merely indicated a set of absolutely valid principles for conflict resolution. He was categorical that republican constitutions in individual states were the necessary stepping stones to achieving perpetual peace among all nations. His faith in republican ideals of 1776 and 1789 did not waver despite the excesses in France during the reign of terror, ultimately helping in the rise of Napoleon. The overall optimism of the enlightenment, and the rise of republicanism and constitutional liberalism convinced Kant that perpetual peace can be envisioned within the plurality of nation states.

> Moral practical reason within us pronounces the following irresistible veto: there shall be no war, either between individual human beings in the state of nature, or between separate states, which although internally law-governed, still lives in a lawless condition in their external relationships with one another. For, war is not the way in which anyone should pursue their rights... . It can indeed be said that this task of establishing a universal and lasting peace is not just a part of the theory of right within the limits of pure reason, but its entire purpose (Kant ibid: 17).

The general perception in the eighteenth century was that the transition from monarchical to republican institutions would eclipse wars, and herald in an era of peace and moderation. "Kant and the other liberals were essentially correct about the benefits of democracy. Peace is more likely when societies have adopted non-violent means of conflict resolution, executive authority is constrained by a system of checks and balances, and intertwined commercial interests make conflict uneconomical ... . There has been a dramatic increase in the number of democracies since World War II ... . The pacific efforts of interdependence provide more reason than ever, therefore, to believe that Hobbesian anarchy is being reconstructed to reflect liberal values" (Russett 1993).

Kant believed that the history of human race was a progress towards a perfect political constitution, and considered the republican constitution as the perfect one. He asserted that there was a reason to believe that the natural process supported the ultimate goal of perpetual peace and explained this with reference to the idea of unsocial sociability of human beings, meaning that the personality of human beings was that of a split personality. They could not live with one another and could also not do without one another. In earlier times, human beings spread over the entire surface of the earth to escape others, but the necessities of existence led them to develop trade and commerce and the latter two in turn brings people together. In the same process, he was convinced that nations would be brought together making the dream of perpetual peace a reality. He applied the categorical imperative to the relations of states and rejected any action or policy that would make peace among nations impossible. Like individuals, he insisted that nations must enter into a union of states, which was the only way to establish peace. This would make a permanent congress of nations a practical reality enabling nations to settle their differences in a civil process than by barbarous war. He based the right to a universal peaceful union of all nations on the juridical principle of legal justice, namely that all people have a right to associate with one another as they originally share the entire soil of earth. He also insisted that even though perpetual peace may not be a reality in the near future, but must be worked for, as one's duty and states that "the universal and lasting establishment of peace constitutes not merely a part, but the whole final purpose and end of the science of right as viewed within the limits of reason" (Kant ibid: 69). It was morality itself that vetoed war, as war treats human beings as mere means and persons as mere things. War was rejected by rational citizens out of legal motive of self love and conversely to wage war was to renounce reason.

Kant in his *Idea for a Universal History from a Cosmopolitan Point of View* (1790) stated that nature compelled people to find a cosmopolitan solution making a league of nations the natural outcome of social evolution. Until that was realized human beings would suffer the cruelty of conflicts. The way out was a moral order which can be brought about only through education, as that would help in building character in accordance with moral principles. The justice and conscience within us, and not with help of governments, would enable us to realize our destiny, the sovereignty of God on Earth. Kant lamented that rulers spend very little money on public because they spend it on paying for past and future wars and was convinced that the ever-growing war debt would eventually make war impractical, economically. Reiterating Montesquieu, he highlighted the value of interstate commerce as paving the way eventually for an international government, as commercial activity and material prosperity were a panacea against war.

In 1795, Kant published his major work on peace entitled *Perpetual Peace: A Philosophical Sketch* as a just treaty that could be signed by nations in the background of his indignation at the separate treaty of Basel in which Prussia ceded France territory west of the Rhine so that it could partition Poland along with Russia and Austria. Kant described his proposed peace programme with reference to two steps—the preliminary articles and then, to three definitive articles at not only halting hostilities but also to lay solid foundations of peace. As far as the first was concerned, he stipulated the following:

1. No secret treaty of peace shall be held valid in which there was tacitly reserved matter for a future war.
2. No independent states, large or small, shall come under the dominion of another state by inheritance, exchange, purchase, or donation.
3. Standing Armies shall in time be totally abolished.
4. National debts shall not be contracted with a view to the external friction of states.
5. No state shall by force interfere with the constitution or government of another state.
6. No state shall, during war, permit such acts of hostility which would make mutual confidence in the subsequent peace impossible: such are the employment of assassins, breach of capitulation, and incitement to treason in the opposing state. He added that a state had no right to wage a punitive war because just punishment must come from a superior authority and not an equal. Like Bentham, Kant emphasized that justice must be delivered publicly and open to scrutiny.

For enduring peace Kant suggested the need for three definitive articles. They are as follows: (i) the civil constitution of every state should be republican in which laws apply to everyone universally and fairly, as that means a government by law and not by favoured persons. His hope lay on the mechanisms of checks and balances within a democratic setup which was absent in authoritarianism. The public opinion would be the restraining element in a republic. His reasoning was that majority of the people would go to war only in self defense and not otherwise. Therefore, if all nations were constitutional republics it would signal the end of war and aggression. For perpetual peace, constitutional republics were the only one of several necessary conditions. (ii) The law of nations shall be founded on a Federation of Free states. If all wars have to be ended forever, then there must be a league of peace and if more republics associate with one another the more practical a federation becomes. (iii) The law of world citizenship shall be limited to conditions of universal hospitality. He also conceded that realization of this ideal would be slow and long but was confident that intensive education of all citizens in every country would make possible the ideal. Eventually, the conflict between the individual's obligation *qua* citizen to obey the law of the state and his obligation *qua* man to obey the cosmopolitan law will cease as the member states of the universal confederation cease to contravene the cosmopolitan law. As a result, the moral responsibilities of citizen and man will coincide and citizenship would assume a universal status. Kant's argument for perpetual peace rested on the assumption that human beings have the singular potential for reasoning and moral development. But Kant did not advocate world government as centralized authority was detrimental to individual freedom.

Kant's doctrine of perpetual peace was one of the most influential aspects of his political philosophy, and has inspired many subsequent thinkers. Herbert George Wells (1866–1946), writing in the early days of World War I, believed that this War would be the war to end all wars on the grounds that once popular government replaces Prussian militarism and autocracy there would be no war among European nations. In 1909, Sir Ralph Norman Angell (1872–1967) reiterating Kant pointed out that war had become unprofitable due to modern commerce even for the technically victorious country and an interdependent European community based on economic self interest then political wars would cease in the same way as religious wars had stopped in the West (Angell 1910: 335). Angell rationalist, believed that war could be eliminated through the growth and progressive application of human reason to international affairs. He pointed out that once human beings were convinced that war was mutually destructive with no winners, disarmament and peace would become possible. However, Angell failed to realize that most of the modern wars, including the first World War, were not necessarily due to economic reasons. Schumpeter argued that modern states were inherently peaceful and opposed conquest due to capitalism's success in ensuring prosperity. Clarence Streit in *Union Now* (1938) proposed a federal union of democratic states modelled after the US constitution on the grounds that trade and peaceable ways of democracy would keep this union perpetual. It included common citizenship, a defense force, a tariff-free market, and a common currency. In recent times, on the basis of the Kantian doctrine of perpetual peace, a thesis has emerged that democracies do not fight one another as peace has its dividends; that commerce and trade are much better alternatives than war and conflict.

Women and Family

Kant regarded women as passive citizens, but did not mention the reasons for not regarding them otherwise. He merely assumed that reason dictated that men transmit their titles of nobility to their wives and not the other way around. He defined a citizen as one who was free, independent and equal, but not everyone in the state had the independence for being a citizen. So, even if all were free and all were equal they might not be independent. They might not have an equal say in framing laws though they were subjects of the law. He emphatically asserted that all were not equally qualified within the constitution to possess the right to vote, i.e. to be citizens and not just subjects.

As passive members, women might be treated in accordance with the laws of natural freedom and equality, but they would not have the right to influence or organize the state itself as active members, nor could they cooperate in introducing particular laws. The distinction between active and passive citizenship was important as it explained the reason for disenfranchisement of certain sections of society. Passive citizens were mere auxiliaries of the commonwealth receiving order or protection from other individuals, but would not enjoy civil independence. An active citizen was one who would be independent and not subject to the will of others. A labourer could not be an active citizen. Other passive citizens included merchants or tradesman, servants not employed by the government, minors, women and all those people, who depend on their living on the offices of others, other than the state. Since they lacked economic independence political subordination was justified.

Kant regarded sex as incompatible to human dignity and worth. It was an animal function even in monogamous relationships, and had nothing to do with moral love. Sexual gratification was a form of exploitation. He regarded men to be naturally superior to women and did not espouse sexual equality. In certain places, he regarded men and women as equal, but then asserted that the latter forgo their equality for the sake of peace and tranquility within households. This inequality was reciprocal for women were granted domination within the private sphere for lack of political power. Through marriage the woman lost her civil independence. There was no coercion, for it was done voluntarily. He regarded women as irrational and lacking in capacity to be autonomous which was necessary for a moral being. Women tended to be emotional and liked to please and were not rational. Moreover, it would be foolish to grant them political power or authority for they tended to be quarrelsome, jealous and domineering.

KANT AND HEGEL

If the contemporary reality was not based on reason, then the reality had to be altered. This general framework of German political theory was given a highly sophisticated personal touch by Hegel with his twofold argument that, first, history was not merely a chronological table, but had a meaning which was both profound and purposeful, the particularly important thing for him being to recreate Greek harmony within the context of modern society based on individualism and reason. Second, as MacIntyre (1971: 199) observed, it was Hegel who was the first thinker to have understood very clearly that questions concerning morality changed from one particular place and time to another, and as such there was nothing called a permanent moral question. This led to the important assertion of Hegel that the history of philosophy was at the core of philosophy. What logically followed was the important conclusion that all history represented particular levels of development, and had to be judged on the basis of advancement towards the realization of reason. Hegel was convinced that reason, truth and freedom were identifiable, that the process of reaching the final stage and even a blueprint of the final stage was conceivable, as history as a quest of development had a definite beginning and a certain end. Hegel's thought, by the time he was writing the logical culmination of the different periods of history, was coming to an end, and because of this historically-determined situation, reconciliation of the first principles of philosophy could match the contemporary reality. It was this confidence that led Hegel to prepare his elaborate scheme to deal with the complexities of modern civilization, which he believed had reached the climax of its evolution.

> Hegel's system is necessarily associated with a definite political philosophy and with a definite social and political order. The dialectic between civil society and the state of the Restoration is not incidental in Hegel's philosophy, nor is it just a section of Philosophy of Right; its principle already operates in the conceptual structure of his system. His basic concepts are, on the other hand, but the culmination of the entire tradition of Western thought. They become understandable only when interpreted within this tradition (Marcuse 1954: 16).

During the time of Hegel, the flowering of German culture was at its best. It was the period of the golden age of German literature. Hegel was 20 years younger than Goethe, and 10 years younger than Friedrich von Schiller (1759–1805). This age difference enabled him to appreciate their works. A similar parallel could be made between Rabindranath Tagore (1861–1941) and Bankim Chandra Chatterjee (1838–1894) in India. Tagore, who was 23 years younger than Bankim, grew to maturity under Bankim's literary genius. The German romantic movement influenced Hegel considerably, though he rejected the ideas of the movement. But the combined influence of all these was much less than the influence of one single philosopher, Kant, whose famous work *Critique of Pure Reason* made a synthesis of the two different ideals of the enlightenment—Newtonian physics and Helvetian empiricism. Newton offered definite and unalterable laws for all occasions and places. On the other hand, Helvetius and Hume argued that rational belief emanated from our own sensual encounters. Kant's important contribution emerged with his assertion that these two different perceptions could be reconciled by the fact that all our experience ended in a Newtonian certainty, by the nature of the concepts and categories with which we understand the world. This interrelationship was crucial, as "concepts without perceptions are empty; perceptions without concepts are blind" (MacIntyre 1971: 191).

Moral and simple goodness like Newtonian mechanics and arithmetic was self-evident. Kant was an exponent of practical reason, which was based on God, freedom and immortality which he described as the categorical imperatives. Within this framework, any meaningful moral category had to have a universalistic basis. The Kantian logic was based on the primacy of the individual's moral perception, without any reference to any external constraint. His *Critique of Pure Reason* ended on a note of optimism as it predicted that it might be possible before the end of the eighteenth century to achieve what had eluded humankind for all the previous centuries, to give human reason complete satisfaction about that what has always engaged its curiosity, but so far in vain. This optimism, which was a total negation of Malthus' pessimism created a new dimension in human thinking by projecting the present and the immediate future as a great leap forward. The condensation of history and the rejection of the past as essentially incomplete resonated in the writings of Hegel, and subsequently in those of Marx. The latter's assertion that "one hundred years of capitalism did more wonders than all the preceding history taken together", echoed the optimism and confidence that Kant and Hegel exuded.

CONCLUSION

MacIntyre points out that Kant's intention was to depict the individual as being superior and standing outside the existing social order. His sympathy lay with the French Revolution. With his firm conviction of human rationality, he condemned servility and cherished independence of mind. The worst form of despotism for him was paternalism. In the context of the subsequent German history MacIntyre found Kant's ideas as illusory mainly because of his attempt to develop a "moral standpoint completely independent of the social order" (MacIntyre 1971: 198). Unlike Kant, both Hegel and Marx built a theory of history in the context of the present societal formation linking it with a philosophical explanation of the past.

Kant belonged to the age of reason, the glorious period of the enlightenment and like many other contemporary thinkers, wanted to reconstruct society on the principles of reason. His quest was for a more plausible social order based on the analysis of human nature. He permitted maximum individual freedom as well as competition with the state have enough power to regulate this freedom. In other words, if the realization of freedom was threatened, resulting in disorder, then the state by its intervention could maximize equal freedom. His social theory was based on the concept of progress whose source was the inherent tension between human sociability and his selfishness. Kant called this antagonism, the unsocial sociability. He believed not only in political progress, namely, the attainment of a perfect political constitution but also in moral progress. Civilization would be attained when human beings broke away from natural state and accepted externally imposed law and this would pave way for moral autonomy when human beings perform duty for the sake of duty.

Kant's attempt to formulate rational principles in politics to which all men could and even ought to, agree on the importance of reason in public life. His continued attraction even in our times has been because of his attempt to construct a political philosophy on the basis of what ought to be. This, being an integral component of normative political theory is still alive in contemporary political theory. However, he differed considerably from the Anglo-Saxon tradition of liberalism which rejected the Kantian notion of human perfectibility and ideas about achieving a perfect political order both within the nation state and among nation states. What attracted contemporary liberals to Kantian ideas was his emphasis on individual autonomy, human rationality, and rights based constitutional order. But still there is no denying the fact that his major emphasis was on the ideal and not the real, and that explained why Hegel and not Kant determined the debates within political theory till the early part of the twentieth century.

Hegel in contrast to Kant accepted within his paradigm competing nation states. Unlike Kant, for whom the absence of republics made possible both international conflict and war, for Hegel war was the result of the distinctive nature of the nation state reflecting the common identity of people. There was a particularity of social and political rules moulded by many particular characteristics like history, language, customs and passions. All these scattered identities could not incorporate the entire human kind. These differences in the way of life were the real causes of conflict and war. Even the cooperation among states was based on advancement of national interest and goals of each uniting nation. As a consequence, in the international arena, the treatises and alliances continue as long as these cater to the need of the contracting states. The international system is inherently fluid and unstable because of the perennial presence of more than one right. The difference between Kant and Hegel was fundamental as their world views were diametrically opposite and unbridgeable. However, in the scale of history the real contest of ideas has ended with the collapse of communism and the triumph of liberal democracy (Fukuyama, 1992). If Fukuyama's prediction becomes a reality worldwide then perhaps Kantianism could triumph over Hegelianism.

9

Edmund Burke

> Burke is still worth our attention because his is a classic statement of conservatism. It has the classic strengths and weaknesses of that position. He offered eighteenth-century solutions to problems. But those problems belong to a family whose descendants live still among us. We still do not have very good solutions. We must therefore come to grips with his (Freeman 1980: 230).

> Burke's writing is an articulated experience, and as such has a validity which can survive even the demolition of its general conclusion (Williams 1958: 25).

> Edmund Burke has been described as one of the greatest men, and—Bacon alone excepted—the greatest thinker who ever devoted himself to the practice of English politics (Hearnshaw 1931: 45).

Edmund Burke (1729–1797) was the most important conservative political thinker, and though there were conservatives before him, conservatism as a school of political theory, as a distinct political creed, began with him. He has been described as an ultra conservative by Berlin (1969) while Cruise O'Brien (1968) viewed him as a liberal and pluralist opponent of the French Revolution. Laski (1920) called him a liberal because of his sympathetic attitude to the USA, Irish and Indian causes. Some saw him as a progressive conservative, for "he supported political and economic progress within the framework of England's established institutions" (Miller 1997: 562). He was described by Kramnick (1977) as "the gravedigger of the Enlightenment" for his virulent anti-clericalism and disembodied rationalism. It is difficult to classify Burke for two reasons. First, there are no clear preferences in him. There are liberal as well as conservative elements, as evident by his support to the American Revolution and his opposition to the French Revolution. Second, Burke was a prolific writer in the long course of his political career. The bulk of his writing was situational, not well-formulated political theory texts.

Burke's most important political tract emerged as a reaction to the French Revolution of 1789, endorsing the adage that there was a clear correlationship between crisis and significant developments in political theorizing. Many, like Kant, looked at the French Revolution as a liberating development. This was not the case with Burke. Even before the rise of terror, and at a time when the French Revolution was regarded in England as a follow-up of the Glorious Revolution of 1688, Burke attacked its entire basis and ideology. He criticized Rousseau for lack of moderation. He described the Encyclopaedists as men of "cold hearts and muddy understandings ... [with] vulgar, base and profane language". He thought that the revolutionaries by their "cant and gibberish of hypocrisy" produced a black and savage atrocity of mind for the French people.

Burke's well-known parliamentary speeches in the House of Commons remain incomparable even today. His major work was the *Reflections on the Revolution in France and on the proceedings of certain societies in England relating to that event* published in 1790, in which he attacked the theories of natural rights, revolutionary change, and concepts of absolute liberty, equality, and democracy as abstract and untested principles. Championing the values of tradition and continuity, Burke advocated a process of orderly, evolutionary and gradual change. Emphasizing the complexities of the entire societal and political processes, he was critical of any plan of rationalism in politics. Like Hegel, Burke pointed to the complexities of the entire social and political processes. Thomas Paine (1739–1809) took the opposite view, and the Burke-Paine debate was one of the most interesting ones regarding the limits and rationale of drastic changes.

LIFE SKETCH

Burke was born in Dublin, Ireland on January 12, 1729. There is considerable controversy regarding his date of birth, for there are as many as six dates that have been given. He was a son of a well-known attorney, Richard Burke. He was sent to Baltimore School in County Kildane. He then studied in Trinity College, Dublin, receiving an AB in 1748. In 1750, he went to London to study law at the Middle Temple, which he abandoned. He remained in London to pursue his literary interests. In 1757, he married Janes Nugent.

Burke published *A Vindication of Natural Society* in 1756. He contended that civilization was built gradually, spread over many ages, and with the efforts of many minds. He rejected the idea of any attempt to remake all the laws and customs at one stroke, a theme with which he persisted in his subsequent writings. His next work, A *Philosophical Sublime and Beautiful* (1757), was the only theoretical work that he attempted, inspired by the writings of Locke and Montesquieu. It was praised by Kant. In 1789, Burke established the *Annual Register*, which is still considered to be one of the best source materials of that period.

Burke joined politics and got elected to Parliament in December 1765. His greatest success lay in oratory and he was regarded as one of the greatest orators of his time. Besides being a skilled orator, Burke was also a political pamphleteer and his most popular and famous writings were all pamphlets and written speeches on contemporary political issues. Burke always took enormous pride in his consistent stand on various issues, which he defended in his well-known writing, *An Appeal from the New to the Old Whigs* (1791). In his *Thoughts on the Cause of the Present Discontents* (1770), he pointed out that the constitution was being subverted by the king's friends, a group which always supported the government and took pride in its non-partisanship. He was the first great defender of the role of political parties in the modern political process. He served his party well from 1765 till the French Revolution of 1789. But when the leader of his party, Charles James Fox, a descendent of both Charles II and James II, lent his support to the cause of the revolutionaries, Burke decided to snap ties with Fox in Parliament on May 6, 1791.

In 1774, Burke delivered his famous speech on American taxation, raising the entire level of discussion from conflicting arguments on constitutional rights to the higher level of prudence or imprudence of exercising these rights. In 1775, he gave a speech on conciliation with America, a masterpiece in the art of oratory, which for generations is still studied by every American schoolchild. In this speech, he advised the English Parliament to avoid the "Great Serbonian Bog" of theoretical rights and instead practice tolerance and magnanimity, as a "great empire and little minds go ill together".

Ireland was of special concern to Burke, for he was critical of the oppressive English rule though he defended British sovereignty. He used Cicero's natural law as principles of superior law to plead the Irish and Indian cases. In 1774, Burke stood for an election at Bristol and won the contest by his famous observation that though it was imperative for a representative to reflect the feelings of the people, the representative had the freedom to differ from his voters in view of the common good. Subsequently, he was forced to withdraw from Bristol in 1780, and thereafter he was elected from Lord Rockingham's borough of Malton till he retired in 1794.

Burke pleaded for administrative reform in his speech on *Economical Reform* (1780). He wrote down his economic views in *Thoughts and Details on Scarcity* (1795). He dealt at length on Indian affairs, and commented that "let everything I have done, said or written be forgotten but this". He argued for a just treatment for Indians under natural law, even if that harmed British trade and rule in India.

Burke is mostly remembered for his defence of the British constitution and his vehement denunciation of the French Revolution as a threat to Western civilization itself. His *Reflections* was an immediate best-seller. This led to the famous controversy between the Conservative Burke and the Radical Paine. His main purpose was not description but persuasion, for he defended traditional British institutions as being a far more preferable arrangement than the abstract French Revolutionary values of liberty, equality and fraternity.

The best orator in an age of talk died on July 9, 1797.

FRENCH REVOLUTION AND ENGLAND

The French Revolution exerted a great deal of influence on contemporary Britain. "Apart from the Industrial Revolution there was no profounder influence than the French Revolution in moulding the course of English history in the eighteenth century, and the development of its political expression in the nineteenth" (Plumb 1967: 155).

The Revolution initially received a great deal of favourable response both in Britain and the United States. The Revolution was a result of multiple factors, for there were serious social, economic, political and administrative anomalies. The *ancien regime* in France was unable to deal effectively with widespread and visible injustices. The Revolution was inspired by the writings of the Enlightenment philosophers who were confident and optimistic about progress, science and reason as shaping and inaugurating a new society. It would be an "age of common sense, reason and humanity" (Torrey 1960: 9). It was a vision of a new, emancipated man, and the establishment of a rational society. "It injected into the early stages of the French Revolution a hope, a new sense of new human horizons, which is difficult now to conceive" (Parkin 1969: 120).

Such unparalleled optimism and the sordid affairs in France led to a positive response in the English-speaking world. The fall of the Bastille was described as the best news since the British defeat at Saratoga by Fox. Even the French Revolutionaries thought that they were repeating the Puritan Revolution, seeing a parallel between the execution of Louis XVI and that of Charles I, for both met similar fates because they disregarded the wishes of the people and the parliament.

A section of the intelligentsia not only welcomed the Revolution as being similar to the Glorious Revolution of 1688, but also urged fellow Englishmen to press for more reforms in Great Britain itself. Richard Price (1723-1791), a dissenting Unitarian minister and "perhaps the most important of Hume's immediate successors" in a sermon on *The Love of Our Country* at a meeting of a body called "The Revolution Society" consisting of dissenters and radical Whigs, pointed out:

> What an eventful period is this! I am thankful that I have lived to it, and I could almost say, Lord, now lettest thou thy servant depart in peace, for mine eyes have seen thy salvation. I have lived to see the rights of men better understood than ever, and nations panting for

> liberty, which seemed to have lost the idea of it. Be encouraged, all ye friends of freedom, and writers in its defence. The times are auspicious. Your labours have not been in vain (Parkin ibid: 120; MacIntyre 1971: 175).

The Revolution Society of Price met every year to commemorate the landing of William of Orange in 1688. Price desired to restate the principles of 1688 by highlighting the rights to liberty of conscience and to resist authority if it abused power. He thought that the impact of the French Revolution would lead to the furtherance of the principles in England, initially accepted in 1688.

One major influence of the French Revolution in Great Britain was the consolidation of lower-class radicalism, which the government viewed with considerable alarm. In 1790, the Habeas Corpus Act was suspended, and in 1794 many radical leaders were arrested. Treason and sedition acts were passed in 1795 and 1799. These acts prevented the radicals from penetrating the mainstream of British political life. "Time and time again, these acts were involved to suppress savagely and indiscriminately the movement towards trade unionism" (Plumb 1967: 158).

POLITICAL IDEAS

Burke's political ideas were spread over his speeches and pamphlets, which originated in response to specific events. He had no philosophy beyond them, and had little knowledge of the history of philosophy. In this, he compared more favourably with his severest critic Paine than with Hume, who, like Burke, was a conservative thinker, but more profound than Burke in his grasp of philosophical problems. But this inadequacy was overshadowed by his strong common sense, analytical and persuasive powers and influence. What Locke was to liberalism, Burke is to conservatism.

Burke's concerns before his critique of the French Revolution could be grouped under the following sub-headings.

Restraining Royal Authority

In the tradition of Whiggism, Burke was a vocal opponent of arbitrary monarchical power and patronage. However, he was also conscious of the importance of the institution of the monarchy as a natural attraction for obedience and reverence. It also strengthened the principle of continuity. But these positive aspects were minor compared to the important role of monarchy for developing a mixed and balanced government, for which it had to be streamlined. In this, the influence of Hooker, Locke and Montesquieu was apparent. Burke was an admirer and defender of the

British constitution which adequately ensured good government and fulfilled the liberty connected with that order.

Ireland

Burke stood with the cause of Ireland, though expediency and the interests of a successful political career compelled him to sacrifice theoretical consistency. Furthermore, his open and public stand was cautious, compared to his private correspondence. But in spite of this limitation, which was understandable because of the prevailing mood and consideration for his political survival, he always emphasized the desirability of the emancipation of the Roman Catholics of Ireland. He also spoke of the inevitability of Irish emancipation.

The East India Company

For about a decade, Burke spoke extensively against the oppression, exploitation and misrule of India by the East India Company. "There is nothing nobler in Burke's career than his long attempt to mitigate the evils of company rule in India" (Laski 1920: 35).

Burke criticized the British rule in India, an ancient civilization, much older than Britain, and hence its traditions and customs were to be respected. Interestingly, Henry Maine used these arguments to challenge Austin's theory of sovereignty. Burke's interest in Indian affairs continued with his primary initiative in launching impeachment proceedings against Warren Hastings in 1787. He challenged Hastings' assertion that it was impossible to apply Western criteria of authority and legality to oriental societies. The proceedings continued for eight long years, though in the end Hastings was acquitted.

American Colonies

Burke championed the cause of the American colonies. In the midst of emotional and angry debates like the right of Parliament to tax colonies and the right of resistance to American settlers, he lifted the entire controversy to a different and higher level altogether. He refused to analyze the problem from the point of view of abstract rights, and raised some very serious and fundamental questions, which were reiterated in the course of his critique of the French Revolution. Furthermore, he charged that the British policy was inconsistent, and emphasized the need for legislative reason.

CRITICISM OF THE FRENCH REVOLUTION

The intellectual challenge of providing a well-reasoned and popular critique of the French Revolution and countering positions like that of Price was provided by Burke. His vehement criticism surprised many, destroying many of his close friendships. Equally shocking was the clear difference between the young and old Burke.

Burke's earlier criticism of the king's control over the parliament, his efforts of more than a decade to expose oppression, exploitation and misrule in India by the East India Company, and his championing the cause of the American colonies was out of tune with the total denunciation of the French Revolution. Unlike many other contemporaries, he refused to draw any parallels between the French events and the Glorious Revolution of 1688.

Burke's *Reflections* was written during the revolutionary years. Macpherson pointed out that one should not overlook the second part of the title of the book, because it was very significant, i.e. his immediate concern was the perceived danger of the French Revolution's impact on England and in other parts of Europe.

> The destruction of the old order in France had it been confined to France might have made Burke weep but it would not have moved him to the measured arguments of the *Reflections* nor to the increasing fury of the writings of the last eight years of his life (Macpherson 1980: 38).

In the *Reflections*, Burke made a detailed criticism of both the theoretical and practical aspects of the Revolution. He pointed out the dangers of abstract theorizing, but was realistic enough to provide for an alternative mode of social progression. Unlike Joseph de Maistre (1753–1821) and Louis Gabriel de Bonald (1754–1840), who outrightly defended orthodoxy and absolutism, Burke provided a framework for change with continuity, for "a state without the means of some change is without the means of its conservation ... without such means it might even risk the last of that part of the constitution which it wishes to most religiously preserve" (Burke cited in Curtis 1961: Vol. II: 49).

As Burke pointed out, these two principles of conservation and correction operated in England during the critical periods of the Restoration and the Revolution, when England did not have a king. But in both these critical times, the entire edifice of the old order was not replaced by a totally new one. Instead, a corrective mechanism was achieved to rectify the deficiencies within the existing constitutional framework. As such, it balanced the old and the new.

Burke criticized Jacobinism for its wholesale attack on established religion, traditional constitutional arrangements and the institution of property, which he saw as the source of political wisdom in a country. He often used the term "prejudice", by which he meant attachment to established practices and institutions. These provided a bulwark against sweeping changes, particularly those that followed from a rational critique. He did not support everything that was ancient, only those that held society together by providing order and stability.

Burke's main audience in the *Reflections* was the aristocracy and the upper middle class of English society, which he perceived to be the upholders of stability and order. He challenged the English ruling class to respond appropriately to the plight of the French queen, otherwise it would reflect lack of chivalry and demonstrate that the British political order was not superior to that of the Continent. Eighteenth-century English culture projected itself superior to ancient republicanism, for the manners begot by chivalry had softened the harsher and more austere qualities associated with the classical model of virtue (Pocock 1985: 193–212).

Burke further argued that the period of the *Magna Carta* 1215 to the *Bill of Rights* of 1688 was one of slow but steady consolidation, reflecting continuity and change. This enabled the British constitution to preserve and provide unity within the context of diversity. Inheritance was cherished as a political necessity, for without it both conservation and transmission were not possible. Drawing a parallel between the natural process and the political one, he wrote: "... by preserving the method of nature in the conduct of the state, in what we improve, we are never wholly new; in what we retain we are never wholly obsolete" (Burke cited in Curtis 1961: Vol. II: 50–51).

Pointing out the enormous difference between the patterns of change in Britain and France, Burke said that in sharp contrast to the process of gradual change in British constitutional evolution, the French attempt had been to achieve a complete break with the past with a new emphasis on equality and participation. With his inherent belief in natural aristocracy, he debunked the very attempt to create a society of equals. "The Levellers passionately only change and pervert the natural order of things; they load the edifice of society by setting up in the air what the solidity of the structure is required to be on the ground" (Burke cited in Curtis ibid: 52).

Burke emphasized the necessity of a well-ordered state, to be ruled by a combination of ability and property. Such an order was inherently based on inequality. He linked the perpetuation of family property with that of society's. There was no place for either proportionate equality or democratic equality in his preference for aristocratic rule.

CRITIQUE OF NATURAL RIGHTS AND CONTRACT

Burke pointed out the intricacies of human nature and the complexities of society, and because of such considerations no simple analysis of human nature or power was possible. Rejecting any claim of either economic or political equality, he provided a theory of rights within this large framework of his political philosophy. He emphasized partnership, but denied any corresponding equal rights in the enjoyment of economic and political privileges. In understanding and perpetuating this philosophy, the British constitution had stood the test of time. Distinguishing the singular characteristics of the British, he sarcastically remarked, "We are not the converts of Rousseau; we are not the disciples of Voltaire; Helvetius has made no progress amongst us" (Burke cited in Curtis ibid: 55).

Emphasizing the utmost need of continuity, Burke pointed out that in the areas of morality, principles of government and ideas of liberty, there was no need to make a fresh beginning every time. Giving the example of the English achievement, he pointed out the inevitability of a continuous process of adaptability and change within the larger structure. Rejecting atheism and pointing out the enormous importance of religion for a proper functioning of civil society, he characterized the individual as a religious animal. He saw no conflict between the existence of an established church, an established monarchy, an established aristocracy and an established limited democracy. The point that Burke made was that in a modern age the coexistence of institutions was of utmost importance for effective functioning and efficiency. He stressed the fact that all authority was to be exercised as a trust, and in this his philosophy was akin to that of Locke, but he emphasized that the continuity of society had to be preserved at any cost. The overall structure of society could not be just reduced to a mere contract between two or more parties. It was not a trade agreement involving paper, coffee, calico or tobacco. Such agreements reflected only transient interests, which could be dissolved by the parties involved. It reflected "the gross animal existence of a temporary and perishable nature". The intricacies of social relationships had to be understood on a very different plane. To quote his memorable words:

> ... It is a partnership in all science, a partnership in all art, a partnership in every virtue and in all perfection. As the ends of such a partnership cannot be obtained in many generations, it becomes a partnership not only between those who are living, but between those who are living. those who are dead and those who are to be born. Each contract of a particular state is but a clause in the great primeval contract of eternal natures, connecting the visible and invisible world, according to a fixed compact sanctioned by the inviolable oath which holds all physical and all moral natures, each in their appointed place (Burke cited in Curtis ibid: 59).

Along with the rejection of the contract, Burke rejected the other Lockeian fundamentals—natural law, the rights of the individual and the separation of the Church and the state. The only laws that he recognized were the laws of God and the laws of a civilized society. For Burke, any parallel between the English Revolution of 1688 and the French Revolution of 1789 was totally misleading. The former was an acceptable and desirable change within a constitutional framework, whereas the latter was based on a rationalist and untested theory of *The Rights of Man*. It was an attempt to create a new order by making a total break with past practices.

> They have *The Rights of Man*. Against these there can be no prescription; against these no agreement is binding, these admit no temperament, and no compromise; anything withheld from their full demand is so much of fraud and injustice. Against these their rights of men let no government look for security in the length of its continuance, or in the justice and levity of its administration. The objections of these speculatists, if its forms do not quadrate with their theories are as valid against such an old and beneficent government as against the most violent tyranny or the greatest usurpation (Parkin 1969: 121).

Burke did not reject the argument of human rights, except that he sought to rescue the real rights from the imagined ones. He shared with Locke the view that political philosophy was based on theological foundations, but rejected the derivative of political and juridical equality from the argument that all human beings were created equal by God. He also rejected the idea of creating order with the help of human reason. He charged the doctrine of natural rights with "metaphysical abstraction". It failed to take into account the differences that existed between societies. Following Montesquieu, he insisted that different countries merited different legal and political systems, keeping in view the differences pertaining to climate, geography and history. The universality of the natural rights doctrine overlooked national, geographical and cultural distinctions.

Burke also emphasized that there were no simple answers in politics, and that nothing could be stated in axioms valid for all times and places as envisaged by the *Declaration*. He called for an Aristotelian mean in each society. "Political reason is a computing principle: adding, subtracting, multiplying, and dividing, morally and not metaphysically or mathematically, true moral denominations" (Burke 1969: 107).

Though Burke's criticism of natural rights seemed similar to that of Bentham, there were significant differences. Burke's conception of human well-being was not hedonistic as in the case of Bentham. In fact, it was more like Aristotle's idea of "eudaimonia", linking moral virtue and duty with that of political morality and duty. Furthermore, Burke suggested maximization, but by stressing the moral to the mathematical he was closer to Aristotle's "phronesis". He also rejected the utilitarian idea of trade-offs. Unlike Bentham, Burke was also cautious about endless new schemes, as evident from the following statement.

> The science of constructing a commonwealth, or renovating it, or reforming it, is, like every other experimental science, not to be taught *a priori*. Nor is it a short experience that can instruct us in that practical science; because the real effects of moral causes are not always immediate; but that which in the first instance is prejudicial may be excellent in its remoter operation; and its excellence may arise even from the ill effects it produces in the beginning. The reverse also happens; and very plausible schemes, with very pleasing commencements, have often shameful and lamentable conclusions. In states there are often some

obscure and almost latent causes, things which appear at first view of little moment, on which a very great part of its prosperity or adversity may most essentially depend (Burke ibid: 106).

Besides emphasizing political virtue, Burke also stressed the need of an elite which enjoyed a privileged position because of its contribution to the common good. He placed aristocracy under this category. In parliament, this elite could be distinguished from others with reference to ownership of property, for inheritance was a sure reason for conservation. In this context, the French National Assembly did not consist of men of property. Instead, they were lawyers who earned their livelihood, "depended upon whatever rendered property questionable, ambiguous and insecure, and country curates, who, immersed in hopeless poverty could regard all property, whether secular or ecclesiastical, with no other eye than that of envy. Nothing lasting, and therefore in human life nothing useful, could be expected from such men" (Burke ibid: 131-134).

It was interesting that, apart from emphasizing the real nature of the aftermath of the Revolution, Burke also took note of the significant fact that the Revolution had been led by a new class of people with no previous experience of politics, namely lawyers, writers, philosophers, city-based financiers and projectors, whom he called the "swinish multitude". In contrast to the established elite of society, who were sober and experienced, these counter-elite were just the opposite. Of these counter-elite, the most important were the lawyers, for they were "artful men, talented, aggressive, ideologically inclined, impractical and dangerous if not alienated".

The basic problem was that the talent that made a good lawyer was not enough to make a good ruler and a part of the natural aristocracy. The basic shortcoming of a lawyer was that his experience had a very narrow base, which meant that both the diversity of humankind and complexities of public affairs were beyond his grasp. Tyranny was inevitable if power got concentrated in such hands after the revolution, because destruction and despotism followed, as good and rational reform could be brought in by people who had the necessary experience and expertise. Burke realized the link between revolutionary change, destruction and tyranny, not because of the French Revolution, but as early as 1780 (Freeman 1980: 207). He dismissed radicals as both "hot" and "zealous", never considering the long-term effects of what they did.

LIMITS OF REASON

Burke questioned the very basic argument that a stable political structure could be established only on the basis of reason. He pointed to the limits of reason and its role in understanding society. In fact, Burke questioned the whole style of rationalistic thought, an argument reiterated by Oakeshott.

Quoting Aristotle, he cautioned against *a priori* deductive reasoning in moral arguments. The philosophy of the French revolutionaries was a "false philosophy", because of its insistence that all authority derived its sustenance from reason. Reason was pitted against prejudice, and the consequence was that "by what they call reasoning without prejudice, they leave not one stone upon another in the fabric of human society. They subvert all the authority which they hold, as well as all that which they have destroyed" (Freeman ibid: 208). As opposed to reason, Burke emphasized wisdom as something more than prejudice.

The philosophy of natural rights based on the new principles of liberty and equality was not conducive to the establishment of order. Veneration of authority developed over a period of time, and the denunciation of one authority by a different group led to its denunciation as well. The abstract revolutionary ideology inevitably led from subversion to anarchy, because it brought a consciousness of rights but not of duties of order, discipline and obedience to authority.

Burke repeatedly stressed that societies needed awe, superstition, ritual and honour for their stability, and to be able to secure the loyalty and support of those on whom it depended. He warned that a state which dismissed these entire aside in the name of rational enlightenment would ultimately be a state based merely on a lust for power.

> On the scheme of this barbarous philosophy ... laws are to be supported only by their own terrors, and by the concern, which each individual may find in them, from his own private speculations, or can spare to them from his own private interests. In the groves of their academy, at the end of every vista, you see nothing by the gallows. Nothing is left that engages the affections on the part of the commonwealth. On the principles of this mechanic philosophy, our institutions can never be embodied, if I may use the expression, in persons; so as to create in us love, veneration, admiration or attachment. But that sort of reason which vanishes the affections is incapable of filling their place (Burke 1969: 111).

Burke emphasized that the dignity of the human being came through socialization. One rendered obedience to society not because it benefited us, or that we had promised to obey it, but because we saw ourselves as an integral part of it. Though he rejected the divine rights of kings, he affirmed, like Cicero, that nothing was more pleasing to God than the existence of human "civitates". He accused the natural rights theorists of not merely "imprudence and intellectual arrogance but of blasphemy and impiety as well" (Waldron 1987: 95).

Making a distinction between legitimate civil authority and the use of force, in 1790 Burke wrote: "Everything depends upon the army in such a government as yours ... you see by the report of your War Minister that the distribution of the army is in a great measure made with a view of internal coercion" (Burke cited in Curtis 1961: Vol. II: 211).

Burke later clarified the nature of this military dictatorship. The arbitrary erection of a new order led to sending "for an army to support their work", and after a prolonged and savage struggle, "the troops prevailed over the citizens". The number of soldiers involved was alarming, as 20,000 troops were involved in garrisoning Paris, the consequence of which was that "a complete military government was formed". Burke added significantly that "every other ground of stability, but from military force and terror, is clean out of the question". The entire French revolutionary government "in its origination, in its continuance, in all its actions, and in all its resources, is force and nothing but force" (Burke cited in Curtis ibid: 211).

This tyrannical nature of the revolutionary government was further exemplified by the fact that in revolutionary France,

> ... committees, called of vigilance and safety, are everywhere formed, a most severe and scrutinizing inquisition, far more rigid than anything ever known or imagined. Two persons cannot meet and confer without hazard to their liberty and even to their lives. Numbers scarcely credible have been executed, and their property confiscated (Burke cited in Curtis ibid: 211).

CITIZENSHIP AND DEMOCRACY

Burke was also perturbed by the democratic aspirations of the French Revolution, in particular by the doctrines of popular sovereignty and general will. He regarded democracy as the "most shameless thing in the world" (Burke 1969: 190). He was skeptical of the political ability of the ordinary people. He was an elitist, totally unconcerned about the plight of the masses. For him, the best form of political practice was one that was played by a few of the enlightened and aristocratic elite.

Burke believed that elections gave an opportunity for the enfranchized citizens to choose the wise elite to govern them. The task of a citizen was "to deliver an opinion while a MP should use his 'mature judgement' and 'enlightened conscience'". Like Aristotle, he favoured citizenship limited to a segment of adults who had the leisure for discussions and information, and were not mentally dependent. Ownership of property as a necessary condition for citizenship was favoured by the Whigs in England and America. In view of the fact that average individuals were guided by their baser instincts, governments had to keep them apathetic so as to prevent their selfishness from undermining communal life. Burke was a precursor of the twentieth-century advocates of elitist democracy.

> Society requires not only that the passions of individuals should be subjected, but that even in the mass and body as well as in individuals, the inclinations of men should frequently be thwarted, their will controlled. and their passions brought into subjection. This can only

> be done *by a power out of themselves;* and not, in the exercise of its function, subject to that will and to those passions which it is its office to bridle and subdue (Burke ibid: 69).

Burke accepted inequalities as natural and unavoidable in any society, and that some would enjoy an enhanced status. In a well-ordered society, this ruling elite was a genuine one, a "natural aristocracy", for the mass of people were incapable of governing themselves. They could not think or act without guidance and direction. For Burke, government was not based on general will, but wisdom. He told his Bristol constituency: "If government were a matter of will upon any side, yours without question ought to be superior. But government and legislation are matters of reason and judgement" (Burke cited in Canavan 1960: 94). This was because government had to do with duty and morality, and that "... neither the few nor the many have a right to act merely by their will, in any matter connected with duty, trust, engagement or obligation ... duty and will are ever contradictory terms, will cannot be the standard of right and wrong" (Burke cited in Canavan ibid: 94).

REPRESENTATION AND PITKIN'S ANALYSIS

For Burke, political representation "is the representation of interests, and interest has an objective, impersonal and unattached reality" (Pitkin 1967: 10). For Burke, aristocracy of virtue and wisdom should govern for the good of a nation. As in other areas, even in representation, there was no clear and well laid-out theory of representation. But out of Burke's speeches and writings some key ideas emerged. He regarded the members of parliament to be an elite group, a group of natural aristocracy. The mass of ordinary people needed guidance and direction from this elite since they could not govern by themselves. Representatives were genuinely superior to the electorate. The representatives had to possess the capacity for rational decision making. They were to be men of practical wisdom. This was a negation of Rousseau's theory. The representatives need not consult or be bound by the views of the voters.

Furthermore, governmental action was guided by obligation and ethical considerations, and questions of right and wrong. Burke championed rational parliamentary discussion, which provided the right answers to political questions. And as a participant, the representative need not consult the voters. They enjoyed complete freedom, for they had no interest other than the national interest. In a famous passage, Burke observed:

> Parliament is not a Congress of ambassadors from different and hostile interests, which interests each must maintain, as an agent and advocate, against other agents and advocates; but Parliament is a deliberative assembly of one nation, with one interest, that of the whole—where not local prejudice ought to guide, but the general good, resulting

> from the general reason of the whole. You choose a member indeed, but when you have chosen him he is not a member of Bristol, but he is a Member of Parliament (Burke 1774: 116).

With contempt for the average voter, Burke advocated restricted suffrage so that the selection of the natural aristocratic group of parliament became foolproof. He also distinguished between *actual representation* and *virtual representation.* Since an area would have one dominant interest, he saw the merit of virtual representation against actual representation. Virtual representation was based on common interest. By this logic, even people who did not vote were represented. The localities which did not have actual representation by this criterion would have virtual representation. Burke was careful in noting that this logic of virtual representation did not hold for the disenfranchised Catholics of Ireland and the people of the American colonies.

Pitkin (1967: 169–170) rightly pointed out that Burke's position was highly inconsistent. His view of representation endorsed the seventeenth-century notion of representation, and had very little relevance in contemporary times. However, it helps us to understand the anti-democratic bias prevalent during Burke's period. The Burkean theory centred around the parliament. Conniff (1977: 331–332) tried to refute Pitkin's analysis by questioning the theory of objective interest and a commonly-held agreement of the parliamentary elite on what constituted the common good. However, since Burke was clear that every recognizable constituency had one dominant interest, and that a consensus could always emerge out of parliamentary discussion, Pitkin's criticism was not on firm ground.

RELIGION AND TOLERATION

Burke's views on religion exhibited both liberal and conservative perceptions. He defended traditional practices of the established church, unless there was an "intolerable abuse". He equated attack on the established Church of England as tantamount to an attack on England's constitutional order. He was convinced that the established church would foster peace and dissuade civil discord. His liberal temperament made him advocate and defend toleration for most religious sects, including non-Christians. He was perturbed that the Protestants did not support toleration for the Catholics. He did not believe in the truth of any particular religion, but was concerned about the effect of changes in traditional religious practice on political stability. Only on the grounds of civil peace could toleration and religious freedom be refused.

Burke believed that atheists posed a grave threat to civil peace. He looked upon atheism as complementary to political radicalism. He was condescending towards Rational Dissenters as being better than atheists, for at least they believed in God, though not in the divinity of Christ.

However, he castigated all those who corrupted and attacked religion as being destructive of all authority, thereby undermining equity, justice, and order—the foundations of human society.

Burke did not quarrel with the atheists as long as they did nothing to publicly attack or subvert religion. While he began to dislike Hume for his open contempt of religion, he remained friendly with the irreligious Smith, even though the latter blamed Roman Catholicism for impeding economic and political progress, but there was no denunciation or revolt against religion.

Burke's critique of the French Revolution was also due to the latter's anti-clericalism. The famous cry "hang the bishops from the lampposts" during the early days of the Revolution was an indication of the "insolent irreligious in opinions and practices". The nationalization of the Church's property by the National Assembly in 1790 was a move against traditional religion, and represented the larger goal of subverting established authority and civil society. The revolutionary fervour only fostered hatred, animosity and suspicion, rather than affection and trust. It undermined the traditional civilizing ties of the French citizens. Burke placed a great deal of emphasis on manners that controlled passions and will.

THE ACTUAL REVOLUTIONARY PROCESS AND BURKE

Burke analyzed the French revolution when the revolutionaries seized **control** of the capital and stormed the Bastille in July 1789. By 1790, the situation in France stabilized when the assembly of deputies declared martial law to prevent disorder. The king agreed to the Declaration of Rights in August 1789. Under the new moderate constitution, the king would enjoy the right to appoint ministers, who in turn were responsible to an elected assembly. The king had a veto on legislation up to four years, and the assembly enjoyed a veto on declaration of war. Suffrage was conferred on males over 25 years of age paying minimum taxes. This meant that 75 per cent of the population had the right to vote, but only one in a hundred possessed the wealth to qualify as a deputy. Aristocratic titles were abolished. Law courts were reformed, and the more barbaric instruments of law (branding, torture and hanging) were abolished. Capital punishment was retained. The majority of the French people viewed these measures as moving towards a constitutional monarchy based on personal freedom and the rule of law. The rule of the king still continued: his subsequent execution, the reign of Terror and the rise of Robespierre had yet to come.

> Burke's lucid description of the Revolution has seemed to many prophetic yet for the most part Burke claims to be describing the events which have already taken place. Indeed it can be argued that the hysteria and international opposition to the Revolution which Burke was instrument in creating contributed to its eventually violent path (Hampsher-Monk 1987: 158).

The exact impact of Burke's tract on the subsequent events in France was difficult to tell, but the fact remained that he really grasped its historic significance. He wrote:

> It appears to me as if I were in a great crisis, not of the affairs of France alone, but of all of Europe, perhaps of more than Europe ... . The beginning of confusion with us in England are at present feeble enough, but ... we have seen an infancy still more feeble growing by moments into a strength to heap mountains upon mountains and to urge war with heaven itself. Whenever our neighbour's house is on fire, it cannot be amiss for the engines to play a little on our own (Burke cited in Spragens 1976: 36).

Burke was also perturbed about the effects' of the Revolution on Britain. He attacked the pro-Revolution speech by Price. His friend Gibbon too agreed with Burke about the Revolution. Gibbon welcomed Burke's critique of the French Revolution enthusiastically, and characterized the revolutionaries as "fanatic missionaries of sedition" and as the "new Barbarians who laboured to confound the order and happiness of society". He dubbed the Jacobins as those who darkened the Christian world. Similar sentiments can be found in Smith's *Theory of Moral Sentiments* (1759). When Burke attacked the Revolution, he was accused of being a friend of Catholicism and a crypto-Jesuit. A cartoon that appeared in 1790 portrayed Burke as a Jesuit Don Quixote: "The Knight of the Woeful Countenance Going to Extirpate The [French] National Assembly". Many within Burke's party (including Fox) felt that Burke's anti-French stance was partly due to his desire to get a pension from the Pitt government.

THE BURKE-PAINE DEBATE

The fact remained that the French Revolution generated a great deal of debate in England. Burke's *Reflections* itself began as a letter to M. Dupont, replying to the latter's request for Burke's opinion. Subsequently, a pamphlet developed which sold 12,000 copies in England and a similar number in France in the first month of its publication. Within seven months, German and Italian translations appeared in the market. Burke's position was criticized by Paine in his *Rights of Man* (1791), which Paine described "had the greatest run of anything ever published in this country" (Paine cited in Jackson 1969: 108). The enormous popularity of these two divergent tracts reflected diametrically opposite views on society.

Paine, in his reply, defended Enlightenment liberalism and tried to correct "the flagrant misrepresentations which Mr Burke's pamphlet contains" (Paine 1973: 270). Both agreed that in contemporary European society there existed in very large proportion illiterate and unenlightened people. Burke, following Aristotle, argued that individuals differed in their capacities, which was why any attempt to level would never succeed.

Paine, on the contrary, attributed the large numbers of illiterate people in the "old" world to bad governments. In total contrast to Burke, he championed the cause of universal suffrage, representative government, the rule of law, and a sympathetic attitude to the poor. He denounced the hereditary system, whether in the name of monarchy or aristocracy, for a "hereditary governor is as ridiculous as an hereditary author" (cited in Jackson ibid: 111). Unlike Burke, Paine, following Locke, justified government as an outcome of a social contract between the people themselves. He was critical of the British constitution for being unwritten, making it unhelpful as a reference point. Its precedents were all arbitrary, contrary to reason and common sense. He defended the French *Declaration of the Rights of Man*. He refuted the entire anti-democratic argument of Burke in the following words.

> It has been thought a considerable advance towards establishing the principles of freedom to say that Government is a compact between those who govern and those who are governed but this cannot be true, because it is putting the effect before the cause for as man must have existed before Governments existed. There necessarily was a time when governments did not exist, and consequently there could originally exist no governors to form such a compact with. The fact therefore must be that the individuals themselves each in his own personal and sovereign right, entered into a compact with each other to produce a Government; and this is the only mode in which governments have a right to arise, and the only principle on which they have a right to exist (Paine cited in Cobban 1950: 31).

Burke and Paine were representative symbols of the conservative and the radical responses to the French Revolution. It was noteworthy that both of them championed the American cause, but were on opposite sides with regard to the French experiment. Their basic disagreements could be understood in light of their support to the American cause. For Burke, "Taxation without representation" violated traditional English rights and liberties and that the English were on the wrong side of history, because they violated their own well-established practices. For demanding redress, the Americans did not base their arguments, like the French did, on a notion of natural rights. Paine, on the other hand, found that the British action in America was a violation of universal reason and natural rights. He declared that "the cause of America is in great measure the cause of all mankind" (Paine ibid: 42). It was an appeal to create a new world. Paine rejected hierarchical authority, and asserted that "setting up and putting down kings and governments is the natural right of citizens" (Paine ibid: 42). "It was not Tom Paine's common-sense but rage that turned hundreds of thousands of Americans to thoughts of independence in the winter of 1776" (Kramnick 1976: 45).

Burke himself wrote of Paine that he wanted to destroy in six or seven days "the feudal and chivalric order which all the boasted wisdom of our ancestors has laboured to bring to perfection for six or seven centuries" (Burke cited in Kramnick ibid: 46). Paine looked down on aristocracy as a class of unproductive idlers and parasites, who lived off the surplus and the exploitation of the industrious classes. As such, in a rational, reconstructed society they would not be missed at all. The striking similarity between a radical Paine, a liberal Mill and a socialist Saint Simon was too clear to be missed. With a direct question to Burke, Paine made his point.

> Why then does Mr. Burke talk of his house of peers, as the pillar of the landed interest? Were that pillar to sink into the earth, the same landed property would continue, and the same ploughing, sowing, and reaping would go on. The aristocracy are not farmers who work the land, and raise the produce, but are the mere consumers of the rent and when compared with the active world are the drones ... who neither collect the honey or form the hive, but exist only for lazy enjoyment (Paine cited in Cobban 1950: 47).

Knowing Burke's influence, in the summer of 1789 Paine wrote to Burke from Paris to solicit his support for introducing in England "a more enlarged system of liberty" (Kirk 1960: 30). Furthermore, Honore Gabriel Riquetti, Comte de Mirabeau (1749–1791) quoted long passages from Burke's speeches in the National Assembly. The reason for this, as Cobban pointed out, was that at least five separate rebellions against authority could be cited as meeting with Burke's specific approval. These were the Glorious Revolution of 1688, the American War of Independence, the struggle of the Corsicans for freedom, the attempt of the Poles to preserve their national independence, and various revolts against the minions of Warren Hastings in India (Cobban 1960b). Whiggism, in the context of the eighteenth-century, was progressive with its opposition to arbitrary monarchical power, advocacy of internal reform in administration, skepticism of England's adventures abroad, a considerable degree of religious toleration, and freedom under the law. All of them, as Kirk remarked, were the intellectual legacies of 1688 (Kirk 1960: 14–15). Burke enthusiastically supported these principles. "Burke was liberal because he was conservative. And this cast of mind Tom Paine was wholly unable to appreciate" (Kirk ibid: 21). But the virulent Burkean onslaught on the French Revolution had to be understood from the fact that "he was always a liberal, never a democrat and that he dreaded a modern democratic state" (Kirk ibid: 20). It was Burke's insight that he could really grasp the historic departure that French revolutionary ideas held for mankind, which were totally out of tune with his philosophy of cautious reform and the rule of the natural aristocracy. Moreover, he emphasized the importance of prudence in political affairs, which was why he supported the American but not the French Revolution.

Another refutation came from James Mackintosh's *Vindiciae Gallicae* in 1791. In it he insisted that Burke had trampled upon the ideals of Whiggism and aligned himself instead with Tory superstition and chivalry. In opposition to Paine, Mackintosh invoked the ideals of 1688 in explaining the events in France. He supported the Revolution, for it attempted to make France a commercial society.

Catherine Sawbridge Macaulay-Graham (1731–91) also furnished a rejoinder to Burke regarding the French Revolution as something new and unique spreading the message of enlightened spirit. Like Price she sees benevolent providence in it and not a repetition of the English developments. The most scathing from a feminist perspective was provided by Wollstonecraft.

CONCLUSION

If one analyzed the costs involved in the revolutionary process, the question that arose was: Was the Revolution justified? Two million people died in the Revolution, a number which was higher than the casualties in the First World War with one-third of its twentieth-century population. Politically, it led to terror and ultimately to the rise of Napoleon. With the exit of Napoleon, the political leadership of Europe moved away from France. On the economic front, the consequences were worse. The population growth rate slowed down. Between 1789 and 1815, the French population increased only by 9 per cent, compared with England's 23 per cent. The French grain production of 1815 was the same as in 1789. In sharp contrast, English agriculture was ahead of that of France before the Revolution, and went further ahead after Waterloo. Industrially, England became the centre of the world. In 1789, the French deficit was 125 million francs; in 1814 it increased to 2275 million francs. The poor and the sick suffered. Established institutions were blindly destroyed, and there was nothing more inhuman than the systematic execution of opponents and critics of the regime. In comparison, Britain established its naval supremacy throughout the world, and also secured the overseas possessions of France. In retrospect, the French Revolution proved to be a good thing for Britain but not for France. Burke dismissed the revolutionaries as radicals, as they were not for reform. In 1795, he said, "I wished to warn the people against the greatest of all evils: a blind and furious spirit of innovation, under the name of reform." This view of Burke was endorsed by Arendt (1973), who demonstrated that for a revolution to succeed in protecting liberty and avoiding terror, it is to be limited in its ambit. It had to be a political revolution like the American one, not a social one as were the French and Russian.

Burke was not only worried about the situation in France, but also concerned with the state of affairs in Ireland. He despised the Irish ruling class for its "armed and systematic tyranny" propped up by the established Protestant Church. He condemned the desire of the Irish to separate from England, which he called "unnatural", and if it happened, then Ireland would lose its tranquillity and prosperity. He had immense faith in English institutions and customs, and saw them as crucial for the well-being of both Great Britain and Ireland. He hoped that the Protestants and the Catholics, being Christians, would unite against their common enemy—atheistic French Jacobins. Of course, he was aware of the fact that the Irish-English distrust and animosity was more historical and less religious. Burke was inherently skeptical as to whether secular faith could bring about progress.

For Burke, the political ends to be secured were stability and the natural hierarchical order by means that would ensure good government and the realization of individual's good within one's station in life. He repeatedly emphasized obedience to be part of a citizen's duty. If there was a likelihood of subversion of the natural order of things, then the natural aristocracy, the *noblesse qui oblige,* should take the lead and set things rights. When such a situation did arise, then violence by necessity became a technique. Burke's caution against the resort of extreme steps like revolution revealed not only his fear of destructive means, but also his reverence for established ends. He preferred peace to freedom, yet he did not support absolutism in the way the Continental reactionary Conservatives did.

Burke used the historical perspective to understand politics. The state to him was a product of historical growth, and he compared it to a living organism. The state represented the whole, and hence was more complex and large than the parts that constituted it. Burke's conservatism rested on a philosophically-backed skepticism about the possibilities of discerning the historical processes by which societies developed. It was not concerned, as in other forms of conservatism, to discover an ideal in the past to which one must go back. His reputation was that of a reformer, for he held that one must reform in order to preserve, and that a society without the means of reformation could not have the means of preservation. However, Burke emphasized limiting the ambit of reforms to eradicate the present evil, and not aimed at realizing a blueprint that would conform to rational standards. The British in 1688 changed persons but not institutions, whereas the French destroyed the institutions, keeping intact the persons.

It would not be wrong to call Burke the chief architect of conservative philosophy and outlook. His political writings were by and large polemical. His speeches in the House of Commons were among the most memorable, and the range of his political oratory was amazing. It included the struggle for a most favourable treatment of the American colonies, the impeachment of Warren Hastings, the opposition to electoral reform, the right of a member of parliament to an independent judgement free from the control of the constituents, and above all a virulent attack on the French Revolution.

The *Reflections* contained the core of Burke's philosophic ideas. He attacked the theory of natural rights, absolute liberty, equality, democracy, popular sovereignty, general will, and abstract principles of change and revolution based on reason. He placed primary emphasis on prescription, presumption and prejudice as being more important than reason for the functioning of government. Reason was inherently limiting, incapable of unravelling the mystery of the universe, for it discounted the roles played by passion, prejudice and habit. He also emphasized that society was not a process of conscious creation, but represented continuity and partnership between generations. He also dismissed atomistic individualism as hollow, for individuals were born within a society. The individual found fulfilment and a sense of belonging only in a society, hence, more than the individual, it was the family which was seen as the basic social unit. He also defended inequality among human beings, and supported the natural ordering of things. Like Smith, he stressed the importance of preserving and protecting property. He favoured accumulation of wealth, rights of inheritance and the need to enfranchise property owners. While Burke was socially conservative, he was a liberal in economics, the two being fused together uneasily.

Burke had to be understood as a "philosophic conservative, opposed equally to unchanging reaction and to revolutionary change. Revolution was undesirable because it would sweep away the sound principles of political action and discard the guidance of nature" (Curtis 1961: Vol. II: 46). Revolutionary change was undesirable not only for the uncontrollable violence it unleashed, but also because it invariably led to seizure of power by those who were unable to use it harmoniously or renounce it peacefully. Reforms, on the other hand, could also be dangerous if they were taken to extremes, making them obtuse and unacceptable to their participants. Change could be enduring and feasible only if it attempted to conserve. Burke impressed upon the importance of acting prudently, improvement by preserving and reform by changing, and not by embarking upon a complete break with the past and traditions. He respected institutions that had worked reasonably well over a period of time, but he did not favour the *status quo*. His respect for prescription was applied to tested schemes and not to untried ones. He favoured penal reforms, abolition of slavery, and reduction in the number of governmental sinecures. "I do not like to see anything destroyed; any void produced in society; any ruin on the face of the land" (Burke cited in Bromwich 1998: 4).

Burke's most important and uncontroversial legacy was his naturalism. He did not, like Locke, believe that conveniences were created when human beings mixed their labour with the earth and its raw materials.

> We are humanized by the time it takes to grow used to our own responses to things, and we do not have enough time if the stimuli change at too rapid a rate. As for society, no single person has made it, nor has the latest living generation; and by seeking to reform it quickly and efficiently, we wish the creation of a mechanism void of the conditions that made us possible. The self-contempt that is latent in such a policy will always be legible in its effects (Bromwich 1998: 4).

He did not see any contradiction in the expansion of commerce and the importance of prescription, though he admitted that it was not easy to strike a balance between the roles of the market and the state. The state was necessary to ensure political stability.

Burke like other political thinkers was a child of his times, and as Laski and Williams (1958) rightly contended, he was opposed to democracy. Williams also stated that he did not experience a mass society which explained his reverence for the past and for the confusion between the state and society. Williams (imbid: 31) also added that Burke "seemed blind to many changes which, even as he wrote, were transforming England". The economic forces were breaking down the organic society which he sought to defend. MacIver (1926: 148) criticized Burke for doing a disservice to humankind when he "enveloped once more in mystic obscurity the office of government and in the sphere of politics appealed once more against reason to tradition and religion". However, "Burke's prejudice in favour of prejudice makes it possible to eulogize the normal practices of any society not founded on coercion. That he is therefore a precursor of John Stuart Mill and not of Joseph Maistre" (Bromwich ibid: 4).

Burke laid down a list of the minimum common rights of individuals which were essential prerequisites for a decent society. These were:

> ... rights to the fruits of their industry; and to the means of making their industry fruitful. They have a right to the acquisitions of their parents; to the nourishment and improvement of their offspring; to instruction in life, and to consolation in death. Whatever each man can separately do, without trespassing upon others, he has a right to do for himself; and he has a right to a fair portion of all which society, with all its combination of skill and force, can do in his favour (Burke cited in Bromwich ibid: 4).

Burke made politics dignified and efficient. He deliberated judiciously on important issues, and because of this achievement he "has endured as the permanent manual of political wisdom without which statesmen are as sailors on an uncharted sea" (Laski cited in Kirk 1960: 23).

10

Jeremy Bentham

> Jeremy Bentham applied utilitarian principles to the discussion of a great variety of political, legal and administrative problems with a thoroughness unrivalled by anyone else... He was not so much a moral and political philosopher as he was a theoretical reformer. It was he who devised some of the best arguments in favour of many of the most impor-tant reforms undertaken in this country during the nineteenth century (Plamentaz 1966: 59).

> Jeremy Bentham was not, I think, in any sense of degree an originator of ideas. He was a man of highly distinctive temperament, highly independent in thought, and of great mental activity. There was, indeed a certain originality in the mere conception of a life devoted to the construction of perfect codes of law based on a few simple principles. But those principles were no discoveries of Bentham's; on the contrary, either they were assumptions common and fashionable among the educated at the time or they were such as Bentham had absorbed from Hume to Helvetius (Allen 1931: 184).

> Jeremy Bentham stood out as the dominating political philosopher of the radical reform group. He did not seek like Rousseau to escape from grim actualities into mysticism. He approached his problem in the spirit of a scientist firmly convinced that the wrongs of the people were commensurable, that their happiness could be assured when once its measurements were ascertained (Doyle 1963: 228).

Jeremy Bentham (1748–1832), the founder of Utilitarianism, combined throughout his active life the careers of a philosopher, a jurist and that of a social reformer and an activist. Though trained to be a lawyer, he gave up the practice of law in order to examine the basis of law and pursue legal reforms. His utilitarian philosophy based on the principle of the "greatest happiness of the greatest number" was aimed "at rearing the fabric of felicity by the hands of reason and law" (Sabine 1973: 617). He championed reforms of prison, legislation and parliament, and stressed the need for a new penal code for England. It was for these reasons that he has been regarded by J.S. Mill as a "progressive philosopher", "the great benefactor of mankind", "an enemy of the *status quo* and the greatest questioner of things established" (Mill 1950: 78).

Bentham had his share of critics as well. Goethe described him as "that frightfully radical ass" Keynes characterized his ideas as the worm which had been gnawing at the insides of modern civilization responsible for its present moral decay. Oakeshott regarded him as a reformer of law and the first significant English writer, but uncharitably dismissed his influence as a thinker. Emerson characterized his philosophy as "stinking". Schumpeter considered his ideas as the "shallowest of all conceivable philosophies of life". J.S. Mill described him as a "boy" to the end, for he had "neither the internal experience nor the external, and had lived a quiet eunuch's life on a private income without ever growing up". Marx regarded him as "the arch-philistine, the insipid, leather tongued oracle of the commonplace bourgeois intelligence". Nietzsche (1955:155–156) mocked at him with a little verse.

Soul of washrag; "face of poker"
Overwhelming mediocre,
Sans genie et sans esprit.

Leon Trotsky (1879–1940) referred to utilitarianism as "a philosophy of social cookbook recipes" (Mack 1962: 2–5).

LIFE SKETCH

Bentham was born on February 15, 1748 in London in a prosperous middle-class family. He lost his mother at the age of 10. His father Jeremiah Bentham, generally strict and demanding, ensured a thorough education for his son, making the latter's childhood monotonous and gloomy. As a child, Bentham's major source of enjoyment was reading books, with no inclination to play. This explained his serious outlook. Bentham started to learn Latin at the age of three and went to Queen's College, Oxford, at the age of 12, learning to dislike, rebuke, suspect and hate anything that was ancient or traditional, both in ideas and institutions.

Bentham studied law and was called to the Bar in 1769. He never pleaded a single case and gave up the idea of practising law in the conviction that the whole system of law needed overhauling. Like Hobbes, he was deeply interested in science, especially chemistry and botany. The French philosophers Claude-Adrien Helvetius (1715–1771) and Cesare Bonesana, Marquis of Beccaria (1738–1794), inspired and influenced him. It was generally believed that he came across the phrase "the greatest happiness of the greatest number" with which his name was intrinsically associated in the 1767 English translation of Beccaria's *Essays on Crimes and Punishments* (1764). Some other biographers contended that he borrowed the idea from Joseph Priestly (1733–1804). In 1770, Bentham acknowledged with a sensation of Archimedes the full import of Priestly's phrase as being a possible foundation of morals and legislation.

Bentham was profoundly impressed by Feneton's *Telemaque,* given to him by his French tutor. In Feneton's version, Mentor and Telemachus, in search of Ulysses came to Crete at a time when elections were to be held to fill a vacant throne. After an athletic competition, the victorious candidates were asked three questions: What Man was most free? Who was most unhappy? Which of the two ought to be preferred, a king who was invincible in war or a king who, without any military experience, could administer civil government with great wisdom in times of peace? Telemachus won the contest by arguing that the happiest ruler was one who made others happy. Bentham was profoundly influenced by this tale. In this sense, his greatest happiness principle was the rationale of his "childish, romantic idealization of Telemachus" (Mack ibid: 32).

From Helvetius, Bentham realized that legislation was the most significant of all worldly pursuits. Legislation could bring about suitable reforms, since all human beings were fundamentally alike and their differences were due to their upbringing, environment and education. He proclaimed "... what Bacon was to the physical world, Helvetius was to the moral. The moral world has therefore had its Bacon, but its Newton is yet to come" (Bentham cited in Halvey 1928: 19).

Bentham hoped to be that Newton. He also credited Helvetius with providing him an answer to the meaning of "genius", a word that bothered him ever since he was introduced as a "prodigy" by his father to the headmaster of Westminster School, Dr Markham. Unable to answer the meaning of "genius" when queried by the headmaster, Bentham was embarrassed. A genius meant to produce. On learning its meaning, he began to wonder whether he had a genius for anything? After enough soul-searching he realized that he had a gift for codifying laws.

From the early 1770s, the study of legislation became Bentham's most important preoccupation. He did not practise law, but concentrated on writing about what the law should *be,* rather than what it *was.* The period from the early 1770s to the mid-1780s was of great significance in the development of Bentham's ideas. During this time he devoted his energies to understanding the rational basis of law, both in England and other countries. In his earliest project, called "Preparatory Principles", he set upon himself the task of making a set of new and systematic legal terms which could be used for studying the theory and practice of law. His manuscripts consisted of definitions and analyses of basic terms and concepts in jurisprudence.

In the mid-1770s, at 28 years of age, Bentham wrote a lengthy critique of William Blackstone's (1723–1780) *Commentaries on the Laws of England*

(1765–1769). A portion of this critique was published in 1776 as *A Fragment on Government,* arousing the interest of the Earl of Shelbourne, a Whig aristocrat. Impressed by Bentham's work, the earl invited him to stay in his country house at Bowood, Wilshire. This was the beginning of a close relationship, based on common ideas and purpose.

Interestingly, *A Fragment on Government* was first published anonymously, encouraging considerable speculation about its authorship. Its sales plummeted when the author's name was accidentally revealed. Coincidentally, 1776 was the year of publication of Smith's well-known book. *The Wealth of Nations,* the adoption of the Declaration of Independence by the American colonies, and the announcement of Major Carthwright's charter for universal suffrage and annual parliaments. It was noteworthy that the Declaration referred to the "pursuit of happiness", motivating Bentham to discover the laws governing human action.

During his close association with the Earl of Shelboume, Bentham got attracted to Lady Shelbourne's niece, Caroline Fox. This was his second love, the first being Mary Dunkley. However, neither of the relationships culminated in marriage and Bentham remained a bachelor. Bentham showered all his affections on his brother Samuel, nine years younger to him. He took a keen interest in his education and career, without being overbearing. He encouraged Samuel to visit Russia. He subsequently decided to visit Russia in 1780, and that visit proved to be a turning point in Bentham's life, for he began to take greater interest in legislation and reforms.

Bentham began to devote his time and energies to practical areas like public administration, economics and social policy, apart from concentrating on developing a theory of law and legislation. One reason for this shift was because of his involvement with Samuel's industrial concerns, devising details on the construction of a prison (or factory or workhouse) in a circular way, enabling the supervisor to monitor the place continuously. This came to be known as the Panopticon, or the inspection house.

Bentham viewed the Panopticon, derived from the Greek word meaning all seeing, as the capstone of Utilitarianism, for it would scientifically mete out felicific calculus by measuring pain justly. Having written a dissertation on punishments, in which he developed and systematized Beccaria's ideas, he was convinced that pain could be scientifically administered by experts. He devoted most of his time to devising the scheme, planning meticulously right down to the governor's urinal. He hoped to be appointed the first governor of the panopticon, and was confident that it would give him £37,000 a year. Like his brother, he believed unflinchingly in contraptions. "[M]orals reformed, health preserved, industry invigorated, instruction diffused, public burthens lightened, economy seated as it were upon a rock, the gordian knot of the poor laws not cut but untied, all by a simple idea in architecture" (Bentham cited in Semple 1992: 153).

In 1791, Bentham sent his plan to English Prime Minister Pitt, but the Panopticon never really materialized, forcing him to admit defeat 20 years later. A jail was built, but not on the design that Bentham recommended. Bentham was awarded compensation for his sincerity and effort, which did not cheer him. He confessed in his old age to John Bowring, the editor of the *Westminster Review* and his literary executor, that he did not like looking into panopticon papers, for it was like entering a haunted house.

Bentham recommended "Big Brother" supervision with 14 hours a day, long hours on the treadwheel accompanied by martial music, totally rejecting solitary confinement as abhorrent and irrelevant. In his utilitarian mission to prevent crime, he advocated punishments like castration for rape and mild kebabbing for arsonists. Subsequently, he applied the principles of the panopticon to poultry, devising the first battery farm.

Foucault presented the panopticon as the quintessence of the disciplinary apparatus of the bourgeois state. He assailed the oppressive totalitarianism that supported self-seeking liberalism. It epitomized repressive rationality. This assessment was far from true. Bentham's proposal never really materialized for it to be considered a prototype of the illiberal capitalist state. He did not prescribe systematic solitary confinement for long-term convicts. He was not the sole ideological father of Victorian social engineering, for the Victorian conception of prison differed considerably from that of Bentham's plans. While Bentham proposed public inspection of the Panopticon, the Victorians wanted the gates of the jails to be closed. He was also against state-run prisons, for they would only lead to corruption and jobbery. Contract prisons, on the contrary, managed by tender and private initiatives would ensure efficiency and profitability. Though he pondered over the rationale for punitive measures, he accepted punishment as long as it served the high goals of utilitarianism (Semple ibid).

Bentham welcomed the French Revolution and sent his reform proposals, though none were adopted. But he was made an honorary citizen of France in 1792 for his *Draught of a New Plan for the Organization of the Judicial Establishment of France* (1790). In the early 1800s, his reputation started to spread, attracting attention even in far-off places like Russia and countries in Latin America.

In 1809, a close relationship between Bentham and James Mill (1773–1836) began, with Mill being convinced of the urgency for reforms. Under Mill's influence, Bentham became more radical. In 1817, Bentham published *Plan of Parliamentary Reform* in the form of catechism. In 1819, he completed the draft proposals of the Radical Reform Bill. An attack on the established church came in *Church of Englandism* in 1818. The codification of law became his primary concern from the 1780s to the 1830s.

Even in his old age Bentham remained in good health. He became financially well-off, with the English Parliament compensating him with £23,000 in 1813 for the non-implementation of the panopticon. He led a simple life, never seeing anyone except for some specific purpose. He relaxed by listening to music, and his favourites were Handel and Corelli. His main hobby was gardening, for that gave him supreme pleasure. He played badminton for physical fitness. He continued with his lifelong devotion to legal reform, looking upon it as a game. In 1819, he wrote:

> [W]hat sacrifice did I make ... ? None at all. I followed my own taste. Chess I could not play without a partner ... codification was a little game I could play at alone ... codification, when I am dead, who can say how many other persons may be the better for (Bentham cited in Mack 1962: 8).

Bentham invented devices like primitive telephones, suggested reforms for the London police, the London sewage and drainage systems, devised a central heating system, ran a law school from his home, worked on schemes for lowering the national debt, secured low interest loans for the poor, planned a national public education system, a national health service, and a national census, conceived a refrigerator for storing goods at low temperatures, and recommended a canal to be dug through Central America to connect the Atlantic and Pacific Oceans. He called himself "The Hermit of Queen's Square Place". Because of his simplicity, he attracted many disciples and followers. A modern counterpart of Bentham was Gandhi (Bronowski and Mazlish 1960: 432). His disciples venerated him as their spiritual leader and teacher. Though he led an ascetic life himself, he regarded asceticism with contempt, for saints were idlers. Bentham scorned spiritualism, for it glorified unhappiness and distrusted pleasures. Spiritualism negated his unflinching belief in happiness as the goal of all individuals.

Bentham helped in founding the University of London. He donated 170 boxes and bundles of his books and writings. The offices at South Kensington have his bust till today. The college has his skeleton dressed in his favourite clothes, holding his walking stick "Dobbin", with which he used to stroll every morning in his Westminster garden. Being fond of inventing playful names for objects of daily use, he called his dining room "the shop", his teapot "Dick", and work desk "Caroccio". His table was raised on a platform and surrounded by a sunken walking passage, which he called the "vibrating ditch" or the "well". He composed humorous songs and was fond of rituals. Before going to bed, he spent an hour preparing for it. As he grew older, he became more light-hearted and casual.

Bentham started and financed the *Westminster Review* in 1824 with the idea of propagating his utilitarian principles. One of his critics wrote in 1830 that Bentham's exposition of the defects of the legal system was the greatest service that he or any other English political philosopher had ever rendered. Bentham's "new science", which would enable a legislator to mathematically measure and administer happiness, helped England to avoid the excesses, terror and tears of a violent revolution. This largely explained why Marxism and other radical doctrines did not have much influence in England.

Bentham lived till the age of 84, "codifying like any dragon", a phrase which he used to describe himself. His writings were voluminous, considering they ran into 11 stout volumes in close print, in double columns. His other famous works (not mentioned so far) include *An Introduction to the Principles of Morals and Legislation* (1789), *Anarchical Fallacies* (1791), *Discourse on Civil and Penal Legislation* (1802), *The Limits of Jurisprudence* (1802), *Indirect Legislation* (1802), *A Theory of Punishments and Rewards* (1811), *A Treatise on Judicial Evidence* (1813), *Papers upon Codification and Public Instruction* (1817), *The Book of Fallacies* (1824), and *Rationale of Evidence* (1827). The last one was edited by J.S. Mill.

Bentham described himself as "J.B., the most ambitious of the ambitious". He desired to preside over an empire consisting of the whole human race that included all cultures, all places, present as well as future. He expressed a desire to awaken once in a century to contemplate the prospect of a world gradually adopting his principles and making steady progress in happiness and wisdom. Towards this end he laboured hard, directed by one guiding principle of laying down the fundamentals of a "new science" whose knowledge held the key to all of humankind's problems. Miranda, Rivadavia, Bolivar, Santander, Jose de Valle and Andrade were Bentham's disciples, adopting and implementing his principles in the constitutions of their respective countries in South America. Edward Livingston, the outstanding American codifier, described Bentham as one man, both in ancient and modern times, to have thrown light on the science of legislation.

Bentham befriended and corresponded with Rammohun Roy. Rammohun himself picked up from Bentham the rejection of the natural rights theory and the distinction between law and morals. He was also influenced by the principles of Utilitarianism. But unlike Bentham, who was more rigid, Rammohun accepted a wider variety with regard to principles governing different societies. Besides, Rammohun was an ardent champion of freedom of the press, for that would promote freedom to think and express, and thus anticipated many of the arguments of J.S. Mill on the importance of liberty in a modern liberal society.

Bentham was a compulsive writer and a reviser. He would constantly get diverted from his study to clarify something written earlier. One of his contemporaries remarked that he could not play a game of badminton without attempting to redesign the shuttlecock.

> Bentham himself was always of a practical bent, not wanting to weave fantastical schemes but to get actual proposals into effect. His great propensity for detail gives some of his proposals a mad or impractical aura. He could not design a poorhouse without designing the inmate's hats; similarly he could not design an electoral system without planning the size of the ballot box (Harrison 1983: 89).

As a result, many of Bentham's works remained incomplete, and very few got published (Leigh Hunt cited in Harrison 1983: 131). This constant reworking made it difficult to establish the textual integrity of his thought, which became evident while reading the actual manuscript and the published work by his nineteenth-century editor, Bowring. Another related problem was the difficulty in discerning Bentham's original ideas from those of his followers, who invoked his name for much that they conceived (Dinwiddy 1975: 685–686).

Bentham died on June 6, 1832.

MEANING OF UTILITARIANISM

Utilitarianism as a school of thought dominated English political thinking from the middle of the eighteenth century to the middle of the nineteenth. Some of the early Utilitarians were Francis Hutcheson (1694–1746), Hume, Helvetius, Priestly, William Paley (1743–1805), and Beccaria. But it was Bentham who systematically laid down its theory, and made it popular on the basis of his innumerable proposals for reform. "Bentham's merit consisted, not in the doctrine, but in his vigorous application of it to various practical problems" (Russell 1961: 741).

Through James Mill, Bentham developed close links with Thomas Malthus (1766–1834) and David Ricardo (1772–1838), getting acquainted with the ideas of the Classical economists. This group collectively styled themselves as Philosophic Radicals, with the aim of transforming England into a modern, liberal, democratic, constitutional, secular, and market state. Utilitarianism was used interchangeably with philosophic radicalism, individualism, laissez faire and administrative nihilism (Mack 1955: 77).

> Only in England, which throughout the nineteenth century was the most highly industrialized country in the world, did liberalism achieve the status at once of a national philosophy and a national policy. Here, contrary to the expectation implied by Marxism, it provided the principles for an orderly and peaceful transition, first to complete freedom for industry and the enfranchisement of the middle class and ultimately to the enfranchisement of the working class and their protection against the most serious hazards of industry. This was possible because the cleavage between social and economic classes in England never coincided exactly with the lines between political parties. Even in its earlier stage, when its economic theories in particular represented clearly the interest of industrialists, English liberalism in intention at least was always a theory of the general good of the whole national community.... It was the Philosophical Radicals, however, who provided the intellectual structure of early liberalism and therefore its programme (Sabine 1973: 610–611).

The basic premise of Utilitarianism was that human beings as a rule sought happiness, that pleasure alone was good, and that the only right action was that which produced the greatest happiness of the greatest number. Bentham and the Utilitarians reiterated the ideas of the Greek thinker Epicures, who had stated that individuals sometimes pursued pleasure wisely and at other times unwisely.

In the hands of Bentham, the pleasure-pain theory evolved into a scientific principle to be applied to the policies of the state, welfare measures and for administrative, penal and legislative reforms. He shared Machiavelli's concern for a science of politics, not in the sense of understanding the dynamics of political power, but in the hope of promoting and securing the happiness of individuals through legislation and policies.

Utilitarianism provided a psychological perspective on human nature, for it perceived human beings as creatures of pleasure. Using the yardstick of utility, Bentham and his followers desired the restructuring of government and legal institutions so as to maximize individual happiness. In the process, they realized the imperative need to codify laws, making them instruments of reform and happiness.

Bentham was confident that his utilitarian principles could be the basis of law. At one point, he even advertised that he could draw up a new code of law for any nation on earth, cutting across diverse cultural and psychological contexts. In *An Introduction to the Principles of Morals and Legislation,* Bentham wrote:

> Nature has placed mankind under the governance of two sovereign masters, pain and pleasure. It is for them alone to point out what we ought to do, as well as to determine what shall we do. On the one hand the standard of right and wrong, on the other the chain of causes and effects, are fastened to their throne. They govern us in all we do, in all we say, in all we think: every effort we can make to throw off our subjection, will serve but to demonstrate and confirm it. In words a man may pretend to abjure their empire: but in reality he will remain subject to it all the while ... the principle of utility recognizes this subjection, and assumes it for the foundation of that system, the object of which is to rear the fabric of felicity by the hands of reason and law (Bentham 1962: 1).

Bentham contended that human beings by nature were hedonists. Each of their actions was motivated by a desire to seek pleasure and avoid pain. Every human action had a cause and a motive. "Take away all pleasures and all pain and you have no desire and without a desire there can be no action" (Bentham ibid: 40). The principles of utility recognized this basic psychological trait, for it "approves or disapproves every action whatsoever, according to the tendency which it appears to have to augment or diminish the happiness of the party whose interest is in question ... not only of every action of a private individual, but of every measure of government" (Bentham ibid: 40).

Bentham viewed hedonism not only as a principle of motivation, but also as a principle of action. He listed 14 simple pleasures and 12 simple pains, classifying these into self-regarding and other-regarding groups, a distinction that J.S. Mill borrowed in elaboration of the concept of liberty. Only two, benevolence and malevolence, were put under other-regarding action. Under self-regarding motives, Bentham listed physical desire, pecuniary interest, love of power and self-preservation. Self-preservation included fear of pain, love of life and love of ease.

In addition to these, Bentham also laid down social and dissocial categories. The social category was subdivided into social and semi-social. Social motive based on goodwill was associated with the pleasure and pain of sympathy, the pleasure and pain that an individual derived from contemplating the (un)happiness of others, without being affected personally. Semi-social motives included the love for regulations, the desire for amity, and a feeling for religion. Each had a social connotation, namely the overall happiness of others, but these were primarily self-regarding. The dissocial motive was essentially one of displeasure, associated with the pleasure and pain of antipathy and resentment. For Bentham, there was an interest corresponding to every motive.

Bentham described four sanctions or sources of pain and pleasure. The first of these was physical sanction: the source of constraints which arose from human nature and natural circumstances. The second was political and legal sanction: the source of constraints was in the form of rewards and punishments that were meted out by the political authority. The third was moral or popular sanction, meaning the influence(s) on individual behaviour exerted by collective opinion, or by the (dis)approval of those the person was in contact with. The fourth and final sanction was religious sanction, stemming from the hope of divine rewards or the fear of divine punishment.

Bentham was confident that a society in which the individual tried to maximize his *own happiness* would be far better than one in which he had to maximize the happiness of others. In this context, he believed that Christianity placed excessive reliance on altruism, for if the precepts of Jesus were taken literally, that would lead to the destruction of society. Like Epicures, Bentham regarded security as the ideal. For Bentham, security preceded liberty. They were both anti-religion. Bentham's dislike, or even hostility, towards religion, and the Church of England in particular, was because of his awareness of the superstitious and irrational side of human nature. It was for this reason that he regarded religion as an enemy of reason. In this, he voiced the views of the mainstream eighteenth-century philosophers. He was convinced that every reasonable person would accept the principle of the greatest happiness as a basis of society. He also expected that each individual would pursue his own happiness rather than something else. To tell the individual to behave differently, contrary to one's disposition, would be futile.

Bentham realized that a self-interested person would perform his duties, as his main concern was in discerning factors influencing particular behaviour. He refused to be judgemental about human behaviour and action per se. He hoped to provide the legislator with an exhaustive list of pleasures and pains, motives and sanctions, and factors that influenced human conduct and behaviour, with the purpose of changing social arrangements and individual actions. Bentham emphasized the fact that the individual either pursued his happiness without hurting anyone, or pursued actions that were actually conducive to the happiness of others. The legislator on his part, through rewards and punishment, could secure such behaviour, so as to ensure that the stock of happiness in the community did not diminish.

Bentham was sanguine that an adult individual was the best judge of his own happiness, fully capable of pursuing it without harming the happi-ness of others. He saw an integral link between the happiness of an individual and that of the community, and offered the principle of utility as a yardstick to a legislator to frame laws in order to obtain the overall happiness and welfare of the community. He repeatedly stressed that a person's actions and policies had to be judged by his intention to promote the happiness of the community. The end and the goal of legislation was to follow the rule, "each is to count for one and no one for more than one", suggesting that in spite of his repeated emphasis on the community, his was essentially an individualistic philosophy, for he understood social community as a fictitious body of individuals. He was concerned with the *distribution* of happiness as much as the *amount* of it.

Bentham distinguished pleasures quantitatively rather than qualitatively, regarding pushpin as good as poetry. He did not differentiate between pleasures, and in that sense he was not an elitist. He did not assign any inherent grading to activities and treated them at par in terms of their contribution to individual happiness. Interestingly, Rawls, though a critic of Benthamite Utilitarianism, retained Bentham's outlook in judging human contentment and excellence by asserting that even an individual who enjoyed counting the blades of grass was essentially fulfilling his moral nature.

In his desire to emulate Newton Bentham laid down principles in morals and legislation. By doing so, he disproved Burke's assertion that a "science of politics did not and could not exist" (Doyle 1963: 231). He was convinced that pleasures and pains could be measured mathematically by taking into consideration factors like intensity, duration, certainty and propinquity or remoteness. Such a formula was called the "felicific calculus". Bentham conceived the principle of utility as having the same status in the moral world, as axioms in geometry have in the world of mathematics. This was because Arithmetic, as noted by Hobsbawn, was the fundamental tool of the Industrial Revolution and for Bentham and his followers happiness was the object of policy. Every man's pleasure could be expressed (at least in theory) as a quantity and so could his pain. Deduct the pain from the pleasure and the net result was his happiness. Add the happiness of all men and deduct the unhappiness, and the government which secured the greatest happiness of the greatest number was the best. The accountancy of humanity would produce its debit and credit balance, like that of business" (Hobsbawn 1968: 79).

> He taught men to govern by the simple rule of the "greatest happiness of the greatest number" which, in practice, could be discovered by a "felicific calculus". Thus, he sought to establish an external standard, mathematically calculable, whereby to measure the legislator's accomplishment. His contention was that he had made legislative reform a matter not of "caprice" or of unenlightened benevolence, but of logic (Bronowski and Mazlish 1960: 431).

Curiously, the phrase "greatest happiness of the greatest number" used for the first time in 1776, and frequently associated with Bentham, did not reappear for the next 40 years. Though he did not invent the phrase, he was undoubtedly its best popularizer. Initially, he used the phrase "greatest happiness of all", which he gave up, for it suggested that the interests of some could be subordinated to those of others. It also implied that the happiness of the majority was all that mattered. If the suffering of one person was greater than the accumulated happiness of many, that was not acceptable. Therefore, he substituted the phrase with "greatest happiness of the greatest number", using it with greater frequency in the 1820s in his crusade for radical reforms. Bentham was categorical that since persons differed very little in their capacity to experience pain and pleasure, they had to be treated equally in a manner that gave their pleasures due regard and consideration. In fact, Bentham was not happy about the word "utilitarian", but continued to use it for want of any other alternate and effective word. For a while, he thought of using 'eudaimonologist' or 'felicist'.

Bentham remained convinced throughout his life on the science of legislation, retaining his belief that an expert legislator could skillfully legislate with a view to ensuring the greatest happiness of the greatest number. In order to do this, a legislator should be able to understand human actions and encourage those with appropriate sanctions that could contribute to the greatest happiness.

> The medieval conception of the magistrate administering the law of God by a system of rewards and punishments according to a divine scale of good and evil reappeared in Bentham's philosophy in the guise of a legislator determining good and evil according to the criterion of human happi-ness now accurately ascertained by scientific methods (Doyle 1963: 235).

Bentham also discussed indirect legislation, namely public instruction and propaganda, through which the legislator could influence human conduct, strengthen moral or popular sanction (i.e. general opinion), and change people's behaviour via their love for reputation. "Since according to Bentham 'society' was nothing but a convenient fiction for an aggregate of individuals, the recipe for success consisted of knowing how to manage 'others'. A man must keep well with public opinion" (Wolin 1960: 346). For instance, drunkenness and idleness, which caused crime, could be tackled by promoting the consumption of non-alcoholic drinks, cultivating innocent amusements like gardening, music, athletic and sedentary games.

Unemployment could be prevented by providing for public works. In this, he was a predecessor of Keynes. Moreover, the love of reputation in a human being could be cultivated by inculcating the value of virtue through stories and literary works that presented good in attractive and vice in ugly terms. Bentham's schemes of the panopticon, and the National Charity Company aimed to balance the claims of humanity with those of the economy, to ensure human welfare without incurring heavy expenses, wastage, inefficiency and patronage.

Besides laws and indirect legislation, Bentham regarded private ethics as the third mode of influencing human behaviour. Its purpose was not to judge or arbitrate morals, but to teach and instruct individuals to maximize their own happiness. In this context, he suggested the use of a savings bank or General Goodwill Fund, where acts of beneficence that did not benefit the agent could be deposited and from which they could be withdrawn in due course. Unlike the moralists, Bentham did not emphasize the need to make sacrifices with a view to promoting general happiness. In general, he recommended economy of sacrifice. Though one could argue that it was desirable to sacrifice a lesser quantity of happiness for attaining a greater quantity, it was equally true that a large amount of happiness would remain intact if less quantity was sacrificed. Bentham's view of human nature was guided by a favourite statement from Helvetius, that "to love one's fellowmen, one must not expect much from them".

Bentham regarded punishments as both reformatory and deterring, controlling the actions of human beings. Fond of moral arithmetic, and for the purpose of laying down ground rules, he stated nine points. By stating these simple ground rules, Bentham hoped that they would become guidelines for both legislators and judges. The nine points were as follows.

(1) The punishment must be great enough to outweigh the profit of the offence to the offender.
(2) The greater the mischief of the offence, the greater the punishment should be.
(3) and (4) are corollaries of (2).
(5) Punishment should never be greater than the least amount required to make it effective.
(6) The sensibility of the offender must always be taken into account.
(7) The more uncertain it was that the offender would suffer it, the greater the punishment should be.
(8) The more distant it was, the greater it should be.
(9) If the offence was of a kind likely to be habitual with the offender, the punishment should be increased to outweigh the profit not only of the immediate offence but also of the other offences probably committed with impunity.

> Bentham's concern to define punishment as precisely as possible, to establish a definite ratio between the degree of punishment and the magnitude of the crime, emanated from the hope of confining pain as narrowly as possible by making it more objective (Wolin ibid: 328).

Bentham's defence of the principles of utility led him to plead a case for democracy, manhood, and later on universal suffrage, including female enfranchisement. Suffrage and democracy were crucial for the realization of the greatest happiness principle. In his *Plan for Parliamentary Reform,* he contended that community interest would emerge the moment the government took cognizance of the people, for they would not wish to be governed badly, nor would they desire a sacrifice of universal interest for something narrow and sectarian.

It was for this reason that Bentham supported universal suffrage, for it not only safeguarded people's interests, but also checked governmental abuse of that interest. Universal suffrage would make governments more accountable and less whimsical. As a result, he drafted a complete scheme of parliamentary democracy in his *Constitutional Code,* pleading for secret ballot, delineating a scheme for elementary, secondary and technical public education, and rejecting plural voting. He was convinced that a good government was possible only by what he called the "democratic ascendancy". He recognized that misrule in England was due to many reasons, including defects in the electoral system. He was equally concerned with the need to explore and combat methods by which the "subject many" were not dominated by the "ruling few". In *Church and Englandism,* he attacked the established church as a close ally of the political elite, for it taught intellectual submissiveness among its followers.

From 1809 to 1823, Bentham devoted his time and energies to weeding out religious beliefs and practices, and eventually religion from the minds of individuals. He was an atheist and a denouncer of organized religion. He subjected religious doctrines, rituals and practices to the test of utility, and found them inadequate, reconfirming his atheism and his desire to build a rational society according to secular notions. He confidently and outrightly denied the truth of religion, of the existence of an-immortal soul, of a future life and of the existence of God. Here, he was influenced by his radical friend Francis Place (1771–1854). He had immense faith and confidence in the power of reason to tell us what *was,* and what was to be *expected.* In this, he was influenced by the thinkers of the French Enlightenment (Voltaire, Helvetius and Paul Henri Thiry, Baron d'Holbach (1723–1789)), and like them, believed that in order to recreate it was necessary to destroy. His hatred for religion, like Voltaire, increased with the passage of time. He was anti-clergy and disagreed with religion as an instrument of moral improvement. Like Holbach, he regarded religion as a source of human misery.

Bentham sought to use the institutions of conventional religion to serve secular ends and public service. He advocated that the clergy could serve as disseminators regarding job vacancies, or compile statistics to aid endeavours at poor relief. The church could be used as a bank for the poor after the Sunday services. The clergy could become moral instructors in the panopticon. He believed that people had a right by law to leave their bodies for dissection.

In a secular utilitarian society, there would be no God and no idea of an immortal soul. There would be no supernatural sanction for morality. A good deed would be remembered for one's family and commemorated by one's fellow citizens. Instead of religious rewards and punishments, there would be verdict by future generations, renewable every century in the case of great men.

THE MODERN STATE

Bentham regarded the notion of a modern state as an ideal, an aspiration, and examined the techniques of state building and methods that would promote modernization. He regarded diversity and fragility within political order as inevitable. For Bentham, the state was a legal entity with individualism as its ethical basis. He was categorical that modernization required two things: first, it needed a broad-based and diversified legal system which would take into account individuals' desires; and second, institutions that would support the legal system, namely bureaucratization of public service and legislation as a continual process, accommodating both change and diversity. Bentham characterized the state as a legal entity, with individualism as its ethical basis. "Bentham's theory brought together in a particular way the two great themes of modern political thought: individualism and the modern sovereign state" (Hume 1981: 238).

Bentham preserved the individualist notion of moral autonomy, with priority to individual interests. He also recognized that these autonomous individuals, governed by their interests, constituted themselves into fragile groupings which the state had to maintain through discipline and cohesion, if it had to be an effective body. Through institutions and other techniques, the community was made responsive to the state, but the state was not allowed to trample on individual interests and wills. It would have to *protect* them by getting the individuals involved in the state through consent, or by representing them as masters and judges of the state's actions. Bentham thought of ideas and devices to guarantee governmental protection of individual interests, namely that public happiness should be the object of public policy, government was a trust (as it was in the case of Locke), with legislation as the primary function, and that uniformity, clarity, order and consistency were essential to both law and order. He was equally conscious of the need for institutional safeguards to ensure that the government pursued public interest. He contended that the reason for misrule was that the government was controlled by those whose interests it was to perpetuate bad governance. This could be changed if people who desired good government were made to take charge.

Bentham was confident that representation would ensure congruence between the interests of the government and those of the community as a whole. It was for this reason that he championed universal adult franchise, and as early as 1790 recommended it to all those who could read the list of voters. His association with James Mill, whom he met in 1809, reinforced his intrinsic faith in democracy.

As opposed to natural rights and natural law, Bentham recognized legal laws and rights that were enacted and enforced by a duly constituted political authority or the state. A state was sovereign, being primarily a law making body. He defined the state or political society as

> a number of persons (whom we may style subjects) are supposed to be in the habit of paying obedience to a person, or an assemblage of persons, of a known and certain description (whom we may call governor or governors) such persons altogether (subjects and governed) are said to be in a state of political society (Bentham 1977: 140).

Bentham defined law as the command of the sovereign. He considered the powers of the sovereign as indivisible, unlimited, inalienable and permanent. His views on sovereignty were reiterated by Austin, though the latter's *Lectures on Jurisprudence* (1832) contained a more rigid statement on sovereignty than the one provided by Bentham (Plamentaz 1966: 65). Benfham's theory (unlike that of Austin) was more sophisticated, for it took into account factors like federalism and written constitutions (Barry 1995: 43). Austin's theory, on the contrary, was legalistic.

Bentham, unlike Austin and Hobbes, did not think that the powers of the sovereign were to be unlimited or illimitable. Instead, he dismissed talk of illegality of actions of government as absurd, unless it was possible to limit these actions by conventions. He did not define law in terms of statute, and accepted the division of sovereignty as in federal systems. He also envisaged the possibility of constitutional law, for morality and religion bound the sovereign's power.

Bentham's greatest contribution was in the field of jurisprudence and government (Sabine 1973: 617). He was critical of Blackstone for regarding tradition as sacrosanct, conferred by time as the basis of law. He opposed the delays in laws, the obscurity and incomprehensibility in its language, its arbitrariness, the undue expenses that it entailed, and the cruel punishments that were recommended as a remedy. Instead of law being a product of the judiciary, contributing to its ambiguity, he wanted it to be carefully drawn and coherently spelt out by a legislature, giving little scope for judicial interpretation and elaboration. The codification of the law had to be such that it would be understood by an average individual. One basic reform that he suggested was replacement of lawyers' fees by salaries, for that would stop endless litigation. He tried to introduce an informal, inexpensive and simple procedure in law courts. He recommended oral testimony and cross-examination before a judge in a public court. He advocated that the proceedings of these courts should be modelled in a way a father conducted his inquiries within a family when there was a dispute or a feud to settle. He emphasized that everyone who was likely to know about a case, and in particular the parties, should be heard. Punishment was to be in accordance with the consequence of the crime, namely the number of people affected by it. If the social pain was less, then the punishment should be less severe.

Like Montesquieu, Bentham argued that a legislator should take into cognizance factors like people's customs, prejudices, religion and traditions while codifying the law. In 1811, he wrote to US President Madison, offering to draw up a comprehensive code for the United States, and in 1814 made a similar offer to Alexander I of Russia. From 1824 to 1832, he wrote *Constitutional Code,* outlining a new system of English government. A substantive part of it became the basis of the 1832 Reform Bill. It was for this reason that in 1844 the *Westminster Review* rightly proclaimed that "we live in an age of Benthamism".

Bentham stipulated happiness, and not liberty, as the end of the state. The state was a contrivance created for fulfilling the needs of the individual. In order to promote happiness, he recommended the need to establish Poor Laws, construct hospitals for the indigent, create workhouses for the unemployed, levy taxes for the purpose of redistribution, decrease direct taxes, recompense victims of crime for damages when the perpetrator was an indigent, safeguard national security, establish courts and internal police, disseminate useful information to industry, label poisonous substances, guarantee marks for quality and quantity of goods, set a maximum price for corn, provide security and subsistence by stockpiling grain or giving granary bouts to producers, encourage investments in times of unemployment, grant patents to inventors, regulate banks, establish and enforce government monopoly on the issue of paper currency, engage in public works to make the unemployed work, establish boards, institutes, universities and savings banks, provide cheap postage, appoint a public prosecutor, and support the selection of the young against the interference and asceticism of the old.

Bentham was categorical that a government and a state had to be judged by their usefulness to the individual. He also insisted on a need for a watchful and interested government, which would readily and willingly act whenever and wherever necessary for the happiness of the individual. Sovereignty rested with the people, and had to be exercised by what he called the "constitutive authority", i.e. the electorate. The task of a sovereign was to harmonize different individual interests and promote social cooperation through legislation in form of punishment, rewards, encouragement and incentives.

In his *Constitutional Code,* Bentham granted the power to the people to select and dismiss their rulers, and to ensure that the interests of the rulers were closely linked with those of the people. Towards this, he recommended the abolition of monarchy and the House of Lords, checks on legislative authority, unicameralism, secret ballot, annual elections, equal electoral districts, annual parliaments and election of the prime minister by the parliament. He also recommended the need for central inspection, a public prosecutor, recruitment of the young in the government, and competitive civil service examinations.

The idea behind annual elections was to maximize aptitude and minimize expenses, in order to ensure high-quality officials and representatives. The threat of dismissal would ensure accountability and responsibility. Unlike James Mill, Bentham insisted on a code of penal sanctions, and attached considerable importance to public opinion. Bentham accepted that democracies would also be subject to the "iron law of oligarchy", and that government would always be that of the many by the few, but there was nothing negative about this, for it ensured representation and expertise.

Bentham viewed representative government as a solution to the problem that Plato raised, namely finding experts to rule. He accepted that all individuals could be corrupted. The only precaution was to give power to the people, for that would ensure the greatest happiness of the greatest number. Like Plato, he accepted that governing was a skill, and that all were not capable of ruling, which was why representatives were needed. Democracy ensured good rule and control of governors.

Bentham rejected the idea of mixed or balanced constitutions representing interests, which was central to the Whig view as exemplified by Burke. This was because interests change, and with it representation would also change. The Utilitarians proposed representation of the people. Everyone as an individual had the right to be represented, and therefore should have the right to vote. In *A Fragment on Government*, Bentham used the criterion of circumstances to distinguish between a free and a despotic government. Free government depended

> ... on the manner in which that whole mass of power, which taken together, is supreme, is in a free state, distributed among the several ranks of persons that are sharers in it: on the source from whence their titles to it are successively derived: on the frequent and easy changes of condition between governors and governed; whereby the interests of one class are more or less indistinguishably blended with those of the other: on the responsibility of the governors; or the right which a subject has of having the reasons publicly assigned and canvassed of every act of power that is exerted over him: on the liberty of press; or the security with which every man, be he of the one class or the other, may make known his complaints and remonstrances to the whole community: on the liberty of public association; or the security with which malcontents may communicate their sentiments, construct their plans, and practice every mode of opposition short of actual revolt, before the executive power can be legally justified in disturbing them (Bentham 1977: 485).

Interestingly, Bentham opposed the concept of division of powers for three reasons. First, he argued that if the rulers were already accountable to the people, there was no need for additional checks. Division of power by itself did not secure and protect constitutional liberty. Second, even with the division of power, it was possible to replace majority rule with that of a minority. This was because divisions would give the minorities the right to veto legislation. He could foresee evil consequences in the displacement of majority rule. Third, he argued that in the absence of effective opposition, division of power would be redundant. He emphasized the importance of accountability of the rulers, instead of division of powers, as not only good in itself, but also good as a means of constitutional liberty.

It was during the French Revolution that Bentham developed his theory of constitutional government. Impressed by the strides made by American democracy with its broad-based suffrage and security of property, he was convinced of the inherent value of democracy, hoping that England would take a leaf from the American experience. He regarded constitutional representative democracy as an overall political arrangement safeguarded by measures like widespread suffrage, an elected assembly, frequent elections, freedom of the press and of association as a guarantee against misrule. It would also protect the individual from arbitrary and despotic governments. He regarded constitutional democracy as being relevant "to all nations and all governments possessing liberal opinions" (Bentham 1983: 1). Initially he desired to make Britain a republic but after witnessing the excesses of the horrors of the French Revolution he was cautious about recommending the abolition of the monarchy.

Bentham doubted the efficacy of a revolution to ensure individual and political emancipation. He insisted on gradual change, based on the overall security of the individual in society. He was enthused initially by the impetus of the French Revolution, seeing in it a hope for his reform proposals and the panopticon scheme. But subsequently he himself was disappointed at the turn of events in France, which led to violence and the "reign of terror".

Bentham urged a more universal and centralized system to register births, marriages and deaths, inspiring the 1836 Registration Act in England. He also suggested that the government should undertake responsibility in matters like education, care of the insane, and provide protection against intentional offences and accidental dangers. He recommended a Preventive Service Minister to mitigate calamities like floods, epidemics, landslides and conflagrations, by providing fire-fighting equipment, enforcing fire regulations and other safety measures in factories and mines, survey bridges, dykes, and embankments, and undertaking repair or demolition of unsafe buildings. He recommended the establishment of a permanent police, separate ministers for education, health and "indigence relief. He sought assurance for adequate and uncontaminated drinking water, hospitals to take care of the sick, vaccination during epidemics, and proper drainage and sewage systems. It was for these recommendations that Joe Roebuck spoke of the silent revolution that became largely possible due to the diffusion of Bentham's ideas.

Bentham's followers helped in the founding of the Anti-Corn Law Association in 1836. Many of them invoked his name to legitimize their cause. Bowring and Archibald Prentice, a Manchester journalist and an admirer of Bentham, praised his monumental efforts towards the Corn Law agitation, describing him as the "father of practical free traders". Benthamite civil functionaries like Edwin Chadwick and James Key-Shuttleworth introduced the principles of central control and inspection. They enacted the Metropolitan Police Act of 1829, the Education Act of 1833, the Factory Act of 1833, the New Poor Law Act of 1834, the Municipal Reform Act of 1835, the Act for Scientific System of Vital Statistics in 1836, the Railway Regulation Act of 1840 and the Public Health Act of 1848. Appropriately and rightly, he "furnished the philosophic banner under which the 'legislative revolution' was carried on" (Bronowski and Mazlish 1960: 430).

ECONOMIC IDEAS

Bentham appreciatively read the works of Smith, a champion of free trade. He considered Smith "a writer of great and distinguished merit", pointing to the similarities between the views of Smith with those of his own, as expressed in *Manual of Political Economy* (1793-1795). Like Smith, Bentham defended laissez faire-ism but pleaded for the government's non-interference in regulating interest rates in his *Defence of Usury* (1787). This was seen by many as criticizing Smith from an extreme laissez faire position as the one articulated by Smith. Smith evidently suggested that interest rates should not be determined by market forces alone.

Bentham's laissez faire leanings were clear in his criticism of active and interventionist foreign policy. In 1789, he maintained that international harmony among people was possible only if existing economic interdepen-dence was recognized and accepted, for people would then realize the truths of political economy. He was categorical that as in political economy, even in foreign affairs, the government should observe "the great secret and do nothing". While Smith defended laissez faire by appealing to the guiding hand of providence, Bentham justified it on the grounds of utility (Bronowski and Mazlish I960: 441).

Though Bentham was a defender of laissez faire and free trade, it would be misleading to conclude that he stood for a non-interventionist government and a minimal state. He was not a dogmatic laissez faireist. He believed that government was an undeniable evil, but the evil could be minimized if it could be used for the production of happiness, which meant security, abundance, subsistence and equality identified as its ends. Of these four ends, security and subsistence were regarded as the most important, while abundance and equality were "manifestly of inferior importance". He linked these ends with the proposals of Smith, and the result was a welfare state with free education, guaranteed employment, minimum wages, sickness benefit and old age insurance (Mack 1955: 85).

Bentham contended that there could be neither abundance nor equality without security, and therefore the chief concern of the law was to ensure security. Without some assurance that property would be protected, individuals would not strive to create new wealth. According to Bentham, the fundamental institution of private property was itself "only a foundation of expectation". He regarded the concept of expectation as a distinctive quality in human beings, for it played a significant role in determining his decisions. Therefore, the purpose of the law was to secure expectations, for it was a precondition not only to peace of mind and to the pleasure of anticipation, but also to any general plan of conduct or forward looking activity. It was also the basic precondition for economic enterprise and investment.

> So crucial to liberal mind was the sense of secure expectations that ultimately the satisfaction of expectations was identified with justice. In Bentham's jurisprudence justice was defined as the "disappointment-preventing principle" and the whole system of civil law was dedicated to the exclusion of disappointment (Wolin 1960: 329).

Bentham was equally convinced that the mass of the national wealth would increase if the wealth of individuals increased, for, like Smith, he too believed that each person being the best judge of his own interests would be most effective in producing it. He contended that government inaction was required with regard to subsistence and economic abundance, for that would give the individual freedom to pursue the best economic opportunities. Equality was problematic, for in the process of equalizing the fortunes of the wealthy, it might stifle individual initiative. Moreover, security preceded equality, for the pain that would be produced by social levelling would be more than the pleasures of those whose position was alleviated. He was consistent in seeing economic levelling as being impractical. To establish equality on a permanent basis was to undermine not only security and abundance, but also subsistence, for that would subvert individual initiative.

Interestingly, Bentham insisted that a government should provide for subsistence for the indigent through public works projects. He also proposed a system of agricultural communes and industry houses to take care of the indigent, as distinguished from the working poor. Under both projects, through strict supervision the indigent would be encouraged to become a part of the normal labour market as soon as possible. Care was to be taken to ensure that the lot of the indigent was not more beneficial than of those who were poor, for that would amount to rewarding shirkers, becoming a positive disincentive to the industrious poor.

Rawls, in his *A Theory of Justice* (1971), reiterated the Benthamite principle of ensuring a fair and just system, whereby both the free riders and the shirkers were not allowed to take advantage of the system. Through his principle of fair equality of opportunity, the industrious individual and his contributions to society were safeguarded, while the difference principle cared for those below the accepted social minimum, thus ensuring productivity and efficiency of the economy without being callous and heartless.

Bentham insisted that workers in the free market were to receive higher wages than those in the industry houses, with the permission to spend freely, something that would be denied to the indigent. The government would be restrained from providing for the indigent by making available non-alcoholic beverages, uniform dress and any other rules which in its own judgement, were conducive to the benefit of either a particular individual or the community at large, at whose expense he was to be relieved.

Bentham demanded a ceiling on the price of grain during shortages, favoured protection of small groups of producers and desired government action to control inflation. He contended that whenever it could be proved and shown that the advantages accrued from interference outweighed the costs, the measure should be regarded as good rather than bad. While he preferred an interventionist state in a backward country, he was generally for private enterprise in advanced countries. He favoured an attentive and active government, and as long as the government promoted happiness, he did not fear the horrible hand of the government. Government interference was not as abhorrent as its negligence. He repeatedly asserted that it was "incumbent on government to make sure that the community pursued courses of actions conducive to the maximum well being" (Bentham 1962: 75).

Bentham was the first to realize the difficulties in applying the principle of utility to social and political problems. After slogging for 10 years in trying to collect correct statistics for the gross national income, tax revenues, and agricultural production, he realized the complete unavailability of reliable economic and social statistics in the late eighteenth-century. In fact, it was not until 1801 that the first elementary census data were available in England. The second obstacle was the inertia and apathy of the British bureaucracy. The third reason was the ambiguity of the meaning of the principle of utility. He kept expanding the phrase and redefining its fundamental tenets. The principle of utility was rephrased as the "greatest happiness principle", and subsequently as the "universal self-preference principle" and "interest function prescribing principle".

> He was no longer so assured of the infallibility of his hypotheses; he was no longer so confident of the parallel between the physical and moral sciences, Newton and Bentham. Yet he did not give up the expectation of founding a new moral discipline, a unique conjunction of art and science (Mack 1955: 83).

NOTION OF LIBERTY, RIGHTS AND LAW

Bentham defined liberty as absence of restraints and coercion. Fundamental to his concept of liberty was the idea of security linking his idea of civil and political liberty. A legislator established a framework of security through law, within which the individual enjoyed liberty. At the level of civil law, a legislator secured right to property, prevented interference, simplified judicial proceedings and encouraged healthy commercial competitiveness. In the realm of criminal law, a legislator protected the individual against crime through a system of a rational criminal code, a strong effective police force and a judiciary. At the level of constitutional law, a legislator guaranteed against misrule, abuse and arbitrary exercise of power.

For Bentham, the principle of utility provided the objective moral standard noticeably different from other theories that supplied purely subjective criteria. Like Burke, he was particularly scathing in his criticism of the concepts of natural law and natural rights. Like Hume, he criticized these notions on pragmatic and conceptual levels. But, unlike Hume, he had immense faith in the power of reason, regarding it as a guardian and director of morals. He dismissed natural law as "nothing but a phrase". It lacked substance.

Since law sprang from human will, law-making (like human conduct) would have to be evaluated in its capacity to promote happiness. From this point of view, a jurist had two duties, one to find out the effects and consequences of the existing laws on society. Second, to devise the implications of utility in a given situation of a given society and frame rules, procedures, schemes and institutions for actualizing these demands, and persuade sovereigns to give effect to the proposals as part of their sanctioned commands.

On normative grounds, Bentham pointed out that natural rights impelled an individual to rise up in arms against whatever one did not like. Talk of natural rights and natural law, he contended, was like using "terrorist language". It incited a "spirit of resistance to all laws—a spirit of resistance against all governments" encouraging chaos and disorder. On a conceptual plane, he dismissed the notion of natural rights as mischievous and "simply nonsense upon stilts", for "there is no such thing as natural rights opposed to, in contradiction to legal" (Bentham 1965: 500, 501).

Bentham dismissed natural rights as nonsense for two reasons. First, they did not mean anything. His dismissal of natural rights as meaningless was similar to the arguments of the Vienna Circle when they claimed that theology and metaphysics lacked meaning (Waldron 1987: 34). Second, the sentences of the natural rights text guaranteed their falsity. Like Hobbes, he was insistent that words be defined precisely and clearly, for ambiguity and confusion contributed to much of the conflicts in politics. Accordingly, the French Declaration of the Rights of Man (1791) was purported to be the penning of a

> ... cluster of truths on which the fate of nations was to hang, was in fact written more like an oriental tale or an allegory for a magazine... it contains stale epigrams, trite sentimental conceits and flippery ornaments rather than necessary destinations and the majestic simplicity of good sound sense (Bentham 1965: 497).

Bentham regarded the principles of the Declaration as fallacious but not pernicious, as Burke did. Interestingly, like Burke who sympathized with the cause of the American colonies, Bentham too was less harsh on the American Declaration of Independence (1776). Both favoured change without undermining security, continuity and order. Neither was Bentham enamoured of Paine's logical defence of the Revolution. Bentham rejected natural rights and natural laws because of his conviction that every aspect of social phenomena could be calculated and measured mathematically by an expert and skillful legislator, becoming an instrument of happiness.

Like Burke, Bentham believed that rights were to be protected by existing laws, but he differed from Burke in his perception of English law. Unlike Burke, he was not so reverential about English law just because it was an "ancient collection of unwritten maxims and customs". Law, according to Bentham, had to be codified, simple, systematic and logical, based on the principle of the "greatest happiness of the greatest number".

> Bentham's objections to natural rights was both philosophical and political. As a legal positivist of the command school Bentham could accept that statements about natural rights were even meaningful... . Rights were co-related with duties and to be under a duty was to be liable to sanctions in the event of failure to perform an action... . Bentham's political objection to natural rights was that they were in fact reactionary, and that their alleged existence retarded the application of science to social reform (Barry 1995: 248).

Interestingly, even though Bentham undermined the sanctity of natural rights formulations, he recognized the importance of rights as being crucial for the security of the individual. He rejected not only the idea of natural and inviolable right to property, but also the idea of absolute right to property, as the government had the right to interfere with property in order to ensure security. Bentham distinguished between sudden and critical attack on property from the fixed, regular and necessary deductions from the wealth of the people, which were needed to finance and support the functions and services rendered by governments. He defended the need for adequate compensation in case of a violation of the individual's right to property. Property was neither natural, absolute nor inviolable.

Bentham defined "right" and "duty" in the context of positive law. Unlike "right" and "duty", "law", "sovereign" and "sanctions" were concrete terms, for they were tangible and could be identified. "Right" and "duty" assumed sense only if translated into propositions about laws and sanctions. When one talked of duty, it implied an action by the sovereign on pain of some sanction. Talk of "right" meant the beneficiary of a "duty", meaning that one benefited from another's performance of an action which was required of him by a sovereign on pain of sanction. Right and law were correlative terms. Without a lawgiver there could be no law, no right and no duty. A natural right was like a son who never had a father.

Bentham applied his celebrated distinction between "descriptive" and "censorial" jurisprudence, namely what the law *ought* to be or whether a particular law was bad or good, to establish the validity of moral propositions about legal rights. It made sense if one contended that an individual ought to have a particular legal right. It became nonsensical when claimed that an individual already had some natural right in virtue of which the legal right was called for. Moreover, there could be no absolute claim to rights and liberties. There was need for some constraints, so, at best, one could speak of a clearly qualified commitment to liberty, property, democracy, and so on.

> In vain would it be said, that though no bounds are here assigned to any of these rights, yet it is to be understood as taken for granted and tacitly admitted and assumed that they are to have bounds; viz. such bounds as it is understood will be set them by the laws. Vain, I say, would be this apology; for the supposition would be contradictory to the express declaration of the article itself... . It would be self-contradictory, because these rights are, in the same breath in which their existence is declared, declared to be imprescriptable; and imprescriptable ... means nothing unless it excludes the interferences of the laws (Bentham 1965: 502).

Once qualifications on rights were revealed, they undermined the initial thrust of the argument. There was a need to mention modifications and exceptions to rights by law.

Bentham believed that without positive law human life would be intolerable, insecure, dismal and miserable, resembling Hobbes' stale of nature. Law ensured security, society and economy. If the law itself was attacked, then it was likely to result in chaos and insecurity, similar to the Terror of the 1790s. In the background of this, it was imperative that irrespective of the way a government was established, nothing was to be done to undermine the fabric of the law. Furthermore, the happiness of the subjects was to be always kept in mind. Both these imperatives were ignored by the proponents of natural rights. Bentham found the natural rights argument distasteful, not because it was non-compliant, but because it encouraged rebellion, which was associated with anarchy, terror and insecurity—his primary concerns. He emphasized that disobedience and revolution were two different things.

Bentham was equally critical of the notion of equality of rights, for that ignored the distinctions that society had found useful to make. He also pointed out that the absolutism inherent in the doctrine of natural rights was based on the Utopian presumption that government could fulfil all aspirations.

The final reason for Bentham's indictment of natural rights was that they threatened social solidarity and attenuated selfishness in society.

> The great enemies of public peace are the selfish and the dissocial passions—necessary as they are—the one to the very existence of each individual, the other to his security. On the part of these affections, a

> deficiency in point of strength is never to be apprehended: all that is to be apprehended in respect of them, is to be apprehended on the side of their excess. Society is held together only by the sacrifices that men can be induced to make of the gratifications they demand: to obtain these sacrifices is the great difficulty, the great task of government. What has been the object, the perpetual and palpable object, of this declaration of pretended rights. To add as much force as possible to these passions, but already too strong, to burst the cords that hold them in, to say to the selfish passions, there—everywhere—is your enemy. Such is the morality of this celebrated manifesto (Bentham ibid: 495).

Bentham, unlike Burke and Marx, identified self-interest as the core of human nature, but like them, visualized the possibility of human society depending on people pursuing interests other than those that were narrowly self-centred. All three attacked the natural rights doctrine on the premise that it sought to provide instant and unconditional gratification of purely selfish individual desires. They were not willing to organize a community exclusively on the principle of self-interest.

> Each of them offered a wider vision—the altruism of Bentham's principle of utility, the intergenerational wisdom of Burke's traditions and the cooperative fulfillment of Marxian species-being. For all of them, human life, to be bearable, involved a substantial commitment to living together in community that is belied by the abstract egoism of a theory of human rights (Waldron 1987: 44–45).

Bentham also rejected the idea of the social contract as pure fiction, a falsehood, on the premise that the binding force of a contract came from a government, from the habit of enforcement and not vice versa. Following Hume, he dismissed the social contract as a chimera, a fiction never entered into. "The notion of an actually existing unconnected *state of nature* is too wild to be seriously admitted" (Bentham 1962: 36). He asserted that the social contract argument, along with the notion of natural law and natural rights, led us to an "unavoidable inference that all government ... that have had any other origin ... are illegal" and "resistance to them and subversion of them, lawful and commendable" (Bentham 1965: 500, 501). For Bentham, the principle of utility provided the basis of all political and moral obligations.

WOMEN AND GENDER EQUALITY

Bentham argued for women's right to vote and the right to participate as equals in the government. In *Introduction,* he attacked the presumption that women should be accorded a subordinate status because of their inferior minds. Under the influence of Helvetius, Bentham paid attention to the needs of women. However, he was critical of Helvetius for condoning the practice in "certain barbarous or half civilized nations" where warriors were rewarded with favours of women. Interestingly, he tried to absolve

Helvetius by alleging that perhaps "Montesquieu had led him into this error". Even then, Bentham commented that both Helvetius and Montesquieu were,

> ... philosophers distinguished for their humanity—both of them good husbands and good fathers—how could they have forgotten that favours not preceded by an uncontrolled choice and which the heart perhaps repelled with disgust afforded the spectacle rather of the degradation of woman than the rewarding a hero ... both of them were eloquent against slavery, how could they speak in praise of a law which supposes the slavery of the best half of the human species (Bentham cited in Boralevi 1984: 9)

In his *Plan for Parliamentary Reform,* Bentham favoured women's suffrage, but in *Constitutional Code* he realized that though there was nothing wrong with women's suffrage, the time was not ripe for it. His reluctance was not because women lacked the capacity and rationality to vote, but because men would oppose it so stiffly that it could jeopardize the very cause. As for women's involvement in government, he felt it would lead to "nothing but confusion and ridicule". Bentham rejected the idea of women's enfranchisement and participation in government on the grounds that men were immature and would refuse to allow women amidst them. This had nothing to do with the fact that women lacked either talent or ability.

Bentham found no evidence to support the view that social inequality had its roots in natural inequality. Natural differences between men and women could not be the basis for oppressing women. If women appeared less fit for intellectual activities than men, it was because of their education, which from their early years was devoted to cultivating qualities like modesty, delicacy and chastity.

Bentham was equally sensitive to the marital and sexual rights of women. He argued for the right of a woman to obtain a divorce in case of an unhappy marriage. He dismissed the idea of an irrevocable marriage contract as "absurd and cruel". Like slaves, women were oppressed and not treated as autonomous individuals in society.

It was noteworthy that J.S. Mill reiterated a similar sentiment, and equated the position of women to that of slaves, and in some respects worse than that of slaves. The analogy between slaves and women appeared throughout Bentham's writings. In *An Introduction,* he perceived a close link between Aristotle's defence of slavery and his anti-women posture. Clearly Bentham, like Hobbes, had very little respect for classical antiquity. For Bentham, both women and slaves were oppressed, and their oppression was justified by prejudice. In 1789 he commented:

> As to the Negro and the Woman, were they by some strange accident to overcome the body of prejudice which opposes their admission with so much force, there could not be a stronger proof of a degree of merit superior to any that was to be found among whites and among men (Bentham cited in Boralevi ibid: 10).

Bentham also lamented on the limited legal personality that English laws of his time conferred on women. He desired the removal of these laws, and of treating women's interests as separate from those of men, whether father, husband or son. Bentham attacked the practice of legal separation, for it would condemn persons to the "privations of celibacy" or "to form illicit connections". He contended that women had equal claims to happiness as men, if not more, because they were subject to physiological pains unique to their sex.

Bentham did not regard sexual differences between men and women as innate or natural. He was equally concerned about the plight of unwed mothers, their feminine delicacy and reputation, and devised the Sotimion along the lines of the Panopticon. He invented the Nothotropftium to take care of illegitimate children. He supported abortion and infanticide. He even pleaded for proper rules that would prevent a stronger mate from maltreating the weaker one in a marital relationship. He recommended severe punishment for those who perpetrated violence against women. He regarded prostitution as an evil but ruled out a legal ban as it would be useless and extremely harmful. He proposed short-term marriages for sailors and soldiers, so that their women would not be humiliated and their children would not be illegitimate. This was suggested as a remedial measure and not as a rule.

For Bentham, the question of autonomy—suffrage and divorce are two important issues that have an intimate link with women's legal personality. The two belonged to the public and private spheres respectively of the individual, and were based on the premise that women were aware of their interests and the means to safeguard them. The right to vote and the right to seek a divorce guaranteed and secured women's interests independent of men.

> Thus while he himself stopped short of demanding radical changes in the status of women, he furnished the philosophy that inspired John Stuart Mill to take up the gauntlet for the cause of women in the Victorian era. Playing the role of gadfly, Bentham wrote, discussed and argued. In his day the time was not ripe, but he caused another generation to seek for women an end to the inequities he so eloquently described (Williford 1975: 176).

Bentham also supported education for women, and proposed a new curriculum called *Christomathia* (1816). This formed the basis of the University College, the first English university to admit all students without discriminating on the basis of race, class, religion or sex. Education and suffrage would enable a woman to be a morally autonomous person and a politically enlightened citizen.

Ball disagreed with the lavish praise that was showered on Benfham for his pro-feminist views (Halvey 1928: 20; Mack 1962: 112; Williford 1975: 168). He pointed out that Bentham was regarded as pro-woman in the light of his critique of James Mill's *Essay on Government* (1820), written in the context of the debate leading up to the Reform Bill of 1832. Bentham fell out with James Mill in 1818, and since then had few kind words for his former associate and friend. The differences were personal, but they cast their shadow on his assessment of Mill's *Essay* (Ball 1980: 105).

Bentham, according to Ball, shelved his initial demand for enfranchisement of women and their political representation on the grounds of principle and practice. In practical terms, as pointed out, he realized that society was not yet receptive to his radical demand. In principle, he too believed that the home was the natural domain for the woman. Her nature was so constituted as to preclude rational political judgements and be prone to superstition. Women were subordinate to men because they were weaker. He also granted the man the right to be the guardian of his wife's interests, but rejected the idea of making them absolute masters. Women, because of their weakness or gentleness, could not be reduced to the position of slaves. He warned that at all costs the "dangerous snare" of "absolute equality" between the sexes was to be avoided. While J.S. Mill believed in sexual equality, Bentham did not entertain that possibility. "If on some occasions Bentham was an ambivalent feminist, he was, on many more, an ardent anti-feminist" (Ball ibid: 107).

In his *Autobiography* (1873), J.S. Mill acknowledged the influence that Bentham had exerted on his thinking, giving sufficient reasons for projecting Bentham as a champion of women's causes. Curiously, he failed to mention his subsequent rejection of women's suffrage.

AS A HUMANIST

Bentham was against colonialism, and argued that it was bad both for the colonizers and the colonies. He wanted England to create a "mass of happiness" by adopting the principle of self-government within the empire. In arguing on behalf of the colonial peoples, he was against the prevailing view in the eighteenth and nineteenth centuries which differentiated between "they" (colonized) and "us" (colonizers). He became interested in the Indian reform movement when James Mill became an official in the English East India Company. He inspired Lord William Bentinck, the Governor General of India in 1827, to support and initiate reforms in India. In 1793, Bentham asked France to liberate its colonies.

Bentham, inspired by the reform proposals with regard to education, formed a committee and drew up plans to establish a school in London patterned on the ideas suggested by Bell and Lancaster. Bell, by training advanced students to teach younger schoolmates, hit upon an inexpensive method of education. This was the first practicable programme for extending education to the lower classes, and eventually abolishing illiteracy altogether. Though the idea never concretized, it enthused Bentham to write his *Christomathia,* a minute compendium on education, covering everything from a pupil's diet to an encyclopaedic table embracing all knowledge. In 1825, James Mill established the Society for the Diffusion of Useful Knowledge with a view to distributing cheap or free utilitarian tracts.

Bentham championed humane treatment of slaves and animals, favouring the abolition of slavery. He was against capital punishment. In line with his conviction that happiness was the motive force in human behaviour and action, he sketched an Encyclopaedical Tree as a master plan for all the arts and sciences in accordance with their contribution to human happiness. He contributed towards evolving an international language, by classifying 17 properties that were desirable in a language. He also outlined the principles of universal grammar. He coined new words like *international, codify, maximize, minimize, rationale, demoralize, deontology, eulogistic* and *false consciousness.* In spite of his dislike for Aristotle, he emphasized, like the ancient master, that mastery of language and the ability to use the right word were essential to serious thinking.

Bentham also suggested "Dialogues with the Dead" for their educational and theatrical value. He prepared snippets of conversations that could take place between Socrates and himself on the subject of happiness; with Bacon on the philosophical developments of the past 2000 years; with Jean le Rond d'Alembert (1717–1783) on the Encyclopaedical Tree; with Etienne Dumont and Montesquieu on the law as it ought to be; with Locke on the fiction of the original social contract; with Porphyny, Locke and Bishop Sanderson on logic; and with Euclid, Appollonius, Diophantus, Newton and La Place on mathematics. He suggested that people should go to pilgrimages to the shrines of dead philosophers as opposed to pilgrimages to the shrines of saints and martyrs. He wanted religion, like political and legal institutions, to serve the public and promote Utilitarian ideals".

In his *Plan for an Universal and Perpetual Peace,* Bentham considered war as the chief cause of suffering and proposed two planks for its elimination,: that of reducing military forces in Europe and to emancipate colonies. For the welfare of all civilized nations he suggested three goals—simplicity of government, national frugality and peace. He opposed international treatises and trade barriers and pointed out that trade was always advantageous to both parties but war, ruinous to all the participants in modern times. He desired the establishment of a common court of judicature to decide differences among states but did not want, unlike St. Pierre and Rousseau, the court to be armed with coercive powers. Establishing a judicial court was in the interest of all. Bentham recommended a congress of deputies from each country whose proceedings would be made public. He distrusted secret diplomacy, had enornmous faith in the efficacy of public opinion and was more optimistic than Kant, about achieving lasting world peace and happiness if people are allowed personal contact with one another than through the abrasive relations between governments thus anticipating the contemporary thrust on people to people diplomacy as the basis of building amity and peace. The cybernetic school of integration led by Karl Deutsch after the Second World War made it the most important plank for achieving regional integration and thereby peace.Bentham's plan is quite sketchy and obviously not comprehensive. However, he demonstrates the usefulness of disarmament and warns about the dangers of colonialism and secrecy. Though he alludes to the power of public opinion in international affairs he was also conscious as to how it could be stifled. He also coins the word 'international'. "The basic Benthamite idea has persisted to this day that the ordinary citizen can have a vision of a more peaceful, just and happy world and has both the right and power to coerce his own government to policies consonant with this ideal" (Heater 1990: 55–56).

CONCLUSION

Bentham advanced numerous ideas which have become central to the liberal creed of the nineteenth century. These were liberty of speech and of the press, liberty of association, freedom of trade, freedom to emigrate from one country to another, support for the rule of law, faith in public opinion, and freedom from arbitrary and despotic government. His commitment to political and constitutional democracy, his support for the extension of suffrage, his belief in the need to widen the ambit of participation to cover as many people as possible and his faith in gradual reforms based on the individual's expectations of security injected new ideas into the traditional notion of liberalism.

Bentham retained the Lockeian idea of liberty with due regard to property, but suggested gradual redistribution of wealth through taxation of inheritance, to ensure a society where the poor enjoyed minimal security and the rich did not feel threatened. In this sense, he laid down the economic basis of the welfare state.

> Bentham's concentration on security—on the instrument of good government—enabled him to move beyond the Lockean conception of the minimal state towards one more appropriate for a modern democratic society where security would be conceived more widely in terms of education, health and welfare as well as real property and wealth (Rosen 1990: 68).

Bentham was a firm believer in gradual reform. He had no faith in the violence of a revolution. His detailed reform package played a crucial role in transforming early liberalism into something that was "socially beneficent and never in intention merely exploitative" (Sabine 1973: 612). His contributions to the development of liberalism were varied and manifold. He used ideas inherited from Locke, Hume, Montesquieu and Helvetius to mount a thorough attack on outmoded ideas and practices. After Bentham, the most vocal strand in liberal thought was based on

Utilitarian principles. "Utilitarianism was essentially a British phenomenon, a philosophy based on empirical investigation, hedonism, the association of ideas and a liberal and humane approach to political and economic affairs" (Curtis 196L Vol. II: 102).

Bentham's Utilitarian principles not only dominated the liberal discourse, but also influenced the early socialist writings of William Thompson (1785–1833). In fact, Beatrice Webb (1858–1943) acknowledged Bentham as Sidney Webb's (1859–1947) intellectual godfather, though the Fabians did not accept the principle of the greatest happiness of the greatest number. Like Bentham, the Fabians realized the urgent need for institutional inspection and criticism before social reconstruction. They were empiricists. Like Bentham, they regarded education as the "keystone of reformation". The Fabians, like the Utilitarians, organized a research society patterned after the Society for the Diffusion of Useful Knowledge, which gradually became the pivot of the Fabian society. They were associated with the University College, and in 1895 established the London School of Economics. In 1912 they started the *New Statesman.* Both the Utilitarians and the Fabians believed in infiltration of the parliament and conversion of existing members. But the Fabians dismissed Bentham's economic understanding as weak. However, this was not surprising, for Bentham never thought highly of his powers of economic analysis. Both rejected the theory of natural rights. While Bentham wanted to emulate Newton, the Fabians, like Marx, were inspired by Charles Robert Darwin (1802–1885), and both sought to build a counterpart of the natural sciences.

> Thanks to the efforts of many current scholars, it is at last becoming clear that Bentham may with more truth be called the patriarch of British collectivism than the father of individualism. The Fabians were direct descendants of Bentham via Chadwick and Forster. Indeed, as J. Bartlet Brebner, one of the pioneer debunkers of the utilitarian myth, pointedly asks, what were the Fabians but the latter day Benthamites? (Mack 1955: 88).

In the 1820s, Bentham provided a new approach to constitutional theory, which advanced the precepts and absorbed the criticisms of the great period of constitutional thought and practice around the time of the American and French Revolutions. He gave to this existing theory not only a new foundation, but also a new emphasis on administrative and judicial organization with regard to responsible exercise of power. By conceiving the ends of legislation to include security, subsistence, abundance and equality, and by envisaging political structures to advance these ends, Bentham could foresee the needs and aspirations of the modern democratic state (Miller 1987: 39–40).

The thrust of Benthamite Utilitarianism was on relieving pain and providing security, on insisting that the pleasures of all individuals deserved equal respect and consideration, and that they should not be interfered with unless it interfered in the pleasure of others. It was true that he did not delve into the spiritual or intellectual dimensions of the individual's pursuit of pleasure, but that shortcoming, if it was one, was made up by J.S. Mill, who offered a conception of liberty that was spiritually and intellectually satisfying to the individual. Mill revised and improvised Benthamite Utilitarianism, but

> Bentham is truly the founding father. As anyone who has written on Mill knows, he cannot be understood except in terms of Bentham—and not only genetically, formatively, but at every point and turning of his life and thought. Mill may have refined, corrected, amplified, even transcended Bentham; but it is only by reference to Bentham that we can appreciate what he tried to do, what he did do, and what, perhaps he finally failed to do (Himmelfarb 1970: 74).

11

Mary Wollstonecraft

> Wollstonecraft's achievement was to extend the commonwealth analysis of male corruption and programme for male reform to women (Baker-Benfield 1989: 95).

> While Mary Wollstonecraft's *A Vindication of the Rights of Woman* is rightly regarded as a classic text of liberal feminism, it had little practical influence on mainstream political or the liberal tradition (Leach 1991: 182).

> What Mary Wollstonecraft herself advocated were not so much political rights as emancipation from the drudgery, the social and economic inferiority, which was women's lot. If that could be achieved they could contribute in their own ways more fully to society (Heater 1991: 42).

In understanding the British political tradition, Whiggism was of crucial significance as liberalism essentially developed out of the Whig tradition. It was not primarily an economic doctrine though it definitely served the economic interests of the middle class. Whiggism forcefully pleaded for parliamentary supremacy, consent as the basis of legitimate government, freedom of conscience and religious toleration, and the famous slogan that mobilized the American people in their fight for independence 'no taxation without representation'.

Alongside this Whig tradition developed the radical opinion that shaped and influenced British liberalism. "These radicals considered themselves to be 'Real', 'True' and 'Honest' Whigs and tried to evoke the spirit of commonwealthmen of the English revolutions of the seventeenth century" (Baker-Benfield 1989: 95). However, unlike Whiggism, which emerged as a coherent doctrine and with a party to advance its ideas the radicals were an amorphous group without a common binding force. The term 'radical' came to signify a wide range of thinkers, politicians, non-conformists and pioneers. The most important among these radicals was Paine.

> Although the mainstream Whig politicians of the eighteenth and early nineteenth centuries tended to interpret their proclaimed principles in ways which preserved their own property and privileges, it was always possible to give these same principles a far more radical interpretation as Thomas Paine did" (Leach 1991: 65).

Paine carried forward the egalitarian and rationalistic assumptions of Locke by pleading convincingly for political equality and full manhood suffrage without any kind of property restrictions. Many within Britain advocated the need for a more democratic constitution. From the 1760s to 1790s, there were demands for democratization of the parliament, abolition of second class status to Dissenters and by some, to women. These demands got strengthened and influenced by the revolutionary events in France in 1789. Through arguments like Locke's natural rights theory, the nature of a freer and more equal Anglo-Saxon age and the utilitarian belief that political enfranchisement would lead to a rational and just society, the reformers defended the widening of suffrage. Their other demands included annual elections, equal electoral districts, secret ballot, abolition of property qualifications for MPs, payment to MP's and manhood suffrage.

It was in this context that Mary Wollstonecraft (1759–97) advocated rights for women being close to the leading Protestant Dissenters, Price and Priestly. Wollstonecraft's *A Vindication of the Rights of Woman* (1792) henceforth referred in the text as *A Vindication* has been aptly described as the first classic work in feminist thought. For the last two hundred years, it has generated many debates and controversies and, has been vilified and eulogized. In the background of the enlightenment and the French Revolution, Wollstonecraft extended the radical opinion of the Dissenters like Paine and Price and brilliantly exposed the myth of equality which had ignored half of the human race. Even the mighty Rousseau did not escape her well-reasoned criticisms, as she skilfully demolished his arguments in his treatise on education *Emile*.

> The whole extent of the feminist ideal is set out and the whole claim for equal human rights is made; and ... it has remained the text of the movement ever since (Strachy 1978: 22).

LIFE SKETCH

Wollstonecraft was born on 27 April 1759 in a house in Primrose Street, Spitalfields in London. She was the second child and eldest daughter in a family saddled with difficulties. Her mother Elizabeth Dickson Wollstonecraft bore seven children. Though submissive to her husband she was domineering towards her children. Edward John Wollstonecraft never settled down to a regular job with a steady income. He quit his job after receiving an inheritance. He drank a lot and became increasingly violent and brutal at home. In 1768, the family moved to a farm in Yorkshire. Wollstonecraft's formal education was meagre and she was self taught. In 1788, she left home in search of financial independence. She became a journalist and also a paid companion to an elderly widow Mrs. Dawson at Bath. She returned home to nurse her ailing mother in the later part of 1781. After her mother's death in 1782, she lived with the Bloods, the impoverished family of her dearest friend Fanny. She left them in 1783 to attend to her sister Eliza and her newly born daughter. In January 1784, the two sisters went into hiding leaving behind Eliza's baby. Wollstonecraft took on the responsibility of taking care of her father. She also financed the education of her younger brothers and sisters and found them suitable employment.

In 1784, Wollstonecraft established a school at Newington Green in London with the purpose of providing informal education for young untrained teachers. This venture enabled her to grow intellectually even though she was beset with personal problems and economic instability. Her close friend Fanny Blood died of tuberculosis. She found out that the school did not do well. She was also in serious financial difficulties. On a suggestion by her neighbour she took to writing and publishing in order to settle her debts. She published *Thoughts on the Education of Daughters: With Reflections on Female Conduct in the More Important Duties of Life* in 1787. Meanwhile in 1786, she took up a job as a governess in Kingsborough family with large tracts of estates in Ireland. This was her first encounter with the leisurely class. In 1788, she published her first novel *Mary*.

In 1787, Wollstonecraft returned to England. In the same year, she wrote for the *Analytical Review* of Joseph Johnson and translated *The Female Reader*. In 1790, she became an editorial assistant to the *Analytical Review* and wrote *A Vindication of the Rights of Men*. She began writing *A Vindication of the Rights of Woman* in 1791, which was published in 1792. In December 1791, she met William Godwin (1756–1836). In 1792, she met Talleyrand and travelled to France. In 1793, she met Gilbert Imlay with whom she shared a happy but stormy relationship. She began writing *A Historical and Moral View of the Origin and Progress of the French Revolution* (1794). She registered herself in the US Embassy as Mrs. Imlay and gave birth to a daughter, Imlay's child in 1794. In 1795, she returned to London and attempted a suicide. She left for a long tour of Scandinavia as Imlay's agent. In 1796, she published *Letters Written during a Short Residence in Sweden*. Having parted with Imlay, she resumed her contact with Godwin and became his lover. They married in 1797, at St.Pancras Church, after realizing that Wollstonecraft was pregnant with Godwin's child. She wrote *The Wrongs of Woman* during this phase. Their daughter, Mary, was born on 30 August 1730. Mary was the future wife of Percy Bysshe Shelley (1792–1822) and the author of *Frankenstein*. On 10 September 1797, Wollstonecraft died of septicemia.

Many of Wollstonecraft's contemporaries were critical of her personal life. She was called a 'shameless wanton' a 'hyena in petticoats' and 'a philosophizing serpent'. They worried that her controversial personal life might hinder the cause of women that she was espousing in public. However, in the twentieth century, Wollstonecraft was described as 'God's angry woman' a 'man hater'. Emma Goldman paid tributes to Wollstonecraft by acknowledging her as the 'pioneer of modern womanhood'.

PRICE AND THE SUFFRAGE QUESTION

Wollstonecraft became acquainted with Price when she moved to Newington Green, a town north of London, and through Price, came to know other men and women who were liberal in their orientation. "She came to see her personal struggle for independence as part of a larger political struggle and through Price, to understand that a person required freedom to cultivate reason and so achieve true humanity" (Todd 1989: 4). These Protestant Dissenters debated on the meaning of popular sovereignty and equality. The crux of the debate was that if men were equal and entitled to full citizenship rights, and if people were sovereign, then who could be denied suffrage and on what grounds. Price at a meeting of a body called *The Revolutionary Society* consisting of dissenters and radical Whigs remarked,

> What an eventful period is this! I have lived to it, and I could almost say, lord, now lattés thou thy servant depart in peace lived to see the rights of men better understood than ever, nations panting for liberty, which seems to have lost the idea of it.... Be encouraged, all ye friends of freedom, and writers in its defense. The times are auspicious. Your labours have not been in vain (Parkin 1969: 120).

Thus, it was during the enlightenment and the French Revolution that the vocabulary and principles of what came to be subsequently styled as 'feminism' emerged. It could be described as a struggle for recognition of the rights of women, for equality between sexes and a re-definition of womanhood. Wollstonecraft's *A Vindication* was the first tract to trigger off a debate centering on the theme of 'equality versus difference'. She regarded sexual distinctions as arbitrary, a product of the patriarchal society, defended the need for equal and similar education for both men and women, glorified reason as the main tool for women's emancipation and attacked the notion of women as sexual beings.

> Wollstonecraft was the first major feminist and *A Vindication*, written when the issue of the rights of men was bringing revolution to the United States to France, and threatened to shake the venerable English Parliament, is the feminist declaration of independence. She dared to take the liberal doctrine of inalienable human rights, a doctrine which was inflaming patriots on both sides of the Atlantic (Kramnick 1982: 7).

Wollstonecraft questioned the male bias in their notions of rationality and citizenship and demanded equal opportunity for women. She highlighted women's oppression even though she lent her support to the new bourgeois order and its liberal political principles, and thus laid the foundations for her feminist political philosophy. She desired the extension of liberal value of economic independence, individual achievement, and personal autonomy to women in general and to the middle class women in particular. She established a close link between liberalism and feminism by accepting the liberal challenge to aristocratic and patriarchal rule (Eisenstein 1986: 90).

The Dissenters believed that only a free individual could be virtuous and, therefore, considered independence of mind as an essential right. They equated independence with reason. Reason was elevated to the status of a religion for it could mitigate most of the shortcomings of the society. True wisdom could be only achieved through rational thinking for knowledge could rectify prejudices and remedy social injustices. The Dissenters, unlike Burke, considered the middle class as a repository of morality and civic virtue. They defended freedom of religious conscience. The rational Dissenters as they came to be referred to were also described as a 'pack of dirty Jacobins' or 'William Godwin and His Circle' in English cultural history included besides Godwin, John Wilkes, Paine, Thomas Holcroft, William Blake, Henry Fuseli and Wollstonecraft. They represented the "radical elements in English religious dissent, moving towards rationalism; ... as a radical political grouping, concerned with parliamentary reform, the extension of education and the removal of obstacles to free intellectual inquiry... . This ... is directly connected with the most progressive elements of the industrial bourgeoisie, with their attachments to free enquiry and to a rational science (Williams 1981: 75). The Dissenters saw themselves as the true inheritors of the Lockeian heritage and were enthusiastic supporters of the American and the early phases of the French Revolution for these revolutions embodied the spirit of liberty. Price, in a letter to Burke wrote,

> In order that liberty should have a firm foundation it must be laid either by poor men or philosophers (Nixon 1971: 51).

Liberty and reform were on the agenda of many writers of that time: Rousseau in France, and, Wilkes and Paine in England. In fact, Paine completed his survey of the working class in England, the defects and deficiencies of a hereditary system of government, the unequal tax structure and the impressment of sailors and soldiers in wars faced with its consequences, namely, poverty as material deprivation without any hope of relief. He championed equal rights for men, representative government and the rule of law. He debunked the hereditary system whether monarchy or aristocracy and supported a government based on a social contract between people themselves. He was critical of the British constitution for being unwritten making it unhelpful as a reference point. Its precedents were all arbitrary contrary to reason and commonsense. Though the radical intelligentsia advocated restructuring of the existing political and administrative systems, as it was unjust, yet "it was rare to find a radical agitator of really humble origins in England" in the 1780s, as England was relatively more prosperous than France and the rest of Europe. The average Englishman led a decent standard living. As a result, "revolutionary thinking was almost totally the preserve of the bourgeois intelligentsia of whom Mary was one" (Nixon ibid: 150).

Criticism of Burke

In her reply to Burke, Wollstonecraft pointed out the apparent and as it appeared to many contemporaries of her time, the contradictions of a liberal Burke supporting the American cause and the conservative Burke opposing Jacobinism in France and England, making him a virulent critic of the French Revolution. Burke's praise of tradition and hereditary rights and his emphatic stress on the conservation of existing political relations indicated according to Wollstonecraft, a lack of reason and predominance of sentiment leading to social stagnation hindering the progressive and dynamic nature of social and political life. She primarily criticized Burke's *Reflections* though she also took exception to one of his earlier and influential book on aesthetics, *A Philosophical Enquiry into the Origin of Our Ideas of the Sublime and Beautiful* (1757) in which he associated beauty with women and sublimity with men. Wollstonecraft accused Burke for championing "the maintenance of unequal property, and if necessary, of despotism and tyranny'. Property, according to Wollstonecraft, not only restricted liberty by creating inequalities but also undermined sociability for 'among unequals there can be no society, meaning friendship and mutual respect'. Burke's conservatism and Wollstonecraft's radicalism were at the opposite ends of the ideological spectrum. Wollstonecraft's views were in congruence with that of the radicals of her time. Being close to Price, her mentor, she articulated instinctively and with conviction the ideas of the Dissenters.

Burke's defence of the hereditary principle and traditional values, according to Wollstonecraft, impeded the progress of civilization for individuals were respected according to their station in life. Moreover, because of the institution of private property which she described as 'demonic', parents treated their children like slaves sacrificing the younger ones to the eldest son and restricting early marriages, thereby injuring the minds and bodies of young people by producing 'lax morals and depraved affections'. Furthermore, property spreads discontent among the middle class who try to imitate the lifestyles of the rich. Wollstonecraft saw the church that Burke praised as an institution upholding the sacredness of traditional values, as fundamentally corrupt having secured vast property from the poor and ignorant. With the help of Hume's *History of England* (1754–62), she tried to show that English laws were a product of contingencies rather than the wisdom of the ages. She insisted that only those institutions, which would withstand the scrutiny of reason and in accordance with natural rights and God's justice, deserved respect and obedience. Furthermore, she assailed Burke for defending a 'gothic affability' more appropriate for a feudal age than the burgeoning commercial age marked for its 'liberal civility'. As against Burke's theory of prescriptive rights, Wollstonecraft contended that human beings by birth as rational creatures have inherited certain rights, especially the equal rights to liberty compatible with that of others. She was critical of Burke's views on women as a "symbol of man's need for a feminine ideal, not woman for herself". His description of women as "little smooth, delicate, fair creatures, never designed that they should exercise their reason and that they should lisp, to totter in their walk and nick-name God's creatures", was the view of a strong prejudiced mind. He was not a great humanist for he was indifferent to the plight and cause of women (Wollstonecraft 1970: 113 and 112).

Paine, like Wollstonecraft, was critical of inadequate parliamentary representation, primogeniture and aristocracy, and state religion and denied reverence to the settlement of 1688 and its 'Bill of Wrongs' enacted by a non-elected Commons. Like Wollstonecraft, he did not wish to destroy property rights completely but insisted that on the division of large estates. In 'An Occasional Letter on the Female Sex' (1775) Paine examined the French *Declaration of the Rights of Man* but "did not think to annotate the document to show the systematic exclusion of women from its principles, as the feminist Olympe de Gouges did in France. It was Wollstonecraft's distinction that, without being the first to do so at the time, she brought the issue of women's rights for a short moment in the 1790s into the general debate about civil rights", (Todd 1989: xiv).

Both, Paine and Wollstonecraft, portrayed Burke as a brilliant but misguided voice of the past. Paine's criticisms of Burke were more effective and well known, as evident from his famous phrase that Burke "pitted the plumage but forgot the dying bird" but it was Wollstonecraft who advocated a more radical stance for ameliorating the plight of the poor. Paine did not have any plan for social levelling other than taxing the rich and insisting "that the appalling conditions of the poor must be improved, but he failed to offer any economic solution to the problem" (Dickinson 1977: 267). On the other hand, Wollstonecraft suggested economic means for improving the condition of the poor by dividing estates into small farms (Wollstonecraft 1970: 140). She endorsed plans for the betterment of the working class.

Response to the French Revolution

The French Revolution, for Wollstonecraft, represented the first expression of humankind towards general emancipation and liberation. The storming of the Bastille translated abstract rights into reality. The Revolution itself vindicated some of her liberal beliefs on the brotherhood of man and the equality of sexes. In the process, she transplanted the principles for women's rights from France to England. Within France, there were arguments for women's equality. This was evident in Condercet's *Sur l' Admission des femmes au droit deute* (1790), Diderot's *Sur les Femmes* (1772) and Holbach's *Des Femmes* (1773). Condorcet argued that to deprive women of their right to vote was contrary to the notion of natural rights since women as rational sentient beings deserved the same rights that men claimed for themselves. If women appeared inferior to men in intelligence it was because of poor education. He coaxed his fellow revolutionaries to adopt a more enlightened attitude towards women. His advocacy of women's rights was part of his plan of a rational political order based on complete equality between the sexes in political rights and educational opportunities. He showed "how the radical opponents of monarchical despotism and aristocratic privilege are themselves still prisoners of prejudices who will ignore or even explicitly endorse the despotic powers exercised by men over women" (Evans 1986: 23). Condorcet desired to give women self-respect and dignity, which could be possible only by public recognition of their equal rights. In 1793, he wrote his *Sketch for a Historical Picture of the Progress of the Human Mind* where he was more forthright about the status of women. He consistently insisted on the need defend sexual equality and observed,

> Some philosophers seem to have taken pleasure in exaggerating these differences; in consequence they have assigned to each sex its rights, its prerogatives, its occupations, its duties, and practically its tastes, its opinions, its sentiments, its pleasures; they take the dreams of a romantic imagination as the will of nature, they have dogmatically pronounced that all *is the best possible* for the common good; but this optimism, which consists in wondrously finding in nature everything as one invented it ... must be banished from philosophy (Proctor 1990: 29).

Initially, Condorcet seemed more concerned about political rather than social rights but subsequently, began to articulate a viewpoint similar to that of Wollstonecraft. He wrote,

> Among the causes of the progress of the human mind that are of utmost importance to the general happiness, we must number the complete annihilation of the prejudices that have brought about an inequality of rights between the sexes, an inequality fatal even to the party in whose favour it works. It is vain for us to look for a justification of this principle in any differences of physical organization, intellect, or moral sensibility between men and women. This inequality has its origin solely in an abuse of strength, and all the late sophistical attempts that have been made to excuse it are vain (Todd 1989: xv–xvi).

Like Wollstonecraft subsequently, Condorcet believed that women's equality would improve human relations within the family. Except for brute strength women were equal to men. The brightest of women were superior to men of limited talents and that improvement in education would narrow the existing gaps. A more rational government would work towards ensuring a better status for women. Thus the radical liberal opinion within France inspired Wollstonecraft though she did not discuss or read Condorcet's works. However, he paid tributes to her as a historian who ought to express her views in the Parliament rather than remain a writer of women's rights and education. Wollstonecraft, unlike Condorcet in his early writings, focused more on social rather than political degradation. By doing so, she "suggested a more intractable problem than Condorcet addressed in his earlier works and was forced to castigate not only male intransigence but also women's collusion in their own oppression" (Todd ibid: xvi).

Jean Le Rond d'Alembert (1717–83) reacted sharply to Rousseau's tirade against women. He attributed the cause of their apparent inferior condition to "slavery and type of disparagement" that women were subjected to. The other advocates for women's rights in France included Madame de Stael, Marie-Jeanne Philipon (1754–93) also known as Madame Roland remembered for her famous statement while facing the guillotine 'Oh! Liberty what crimes are committed in thy name?, Olympe de Gouges (1748–93) (who dedicated her book *The Declaration of the Rights of Women—La declaration des droits Des femmes*—to the Queen) and Theroigne de Mericourt Poulain de la Barre accepted the intellectual equality of the sexes and that a woman ought to play a more active role in the society since their natural powers were so far uncontaminated. Condorcet and Voltaire used logic and biting satire to critique the French unequal adultery laws and pleaded for the need of divorce laws.

De Gouges tries to organize women's societies that were both intellectual and political. Her *Letter to the People or Project for a Patriotic Coffer by a Female Citizen* (1788) urged women to demonstrate their patriotism by voluntarily contributing to the state coffers for that would bring about an egalitarian redistribution of wealth and repay the national debt. Her *Reflection on Black Men* (1788) argued that there were no innate differences between blacks and whites, and hence, no justification for slavery. In the *Project for a Second Theatre and for a Maternity Hospital* (1789) she insisted on a need to set up a women's hospital. In *The Call of the Wise by a Woman* (1789) she instructed the clergy, nobility and land owners convened by Louis XVI not to take covertures for granted. Her well-known and philosophical tract *The Rights of Woman* (1791) laid down the constitutional principles—natural law and laws of logic as the basis of the rights of women. She advocated full political equality, equal opportunity for employment, education and holding public offices, equal access to women to public programmes, right to outright ownership and control of property if married. She called for a marriage to replace conventional marriage vows as a way of proving legal paternity of illegitimate children. *The Well-being of the Nation* (1793) formed the basis for her advocacy of general social reform. This pamphlet was seized and de Gouges was imprisoned for her criticisms of the revolution and the subsequent terror. She was declared a reactionary royalist and guillotined the next day after the trial ended.

Marquis de Sade, a defender of the woman's question raised some psychological and ethical questions regarding man's nature thereby undermining preconceived notions about sexuality and the 'natural' relations of the sexes. He defended the need for absolute equality of right in sexual matters between men and women. Being a militant atheist and a philosophical materialist, he opposed the tyranny of the church and the repressive Christian doctrines. The Christian God with his threat of divine retribution in his opinion was too immoral and base to be acceptable. He replaced God with Nature and looked upon the latter as the prime mover of the Universe. Anticipating Pierre Joseph Proudhon (1809–65) De Sade defined property 'as a crime committed by the rich against the poor'. Property originated in usurpation and theft with law protecting the wealthy. He rejected laws as being detrimental to human passions. He had a poor opinion of individuals with weak passions regarding them as mediocre beings. He regarded crime as an outcome of passions or want and that kindness and honour could provide an effective deterrent. He advocated the abolition of death penalty. He defended women's equal opportunity with men to satisfy their desires and wrote,

> No act of possession can ever be exercised on a person; it is as unjust to possess a woman exclusively as it is to possess slaves; all human beings are born free and with equal rights; let us never forget that, consequently no sex can have a legitimate right to the exclusive possession of another and no sex or class can possess the other exclusively (Marshall 1992: 148).

Interestingly, the French *Declaration of the Rights of Man* of 1789 referred only to universal manhood suffrage. The National Assembly recognized male voters. On 28 October 1789, it refused to entertain a petition from the Parisian women who demanded universal suffrage in the election of national representatives. In fact, the revolution withdrew some of the rights that a woman enjoyed under the *Ancien Regime*. For example, a noble woman as a landowner had rights similar to those enjoyed by feudal lords. She could raise and levy taxes, and administer justice. Women could become peers, diplomats and own large tracts of land. In the guilds, women exercised their professional rights as voters. The abbesses enjoyed the same powers as the abbots. The French Revolution, though libertarian in most respects, was conservative on the gender issue. The proponents of gender inequality studied the animal kingdom to support their contention that everywhere it is the male who reigned supreme. Men in the revolution continued to regard the home as the rightful place for the woman since the domestic environment offers the best possibilities for freedom. The revolutionary ideals of liberty, equality and fraternity did not include women. The position of the women became more restrictive in post-revolutionary period. The civil and criminal codes that Napoleon promulgated placed the woman under the guardianship of a man, which meant that she could initiate legal transactions only under his tutelage. Only after 13 July 1807, could a married woman have an independent control over her earnings and savings. The July 1830 revolution and the February 1848 revolution took a more favourable view regarding the question of women's rights. Women finally secured suffrage under the Fourth Republic (1946–58).

In volume one of *An Historical and Moral View of the Origins and Progress of the French Revolution*, a narrative account of the events in France written in 1793–94, Wollstonecraft cautioned her readers to rationally judge the revolution. She empathized with the poor and the politically underprivileged, and opposed tyranny of all hue and colour. In spite of the 'reign of terror' in France, she continued to retain the belief that the revolution represented the culmination of the intellectual movement towards general social advancement. She remained still convinced of the intrinsic rightness of the principles of the revolution and blamed the French people for not having sufficient strength of character to carry forward the task of liberating humanity. She agreed with Price when he observed,

> I see the ardour of liberty catching and spreading, a general amendment beginning in human affairs; the dominion of kings changed for the dominion of laws and dominion of priests giving way to the dominion of reason and conscience (Wardle 1952: 112).

Wollstonecraft, like Paine and Price, regarded the French Revolution as the beginning of a new dawn in the chapter of human history. "Mary can be called a child of the French revolution. Its philosophy inspired her and was the foundation of her hopes for the future" (Nixon 1971: 250). In her classic *A Vindication*, she extended the prevailing arguments on the rights of man to include women and affirmed the principles of "true whiggery and political radicalism" (Barker-Benfield 1989: 106). This singular achievement of Wollstonecraft was of major significance in comprehending the gender question in political philosophy.

WOLLSTONECRAFT AND CONTEMPORARY FEMINISTS

Wollstonecraft's tract was rightly hailed as the "first classic work in Feminist thought" (Charvet 1982: 6). She applied Locke's individualistic political and social theory as modified by his radical and dissenting followers in the eighteenth century to the woman's question. She was not the first in this endeavour as there were others but hers remained the most substantive effort and contribution to individualist Feminism (Charvet 1982).

Mary Astell's (1666–1731) *Reflections upon Marriage* (1700) was historically recognized as one of the earliest tracts on education and women's rights. Astell noted that male arrogance and pride were responsible for women's oppression and subordination. Influenced by Locke she argued that there were innate ideas which men and women possess in equal capacity. Astell had an interesting exchange in print with Lady Damaris Cudworth Masham (1658–1708), the daughter of Ralph Cudworth, an eminent Cambridge Platonist on the relative merits of Locke's empiricism and Platonism. Like Locke, Astell contended that judgement was usually on the basis of what was perceived so it was not the idea but the judgement that was false. She accepted Descartes' definition of clarity and distinction and claimed that one had a clear but not a distinct idea of God and individual souls. She agreed with Locke that 'not all truths are equally evident because of the limitations of the human mind'.

Astell contended that there was absolute authority in the patriarchal family and in *An Essay in Defence of the Female Sex* (1694) she observed that conjugal power was based on force and not on the Law of Nature or 'natural' inequalities of capacities. She argued that if more attention was given to women's education then 'marriage might recover the dignity and felicity of its original institution' and men would be very happy in a married state. Marriage failed because most men did not look for proper qualifications in their wives. She instructed women to marry not because they wanted to please their friends or escape from the hardships of life but because they could enjoy an equal status in marriage. She wanted women to regulate their wills and be governed by right reason. Subjection would only enhance the pride and vanity of those who wield power. If all were born free then it did not make sense to treat women as slaves of men. Since arbitrary power was protested against when exercised in the public realm there was no justification of it as a governing principle in the private sphere.

Masham was critical of the inferior education provided to women as that made them unfit for educating their children. Ill education made women and children take to Christianity out of habit or rote rather than out of understanding. She blamed men for feeling threatened by educated women and that explained the dismal state of affairs. She was critical of the double standards in sexual morality seeing women's virtue as primarily in chastity. To give undue importance to chastity lowered the self-esteem of women and made them think of men as unjust. It also made women vain and conceited. True virtue for Masham was action in accordance with 'right reason' and not the strict observance of customs or civil institutions. Virtue was not mere adherence to rules.

Catherine Trotter Cockburn (1679–1749), initially a playwright turned to philosophy with *A Defence of Mr. Locke's Essay of Human Understanding* (1702). She prepared the case for justifying equal rights for women and men towards perfectionist goals of self-development. She argued from liberal principles for equal and fair treatment of women. Lady Mary Wortley Montagu (1689–1762) was another theorist who upheld the right of education for women. These accounts for equal civil and educational rights for men and women remained peripheral and never formed a part of mainstream eighteenth century political theory.

Wollstonecraft did not acknowledge anywhere that she had read the views of her predecessors even though her views resembled theirs in a striking manner. She acknowledged Macaulay's views on the need for women to have a rational education before they could be judged, as moral beings for the cultivation of the female intellect would eradicate feminine frivolity and triviality. Macaulay recommended a liberal upbringing for children with ample play-time, opportunities for physical activity to develop confidence and strength and shouldering responsibility of pets in order to develop care and kindness for dependent creatures. She defended women's equality and criticized the idea of sexual incompatibility as it ignored the immorality of the unequal treatment given to women. She regarded slavery as immoral and condemned the British slave trade in the West Indies. She was critical of the anti-libertarian and pro-monarchical philosophies of Hobbes, Rousseau and Hume and adopted a contractarian view. Her most famous and monumental work was *The History of England from the Accession of James I to that of the Brunswick Line* published over twenty years in eight volumes. It detailed the abuses and failures of the English monarchy at the time of its political decline leading to scathing criticisms from both Samuel Johnson and Hume. She firmly believed in the doctrine of equal individual rights, which included women also. She demanded equal educational opportunities for women. Her opposition to royal authority and rejection of any mode of dominance led her to travel to the United States to meet the anti-monarchial revolutionaries, Benjamin Franklin, John Adams, George Washington, Martha Washington, James Otis Warren and Mercy Otis Warren.

Unlike Macaulay, a Whig historian who saw progress in history, Wollstonecraft believed only in individual progress on the premise that change would improve the life prospects for everyone. Society could not progress if half of its population remained backward. For this purpose, women would have to be regarded first and foremost as human beings and then as women for the soul is unsexed. The inequality and oppression that women suffer corrupted both men and women equally. Essentially believing in the importance of environment she rejected heredity. Professing faith in the libertarian principles of the French Revolution, Wollstonecraft felt the need to extend the same to women whom she considered as the cradle of the human race. The basic ideas of human perfectibility, equality of individuals and the natural right of each to determine his destiny would enable society to overcome its oppressive and unequal ways. "In doing so, she linked feminism to the general struggle for political and social reform, arguing that the abstract rights of woman were inextricably linked with the abstract rights of men and that the tyranny of man, husband, king, primogeniture and hereditary privilege must all cease, in the name of reason, a reason that was woman's as well as man's" (Todd 1989: xvii). Wollstonecraft basically contended that only women with independent minds could make good wives and become good mothers.

"Meek wives make foolish mothers... . Speaking of women at large, their first duty is to themselves as rational creatures and the next in point of importance, as citizens, is that of a mother" (Wollstonecraft cited in Nixon 1971: 120). If women have to rise they would have to imbibe middle class values, attitudes and virtues. The domestic revolution that she aspired for ought to emulate the French Revolution and be middle class in its orientation and ideas. "The women she hoped to reach first and foremost belonged to the middle class. Her ambition was to stop them from aping their social superiors, to divert their attention away from the world of fashion to that of learning, and thereby to emancipate them from their dependence on the opinion of other vain and superficial beings" (Tomaselli 1995: x–xi).

Views on Women

Wollstonecraft believed that fulfilment, maturity and eventual emancipation would come only if women were treated as persons and not merely as sexual beings. Women like men were endowed with reason enabling them to make rational decisions and were entitled to natural rights. Extending the argument of the natural rights theorists. Wollstonecraft pointed out that the chief distinguishing trait that separate human beings from animals was the fact that they possess a reasoning faculty. If this proposition applied to men then it was equally true for women also. Women were not inferior to men and if they appear so it was because they were denied rights and training of their talents and skills. She instructed women to develop their inner resources to make themselves interesting not for others, but for themselves. She accepted that the result of generations of neglect, women's capacities and skills have been stunted which could be remedied with sufficient opportunities, freedom and education.

Having very little faith in the women of her time, Wollstonecraft looked to assistance from enlightened men as being crucial to bring about a first generation of independent women. Subsequent generations would find it easier for they would have role models for emulation. A disciple of Locke, Wollstonecraft regarded nurture as being more important than nature for education could temper and shape human beings. Within this broad framework a major portion of *A Vindication* (1792) was directed to the prevailing perceptions on women and their role in society. Wollstonecraft made Rousseau, Burke, Dr. Gregory, Dr. Fordyce and Lord Chesterfield her targets for in her opinion, their texts and views presented a 'sexual character to the mind'. These theorists saw women as artificial beings meant to pander to the egos of men, which unfortunately was endorsed by many women themselves. To this, Wollstonecraft observed

> All the causes of female weakness as well as depravity, which I have already enlarged on, branch out of one grand cause—want of chastity in men (Wollstonecraft 1985: 152).

Wollstonecraft was equally critical of women for accepting their artificial and subordinate status. She asserted that they were not merely confined to household work, but were corrupted by it for making them servile as the dependent class, and arbitrary and irrational as tyrants in their sexual relationships with men. She found the idea of chaste wives and sensible mothers as absurd. As far as chastity was concerned, if discarded by their husbands they tended to look for admirers and lovers elsewhere. As far as the upbringing of their children was concerned they had no rational plan for conducting it. It was done through trial and error, by perpetuating the same techniques and values with which they were brought up without critically examining its appropriateness or effects.

Wollstonecraft was critical of Rousseau for assuming that men and women differed in their capacity for virtues. While a man's virtue was considered to be his rational capacity a woman's virtue was her chastity, gentleness and obedience. Rousseau was prepared to keep women in ignorance by not allowing them to gain knowledge and in the process, according to Wollstonecraft, was prepared to debase one-half of humanity without any consideration for the future of humankind. She was critical of Rousseau for regarding women as sexual beings and, therefore, not free. A man, on the contrary, was sexual only at certain times, but was free and equal for the rest of the time. Rousseau recommended little liberty for women so that her nature was good and that she could bear the insults and injustices of her husband, an imperfect being. She was supposed to be timid, weak and try and develop her beauty. To this, Wollstonecraft replied:

> The being who patiently endures injustice, and silently bears insults, will soon become unjust; ... of what materials can that heart be composed which can melt when insulted, and instead of revolting at injustice, kiss the rod... . Greatness of mind can never dwell with cunning or address; for I shall not boggle about words ... but content myself with observing that if any class of mankind be so created that it must necessarily be educated by rules not strictly deducible from truth, virtue is an affair of convention... . Men have superior strength of body; but were it not mistaken notions of beauty, women would acquire sufficient intelligence to enable them to earn their own subsistence, the true definition of independence; and to bear those bodily inconveniences and exertions that are requisite to strengthen the mind. Let us then, by being allowed to take the same exercise as boys, not only during infancy, but youth arrive at perfection of body, that we may know how far the natural superiority of man extends. For what reason or virtue can be expected from a creature when the seed-time of life is neglected (Wollstonecraft 1985: 92, 94).

Wollstonecraft was also critical of the legal and educational aspects of women's place in society, a fact that Rousseau accepted as natural. It is interesting that Rousseau was radical in many other areas of human knowledge except sexual relations. The crux of her criticisms of Rousseau was that if women did not pursue the false idea of securing beauty then they could acquire sufficient strength to be able to earn their living without which genuine independence was not possible. Like Plato, Wollstonecraft affirmed the principle of sexual equality between men and women but strove to achieve freedom, equality, and independence within the realm of the family and home. The early feminists of the nineteenth century like Fuller and Wollstonecraft respected the traditional functions that a woman performed within her home as a wife and as a mother. She not only rejected Rousseau's *Emile* but also James Fordyce's *Sermons* perceived as a guide to good girl's behaviour as it does "little more then sentimentalize the teachings of Rousseau".

> I should instantly dismiss them from my pupil's attention if I wished to strengthen her understanding (Wollstonecraft ibid: 103, 102).

Wollstonecraft was more sympathetic towards Dr. Gregory's *A Father's Letters to his Daughter* (1774) though she did not agree with his advice, for that made women lead a life without independence and dignity. She found Lord Chesterfield's *Letters to his Son* (1774) "unmanly and immoral" and for making the "vain attempt to bring forth fruit of experience, before the saplings has out-thrown its leaves" (Wollstonecraft ibid: 116). She questioned the proposition in the *Bible* that a woman was created solely for man's convenience. A dependent woman would be docile with very little desire and understanding that was necessary to lead a social, a happy and a useful life. As a teacher, Wollstonecraft was interested in the practical implications of Locke's theory of education. The latter's emphasis on good example, learning through pleasure rather than the rote, sympathy, tolerance, virtue and wisdom as goals of liberal spirit were repeated with variations throughout the eighteenth century. To Wollstonecraft, the purpose of education was to cultivate the spirit of reason, an innate quality in individuals, men and women.

Role and Importance of Education

Having examined the masculine views on women, Wollstonecraft pointed out to the positive and constructive role of education in correcting these distorted views. She contended that right education would lead to creativity, critical thinking, individual excellence and a proper understanding that was nourished by experience. This would be possible only with economic freedom and self reliance. The human spirit in order to find its fullest and freest expression ought to be liberated from the claims of prejudice, greed and financial insecurity. She rejected classical education in 'dead languages' and rote learning, and desired a combination of information and development of rational skills.

Wollstonecraft observed that women's education lacked the needed order, and as a result women did not have the capacity to generalize their thoughts and develop their understanding. This had led to excessive emotionalism, which was further reinforced by a lifestyle that they were made to lead. They were confined to household work and unlike men had to pursue activities and jobs that did not lead to an enlargement of understanding. She contended that an activity that one pursued shaped one's essential character and outlook. The rich and women were generally insipid. While the rich were born with wealth and status for which they were admired, women were appreciated for their sexual charm. Reason was acquired only if engaged in the exercise of ability and virtue in useful employment. In this she differed from those politically diverse thinkers as Godwin, Coleridge, Hannah More (1745–1833) and Jane Austen who stressed on sensibility as a female quality. More accepted sexual differentiation, but rejected the idea of amoral self-indulgence that was inherent in it. In *Strictures on the Modern System of Female Education* (1799). More argued for improved education for women to enable them to achieve 'purity of conduct' and hoped that women of rank and fortune would show the way for the revival of morality and religion in Britain. She advocated a serious, rigorous intellectual training for women, but espoused a conventional view with regard to women's role in society. She denounced advocates of women equality in employment and politics.

In the eighteenth century England, besides More and Macaulay, many like Maria Edgeworth, and Wollstonecraft wrote and stressed on the need to change and revitalize the intellectual and moral education imparted to the young ones, and in particular, to girls. Though these writers differed considerably in their philosophical outlooks they agreed that education was a rigorous process and that children needed a strong female figure of authority. In her review of Macaulay's *Letters on Education* (1790), Wollstonecraft once again reiterated the importance of education in moulding and developing the rational element in human beings and as a remedy, to most social ills. She also defended education for the under-privileged women and for all those who desired it. Education was pivotal in shaping the character and personality of the individual. She was convinced that children exposed to right and correct values would abstain from vices and other evils. Her own experience as a school teacher and governess, and, in her later years, her care in the upbringing of her daughter Fanny, further reinforced her commitment and concern in education. *Thoughts on the Education of Daughter* (1786), *Original Stories from Real Left* (1788), *The Female Reader* (1789), *A Vindication* (1792) and the unfinished manuscript *Letters on the Management of Infants* (1797) voiced her main concerns like the need to develop women as rational beings, the importance of entering into marriage for friendship and partnership, and the imperfect existing education system that neglected girls. She was equally concerned with social and physical misery and asserted the need to avoid misery rather than suffer it.

Educational Reforms

A Vindication was dedicated to Charles Maurice de Tallyrand-Perigord, the Bishop of Autun who had formulated the idea of free national education for boys and had placed the proposal before the French National Assembly for consideration and action. Wollstonecraft hoped that by making this dedication she could make Talleyrand extend the scheme to include girls, which did not happen. She felt that education of both boys and girls would only strengthen the New Republic and observed

> If women are to be excluded, without having a voice, from a participation of natural rights of mankind, prove first, to ward off the charge of injustice and inconsistency, that they will ever show that man must, in some shape, act like a tyrant, and tyranny, in whatever part of society it rears its brazen front, will ever undermine morality (Wollstonecraft 1985: 11–2).

Wollstonecraft contended that women must be independent of men to some degree or they will never be virtuous persons or even good wives and mothers. The meaning of independence meant that both girls and boys were to be subjected to the same discipline and study in the same school taught by the same set of teachers. She advocated co-educational schools and firmly believed that segregation between boys and girls at the level of schooling leads to acquisition of bad habits. She advocated a committee to choose teachers who were to be accountable for their performance. Children ought to dress alike for that would undermine unnatural class distinctions. Besides being a staunch exponent and defender of gender equality, Wollstonecraft also advocated class equality. Children must be allowed to play or be at the gym after each hour of sedentary work. They would be encouraged in peer inquiry of every form. The curriculum would emphasize thinking and formation of character to enable children to grow into good citizens. She also insisted on the importance of establishing early habits of reading and writing and the need to have simple attire and unaffected manners. She preferred education at home, but warned against the adverse effects of ill educated and devious servants. She also recommended a 'course in sexual education' during which children would be made familiar with reproductive organs and made aware of the implications of sexual intercourse. For expounding these views, Wollstonecraft was branded as an immoral author. Thomas Taylor published a rejoinder entitled *A Vindication of the Rights of Brutes*.

Wollstonecraft recommended that primary school teaching ought to be made more interesting and explanatory, methods employed by kindergarten schools of today. For older classes she prescribed the Socratic method of education through dialogue and discussions. Personal opinion of the students ought to be brought into play while discussing matters relating to history, politics, and religion, thus ensuring their relevance and validity. She also prescribed sports for boys and girls, an hour of sedentary employment, and wide ranging curriculum that included the

3 R's of education (Reading, Writing, Arithmatic), botany, mechanics, astronomy, natural history and natural philosophy. Wollstonecraft's educational reforms took into account the different endowments and talents in different individuals. She recommended a selection process at the age of nine to separate the mechanically minded from those with logical abilities. Education would be imparted according to one's skills, but boys and girls would study together at all times. She wanted children to be resilient so that they could face the ups and downs of life courageously. She knew that it would take a long time before "the world will be so far enlightened that parents, only anxious to render their children virtuous, shall allow them to choose companions for life themselves" (Wollstonecraft ibid 1985), and hence, was pessimistic. She was critical of the kind of education women received for it ruled out the possibilities of a life based on reason. A proper education would train girls to undertake some profession. Writing about the existing scheme she observed

> the education which women now receive scarcely deserves the name. My very soul has often sickened at observing the sly tricks practiced by women to gain some foolish thing on which their silly hearts were set. Not allowed to dispose of money or call anything their own, they learn to turn the market penny (Wollstonecraft ibid: 181–2).

Wollstonecraft accepted Talleyrand's *Report on Public Instruction,* which recommended that children and youth could make their own independent decision regarding punishment. This, according to her, would instil a sense of justice, which would lead to their happiness and well-being. Many opposed this proposition particularly if it applied to women for that would make them unsexed. Wollstonecraft disagreed and observed:

> It was not freedom that would unsex women...Reason and experience convince me that the only method of leading women to fulfill their peculiar duties is to free them from all restraint by allowing them to participate in the inherent rights of mankind (Wollstonecraft ibid: 194).

Faith in Reason

Wollstonecraft perceived a woman to be a rational human being with virtues that were fundamentally the same as those of a man. It was reason that enabled a human being to understand one's virtue. Reason distinguished human beings from other living creatures and was common to both men and women. If there were human beings who did not exhibit cultivate reason this might be due to neglect or wrongful socialization by society and its institutions. She was convinced that neither sex nor class was relevant to the initial birthright of human beings as reasonable. Like Condorcet, she believed in asexual rational woman. To believe otherwise would be to believe that either human beings were not made in the image of God or that God was unreasonable. She wrote in *A Vindication of the Rights of Man*:

> But I was not with an individual when I contend for the *rights of men* and the liberty of reason. You see I do not condescend to cull my words to avoid the invidious phrase, nor shall I be prevented from giving a manly definition of it, by the flimsy ridicule which a lively fancy has interwoven with the present acceptance of the term (Wollstonecraft 1970: 230).

Wollstonecraft recognized that the female was inferior to the male in physical strength. All the other distinctions were a result of education and socialization. She consistently asserted that if women did not think for themselves, if they were weak-willed and vacillating or if they were preoccupied by externals of clothing and manners it was because of their training. Reason ensured the perfect development of human nature and should be the basis of human happiness. Reason according to Wollstonecraft "is the grand blessing of life, the basis of every virtue" and the key to independence. Education ensured the development of this reason, and therefore, perfect education was one that enabled the individual to achieve this independence. She believed that the advancement in human reason would lead to constant and uninterrupted progress and that for the first time technology would be able to ensure alleviation of mass miseries.

Wollstonecraft explained how existing social norms and outlook prevented the development of human capacities and virtues in women. Since women were primarily visualized as sexual beings they were educated in a manner to acquire qualities that ensured a relationship of dependence vis-à-vis men. They were brought up to learn to please men, to be charming, graceful and beautiful for men and to cultivate virtues like gentleness, docility and spaniel-like affection making them weak, dependent and emotional creatures. They were an artificial, product of male ideas and arrangements. Wollstonecraft believed in the power of education and environment as powerful and as potent determinants of human character. Individuals for her were inherently free and rational beings, and it was this potential that had to be brought to fruition.

In *A Vindication* Wollstonecraft appealed to the reason in men rather than in women. She told Talleyrand that from her own analysis of the social and political status of women she aimed "to prove that the prevailing notion of respecting a sexual character was subversive to morality" (Wollstonecraft 1985: 10). By relying on reason she proved the emotive and prejudicial view of sexuality. She contended that reason did not recognize sex and the mind was unaware of sex. Sexual distinction was relevant only with regard to reproduction. In keeping with the spirit of her times characterized as 'the Age of Reason', Wollstonecraft hoped that reason would be the governing principle of human endeavours and actions. A society to be truly rational had to be based on the needs and character of human beings allowing for the fullest development of one's potential. She bestowed faith in the ultimate triumph of reason. She claimed that reason could help in scaling new heights. In this she is a true follower of Paine, whom she never met, but is nevertheless inspired by his ideas.

Ironically, Rousseau of whom she is very critical for his sexist views also influenced her tremendously.

> Rousseau and Paine were new men, Mary was the new Woman. Paine was conscious of the prison of class and ignorance in which the poor were confined, and dedicated himself to their liberation, just as Mary was to dedicate herself with equal vigour and passion to the freeing of women (Nixon 1971: 35).

Wollstonecraft was convinced that a reasonable and virtuous human being was spiritually rich. Virtue for her was to act reasonably, to use one's own freedom and respect the freedom of others, to do productive work and to parent wisely. To fail in these virtues would be to fail in one's duty as a human being. She was critical of both men and women if they failed to fulfill their duties. She was particularly critical of men as a group and specific thinkers for employing "their reason to justify prejudices" and for avoiding "close investigation of their vices or the partiality of European civilization. She criticized rulers who set themselves apart and limit the freedom of ordinary people; ladies and gentlemen from the upper class as being unproductive and parasitic; and parents who did not enable their children to become independent and productive, or if they neglected in their care of their children. She condemned the system of arranged marriages for it sacrificed the happiness of the children for the sake of material and social advancement of the family. She disproved of late marriages and marriages of convenience as it encouraged sexual immorality. Like Macaulay, Wollstonecraft argued that parental rights derive from a natural sentiment of care. Just as parents have a duty towards their children, similarly adult daughters and sons have a reciprocal duty to care for their aged parents unless of course parents have neglected theirs.

Liberty and Equality

Like her liberal predecessors and contemporaries, Wollstonecraft regarded the liberty of the individual as of paramount importance. She accepted Rousseau's famous axiom that 'Man is born free' but was quick to realize the oversimplification of the statement, for an individual's conduct was inevitably subject to the exigencies of society, to questions of traditions, behaviour and prevalent morality. She defined rights as 'a degree of liberty, civil and religious, as is compatible with the liberty of every other individual with whom he is united in a social compact'. She opposed blind obedience of any kind and believed that obedience should be based on reasoning and a conscious awareness of one's rights. She was certain that reason and progress would make it possible for the realization of universal benevolence which she regarded as the first virtue of a rational person. But she could understand that generosity could not emerge out of a situation of deprivation and slavery.

Wollstonecraft was convinced that equality was the key to reform of society in general and of women in particular. Equality meant absence of dependence of one person over another either through the existence of privileged ranks, which legally subject some to others, or through extremes of wealth and poverty which reduced formal equality of rights to a farce. Like Rousseau, she gave a passionate call for human equality not only incorporating both the sexes but also the poor and the deprived. Equality would lead to the creation of better human beings and citizens. Equality of civil rights, equality of opportunity for persons to develop their talents and exercise them in any profession or activity of their choice was a fundamental requirement of a progressive free society. Wollstonecraft accepted Rousseau's propositions with regard to narrowing the material gap between the rich and the poor, but rejected his hostility to commercial life and the market society. She was more with Locke and Smith for she supported and encouraged the spirit of free enterprise and had immense faith in the progressive outlook of the middle class. She was frank in her support for the middle class as being fully virtuous, independent, and rational.

Wollstonecraft insisted on equitable distribution of property among all the children in a family for that would ensure happiness and virtue. A property acquired by an individual's singular efforts could be disposed off in a manner that the owner saw fit. She suggested division of estates into small farms, and forests and common land to be given to the poor for that would solve problems like lack of work, ill health and poverty. She was anguished by Burke's contempt for the poor and the deprived and pleaded for legal reforms for that would give them a better deal. She was skeptical of large-scale capitalism, but preferred small-scale mercantilism linking it with women's emancipation. She was appreciative of the merchant who without any aristocratic privilege succeeded by his own hard work and tenacity of purpose. She wanted the same for women too. Like Price, she feared the harmful effects of commerce, namely luxury and selfishness setting her apart from the Whig liberals who regarded trade and republicanism as compatible, or Paine, who saw commerce as an instrument of liberty. Under the influence of Wollstonecraft, Godwin revised his extreme views and conceded a right to property in the second edition of *Political Justice* (1796). Initially he regarded property as a positive evil and that hereditary property not only caused robbery and war, but also inculcated qualities like vice, envy, malice and revenge.

Wollstonecraft thus desired an egalitarian society and was critical of every kind of institutionalization of privilege, namely, the monarchy for hereditary rule introduced idiots into the noble stem, and a standing army being disciplined and hierarchical was inimical to freedom. She questioned every non-egalitarian arrangement in society which included the British and European schools, private and public schools for they dulled the inquisitive minds of the youngsters and corrupted their moral character. She was critical of dogmatism and classics in the educational system.

> Hers was not a moral critique directed at various individuals or even at the female sex as a whole, but a more fundamental attack on the mores of her day and the institutions which she thought sustained them (Tomaselli 1993: xi).

Rights and Representation

While women according to Wollstonecraft would be able to enjoy civil rights she was not clear with regard to their political rights. She remarked that "women ought to have representatives, instead of being arbitrarily governed without having any direct share allowed to them in deliberations of government" (Wollstonecraft 1985: 212). But she did not explain the kind of representation she had in mind and whether it would establish a straightforward equality of political rights with men. This question, she hoped to pursue subsequently which however remained unfulfilled due to her untimely death at the age of thirty eight. She tried to enquire into the effectiveness of formal equal civil rights within the confines of marriage and family and as to how to achieve equality and independence in marital relationships.

Moreover, Wollstonecraft's awareness of the many difficulties that lie in securing even the elementary rights for women stopped her from campaigning for equal rights for women. She was aware that even amongst the radicals there were only a few who would support the extension of suffrage to women. Most of them equated women with children and domestic servants dependent on their masters, the men, and hence as incapable of exercising their free and rational choice independently (Dickinson 1977: 252). Thus, she saw the rights of women in the larger context of human rights. The idea of liberty, equality and fraternity were to apply to women equally. The cause of women was related to the cause of men and his relationship to the state. While women were subjugated to men, men themselves were subjugated. Therefore the liberation of women was linked closely to the liberation of men. In the 1790 tract, Wollstonecraft did not discuss the role and rights of women, but she saw women as parties to the social compact. The idea that men and women did not enjoy identical social and political rights was more clearly stated in the 1792 tract.

Rejection of Patriarchy

Wollstonecraft accepted the formulation of the enlightenment that political authority was artificial and conventional, but refused to accept filial and sexual relationships as natural. She insisted on the need to extend the belief in reason as an ordering principle in all matters and in all aspects of human existence. She was not willing to divide the private from the public sphere of human activity. The authority and the power of the male which manifests itself in a father and in a husband in the private realm were as artificial as the authority and power asserted by the royalty in the public sphere. Here, like Locke, she separated political and paternal power.

Wollstonecraft regarded royalty and aristocracy as 'pestiferous purple' and was opposed to it, as it limited the freedom of individuals to development and in turn, restricted the progress of society. A human life was not worth living and it would not be truly a human life if the opportunity for growth and self-improvement was not guaranteed. She essentially believed in the "Protestant notion of self-improvement" (Barker-Benfield 1989: 110). Therefore, she realized that political enfranchisement was not a singular solution. Women had to be liberated within the private sphere also. "The task undertaken by Wollstonecraft was far more complicated than those political philosophers who defended a case of equal rights for men" (Gatens 1991: 112).

Role of Women and Prescription for Change

Wollstonecraft accepted that women would have to fulfill their roles as wives and mothers. She stressed on the need for women to be granted 'the protection of civil laws', the freedom to follow careers that were compatible with their natural duties (for example, nurses, midwives, physicians, etc.). She was convinced that only women of superior quality would be able to lead independent and useful lives. For the majority of women the family would be the arena where they would realize equality and independence. She, like Rousseau, considered the family as the foundation of the state and marriage as the 'cement of society'. This could be achieved by the following measures: (i) The wife would have to be considered an equal and a responsible person and not be totally dependent on her husband with regard to property rights. (ii) If women have the capacity to look after themselves by earning their living then marriage would not be seen as the only source of livelihood. Moreover women as wives would not be dependent on their husbands during their lifetime and after their death. (iii) In managing their households and in rearing their children, in the exercise of their traditional roles as mothers and as wives, they would have sufficient scope for realizing their human nature and virtues.

Both the partners in a marriage would be equal and independent and would need one other. Each of them would fulfil the duties assigned to one's station in life—the husbands as providers and the wives as managers of their households, and rearing their children. The ideal middle class family life, for Wollstonecraft, was one where the woman brought up her children with a maid to attend to domestic chores and the husband would come home after a day's productive work to a clean household and happy children. She did not focus on poor working women except in her novel *The Wrongs of Woman*, wherein she described their oppression and weakness and prescribed possible solutions.

Wollstonecraft did not remove the woman out of the context of her family for she considered child rearing a unique function that a woman performed. However, this function could not be performed adequately, for the present education system did not prepare a woman for its discharge. They were not trained to rear their children because many of them were ignorant with undeveloped reasoning powers and excessive sensibilities. She wrote:

> The great Principle and Foundation of all Virtue is placed in this that a man is able to follow what reason directs as best. The object of education is to make men virtuous and through virtue happy. Women should acquire human virtues by the same means as men, instead of being educated like a fanciful kind of half being. Gentle women are literally speaking slaves to their bodies and glory in their subjection .... The power of generalizing ideas, of drawing comprehensive conclusions from individual observations is the only acquirement for an immortal being that really deserves the name of knowledge. Merely to observe without endeavouring to account for anything may serve as the common-sense of life, but where is the store laid up that is to clothe the soul when it leaves the body (Wollstonecraft 1970: 208).

Wollstonecraft's model woman was one who would be educated with a well-developed mind, independent character and a capacity for self-reliance. She was the one who would earn her husband's respect and affection rather than be idolized as a chaste and a weak being. This new woman would make a better companion to her husband and mother to her children. On the whole, her views on marriage as a relationship were based on compassion, partnership and companionship. She wrote

> Marriage will never be held sacred till women by being brought up with men are prepared to be their companions rather than their mistresses. I venture to predict that virtue will never prevail in society till the virtues of both sexes are founded on reason, and till the affections common to both are allowed to gain strength by the discharge of natural duties (Wollstonecraft ibid: 183).

Wollstonecraft regarded motherhood as more important than wifehood. Marriage was the means for reproduction and child-rearing and not the opportunity for contractual sex. The purpose of sex was not personal gratification, but to ensure a bond between a husband and a wife for child-rearing and for creating immortal spirits. It is interesting that in her early days, observing on the relationship between her parents, she came to look upon marriage as 'servitude-unrelieved and hopeless'. Looking to the abject position of her mother, she decided never to marry. Her views on the subject swung from virulent criticism to intense idolization. Godwin was equally critical of marriage though his ideas were not based on first hand witness to its working. It was more intellectual, derived from his concern with an individual's liberty of action and the ability to act in society and with his progress in society, all of which depended on being free from the interference of the Church or the state. At the same time, he opposed promiscuity even though he rejected the institution of marriage as 'the worst kind of property'. An anarchist by persuasion, he believed that the vices in the individual were wholly due to the restraining influences of the law, and, if these restraints were eliminated the natural goodness in the human person would triumph. It was for their views on marriage that both Wollstonecraft and Godwin keep their marriage a private affair and led separate lives. In fact, the news of their marriage was met with ridicule.

Wollstonecraft failed to see the sexual division of labour as socially constituted rather than dictated by nature. The picture of domestic bliss that she painted ignored class distinctions and sexual differences thereby leaving "the asymmetry between the citizen/husband/father and the citizen/wife/mother unaddressed" (Gatens 1991: 121). In the Lockean tradition, she defended the rights of women as a wife, a mother and a citizen. Like J.S. Mill subsequently, she desired to give women the freedom to choose and not accept marriage as the only option. She also realized that the law in the eighteenth century did not defend women and give them legal rights. She had an uphill task before her, a giant campaign to lead. She desired for all women a life of freedom and independence, "to be herself without any hindrance, to follow the way of her own understanding, to ask protection of no one, to depend only on the law for her rights" (Nixon 1971: 8).

CONCLUSION

The seminal importance of Wollstonecraft's tract was in the fact that she wrote at a time when the majority of contemporary radicals were concerned with the liberty of adult males only. Hers, along with Lady Macaulay, represented the only voices that articulated the need for women as much as men for equal rights and to rectify prevailing opinions and prejudices that supported women's subordination. The enlightenment which grappled with issues like citizen's rights against arbitrariness, the relationship between law and liberty ignore women's issues. In that context, Wollstonecraft's efforts represented the first beginning in an exercise that turned out to be a long drawn one. Hers remained the first voice to espouse the cause of women's rights, self-worth and independence.

> *The Vindication* contain a good number of social and political proposals, which range from a detailed outline of necessary changes in school curricula to the suggestion that women not only be granted civil and political rights, but also have elected representatives of their own.

It argues that women should be taught skills so as to be able to support themselves and their children in widowhood. It seeks to reclaim midwifery for women, against the encroachment of male accoucheurs, and contends that women could be physicians just as well as nurses. It urges women to extend their interests to encompass politics and the concerns of the whole of humanity... . But what is clear is that the extent to which she is relevant today depends on the degree to which we are prepared to conceive of reason as being genderless, to accept that the pursuit of virtue is the good life of all human beings, and to cease to regard the upbringing of children as a lesser form of existence. Above all Wollstonecraft requires us to think not only of rights, but of duties, and to examine the nature of the framework in which to conceive of them both. Hers, was most definitely not a world of selfish gratification" (Tomaselli 1993: xxvii, xxix).

Most of Wollstonecraft's tracts were polemical. Many of her arguments were repetitive. Her essential mission was to look for the first principles of truth to dispute prevailing prejudices. She agreed with Rousseau and Paine that civilization in contemporary Europe was partial because of the many discriminations and inequities. She was equally conscious of the imperfections of her time and noted that the science of politics was very much in its infancy. She also agreed that force had been the guiding principle in the governance of the world till the modern times. But sharing the optimism of the enlightenment thinkers she was confident that a better level of politics would lead to greater diffusion of liberty and the entire humankind—men and women—would become more virtuous, free and independent. "Through all her works ran the thread of disgust at the genderizing of all people according to sex ... and by her hatred of the familial metaphors that enforced the fixed gendered view in writers such as Burke" (Todd 1993: xxv).

Wollstonecraft could easily see that the quest for the dignity of women was part of the larger process of reform that society needs. She was able to identify the two major maladies of contemporary reality—wealth and non-acceptance of the fact that women like men were rational creatures. She was equally aware of the effects of luxury, idleness and the maldistribution of power and property on the lives of men and women. The degradation of women was reflected in the trivialities by which their values were judged and in the fact that they were left out in most of the important human activities like gallantry, poetry, music, etc. She was "the first political theorist systematically to highlight and criticize the interrelationship between sexuality, marriage, the sexual division of labour and citizenship" (Pateman 2009: 339).

Interestingly, Wollstonecraft also understood that the arguments that were generally put forward against educating women was similar to those used against educating the poor. She was categorical in stating 'respect for man, as man, is the foundation of every noble sentiment' (Wollstonecraft 1985: 137). She asserted that even duty could be considered to be binding only when it was based on reason. She defended the cause of women cogently and proved beyond doubt, that subjugation of women was unjust even in a situation when men believed and took actions best calculated to promote the happiness of women.

Wollstonecraft as a critic was descriptive rather than prescriptive. She tried to show what was wrong with society than suggest alternatives. She "brought no women to the barricades, but she inspired passion in all her readers" (Kramnick 1972: 7). It was her controversial personal life that brought her disrepute. The Victorian feminists like Millicent Fawcett (1847–1929), France Power Cobbe (1822–1904) and Josephine Butler (1828–1906) generally ignored her. Fawcett while introducing *A Vindication* did not even grant her the status as a founder of Victorian feminism. However, this was adequately compensated when one of the greatest minds of the nineteenth century, J.S. Mill reiterated many of Wollstonecraft's formulations. He praised her contributions to the growth of the women's movement. It is a tribute to Wollstonecraft that many of her major formulations formed the core arguments of Mill's classic work on the gender question *The Subjection*. Wollstonecraft not only inspired Mill but also the Owenite feminists and Wheeler. Her ideas influenced Jane Austen (1775–1813) who through her novels took up the issues of women's equality, the plight of single women, women's financial dependence and lack of education, women's suffering through the English system of primogeniture, and the double standards in sexual matters. Austen did not refer to Wollstonecraft directly, but elaborated and developed many of the themes that the latter wrote about. Besides Austen, others like Elizabeth Barrett Browning (1806–61) and George Eliot (1819–80) also acknowledged having read *A Vindication* and being inspired by it.

Liberal feminism of Wollstonecraft and J.S. Mill traced women's oppression to unjust laws. It focused on the subjugation of women in the private domain, which was insulated from the ideals of freedom, equality and justice that dominated the public sphere. The aim of liberal feminists' emphasis on equal rights was to gain access to the public sphere on the same terms as men. The liberal feminists sought to reform the traditional family and accord women dignity, self-respect and independence by demanding rights of marriage, property, inheritance and custody of children. Pateman (1988) accused liberal feminism of harbouring a masculine bias, and not being gender neutral in their conception of individuality. She observed in a patriarchy, the laws reflected the basic patriarchal principle that men had sexual rights over women and this was the sexual contract. Thus, marriage contracts and the law of couverture guaranteed the control of the husbands over their wives and the latter's subordination. The marriage contract was not one freely determined by free agents; but it was the state that prescribed its terms. It was for this reason that many feminists in the nineteenth century called for the abolition of marriage as a state certified institution. As a result, feminist jurisprudence debates on the private-public division and the traditional ascription of women to certain functional roles within the private sphere. The focus of the liberal theory was on the public sphere and on individual citizens and their rights which was why feminist theory continued to focus on the consequences of fundamental contradictions within the private sphere. Traditional liberal theory which was largely the basis for American jurisprudence did not work as it is accepted the public-private divide and the roles which women performed in the private sphere. The private-public distinction was criticized for not only excluding women from public activities like voting or holding public office but at the same time covering up what went on within the home, including violence against women and children from public scrutiny. In *Feminist Challenges* (1986) edited by Pateman and Elizabeth Gross, many of its contributors noted that not just liberal political theory but much of western philosophy was predicted upon women's subordination. "Existing patriarchal theory has no place for women as *women*; at best, women can incorporated as pale reflections of men" (1986: 8). Thus, many 'gender-neutral' laws have failed to benefit women as it neglected the contingencies of most women's social situations. There was, therefore, a need for a new feminist theory, according to Pateman and Gross, one that began from a recognition of difference, from an acceptance "that individuals are feminine and masculine, that individuality is not a unitary abstraction but ... embodied and sexually differentiated" (ibid: 9). Pateman pointed out that sexism and the assumption of male superiority permeated the dominant culture and the political arena embodied patriarchal power. She lamented that household work that constituted the major chore for most women had no value for citizenship. Women, by and large lacked the means to be recognized as worthy citizens as they were considered as men's dependents by the welfare state as in the case of the National Insurance Act of 1946. "Most women's jobs are unskilled and of low status; even in the professions women are clustered at the lower end of the occupational hierarchy" (Pateman 1988: 191). The welfare provisions have been established within the two-tier system of husband/wife and worker/housewife. There were benefits that were available to individual workers and usually men claimed these benefits. There were benefits that were available to dependents of the individuals which are claimed by women, mostly as wives or mothers. Women were the majority of recipients of many welfare benefits for they were most likely to be poor and single mothers and the reason that they were poor was because most women found it difficult to secure a job that would give them a decent salary. This was because the occupational structure was sexually segregated in spite of equal-pay legislation. It was with the elimination of the patriarchal dichotomy between women and independence-work-citizenship that a welfare state could truly become a welfare society.

Across the Atlantic, long before Wollstonecraft's tract appeared, many American women reflected on the issues that *A Vindication* raised namely the place and role of women in the political system and the extent to which women must be encouraged to be independent. A conservative

Quaker, Elizabeth Drinker remarked after reading *A Vindication* "In very many of her sentiments, she...speaks my mind" (cited in Kerber 1980, xi). *A Vindication* was printed in Philadelphia shortly after its publication in 1792. Wollstonecraft also inspired Stanton and Mott's discussions at the World Anti-Slavery Convention in London in 1840. But Wollstonecraft did not fit as the role model for the American women as most of them rejected their homes on assuming a public role. The American Revolution was purely a 'male' affair, but it expedited the integration of women into the civic polity. Education of women was given premium as educated mothers preserved family stability and educated future generations of sensible republicans. Women had a distinct political role but within their homes. Covertures, the absorption of a married woman's property under the control of her husband were retained indicating that a married woman did not enjoy independent political capacity.

Wollstonecraft was critical of political legislators, preachers, school teachers, tutors and authors such as Rousseau, Dr. Gregory, James Fordyce and Lord Chesterfield. She was equally critical of women for she did not like them the way they were. She desired a complete transformation of women and be the opposite of what they were. She wanted them to be rational and independent with a sense of confidence stemming from inner perceptions of their self control. She hoped for them full citizenship. She deserved rightfully the place of a pioneer in making the women's issue not only as a part of mainstream political theory but also in bringing it to the forefront of the political agenda.

12

George Wilhelm Friedrich Hegel

> Hegel's system claims to be a system of "absolute idealism". Hegel appears as the heir of the great idealistic tradition. He is believed to complete that great process of thought that begins with Plato and that in modern philosophy reaches its culminating point in Kant's critical philosophy... . Its greatest achievement ... depends on the fact that here the fundamental presuppositions and principles which were already involved in the Kantian system are brought to an explicit statement, to a full consciousness of all their systematic complications (Cassirer 1946: 245).
>
> By Hegel's time all the fundamental positions have been taken up; after Hegel they reappear in new guises and new variations but the re-appearance is a testimony to the impossibility of fundamental innovation (MacIntyre 1971: 199).
>
> The transition from philosophy to the domain of state and society had been an intrinsic part of Hegel's system (Marcuse 1954: 251).

Epoch-making events lead to important political theorizing. One of the finest examples of the co-relationships between a major event and its tremendous impact on an entire generation in a country is exemplified by the impact of the French Revolution and German political theorizing for the coming half a century. The French Revolution had its impact throughout Europe, and Wordsworth wrote

Bliss was it in that dawn to be alive,
But to be young was very heaven

George Wilhelm Friedrich Hegel (1770–1831) and all the other important German thinkers, Kant, Fichte and Schelling were the children of the French Revolution. Compared to both England and France, Germany was much more backward and feudal, consisting of more than 300 states loosely linked to the Holy Roman Empire with leadership provided by Francis I of Austria. It came to an end when Napoleon defeated this 1000-year-old empire, and subsequently in 1806 defeated another powerful German state, Prussia. Hegel was a resident of Prussia at the time of the defeat, and in the normal course the expectation would be that the support and the sympathy of the young Hegel would be for Prussia. But, surprisingly, his admiration was for Napoleon; he welcomed the conquests and domination of Napoleon. The admiration for Napoleon was total, for he wrote in a letter, "The Emperor—this world soul—I saw riding through the city to review his troops, it is indeed a wonderful feeling to see such an individual who, here concentrated into a single point, sitting on a horse, reaches out over the world and dominates it" (Hegel cited in Singer 1983: 1–2).

When Napoleon ruled, he earned Hegel's acclaim, and when he was defeated in 1814, for Hegel it was a tragedy, a genius vanquished by mediocrity. This admiration of Napoleon highlighted a very significant component of German political theory of this period, with its primary focus on dealing with the question of organizing the modern state and society on the basis of reason, and that meant protection of the freedom and interests of the individual. The Enlightenment philosophy was actualized by the temper and ideas of the French Revolution. Even the subsequent terror did not lead to this adulation of the spirit of the revolution, though the terror itself was severely criticized by German thinkers. The well-known sentence that "issues become political at a particular time and place" was exemplified by the quest of the German thinkers to create a modern order with the abolition of feudalism, and putting the middle class and individual at the centre stage. With confidence in science and knowledge, a political order based on reason looked both plausible and desirable. The setting of the formulation came out of an awareness of the relative backwardness of Germany, and the acceptance that an external agency was necessary to bring about the desired change in Germany and hence the adulation for Napoleon in Hegel, one of the three heroes, the other two being, Socrates and Julius Caesar. Hegel regarded Napoleon as the person who carried forward the real progressive element of the French Revolution, by liquidating the extremities and excesses of the revolution, exemplified by Robiespierre's terror and by providing the necessary order and rule of law which allowed industrial production to grow at great speed. Hegel grasped what later Socialists and Marxists put at the central stage of analysis, the capacity of the modern industrialized civilization to meet the needs and aspirations of every single individual. Saint Simon, whom Friedrich Engels (1820–1895) described as the second-most encyclopaedic mind after Hegel, was also popularizing the possibility of the establishment of a free and rational society, based on reason as a positive outcome of this revolutionary and industrial process. Hegel's emphasis on human reason had to be understood in the context of this new temper and optimism, created by the possibilities of the creation of a new and prosperous societal order. All his important concepts—freedom, subject, mind and notion—were based on this unshakeable faith in human rationality. His eulogy of the French Revolution also emanated from the conviction that both reason and right were established by the philosophical basis of the revolution.

One significant change that could be found in this kind of understanding from the pre-revolutionary belief-structure was that there was no automatic or uncritical acceptance of the contemporary reality, as it was recognized that a minimum standard was expected from a given political and societal structure, and what logically followed was that if that structure did not have the capacity to absorb the positive aspects of this new epoch, then that structure had to be replaced with a more modern one which was conducive to the needs and aspirations of the contemporary situation. The first important thing that was regarded as being an obstacle to this modern Germany was the continuation of feudalism, seen as a structure that did not allow healthy and free competition which was the basis of progress and affluence. It was also an obstacle to the establishment of a modern political order that was based on equality before law.

LIFE SKETCH

Hegel was born in Stuttgart, Germany on August 27, 1770. His father was a civil servant, and most of his relatives were either teachers or Lutheran ministers. He was 19 when the French Revolution broke out. By the time he was 21, the revolutionary wars had begun. This was also the golden age of German literature.

Hegel was a brilliant student, and at school he excelled and won a scholarship to a reputed seminary at Tubingen in 1788, where he studied philosophy and theology. After completing his studies, he accepted the position of a family tutor with a wealthy family in Switzerland from 1793 to 1796. This was followed by a similar position at Berne and Frankfurt from 1797 to 1800. His philosophical speculations began at this time.

Hegel's father died in 1799. His inheritance was modest. He gave up tutoring and took to writing. He published a book differentiating the philosophies of Fichte and Schelling. In collaboration with Schelling, he edited the *Journal fur Philosophie*. His well-known *Phenomenology of Mind* appeared in 1807. He was a university lecturer at Jena from 1801 to 1807. After working for a year as a newspaper editor in Bamberg, he moved to Nuremberg as headmaster of a high school in 1808, and continued in this position till 1816. His long work, *Science of Logic* in three volumes, appeared in 1812, 1813 and 1816. By this time he became quite well-known, and in 1816 he was invited to take up the post of professor of philosophy at the University of Heidelberg. Here he wrote the *Encyclopedia of the Philosophical Sciences*.

By this time, Hegel became quite famous, and the Prussian minister of education offered him the prestigious chair of philosophy at the University of Berlin, succeeding Fichte. Berlin was the intellectual centre of Germany, and Hegel accepted the offer and taught at Berlin from 1818 till his death in 1831. This period was the most eventful in his life. He wrote his famous work *Philosophy of Right*, and lectured on the philosophy of history, religion, aesthetics and the history of philosophy. In all these diverse areas, he covered many aspects of political theory.

Hegel was the founder of modern idealism and the greatest influence in the first half of the eighteenth century, when the entire academic community in Germany was divided between Hegelians, the Left Hegelians and the Right Hegelians. He formulated the theories of dialectic and of self-realization. He gave a new theory of history, which, according to him, was the human spirit writ large, the "march of reason in the world". He was critical of purely reflective knowledge, as "the owl of Minerva spreads its wing only at the gathering of the dusk". Hegel's *Philosophy of Right* published in 1821 dealt with key issues of law, politics and morality, and made an important distinction between the state and civil society.

Towards the end of his life, Hegel started attracting large audiences from the entire German-speaking world. It was his disciples who published several of his lecture notes after Hegel's death. Some of Hegel's other well-known works include *Lectures in the Philosophy of History, Lecture on Aesthetics, Lectures on the Philosophy of Religion* and *Lectures on the History of Philosophy*. In 1830, in recognition of his works, Hegel was elected rector of the university. The following year, he suddenly died on November 14, at the age of 61.

IMPORTANCE OF REASON

Hegel was critical of Kant's handling of reason while dealing with the challenge of empiricism. If things in themselves were beyond the scrutiny of reason, then reason remained merely subjective, without control over objective reality, leading to an unacceptable division of the world between subjectivity and objectivity. The relation between subject and object was a complex but interrelated one, with unity of the opposite subjects or matters both in theory and practice leading to *praxis*. This conflict was of crucial importance to Hegel, as his seminal contribution of alienation originated with this formulation. The alienation of mind originated when the objective factors which were originally produced by human labour and knowledge became detached and unrecognizable to man. In such a situation, theory did not reflect reality, and truth had no meaning in the real world. As a result, human frustration and helplessness increased. To end this separateness in all its manifestations, the entire framework of enquiry was brought within the ambit of reason. Separateness had to be ended by a theory of unity of totality in philosophy.

This utmost emphasis on reason was of tremendous importance to Hegel, as human emancipation—a distinct possibility in the modern period—could only be realized on the basis of reason. "Man could be free, could develop all his potentialities, only if his entire world was dominated by an integrating rational will and by knowledge. The Hegelian system anticipates a state in which this possibility has been achieved" (Marcuse 1954: 24). This was how, in Hegel's theory, reality merged with rationality.

Hegel, however, was well aware that the present reality in many of its manifestations was far from reason and perfection. But what he emphasized was the human capacity to cherish freedom, and in that sense had the capacity to transcend the imperfections of contemporary nature and society by the process of mediation. Reason and human action led to mediation, by new concepts and categories replacing old ones, which at one time looked stable. This was the driving force of the Hegelian dialectic, which made his philosophy a negative one. Marcuse remarked:

> It is originally motivated by the conviction that the given facts that appear to commonsense as the positive index of truth, so that truth can be established by their destruction. The driving force of the dialectical method lies in this critical conviction. Dialectic in its entirety is linked to the conception that all forms of being are permeated by an essential negativity, and that this negativity determines their content and movement. The dialectic represents the counter thrust to any form of positivism (Marcuse ibid: 27).

PHILOSOPHY OF HISTORY

To convince that the present was really different from the past, capable of actualizing reason and ending the negative and critical roles of philosophy, Hegel had to dissect the historical process of humankind critically and comprehensively. In attempting to perform this gigantic task, there was also a marked difference between Kant and Hegel. Kant argued with the help of philosophical reasoning that human nature was permanent and unchanging. Hegel pointed out that human nature, like everything else, changed from one historical epoch to another. Employing his dialectical method, Hegel developed one of his most enduring achievements, a philosophy of history based on change. "It was Hegel who established the history of philosophy as a central academic discipline as part of the core of any philosophic education" (Kaufmann 1965: 21–22).

Commenting on the enormous influence of Hegel, Engels wrote:

> What distinguished Hegel's mode of thinking from that of all other philosophers was the exceptional historical sense underlying it. However abstract and idealist the form employed, the development of his ideas runs always parallel to the development of world history, and the latter is indeed supposed to be only the proof of the former (Engels cited in Singer 1983: 9).

Engels' clear statement revealed that for him and Marx, no other philosopher could match Hegel's sense of history, as it truly reflected the process of world history. Such a claim emerged because the Hegelian scheme of analyzing history had both a reflection of accumulation of a good deal of facts encompassing a large portion of world history, and a novelty of the method of the dialectic in understanding the hidden meaning of the process of history. His canvas included the ancient and important civilizations of India, China, and Persia, linking them to the ancient civilizations of Greece and Rome, ultimately stressing the development of the modern period of European history reflecting on European feudalism, the Protestant Reformation and ending with the Enlightenment and the French Revolution. But what distinguished Hegel's enterprise from other historical accounts was the important fact that the philosophy of history was not purely a historical account, but a way to comprehend the entire evolution of human civilization in a comparative perspective, with a view to understanding the meaning and rationality behind the evolution.

This rationality of world history was the progress of the consciousness of freedom. Since the concept of freedom was the pivot around which the entire political philosophy of Hegel hinged, it was important to find the link between the realization of freedom and the process of history, not only of Europe but also of the Orient.

The beginning for Hegel was the oriental world, consisting of China, India and Persia. China and India were static, i.e. stationary civilizations, in which no change worth the name had taken place for thousands of years. They were non-dialectical, and, for Hegel, outside the framework of world history. The most important reason for the unchanging nature of these civilizations was that they did not comprehend the idea of freedom, since a single person (the ruler) was supreme, subordinating all others under the rule of oriental despotism. This despotism was not just based on the fear of persecution and cruelty, as that would mean that the subjects had a consciousness of their own. However, this was not the case. The subjects lacked consciousness.

Both law and morality emanated from an external authority. Since individual consciousness was lacking, individuals did not have the capacity for moral judgements of right and wrong. Nothing was questioned, and subservience to the despot was total. However, Hegel conceded that this lack of individual consciousness manifested itself differently in other cultures and civilizations. The Chinese state was governed on the model of a family, and the emperor was looked to for providing the basis of their paternal order, the subjects being like children. In India, despotism was naturally ordained by the caste system, and that explained its static and unchanging nature. Both China and India were outside the process of history, as both reflected arrested development.

Among the oriental states, Persia was distinctly different. The modern process of history that Hegel spoke of begins here. The Persian emperor was similar to the Chinese one, for both enjoyed absolute power. But they differed in actual position. In Persia, the loyalty to the state was not akin to that within a family. The relationship between the ruler and subject was based on general category. Persia was a theocratic monarchy based on Zoroastrianism, which believed in worshipping the light. For Hegel, light, like the sun, was a universal category as its benefit was shared equally by all. Still, the ruler was an absolute ruler and his rule was based on a general criterion which was not a natural one. This was not possible in China and India. As a universal principle or rule was the basic necessity for acquiring the consciousness of freedom, true history began with ancient Persia.

Within Persia, though the consciousness of freedom existed in its rudimentary form, its realization within the Persian Empire remained unfulfilled. Because of proximity and desire for expansion and domination, it developed contacts with Athens, Sparta and other city states of ancient Greece. The Persian emperor wanted the Greeks to accept his authority, which the Greek city states refused. Consequent to the refusal, the Persian emperor sent a huge army and a fleet of ships to subdue the Greeks. The Persian and the Greek fleets fought an epic battle in 480 BC at Salamis, a Greek island in the Aegean Sea, west of Athens. The Greeks won on account of their smaller ships. Hegel perceived it to be a contest between an oriental despot who wanted to conquer the Greeks and establish his own authority, and the separate Greek states committed to "free individuality". The Greek victory shifted the focus of world history from oriental despotism to the Greek city states.

However, like Marx's notion of primitive communism, the Greek notion of freedom was only partial and not total. This limitation arose out of two reasons. First, the Greeks used slaves, which meant that they had only a partial realization of freedom, as a universal philosophy could not exclude any section. But Hegel also acknowledged that the limited democracy of the Greeks needed slavery for its success. It was a necessary evil, as political participation meant that somebody else would have to provide for the necessities of life. The base of *working non-citizens* made possible the public activities of *non-working citizens*. This functionalist attitude was very similar to the defence of slavery by Aristotle, who could postulate the end of it only when some other mechanism of work could be established. This incompleteness was also reflected in another way, as the Greeks did not have any conception of individual consciousness. But the difference with the oriental world was that whereas in the Orient obedience came from external agencies, for the Greeks it was derived from within. It was habitual obedience, without a universal or impersonal principle. They identified totally with the city state, without distinguishing their own interests from those of the community. It was incon-ceivable for them to think of an existence without or in opposition to it. The motivation was natural, as it was in Henry Maine's criticism of Austin's theory of sovereignty. The basic precondition for freedom for Hegel was the existence of two qualities (the capacity for critical insight, and reflection), and since the Greeks lacked it, their realization of freedom was only partial.

In understanding this true basis of freedom, Socrates played a pioneering role. He symbolized the spirit of the Greek god Apollo, "Man, know thyself. Socratic dialogues were a reflection of this spirit of free enquiry, in which Socrates gave his own views in contrast to those of others, on subjects like "good", "just" or "education". In each one of them, the customary belief or common-sense tenets were questioned by critical reasoning. "This critical reflection makes reason, not social custom the final judge of right and wrong" (Singer ibid: 15).

Socrates' revolutionary appeal against the ideological basis of the Athenian state was highlighted by Hegel. From the perspective of the Athenian state, the death sentence against Socrates was an essential and correct act, as his critical reasoning eroded the basic foundation of the existence of the state and commonality based on customary morality. The death of Socrates, argued Hegel, did not, however, put an end to the dialectics which had taken firm intellectual roots. As a result, the executioners were seen as villains and Socrates emerged as a hero, though a tragic one. Hegel also added that the independent line of thinking that Socrates encouraged led to the subsequent downfall of Athens and the collapse of the city states.

The achievement of the Greeks was their essential homogeneity, and this stood in sharp contrast to the Roman Empire, which was heterogeneous and diverse. There was neither a natural patriarchy as in the Orient, nor a customary bond of the Greeks which enforced strict discipline, backed by force, among them. The Roman Empire resembled the oriental world more than the Greek one, but that was only in appearance. Hegel had tremendous respect for Aristotle, whom he looked upon as a kindred spirit. Contrasting Plato with Aristotle, he pointed out that while Plato laid down the general in abstract form as a principle, in Aristotle thought became concrete.

Hegel's philosophy of history was based on the assumption that the process had to be interpreted dialectically, which made going back to an earlier situation impossible. There was also a progressive side of history, though it was never smooth and even. As such, there were bound to be differences between the earlier experience of the Persians and the later development of the Romans. The Socratic notion of critical judgement was not relegated to history, and the Roman constitution and legal system sanctioned individual rights as one of the basic precepts. This was the basic difference between the Persian and the Roman Empires. But even in the Roman Empire, such guarantees formed the "abstract freedom of the individual as the real freedom based on diversity of ideas reflecting concrete individuality" was never allowed by the brutal power of Rome. This led to constant tension between an absolutist state power and the spirit of individual freedom, which made the Roman civilization an unhappy one. The true spirit of the Greeks was replaced by enforced conformity, which meant a retreat from the public to the private domain, leading to the non-political philosophies of Stoicism, Epicureanism and Skepticism. These diverse philosophies were based on the negation of the real world by avoiding affluence, political power and glory, substituting them with utter indifference to such values. These philosophies of withdrawal arose out of helplessness in influencing the political process. This negative response by itself was not enough, and a more positive solution emerged from the rise of Christianity. The difference between animals and humans was that the former lived only in a natural world, whereas human beings had a spiritual side to their existence. When the natural world of material surroundings became an impediment to their urge for freedom, a positive response emerged, as it happened with the rise of Christianity during Roman rule.

The uniqueness of Christianity lay in the fact that Jesus combined in him a human body with being the Son of God. This linked human beings to some infinite values, an eternal destiny, "religious consciousness" which made the city of God the spiritual world, the individual's true home (and not the natural world of the present) the city of humans. A link is established between the life in the material world and that in the spiritual one. However, placing the entire argument within his progressive knowledge of history, he asserted that the movement towards this cosmic unity began with the Romans and reached culmination only in the contemporary world. The rise of Christianity allowed the re-creation of the spirit of freedom of the Greeks in the contemporary world. But unlike the Greeks, the Christian doctrine opposed slavery and replaced the customary morality of the Greeks by a universal spiritual idea of love and fellow feeling.

By the time of Constantine, Christianity became the official religion of the Roman Empire, and continued for 1000 years of the Byzantine Empire, though the western part was detached from it by the barbarian invasions. But this Christianity for Hegel was both decadent and stagnant, and led to the rise of the contemporary world—what Hegel called the Germanic world.

Hegel referred to the entire period of history from the fall of the Roman Empire to his times as the Germanic period. He used it broadly to include the Scandinavian countries, Holland and also Great Britain. He also took note of the developments in Italy and France. But all these paled into insignificance in what Hegel perceived to be the most important happening after the fall of the Roman Empire: the Reformation, which began in Germany. The German nations "were the first to attain the consciousness that man, as man, is free, that it is the freedom of spirit which constitutes its essence". The thousand years that elapsed between the fall of the Roman Empire and the Restoration was a tragic period of history. There was a total degeneration of the Church and the true religious spirit, for there was more insistence on blind obedience, and that was a sad development of a faith which started with great promise. The Middle Ages, noted Hegel, were "a long, eventful and terrible night"; that night ended with the dawn of the Renaissance, "that blush of dawn which after long storms first brokers the return of a bright and glorious day". Hegel saw the Reformation as being more important than the Renaissance, and described it as "the all enlightening Sun". With the Renaissance and Reformation began the happy period of the modern age.

The Reformation ended the corruption of the Church, symbolized by Luther's protest. But it was not just the achievement of one single individual, rather the lasting achievement of the entire Germanic people. The two key words that Hegel used for the Reformation were "simplicity" and "heart". The Reformation swept away the hold of the Catholic Church with the simple but revolutionary and explosive formulation that the individual had a direct spiritual relationship with God (Christ), and as such did not need the mediation of anybody else. The replacement of Roman Catholicism with Protestantism was not merely a revolt against the oppression of the old Church, more important, it established the idea of individual identity and salvation. This set aside the interpretation of scriptures, and there was no compulsion to perform rituals. The judgement of truth, justness and goodness would be moulded by one's self. This was the assertion of the free spirit, which Hegel asserted was the destiny of humankind. The acceptance of individual freedom based on human rationality and free choice was the crowning glory of modern times.

Hegel saw the aforesaid aspect bringing about significant changes, such as rationalization of standards to accommodate multitudes of rational people. As such, any claim to universality had to first satisfy the claim of rationality in all the spheres of social institutions, legal structures, property, social morality, governmental organizations and the constitution. Since individuals had the right of free choice, support would emerge only when institutions were based on rational foundations. In such a situation, arbitrary rules and abuse of power could not exist, thereby creating a world of harmony between the individual and the real world that he encountered.

Hegel, like other thinkers of the Enlightenment in general and Diderot and Voltaire in particular, looked upon reason as a guide to human existence. The French Revolution was the culmination of these developments, representing the philosophers' critique of the existing order. The French nobility lost its rational basis, and that explained the emergence and popularity of the doctrine of the Rights of Man. Hegel hailed the Revolution as a "glorious mental dawn" which had to be welcomed by all thinking people. However, the euphoria was short-lived, for it led to revolutionary terror, with the guillotine institutionalizing punishment without any legal basis. This deterioration took place because the revolution wanted to implement purely abstract philosophical notions, without ascertaining what the people really wanted. It was not directed by reason, as it never took note of the totality of the situation, and relied more on isolated acts, which never succeeded. As a result, the revolution remained a promise unfulfilled.

The significance of the French Revolution was to be understood in the context of its influence elsewhere in Europe, and in particular, in Germany. The brief periods of Napoleonic victories and rule brought in the desired changes in Germany, like giving it a series of rights, establishment of freedom of the individual, freedom of property, opening of state jobs to the most talented, and the end of feudal obligations. Hegel took note of the fact that monarchy still remained at the apex, and its decisions were important, but because of well-established laws and efficient rule-based state organizations, personal discretion hardly mattered.

The movement of world history, for Hegel, had reached its destination and this was made possible by two factors. The first was the capacity and the circumstances in which the individual acted according to his own conscience and convictions. This was the individual spirit which sought happiness and provided energy. The second factor was the corresponding social and political institutions of the real world, which was based on reason. This was the world spirit which tried to reach a higher freedom which came with the knowledge of the self, providing the necessary direction. Both were necessary, as one was incomplete without the other, and the absence of one signified conflict and not harmony. Hegel was explicit in his emphasis that in history, nothing was achieved without individuals, each pursuing his own goals, whatever those goals might be. But for knowing whether the actions were in conformity with the dialectic of the universal, "the cunning of reason" played its role, and "sets passions to work for itself".

The individuals broadly fell under three categories with regard to their roles in history: (a) the category of persons in whom the customs and beliefs of a particular civilization were realized, signifying the rights and duties of that particular order, resisting the process of historical change and becoming chief victims of history; (b) the category including the world-historical individuals (like Julius Caesar), who, though seeking their particular ends, possessed the insight to grasp the truth of their age; and (c) the category consisting of moral reformers who continuously evaluated things from "is" to "ought", Hegel being very critical of such persons, as in the name of reason, liberty and justice, they took up a "position not merely of discontent, but also of open revolt against the actual condition of the world".

In Hegel, both the subjective idea of freedom of the individual, as also the notion of freedom towards which the spirit was destined to move, were abstractions. These abstractions became concrete in the social life of man, which for Hegel was the state, the bearer of freedom. Rejecting the idea of natural rights, he also criticized the very basic premise of the Enlightenment theory, the cherished ideal of individual rights, making the state the means to the end for the realization of these rights. The state was the "embodiment of rational freedom, realizing and recognizing itself in an objective form".

Hegel, however, did not work out the details of the nature of the rational state in the *Philosophy of History*. This had been provided in the *Philosophy of Rights*, where he spelt out the details of a rationally organized state based on the enjoyment of individual freedom. Hegel's fundamental conviction was that Western civilization was built by two important forces: (a) the harmonious Greek Institutions, and (b) Christianity. He was convinced that human history had culminated in Germany, and there was no more forward march to be made, which explained his reluctance to speculate about the future.

Hegel, like Kant, was concerned with historical analysis, but differed from him in his ideas and methods of analysis. Like Kant, he viewed history as the progressive manifestation of man's reason, but unlike Kant, he was disinterested as far as the future was concerned. His purpose was to show that human history had been progressive till the present, and beyond that he had very little to say. In a sense, Hegel believed that the philosophy of history was some kind of theodicy. He agreed that from very early times, humans had speculated about God's providence and the power of reason. However, all those who had done so always thought that the logic of such providence was beyond the comprehension of ordinary human beings. On the contrary, Hegel thought that he was capable enough of demonstrating the basis for eternal reason and giving an adequate reply to the question of manifestation of universal reason first in nature and then in history, which was a record of human progress from one state to another, towards the individual's essential goals. He differed from Kant insofar as taking into account the basis of the human condition that varied from one historical era to another was concerned. Kant, on the other hand, treated freedom purely on philosophical grounds.

The idea of progress was of crucial importance to Hegel, as by this he stressed the development from the rudiments to the final form of perfection. This progressive unfolding of human history was explained by the idea of the dialectic—in essence the idea of the dialectic goes back to Socrates, Hegel's great hero—by which all the different concepts were bound together. These concepts were not static, but dynamic, in the sense that when one fulfilled its role, it generated from within another, which was in opposition to the first concept. The conflict between the two concepts produced the third, which within its fold united the first two. This dialectical progression had to be found in virtually everything: logic, nature and spirit.

One could notice striking differences in Hegel's *Philosophy of Right* and *Phenomenology* regarding the progress of the Mind and the object of its attainment. In the *Phenomenology*, Hegel did not mention specific countries, periods, dates, events or people. The emphasis was on the general process of development of the mind, compelled by its inner necessity of realizing itself. The analysis was on an abstract level. In the *Phenomenology*, Hegel described the progress of the mind as developing towards absolute knowledge, while in the other two works he described the course of history as progress towards the attainment of freedom. The inference one could make was that, for Hegel, absolute knowledge and true freedom were intrinsically linked. In the *Phenomenology,* Hegel saw all human history as the necessary path of the development of the mind. Freedom, for Hegel, was not the ability to do what one pleased, but lay in developing an autonomous, free mind. It meant rational choice. Reason was regarded as something universal, and hence the mind was also inherently universal. For the human being to be free, he must fully comprehend the rational and universal nature of his intellect; hence the link between freedom and knowledge in Hegel's paradigm.

However, in spite of the unique influence and the impressive structure of history that Hegel built, it was one of the most severely criticized concepts. Plamentaz (1963: Vol. II) inquired as to why the spirit should be ultimately tied to the nation states when a synthesis in the universal process looked more logical, when the process of history itself was universal. Hegel had no satisfactory answer to this fundamental question, and his theory of the culmination of human history in the nation states was not a very cogently argued case. MacIntyre pointed out that the Greek life was far from being harmonious, and in fact was ridden with violent conflicts, which Hegel ignored.

Thus, for Hegel, history had a certain meaning, purpose and significance. It was not just a record of the past. On the contrary, it was a progressive evolution and the world-historical individuals were decisive influences on this evolution. However, history was not made by states or for states, or by world-historical individuals. It was made by people for people, by ideas of intellectuals like Hegel. Marx made Hegel's philosophy of history the starting point of his analysis, and thereby transformed the very nature of the subject.

> Hegel himself was unsurpassed among modern philosophers in his knowledge of the history of Western culture. The history of religions, the history of philosophy and the history of law were created as special subjects of investigation largely under the influence exerted by his philosophy (Sabine 1973: 582).

PHILOSOPHY OF RIGHT

Once Hegel became confident that the present reality was the ultimate one, he concentrated on guiding enlightened citizens for the purposeful conduct of public life. Like Aristotle's *Politics* and *Ethics,* the material that we find collected in the *Philosophy of Right* comprised the lecture notes that he delivered at the University of Berlin. Significantly, unlike his other works which were compiled from the notes of his students; the *Philosophy of Right* was painstakingly prepared for publication by Hegel himself. It was supposed to be a "compendium", the purpose of which was "the need for putting into the hands of my audience a text book for the lectures on the *Philosophy of Right* which I deliver in the course of my professional duties" (Hegel 1969: Preface, 1). Many scholars raised the question regarding the impact of the prevailing strict political control of the university publication on the text itself, thereby implying that there were important differences between his lecture notes and the published version, the latter obviously being a more careful and perhaps a doctored exercise. We are not quite certain about this. But it was clear that the purpose of the publication by Hegel was to "create a public minded ruling class, a sort of ideal civil service, fully committed to the values of civility, impartiality and honourable conduct" (Smith 1989: 140). It was a long-term educational project beginning at the universities and then spreading to other spheres. As such, it was a guide to action to conduct the complex affairs of the state. With this overriding concern for harmony, the text was supposed to create the basic framework of the detailed functioning of the modern state, for which Hegel had to discuss the roles and functions of various components like the family, civil society, the legal apparatus, representative assemblies, bureaucracy, the monarchy and questions involving international relations and war.

Family, Women and Children

Hegel had a much idealized view of the family. He characterized it as an arena of love based on a sense of fulfillment and unity. Within the family, individuality flowered, not independently but as a part of the larger whole. Hegel dealt with all the important aspects of family formation like marriage, family, property and capital, the education of children and the dissolution of the family. Marriage, for Hegel, was essentially an ethical relationship. It was a special kind of unity, whose "objective source lies in the free consent of the persons, especially in their consent of the persons, especially in their consent to make themselves one person, to renounce their natural and individual personality to this unity of one with the other". The bond of marriage was based on love, trust and commonality. Recognition and confirmation by the family and the community were equally important.

Hegel reflected the prejudices of his time, for he reinforced the traditional sexual division of labour within the family and the stereotyped image of the woman. In external matters, man was supposed to be powerful and active, while the woman was to be both passive and subjective. The arena of civil society was an exclusively male preserve, whereas for the female her substantive destiny was with the family. Hegel gave the example of Sophocles' *Antigone* in defence of his thesis.

Hegel regarded women as inferior, with less reasoning abilities, reinforcing the argument that the natural differences between the sexes were immutable and basic. This did not deter him from giving women a significant role. He discussed women while analyzing the role of the family, which he described as a "natural ethical community" and an "ethical mind in its natural or immediate phase". The family was natural because its bonds were based on feelings that were intuitive and immediate. It had an ethical quality because the love that it imparted had a universal and spiritual quality. It was not based on brute force or unmediated egoism. It contained reason in its embryonic form.

Like Aristotle, Hegel regarded marriage as necessary for procreation of the human race, which was natural, outside history. He moved beyond this initial formulation and regarded marriage as "a union of mind", dismissing the arguments that it was purely sexual, contractual and emotional. Marriage symbolized reason and unity, attributes which were essential for the state.

Within the family, men had the capacity for conceptual thinking, granting them universality and real freedom, enabling them to make history and engage in politics and learning. Men were powerful and active, while women were passive and subjective, because they were self-conscious and lacked the capacity for reflection. They could be educated, but lacked the ability for science, philosophy or art—subjects that guaranteed access to the Ideal. They continued to therefore remain creatures of experience, unable to transcend it altogether. Since women lacked the universal faculty, they were prohibited from participating in the public domain. Men could attain individuality, reason and universality, while women were denied personal autonomy, since individuality and family life were incompatible.

For Hegel, like Rousseau, women were enemies of the community, for they identified their interests with those of their family. Unlike Rousseau, Hegel did not prescribe separate educational curricula for boys and girls, but even if they were equally educated, they would grow up representing unequal interests. Sons became heads of new families. Through marriage, the parties surrendered their individual personalities and formed a union, which was why the family was a basic element in human life having an ethical form and a legal persona. The man became the representative of the family in law. Natural and biological differences generated social differences. Hegel did not recognize domestic work as worthwhile. Women enjoyed an ethical status only because of the marital bond that they had with their husbands. Men could enjoy the same because of their public transactions in civil society and the state. He regarded marriage as a girl's destiny while a promiscuous man could regain his honour *qua* citizenship. Hegel contended that if women held public positions or participated in government, it would be disastrous, for they lacked universality and were bound by arbitrary inclinations and opinions. They would bring into the public domain a morality and a sense of justice that was appropriate within the private sphere. They could not be impartial, since they were not detached and lacked the capacity for abstraction.

Hegel placed a lot of importance on marriage and argued that the ethical life of the community depended on it. He discouraged marriages among the well-known, and favoured that "the parties should be drawn from separate families and their personalities should be different in origin" (Hegel 1969: 168). He was against marriage between blood relations. The husband was the head of the family. Family property was described under no single individual's exclusive preserve, while each had a right to the common fund or property. Hegel emphasized the importance of self-subsistence and independence of the family unit.

Hegel, like Locke, argued that children had a right to maintenance and education, and that parents were responsible for their discipline and education. The punishment of children was essentially moral, "to deter them from exercising a freedom still in the toils of nature and to life the universal into their consciousness and will" (Hegel ibid: 174). Children were potentially free and could not be treated as property by parents. In the formative years the emphasis was love, trust and obedience. The purpose of education was to make children self-reliant, so that they could enjoy the freedom of personality. This would enable them to gain power in order to leave the natural unity of the family. At this stage, the children became adults and were capable of having property and families of their own. The individual, at the end of the family relationship, had total freedom to dispose of his property in a manner he deemed fit.

Hegel ended the discussion of the family when families grew to form parts of the larger civil society. The disintegration of the family was a natural occurrence, and with it the larger formations emerged. Here also, dialectics was in operation, as the unity of the family provided the ethical basis of life, which, while disintegrating, captured the universal principles of life. The expansion of the family was the key to the understanding of the larger formations like a nation or a federation of different groups on a voluntary basis with a power centre. But the bases of this larger formation remained the same: needs and reciprocity.

Civil Society

In the ethical connotation of Hegel, the important formation between the family and the state was the arena of civil society, which he stated categorically was of modern origin. This was because of the fact that the modern understanding of what constituted social was very different from the ancient perception; for instance in Aristotle, civil society was identical with the political community. Cicero described "civic" as an attribute of civility, or knowledge of civic affairs and prudence. In Hegel, the nature and basis of civil society were very different from those of the family and the state. The bases of the family were love and affection. On the other hand, the state was governed competently and impartially by a universal class—the civil service. Civil society, for Hegel, reflected a "system of needs" where the individual pursued his own interests according to his inclinations and abilities. This was an achievement of the modern world, reflecting division of labour and the actualization of a new science—political economy. This new science was of enormous importance, as it had discovered the laws which governed an individual's behaviour in civil society—the major arena for the bulk of the people for the major part of their time. Hegel regarded the theories of Smith and Ricardo as important as those of Kepler and Galileo.

Civil society, in Hegel, contained three different but interrelated things: (a) the system of needs, (b) the administration of justice, and (c) need of police and cooperation. Regarding the first, Hegel said that these were particular needs of particular individuals, which existed in contrast to universal principles. They were subjective needs. Hegel argued that the needs of animals were limited in scope, whereas those of human beings multiplied. Division of labour was one of the major means of their attainment, as by this the individual's work became simpler and his skill increased with growth in output. They became interdependent, leading to a "dialectical advance" as self-interest generated a situation where everyone else's needs were also satisfied. The cumulative effects of the particular motivations led to a universal minimum in which each person's enjoyment led to similar enjoyment by all others out of this complexity of interdependence. By education and the skills of multitudes of people, the general wealth of civil society also increased.

Civil society inevitably got divided into various classes and estates. This division was bound to take place because of the different levels of skills, outlooks, interests, ways of life, opportunities and other factors like risk or fortune. The three broad groupings of the peasantry, the business class and the universal class of bureaucracy mediated between the family and the state. The state being very large and impersonal, the individual's public spirit and feeling for the community had to grow within the ambit of civil society. Hegel's corporation was the mechanism to achieve this by the flowering of professional associations and voluntary organizations. Here, Hegel sounded like Tocqueville, and accepted that freedom of association was one of the key rights of the modern world. Corporatism was to perform a number of crucial functions. It was an essential requirement for actualizing freedom. He could even go to the extent of arguing that freedom of association was more important than freedom of speech and opinion. Freedom of association was important for furthering different human capacities and for identification of a particular individual for a particular kind of grouping of one's liking or interest. Associations helped not only in preventing over centralization of the state but also in preventing fragmentation of the market at a particular level. They also provided for the development and recognition of particular skills, abilities, and talents. People also learnt how to cooperate, and gain by such cooperation. Membership entailed acceptance of a code of conduct which inculcated a sense of discipline. It allowed for the growth of pride and integrity, giving the individual dignity, second only to the family.

Another important aspect of corporatism was its welfare functions for the underprivileged. The state, in Hegel's theory, was not a welfare state nor was Hegel an advocate of a planned economy. But he was opposed to social indifference to poverty and the idea that people should fend for themselves. With concern for social stability, he suggested that a safety net be provided by the corporation for all those who suffered in the market. However, he recommended foreign markets and thought that domestic problems could be solved by external involvement. For him, society consisted of three classes: the agricultural, governmental and business class. The last one incorporated all craftsmen and producers.

The corporation also played the role of a mediator between the state and civil society by facilitating political representation for its members. Like other political thinkers of his time, Hegel opposed universal franchise, arguing that it would lead to fragmentation and apathy. But he was also conscious of the need for representation, and preferred corporate representation in the legislative assemblies or states. The representation was not geographical but interest-based. Participation in the political process would protect interests better. Hegel's idea was very similar to Burke's theory of representing interests. For Hegel, it was a kind of functional representation leading to class cooperation and harmony. This political recognition was essential to prevent people from forming an organized group of disgruntled people against the state.

> The consideration behind the abolition of Corporations in recent times is that the individual should fend for himself. But we may grant this and still hold that corporation membership does not alter a man's obligation to earn his living. Under modern political conditions, the citizens have only a restricted share in the public business of the state, yet it is essential to provide men—ethical entities—with work of a public character over and above their private business. This work of a public character, which the modern state does not always provide, is found in the Corporation (Hegel ibid: 278).

In the twentieth century, corporatism was looked upon with suspicion because of Italian Fascism, and also because military and authoritarian rulers of South America had used this term in the context of total governmental control and direction of business enterprises and labour movements to secure unity, discipline, order, efficiency and to crush any opposition. It was supposed to create a state-supported consensus between different and even conflicting social groups, by controlling market competition. Hegel's corporatism was very different from this. It was more akin to the idea of liberal corporatism, meaning self-regulation by quasi-autonomous social groups within the ambit of constitutional government. It was still not democratic, as by preferring organized groups and elite, it would negate the representational process.

State

For Hegel, the state represented universal altruism. It synthesized dialectically the elements within the family and civil society. As in the case of the family, the state functioned in a manner that the interests of everyone were furthered and enhanced. It represented the universal tendencies within civil society, thus giving rise to the notion of citizenship. The state had "its reality in the particular self-consciousness raised to the place of the universal". The state was "absolutely rational" and had "substantive will" for realizing itself through history, and was therefore eternal. "This substantive unity is its own motive and absolute end. In this end freedom attains its highest right. This end has the highest right over the individual, whose highest duty in turn is to be a member of the state" (Hegel cited in Bondurant 1958: 212–213).

Hegel perceived the state as an end in itself; it was Mind realizing itself through history. As an idealist, Hegel viewed the state as an organism having "the highest right over the individual, whose highest duty in turn is to be a member of the state" (Hegel cited in Bondurant ibid: 213). Hegel emphasized the public nature of the state, yet he did not distinguish between the private and the public spheres. Hegel examined the different components of the state like the rule of law, the bureaucracy, and the monarchy.

Rule of Law

The rule of law was one of the key formulations in the *Philosophy of Right*. Hegel did not see law as a hindrance to freedom: it was a characteristic of freedom. He had both a broad and a narrow conception of law. In the wider sense, it was one of the instruments for realizing social cohesion. Here law was seen not as a code, but one that reflected ethical values which governed cultural life. In this holistic concept, justice was linked to the institutional ordering of entire society.

In the narrower sense, law was linked to positive legal justice. In an important clarification, he stated in the context of positive law, "it is the legal which is the source of our knowledge of what is right or more exactly of our legal rights". The emphasis on the conventional principles of law made him reject a conception of higher or natural law. The basis of this argument stemmed from the fact that modem civil codes were becoming more rational and public. The dignity of the rule of law had to be honoured.

Laws were for universal application, and had to be based on impersonal and universal values. Under such a system, every person was a legal entity who was entitled to dispose of the objects which were his property. The quantity of that property was a question of legal indifference.

What mattered was the legal authority to acquire, use and exchange property with others, based on the principle: "Be a person and respect others as persons".

An interesting aspect of the Hegelian legal system was that it lacked the idea of command normally associated with Hobbes. The determining characteristic of a legal norm was its form, which had its basis in practical rationality. The embodiment of a rule was more important than command. It was this rule that gave meaning and shape to the rule of law, and distinguished it from arbitrary power. In an important distinction between command and law, Hegel asserted that commands and orders were specified purposes for identified people, whereas the ambit of law was much wider, as it addressed a larger and unknown audience, and was equally applicable to all within its jurisdiction. Command was from a superior to an inferior. The basis of rational authority had to have the sanction of law.

Hegel also rejected the notion that the purpose of law was the realization of a lofty ideal of human excellence, or the full development of human capacities. The ancient view on this was rejected by Hegel. For instance, in Aristotle, the purpose of law was to instil in citizens a very high level of civic virtue. But in Hegel, all such issues were left to the private discretion of the individual. One major difference between the ancient and modern formulations was that in the former, the emphasis of law was on determining details of conduct and behaviour, whereas the modern perception was on the generality of the law, as it provided personal initiative and freedom. Hegel was critical of "the legislation of the ancients", as it is "full of precepts about uprightness and integrity which are unsuited by nature to legal enactment because they fall wholly within the field of the inner life" (Hegel 1969: 213, 272). In contrast, the modern rule of law consisted of a few necessary features, which were common to all. Laws were established by the rationality of free individuals. Laws were impersonal. They had to be rational and written. Burke's appeal to tradition and custom was rejected by Hegel, as such attitudes developed ill feeling and hatred for all laws and legislations. For conferring legitimacy to tradition, one had to go back to a situation that existed before tradition began, namely the animal kingdom of the state of nature, where only the law of the jungle prevailed. All traditions were based on "the irrational power of brute force". The purpose of written and codified law was that people would know about it. For getting conformity and consent of the governed, laws had to reflect intelligible rules.

> ... rulers who have given a national law to their people in the form of a well-arranged and clear cut legal code ... have been the greatest benefactors of their peoples, [and that] to hang the laws so high that no citizen could read them ... is injustice of one and the same kind as to bury them in row upon row of learned towns, collections of dissenting judgements and opinions, records of custom, etc., and in a dead language too, so that knowledge of the law of the land is accessible only to those who have made it to their professional study (Hegel ibid: 138).

The Universal Class

One of the most important components of the Hegelian state was the class of civil servants or the bureaucracy. This class became the universal class because of its commitment to impartiality. Unlike the other groups of civil society, which were primarily interested in their own progression or business, the civil service performed the stupendous service of supervising the entire societal apparatus, which Hegel called the public business. This class of people would not be recruited from the nobility, but from the modern middle classes, which symbolized "the consciousness of right and the developed intelligence of the mass of people". For this reason, it becomes "the pillar of the state so far as honesty and intelligence are concerned" (Hegel ibid: 190). Not heredity, but "knowledge and proof of ability" were the criteria for recruitment (Hegel ibid: 190).

Hegel, in developing this philosophy of the civil service, differentiated the modern constitutional state from the *polis* and oriental despotism, and pointed to the relative impersonality of the bureaucracy. The constitutional state retained its independence from its ruling groups by the mechanisms of free institutions and a civil service. The state was not the personal property of an individual or a group. It placed more emphasis on institutional constraints, defining and limiting the power of government rather than depending on virtues of statesmen or citizens. This was because modern constitutionalism was suspicious of the abilities of men in power to control their passions, and prevent abuse of power by the rulers. The rule of law and not rule of men reflected the concern of modern societies. The modern constitutional state could not act in a partisan manner.

The civil service, like Plato's Guardians, had the interests of the commonwealth in mind. Hegel was categorical that the bureaucracy should be open to all citizens on the basis of ability and citizenship. Civil servants should have fixed salaries so that they could resist the temptations of civil society. Unlike Plato's guardians, the universal class functioned within a framework where the special interests expressed themselves legitimately within the Assembly of Estates and autonomous corporations.

The indispensability of the state was demonstrated by the fact that the individual qualities and potentialities of good life could be realized only through the state. It was the destiny of the individual to identify with the universal and the truth, and not with incorrect notions of individuality that rejected social values and championed the cause of individual eccentricities. The state, in Hegelian terms, was the divine will, "in the sense that it is mind present on earth, unfolding itself to be the actual shape and organization of a world". The state was the most sublime of all human institutions, the final culmination which embodied both mind and spirit. Its strength was in providing the mechanism for the realization of the ideal—the synthesis of the individual interest with that of the state. In case of conflict between the individual interests and those of the large whole, the citizen would identify with those of the state, rather than pursue one's own interests. The state was the individual writ large.

The Monarchy

The monarchy, for Hegel, was a functional requirement of the modern constitution. This modern constitution accepted separation and division of powers. He went to the extent of saying that division of power guaranteed freedom. Hegel differentiated between the doctrines of the separation of powers from his own innovative theory of inward differentiation of constitutional powers. Separation of powers was rejected as a false doctrine, as it supported total autonomy and the independence of each functioning category. His model portrayed all these categories as mutually supporting aspects of the same totality.

> ... the constitution is rational in so far as the state inwardly differentiates and determines its activity in accordance with the nature of the concept. The result of this is that each of these powers is in itself the totality of the constitution, because each contains the other moments and has them effective in itself (Hegel ibid: 174).

Hegel's supreme concern was to find a method by which he could secure the unity and integrity of the state. Absolute separation of powers led either to a stalemate, or to self-destruction of the state. To avoid this, Hegel's prescription was that the crown, the executive and the legislative body would have legally differentiated spheres, with harmony and cooperation among these bodies as necessary for guaranteeing freedom to its citizens. "Sovereignty depends on the fact that the particular functions and powers of the state are not self-subsistent or firmly grounded but have their roots ultimately in the unity of the state as their single self (Hegel ibid: 186).

Interdependence and a cooperative attitude of the three important branches were the preconditions of continuance of the sovereign state. Monarchy at the apex was supposed to signify this unity. The monarch was the tangible expression of all the features of the constitution. Hegel opposed the idea of an elected monarchy or the American-style presidency, for even though it might be an expression of the popular will, it was merely a small portion of the constitution. That was an insufficient basis, as the monarch in his own self-embodied the entire constitution and not just one portion of it.

> The power of the crown contains in itself the three moments of the whole, viz. (a) the universality of the constitution and the laws, (b) counsel, which refers the particular to the universal; and (c) the moment of ultimate decision, as the self determination to which everything else reverts and from which everything else derives the beginning of its actuality (Hegel ibid: 179).

Monarchy was an important institution for Hegel, as it solved the problem of identifying national sovereignty. It was a legalistic argument, for it tried to locate where the sovereignty resided. Since this task could not be performed by popular sovereignty, it was rejected. The people represented a mere abstraction. Following Hobbes and Austin, Hegel argued that since the manifestation of the state was one, its head should also be an identifiable one. This guarantee was not provided by any single person, but by the *institution* of monarchy. The deeper meaning of this was that it was immaterial who that person was, and because of this, hereditary succession was the best plausible one. Hegel's monarch was "in essence characterized as the individual in abstraction from all his other characteristics, and this individual is raised to the dignity of monarchy in an immediate natural fashion, that is, by accident of birth" (Hegel ibid: 155). For holding this symbolic office of unity, physical power or intellectual gifts were not necessary.

Sovereignty, both in the *de jure* and *de facto* senses, rested with the state. However, sovereignty, which stipulated that all functions were ultimately rooted in the state, was not to be found in despotic rule or in a feudal state. Hegel had very little faith in popular sovereignty. Instead of a democratically elected legislature, he conceived of an Assembly of Estates which would represent the different interests with some link in matters of public concern.

Hegel's defence of monarchy had to be understood on the basis of his philosophical framework to find out rational arrangements within the existing institutions. It was not a descent into mysticism as Marx thought, nor did Hegel provide "the most specious reasoning that ever disgraced a philosopher" as he tried to prove by dialectical logic that state sovereignty was to reside in a hereditary monarch, but rather to concretize functional differentiation with unity (Hook 1958: 156). Hegel was not interested in finding a philosophic ruler, like Plato nor was he trying to depict a future based on human emancipation within a framework of true democracy like Marx. Such ideas were negations of the entire approach of Hegel, which is based on the assumption that the *real is rational,* and that the *immediate present* and not the future is the concern.

War and International Relations

One of the most controversial aspects of Hegel's political philosophy, in sharp contrast to the optimism of the Enlightenment, was his assertion that war "preserves the ethical health of peoples". He repudiated the liberal theory of obligation for confusing civil society with the state. He commented:

> ... an entirely distorted account of the demand for this sacrifice results from regarding the state as a mere civil society and from regarding its

> final end as only the security of individual life and property. This security cannot possibly be obtained by the sacrifice what is to be secured on the contrary (Hegel 1969: 209).

Civil society was an arena of life motivated by subjectivity, a creation of the modern world created by Christianity, and the doctrine of natural rights which did not perceive the human individual as a political animal but as possessors of certain inalienable rights which the state had to protect. Self-interest was the guiding force of civil society, with Smith's "invisible hand" as the controlling agency of economic transactions and of ensuring the mutual satisfaction of individual needs. Unity of civil society developed unconsciously by exchange of goods and services at the market place. Hegel's essential argument was that the aim of civil society was different from that of the state, and this differentiation was the key to understanding Hegel's theory of war and international relations.

The state, i.e. the "political state", was an ethical community. It was not an instrument for advancing one's material interests. It was not based on brute force, where obedience came out of coercion and fear. It was a union much above all these, which emphasized shared values and demanded common sacrifice. Obligation to such an entity flowed not from fear, but from a shared view of good life. The emphasis was on the ethical, spiritual and material characters of the state. Hegel's defence of war was derived from the argument that the ethical nature of the state was preserved by war. As an ethical entity, it could resort to war in order to maintain itself. War was a moment in the ethical life of the state.

> War is not to be regarded as an absolute evil and as a purely external accident, which itself therefore has some accidental cause, be it injustices, the passions of nations or the holders of power, etc., or in short, something or other which ought not to be. It is to what is by nature accidental that accidents happen, and the fate whereby they happen is thus a necessity. Here as elsewhere, the point of view from which things seem pure accident vanishes if we look at them in the light of the concept and philosophy because philosophy knows accident for a show and sees in it its essence, necessity (Hegel ibid: 209).

War raised the level of consciousness from mere material possessions and interests. During wars, common values and commitments were not only preserved, but also enhanced. Prolonged peace led to the mistaken belief that the state existed only for civil society. War had both a negative and a positive utility. Negatively, it demonstrated the limitations of the material world, and positively, it united people for a common goal. The argument was as follows.

> In order not to let them get rooted and settled in this isolation and thus break up the whole into fragments and let the common spirit evaporate, government has from time to time to shake them to the very center by War. By this means it confounds the order that has been established and arranged, and violates their right to independence, while the individuals ... are made, by the task thus imposed on them

> by government, to feel the power of their lord and master, death. By thus breaking up the form of fixed stability, spirit guards the ethical order from sinking into merely natural existence, preserve the self of which it is conscious, and raises that self to the level of freedom and its own powers (Hegel cited in Smith 1989: 159).

Again:

> War is the state of affairs which deals in earnest with the vanity of temporal goods and concerns—a vanity at other times a common theme of edifying sermonizing. This is what makes it the moment in which the ideal of the particular attains its right and is actualized. War has the higher significance that by its agency ... the ethical health of peoples is preserved in their indifference to the stabilization of finite institutions; just as the blowing of the winds preserves the sea from the foulness which would be the result of prolonged calm, so also corruption in nations would be a product of prolonged, let alone "perpetual peace" (Hegel 1969: 209).

The above two passages had to be integrated with Hegel's overall perception of the state, and not merely as a definite indicator for glorifying war. He was concerned with the actualities of the state. He accepted the fact that a state might be formed by violence. But violence could not be the final quest. A founder's mettle was to be gauged by his ability to create and stabilize political institutions which replaced violence and force. But what Hegel ignored in this formulation was the fact that a relatively peaceful transformation, rather than force, was always more conducive to building stable political institutions. Added to this was also the fact that only those revolutions were able to institutionalize liberty which kept their ambit limited to the political, and not encroached the social.

For Hegel, war performed particular and important functions: first, in establishing a state; and second, when the state was well-established, as a mechanism of preserving the state from the inevitable conflicts generated by a market within civil society. It was necessary to act to create a public spirit and go beyond limited private interests. It was in a warlike situation that courage and honour became important. On this, Hegel wrote:

> Courage to be sure is multiform. The mettle of an animal or a brigand, courage for the sake of honor, the courage of a knight, these are not true forms of courage. The true courage of civilized nations is readiness for sacrifice in the service of the state, so that the individual counts as only as one amongst many. The important thing here is not personal mettle but aligning oneself with the universal. In India five hundred men conquered twenty thousand who were not cowards, but who only lacked this disposition to work in close cooperation with others (Hegel ibid: 296).

Hegel was categorical that since modern political institutions were different from ancient ones in purpose, ambit, scale and mechanism, modern warfare was also totally different from the ancient one. In the ancient heroic societies, individual bravery in war and conquest was one of the important indicators of human excellence. It was an individual glorification. But in the modern period, personal pride was subordinated to a larger impersonal category, the state. Personal honour and bravery were replaced by a larger cause or ideal. The modern hero mingled with the universal.

Hegel also believed that since modern warfare was impersonal, it was destined to become less barbaric and more humane than what it was in the past. He also asserted that the invention of the gun would make wars more rational, rather than based on personal whims and fancies, including personal enmity. He wrote: "It is for this reason that thought had invented the gun, and the invention of this weapon which has changed the purely personal form of bravery into a more abstract one, is no accident" (Hegel ibid: 295).

Hegel explicitly rejected the Kantian notion of perpetual peace.

> Perpetual peace is often advocated as an ideal towards which humanity should strive. With that end in view, Kant proposed a league of monarchs to adjust differences between states, and the Holy Alliance was meant to be a league of much the same kind. But the state is an individual, and individuality essentially implies negation. Hence even if a number of states make themselves into a family, this group as an individual must engender an opposite and create an enemy (Hegel ibid: 295).

Hegel's skepticism of international law emanated from his belief that the causes of war were sown deeply in human nature, and as such no solution could be found on the basis of legal formulations. Another argument against international law was that a state had an inherent right to act as a state, which no contract could curtail. As there was no superior power to enforce international law, states existed in a "state of nature" in relationship to one another. As a result, international law, like the categorical imperative, remained only in the realm of *ought* and not *is*. Hegel wrote:

> The fundamental proposition of international law ... is that treaties, as the ground of obligations between states, ought to be kept. But since the sovereignty of a state is the principle of its relations to others, states are to that extent in a state of nature in relation to each other. Their rights are actualized only in their particular wills and not in a universal will with constitutional powers over them. This universal proviso of international law therefore does not go beyond an ought-to-be and what really happens is that international relations in accordance with treaty alternate with severance of these relations (Hegel ibid: 213).

In the relationship between nations, Hegel discounted tightness or wrong as categories. He recognized the inevitable existence of a variety of regimes or constitutions, without any attempt to grade them. So war reflected a situation of two rights. There was nothing called a "just" war. The only court of appeal for Hegel was the process of history itself, which decided who was right at that moment, "the history of the world is the world's court of judgement". Both Hegel and Hobbes cynically rejected the claim of the bourgeois state to be under international law. As such, "Hegel's idealism comes to the same conclusion as did Hobbes' materialism" (Marcuse 1954: 222).

DIALECTICS

Hegel's dialectical method played a crucial role in his political philosophy. By applying the categories of a *thesis*, an *antithesis* and a *synthesis*, Hegel's major thrust was to solve the problem of contradiction. It attempted to reconcile the many apparent contradictory positions and theories developed by earlier thought processes. As a method of interpretation, it attempted to reconcile the various different traits developed in the past. He never claimed to be its inventor, and even acknowledged that the ancient Greek philosopher Socrates used it.

Hegel's own use of the dialectical method originated with his identification of Kantian critical theory, which meant rejection of the Enlightenment philosophical method based on the scientific approach of studying nature. Crucial to this method was a belief that accuracy came out of a method of reduction, which meant that knowledge emerged out of the detailed study and analysis of parts. Descartes, for example, took recourse to mathematics in search of true knowledge. In Descartes' words, "to divide up each of the difficulties which I examined into as many parts as possible, and as seemed requisite in order that it might be resolved in the best manner possible" (Smith 1989: 165). Critical philosophy questioned the utility of this method in seeking answers to moral problems which arose out of free will and initiation. In this situation, the scientific method became inappropriate.

Hegel's dialectical method presupposed that ideas and beliefs were to be related to their institutions and social structures, i.e. the spheres of the subjective mind and the objective mind had to converge. The categories of subject and object were to go together, as did theory and practice. What apparently looked contradictory were actually dialectical terms, interdependent. This method was to be internally linked to the subject matter. It did not just record and observe, but attempted to build an edifice of a well-connected discourse, which one may accept or reject. It accepted dialogue and conversation, and as R.G. Collingwood pointed out, the very basis of the dialectical method is a "constant endeavour to convert every occasion of non-agreement into an occasion of agreement" (Smith ibid: 168).

For Hegel, dialectics was "the only true method" for comprehending pure thought. He described dialectics as

> ... the indwelling tendency outwards by which the one-sidedness and limitation of the predicates of understanding is seen in its true light...

> the Dialectical principle constitutes the life and soul of scientific progress, the dynamic which alone gives immanent connect and necessity to the body of science (Hegel cited in Smith ibid: 203).

In the *Phenomenology*, Hegel gave an example of its use in human consciousness, but a more comprehensive political use was found in the *Philosophy of Right*, in which the dialectical process reflected the evolution of world history from the Greek world to Hegel's time.

For Hegel, there was a dialectical pattern in history, with the state representing the ultimate body, highly complex, formed as a result of a synthesis of contradictory elements at different levels of social life. However, the relationship between contradiction and synthesis was within concepts shaped by human practices. Marx too discerned a dialectical pattern in history, but then understood contradictions between the means and relations of production at different stages of history.

Praising Hegel's method, Marx wrote to Engels:

> In the *method* of treatment the fact that by mere accident I again glanced through Hegel's *Logic* has been of great service to me ... . If there should ever be time for such work again, I would greatly like to make accessible to the ordinary human intelligence, in two or three printer's sheets, what is *rational* in the method which Hegel discovered but at the same time enveloped into mysticism (Marx cited in Singer 1983: 77).

However, like many other unfulfilled desires of Marx, namely writing a book on Hegel's political philosophy or a book on the theory of the state, he could never find time to provide for this rational explanation of the dialectical method.

Popper argued that it was possible that contradictions remained in our theoretical perception of reality, but it was impossible that such contradictions were a part of reality itself. Popper argued that our perceptions might be incorrect, but that was not true of reality itself. Scientific progress revealed elimination of contradictions from our perceptions till they reached the proper nature of reality itself. Unlike Hegel, Popper believed that the methods of the natural sciences and those of the social sciences were identical. In this observation, Popper was closer to Descartes than to Hegel.

POPPER'S CRITIQUE

Popper launched a frontal attack on Hegel as a major enemy of the open society along with Plato and Marx. He stressed the origins of Hegel's historicism to three ideas developed by Aristotle: (a) linking individual or state development to a historical evolution; (b) a theory of change that accepted concepts like an undeveloped essence or potentiality; and (c) the reality or actuality of any object was reflected by change. The first one led to the historicist method, which in Hegel assumed a form of "worship of history"; the second one linked the underdeveloped essence of destiny, and the third helped Hegel to formulate his theory of domination and submission, justifying the master-slave relationship. Hegel, asserted Popper, was a true disciple of Heraclitus, Plato and Aristotle. His initial success in evolving a new philosophical method of enquiry was mainly due to the underdeveloped nature of German science at that time. It was an "age of dishonesty", in which Hegel became an important philosopher with the backing and patronage of the Prussian state. No wonder Hegelianism was an apology for Prussianism. In the context of subsequent history, Hegelian historicism and the doctrine of modern totalitarianism were identical. Hegel's principle aim was "to fight against the open society, and thus to serve his employer, Frederick William of Prussia" (Popper 1945: Vol. II: 24).

Popper, like Rudolph Haym, was very critical of Hegel's deification of the state. He was also critical of the bureaucracy's role in stabilizing society. He was critical of Hegel for his historicism and approach to the social sciences, which assumed that historical prediction was their principal aim, and which assumed that this aim was attainable by discovering the "rhythm" or the "pattern": the laws or the trends that underly the evolution of history (Popper ibid: 3).

Popper also argued that Hegel's identification of the rational with the actual inevitably led to a philosophy of the pure politics of power, where might was right. The irrational forms of "state worship" led to the "renaissance of tribalism" (Popper ibid: 30–31). Another important fallacy in Hegel was that he admitted that since the process of history was partly controlled by the direction of knowledge, and since that direction could not be predicted, there was a gross underestimation of this factor of openness and unpredictability in Hegel.

Interestingly, immediately after Hegel's death in 1831 (when Hegel was 'canonized' by the Prussian state), apart from the beginning of the two parallel streams of right Hegelianism and left Hegelianism, one important criticism appeared which raised many of the points raised by Popper. In 1839, K.E. Schubart rejected Hegel's doctrine both as a Prussian and a Protestant. He questioned Hegel's insistence that Prussia was a constitutional monarchy, as according to him it was not one since Prussia was a dynastic state. It was an absolute monarchy. "It is always the monarch through whom all others act and can act" (Avineri 1972: 337). Kaufmann, criticizing Popper, wrote, "it would be absurd to represent Hegel as a radical individualist but [it] is equally absurd to claim as Popper does, that Hegel's state is totalitarian" (Kaufmann 1965: 41). Popper ignored the spheres of "subjective freedom" in the Hegelian system.

Singer criticized Popper on the following grounds: (a) all his quotations were not from Hegel's own writings; (b) one of them was a mis-translation; (c) the Hegelian state did not incorporate only the government but referred to the entire social life—there was no glorification of the government against the people; and (d) the Popper quotations needed balancing by others. But in spite of such criticism, Singer acknowledged "that the extravagant language Hegel used to describe the state, and his idea that true freedom is to be found in rational choices, are both wide open to misuse and distortion in the service of totalitarianism is undeniable; but that it is a misuse is equally undeniable" (Singer 1983: 43). Cassirer stated that "Hegel could extol and glorify the state, he could even apotheosize it. There is, however, a clear and unmistakable difference between his idealizations that is the characteristic of our modern totalitarian system" (Cassirer 1946: 42). Similarly, Marcuse also pointed out the many fundamental differences between Hegel's presumptions and National Socialism.

However, all these critics of Popper did not endorse many of the authoritarian implications of Hegel's political philosophy. Their objection was the parallel between Hegel's authoritarianism and twentieth-century totalitarianism, as there was a debate in Marxist theory about the exact relationship between nineteenth-century Marxism and twentieth-century Communism. But here one could point out a serious limitation in Hegelian enterprise, as it was in the Marxist one, that it could not envisage that a serious misuse of its framework was possible. If Hegel was interpreted in this light, then Popper's criticism of Hegel became relevant for our times. One need not always agree with Skinner's argument, "to demand from the history of thought a solution to our immediate problems is thus to commit not merely a methodological fallacy, but something like a moral error" (Smith 1989: 15). A history of political theory was not merely an intellectual history, and the primacy of the political is always there. The continued attraction of the classics was in their handling important themes like justice, education, rights, welfare, international relations and equity, and what we could learn from them and incorporate in enriching our own vision. In this sense, Locke and Kant remain closer to us now than Hegel and Marx. Rawls begins with Kant, and Nozick with Locke, but no such attempt has flown from either German idealism or German Marxism. In this sense, they were both locally dated.

CONCLUSION

In the entire tradition of Western political theory of over 2000 years, no other thinker aroused as much controversy about the meaning of his discourse as Hegel did. Hegel himself was partially responsible for this, as his works were difficult to dissect and because of the critical nature of his philosophy and the operation of the dialectics, the inner essence was always vulnerable to more than one plausible interpretation. As such, the debate as to whether Hegel was a conservative, a liberal or a totalitarian, would continue for the coming years. Complicating the problem was the assertion by Hegel that history as a mode of fundamental shifts and changes had ended during his own time. He looked upon the 1806 war in Jena as the last war, for by then the liberal principles of liberty and equality had become the acceptable principles of a modern state in most advanced countries, and there were no other principles than the ones that liberalism advanced (Fukuyama 1992: 64).

Marx realized the formidable dominance of Hegelian philosophy, and compared it with the philosophies of Plato and Aristotle. He stressed that Hegel's philosophy could be attacked only from within and not from outside, which meant that Hegel could be criticized on the basis of the rational and critical standards that he had evolved. Because of this reason, Marxian materialism was dialectically linked to Hegelian idealism. Marx used all the categories of Hegel and remained a Hegelian throughout his life. Moreover, Marx used Hegelian terms to criticize the liberal state and projected Communism as not only superior, but also perfect. The collapse of Communism raised "the question of whether Hegel's Universal History was not in the end the more prophetic one ... communism did not represent a *higher* stage than liberal democracy, it was part of the *same* stage of history that would eventually universalize the spread of liberty and equality to all parts of the world" (Fukuyama ibid: 65-66). Interestingly, though Marx made a dialectical critique of Hegel on all the major European themes, he accepted Hegel's analysis on the Orient without subjecting it to a dialectical critique. Hegel's Eurocentricism overwhelmed even his bitterest critic.

Hegel was part of the Eurocentric tradition which began with Montesquieu and inspired the entire gamut of thinkers who subscribed to what Edward Said called Orientalism. In spite of his belief in universal history, Hegel remained a child of his times, unable to transcend the prejudices of his time. This was borne out by his criticism of the Reform Act of 1832, the first major electoral reform movement in England. Contrast Hegel's reactions with those of Rammohun Roy, who, coming from a relatively backward colonial country, could comprehend the tremendous progressive content of the act.

Hegel also lacked a proper understanding of the role of science in changing the societal process. Even here, his French contemporary Saint Simon grasped the dynamics of the industrial technocratic society, which enabled him to predict a future European Union. The fact remained that "far from genuinely marking an end of history, Hegel's thesis was itself a key expression of the history of his time and place" (Smith 1989: 230). Though Hegel himself said as a matter of general rule that "all philosophy is its own time apprehended in thought", his own effort was no exception.

Hegel's political philosophy was contained in his *Philosophy of Right*. In his earlier writings he tried to establish a correlation between classical philosophical tradition, particularly the legacy of Kant and Fichte, and the changing scenario that became imminent with the French Revolution. "Hegelian political philosophy goes beyond the idealism of Kant and of Fichte to embody an historical, evolutionary doctrine which transforms the will into an aspect of pure abstract intelligence" (Bondurant 1958: 212).

In an unpublished essay, *The German Constitution* (1801), Hegel attempted to delineate a workable definition of the state in order to counter the radicalism of the French revolutionary wars and the traditional political system in Germany. In the *Phenomenology of Spirit,* he evoked the Greek *polis* as the symbol of political cohesion and compactness, and at the same time expressed his doubts about its realization in the modern world based on subjectivity. In his *Science of Logic* and *Encyclopedia,* Hegel gave us a systematic exposition of the method of dialectics, and integrated it with his political philosophy as outlined in the *Philosophy of Right*.

Hegel rejected the instrumentalist conception of the state as a political community for the promotion and protection of individual aspirations and ambitions. The state therefore "was no utilitarian institution, engaged in the commonplace business of providing public services, administering the law, performing public duties and adjusting industrial and economic interests" (Sabine 1973: 641). The state safeguarded subjective freedom, the hallmark of modern society, but it was an ethical entity whose objectives and goals were rooted in interpersonal relationships that transcended individual wishes and caprice. However, the Hegelian state did not permit individual judgement or choice. It emphasized obedience. "Hegel failed to make clear a belief that the modern state does protect the right of choice. The effect of Hegelian theory emerging in authoritarian systems has been to reaffirm the expressed belief that individual choice is caprice and sentimentality" (Sabine ibid: 640).

The *Philosophy of Right* did not discuss certain important components of the modern political system, like political parties or pressure groups. Though essentially anti-democratic, Hegel placed considerable emphasis on public opinion and advocated limited freedom of the press. The theory did not provide a definite doctrine of political obligation.

The basic problem with Hegel's liberalism was that it was ambiguous and placed a great deal of emphasis on the state. This could be attributed to the fact that liberal institutions did not exist in the Germany of his time. Moreover, liberalism as a creed and way of life was essentially English in character and outlook. However, Hegel was not an enemy of liberalism, for he emphatically defended the idea of freedom. "The connection between freedom and the other virtues is emphasized by Hegel as by no other author" (MacIntyre 1971: 205). He rejected the conception of freedom as absence of restraints as being abstract, for it lacked substance. The primacy of individual preference detached from other factors normally took shape in uncommon situations, and as such that kind of freedom could not be considered genuine freedom. He recognized the incompleteness and weakness of atomistic liberal individualism, and sought to replace it with one where society was the overall framework for the realization of individual freedom and autonomy. Unlike the thinkers of the Anglo-Saxon world who emphasized liberty and individuality, Hegel stressed freedom and rationality. In obeying the state, the individual was acting freely and rationally. Hegel was too authoritarian to be a liberal, and too liberal to be authoritarian.

Hegel exerted considerable influence on subsequent political theory, particularly Marxism and Existentialism. He has been claimed as the philo-sophical inspiration by both Communists and Fascists. The British Idealist T.H. Green adapted Hegelianism to revise liberalism in the late nineteenth century. Hegel influenced Bergson, Croce, John Dewey (1859–1952), Heidegger (1889–1976), Jaspers, Kierkegaard, and Jean-Paul Sartre (1905–1980).

Another important aspect of Hegel was his critical rationality. His questioning of the entire political process opened up a new dimension of the otherwise conservative side of him. His was a searching mind, always looking for answers to new and old questions, essentially accepting Galileo's asser-tion that "still it moves". This only proved that it is difficult to theorize or philosophize without acknowledging *some* debt to Hegel.

13

John Stuart Mill

> If anyone is a liberal, it is surely John Stuart Mill .... In Mill's thought. ... we find in the clearest form all the elements that together make up the liberal outlook. We find in Mill ... a qualified affirmation of the priority of individual liberty over other political goods and the settled conviction that the human lot may be indefinitely improved upon by the judicious exercise of critical reason. Further, the political positions that Mill himself adopted during his lifetime—his support for democratic institutions, for the nascent feminist movement and for individual freedom from a tyrannous public opinion—would seem unambiguously to qualify him as a paradigmatic liberal thinker (Gray 1989: 217).

> Mill ... was a transitional thinker between old and new, *laissez faire* and collectivist forms of liberalism, who imposed a perfectionist teleology of progress upon liberalism. He not only made the negative demand that the state respect the existing capacities of "autonomy, reason and agency" among its citizens, he maintained that it should do what it could, more positively, to encourage their attainment. True liberty, to Mill, was concerned with the full development of independence, self-development, and self-control. It may have been left to Green and Hobhouse to add to the list of actions government could take to create the social conditions for self-realization, but Mill had prepared the way (Gibbins 1990: 107).

> His (Mill's) death was a terrible blow to the Suffragists who lost one of their well known, passionate, staunchest advocates. He was their adviser, friend and a champion and none ever arose to take his place (Strachey 1978: 269).

John Stuart Mill (1806–873) was the most influential political thinker of the nineteenth century. In his political theory, liberalism made a transition from *laissez faire* to an active role for the state, from a negative to a positive conception of liberty, and from an atomistic to a more social conception of individuality. While Mill was a liberal, he could also be regarded, at the same time, as a reluctant democrat, a pluralist, a cooperative socialist, an elitist and a feminist.

Mill's transformative criticism of Benthamite utilitarianism was one of his greatest contributions to political thought. He regarded himself as Peter, who defied his master, for he argued that the principle of greatest happiness of the greatest number was defensible only if a distinction was made between happiness and pleasure. He also replaced the *quantitative* approach of Bentham by a *qualitative* one. Mill also convincingly argued for a defence of basic freedoms by law. The purpose of law was to maximize liberty, as it gave an opportunity for "self-realization". He made an important distinction between the public sphere regulated by law, and the private sphere regulated by morality. He saw the need for a liberal society as a basic precondition of a liberal state and government (Sabine 1973: 642). The reason for this emphasis in the context of the Anglo-American tradition was because the liberal state was already an irreversible reality. He defended free speech and the right of individuality. Mill, unlike many contemporary liberals, championed women's rights, seeing sexual inequality as ethically and legally untenable.

Mill updated Smith's ideas in his *Principles of Political Economy* (1848). He not only defended *laissez faire* but also argued that a just and orderly economic development was possible if trade unions existed, for that would restore a balance in the bargaining process between the capitalists and their employees. His concern for social justice was reflected in his proposals for redistribution, mainly by taxation. He ignored Ricardo's labour theory of value, since price was determined by forces of demand and supply.

LIFE SKETCH

John Stuart Mill was born in London on May 20, 1806. He had eight younger siblings. His father James Mill came from Scotland, with the desire to become a writer. Initially, the senior Mill tried journalism and then concentrated on writing a *History of British India*, which took him 11 years to complete. It remained one of the seminal works on Indian history of the eighteenth century, and is still used as a reference work.

India influenced the life of the young Mill, and subsequently determined his career. All his learning came from his father, and he read the books his father had been reading for writing the book on India. At the age of 11, he began to help his father by reading the proofs of his father's books. Immediately after the publication of *History of British India* in 1818, James Mill was appointed as an assistant examiner at the East India House. It was an important event in his life, as this solved his financial problems, enabling him to devote his time and attention to write on areas of his prime interest: philosophical and political problems.

He could also conceive of a liberal profession for his eldest son, John Stuart. In the beginning, he thought of a career in law for him, but when another vacancy arose for another assistant examiner in 1823, John Stuart got the post and served the British government till his retirement.

As James Mill decided to teach his son all by himself at home, the latter was denied the usual experience of going to a regular school. His education did not include any children's books or toys, for he started to learn Greek at the age of 4 and Latin at 8. By the time he was 10, he had read many of Plato's dialogues, logic and history. He was familiar with the writings of Euripides, Homer, Polybius, Sophocles and Thucydides. He could also solve problems in algebra, geometry, differential calculus and higher mathematics. So dominant was his father's influence, that John Stuart could not recollect his mother's contributions to his formative years as a child. At the age of 13, he was introduced to serious reading of the English classical economists, and published an introductory textbook in economics entitled *Elements of Political Economy* (1820) at the age of 14. From Thomas Carlyle (1795–1881), Samuel Taylor Coleridge (1772–1834), Comte, Goethe, and Wordsworth, he came to value poetry and art. He reviewed Alexis de Tocqueville's (1805–1859) *Democracy in America* in two parts in 1835 and 1840, a book that left a deep impact on him.

From the training that John Stuart received at home, he was convinced that nurture more than nature played a crucial role in the formation of character. It also assured him of the importance education could play in transforming human nature. In his *Autobiography,* which he wrote in the 1850s, he acknowledged his father's contribution in shaping his mental abilities and physical strength, to the extent that he never had a normal boyhood.

By the age of 20, Mill started to write for newspapers and periodicals. He contributed to every aspect of political theory. His *System of Logic* (1843), which he began writing in the 1820s, tried to elucidate a coherent philosophy of politics. The *Logic* combined the British empiricist tradition of Locke and Hume of associational pyschology with a conception of social sciences based on the paradigm of Newtonian physics. His essays *On Liberty* (1859) and *The Subjection of Women* (1869) were classic elaborations of liberal thought on important issues like law, rights and liberty. His *The Considerations on Representative Government* (1861) provided an outline of his ideal government based on proportional representation, protection of minorities and institutions of self-government. His famous pamphlet *Utilitarianism* (1863) endorsed the Benthamite principle of the greatest happiness of the greatest number, yet made a significant departure from the Benthamite assumption by arguing that this principle could only be defended if one distinguished *happiness* from *pleasure.* His essays on Bentham and Coleridge, written between 1838 and 1840, enabled him to critically dissect Benthamism.

In 1826, Mill experienced a "mental crisis" when he lost all his capacity for joy in life. He recovered by discovering the romantic poetry of Coleridge and Wordsworth. He also realized the incompleteness of his education, namely the lack of the emotional side of life. In his re-examination of Benthamite philosophy, he attributed its one-sidedness to Bentham's lack of experience, imagination and emotions. He made use of Coleridge's poems to broaden Benthamism, and made room for emotional, aesthetic and spiritual dimensions. However, he never wavered from the fundamentals of Benthamism, though the major difference between them was that Bentham followed a more simplistic picturization of the human nature of the French Utilitarians, whereas Mill followed the more sophisticated Utilitarianism of Hume. "The distinctive characteristic of Mill's utilitarianism ... was that he tried to express a conception of moral character consonant with his own personal idealism" (Sabine ibid: 640).

Mill acknowledged that both *On Liberty* and *The Subjection of Women* were a joint endeavours with Harriet Hardy Taylor, whom he met in 1830. Though Harriet was married, Mill fell in love with her. The two maintained an intimate but chaste friendship for the next 19 years. Harriet's husband John Taylor died in 1849. In 1851, Mill married Harriet, and described her as the honour and chief blessing of his existence, a source of great inspiration for his attempts to bring about human improvement. He was confident that had Harriet lived at a time when women had greater opportunities, she would have been "eminent among the rulers of mankind". Mill died in 1873 at Avignon, England.

CRITIQUE OF UTILITARIANISM

Mill criticized and modified Bentham's Utilitarianism by taking into account "factors like moral motives, sociability, feeling of universal altruism, sympathy and a new concept of justice with the key idea of impartiality" (Gibbins 1990: 96). He asserted that the chief deficiency of Benthamite ethics was the neglect of individual character, and hence stressed on the cultivation of feelings and imagination as part of good life. Poetry, drama, music, painting was essential ingredients, both for human happiness and formation of character. They were "instruments of human culture" (Mill 1924: 101, 106). He made happiness and the dignity of man, and not the principle of pleasure, the chief end of life. He defined happiness to mean perfection of human nature, cultivation of moral virtues and lofty aspirations, total control over one's appetites and desires, and recognition of individual and collective interests.

> Mill's ethics was important for liberalism because in effect it abandoned egoism, assumed that social welfare is a matter of concern to all men of good will, and regarded freedom, integrity, self respect, and personal distinction as intrinsic goods apart from their contribution to happiness (Sabine 1973: 641).

Mill retained the basic premise of Utilitarianism, but distinguished between higher and lower pleasures, and that greater human pleasure meant an increase not merely in the *quantity* but also in the *quality* of goods enjoyed. He insisted that human beings were capable of intellectual and moral pleasures, which were superior to the physical ones that they shared with animals. He succinctly summarized the difference in his famous "and oft-quoted statement:

> It is better to be a human being dissatisfied than a pig satisfied, it is better to be Socrates dissatisfied than a fool satisfied. And if the fool or the pig is of a different opinion it is because they only know their own side of the question. The other party in comparison knows both sides (Mill 1976: 9).

Mill pointed out that every human action had three aspects: (a) the *moral aspect* of right and wrong, (b) the *aesthetic aspect* (or its beauty); and (c) the *sympathetic aspect* of its loveableness. The first principle instructed one to (dis)approve, the second taught one to admire or despise, and the third enabled one to love, pity or dislike. He regarded individual self-development and diversity as the ultimate ends, important components of human happiness and the principal ingredients of individual and social progress.

Mill used the principle of utility, which he regarded as the "ultimate appeal on all ethical questions" to support his principle of liberty, but then it was Utilitarianism based on the permanent interests of the individual as a progressive being. He made a distinction between toleration and suppression of offensive practices. In case of offences against public decency, majority sentiment would prevail. Beyond these, minorities must be granted the freedom of thought and expression, and the right to live as they pleased.

Mill also tried to reconcile the interests of the individual and society. He spoke of nobility of character, a trait that was closely related to altruism, meaning that people did what was good for society, rather than for themselves. The pleasures they derived from doing good for society might outweigh the ones that aimed at self-indulgence, contributing to their happiness. Mill saw social feelings and consciences as part of the psychological attributes of a person. He characterized society as being natural and habitual, for the individual was a social person. To be less than social was inconceivable. The more these feelings were heightened, private good and public good coincided.

Mill also stated that pleasures could not be measured objectively. The felicific calculus was absurd; one had to rely upon the judgement of the competent and wise. He described the state as an instrument that would bring about transformation of the human being. The state played a crucial role in shaping the ends of an individual through education, an idea that found full flowering in Green's philosophy. Mill was the hyphen that joined Bentham with Green.

DEFENCE OF INDIVIDUAL FREEDOM AND INDIVIDUALITY

In *On Liberty,* Mill stated one simple principle that governed the actions of society and the individual in the way of compulsion and control.

> ... the sole end for which mankind are warranted, individually or collectively, in interfering with the liberty of action of any of their members, is self-protection. That is the only purpose for which power can be rightfully exercised over any member of a civilised community, against his will is to prevent harm to others (Mill ibid: 75).

Mill defended the right of the individual to freedom. In its negative sense, it meant that society had no right to coerce an unwilling individual, except for self-defence. "It is being left to oneself; all restraints *qua* restraints is an evil". In its positive sense it meant the grant of the largest and the greatest amount of freedom for the pursuit of the individual's creative impulses and energies, and for self-development. If there was a clash between the opinion of the individual and that of the community, it was *the individual who was the ultimate judge,* unless the community could convince him without resorting to threat and coercion.

Mill laid down the grounds for justifiable interference. Any activity that pertained to the individual alone represented the space over which no coercive interference, either from the government or from other people, was permissible. The realm which pertained to the society or the public was the space in which coercion could be used to make the individual conform to some standard of conduct. The distinction between the two areas was stated by the distinction Mill made between self-regarding and other-regarding actions, a distinction made originally by Bentham.

> The only part of the conduct of any one, for which is amenable to society, is that which concerns others. In the part which merely concerns himself, his independence is, of right, absolute. Over himself, over his own body and mind, the individual is sovereign (Mill ibid: 76).

Mill defended the right of individuality, which meant the right of choice. As far as self-regarding actions were concerned, he explained why coercion would be detrimental to self-development. First, the evils of coercion far outweighed the good achieved. Second, individuals were so diverse in their needs and capacities for happiness that coercion would be futile. Since the person was the best judge of his own interests, therefore he had the information and the incentive to achieve them. Third, since diversity was in itself good, other things being equal, it should be encouraged. Last, freedom was the most important requirement in the life of a rational person. Mill contended that positive liberty, i.e. autonomy and self-mastery, were inherently desirable and it was possible if individuals were allowed to develop their own talents and invent their own lifestyles, i.e. a great deal of negative liberty. Hence, he made a strong case for negative liberty, and the liberal state and liberal society were essential prerequisites. He warned that pressures of public opinion could turn Victorian Britain into a nation of dull conformists. Mill recommended interference with liberty of action of any person, either individually or collectively on grounds of self-protection: "the only purpose for which power can be rightfully exercised over any member of a civilized community, against his will, is to prevent harm to others. His own good, either physical or moral is not a sufficient warrant" (Mill ibid: 78).

Mill contended that society could limit individual liberty to prevent harm to other people. He regarded liberty of conscience, liberty to express and publish one's opinions, liberty to live as one pleased and freedom of association as essential for a meaningful life and for the pursuit of one's own good. His defence of freedom of thought and expression was one of the most powerful and eloquent expositions in the Western intellectual tradition. "If all mankind minus one were of one opinion, mankind would be no more justified in silencing that one person than he, if he had the power, would be justified in silencing mankind" (Mill ibid: 79).

Mill's defence of freedom of thought and discussion was linked to the persecution of error. Even if an opinion was incorrect, it ought to be articulated, for only through active interaction and dialogue could opinions evolve; otherwise they would lose their vitality and become dead dogmas. Ideas were to be subjected to critical scrutiny from other points of view for arriving at the truth. He supported individuality, for great advances in society were made possible only by creative individuals. Creativity could be effective only if allowed to function freely. The early liberals defended liberty for the sake of efficient government, whereas for Mill, liberty was good in itself, for it helped in the development of a humane, civilized, moral person. It was "beneficial both to society that permits them and to the individual that enjoys them" (Sabine 1973: 641). Mill emphasized the larger societal context within which political institutions and individuals worked.

Mill accepted the observation of Tocqueville that the modern industrial societies were becoming more egalitarian and socially conformist, thereby threatening individuality and creativity. He was fearful "lest the inevitable growth of social equality and of the government of public opinion should impose on mankind an oppressive yoke of uniformity in opinion and practice" (Mill 1924: 177–178). For Mill, the singular threat to individual liberty was from the tyranny and intolerance of the majority in its quest for extreme egalitarianism and social conformity. This made him realize the inadequacy of early liberalism.

> ... when society is itself the tyrant—society collectively over the separate individuals who compose it—its means of tyrannizing are not restricted to the act which it may do by the hands of its political functionaries Protection, therefore, against the tyranny of the magistrate is not enough; there needs protection also against the tyranny of the prevailing opinion and feeling; against the tendency of society to impose, by other means than civil penalties, its own ideas and practices as rules of conduct on

> those who dissent from them; to fetter the development, and if possible, prevent the formation, of any individuality not in harmony with its ways and compels all characters to fashion themselves upon the model of its own. There is a limit to the legitimate interference of collective opinion with individual independence: and to find that limit, and maintain it against encroachment, is as indispensable to a good condition of human affairs, as protection against political despotism (Mill 1976: 68).

Mill pointed out that in the area of thought and discussion the active and inquiring mind had become morally timid, for it concealed the true opinion when discussed in public. "Our merely social intolerance kills no one, roots out no public, but induces men to disguise them, or to abstain from any active effort for their diffusion" (Mill ibid: 93).

The majority projected itself as the controller of social opinion, as the "moral police". Social tyranny was exercised in subtle forms like customs, conventions and mass opinion, which did not make an individual stop and think where and how one had come to acquire these. There was an absence of "individuality". Individuality, to Mill, was not mere non-conformism, but signified the act of questioning, the right to choice. He encouraged eccentricity, "the mere refusal to bend the knee to custom" at a time when mass opinion was exceptionally assertive. On the contrary, when the pressure to conform socially was not so strong, then there was no need to encourage eccentricity. The second qualification was the link Mill established between the desirability of difference and the desirability of independence of character. It was only with moral and mental autonomy that there would be considerable variety of thought and behaviour.

Individuality, to Mill, meant the power or capacity for critical enquiry and responsible thought. It meant self-development and the expression of free will. He stressed absolute liberty of conscience, belief and expression, for they were crucial to human progress. Mill offered two arguments for liberty of expression in the service of truth: (a) the dissenting opinion could be true and its suppression would rob humankind of useful knowledge; and (b) even if the opinion was false, it would strengthen the correct view by challenging it.

> But the peculiar evil of silencing the expression of an opinion is, that it is robbing the human race, posterity as well as the existing generation; those who dissent from the opinion, still more than those who hold it. If the opinion is right, they are deprived of the opportunity of exchanging error for truth: if wrong, they lose, what is almost as great a benefit, the clearer perception and livelier impression of truth, produced by its collision with error (Mill ibid: 79).

For Mill, all creative faculties and the great goods of life could develop only through freedom and "experiments in living". *On Liberty* constituted the most persuasive and convincing defence of the principle of individual liberty ever written. Like his father James Mill, he also believed in the individual's capacity for education, by which he meant not only intellectual training or cultivation of critical enquiry, but also the training of individual character. He regarded individual character as a result of "civilization, instruction, education and culture" (Mill ibid: 115). Happiness, for Mill, was the ability of the individual to discover his innate powers and develop these while exercising his human abilities of autonomous thought and action. Happiness meant liberty and individuality. Liberty was regarded as a fundamental prerequisite for leading a good, worthy and dignified life. "The contention of the essay *On Liberty* is that happiness so conceived is best achieved in a free society governed by the Principle of Liberty" (Gray 1989: 220).

Mill applied the principle of liberty to mature individuals, and excluded children, invalids, the mentally handicapped and barbarian societies in which race itself was considered "nonage". Liberty could be withheld where individuals were not educated. He considered liberty as belonging to higher and advanced civilizations, and prescribed despotism or paternalism with severe restrictions in case of lower ones.

> Despotism is a legitimate mode of government in dealing with barbarians, provided the end be their improvement and the means justified by actually effecting that end. Liberty, as a principle, has no application to any state of things anterior to the time when mankind have become capable of being improved by free and equal discussion (Mill 1976: 75).

Mill also cautioned against sacrifice or infringement of liberty for the sake of making a state strong. Such an action or policy would be inherently counter-productive, for states were made up of the individuals who composed them. His concluding paragraph was a good testimony of the liberal temper and outlook.

> A state which dwarfs its men, in order that they may be more docile instruments in its hands even for beneficial purposes will find that with small men no great thing can really be accomplished; and that the perfection of machinery to which it has sacrificed everything, will in the end avail it nothing, for want of the vital power which, in order that the machine might work smoothly, it has preferred to banish (Mill ibid: 120).

It is generally believed that Mill's essay on liberty was essentially written with the purpose of defending the idea of negative liberty (Berlin 1969). Barry (1995: 216, 227) questioned this assessment, for he contended that Mill understood liberty not only as involving absence of restraints, but also as self-mastery, involving the exercise of choice. It is true that Mill advanced a notion of positive liberty, but he valued choice and individuality as ends in themselves, and not because they promoted general happiness. He did not propose a single overarching principle or values which normally accompanied theories of positive liberty (Berlin 1969). Conscious of the power society and the majority could wield, Mill sought to protect the individual's private space. He was right in observing that a society could be as oppressive as a government. The theme in

On Liberty was not the absence of restraints, but the denial of individual autonomy by the coercion exercised by a moral majority and/or an intrusive public opinion (Berlin ibid).

By individuality, Mill meant the property in human beings that made possible the scrutiny of prevailing ideas and conventions and subjecting them to the litmus test of reason. Freedom meant not only absence of restraints, but also an ability to cultivate some desirable qualities. It was a notion that was rooted in the individual's ability to exercise his choice, for otherwise a human being did not differ from the apes. However, Mill's linkage between individuality and liberty made him conclude that only a minority was in a position to enjoy freedom. The majority of people remained enslaved in customs, and hence not free. In spite of his elitism, he remained an uncompromising liberal, for he ruled out paternalism, the idea that law and society could intervene in order to do good to the individual. He explicitly ruled out interference in self-regarding actions. On this score, he differed from Bentham, who allowed the pleasure of malevolence, namely if the majority abhorred a particular kind of private conduct, then it was similar to the pain it would cause to the individual if such a conduct was prohibited. Mill, disagreeing, explicitly stated that the right of liberty could be sacrificed only for some "other right", a point that has been reiterated by Rawls. However, he failed to analyze and establish a relationship between freedom and responsibility.

> At times he retained the traditional view derived from Bentham that any compulsion of even any social influence is an abridgement of liberty. Yet he never supposed that there could be any important freedom without law and when he identified liberty with civilization, he did not imagine that there could be civilization without society. What Mill's theory required was a thoroughgoing consideration of the dependence of personal liberty on social and legal rights and obligations. It was this which T.H. Green tried to add to liberalism (Sabine 1973: 644).

Mill failed to specify the proper limits of legislation, and was unclear when it came to actual cases. For instance, he supported compulsory education, regulations of business and industry in the interest of public welfare and good, but regarded prohibition as an intrusion on liberty.

Sir Ernest Barker (1950) made an interesting observation when he remarked that Mill, in reality, was a prophet of an empty liberty and an abstract individual. This observation flowed from the interpretation that the absolutist statements on liberty like the rights of one individual against the rest was not substantiated when one assessed Mill's writings in their totality. Mill separated the inseparable. The conduct of any person was a single whole and there could be nothing in it that concerns himself and did not concern others. Bosanquet too advanced a similar point that every action of a person would affect others and the demarcation between self-regarding and other-regarding did not hold good.

Mill qualified his statements, circumscribing his original intent on liberty. For instance, his compartmentalization between self-regarding and other-regarding actions, and the tension between his tilt towards welfarism, which conflicted with individualism, were all indications of this incompleteness. But the point Barker ignored was the fact that the tension that emerged in Mill was an inevitable consequence of attempting to create a realistic political theory which attempted to extend the frontiers of liberty as much as possible. In fact, no political theorist including the contemporary ones like Rawls, Nozick and Raz, are free from this inevitable tension.

EQUALITY WITHIN THE FAMILY AND BETWEEN THE SEXES

Mill's thought and activism could be distinguished from those of his predecessors within the liberal tradition, because of his application of the principles of liberalism to the question of women. For Mill, improving women's position by giving them suffrage, education and employment opportunities was a stepping stone to progress and civility.

Mill rightly regarded improvement in the position of women as a concern not restricted to women alone, but of entire humankind. *The Subjection* therefore made a strong claim for equal status in three key areas: women's right to vote, right to equal opportunities in education, and employment. He acknowledged the tremendous impact the writings of his mentor (Bentham) and his father had on his intellectual development, for both of them had to grapple with the issue in the course of a long-drawn-out debate on the subject. The other intellectual influences on Mill with regard to the women's question had been those of Harriet Taylor Mill, W.J. Fox, William Thompson and the Saint Simonians like Saint-Bazard, Enfantin and Pierre Leroux, from whom he learnt to think in terms of stages of progress.

Liberty and self-determination were two themes that figured prominently in Mill's writings. Freedom, he believed, was the most precious and crucial issue for a human's well-being. In this context, women were the subjugated sex denied access to their own potential, and subjected to the unquestioned prejudices and biases of society. He declared his concern to show that

> the existing relations between the sexes, the legal subordination of one sex to the other is wrong in itself, and now one of the chief hindrances to human improvement, and that it ought to be replaced by the principle of perfect equality admitting no power or privilege on the one side nor liability on the other (Mill 1985: 125).

Equality as a legal right between the sexes was Mill's main concern. He referred to women as both the subject and the enslaved class, for their position was worse than that of slaves. Unlike slaves, they were in a "chronic state of bribery and intimidation combined". Mill's *The Subjection*

> ... is avowedly devoted to condemning the legal inferiority of women in Victorian England, but it ends with an argument from the absolute value of liberty: no country would surrender its independence for any amount of prosperity, and no human being who has tasted freedom would give, it up at any price. What further proof could there be of the supreme value of liberty, for women as well as for men? (Ryan 1987: 342).

Writing to Comte, Mill pointed out that women's capacities were spent seeking happiness not in their own lives, but exclusively for the favour and affection of the other sex, which was only given to them on the condition of their dependence. The parallel between women and slaves was used to depict the reality of nineteenth-century England, where, on marriage, the woman became subservient to her husband both in physical being and property. For women, marriage was like Hobson's choice, either marry and face the abuses and loss of dignity that subjugation and subservience entailed, or remain single and get deprived of educational and professional opportunities. A woman was not free within marriage, nor was she free to remain unmarried. Through the description of Eleanor Garrett (the sister of Millicent Garrett Fawcett, the suffrage leader), Mill explained how unmarried women in the nineteenth century were deprived of avenues for leading a good and independent life. He deplored the lack of freedom of choice for women, and contended that equality should be the ordering principle of societal and personal relationships "The work was a pioneering effort, rightly honoured as one of the first essays to discuss the inequality of women as a political problem and to consider its sources and solutions in a scholarly manner" (Ring 1985: 187).

Mill pointed out that opposition to sexual equality was not based on reason. To dismiss equality of sexes as a mere theoretical proposition did not lend credibility to the argument that women were weaker, and hence subordinate. He agreed that the majority opinion favoured inequality, but this he contended went against reason. The basis for such a supposition was that it was derived from the generality of the practice in the history of humankind, and hence was regarded as good. But Mill pointed out that the subordination of women was only due to the fact that they were physically not as strong as men. In fact, the origins of women's subjection was in physical force, of the allegedly superior bodily strength of men. Consequently, while this had become a virtue in a man, the opposite, namely renunciation, patience, resignation and submission to power, have been regarded as characteristics of a gentle and graceful woman. The subjection of women was similar to slavery. "So true is it that unnatural generally means only uncustomary, and that everything which is usual appears natural. The subjection of women to men being a universal custom, any departure from it quite naturally appears unnatural" (Mill 1985: 230).

Mill pointed out that the rule of men over women was not entirely and altogether based on force. Women also accepted it voluntarily without complaint and became consenting parties to their subordination. Men, on their part, expected not only obedience, but even affection from women. This was ensured through education, training and the socialization process. Women from childhood were taught to be submissive, yielding and accommodating, rather than become independent with self-will and self-control. They were taught to live for others, their husbands and children. Selfless devotion was considered to be the best feminine trait, the glory of womanhood.

> When we put together three things—first, the natural attraction between opposite sexes, secondly the wife's entire dependence on the husband, every privilege or pleasure she has being either his gift, or depending entirely on his will; and lastly, that the principal object of human pursuit, consideration, and all objects of social ambition, can in general be sought or obtained by her only through him, it would be a miracle if the object of being attractive to men had not become the polar star of feminine education and formation of character (Mill ibid: 241).

Sexual relations which were based on force gradually softened, and with the progress of society from status to contract, it came to rest on consent. In case of a pre-contractual social arrangement, birth determined one's position and privileges, while modern society was characterized by the principle of equality. Every individual enjoyed greater freedom of choice to pursue his own life and improve his faculties. However, women continued to be denied this opportunity, for they were still born to a particular place, and were not free to do what they chose to. Paradoxical as it seemed, the modern world accepted the general social practice of human equality, but not gender equality. For Mill, denying women an equal position only demeaned a man.

> A most beneficial change, if the companionship were between equals; but being unequals it produces ... a progressive deterioration among men in what had hitherto been considered the masculine excellences. Those who are so careful that women should not become men, do not see that men are becoming, what they have decided that women should be, are falling into the feebleness which they have so long cultivated in their companions. Those who are associated in their lives, tend to become assimilated in character. In the present closeness of association between the sexes, men cannot retain manliness unless women acquire it (Mill ibid: 111).

Here Mill echoed the sentiments of his father, who too felt that men would be debased if they exercised dominance and power over their women. For both father and son, the ideal was a compassionate marriage between a strong-minded man and a strong-minded woman. Like Wollstonecraft, John Stuart believed that women could earn their liberation with the support of men. Both presented a reasonable critique of male domination within marriage. Mill extended it by pleading for a relationship based on mutual friendship and respect.

Like Wollstonecraft, Mill rejected the contention that the nature of women differed from that of men, and that a woman's nature was contrived and artificial. He dismissed the idea that the nature of women was different, because no one had ever seen a free woman in a free society. If women were the way they were, it was because of years of suppression and domination, and had nothing to do with their natures or dispositions. He subscribed to the view that, by and large, human nature and character were shaped by the circumstances in which individuals were found, and was sanguine that unless and until women were granted freedom, they could not express themselves. The process itself could take longer, but that could not be the basis for denying women the freedom and opportunities for their fullest development.

Like Wollstonecraft, Mill believed that women were as bright and gifted as men, and once granted the same "eagerness for fame", women would achieve the same success. Moreover, a judgement regarding capacities and talent in women could be made only after generations of women benefited from equal opportunities for education and employment. He rejected the idea that it was natural for a woman to be a mother and a wife, and felt that it was the woman who should be able to decide whether to marry and manage a house, or to pursue a career. He contended that it was society, however, that had decided marriage to be the ultimate aim of a woman.

> Marriage being the destination appointed by society for women, the prospect they are brought up to, and the object which it intended should be sought by all of them, except those who are too little attractive to be chosen by any man as his companion; one might have supposed that everything would have been done to make this condition as eligible to them as possible, that they might have no cause to regret being denied the option of any other. Society, however, both in this, and, at first, in all other cases has preferred to attain its object by foul rather than fair means (Mill ibid: 315).

Like Wollstonecraft and Margaret Fuller (1810–1913), Mill articulated and defended the right of women to be considered as free rational beings capable of choosing the life they would like to lead for themselves, rather than being dictated by what society thought they *should* be or do. Mill was confident that women, even if granted freedom and opportunities, would not fail to perform their traditional functions. It was not a question of a choice between domesticity and a career. The reason why men shied away from granting equal status to women was because *they were afraid of marriage on equal terms.*

As a member of the English Parliament, Mill supported a Married Women's Property Bill. He contended that England had to move beyond the "savage state" where marriage was based on the idea that one had to have absolute power over the other. He pointed out that the position of the wife under the common law of England "is worse than that of slaves in the laws of many countries; by the Roman law, for example, a slave might have his peculiar status which to a certain extent the law guaranteed to him for his exclusive use" (Mill ibid: 225).

Mill further pointed out that marriage did not give the woman the dignity and equal status that she ought to get. Once married, she was totally under the control of her husband. She was denied by law right to her children and property. Hence, they must have the rights to property, inheritance and custody. The woman, according to Mill was worse than a slave, a "personal body-servant of a despot for her husband may compel her, claim from her and enforce the lowest degradation of a human being, that of being made the instrument of an animal function contrary to her inclinations" (Mill ibid: 250). The law also granted the husband rather than the wife the right over her children. A mother did not become a legal guardian of her children in the event of the death of their father, unless expressly desired in the will of the deceased. If a wife decided to leave her husband, she could not claim anything, including her children. Mill pleaded, therefore, for equality of the sexes before the law, for that was crucial to ensuring a just arrangement. This, he felt, would be beneficial to all. Here he made an interesting point, that normally institutions such as slavery, political absolutism or the autocracy of the head of the family were judged by giving the *best examples in their support*, as the purpose of the law and institutions was not for good, but for bad persons. Moreover, any good law should take into account domestic oppression and personal violence, considering the high incidence of such crimes. The only option was that

> ... the equality of married persons before the law, is not only the sole mode in which that particular relation can be made consistent with justice to both sides, and conducive to the happiness of both, but it is the only means of rendering the daily life of mankind, in any high sense a school of moral cultivation (Mill ibid: 280).

A marriage contract based on equality of married persons before law was not only a sufficient, but a necessary condition for full and just equality between the sexes. For Mill, equality was a genuine moral sentiment that ought to govern all relationships, including the marital one. Such a sentiment could be instilled and nurtured within a family that had been justly constituted. Mill acknowledged the family as the real school for learning the virtues of freedom and liberation, yet it was here that sentiments of injustice, inequality and despotism were taught. The boy, by virtue of being a male, was treated and reared as if he was superior and better, thus dismissing the needs and interests of one-half of humankind to bear the consequences of subordination and inhumanness. The self-worship of the male in a traditional family, described by Mill as a school of despotism, was contrary to the modern principles of individuals being respected for what they *did*, rather than what they *were*.

A just family would nurture feelings of sympathy in equality and love, rather than subordination and command. Mill desired a transformation of the family to suit the temperament and spirit of the modern age, namely the spirit of equality and justice, and in the process bring about a moral regeneration of humankind. The relationship between a man and a woman in marriage should be based on mutual respect and mutual love, giving due regard to one another's rights. This would make them self-reliant and self-sufficient. Unless the equal and just worth of every human being was recognized, he could not enjoy equal rights nor realize his full potential. A life of rational freedom devoted to the release of their full creative potential was as much a requirement for men as for women.

> Mill's essay emphasizes the value of non-instrumental relationships in human life. His depictions of both corrupt and well ordered marriage trace the relationship of family to right political order. His vision of marriage as a locus of mutual sympathy and understanding between autonomous adults stands as an unrealized goal for those who believe that the liberation of women requires not only formal equality of opportunity but measures which will enable couples to live in genuine equality, mutuality and reciprocity (Shanley and Pateman 1991: 165).

Mill argued that men should not be trusted with absolute power. Such absolute power within the family and marriage only led to brutalization of women. He denied the need of one having the power of decision making within the voluntary association between two persons, and cited the example of commercial partnerships. In matters where quick decisions were needed, it would make sense to have division of power, but one that involved changes of system or principles would need the consent of both parties. The division of affairs for practical purposes would depend on the *comparative qualifications of the couple. The man had an advantage,* being the older of the two, the breadwinner and provider of his family. In spite of his insistence on the need to restructure family relationships based on equity and fairness, Mill continued to perceive the family as one where a man earned the family income, and a woman would take care of domestic affairs.

Eisenstein (1986) noted that Mill reiterated the conventional assumptions about the woman's role in a patriarchal family. In bearing and rearing children, the woman contributed more to the household and its common life. In *addition* to these chores, if she went out and worked, it would impair the proper discharge of these functions. *The Subjection* toned down the assertions made by Mill in 1832 that in the absence of servants at home, women would do all the work that a servant would have done if there was one and at the same time be a mother and a natural teacher to her children. Moreover, if the woman was well-protected and enjoyed an equal status within marriage, she would not feel the need to labour outside her home, for when she married she chose a profession, that of managing her home and bringing up her children.

> Like a man when he chooses a profession, so, when a woman marries, it may in general be understood that she makes choice of the management of a household and the bringing up of a family, as the first call upon her exertions, during as many years of her life as may be required for

> the purpose; and that she renounces, not all other objects and occupations, but all which are not consistent with the requirements of this (Mill 1985: 289).

Mill was also convinced that if suitable domestic help was made possible, then women, and in particular the talented and exceptional ones, could take up a profession or a vocation. Like Wollstonecraft and Fuller, he argued that *the dignity of a woman was guaranteed if she had the power of earning her own living.* A married woman would have full right in her property and earning. She would have the right to enter a profession or take up a career. Women, he pointed out, were fully capable of becoming business partners, philosophers, politicians and scientists.

Mill has been criticized for recommending that women continue being confined within the family and home, which implied that they would not be able to develop the sense of justice to sustain public spirit, and continue to be selfish and narrow in their outlooks (Kramnick 1982: 68; Pateman 1987: 27; Tulloch 1989: 27). In this perception, he could not transcend the nineteenth-century image of women as primarily homemakers and mothers. His focus was also restricted only to middle-class women (Okin 1979: 226; Coole 1993: 111).

Mill questioned the Lockeian separation of paternal and political power, and raised the larger question about the status of the family. He treated the family as a conventional rather than as a natural institution, yet he did not regard the family as political. In *On Liberty,* he solved the private-public divide and suggested personal judgement as a solution, but did not tackle the other important public-private dichotomy of the family versus the civil sphere (Tulloch 1989: 8).

Mill's position got further reinforced by his emphasis on the inherent incompleteness of mid-nineteenth-century England in particular, and Europe in general, because of the exclusion of women from the public realm, which made his position very similar to that of Paine, who highlighted the hollowness of British democracy at the end of the eighteenth century because of the exclusion of the majority of the people from the political process.

> *The Subjection of Women,* challenged much more than Victorian decorum, however, it was a radical challenge to one of the most fundamental and precariously held assumptions about marriage in the modern era, which is that it was a relationship grounded on the consent of the partners to join their lives. Mill argues to the contrary that the presumed consent given to women to marry is not, in any real sense, a free promise, but one socially coerced for the lack of meaningful options (Shanley and Pateman 1991: 168).

In the *Principles of Political Economy,* Mill argued that women received low wages because of the prejudices of society, thereby making them appendages of men and giving the latter a greater share of "whatever belongs to both". The second reason for low wages was surplus female labour for unskilled jobs. Both law and custom prohibited women from seeking any means of livelihood, other than being a mother and wife.

Mill pointed out that if women were allowed to exercise their faculties freely and fully, the real beneficiary would be society, for it would be able to draw from a larger pool of mental resources. If women were properly educated it would not only brighten their dull and impoverished lives, but also enhance society in general. He understood the important point that *equal opportunities in education* meant equal opportunities in employment. If women were denied the latter, it was because men could not think of them as equals, and only desired to confine them to their domestic chores. He also pleaded for political rights to vote and to participate in government as administrators and as rulers.

In the *Representative Government,* Mill commented that difference of sex could not be the basis of political rights. Citing examples like Joan of Arc, Elizabeth and Margaret of Austria, he argued that these women and others had proved that women were as competent as men to participate and manage political offices. In granting the right to vote, Mill hoped that women would be able to bring about legislation to remedy domestic violence. He objected to women being prevented by law to compete and contribute to society. He desired that the subjection of women be ended not merely by law alone, but by education, opinion, habits, and finally a change in family life itself.

In the *Principles,* Mill observed the need to open industrial occupations freely to both sexes, but a shortcoming of *The Subjection* was the neglect of the question of how women of all classes could find and keep their jobs. Mill failed to address the problems of women in the market place and as part of the labour force. Mill's concern was with the removal of the legal barriers erected by patriarchy that prevented the possibilities of a compassionate and interdependent relationship between a husband and wife, ensuring political equality for both men and women in the political sphere. At that time, skilled female labour in the market place was still a remote possibility, whereas suffrage was the burning issue. The question of whether to grant women the right to vote and citizenship was linked to their subordinate and inferior status—a prejudice that Mill felt was imperative to confront and combat.

Many of Mill's contemporaries acknowledged his importance because of his eminence, but did not regard him their leader, for in their opinion he had ignored the plight of daughters, sisters or single women living alone or under the parental roof in *The Subjection.* His focus was on the wife and mother. Most Victorian Feminists voiced concern about the status and problems of single women. They focused on the problems that daughters faced, a relationship that all women shared and the most crucial problem in a society that did not give them independence. This seemed an appropriate framework for discussing the power of fathers and in delineating the basis of patriarchy (Caine 1992: 36).

However, the scope of *The Subjection* was much more wide than alleged by the Victorian Feminists, for Mill did see the plight of single women in a society that gave undue importance to marriage. This was clear from his concern and description of Eleanor Garrett, who was denied the opportunities of leading a decent, independent life. The solution, according to him, was in giving freedom of choice to women, whether married or single. He could perceive clearly that the problems women faced were not merely those of misconception or false social notions, but of *systematic domination,* which was why he constantly used the language of justice, freedom and slavery to improve their lot.

Mill defended the right of individual women who wanted the opportunity to choose a life other than that of motherhood and marriage. He did believe that most women would not make that choice, but he certainly did not want *to force* women into marriage by not offering them alternatives. He also defended the right of exceptional women to have their freedom of choice, and to make the home a dignified and honourable place for those who preferred domestic work. He believed that ordinary men and women were slaves to custom, and it was necessary to remove the legal barriers which restricted women's opportunities.

DEMOCRACY AND REPRESENTATIVE GOVERNMENT

Mill regarded representative democracy as necessary for progress, as it permitted citizens to use and develop their faculties fully. It promoted virtue, intelligence and excellence (Mill 1976: 193–195). It also allowed the education of the citizens, providing "an efficient forum for conducting the collective affairs of the community" (Mill ibid: 196). Interaction between individuals in a democracy ensured the possibility of the emergence of the wisest and recognition of the best leaders. It encouraged free discussion, which was necessary for the emergence of the truth. He judged representative democracy on the basis of how far it, "promotes the good management of the affairs of the society by means of the existing faculties, moral, intellectual and active, of its various members and by 'improving' those faculties" (Mill ibid: 208).

Mill tried to reconcile the principle of political equality with individual freedom (Hacker 1961: 573). He accepted that all citizens, regardless of their status, were equal and that only popular sovereignty could give legitimacy to the government. Democracy was good because it made people happier and better.

Mill laid down several conditions for representative government. First, such a government could only function with citizens who were of an "active, self-helping character". Backward civilizations, where citizens were primarily passive, would hardly be able to run a representative democracy. Second, citizens had to show their ability and willingness to preserve institutions of representative democracy.

Influenced by de Tocqueville's thesis on majority tyranny, Mill advocated a liberal democracy which specified and limited the powers of legally elected majorities by cataloguing and protecting individual rights against the majority. He pleaded for balancing the numerical majority in a democracy by adjusting franchise. Even though he advocated universal adult franchise in 1859, he remarked in 1861: "I regard it as wholly inadmissible that any person should participate in the suffrage without being able to read, write, and I will add, perform the operations of arithmetic" (Mill 1976: 280).

Mill prescribed registration tests for checking performances, universal education for all children and plurality of votes to the better educated, in order to balance the lack of voting rights to the uneducated. "No one but a fool, and only a fool of a peculiar description, feels offended by the acknowledgement that there are others whose opinion, and even whose wish, is entitled to a greater amount of consideration than his" (Mill ibid: 284).

Mill also recommended the disqualification of three other categories of dependants: (1) those unable to pay local taxes; (2) those dependent on public welfare would be excluded for five years from the last day of receipt, for "by becoming dependent on the remaining members of the community for actual subsistence, he abdicates his claim to equal rights with them in other respects" (Mill ibid: 282) and (3) legal bankrupts and moral deviants like habitual drunkards. He, however, championed equal voting rights for all irrespective of their sex or colour.

Mill looked upon equal voting rights, universal suffrage, democracy and liberty as conditionally good. They had to be conferred only on those who had the character for self-control, and the ability and interest in using them for the public good. The policy of a government in franchise reform should be

> to make participation in political rights the reward for mental improvement .... I do not look upon equal voting as among the things which are good in themselves, provided they can be guarded against inconveniences. I look upon it as only relatively good, less objectionable than inequality of privilege (Mill ibid: 288).

Mill also recommended open rather than secret ballot, for voting was a public trust which "should be performed under the eye and criticism of the public" (Mill ibid: 286). Open voting would be less dangerous, for the individual voter would be less influenced by the "sinister interests and discreditable feelings which belong to himself, either individually or as a member of a class" (Mill ibid: 289).

Mill believed that citizens developed intellectual qualities of reason and judgement only through political participation. "Civil participation enhances autonomy and altruism: autonomy from self-government; altruism from judging the interests of the community" (Heater 1990: 199). This enabled the participant to attain moral maturity, for when an individual undertook a public action, he felt that "not only the common weal is his weal, but that it partly depends on his exertions". People had to be free to be able to participate in the government of their country, the management of their workplace and to act as bulwarks against the autocracy of modern day bureaucracy. This feeling of belonging to a community could only come about if all were granted the right to vote. He did worry about the consequences of absolute equality that universal adult franchise entailed, namely the trampling of a wise and educated minority by the mass of people. He recommended compulsory elementary education, for that would make individual citizens wise, competent and independent judges (Mill 1902: 575-577). In *On Liberty* Mill recommended education to be established and controlled by the state. In the nineteenth century liberal thinkers relied on state intervention to reduce the dominance of the church and to protect the right to education of children against their own parents but also warned against the dangers of too much state involvement in education. He always emphasized that representative democracy was only possible in a state that was small and homogeneous, an assertion that has been nullified by the success of plural democracies like India.

Through the rights of citizenship an individual became a social person. He acquired both political freedom and responsibility. It was for this concern with the public realm that Mill defended women's civil and political rights. It also constituted one of his major contributions, considering that the argument for the public domain became central to Rawls' theory in *Political Liberalism* (1993).

ECONOMY AND STATE

Mill deviated from the classical economic theory of *laissez faire* and advocated "optional" areas of interference. Other than gender equality, Mill tried to accommodate the other major intellectual streams in Europe within Liberalism, namely Socialism. He realized that unless Liberalism adapted itself to changing times, it would not be able to sustain itself. It was to Mill's credit that he brought about this change without giving up the fundamentals of Liberalism. Interestingly, his *Principles* were published in the same year as Marx's *Communist Manifesto* (1848).

The *Principles* reiterated the principles of Ricardian political economy. In the process, Mill simplified Ricardian economics, making it less deterministic. Second, he preferred *laissez faire,* as a principle, to state intervention in matters of social and economic policy. Third, his acceptance of socialism was within the overall framework of a market economy (Thomas 1985: 78).

The shift in Mill's position was prompted by revolutions in Europe in the 1840s, the Irish famine and the efforts of working men's organizations to improve their wages and conditions of work in the 1870s. Mill viewed the Irish famine and the emigration of population as a result of the systems of hereditary ownership and absentee landlord farming. Hence, he proposed curtailment of the normal right of inheritance and compulsory redistribution of large holdings from absentee landlords to local peasants, for they would then become efficient cultivators. He recommended interference in the market not with the purpose of overruling "the judgement of individuals but to give effect to it" (Mill 1902: 560). He also supported limiting of working hours, state control of monopolies and factory legislation for children.

Mill visualized society as composed of free, equal, independent and virtuous citizens, who contributed their best towards the common good and would in turn receive fair rewards for their contributions. He rejected the hereditary class system, because it was inherently inefficient and obstructed progress. Mill diluted the distinction between the three social classes in the Ricardian system. He did not attack the landowning class for receiving a steady increase in rent, while the capitalist faced diminishing returns and the labourer survived at the bare level of subsistence, a point picked by George Bernard Shaw (1856–1950) later to furnish the economic basis of Fabian Socialism. Mill was critical of idleness and opulence, just as his father was, and attacked the conspicuous consumption of the new middle class in the same way as he castigated the old aristocracy. As opposed to the big bourgeois, he praised the small, landed proprietors for he learnt of their importance from Tocqueville as preservers of American democracy.

Mill insisted that while increased production was important for poor countries, it was *better distribution of existing wealth* that mattered in advanced ones. He visualized a happy society as one that consisted of

> a well paid and affluent body of labourers; no enormous fortunes, except what were earned and accumulated during a single lifetime; but a much larger body of persons than at present, not only exempt from the coarser toils, but with sufficient leisure, both physical and mental, from mechanical details, to cultivate freely the graces of life, and afford examples of them to the classes less favourable circumstances for their growth (Mill 1963: 755).

Mill advocated taxing inheritance above a modest level, rather than industry and the economy, for that would curtail the incentive to work harder and save more than his peers. In case of intestacy or property without a legal will, it would revert to the state after providing enough for the descendants. He opposed taxation on investments, for that would harm those who could not work, and for whose security it was started. He did not like taxing incomes and savings simultaneously, for that would undercut the willingness of those who kept a portion of their money for productive investments, by which wealth was created and "distributed in wages among the poor" (Mill ibid: 816). While he desired to preserve the entrepreneurship of the bourgeois, he attacked the landed aristocracy which grew wealthy "without working, risking or economizing" (Mill ibid: 819–820). It was for this reason that he was against primogeniture. Thus, Mill combined both a production and a distribution view of economics.

In general, Mill believed that the policy of *laissez faire* was the ideal, but it could be set aside for the purposes of education, care of children and the insane, planned colonization, relief for poor, public utilities like water and regulation of hours of work. The state would ensure that none starved. He did not advocate abolition of property or its equalization. He desired general *embourgeoisement* so that everyone worked for a living, enjoyed a decent standard of living and had sufficient leisure to cultivate one's mind.

Mill's "socialism" was essentially libertarian, for it aimed at the full development of the individual's faculties and the liberation of the human potential. "The aim of improvement should be not solely to place human beings in a condition of which they will be able to do without one another but to enable them to work with or for one another in relations not involving dependence" (Mill ibid: 460–461).

Mill was attracted to socialism because of its idea of human cooperation or partnership, but he was equally keen to preserve individuality and freedom. He did not advocate socialization of the means of production. He realized the need to change capitalism by bringing in the ethic of social welfare and cooperation. This was because capitalism, even with the incentive of self-interest, had not been able to eliminate parasitism, for those unwilling to work were able to develop ways to shirk work. Socialism with communal ownership had superior methods, which forced lazy members to produce and work. The difference was that in a capitalist society a employer could dismiss a lazy worker, but in a socialist society he could be reformed by public opinion, which to Mill was the "most universal and one of the strongest methods of control". However, he was aware of potential tyranny within a socialist society, for he rejected all forms of paternalism as anti-progressive. He supported local workers, retail cooperatives and schemes of sharing profits between workers and managers, and other workers' savings, investment and insurance schemes. He cautioned that these schemes, however beneficial to the larger community, should not "dispense with the inducements of private interests in social affairs". This was because there was no substitute for them, nor could one be provided.

Mill, therefore, could be classified as an "unrepentant defender of the *laissez faire* system of the economy and a radical libertarian in his efforts to extend its practice and benefits from capitalist employers and the self-employed to all peasant and industrial workers" (Gibbins 1990: 103). In 1866–1867, he was prepared to serve as a bridge between Gladstonian parliamentary liberalism and working-class causes. He described socialism as educative, but was not hopeful of its success. He classified socialist perception in two distinct categories: (a) a vision of a new society based on free association of small self-governing units; and

(b) a more drastic scheme of managing the total productive resources under a centralized authority. He favoured the first model, mistakenly attributing the second to continental Europe. However, both these trends characterized British socialist thought.

Mill's advocacy of the participation of workers in management and the need for just apportionment in the ownership of property, one that united him with the Socialists of his time, had twofold implications for his views on citizenship. First, it was just that the industrious should be compensated for their contributions to the well-being of society; by not merely making them part of the body politic, but also granting them economic benefits. This view has been reiterated and refined by Rawls, who viewed productive capacities as social assets, but insisted on granting incentives to the well-off to secure efficiency and productivity. Rawls ruled out rewards if they were unearned. This was necessary if the difference principle had to be meaningfully implemented, so that not only was the worst off elevated, but also the interests of the well-off protected. Second, it was through participation, whether in running a factory or workshop or government, that an individual learnt to exercise his judgement and work for the common good. Judgement required thought, considerations of common good required altruism, and participation did away with lethargy.

Mill contended that trade unions not only restored bargaining power between the workers and the captains of industry, but also ensured just and orderly economic development. He was against making membership within trade unions compulsory. Nor did he believe in prohibiting the right to strike.

In 1869, Mill began a book on Socialism, which remained incomplete. He expressed the need to reform the existing property laws, so that everyone could share its benefits. He disliked the exploitation that private property entailed, but was more perturbed by the uniformity that Socialism/ Communism enforced. He did not think that Socialism would solve the problems that capitalism faced. Moreover, capitalism, far from increasing misery and injustice, decreased them in the long run. He was convinced that Socialism would run into a dead end if it renounced its liberal heritage and supported an all-powerful state. He alluded to the problem of maintaining property rights within Socialism. He also warned against the submersion of individuality within Socialism.

> Already in all societies the compression of individuality by the majority is a great and growing evil; it would probably be much greater under Communism, except so far as it might be in the power of individuals to set bounds to it by selecting to belong to a community of persons like-minded with themselves (Mill 1963: 746).

For Mill, Socialism prevented the proponents of *laissez faire* and the free market from becoming complacent. It remained, for him, a set of arguments and was not a viable potent political force. His views on

Socialism were formed by reading Blanc, Fourier, Owen and Saint Simon, rather than Marx and Engels. He presided over the relative merits and demerits of Socialism and capitalism like a referee in a heavyweight boxing context (Thomas 1985: 90).

ON INDIA

Mill's *Autobiography* and his private letters indicated that he looked upon his Indian duties as essentially belonging to his official employment, rather than of personal interest. He wrote very little about India, and was influenced by his father's pessimistic views on Indian culture. He was skeptical, like Comte and the Saint Simonians, about the feasibility and success of representative governments in Asia, including India. The reason was the passivity of its people, which was due to centuries of despotism, preventing them from taking an active posture in the public sphere. While he conceded that Asian countries such as China and India had attained (in the earlier ages) high standards of civilization, presently they were dominated by custom and sufficiently unres-ponsive to the stimulating ideas of individualism and rationalism. This made Eastern societies essentially passive and stagnant, making it difficult for them to progress on their own volition. There is very little difference between a liberal Mill, an idealist Hegel and a socialist Marx, when it came to writing and perceiving the non-European world. All of them remained Eurocentric.

Mill felt that some form of benevolent despotism or rule by a superior people belonging to an advanced society was best suited for India. At the same time, he had reservations about the capacity of a foreign government to act in the best interests of its subjects, especially in the case of India where the British had very little understanding of their subjects, or sympathy for them. In such a situation, it would be better for the rulers to "govern through" a delegated body which would give supreme importance to the best interests of the subject people. Mill's position was very different from the one articulated by Indian reformers. Rammohun had already rejected the idea of a delegated body, and insisted that the British Parliament enact laws for India since Indian society was incapable of changing from within. He defended his view by pointing out that, unlike the West, where the law emerged from a sovereign authority because of the separation of legislative and executive powers, in India all the powers were vested with the executive, which deterred progressive and wholesome legislation. He was sanguine that the British Parliament would have permanent interests which would benefit India. Rammohun's arguments seemed more reasonable and convincing than Mill's.

Mill, like Burke, was opposed to any kind of interference with religious practices in India, though these were abhorrent to humanity in general. He was against the official imposition of the English language and culture, though he regarded it as the duty of the Empire to uproot barbarous practices like infanticide slavery and *sati.* He supported legal reforms in India like the Indian Penal Code and the codes for civil and criminal procedure. Though an ardent champion of educational reforms in India, he was critical of the education policy that was adopted in 1835 by Lord Bentinck and Lord Macaulay. The policy decision to withdraw funds from centres of oriental learning implied a rejection of Indian culture and religion, and that was unacceptable. Mill distinguished between a limited plan of funding colleges to teach English to potential government employees, and the more fundamental idea of spreading Western ideas and knowledge throughout the country. The second could be achieved by disseminating Western ideas through Indian, rather than foreign languages, with the help of the Indian educated class for the masses to understand and learn.

Mill and Harriet championed the cause of European, and in particular Victorian women, but felt that Asian women were not ready for equality, individuality and liberty yet. Mill, even on this score, was Eurocentric. He was willing to use different standards for judging similar practices, particularly on an issue like gender equality, which was close to his heart since the 1860s.

Mill's plea for gender equality was appreciated by Bankim, who felt that there was no need to add anything to what was stated in *The Subjection,* except the fact that Indian women faced "one hundredth degree more of subjugation" than their European counterparts. In fact Bankim abandoned the idea of dissecting the issue, for Mill had stated the case coherently and brilliantly. This in itself was a great tribute, considering Bankim's *Samya* (1879) analyzed the question of inequality in society.

CONCLUSION

Mill's efforts to revise and modify classical Utilitarianism by emphasizing the social aspect of the individual, the need to assess happiness both quantitatively and qualitatively, stating that liberty and not happiness was the chief end of the state, and defining happiness to include liberty, individuality, self-development and self-control, paved the way for many of the changes that were initiated within English political thought and practice. His most important concern was the preservation of liberty within a democratic society as an intrinsic good in itself, and looked down on majority tyranny and mass mediocrity as potent threats to individuality and liberty. By making liberty the chief aim and objective of the state, he established the limits of legitimate interference by society and the state in areas that strictly and exclusively belonged to the individual. He categorically demarcated things that belonged to Caesar, and the things that did *not* belong to Caesar.

The early Utilitarians in general and Bentham in particular, were concerned with the ascendancy of political democracy as a complement to the Industrial Revolution. The Reform Bill of 1832 was seen as securing a good government. Mill perceived the dangers inherent in such an extension: the tyranny of opinion and prejudices, the will of the majority overriding individuality and minority perceptions. He was no longer concerned about the suppression that authoritarianism resorted to. Instead, it was the preservation of individual and minority rights against the democratic state and public opinion. He could foresee the dangers inherent in *laissez faire* commercialism. It was not just the freedom to do as one pleased or willed, but freedom of thought, to think differently (Williams 1958: 71–72). In spite of his passionate advocacy of individuality and liberty for all including the eccentric, Mill remained intellectually an elitist.

Mill, like Coleridge and Burke, regarded cultivation of culture as social and emphasized on the need for institutions that would conform and constitute the individual's personal needs. Applying this framework, he argued that:

> A philosophy like Bentham's ... can teach the means of organizing and regulating the merely *business* part of the social arrangements ... . It will do nothing (except sometimes) as an instrument in the hands of a higher doctrine for the spiritual interests of society; nor does it suffice of itself even for the material interests ... . All he can do is but to indicate means by which, in any given state of the national mind, the material interests of society can be protected; saving the question, of which others must judge, whether the use of those means would have, on the national character, any injurious influence (Mill 1950: 73).

Mill visualized the state as a moral institution concerned with the promotion of virtue and excellence in the individual citizen. He felt that a conception of good life was more important than a life devoted to the pursuit of pleasure. He pleaded for the removal of obstacles in the way of the individual's self-development that made life less mean and less intolerable for the masses. He, however, continued to see the state as a product of wills, though not of interests, and contended that to ignore the state as constituted by human wills was fallacious.

Mill was essentially a critic of the complacency and conventions of Victorian English society, as evident from his three main tracts, *On Liberty*, *Representative Government*, and *The Subjection of Women*. Following the spirit of optimism of the Enlightenment era, he accepted the notion of progressive advancement of human civilization that the theorists of this period espoused. Since an individual did not develop in isolation, for the flowering of a vibrant culture, healthy discourse, diversity and a concern for public affairs, liberty of expression assumed special significance.

Mill was the first male philosopher of considerable stature and repute to consider the "Woman's Question". Mainstream thinkers had either ignored it altogether, or written about women and the role of the family *en passant*, usually endorsing the stereotype image of the woman. *The Subjection*, along with his active support for women's causes, played a pivotal role in advancing the women's movement. He integrated the central themes raised in the tract with his overall political philosophy. The tract raised many issues of continuing relevance to women, namely the alleged differences between men and women, sexual division of labour, the family as an instrument of change, equality and self-worth in family and sexual relationships, freedom of choice for women, and the reasons for women's subordination and oppression. Mill was the first to apply public principles of justice and equality to the private realm of the family, which he characterized as a "sympathetic association" and the very foundation of a just and equitable society. Being an association of equals, it had to reflect true equality.

In the *Principles*, Mill clearly stated that for ending sex and class oppression, paternalistic structures had to be replaced by responsible self-governments. Paternalism, for Mill, was illicit and pre-modern. He was sure of the benefits of public involvement, and rightly pointed out that women languishing in privacy threatened the very spirit of public integrity. Equality within the family would lead to a better and responsible society. It would also eliminate the evils of an hierarchical, patriarchal family system, like selfishness, domination, injustice, unfairness and male-centredness, and contribute to a better and proper development of children. Mill, like Wollstonecraft, rejected the natural distinction between men and women and dismissed women's nature as an artificial thing, a product of what he described as "forced repression in some directions, unnatural stimulations in others". He perceived the subjection of women as a conspiracy hatched by men to keep them ignorant and subordinate.

Mill was convinced that a good society was one which consisted of happy people, and happiness came out of self-reliance, rationality, tolerance, wide-ranging interests and a compassionate temper. For Mill, "coercion is logically at odds with the creation of such a character" (Ryan 1974: 255). Self-development and moral progress were instrumental to such a good life, leading to "the establishment of the life of the individual as a work of art". This was only possible where coercion, in the name of either class or gender, was eliminated, if not minimized. Mill, the rationalist and the Utilitarian, was also the philosopher of human liberation, individuality, equality and fulfilment.

Mill accepted the Industrial Revolution, for it produced a class of energetic and acquisitive entrepreneurs with the sole aim of the profit motive and the accumulation of money. He feared mass democracy because of its collective mediocrity, which would destroy higher civilization. He was fearful of mass conformity and the effect it would have on individual freedom. He favoured a society based on just meritocracy. He was not appreciative of the destruction unleashed by the French Revolution, though he was happy at the decimation of the monarchy and nobility, and at the reduction of the influence and role of the Church. He assigned an important role to the intellectual elite in shaping and making the attitudes and beliefs in a society, particularly in times of transition. He also insisted on the need to correlate political institutions with society.

Mill distinguished between the public sphere of law and the private sphere of morality, and the need to guarantee by law basic human freedoms. He also established the relationship between law and liberty, whereby law as a system maximized liberty, namely self-development. He clearly saw the need to establish a large ambit of freedom, while emphasizing some restraints, both as a condition of social life, and for protecting freedom itself. He was not indifferent to conduct that fell short of accepted standards of private morality. He also advocated proportional representation as a device to protect the rights of the minorities, giving them an opportunity to share power. He championed the right to express one's opinion, it being immaterial whether one was right or wrong. The important thing was free expression and articulation of contesting opinions. He refined and developed Voltaire's defence of free speech and toleration, immortalized by his famous dictum, "I disapprove of what you say, but I will defend to the death your right to say it."

Mill welcomed the idea of socialism winning over private property, but it would have to be a socialism that respected individuality. He wanted the most people to enjoy property, and for this he insisted on restricting the rights of inheritance, limiting the size of the population and increasing the quality and quantity of education.

Mill was also convinced that advancement of democracy would depend on the spread of education and schooling. Following Rousseau, he advocated participation in public affairs as a means of counterbalancing human selfish-ness. Participation maximized responsibility. But for his father, participation minimized oppression. John Stuart's entire focus was on enlarging participation and the individual's freedom of choice.

> Participation was integral to political education. An educated citizenry was vital to the creation and perpetuation of a healthy body politic. The expansive ideal of citizenship inculcated by Mill put a premium on a widely diffused energy, virtue and intelligence. The achievement of a higher politics required, among other things, opportunities for personal growth, which entailed bringing more and better schooling, more civic participation, more material benefits, and more beauty within the reach of more and more people ... . Political development, personal growth, and an increase in the total sum of human happiness were to advance together (Robson, Moir and Moir 1988: lx).

Mill applied liberal principles not only in the public sphere but also in the private realm, and was the only philosopher to emphasize the importance of fairness, equality and independence within the family as well as within the state. He also insisted that the state had to grant the means of self-protection to its people. Towards this end, he advocated women's enfranchisement, quality elementary education for the masses and land reforms for agricultural labourers. A liberal state had the duty to empower the disadvantaged and the dispossessed. Mill humanized and broadened the ambit of liberalism, which made possible its subsequent revision by Green with his doctrine of Common Good.

14

Karl Marx

> It was the power of Marx's vision that it was also a system; the power of his system that it was also a vision (Howe 1972: 5).

> Marx's views on technical change, exploitation, class struggle and belief formation retain an importance beyond the value they may have as instances of the Marxist method, if there is one ... . Even today, not all of his insights have been exhausted (Elster 1986: 3).

> It (Marxism) set out to refute the proposition that ideas decisively determine the course of history but the very extent of its influence on human affairs has weakened the force of its thesis (Berlin 1963: 234).

Karl Heinrich Marx (1818–1883) was truly the last of the great critics in the Western intellectual tradition. His ideas exerted a decisive influence on all aspects of human endeavour, and transformed the study of history and society. They significantly changed anthropology, the arts, cultural studies, history, law, literature, philosophy, political economy, political theory and sociology by establishing a link between economic and intellectual life. By developing a theory of *praxis*, i.e. unity of thought and action, Marx brought about a sea change in the entire methodology of the social sciences. He was "a brilliant agitator and polemicist, a profound economist, a great sociologist, an incomparable historian. Marx was the first thinker to bring together the various strands of socialist thought into both a coherent world view and an impassioned doctrine of struggle" (Howe 1972: 4–5).

However, from its very inception Marxism was faced with a variety of criticism and critical acclaim. In fact, the controversies within Marxism are such that Marxism, like Liberalism, has become an umbrella ideology. In the context of Marx's writings, scholars spoke of two Marx: the young and the old. The young Marx was concerned with alienation, human nature and morality; the old was more deterministic, with his in-depth study of the workings of capitalism (Althusser 1969; McLellan 1971). The link between the two was the *Grundrisse* (1857–1858) and the *Introduction to the Critique of Political Economy* (1859).

Another crucial fact was that four of Marx's writings were written in collaboration with Friedrich Engels (1820–1895), his friend and comrade. After Marx's death, Engels edited and published some of his works as Marx's disciple, raising questions about how much was Marx's original, and what were Engels' interpretations. It is generally believed that Marx generalized on the basis of particular events, i.e. from the particular to the general. Engels on the other hand was more deterministic, analyzing from the general to the particular (Carver 1981). Engels acknowledged Marx as a genius, while, at best, he was talented. Marx was an innovator, and Engels the popularizer.

To comprehend the major thrust of Marx's political philosophy that aimed at human liberation, it is noteworthy to take into account the significant shift that occurred in the late seventeenth century when traditional analysis of the political order based on scarcity was replaced by a philosophy of abundance. This meant that poverty and disparities once seen as natural, inherent and inevitable were now considered man made and hence solvable (Arendt 1973: 22–23). The liberal writings of Locke and Jefferson reflected this libertarian dimension. However, the failure of early liberalism to fulfil its own promise led to the crystallization of socialist ideas (Watkins 1961: 43).

The liberal theory hinged on two principles, namely politics as involving non-coercive solutions to antagonistic interests, and the importance of democratic methods as being effective in making these adjustments. Though it took cognizance of the Hegelian critique of individualism, it did not accept two of its major assumptions. The first was that society moved, balancing the antithetical forces which generated social change by their schisms and strifes, and second, that social history was inherent in the very forces that generated them. These aspects of Hegelian philosophy played a pivotal role in the political theory of the nineteenth century, and later primarily due to the transformation brought about by Marx. Conflict played a crucial role in both Hegelian and Marxist political theory, thereby ruling out peaceful adjustment for the mutual advantage of the contending parties.

Marx interpreted liberalism and classical economics as articulating and defending the interests of the middle class. He proposed to create a social philosophy that was in tune with the aspirations of the rising proletariat. Like Hegel, he looked upon the French Revolution as an indication of the demise of feudalism, but while Hegel contended that the Revolution would culminate in the emergence of nation states, Marx looked upon it as a prelude to a more fundamental and total revolution beyond the nation states. The French Revolution, which brought the middle class to the forefront with the destruction of the nobility, was essentially a *political* revolution. The next step to be undertaken was a *social* revolution which would be brought about by the proletariat. It should be pointed out that Francois Noel Gracchus Babeuf (1760–1797) was the first to point out the contradictions within the revolutionary slogans of liberty and equality. He advocated socialization of industry and land to complete the Revolution that began in France in 1789.

Socialism carried forward the Libertarian element of early Liberalism in its call for total human emancipation. Marx disparagingly dubbed the Socialists who preceded him as "Utopians", for their emphasis on class harmony and non-revolutionary politics. The label "Utopian socialists" was first used by Jerome Blanqui in the *History of Political Economy* (1839). Marx learnt a lot from these Utopian socialists, and borrowed more of their ideas than he ever cared to admit. The relationship between the early Socialists and Marx was similar to the one that Plato shared with the Sophists. Like Marx, Plato disparaged Sophism, but was indebted to its ideas. Marx described his socialism as "scientific". Having studied the laws of social development and of capitalism, he sought to prove that the destruction of capitalism was inevitable, for it had given rise to its own "grave diggers".

Some of the ideas that the early Socialists articulated were a centrally planned economy, equal income, production for use and common good, and not for profit, common ownership of property, and moral indignation at inequities and injustices between the possessing and the non-propertied classes. They looked down on capitalism as a wasteful and inefficient system, for it led to poverty, unemployment and squalor. Capitalism was evil because it produced a class-divided society. It made human beings selfish, acquisitive and ruthlessly competitive, making them lose their natural instincts of compassion, fellow-feeling and solidarity. Their critique of capitalism was both practical and ethical. Many, in fact nearly all these ideas were reiterated by Marx, except that he proved that the destruction of capitalism was inevitable because of certain consequences it produced. The early Socialists, on the contrary, sought to bring about the desired changes by appealing to the feelings of human brotherhood and solidarity. They could not visualize the mechanisms of changing capitalism, as they wrote at a time when it was too early to foresee the course of development of capitalism. Their credit lay in the fact that they did not harp on a golden age of the past of a pre-capitalist period, but were aware of the fact that there was no going back in history. Instead, they chose to humanize contemporary reality. Marx

> was the first spokesman for socialism to remove the earlier Utopian fantasies and eccentricities, the first to present the socialist ideal not as a mere pleasing dream but as a historically realizable goal, indeed as a goal that history had brought to the very threshold of possibility (Howe 1972: 5).

Marx inherited and integrated three legacies—German philosophy, French political thought and English economics—in his theoretical construct.

From the German intellectual tradition, he borrowed the Hegelian method of dialectics and applied it to the material world. From the French Revolutionary tradition, he accepted the idea that apocalyptic change motivated by a "messianic" idea was not only desirable, but also feasible. He applied his method with a view to bringing about large-scale changes within the industrialized capitalist economy, of which England was the classic model in the nineteenth century. He used the writings of the English classical economists to understand the dynamics of capitalism and the Industrial Revolution (Nisbet 1969). He believed that historical movement took place according to laws that were similar to the ones found in the natural world. In the preface to the *Capital* (1861–1879), he spoke of the "natural laws of capitalist production". England, being the most developed society in his time, was the subject of his study. The purpose of his focus was to lay down, the road other societies would travel.

> Intrinsically, it is not a question of the higher or lower degree of development of the social antagonisms that result from the natural laws of capitalist production. It is a question of these laws themselves, of these tendencies working with iron necessity towards inevitable results. The country that is more developed industrially only shows to the less developed, the image of its own future (Marx 1975: 1, 8–9).

The emphasis on action and revolution made Marx a philosopher, a social scientist and a revolutionary. Though he used Hegelian concepts, he gave them very different meanings. The critique of Hegelian idealism and the materialist interpretation of history—the core of Marxism—crystallized in the writings of Marx in the early part of his adult life. His early writings (the poems written to Jenny von Westphalen and his doctoral thesis entitled *The Difference between the Democritean and Epicurean Philosophies of Nature* [1839–1841]) contained the genesis of Marxist theory. He acknowledged Hegel to be a "Giant thinker", but his poems and doctoral thesis showed his dissatisfaction with German (and, in particular, Hegelian) idealism, though in many respects he continued with Hegelian philosophy.

> Marx removed from Hegel's theory the assumption that national cultures are the effective units of social history—an assumption that never had any close logical relation to his system—and replaced the struggle of nations with the struggle of social classes. Thus he took away from Hegelianism its distinctive qualities as a political theory—its nationalism, its conservatism and its counter-revolutionary character—and transformed it into a new and very powerful type of revolutionary radicalism. Marxism became the progenitor of the more important modifications to be, of present day communism (Sabine 1973: 681).

LIFE SKETCH

Marx was born on March 5, 1818 in the predominantly Catholic city of Trier in the Rhineland in a Jewish family. His father Heinrich, a son of

Marx Levi, was a rabbi in Trier. The surname Marx was the abbreviated form of Mordechai, later changed to Markus. The paternal side had an illustrious ancestry. Heinrich's father was a successful lawyer. His uncle Lion Philips was a successful businessman who later founded the famous Philips Electric Company. Heinrich converted himself to Lutheranism in 1817, but did not abandon his religion. His wife Henriette converted herself in 1825. Karl converted himself in 1824. Perhaps it was the consciousness of his Jewish background that heightened his awareness about "his sense of marginality, his ambivalence toward society, and eventually of his conflicting qualities—thinker and prophet, scientist and moralist" (Rubel 1968: 35).

Marx studied law at the University of Bonn in 1835 and at the University of Berlin in 1836. He changed his course to philosophy under the influence of the young Hegelians. He completed his doctorate in philosophy in 1841. The accession of Wilhelm IV in 1840 sealed Marx's prospects for an academic career. Marx married his childhood sweetheart, Jenny, daughter of Baron Ludwig von Westphalen, his spiritual guide since his adolescence in 1843. Jenny (six years older than Marx) and Marx married after a seven-year period of courtship. Together, they led a hard but happy life, though Jenny was known to have remarked that instead of writing the *Capital,* Marx could have made money.

From 1842 to 1848, Marx edited radical publications in the Rhineland, Belgium and France. He became the editor of the liberal *Rheinische Zeitung* which he remained till 1843. In 1844, while in Paris, he became interested in the working-class movement and political economy. Around this time, Marx and Engels began working on the *German Ideology* (1847).

In 1848, Marx and Engels helped in the founding of the Communist League, which existed till 1850. In 1848, Marx was expelled from the Prussian territories, compelling him to move to London, where he stayed till the end of his life. He worked and studied in the British Museum from 1850 to 1860. There was no evidence that Marx actually spoke to peasants, workers or landowners. Though he wrote about industrial and financial processes, he knew only two who were connected with them—his Uncle Philips and friend Engels (Johnson 1988: 60). He wrote for the *New York Tribune,* which paid one pound for each of his articles, and that was his only regular income. He was helped financially by Engels. He lived a life of poverty, the reason being attributed to mishandling of money (Johnson ibid: 73). Three of his six children died of want. His own health did not remain well. Jenny died in 1881. She played an extremely helpful role by editing Marx's manuscripts and preparing them for publication. Marx died on March 14, 1883. He was buried at the Highgate cemetery in London. His death went unnoticed in Britain. It was the London correspondent in Paris who reported his death, which was featured in the *London Times.*

MARX AS A POET

The poetic phase of Marx was short-lived. In his later life he did not show much interest in his own poems, though his interests in poetry in general continued. Marx was well-versed with the works of contemporary German poets and those of Shakespeare. This interest was further reinforced by his father Heinrich Marx and his mentor Baron von Westphalen. During his student years in Bonn University, Marx belonged to the poet's club. Even after he moved to Berlin, his interest in poetry continued. During this time he attempted to write fiction and a tragedy. Unfortunately, the poems written in the autumn of 1836 were lost. The ones that survived, written sometime in the early part of 1837, were also those that were dedicated to Jenny.

Marx's poems were not amongst his well-known works. His overall lack of interest in his poems was because everything seemed vague and diffused. In 1929, about 60 of his poems were discovered and published. However, this did not arouse much interest among Marxist scholars, as Marx had disowned their significance and importance from the point of view of revolutionary activity. These poems, as his early biographer Franz Mehring (1846-1919) admitted, "breathe(d) a spirit of trivial romanticism, and very seldom does any true note ring through".

A dissection of Marx's poems revealed his resolve for purposeful activity, signalling the beginning of Marx the revolutionary. This was evident from the following poem.

Never can I calmly realise,
What steadfastly grips my soul;
Never can I rest in comfort,
Storms forever through me roll.

Continuing with his revolt against abstract thought and his repudiation of German idealism, Marx wrote:

Kant and Fichte like to whirl in the ether,
Searching for a distant land;
While I only seek to understand completely,
What I found in this street.

Some of his epigrams revealed his dissatisfaction with the unrealism of Hegelian idealism, for it ignored realities and depicted the non-existent.

Pardon us creatures of epigram,
If we sing disagreeable tunes;
We have schooled ourselves in Hegel,
And from his aesthetics we have not yet been purged.
Because I have discovered the highest.
And found the depths by pondering;

I am roughen like a god, I hide in darkness, like him,
Long I searched and floated over the rocking sea of thoughts,
And when I found the word, I clung fast to what I had found.
Words I teach in a demonically confused to-do.
At least he will never more be restricted by limiting fetters,
For as out of a roaring flood pouring from a projecting rock;
The poet invents the words and thoughts of his beloved.
And perceives what he thinks and thinks what he feels;
Everyone can sip the refreshing nectar of wisdom,
After all, I am telling you everything because I have told you nothing.

The concept of alienation that was Marx's concern during his early years was clearly depicted in his poem *The Player* (1840), and in *Oulanem*, a poetic tragedy. While in these, he understood alienation as an individual phenomenon, in the *Manuscripts* (1844) he saw it as a feature of society. Though the poems were written in the formative years, they indicated the direction of Marx's subsequent thought.

MARX'S DOCTORAL DISSERTATION

Marx was not a direct disciple of Hegel, but his interest in Hegelian doctrines stemmed from his encounter with the Young Hegelians in the Doctors Club. It was during his discussions in the Doctors Club that Marx got interested in contemporary philosophy. The Young Hegelians were radical in their outlook. They were an amorphous group in Germany in the 1830s and 1840s, consisting of Bruno Bauer, Karl Kopper and Adolf Rutenderg. Among them, Bauer influenced Marx the most. Initially, the Young Hegelians were interested in religious questions, but with the accession of Frederick William IV and the relaxation of press censorship, they renewed their political debates. In philosophy, they could be described as speculative rationalists, for they believed in the continuous unfolding of the power of reason. They professed a deep admiration for the principles of the French Revolution. They were concerned with the individual's self-consciousness and its development. Their position was similar to that of the Epicureans, Skeptics and Stoics, the post-Aristotelian philosophers whom Marx described as rich in spirit.

The Young Hegelians regarded the post-Aristotelian philosophies as providing the foundations of modern thought, as precursors of the philosophy of self-awareness or consciousness. These philosophies emerged at a time when Rome was established drawing from the Greek heritage. The Greco-Roman tradition influenced the rise of Christianity and identified the principles of rationalism, akin to the ones in eighteenth-century Enlightenment. There were similarities between the post-Aristotelian and post-Hegelian philosophies, for both of them were preceded by the "total philosophies" of Plato, Aristotle and Hegel respectively. Marx felt that the choice before the Hegelians was either a feeble imitation of Hegel, or a deflection of the direction of philosophy. The dominant influence of Hegel in the 1830s and 1840s was acknowledged by Engels in the following words.

> ... the Hegelian system covered an incomparably greater domain than any earlier system and developed in this domain a wealth of thought which is astounding even today.... One can imagine what a tremendous effect this Hegelian system must have produced in the philosophy-tinged atmosphere of Germany. It was a triumphal procession which lasted for decades and which by no means came to a standstill on the death of Hegel. On the contrary, it was precisely from 1830 to 1840 that "Hegelianism" reigned most exclusively, and to a greater or lesser extent infected even its opponents (Engels cited in Singer 1980: 11).

Marx's choice of a comparative study of the philosophical systems of Epicures and of the Democritus (460–370 BC) was partly because of the influence of the Young Hegelians (whose company he enjoyed), and partly because of his quest of relating philosophy to the external world with a view to liberating the individual from all shackles through the power of reason. Marx criticized Hegel for belittling the contributions made by the post-Aristotelian philosophies. He contended that these theories held the "key to the true history of Greek Philosophy". In his doctoral thesis, Marx dealt with the relationship between Epicureanism and Stoicism, the concept of the sage in Greek philosophy, the ideas of Socrates and Plato on religion and the prospects of philosophy in the post-Hegelian period. Its appendix included Plutarch's critique of Epicures and two lengthy notes on Hegel and Schelling.

Marx contended that the task of philosophical criticism was to expose the hindrances to the process of free development of human self-consciousness. The idea of human liberation ran through Marxist thought as a guiding force. Marx contended that the human mind was dynamic and capable of comprehending the external world, thereby criticizing those who argued that human beings were incapable of understanding the world around, and therefore had to blindly accept what appeared to be incognito phenomena. Marx was attracted by Epicurean philosophy for the spirit of freedom and independence of thought that it advocated. By this time, Marx began to perceive the transformative power of philosophy to change human society. Philosophy, in the process, would cease to be pure theory, as it would manifest itself in practical activity.

Marx characterized Epicures as a genuinely radical and enlightened mind of antiquity. In contrast to Democritus, Epicures provided energizing principles by introducing an element of spontaneity in the movements of, atoms, rather than regarding nature as inanimate, governed by mechanical laws. The two achievements of Epicures, according to Marx, were: (a) emphasis on absolute autonomy of the human spirit, freeing men from all superstitions of transcendent objects; and (b) emphasis on free, individual self-consciousness. Both these factors helped in circumventing the limits imposed by a "total philosophy". It was the liberating aspect of Epicures that Marx found endearing. Marx tried to refute Plutarch's critique of Epicures, examining each statement with a view to formulating a diametrically opposite conclusion.

DIALECTICS

Dialectics was the key idea in Hegelian philosophy, though Engels credited Heraclitus with its origins when he held that "Everything is and is not, for everything is fluid, is constantly changing, constantly coming into being and passing away. All is flux and nothing stays still. Nothing endures but change." It was Hegel who offered a systematic exposition of the concept. In Hegelian philosophy, dialectics applied to the process, evolution and development of history. Hegel viewed history as the progressive manifestation of human reason, and the development of a historical spirit. History recorded increasing awareness and greater rationality as exhibited in human affairs. Human consciousness and freedom expanded as a result of conflicting intellectual forces, which were constantly under tension. Hegel believed in a movement from a rudimentary state of affairs to a perfect form.

The process of history, for Hegel, was marked by two kinds of causation: (a) *the individual spirit* which desired happiness and provided energy, and (b) *the world spirit* which strived for higher freedom, that came with the knowledge of the self. He emphatically believed that without each individual pursuing his own goal(s), whatever they might be, nothing was achieved in history. But to know whether these actions were in conformity with the dialectic of the universal, "the cunning of reason" played its role by allowing passions to run their full course.

Marx agreed with Hegel that there was a constant movement in the dialectical process, but emphasized the *real* rather than the *ideal*, the *social* rather than the *intellectual, matter* rather than the *mind*. For Marx, the key idea was not the history of philosophy, but the history of economic production and the social relations that accompanied it. He acknowledged Hegel's great contribution, which was to recognize world history as a process, as constant motion, change, transformation, and development, and to understand the internal connections between the movement and its development. From Hegel, he also learnt that the various angles of the developmental process could not be studied in isolation, but in their relations with one another and with the process as a whole- Hegel applied dialectics to the realm of ideas. However, Marx as a materialist believed that consciousness was determined by life, and not the other way around. Unlike the latent conservatism and idealism of Hegelian philosophy, Marxism rejected the status quo—capitalism—as intolerable. Social circumstances constantly changed, with no social system lasting forever.

Capitalism arose under certain historical circumstances, which would disappear in due course of time. Thus Marx, like Hegel, continued to believe that dialectics was a powerful tool. It offered a law of social development, and in that sense Marx's social philosophy (like that of Hegel) was a philosophy of history. Both perceived social change as inevitable.

MATERIALISM AND HISTORY

Marx applied his dialectical method to the material or social world that consisted of economic production and exchange. A study of the productive process explained all other historical phenomena. Marx noted that each generation inherited a mass of productive forces, an accumulation of capital, and a set of social relations which reflected these productive forces. The new generation modified these forces, but at the same time these forces prescribed certain forms of life, and shaped human character and thought in distinct ways. The mode of production and exchange was the final cause of all social changes and political revolutions, which meant that for minds or thoughts to change, society would have to change. Marx considered matter as being active, capable of changing from within. It was not passive, needing an external stimulus for change, a conception found in Hobbes.

> Our conception of history depends on our ability to expound the real processes of production, starting out from the simple material production of life, and to comprehend the form of intercourse connected with this and created by this (i.e. civil society in its various stages), as the basis of all history; further, to show it in its action as state, and so, from this starting point, to explain the whole mass of different theoretical products and forms of consciousness, religion, philosophy, ethics, etc., and trace their origins and growth (Marx 1977a: 35).

While Hegel viewed national cultures as the driving force of history, for Marx it was the social classes whose antagonism supplied the motive power for change. Both regarded the historical course as a rational necessity consisting of a pattern of stages, with each stage representing a step towards the predetermined goal. Both appealed to an emotion above self-interest: in the case of Hegel it was national pride; for Marx the loyalty among workers for a better future. Marx was initially enthused by Darwin's *Origin of Species*, but subsequently dismissed it as strictly an empirical generalization offering a causal theory of change with no implied idea of progress. Hegelian dialectics, on the contrary, offered a law with a definite beginning and an end, "a condition towards which society is progressing, a condition of complete harmony and integration in which man will discover his time fulfilled nature" (Caute 1967: 17).

Marx attacked the formidable Hegelian philosophy from within with the help of the writings of Ludwig Andreas Feuerbach (1804–1872).

Feuerbach, in *The Essence of Christianity* (1843), rejected the theory that subject and object condition influenced each other, declaring that comprehension of things was primarily sensual and passive, and only secondarily active and conceptual. As a result, he saw religion as the basis of all social evils. The more an individual enriched the concept of God, the more he impoverished the self. In his later works, Feuerbach went beyond the criticism of religion, subjecting Hegelian philosophy to a critical analysis. Hegel viewed the mind as the moving force of history, and humans as its manifestations. This, according to Feuerbach, located the essence of humanity *outside* human beings, and thus, like religion, served to alienate humanity from itself. He emphatically insisted that philosophy had to begin with the finite and the material world; thought did not precede existence, it was existence that preceded thought. In Feuerbach's philosophy, it was neither God nor thought, but the individual who was the focus.

The atheistic bent of Marx was reinforced by Feuerbach's humanistic critique of Hegelian dialectics, enabling him to move away from idealism towards materialism. Using Feuerbach's transformative method, Marx criticized Hegel for inverting the relationship between the predicate and the subject. The individual, in Hegel's philosophy, instead of remaining a real subject was turned into a predicate of universal substance. Marx pointed out that belief in God derived from attributing human virtues to an illusory subject, rather than to the human being. Just as religion did not make people, similarly a constitution did not shape people. On the contrary, both religion and constitution were made by the people. By this logic, the material world could be *transformed*, rather than just being *understood*. The task of philosophy was to be critical, and participate in that transformation. As he observed in the eleventh *Theses on Feuerbach* (1845) "The philosophers have only interpreted the world in various ways; the point, however is to change it" (Marx 1977a: 125).

Marx criticized Feuerbach for reducing religion to its secular origins, without offering an explanation of the duality in human existence. He rejected Feuerbach's materialism as passive, for objects were seen in a contemplative way rather than as "sensuous, practical human activity". Since materialists like Feuerbach failed to offer an effective cure, idealism developed the active side of matter in an abstract way. The mind could be freed from mystification only if the negativities of social life were removed through practical action. Hence Marx began with the conception of socialized humanity, rather than the civil society of old materialism. He replaced God with money in *On The Jewish Question* (1848).

> Money is the universal, self contained value of all things. Hence it has robbed the whole world, the human world as well as nature, of its proper value. Money is the alienate essence of man's labour and life, and this alien essence dominated him as he worships it (Marx ibid: 60).

From a materialist perspective, Marx analyzed the economic mode of production the way people actually lived and engaged in production. In the *German Ideology,* Marx and Engels wrote:

> We must begin by stating the first premise of all human existence, and therefore of all history, the premise namely that men must be in a position to live in order to be able to "make history". But life involves before everything else eating and drinking, a habitation, clothing and many other things. The first historical act is thus the production of the means to satisfy these needs, the production of material life itself. And indeed this is an historical act, a fundamental condition of all history, which today as thousands of years ago, must daily and hourly be fulfilled merely in order to sustain human life (Marx ibid: 238).

Marx, in his analysis of history, mentioned the important role of ideology in perpetuating false consciousness among people, and demarcated the stages which were necessary for reaching the goal of Communism. In that sense, both the bourgeoisie and the proletariat were performing their historically destined roles. In spite of the deterministic interpretation of history, the individual had to play a very important role within the historical limits of his time, and actively hasten the process.

Marx was a revolutionary with a belief in the philosophy of praxis. Implicit in his belief was an underlying assumption of a law operating all the time which led to Engels' formulation of the dialectics of nature. This alteration changed the very essence of Marx's method of arriving at a conclusion from a particular event or a happening, to a general theory or framework determining even the small happenings.

Marx had a very powerful moral content in his analysis, and asserted that progress was not merely inevitable, but would usher in a perfect society free of alienation, exploitation and deprivation. His materialistic conception of history emphasized the practical side of human activity, rather than speculative thought as the moving force of history. In the famous funeral oration speech, Engels claimed that Marx made two major discoveries—the law of development of human history and the law of capitalist development.

ECONOMIC DETERMINISM

Marx and Engels developed the materialistic conception of history to explain the law of human development. Engels specifically linked the enterprise to Darwin's theory of evolution. The underlying assumption of the materialistic conception was the role played by economic factors, which formed the base. Everything else belonged to the superstructure, which consisted of the state, the law, government, art, culture and philosophy. Like Hegel, Marx saw history as progressing towards a definitive and inevitable goal. In the sequence of world history, England represented the "unconscious tool of history".

> Our conception of history depends on our ability to expound the real processes of production, starting out from the simple material production of life, and to comprehend the form of intercourse connected with this and created by this (i.e., civil society in its various stages), as the basis of all history; further, to show it in its action as state, and so, from this starting point to explain the whole mass of different theoretical products and forms of consciousness, religion, philosophy, ethics, etc., and trace their origins and growth (Marx 1975: 35).

Marx regarded the mode of production as the economic base, the real foundation of society. The mode of production consisted of the means or techniques of production, and the relationships that people entered into with one another for production of goods and services. The economic base conditioned and determined the superstructure. Writing in the *German Ideology*, he observed: "It is not the consciousness of men that determines their existence, but, on the contrary, their social existence determines their existence" (Marx 1977a: 242).

When the economic basis of society changed, there was a change in consciousness. Changes within the economic base brought about consequent changes within the superstructure. Marx observed:

> At a certain stage of their development the material forces of production in society come into conflict with the existing relations of production, or—what is but a legal expression for the same thing—with the property relations within which they had been at work before. From forms of development of the forces of production these relations turn into their fetter. Then comes the period of social revolution. With the change of the economic foundation the entire superstructure is more or less rapidly transformed (Marx ibid: 248).

Marx's materialism referred not only to matter, but also to economic and social relations. He said the material forces of production came into conflict with the relations of production, but did not explain the nature of that conflict, other than alluding to the fact that it could be a moral one. It was moral, for it desired to create a humane and decent society free of exploitation, domination and oppression.

Marx identified five stages of economic development known to history. These were Primitive Communism, Slavery, Feudalism, Capitalism, and Communism. In each of these stages (except for the final one), there were forces of contradiction which made revolutions inevitable. The given status quo would be the thesis with conflict(s) symptomatic of an antithesis, and a solution in the form of a synthesis. The synthesis in turn would become the thesis, and the process continued till a perfect society was attained.

For Marx and Engels, it was not enough to understand the general processes of history, but also the way these processes worked themselves out in the present. If one desired to transform the world, then a correct diagnosis of the prevailing social conditions was necessary. In the nineteenth century, this meant an understanding of the working of bourgeois society, a study of the sociology of capitalism. Capitalism created unavoidable suffering, which ought to be replaced first by Socialism and then Communism.

CLASS STRUGGLE AND SOCIAL CHANGE

Marx articulated the idea of human liberation distinct from political emancipation. The aim of human liberation was to bring forth the collective, generic character of human life which was real, so that society would have to assume a collective character and coincide with the life of the state. This would be possible if individuals were freed from religion and private property. The proletariat, by being the universal class in chains, would liberate itself and human society. Relations of production in reality were class relations. Class antagonisms were crucial to the workings of all societies, as Marx observed that, "the history of all hitherto existing society is the history of class struggles" (Marx 1977b: 109).

In every society there were two classes, the rich and the poor, one that owned the means of production, and the other that sold its labour. During different historical phases, these two classes were known by different names and enjoyed different legal statuses and privileges, but one thing was common, that in the course of all these phases, their relationship had been one of exploitation and domination. Marx wrote: "Freeman and slave, patrician and plebeian, lord and serf, guild-master and journeyman, in a word, oppressor and oppressed, stood in constant opposition to one another" (Marx ibid: 109).

Marx objected to the idea of the middle-class historians that class struggle had ended with the rise of the bourgeoisie, just as he opposed the perceptions of the Classical economists that capitalism was eternal and immutable. He harnessed the rising consciousness and power among the industrial proletariat, and emphasized that it was their desire to bring about economic equality that kept class struggle and revolutionary change alive. He summed up his own contributions to the notion of class struggle in a letter to Josef Weydemeyer in 1852, wherein he confidently declared that class struggles would not be a permanent feature of society, but were necessitated by the historical development of production. Class struggle would end with the destruction of capitalism, for Communism would be a classless society.

Class, for Marx, symbolized collective unity in the same manner as the nation in Hegel's theory. Each class produced its own ideas and beliefs, and operated within a particular economic and social system. The individual was important with respect to his membership within a class, which determined his moral convictions, aesthetic preferences and every kind of reasoning.

For Marx, ideology played a pivotal role in controlling the oppressed. There were three main features of ideas. First, they depicted the existing order as entrenched in forces that were beyond human control. Things were not arbitrary, but instituted by certain sections of people for their own benefit. Second, ideas explained how the existing order benefited everyone in society. Third, ideas depicted the existing order as beneficial in a particular way, namely to promote the interests of the dominant economic class and protect class privileges. The actual reality was hidden, which Marx described as "false consciousness".

> The ideas of the ruling class are in every epoch the ruling ideas: i.e., the class which is the ruling material force of society, is at the same time its ruling intellectual force. The class which has the means of material production at its disposal, has control at the same time over the means of mental production, so that thereby, generally speaking, the ideas of those who lack the means of mental production are subject to it. The ruling ideas are nothing more than the ideal expression of the dominant material relationships, the dominant material relationships grasped as ideas; hence of the relationship which make the one class the ruling one, therefore the ideas of its dominance (Marx 1977a: 245).

Ideology, along with economic determinism and class struggle, provided the strategic guide to the working class in its efforts to bring about a social revolution.

ANALYSIS OF CAPITALISM

Marx defined capitalism by two factors, first, by the use of wage labour. In the *Capital,* he pointed out that "capitalism arises only when the owners of the means of production and subsistence meet in the market with the free labourer selling his labour power". The basis of capitalism was wage labour. The second defining characteristic of capitalism was private ownership of the means of production, which was distinct from personal property, like household effects and home. The ownership of the means of production was the crucial feature of capitalism, for it was restricted to a few. Those who did not own anything were forced to sell their labour power and became wage earners. The idea that labour was only the property of the poor was derived from William Cobbett (1763–1835). Unlike the medieval guildsmen, they did not work for themselves but for others. Marx observed:

> The man who possesses no other property than his labour power must, in all conditions of society and culture, be the slave of other men, who have made themselves the owners of the material conditions of labour. He can work only with their permission, hence live only with their permission (Marx ibid: 228).

In the *Critique of the Gotha Programme* (1875), Marx implied that even if the state owned the means of production, wage labour would still continue. This was not real Socialism, but a new variation of capitalism, namely state capitalism. Many critics often argued that the former Soviet Union was not a true Socialist state, but a tyrannous form of state capitalism.

In the *Communist Manifesto* (1848), Marx paid handsome tributes to the bourgeoisie, while highlighting its negative side. There were three reasons that made capitalism attractive. First, it brought remarkable economic progress by revolutionizing the means of production and developing technology as never before. It built and encouraged the growth of commerce and factories on a scale unknown before. It instituted cooperative social production. Writing about the role of the bourgeoisie, Marx observed:

> The bourgeoisie, during its rule of scarce one hundred years, has created more massive and more colossal productive force than have all preceding generations together. Subjections of Nature's force to man, machinery, application of chemistry to industry and agriculture, steam-navigation, railways, electric telegraphs, clearing of whole continents for cultivation, canalization of rivers, whole populations conjured out of the ground—what earlier century had even a presentiment that such productive forces slumbered in the lap of social labour?
>
> It had accomplished wonders far surpassing Egyptian pyramids, Roman aqueducts and Gothic cathedrals; it has conducted expeditions that put in the shade all former exoduses of nations and crusades (Marx 1975: 35).

By the very range and extent of its activity, capitalism made its second contribution. It undermined national barriers. In its search for markets and raw materials, capitalism and the bourgeoisie crossed national boundaries and penetrated every corner of the world, drawing the most backward nations into their fold. Capitalism was cosmopolitan and international.

Being worldwide, the third achievement of capitalism was within its territorial confines. It eliminated the distinction between the town and country, and enabled the peasants to come out of what Marx called "the idiocy of rural life". In summation, capitalism revolutionized the techniques of economic production, reduced international barriers and created an urban civilization. In spite of these achievements, Marx contended that capitalism had outlived its use because of the sufferings and hardships it caused. It would have to yield itself to a new socialist organization of production.

Marx examined the sufferings within capitalism, which were rooted in its origin: the eviction of peasants from their land, the loss of their sources of income, their vagabondage, their assembling in cities where they had become dependent on starvation wages, and, most significantly, the creation of the proletariat.

> The historical movement which changes the producers into wage-workers appears, on the one hand, as their emancipation from serfdom and from the fetters of the guilds, and this side alone exists for our

> bourgeois historians. But, on the other hand, these new freemen became sellers of themselves only after they had been robbed of all their own means of production, and of all the guarantees of existence afforded by the old feudal arrangements. And the history of this, their expropriation, is written in the annals of mankind in letters of blood and fire (Marx 1977b: 272).

The suffering required for the creation of the free-wage labourer was the first cost of capitalism. The exploitation of the proletariat could be measured with the help of surplus value—the difference between the wages paid to the labourer, and the final price for which the product was sold. The rate of profit indicated the degree of exploitation. The capitalist squeezed the working class like a sponge to extract the last drop of profit. Exploitation, therefore, was the second disadvantage of capitalism.

The third was the alienation of the worker. To Marx, labour had to be satisfying and fulfilling, which was not possible under capitalism. The reason was the lack of control the worker had over the productive process. The worker had no voice to decide when, how and where to work, but merely obeyed the boss' commands. Division of labour and specialization of skills had made the worker a specialist, preventing the full development of all his talents, thereby stifling his potential. A labourer had no control over the final product of his labour. The nature of the productive process divided workers and set them against one another; they no longer conceived of their work as a great, collective, human project. Moreover, human beings lost the ability to see their own products for what they were, and were willing to be enslaved by them. This was what Marx meant by commodity fetishism. All this criticism rested on an implicit Utopian premise, that individuals were fully human only when they developed and expressed their potential through satisfying labour. Linked with this premise was the second remarkable assumption, that the modern industrial system afforded opportunities for all to engage in rewarding labour. In the socialist Utopia, division of labour would be abolished ending alienation and monotony.

The early Liberals were confident that economic inequality could be obviated with constant growth, which would percolate downwards and raise the standards of living. Marx, however, pointed out that the gulf between the rich and poor forever widened. Capitalism encouraged inequality and consumerism. Commodities assumed personalities of their own. Poverty and affluence were relative categories, for human needs were by and large social in nature.

> A house may be large or small; as long as the surrounding houses are equally small it satisfies all social demands for a dwelling. But let a palace arise beside the little house, and it shrinks from a little house to a hut ... however high it may shoot up in the course of civilization, if the neighbouring palace grows to an equal or even greater extent, the occupant of the relatively small house will feel more and more uncomfortable, dissatisfied and cramped within its four walls (Marx ibid: 259).

To Marx, exploitation and alienation made possible the revolutionary transformation of capitalism. It was the individual as a producer who rebelled against society to free himself from exploitation and oppression. The basis for change was therefore moral. Unless private property was abolished, the worker could not be truly free. But once this was achieved, human nature would undergo a transformation, for a true Communist society was one of socialized humanity.

Capitalism divided society into two hostile camps. The proletariat grew larger and larger, with their miseries and pauperization attenuated, while the bourgeoisie would become numerically small, prosperous and well-off. With wages pushed low, small entrepreneurs were forced to join the working class or merge with giant monopolies. The ever-increasing appetite of the capitalist class led to an ever-increasing demand for markets, raw materials and profits, representing a crisis within capitalism. Marx argued that the increase in productivity did not benefit the worker, who only received *exchange,* and not *use value.* The surplus value was appropriated by the capitalist. With polarization of society, class struggles became sharper, making a revolution on a world scale inevitable. Marx conceived of a worldwide transformation, for capitalism was truly international and global in impact.

Marx asserted that capitalism contained within itself seeds of its own destruction. He rallied the working class under the call "Workers of all countries unite", a phrase that he borrowed from Karl Schapper. Within capitalism, increase in monopolies led to growing exploitation, misery and pauperization of the working class. Simultaneously, as the working class increased in number, it became better organized and acquired greater bargaining skills. This initiated a revolutionary process, leading to a new socialist arrangement in which common possession replaced private ownership of the means of production. The clarion call given to the workers was to unite, shed their chains and conquer the world. In fact, it was "Marx's journalistic eye for the short, pithy sentence which ... saved his entire philosophy from oblivion ..." (Johnson 1988: 56).

Subsequently, in 1895 Engels questioned the efficacy of revolutionary insurrection of society by the proletariat, for he observed that "history has proved us, and all who thought like us, wrong ... has also completely transformed the conditions under which the proletariat has to fight. The mode of struggle of 1848 is today obsolete in every respect". This observation by Engels set the tone for Revisionism led by Eduard Bernstein (1850–1932) (Elliot 1967).

ASSESSMENT OF MARX'S PREDICTIONS

Marx's analysis of capitalism led him to predict the following:

1. The income gap between the capitalists and the workers would increase. More and more independent producers would be forced

down into the proletariat, leaving a few rich capitalists and a mass of poor workers.

2. Workers' wages, with short-lived expectations, would remain at a subsistence level.
3. The rate of profit would fall.
4. Capitalism would collapse because of its internal contradictions.
5. Proletarian revolutions would occur in the most industrially advanced countries (Singer 1980: 67).

Many (nearly all) of these predictions, did not come true as Marx failed to take into account the changes within capitalism. He did not anticipate or comprehend its tremendous resilience. By the late nineteenth century, capitalism stabilized itself. Historical developments did not validate many of Marx's observations, which became increasingly obsolete in the twentieth century. Besides these, there was a basic error in the model which was that he failed to take cognizance of the fact that "a hatred of capitalism need not lead to socialism" (as it could) "take other political directions" (Shklar 1998: 86). The operationalization of democracy, extensive social security cover and labour welfare laws had improved the working conditions and the position of the working class. "The proletarian class no longer exists in its previous stage. Workers have rights in developed countries, they are proprietors" (Djilas 1990: 7).

In the 1890s, Bernstein rightly perceived that many of the Marxist predictions became obsolete. He pointed out that the peasantry and the middle classes were not disappearing. Small business organizations did not get eliminated, and the industrial working class was not becoming the overwhelming majority of the population. Instead, the substantial portion of the population was neither bourgeois nor proletarian. Rather, the middle class was on the increase. Among the members of the working class, the rapid growth in membership and votes for social democratic parties did not necessarily indicate any desire for Socialism. The workers voted and joined social democrats for many reasons other than purely a commitment for Socialism. Bernstein also questioned the capacity of the working class to assume control of the means of production.

Taking a cue from Webb, who had pointed out that the poor performance of the cooperative was because of its democratic character on the one hand, and the need for functional differentiation and hierarchy of authority on the other hand, Bernstein asserted the impossibility of the idea of the manager being "the employee of those he manages, that he should be dependent for his position on their favour and their bad temper" (Bernstein 1961: 65). Based on these observations, Bernstein pointed to the lack of revolutionary ardour among the workers. Instead of analyzing the economic and political implications of Revisionism, Vladimir Illyich Ulyanov Lenin (1870–1924) reiterated and supported the Marxist critique of capitalism, which had lost its relevance by the end of the nineteenth century, and more so by the beginning of the twentieth.

It would be tempting to denigrate the degeneration of the Marxist doctrine because the revolution that Marx predicted occurred in a relatively backward country in Europe, with no prior tradition of democracy. But it was equally true that there were no possibilities of a real Marxist revolution in any of the advanced industrial democratic regions of Europe. "Marx's economics has been characterized as a reaction to the specific evils of the nineteenth century of capitalism" (Dahl 1986: 69).

ANALYSIS OF THE STATE

Marx critically dissected the Hegelian theory of the modern state and its institutions in his *Critique of Hegel's Philosophy of Right* (1843). Hegel's separation of civil society and the state was only relevant in his perception of a particular historical context. The state was not eternal. It would eventually disappear. Marx was also critical of Hegel's analysis of the state. The state was not, as Hegel described, a "march of God on earth", but an instrument of the dominant economic class exploiting and oppressing the other sections of society. Marx rejected the dichotomy between civil society and the state in Hegelian philosophy, and concluded that the state and bureaucracy did not represent universal interests.

Marx regarded the state, regardless of the forms of government, as an evil, because it was a product of a society saddled with irreconcilable class struggles. It belonged to the realm of the superstructure, as it was conditioned and determined by its economic base. In the course of history, each mode of production would give rise to its own specific political organization, which would further the interests of the economically dominant class. In a capitalist society, the state, as defined in the *Manifesto*, was "the executive committee of the bourgeoisie".

Unlike Hegel, who had worked out the details of a modern state by his distinction of the realm of the state and the realm of civil society, Marx's account was sketchy. This was in spite of Marx's professed aim to provide for an alternative to the Hegelian paradigm as outlined in his *Critique of Hegel's Philosophy of Right*. The alternative that Marx envisaged was a classless, stateless society of true democracy and full communism, in which the political state disappeared.

For Marx and Engels, the state expressed human alienation. It was an instrument of class exploitation and class oppression, for the economically dominant class exploited and oppressed the economically weaker class. The state apparatus served the ruling class, but acquired independence and became autonomous when the adversary classes were in a state of temporary equilibrium. This phenomenon was described as Bonapartism. In such a situation, the dictator, with the support of the state apparatus, became its guardian.

In the *Anti Duhring* (1878), Engels regarded the state as an unnatural institution arising when society was divided into "two irreconcilable and antagonistic classes". In such a situation, a state could not be democratic, for *a true democratic society would have to be both classless and stateless.* The instruments of the state, like law, government, police and bureaucracy, served the interests of the dominant economic class, and not the whole of society as contended by the liberals.

Bonapartism

In the *Eighteenth Brumaire of Louis Bonaparte* (1852), Marx denounced the bureaucratic and all-powerful state advising the proletariat to destroy it. His views on the state were determined largely by his perceptions and analyses of the French state, the Revolution of 1848 and the *coup d'etat* of Napoleon III. As a result, Marx advocated a violent revolutionary seizure of power and the establishment of the dictatorship of the proletariat. However, in countries with democratic institutions, the transition from capitalism to socialism could be peaceful. In 1872, Marx noted such a possibility in America, England and Holland, where the state was not as highly centralized and bureaucratic as in France.

In the *Eighteenth Brumaire,* Marx and Engels referred to Bonapartism as a regime in a capitalist society in which the executive branch of the state, under the rule of one individual, attained dictatorial power over all other parts of the state and society. Bonapartism was an extreme manifestation of what, in recent Marxist writings, was described as relative autonomy of the state (Poulantaz 1973). An example of such a regime during Marx's lifetime was that of Louis Bonaparte, the nephew of Napoleon I, who became Napoleon III after his *coup d'etat* of December 2, 1851. Engels found a parallel with Bismarck's rule in Germany.

Bonapartism was the result of a situation where the ruling class in capitalist society was no longer in a position to maintain its rule through constitutional and parliamentary means. Neither was the working class able to wrest control for itself. It was a situation of temporary equilibrium between the rival warring classes. In the *Civil War in France* (1871), Marx described Bonapartism as a "form of government possible at a time when the bourgeoisie had already lost, and the working class had not yet acquired, the faculty of ruling the nation" (Marx 1977b: ch. 3).

In the *Origins of the Family, Private Property and the State* (1884), Engels remarked that the state was generally a tool of the ruling class, but there were exceptional times when the warring classes balanced one another, giving it sufficient independence. The independence of a Bonapartist state, and its role as the "ostensible mediator" between the rival classes did not mean that the state was in a position of suspended animation. The Bonapartist state, in reality, ensured the safety and stability of bourgeois society, guaranteeing its rapid development.

In opposition to the German Federalists, in 1848 Marx and Engels contended that a strong centre was a prerequisite of all modern states.

They criticized the Frankfurt Assembly for not creating a sufficiently strong central government, and, conversely, praised the Jacobins during the French Revolution for overriding the powers of the elected local authorities and establishing a centralized administration. Subsequently, Lenin pointed out that the essential difference between the Marxists and the Anarchists was on the question of centralism.

Both Marx and Engels had mixed feelings about parliamentary institutions. Whether the proletarian revolution would be violent or peaceful would depend on the level and maturity of democratic political institutions, but they were categorical that it would be democratic by virtue of being majoritarian. In the light of the severe restrictions on suffrage in their times, they had qualms about whether parliamentary means could act as instruments, or even as catalysts, for profound social and economic changes. Hence, the *Manifesto* stressed the need to introduce democratic institutions once the proletarian revolution was accomplished. The preliminary draft contended that the revolution would "inaugurate a democratic constitution and thereby directly or indirectly the political rule of the proletariat" (Marx 1975).

Future Society

For Marx and Engels, Communist society eliminated all forms of alienation for the human individual, from nature, from society and from humanity. It did not merely mean consumer satisfaction, but the abolition of all forms of estrangement, the liberation of human forces and enhancement of personal creativity. The institution of private property and division of labour, identified as the source of alienation, would be destroyed as a prerequisite for the new and truly human phase in history. Marx and Engels viewed the proletariat as an agent, and not as a tool in history, and with the liberation of the proletariat came the liberation of society.

The transitional phase, the phase between the destruction of the bourgeois state and the inauguration of a communist society, symbolized by the dictatorship of the proletariat, generated a great deal of controversy in Marxist political theory. Interestingly, one of the well-known Utopias was the least delineated. Marx's cautious predictions were imposed by his own epistemological premises (Avineri 1976: 221). Any discussion of the future (which was not yet an existing reality) would smack of philosophical idealism for it would amount to the description of an object that existed only in the consciousness of the thinking subject. Moreover, he did not want to rival those Socialists whom he branded as "utopian", by constructing detailed blueprints for a communist society that would be determined by the specific conditions under which it was established.

The crucial fact was that observations on future society were set forth in cautious tones "as a posthumous analysis of the passing of the bourgeois world" (Avineri ibid: 221). Communism, for Marx, "can never be an ideal to which reality must adjust. It is reality that comes into being" (Hoffman 1977: 208). This was evident in the' *Critique of the Gotha Programme.* "What we have to deal with here is communist society not as it has developed on its foundations, but on the contrary just as it emerges from capitalist society" (Marx 1977c: 17).

In the *Civil War in France*, similar sentiments were stated. "The working class has no ideals to realize but to set free the elements of the new society with which the old bourgeois society itself is pregnant" (Marx 1977b: 224).

There were similar observations in the *German Ideology* and the *Paris Manuscripts* (1844). Marx projected an image of future society from the internal tensions of existing capitalist society, implying that, at the outset, Communist society would be perfect, universalizing those elements of bourgeois society that could be universalized.

DICTATORSHIP OF THE PROLETARIAT

The controversial and ambiguous concept of the dictatorship of the proletariat emerged in the writings of Marx and Engels as a result of a debate with the German Social Democrats, the Anarchists, and more significantly, from the practical experience of the Paris Commune of 1871. These observations had to be put together from the remarks solely made en passant and from different sources. The two major texts, however, were the *Civil War in France* and the *Critique of the Gotha Programme.*

The concept of the dictatorship of the proletariat held the key to the understanding of Marx's theory on the nature of Communist society and the role of the proletarian state. It was a concept that divided the Marxists and Leninists from the Anarchists on the one hand, and the Social Democrats on the other.

The Communist Manifesto

The phrase "dictatorship of the proletariat" was not used in the *Manifesto.* Nor was there any mention of the complete elimination of state power and the state machinery. Marx and Engels spoke about the "political rule of the proletariat", advising the workers to capture the state, destroy all privileges of the old class, and prepare for the eventual disappearance of the state.

> We have seen above that the first step in the revolution by the working class is to raise the proletariat to the position of the ruling class, to win the battle of democracy ... . The proletariat will use its political supremacy to wrest, by degrees, all capital from the bourgeoisie,

> to centralize all instruments of production in the hands of the state, i.e., of the proletariat organized as the ruling class; and to increase the total of productive forees as rapidly as possible (Marx 1975: 74).

Marx and Engels were convinced that existing states, whether as instruments of class domination and oppression, or rule by bureaucratic parasites on the whole of society, would grow inherently strong and remain minority states representing the interests of the small, dominant and powerful possessing class. It was only when the proletarian majority seized the state structure that the state became truly democratic and majoritarian. Whatever might be the form the state assumed, it was powerful and the proletariat would have to contend with while making its revolution. In the later part of his life, Marx was convinced of the imperative need to destroy the state and establish the dictatorship of the proletariat. In the initial stages, bearing in mind the example of the French Revolution of 1789, he anticipated a seizure of the existing state machine by the revolutionary proletariat for he believed that political centralization would assist the revolutionary process.

The initial "capture" thesis of the state, however, yielded to the "smash" thesis subsequently. The former viewpoint was articulated in the *Manifesto,* where the existing state structure would be used for revolutionizing the mode of production. The "smash" thesis was articulated in response to the experience of the Parisian Communards, as evident in the *Civil War in France* and the *Critique of the Gotha Programme.* In a book review written around 1848— 1849, Marx observed that the destruction of the state had only one implication for the Communists, namely the cessation of an organized power of one class for the suppression of another class (Draper 1977: 288).

In the *Manifesto,* Marx described the nature of Communist society as one in which the classes and its antagonisms would have disappeared. The bourgeois society would be replaced by "an association, in which the free development of each is the condition for the free development of all" (Marx 1975: 76). For the purpose of socializing the means of production, a list of 10 measures was outlined, which would vary from country to country, but which were essential prerequisites for a Communist society. These ten measures were as follows.

1. Abolition of landed property and application of all rents of land for public purposes.
2. A heavy progressive or graduated income tax, and abolition of all rights of inheritance.
3. Confiscation of the property of all emigrants and rebels.
4. Centralization of credit in the hands of the state.
5. Centralization of the means of transport in the hands of the state.
6. Extension of factories and instruments of production owned by the state.
7. Equal liability of all to labour.

8. Combination of agriculture and industry.
9. Gradual abolition of the distinction between town and country.
10. Free education for all children in public schools (Marx ibid: 74).

Beyond this, Marx did not delve into the transitional phase. Interestingly, many of these ideas were outlined by Engels in his *Principles of Communism* (1847), which formed the core of the *Manifesto.*

The Class Struggles in France

Marx modified his views on the state between 1848-1852 as a result of events in France, and more significantly after 1871. His ideas were the result of an elaborate misunderstanding of the French Revolution, of the role of classes and of the very nature of the proletarian revolution. The Bolsheviks in Russia imitated France as seen through the prism of the writings of Marx, which seemed to them more real than the actualities of French history (Wolfe 1969: 7–8).

Until March 1850, Marx and Engels did not apply the word "dictatorship" to the rule of the proletariat. The phrase was used as a tactical compromise slogan with the Blanquists, and then as a polemical device against the Anarchists and assorted reformists (Hunt 1975: 334). Before that, they neither mentioned nor discussed the Babouvist-Blanquist conception of educational dictatorship for it contravened their vision of a proletarian revolution based on the faith they had in the masses to emancipate themselves. Hence, they did not feel the need for a period of educational rule by an enlightened minority, or the need to postpone democratic elections.

It was not Louis-Auguste Blanqui (1805–1881), but Louis Eugene Cavaignac, a general and an arch-antagonist of Blanqui, from whom Marx and Engels borrowed the word "dictatorship" and incorporated it into their vocabulary. Engels clarified that the "strictest centralization of state power" was necessary to fill the vacuum as a result of the destruction of the old order till the creation of the new one. Unlike the previous phases, the dictatorship of the proletariat would represent the rule of the majority over the minority. Marx accepted this formulation. Both were confident that it did not mean the permanent rule of one person or group.

In March 1850, the phrase "dictatorship of the proletariat" replaced the habitually used phrase "rule of the proletariat". Marx and Engels stressed the notion of extraordinary power during an emergency for a limited period of time. It was a constitutional dictatorship, like the one suggested by Babeuf and Blanqui, but differed from their conception insofar as it would not be educational. It did not mean the rule of a self-appointed committee on behalf of the masses, nor did it envisage the need for mass terror and liquidation.

Marx did not define, in any specific way, what the dictatorship of the proletariat entailed, and what its relationship with the state was. It was "a social description, a statement of the class character of the political power. It did not indicate a statement about the forms of government authority" (Draper 1977: 294). But for some scholars, the concept was both a statement of the class character of political power, and a description of political power itself. "It is, in fact, the nature of political power which it describes which guarantees its class character" (Miliband 1965: 289–290).

To Marx and Engels, the dictatorship of the proletariat was by the *entire class*, for the revolution would be made by the masses themselves. In a series of articles written in *Neue Rheinische Zeitung*, which were subsequently compiled under the title *The Class Struggles in France* (1848–1850), Marx contended that

> ... the declaration of the permanence of the revolution, the class dictatorship of the proletariat as the necessary transit point to the abolition of class distinctions generally to the abolition of all relations of production on which they rest, to the abolition of all social relations that correspond to these relations of production, to the revolutionizing of all the ideas that result from these social relations (Marx 1977a: 282).

The phrase dictatorship of the proletariat was incorporated into the first of the six statutes of the Universal Society. In a letter to Otta Luning, co-editor of *Neue Rheinische Zeitung*, Marx clarified that he did not find any significant departure from the idea of the dictatorship of the proletariat as articulated in the *Class Struggles*, to the one formulated in the *Manifesto*.

The ambiguous compromise slogan "dictatorship of the proletariat" would have died a natural death, had the Marxists and Blanquists not renewed their contacts in the aftermath of the Paris Commune (Hunt 1975: 305–306). The ramification of the concept was attempted by Marx, when engaged with Michael Alexandrovich Bakunin (1814–1876) during their high-pitched debate in the First International, and in response to the initiatives undertaken by the German Social Democrats.

The Civil War in France

Meanwhile, an important event that helped in the clarification of the concept was the Paris Commune, leading to an immediate amendment of the *Manifesto* in 1872. "One thing especially was proved by the Commune, viz. that the working class cannot simply lay hold of the ready-made state machinery and wield it for its own purpose" (Marx 1975: 8).

Marx was enthused about the Commune, regarding it as a "glorious harbinger of a new society", and observed in his letter to Kugelman in April 1871 that:

> If you look at the last chapter of my *Eighteenth Brumaire*, you will find that I say that the next attempt of the French Revolution will no longer

> be, as before, to transfer the bureaucratic-military machine from one hand to another but to smash it and this is the precondition for every real people's revolution on the continent. And this is what our heroic Party comrades in Paris are attempting (Marx 1977a: 240).

Marx characterized the Paris Commune as the first major rebellion of the modern industrial proletariat, in consonance with his belief that France would set the example in a struggle between capital and labour. In his address in 1868 to the General Council of The International Workingmen's Association or the First International in London, he outlined the importance of the Commune and its lessons for future socialist movements. These were identified as follows.

1. Abolition of the standing army and the institution of the citizen's militia.
2. Election of all officials, subjecting them to recall.
3. Removal of political attributes of the police.
4. Abolition of the monarchy.
5. The role of the majority in directing and performing all functions of the state, which were previously executed by a privileged minority.

With regard to the last-point, Marx emphasized the following measures.

1. Abolition of all representative allowances, all monetary benefits to officials, and reducing the remuneration for officials to the level of "workmen's wages".
2. Abolition of the distance between the governed and the governors, and erasing the labels of "High" dignitaries.
3. Election of judges.
4. Universal suffrage, exercised freely and frequently.

The Commune was regarded as a working, and not a parliamentary, body exercising legislative and executive power simultaneously. It would break down the power of the modern state, as people would be organized on the basis of a decentralized federal system, with dissemination of power at the broadest and largest levels. Its real strength lay in the fact that it represented the working class, and was "the product of the struggle of the producing against the appropriating class, the political form at last discovered under which to work out the economic emancipation of labour" (Marx ibid: 220–225). Subsequently, in the 1891 edition of the *Civil War in France,* Engels eulogized the Commune as the prototype of the dictatorship of the proletariat. This was one of the examples of the different world-views of Marx and Engels (Carver 1981).

The Critique of the Gotha Programme

The Anarchists were critical of Marx for retaining the state after the proletarian revolution, for it would amount to replacing the old despotic rule with a new one. They regarded the Marxist variant as essentially authoritarian and highly centralized, stifling voluntarism and individual initiative. The German Social Democrats, following Ferdinand Lassalle (1825–1864), articulated the possi-bilities of using the existing state for the realization of socialism and for the enhancement of human freedom. They favoured reforms, as opposed to revo-lution, and believed that the spread of suffrage would enable the workers to play a decisive role in parliament and the institutions of the state. These demands were incorporated in the Gotha Programme, which the Social Democratic Party adopted in 1875.

In response to both the Anarchists and the German Social Democrats, Marx wrote the *Critique of the Gotha Programme,* in which he emphasized the transitional nature of the dictatorship of the proletariat. He outlined the two-phased development to full Communism, which could be attained through a revolutionary transformation of society. "Between the capitalist society and communist society lies the period of the revolutionary transformation of the one into another. There corresponds to this also a political transition period in which the state can be nothing but the revolutionary dictatorship of the proletariat" (Marx 1977c: 19).

According to Marx, the first (or the lower) phase would still be "stamped with the marks of the old society from whose womb it emerges". The principle of distribution with regard to consumer goods would still be the principle of performance. In the second phase, production would be abundant, and distribution would be on the basis of one's needs. The principle of distribution would be "from each according to his ability to each according to his needs" (Marx ibid: 18–19). This principle was initially advanced by Proudhon. Lenin characterized these two phases as "socialism" and "communism" respectively.

In the second phase, division of labour would be abolished and each individual would devote himself to a single life task. In the Communist society as portrayed in the *German Ideology,* Marx hoped that "each can become accomplished in any branch he wishes", allowing a person to hunt in the morning, fish in the afternoon, rear cattle in the evening, criticize after dinner, "just as he has a mind to without ever becoming a hunter, fisherman, shepherd, or critic". Individual and private ownership of property would cease to exist, and be replaced by social ownership. The anti-thesis between mental and physical labour would be abolished, for labour would become not only a means of life, but also a prime want of life (Marx ibid: 19). He contrasted the higher form of Communism with Primitive or crude Communism, the first stage in the process of historical materialism. Primitive Communism was signified by the necessity of all to labour, a levelling down of all individual talents, and communal ownership of women, essentially indicating a negation of the human personality. All these features would be absent in the final Communist society.

Marx did not specify the mechanisms of change from stage I to stage II in the post-revolutionary phase of human history, leading to serious doubts as to how stage I would develop into stage II, and whether it would develop as intended (Avineri 1976: 329). Since this process was not explained, the ultimate aim that "free development of each will lead to the free development of all" might not ever be realizable (Wilson 1941: 335–336).

In the *Ami Duhring,* Engels introduced the notion of the "withering away of the state", and the fact that "government of persons would be replaced by administration of things", a phrase borrowed from William Morris (1834–1896). Engels stressed that the state would not be abolished, but it would wither away. Engels did not articulate on the nature of future society, except, like Marx, on insisting that it was the *condition,* rather than the nature and form of the future society that was important. Both Engels and Marx accepted that the proletarian state would be centrally planned and directed, but without coercion and force. However, they failed to resolve the possible conflict between centralized planning and individual freedom in the Communist society. They remained ambivalent on the role of markets, but the inference was that markets had to be eliminated, for they were unequal in their outcomes.

Thus, Marx and Engels reacted sharply to Bakunin's criticism about the statist implications of their conception and Lassalle's 'Free State'. By 1875, it became clear that the German Social Democrats began to think about using the existing state apparatus, and had settled down to a more reformist method. Marx still advocated the revolutionary overthrow of the existing bureaucratic-military state, and replacing it with the truly transitory (but majoritarian and democratic) dictatorship of the proletariat. Bakunin insisted on the immediate elimination of all forms of political authority, replacing them with spontaneous and voluntary organizations. Marx accepted the Anarchist demand of abolition of the state, but emphasized the majoritarian content of the transitional state purely as a temporary measure, hoping to counter both his critics, Bakunin and Lassalle.

REVISIONISM, RUSSIAN REVOLUTION AND DICTATORSHIP OF THE PROLETARIAT

In the 1890s, the German Social Democrats decided on a new programme, which was adopted as the official policy of the Social Democratic Party (SPD) in 1891 for the next 30 years. The Erfurt Programme, as it came to be known, contained two parts. The first part was prepared by Karl Johann Kautsky (1854–1938), known as the Pope of Marxism and the most important Marxist theoretician of the period of the Second International (1890–1914). Reaffirming orthodox Marxist posture, he emphasized economic determinism. The second part was prepared by Bernstein, laying down practical reforms with a view to realizing socialism.

Bernstein rejected the notion of the dictatorship of the proletariat as barbaric, "an atavism" belonging to a lower culture and civilization. He categorically insisted that socialism had to eschew all forms of violence and dictatorial rule. He conceived of a representative democratic state organized on the basis of socio-economic equity. He believed in democracy as ihe only framework for realizing Socialism. It was not surprising that he characterized the Bolshevik regime as a brutal distortion of Marxism. Within Russia, Julian Martov (1873–1923) of the Menshevik group accused the Bolsheviks of undermining the majoritarian content of the dictatorship of the proletariat, as envisaged by Marx and Engels. He contended that Lenin had superimposed on a passive majority the will of an active minority, thereby reducing the former to passive subjects in a social experiment. Martov and the Mensheviks broke away from the Russian Social Democratic Party (RSDLP), for they disagreed with Lenin's conception of the Vanguard Party.

In order to confront the Revisionist challenge, and seizing the observations made by Marx and Engels in 1882, Lenin as a strategist committed himself whole heartedly to effecting a working-class revolution, and explored its possibilities in Tsarist Russia. Taking a cue from Kautsky's formulations in the *Class Struggles* (1892), Lenin elaborated his theory of a party consisting of professional revolutionaries, on the plea that the workers were capable of only trade union, rather than revolutionary consciousness. Looking at the possibility of an outbreak of revolution in Tsarist Russia, to counter the continuous criticism by the German Left and to meet the radical challenge posed by Nikolai Ivanovinch Bukharin (1888-1938) in 1916, Lenin developed his theory of the state in *The State and Revolution,* regarded as the greatest contribution of Lenin to political theory (Colletti 1969: 223–225).

Lenin reiterated the need to destroy the state machinery in a situation of revolutionary seizure of power. The state, per se continued in its socialist phase in the form of the dictatorship of the proletariat with full democracy, exhibiting, like Marx, contempt for parliamentary and representative institutions. However, the suppression of the constituent assembly, universal suffrage, the exclusive monopoly and pre-eminence of the Communist Party and the brutal repressive measures against the Kronstadt rebellion, completed the logic of what was essentially a minority revolution led by the Bolsheviks. The libertarian and majoritarian perceptions of Lenin, in 1916, were subsumed by his authoritarian and undemocratic outlook in *What is to be done!* (1902).

The dictatorship of the proletariat, in practice, was reduced to the dictatorship of the Bolshevik Party over the proletariat. Both Kautsky and Rosa Luxemburg (1871–1919) were critical of the Leninist experiment. Kautsky characterized the Bolshevik revolution as a *coup d'etat,* and its socialism as "barrack socialism", for it had nothing to do with majority rule and parliamentary democracy. Luxemburg expressed solidarity with Lenin and Trotsky for pre-empting a socialist revolution, but was critical of their abrogation of spontaneity, freedom of opinion and socialist democracy.

Lenin and Trotsky reacted sharply to Kautsky's criticism. Lenin dismissed the argument that democracy was not only compatible, but also a precondition for the proletarian rule, as irrelevant. He clarified that democracy was abolished only for the bourgeoisie. Subsequently, in 1921, Lenin acknowledged the lack of culture, and the fact that the Bolsheviks did not know how to rule, as the serious shortcomings of the new regime. Trotsky defended the use of terror, force and violence as means of safeguarding Socialism and its advancement in Russia. Later, Trotsky also turned critical of Stalin for making Socialism repressive and bureaucratic, never acknowledging that along with Lenin, he himself was instrumental for laying the foundations of Stalinism. In fact, Solzhenitsyn (cited in Keane 1988: 267) characterized Stalinism as the malignant form of Leninism.

INADEQUACIES IN THE MARXIST THEORY OF THE STATE

Viewed in this perspective, all the experiments that were carried out in the twentieth century in the name of Marx have totally repudiated his principles. Russia's backwardness, the lack of a coherent theory of post-revolutionary society in Marxism, and Marx's personal fascination with the possibilities of absolute power, attenuated the Blanquism in Lenin and Stalin. If Stalinism was an offshoot of Leninism, then Leninism itself was inspired by Marxism, for Lenin repeatedly affirmed his commitment and faith in Marxist ideology. The distortions in Soviet Communism could be attributed to the shortcomings and inadequacies in Marx's world-view, the fact that Marx had

> pointed out that historical developments are always open to several possibilities. Yet Marx disregarded the possibilities open to his own theory; and here lies its major intellectual blunder ... he overlooked the possibility that one of the alternatives to which the future development of his own theory was open might be the combination of his philosophical and historical theory with the Jacobin tradition of merely political, subjectivist revolutionary action. Thus, if Marx's point of departure was Hegelian, so was his blind spot: like Hegel himself he did not subject his own theory to a dialectical critique (Avineri 1976: 258).

Dahl asserted that Marxism could not be accepted "as an adequate political theory" on the basis of the basic propositions on democracy which were agreeable to all political parties, and defended zealously by them. These were: (a) inevitability of conflict of interests and articulation of wants as a matter of choice in a complex society, (b) resolution of such conflicts by majority rule, but with due concern for minority rights; and

(c) freedom to form political parties, and recognition of free competition (Dahl 1986: 55, 73). The emphasis on harmony in Socialist society was inconsistent with the first proposition of the democratic theory. Marxism did not offer any clue to the distribution of political power in a Socialist society, and was equally ambiguous on the concept of majority rule. The introduction of universal adult franchise in Germany in 1866, the electoral reforms in England in 1867 and 1884, and the mushrooming of socialist parties, weakened the essential proposition of the state as an instrument of oppression, controlled by the bourgeois minority exploiting and oppressing the proletarian majority. The reforms gave the workers an opportunity to control the state by winning the majority of votes, and thereby seats in the parliament. "Marx's politics is based on particular qualities of the bourgeois state in the nineteenth century" (Dahl ibid: 69).

Marxism in theory and practice could never provide a primer for constitution-based representative democracy. The important fact to note was that "neither Marx nor Lenin spoke of a law governed state ... because they considered that the state would inevitably wither away" (Djilas 1990: 7).

Marx never addressed himself to the issue of rights, political freedom, power and the role of authority in a socialist society. For all his libertarian vision, Marx himself was consumed by the idea of having absolute, total, concentrated state power, unrestrained and unlimited. He was contemptuous, of, in fact had very little faith in, a constitution or law, dismissing them as shams, formalities and covers to conceal bourgeois oppression and domination. The attack on formal democracy by promising substantive democracy resulted in reducing formal democracy to the point of non-existence. Marx overlooked the protection that constitutional representative democracy and rule of law gave against arbitrary rule, and the freedom it ensured against physical harm. He failed to understand the dynamics of democracy in empowering people being more revolutionary than a bloody, violent revolution itself. "He profoundly underestimated the capacity of democratic societies to correct or mitigate the injustices that seemed to him built into capitalism. The concept of the 'class struggle' which is central in the thinking of all Marxists seems largely irrelevant in America and Western Europe" (Berlin 1963: xi)

Berlin's last observation about the obsolence of class struggle in advanced industrialized countries can be extended to the developing world now. There is no more talk of revolutionary transformation of society, or that the "East is Red". Moreover, the possibility of using democracy as a means of realizing socialism never moved to the centre stage of his analysis of future society. "The overall sweep of the Marxist historical scheme relegates democracy to a subsidiary role in the drama of human development" (Harding 1981: 157).

This was where the Social Democrats scored over Marx, for they, and in particular Bernstein, insisted on the need to combine democracy (representative parliamentary institutions with universal suffrage) with socialism, bringing about a breach that could never be closed between German Marxism and Russian Communism (Plamentaz 1963: Vol. II).

The idea of Communist society being classless and equal remained a myth. Djilas, in the *New Class* (1959), pointed to the presence of the *nomenklatura* in the former communist societies, namely those who enjoyed privileges and special status because of their position within the hierarchy of the Communist Party, thus confirming the fears of Bakunin that the dictatorship of the proletariat would create *fresh* inequities and *new* forms of oppression and domination. Perhaps no one has captured the myth of a classless society better than Orwell in his *Animal Farm* and *Nineteen Eight-Four*. As Orwell observed succinctly "... so-called collectivist systems now existing only try to wipe out the individual because they are *not* really collectivist and certainly not egalitarian—because, in fact they are a sham covering a new form of class privilege" (Orwell cited in Wykes 1987: 69).

An examination of the development of the idea of the dictatorship of the proletariat revealed a tension between the concept's organizational necessity, though maybe of a transitory kind, with the larger Marxist hypothesis of enlargement of human freedom. The idea of delineating and working out a participatory model of democracy was never completed by Marx. This was also compounded by Marx's inadequate handling of the crucial role of the theory of the state. In tackling the complexities of the modern state, the general descriptions of the ideal as realizing true democracy and Communism have proved to be extremely simplistic in providing the essential institutions of a modern democratic state. Marx's aversion to Utopian blueprinting made him ignore the details that were necessary for managing a society based on equity, just reward and freedom. The terms "true democracy" and "communism" hardly dealt with the complexities of modern times.

WOMEN AND THE GENDER QUESTION

Like in many other areas, even with regard to the question of women, Marx made Hegel the starting point. Hegel regarded women as inferior, with less reasoning abilities, seeing the natural differences between men and women as immutable. Marx did not say much on the role and position of women. He took it for granted that Socialism would bring about their emancipation. In the *German Ideology* and the *Capital*, he spoke of the natural and spontaneous division of labour within the family. The natural relationship paved the way for a social one, and the first property relationship was the one when the man regarded his wife and children as his slaves. The man had power over them, and could do with their labour as he chose, though Marx did not explain how this came about. Marx did not focus his attention on the position and role of women.

Engels, in the *Origins*, provided a materialist account of the origins of patriarchy, and linked women's subordination with the rise of private property. In the *Holy Family*, Marx and Engels observed that the degree of emancipation of women could be used as a standard by which one could measure general emancipation. Marx reiterated this view in a letter to Dr L. Kugelmann in 1868, that social progress could be assessed exactly by the social position of women. In 1845, Marx warned against treating the family regardless of its specific historic setting. In his criticism of Max Stirner (1805–1856), he observed that it was a misconception to speak of the family without qualification. Historically, the bourgeoisie endowed the family with the characteristics of the bourgeois family, whose ties were boredom and money.

THE ASIATIC MODE OF PRODUCTION

Marx's views on the non-European world, like his overall political theorizing, also flowed from Hegelian prescriptions. But in the evolution of these two basic themes, there was an interesting yet contradictory development. The contemporary analysis of Germany that Hegel offered was rejected on the basis of a universalistic criterion, while the notion of the unchanging and static nature of the non-European world was accepted without any critical examination. Marx used the phrase "Asiatic Mode of Production" to describe the non-European societies. In this formulation, there was a clear "discrepancy between the analytical and historical nature of the categories of ancient, feudal and bourgeois modes of production and the mere geographic designation of the Asiatic one" (Avineri 1969: 56).

Prior to 1852, Marx did not show any specific interest in the non-European world. His interest arose as a result of a series of articles that he penned for the *New York Daily Tribune* (1852–1862). The Asiatic Mode of Production assumed importance subsequently, in the theoretical and political debates within Marxist circles. "The debates about the Asiatic Mode of Production has raised questions concerning not only the relevance of Marxist concepts outside the European context, but also the character of materialist explanations of class society, revolutionary change and world history" (Bottomore 1983: 32).

The underlying assumption among many post-Renaissance European thinkers who took an interest in the non-European world was that there was a marked and qualitative distinction between the advanced European cultures and other backward civilizations. Montesquieu was the pioneer of this perception. Using climatic conditions as the yardstick, he noted that tropical climates were unsuited for democracies and individual freedom. Smith clubbed China, Egypt and India together for the special attention irrigation received in these societies. James Mill observed the difference between European feudalism and governmental arrangements in Asiatic societies. Richard Jones used the phrase "Asiatic society" and J.S. Mill used the term "Eastern society" in 1848. Others, like Herbert Spencer (1820–1903), Vilfredo Pareto (1848–1923) and Emile Durkheim (1855–1917), analyzed Asiatic societies from a comparative perspective. Hegel was the most influential among these thinkers, whose philosophy of history not only concurred with this prevailing European perception of the East, but also influenced—to a very large extent—the left Hegelians with respect to perceiving colonization as a modernizing force. For Hegel, with his clear Eurocentricism, India and China did not have any history as these were "stationery and fixed". This was true of all Asiatic societies. Hegel's point that the East lacked history influenced Marx.

Marx described the oriental societies of India and China as lacking in history, incapable of changing from within, and essentially stagnant. Since, by themselves, they would block historical progress, the industrialized West, when it became socialistic, would be the agent of liberation in the less developed areas. In other words, European socialism would have to precede national liberation movements in the Asian societies. Marx identified Europe with progress, and the Orient with stagnation. He looked upon imperialist rule as being simultaneously destructive and constructive. It was degenerative, for it destroyed indigenous institutions and practices; it was regenerative, for it created the modem techniques of production, brought political unity and social changes.

Marx and Engels concluded that the chief characteristic of Asiatic societies was the absence of private property, particularly private ownership of land. In contrast to the state in the European context, which was an instrument of class domination and exploitation, the state in Asiatic societies controlled all classes. It did not belong to the superstructure, but was decisive in the entire economic arena, building and managing water supply and the life breath of agriculture in arid areas. It performed economic and social functions for the whole of society. Social privileges emanated from service to the state, and not from the institution of private property, as was the case in Europe. Asiatic societies had an overdeveloped state, and an underdeveloped civil society. Military conquests and dynastic tussles ushered in changes periodically, without affecting the economic organization, for the state continued to be the real landlord. The unchanging nature of Asiatic societies was also buttressed by self-sufficient autarchic villages, which sustained themselves through agriculture and handicrafts.

In the *Grundrisse,* Marx and Engels developed on these preliminary sketches of Asiatic societies to highlight the key differences in the urban history of the West and the East. In the West, the existence of politically independent cities conducive to growth of the production of exchange values determined the development of a bourgeois class and industrial capitalism, whereas in the East, the city was artificially created by the state, and remained a "princely camp" subordinated to the countryside. The city was imposed on the economic structure of society. Social unity represented by the state lay in the autarchic self-sufficient villages where land was communally owned. Stability was ensured by simplicity of production. The state appropriated the surplus in the form of taxes. Factors like free markets, private property, guilds and bourgeois law, that led to the rise of the capitalist class in the West, were absent in Asiatic societies due to a centralized state that dominated and controlled civil society. For Marx, imperialism would act as a catalyst of change since these societies lacked the mechanisms for change. It was because of its covert defence of imperialism that Marxists have sought to dismantle the concept.

The Anarchists, and in particular Bakunin, defended the right of nations (including the predominantly peasant Eastern nations) to self-determination. The West was based on slavery, and did not prove that it was superior to the "barbarians of [the] Orient". He asserted that all states were constituted by their nature and the conditions of the purpose for which they existed, namely the absolute negation of human justice, freedom and morality. By this logic, he did not distinguish between the uncouth Tsarist Russia and the advanced countries of North Europe, for the former did the same thing as the latter, with the mask of hypocrisy.

The concept of the Asiatic Mode has had a chequered history. In the preface to *A Contribution to the Critique of Political Economy* (1859), Marx considered the Asiatic Mode as one of the "epochs marking progress in the economic development of society". Engels did not refer to the Asiatic Mode in *The Origins of the Family, Private Property and the State.* It was in the context of discussions on revolutionary struggles in Russia, that the concept figured once again. Different political strategies were devised in view of Russia being feudal, semi-capitalist, authoritarian and partly Asiatic. In 1853, Marx and Engels characterized Tsarist Russia as "Semi-Asiatic". In the *Anti Duhring,* Engels viewed the Russia commune as the basis of oriental despotism. Between 1877 and 1882, Marx, in his letters to Vera Zaulich (1852–1919) and Engels, as a member of the editorial board of *Otechestvenniye Zapiski,* examined the prospects of revolution in Russia and whether in such an eventuality the commune could provide the foundations of socialism.

In exploring the possibilities of a world proletarian revolution, Marx and Engels began to show interest in the non-European world. The notion of the Asiatic Mode of Production examined the relevance of Marxist concepts outside the European context. While Marx and Engels were convinced that socialism represented the zenith of capitalism, and that the proletarian revolution would break out only in the advanced industrialized societies, they pointed out in 1882 that if a revolution would break out in Tsarist Russia, it would complement the efforts of the proletariat in the advanced West.

The Asiatic Mode paradigm undermined Marx's universalistic presumption that a ruling class could only be a proprietary class, i.e. a class that owned the means of production. The primary paradigm in the *Manifesto* and other writings did not focus on the class character of the state bureaucracy, which could be one of the reasons why the Asiatic Mode in particular and the theory of the state in general, remained so sketchy in the works of Marx and Engels (Gouldner 1980: 339–342).

ON INDIA

Analyzing India within the framework of the Asiatic Mode, Marx was convinced that Imperial Britain would establish the foundations of Western society in India, for English imperialism represented the only social revolution in Asia. This belief rested on the logic that though colonialism was brutal, it was dialectically important for the world proletarian revolution. Colonialism would unleash forces of modernization which would eventually lead to the emancipation of these areas. Marx's account of British imperialism led to the proposition that the more extensive the forms of imperialism, the more profound would be the consequences for modernization (Avineri 1969: 132–133). Marx and Engels favoured colonialism, as it was a catalyst for modernization, though they did take note of regressive and exploitative side of it.

Marx noted that in India, England had a dual function, one destructive and the other regenerative. Colonization as a regenerative force brought about political unification, introduced railways, a free press, a trained army, Western education, rational ways of thinking, and abolished common land tenures. As for its being destructive, British colonization destroyed indigenous industries and handicrafts. Marx mentioned the exploitative role played by the East India Company, and the increasing resentment English capitalists had against its monopoly, preventing the transfer of surplus British capital to India. All these changes profoundly affected the static nature of Indian society. In this context, he mentioned superstition and narrow-mindedness, which reinforced animal worship, preventing development.

In spite of these insights, the fact remained that like the Conservatives, Marx and Engels favoured colonialism. In the fierce controversy between Marx and Bakunin, the question of the right of self-determination was one of the major issues of disagreement. Moreover, the Marxist view of the non-European world and the dominant streams of twentieth-century nationalist thought did not vindicate the Marxist thesis. Amilcar Cabral (1924–1973) rightly rejected this entire postulate of history, starting with the emergence of class struggle and the consequent thesis that the continents of Africa, Asia and America did not have any history before the colonial period. The factor of nationalism that contributed to the liberation of the colonies was completely ignored by Marx.

Marx, in spite of his erudite scholarship, was a child of his times. He viewed the non-European world through the European perspective. His observations, however profound, reflected a great deal of prevailing

Hegelian prejudices and Eurocentricism. Many of the Indian Marxists did not accept Marx's formulations on the Asiatic Mode, or his observations on British imperialism in India.

CONCLUSION

Marx wrote in the optimistic environment of Victorian England, where the gloomy predictions of Malthus were forgotten. He was a believer in the uninterrupted progress of human civilization and of industrial society. He did not recognize any limits to growth. He was generally hopeful of the liberating and progressive roles of science and human rationality. For their sheer range and breadth of influence, it would be appropriate to say that one could not write without taking into account his writings, and without understanding the full import of his ideas.

Marx claimed that he had turned Hegel upside down, and was initiating his own independent line of theorizing. Though he styled his brand of socialism as scientific, his exposition was not systematic and cogent. His observations and descriptions of the Communist ideal lacked the details that were needed to project a blueprint. The general nature of the descriptions meant different things to different people. Unless one clearly and precisely stated the meaning of a just society, it was not possible to debate and reflect on it. Instead, when "men range themselves under the banner as friends and enemies of the 'Revolution', the only important question which is just and useful is kept out of sight and measures are judged not by their real worth but by the analogy they seem to have to an irrelevant abstraction" (Lasky 1976: 573). This failure to give details led to considerable confusion, for the same words conveyed different things to different people. "... Marx sketched but never developed a systematic theory of the state and hence the idea of a political economy remained overdetermined and undescribed politically" (Wolin 1987: 469).

However, Marx was a revolutionary and a socialist, but above all he was a humanist who believed in genuine emancipation and liberation of human beings. He registered protest against every kind of domination. True, many of his predictions did not materialize, but Marx's genius lay not merely in his ability to predict, but in the new modes of thinking about economic and political issues.

> The doctrine which has survived and grown, and which has had a greater and more lasting influence both on opinion and on action than any other view put forward in modern times, is his theory of the evolution and structure of capitalist Society, of which he nowhere gave a detailed exposition. This theory, by asserting that the important question to be asked with regard to any phenomenon is concerned with the relation which bears to the economic structure ... has created new tools of criticism and research whose use has altered the direction and emphasis of the social sciences in our generation (Berlin 1963: xii).

Undoubtedly, Marx was a genius, but one should not overlook his shortcomings. Weber, in his famous essay *The Protestant Ethics and the Spirit of Capitalism* (1904–1905) points out that capitalism was caused by the habits, beliefs and attitudes of Protestantism, and more specifically, Calvinism and English Puritanism. For Weber, ideas and economic motives were interests too, that "material without ideal interests are empty, but ideals without material interests are impotent" (Weber cited in MacRae 1974: 58). Weber gave importance to concepts and values, for they played a pivotal role in social life.

According to Weber, Marx remained vague about the economic base. He conceded that within the parameters of non-economic factors, purely economic behaviour would occur. In fact, Marx's simplistic analysis precluded such considerations. Weber was not happy with Marx's clubbing of technology with the economic base, for he believed that with any state of technology, many economic orders were possible and vice versa. He criticized Marx for being imprecise about what really constituted economic categories.

Weber criticized Socialism for its attempt to replace the anarchy of the market and achieve greater equity through planning. This, he believed, would result in greater bureaucratization, leading to a loss of freedom and entrepreneurship. Weber was clear that private property and markets were necessary for guaranteeing plurality of social powers and individual freedom.

Marx did not foresee the rise of Fascism, totalitarianism and the welfare state (Berlin ibid: xi). His analysis of capitalism was, at best, applicable to early nineteenth-century capitalism, though his criticisms of capitalism as being wasteful, unequal and exploitative were true. However, his alternative of genuine democracy and full Communism seemed more difficult to realize in practice, for they did not accommodate a world which was becoming increasingly differentiated, stratified and functionally specialized.

Popper's (1945) critique of Marxism on the basis of falsification was equally true and difficult to refute, for Marxism constantly adjusted theory in the light of reality. Popper was suspicious of Marx's scientific predictions, for a scientific theory was one that would not try to explain everything. Along with Plato and Hegel, Marx was seen as an enemy of the open society. Marxism claimed to have studied the laws of history, on the basis of which it advocated total, sweeping and radical changes. Not only was it impossible to have first-hand knowledge based on some set of laws that governed society and human individuals, but Popper also rejected Marx's social engineering as dangerous, for it treated individuals as subservient to the interests of the whole. Popper rejected the historicism, holism and Utopian social engineering of Marxism. In contrast, he advocated piecemeal social engineering, where change would be gradual and modest, allowing rectification of lapses and errors, for it was not possible to conceive of everything. This method also encouraged public discourse and participation, making the process democratic and majoritarian.

Popper claimed that Marx's scientific socialism was wrong not only about society, but also about science. The capitalism that Marx described never existed. Marx made the economy all-important, ignoring factors like religion, nationality, friendship. Society was far more complex than what Marx described. In spite of exaggerating the influence of economics, it was a fact that "Marx brought into the social sciences and historical science the very important idea that economic conditions are of great importance in the life of society ... . There was nothing like serious economic history before Marx" (Popper 1996: 20).

Comforth, in *The Open Philosophy and the Open Enemies* (1968), charged Popper for regarding capitalism and the open society as coextensive, and for believing that capitalism had changed fundamentally. For him, "friends of the open society, who are organizing to get rid of capitalism, are its enemies; and the enemies of the open society, who are organizing to preserve capitalism as its friends". The fight for an open society, in reality, was a fight against anything and everything that was done to prevent exploitation of man by man. He did not accept the charge that Communism would destroy individual freedom, reinforce dogmatism, and undermine science, the arts, culture, and eventually civilization. Communism did not stand for lawless tyranny and violence.

Cornforth's defence of Marxism against Popper was merely polemical, without much substance. He ignored the fact that unlike many other well-known critics, Popper did not attack totalitarian Marxism at its weakest but at its strongest, which led Berlin to acclaim that Popper provided the "most scrupulous and formidable criticism of the philosophical and historical doctrines of Marxism by any living writer" (Berlin cited in Magee 1984: 2) To this, Magee observed, "I must confess I do not see how any rational man can have read Popper's critique of Marx and still be a Marxist" (Magee ibid: 92).

Berlin rejected the deterministic outlook of Marxism, and questioned the entire argument of providing the right goal for all individuals. Instead the focus was on *today,* rather than chase chimerical Utopias of *tomorrow.* The idea of Utopia for Berlin, like Popper, was philosophically dubious, hideously dangerous and logically incoherent. Both ruled out finality in anything. While, for Berlin, a Utopian society meant lack of free choice and Monist values, namely one idea of good life, for Popper, a blueprint of a perfect ideal meant statism and arrested growth. It precluded what he called "unplanned planning".

Like Popper, Berlin attacked the historicism of Hegel and Marx, which he developed in his essay, *Historical Inevitability* (1954). Many of Berlin's arguments were similar to those of Popper, except that Berlin was emphatic that the historicism of Hegel and Marx denied free human will which enabled them to absolve historians from censuring the villains in history. Historicism was some kind of metaphysical mystery. Both Hegel and Marx defined freedom as obedience to a rational will, namely the idea of positive liberty, rather than seeing freedom as choice, as reflected in the writings of Locke, Hume and J.S. Mill. Choice implied conflict among rival goods, whereas rational will suggested one way of life, one life plan that would be the same for most, if not all the people.

Berlin's inherent faith in pluralism led him to defend freedom as choice or negative liberty for each individual, each culture and each nation. Each historical period had its own goals, aspirations and conceptions of good life, and it was impossible to unite them into an overarching, single, theoretical system in which all ends would be realized without any clashes and conflicts. For Berlin, values, however ultimate they may be, did and could exclude one another, and their incompatibility had to be reconciled through a constant process of compromise and trade-offs instead of a false synthesis. Thus, Berlin was a critic of Enlightenment rationalism, which suggested the uninterrupted progress of history and the possibility of synthesizing all values. The master idea for Berlin was pluralism, which suggested that there was no single master idea, meaning that there were many conceptions of good life, a good society, and that these goods were often, at least sometimes, incommensurable and incompatible. A Monist was compared to a hedgehog, who knew one Grand Idea. Marx, Hegel and Plato were hedgehogs. A pluralist knew many things, like a fox.

Rejecting Monism, Berlin attacked the metaphysical content behind positive liberty, that everything could be explained with reference to a single homogeneous principle and discoverable laws. This led to determinism and totalitarianism. He insisted that philosophy had to be humble. It could not offer a set of principles or a theory that would solve all the dilemmas of moral and political life, nor could it straighten the "crooked timber of humanity", a favourite phrase with him, which he borrowed from Kant. He was opposed to philosophy proposing radical social reforms, which explained his hostility towards Marxism. For Berlin, totalitarian ideologies and politics—Fascism, Nazism and Communism—did have different goals between them to pursue, but they shared certain common traits. They viewed the state as being superior to the individual, giving it an overarching role over society and individuals. It directed every aspect of the individual's life, suggesting homogeneity and regarding any deviation as sacrilegious.

Habermas (1991) rejected specifically the nostalgic, romantic and Utopian vision of Socialism, though he remained a committed socialist. He was clear that Socialism would not rise again, but that it was still alive, as a critique. He considered Socialism as a "discourse in exile". He examined Marx's theory of history by focusing on the relationship between crisis and critique, and then on the concepts of reification and alienation. First, Habermas raised doubts about Marx's Hegelian-inspired concept of labour as a human being's self-creative activity. Individuals learnt to control the natural world and acquire technical knowledge, but it was social interaction that established human capacity, namely the development of moral cognitive abilities. This, according to Habermas, could not be explained by the increase in productive forces, implying that class conflict was no longer a motive in history. By focusing on production, Marx failed to see the possibilities for freedom in the realm of social interaction. He mistook command of the external nature of human freedom, and ignored social repression of internal nature. Second, Habermas pointed out that societies were totalities, whose parts were in the end determined by the level of development of their productive forces. He distinguished between life-world and system, which in turn were divided into the private and public spheres. The life-world was the realm of moral-practical knowledge or relations that existed within the families and workplaces (the private), and political actions and opinions (the public). It was coordinated through communicative actions, namely actions involving the self and those of others. In comparison, political (states) and economic (markets) systems were coordinated through the modicum of power and money. Habermas argued that Marx failed to see these distinctions, which was why he could not foresee the stability of capitalism or the bankruptcy of Socialism. Third, Marx defined history as progress, rather than the development of universal principles of morality and justice. Though these did not represent the unfolding of reason in history, "Historicizing the knowledge of an essence ... only replaces the teleology of Being with that of History. The secretly normative presuppositions of theories of history are naturalized in the form of evolutionary concepts of progress" (Habermas 1991: 35).

Habermas pointed out that moral cognitive developments logically created a space for new forms of social organizations, and that fundamental changes occurred when society demonstrated the capacity to adapt and grow. These changes indicated the meaning of freedom, and were defined by the participants themselves. Only with a convergence of knowing and doing, and the self-conscious creation of a socialist society could put an end to human exile. The specific function of critical theory was to identify the formal conditions that made this emancipation possible. Habermas maintained that by visualizing humans as producers, societies as totalities, and history as progress, Marx went back to a Hegelian-inspired theology and anthropology.

According to Habermas, state socialism became bankrupt, but Socialism still nurtured "the hope that humanity can emancipate itself from self-imposed tutelage" (ibid: 45). It remained a "doctrine in exile", for it nourished the possibility, according to Fischman, that "people can be more human than their society permits" (Fischman 1991: 108).

Anthony Giddens observed: "In many respects Marx's writings exemplify features of nineteenth-century thought which are plainly defective when looked at from the perspectives of our century" (1995: 1), and concluded that "Marx's materialist conception of history should be discarded once and for all" (ibid: 105). He pointed out that Marx's greatest failure was the theory of nationalism for Marx was an archetypal modernist. He distinguished between nationalism (symbols and beliefs) and the nation state (the administrative set-up), which were two separate entities, though sometimes they converged. Nationalism was a primordial sentiment "found in tribal and traditional societies", while the nation state was a modern "power container of time and space" (ibid: 193). Capitalism needed the nation state, and as a power structure, promoted the aims of capitalism.

The collapse of Communism proved the serious shortcomings of Marxism, both in theory and practice. It, at best, remained a critique rather than providing a serious alternative to liberal democracy (Harrington cited in Heilbroner 1989: 10). The Soviet experiment, despite its many failings, kept alive the possibility that there was an alternative to capitalism. Its collapse and furthermore the shrinking of the industrial working class and the weakening of the labour movement have underlined the irrelevance of Marxism as a political practice, environmentalism and post-Modernism challenged some of the fundamental assumptions about progress and knowledge that underpinned Marxism (Hobsbawn 2011).

Marxism's dream of creating a classless society beyond conflict and based on equality remained illusory. However, its critique of exploitation and alienation, and the hope of creating a truly emancipated society that would allow the full flowering of human creativity, would continue to be a starting point of any Utopian project. In spite of Marx's Utopia being truly generous, it displayed a potential for being tyrannical, despotic and arbitrary. Centralization of power and absence of checks on absolute power were themselves inimical to true human liberation and freedom. He "offered no good reason to believe that the power politics of radicalism would prove to be less authoritarian in practice than the power politics of conservative nationalism" (Sabine 1973: 682). Commenting on the activities of his fellow comrades, which were in total negation of his ideals, Marx once proclaimed that he was not a Marxist. This proved to be a serious limitation of his theory, even during his lifetime, as it was after his death. He would be remembered at best as a critic of early nineteenth-century capitalism and politics. The limitations and inadequacies within the doctrine are reminders that his blueprint was, as Koestler remarked, "a God that failed".

Appendix

John Rawls
Revival of the Classical Tradition

> *A Theory of Justice* is a powerful, deep, subtle, wide ranging systematic work in political and moral philosophy ... . Political philosophers now must either work within Rawls' theory or explain why not (Nozick 1974: 183).

> Rawls' theory has both the simplicity and the complexity of a Gothic Cathedral (Chapman 1975: 583).

> Rawls' endeavour represents the most comprehensive effort in modern philosophy to justify a socialist ethic (Bell 1973: 444).

John Rawls' *A Theory of Justice* (1971) and a score of articles which constitute the Rawlsian system in the contemporary political philosophy, was a classic example of the contractual approach applied to liberal justice. He wove an intricate and elaborate pattern of inquiry and provided a coherent, systematic and powerful defence of a new kind of egalitarianism that preserved and extended the ambit of individual liberty. The first major review by Hampshire (Rawls 1972: 34) proclaimed it to be the 'most substantive and most interesting contribution' in the post-Second World War period. Commentaries and critical appraisals have assumed the 'status of a Rawls industry' (Ryan 1985: 103). The impact of his theory could be gauged from the fact that *A Theory of Justice* was translated into several European languages—Chinese, Japanese and Korean. Rawls' philosophical edifice elicited responses both immediate and immense, and since 1971, any attempt at moral and political philosophy had to reckon with his conception. Rawls outlined the features of his conception in an article that appeared in 1957, entitled *Justice as Fairness* (also the nomenclature for his theory), culminating in *A Theory of Justice*.

The elaboration and clarification of theory continued even after the publication of *A Theory of Justice* through two more books—*Political Liberalism* (1993) and *The Law of Peoples* (1999).

Rawls was credited with reviving the grand old style of political theory and restoring its grandeur that it commanded in the past, thereby ending the debate about its death and/or decline. During the long gestation period, the Rawlsian theory underwent subtle alterations and changes, making it difficult to discern some of the arguments that have been revamped (Barry 1973: 1–3). Many of the modifications were in response to the critical appraisals though in course of revision most of the core doctrines were retained. The model was the result of meticulous and painstaking research, an example of the Socratic Method reacting to his critics, making the necessary modification and clarification, but retaining the core doctrines. Contemporary discussions on Justice—Ackerman (1980), Dworkin (1977), Nozick (1974), Sandel (1982) and Walzer (1973)—were in response to Rawls' formulations.

A Theory of Justice coincided with the culmination of various movements in the United States in the 1960s and 1970s. The movements for civil rights, liberation of the blacks, equal rights for the minorities, alleviation of poverty through the great society programme and the anti-Vietnam war protests raised questions about individual and minority rights, just and unjust wars and issues of social justice in policy formations and executions. *A Theory of Justice* examined many of these issues while formulating the principles of justice for a well-ordered society that would be governed by a set of permanent principles of justice. These principles were congruent with, 'our common sense and firmest convictions' (Rawls 1972: 19–20) and would provide the moral basis of a democratic society with which the notion of a just society was inseparably linked. Rawls considered justice as the 'first virtue of social institutions as truth is of systems of thought' and that efficiency and stability were equally important but 'justice has a certain priority being the most important virtue of institutions' (Rawls ibid: 3, 6). Initially, in 1958, he applied the principles to practices but subsequently applied it to the basic structure of the well-ordered society. He acknowledged that existing societies were seldom well-ordered, for there was usually a dispute regarding justice and injustice. Rawls referred to his conception as pure procedural, distinguishing it from perfect procedural and imperfect procedural, since there was no independent criterion for the just result. If procedures were fair then the outcome would also be fair. "There is a correct or fair procedure such that the outcome is likewise correct or fair, whatever it is, provided that the procedure has been properly followed...the background circumstances define a fair procedure ... what makes the final outcome...fair or unfair is...a fair procedure (which) translates its fairness to the outcome only when it is actually carried out" (Rawls ibid: 86).

Rawls tried to demonstrate that justice was about rules that govern a social practice, and not about the evaluation of different situations through criteria such as need and desert. He tackled the main criticism of this approach, which was that, following the rules in an exact manner might produce outcomes that were inconsistent with our commonsense notion of justice. Therefore, he purported to show that under certain carefully specified conditions rational agents chose a set of principles that were consistent with their intuitive ideas of distributive justice, and that, when followed, yielded outcomes which, whatever they might be, were morally acceptable. Notwithstanding its procedural features, Norman P. Barry (Barry 1995: 173) regarded Rawls' theory as a contribution to the theory of social justice because of his continual stress that there was a need for rational justification of all departures from equality. Furthermore, there was a strong preference for equality in the theory which contrasted it with other renditions of entitlement theory. Rawls made a clear-cut demarcation between production and distribution. Though he understood the importance of productivity to bring out the natural talents in persons, he realized the importance of controlling the market criteria by principles of social justice. The fundamental needs of all have a moral priority in the distribution of goods and service and that merit and desert did not play a significant role in justice as fairness. He rejected desert and merit on the grounds that skills, talents and endowments were social products. Rawls did not seek to equalize human beings or ignore individual talents and achievements. Rather he believed that inherited advantages and genetic superiority had to serve society and, in particular, the least advantaged.

CRITIQUE OF UTILITARIANISM

Rawls developed a concept of justice that was congruent with liberty and reciprocity. Both these concepts were at variance with utilitarianism, a doctrine that dominated Western moral and political philosophy since the middle of the eighteenth century. Rawls rejected classical utilitarianism of Bentham and Sidgwick by developing an alternative based on Kantianism, a rival school of utilitarianism. He observed that while utilitarianism was an individualistic theory par excellence it ignored the distinctions that exist between persons. He accepted its premise that each individual had a view of his good, which the society had to satisfy provided no one was harmed in the process. Though utilitarianism believed in the idea of the 'greatest happiness of the greatest number', Rawls accused it of ignoring the interests of the least advantaged. He queried about the reasons as to why the greater gain of some should not compensate for the lesser losses of others; or more importantly, why should the violation of liberty of a few should not be made right by the goods shared by many (Rawls 1972: 26, 33). As a result, utilitarianism treated some individuals only as means towards the ends of others, while justice as fairness considered persons as ends and not as means only. Rawls considered the principle of utility as incompatible with the conception of social cooperation among free and equal individuals for mutual advantage and with the idea of reciprocity implicit in a well-ordered society (Rawls ibid: 13). Furthermore, utilitarianism did not distinguish between the 'claims of liberty and rights on one hand and the desirability of increasing aggregate social welfare on the other' (Rawls ibid: 28). In justice as fairness, basic liberties were taken for granted and rights secured by justice were not 'subject to political bargaining or to the calculus of social interests' (Rawls ibid: 28). Utilitarianism was a teleological doctrine while justice as fairness was a deontological theory, for it did not specify good independently from the right or interpret right as maximizing good. The question of attaining the greatest net balance of satisfactions never arose in justice as fairness. Utilitarianism emphasized on the efficient administration of social resources to maximize the satisfaction of the system of desires constructed by the notion of impartial spectator, from which the many individual systems of desire were accepted as given. Rawls rejected the notion of the sympathetic spectator, as it was a device of utilitarian theory for thinking of the interests of society, as if they were the interests of a single individual. This also led to 'impersonality in the conflation of desires into one system of desire' (Rawls ibid: 188). In utilitarianism, the rational and impartial sympathetic spectator took up a general perspective, a position where his own interests were not at stake. He was equally responsive to the desires of everyone affected by the social system. In justice as fairness the parties were mutually disinterested rather than sympathetic.

Rawls pointed out that his two principles of justice were more congruent than utilitarianism with our common sense convictions, and hence, closer to intuitionism as it condemns institutions like slavery and serfdom. Intuitionism was a doctrine that accepted the existence of an irreducible family of first principles, which were weighed against one another to obtain a just outcome that would match with one's 'considered judgement'. It had two defects: first, it was unable to explain as to why its principles should be followed and second, it gave no guidance for decision when two or more of its principles pointed to conflicting courses of action in a particular situation. Rawls dealt with the first defect by proposing a contractual hypothesis as a method of arriving at principles of justice without having to rely simply on intuitionism. Furthermore, justice as fairness explained not only what intuitionism left unexplained, but also resolved a material disagreement regarding the substance of justice. While one might propose distribution based on merit, the other might want it based on need. Rawls pointed out that the contractual hypothesis led to the criterion of need, thus, taking care of the second drawback.

Rawls accused utilitarianism, including that of J.S. Mill, in spite of the latter's revision of the doctrine, for failing to secure individual rights. Despite the revision, Mill continued to see right as maximizing good without sufficient guarantees of securing equal liberties for all. For Rawls, values like individual liberty and dignity had an independent status and could not be derived from the maximization of social good, while for Mill these were derivative. Mill did not show how the distributive ideal could be subsumed under an aggregative one. Like the classical economists, he assumed the greatest good as the maximum total income, but failed to devote himself to the question of what happened if maximizing total happiness leads to extreme inequality. Sen found very little difference between Rawls and Bentham, for both "captured two different aspects of interpersonal comparison—both necessary and neither sufficient as a basis of ethical judgement. The utilitarian procedure is based on comparing gains and losses of different persons and is insensitive to comparisons of levels of welfare. The Rawlsian procedure does exactly the opposite and is based on comparisons of levels only without making essential use of comparisons of gains and losses (Sen 1974: 307–308). Sen rightly concluded that the two theories were incomplete and that Rawls' formulations were a corrective of Bentham's prescriptions rather than a complete theory in itself. Rawls retained utilitarianism's aim of maximizing social welfare, but insisted on separateness of persons so that none were viewed as means to the ends of the society at large. Neither the well off nor the worst off were to make undue sacrifices that were disproportionate to the benefits they received. Recognition of individual distinctiveness enabled him to argue a case for equal rights, making it clearly a right-based theory (Dworkin 1977). A right-based theory of justice was long been overdue in the Anglo-American tradition in light of the critiques of natural rights conception. The Rawlsian theory was attractive to the liberals, for it provided an independent basis to the defense of individual rights.

Besides utilitarianism, Rawls rejected perfectionism since the persons in the original position did not take interest in one another's preferences for they had different conceptions of good. Perfectionism was a moral theory, according to which, certain activities or states of human beings such as knowledge, achievement and artistic creation were good, apart from any pleasure or happiness they bring. Furthermore, what was morally right was what most promoted these human excellences or perfections. Some versions of perfectionism held that the good consisted in the development of qualities central to human nature so that if knowledge and achievement were good, it was because they realized aspects of human nature. Perfectionist ideas featured in pluralist morality where they were weighed against other competing moral ideas. Perfectionism was rejected as a political principle as Rawls' contracting agents chose greatest equal liberty with a similar equal liberty for others. This did not imply that ends, freedom and well-being of different people were of the same worth, but the fact remained that though people's activities and accomplishments differed, all had equal dignity. Rawls' principles were egalitarian, unlike perfectionism, which was a hierarchical doctrine stating its preference for the extraordinary.

Social Contract

Rawls revived the social contract tradition in its Kantian version. This not only aroused others like Barry (1989 and 1995) and Scanlon (1982) to use the contractual tradition, but also prompted a new tradition of anti-contractualists known as communitarians. The contractual approach exemplified consent and voluntarism by trying to show how self-interested persons, with legitimate competing claims arrived at mutually acceptable social arrangements. Unlike the social contract theory that used the device to explain the origins of the state and the nature of sovereignty, Rawls resurrected it to explain principles of justice. These ensured just practices and institutions in a society, viewed as a fair system of social cooperation between individuals fair and equal. A scathing attack by Hume and Bentham put the social contract theory into oblivion till Rawls revived it. Rawls was the not the first to use the idea of contract for outlining what justice is. As explained before, Glaucon also made use of it in Plato's *Republic*.

Rawls began with the assumption that the principles of justice that "expresses our moral sentiments" (Rawls 1972: 130) was a product of an original agreement in the original position, a hypothetical situation, and 'a heuristic device' akin to the state of nature of the traditional social contract theory. The persons in the original position were rational, capable of a conception of good and with a sense of justice. They were rational with a capacity for intelligent pursuit of one's own interests, to enter into agreements that they adhered and fulfilled. Rational persons did not suffer from envy, for envy tended to make everyone worse off and was collectively disadvantageous. Like Kant, Rawls also believed that envy was one of the vices of humankind. Furthermore, the parties were not in a position to coerce any one, thus, ensuring that agreement was voluntary. The parties were mutually disinterested, roughly similar in needs and interests, equal in power, and, moral and autonomous, thereby, making it possible for fruitful cooperation. Like Hume, Rawls characterized society as a cooperative venture of mutual advantage, where there was both identity and conflict of interests. Borrowing from Hume, he specified the circumstances of justice with two background conditions, which gave rise to the conception of justice: first were objective circumstances that made human cooperation both possible and necessary. Individuals coexisting together in the same definite territory were similar in physical and mental power and lived in conditions of moderate scarcity. The second were the subjective circumstances, where parties with roughly similar needs and interests were willing to cooperate for mutual advantage. They had their own life-plans, which obviously led them to have different ends and purposes and made conflicting claims on the available natural and social resources. However, the interests advanced by these plans were not in the interest of the self, for the persons were mutually disinterested with the incomplete knowledge and limited powers of reasoning and memory. Rawls conceded plurality of lifestyles and the possibilities of diverse philosophical and religious beliefs and social and political doctrines. Among the objective circumstances, he stressed on moderate scarcity and as far as subjective circumstances were concerned, he emphasized mutual disinterestedness (limited altruism). The original position based on pure procedural justice was specified to meet these two conditions. The principles of justice chosen were (Rawls ibid: 131–135): (i) General in form, eliminating both first person dictatorship and free rider forms, (ii) universal in application, (iii) publicly recognized as a final court of appeal for carrying the conflicting claims of moral persons, (iv) conflicting claims ought to be ordered with the help of a conception of right and (v) final.

The novelty about the choice situation was the permissible knowledge that was relevant so as to enable the contracting parties to choose principles of justice without prejudice. This was achieved through the device called the veil of ignorance, not mentioned in the 1957 version, but introduced in 1958, to nullify the influences of genetic endowments, superior talents and social contingencies that tempt the individuals to exploit and tailor the principles for their own advantage. Rawls assumed that parties did not know certain kinds of particular facts like their class position or social status, their fortune in the distribution of natural assets and abilities, their physical and mental strengths, their conception of good, particulars of their rational plan of life and special features of their psychological framework, like aversion to risk or their ability to be optimistic or pessimistic. They did not know the economic and political situation of their society or its level of civilization and culture. They had no information as to which generation they belonged to, but knew they were contemporaries. The parties, however, had general facts about human society, "understand political affairs and the principle of economic theory; they know the basis of social organization and the laws of human psychology" (Rawls ibid: 137). This ensured that all would have an equal say. He assured that the principles chosen were in a state of reflective equilibrium. "It is an equilibrium because at last our principles and judgements coincide; and it is reflective since we know to what principles our judgements conform and the premises of their derivation" (Rawls ibid: 20). He introduced the technique of reflective equilibrium as a method of testing rival moral theories and gauge which one would be preferred. This suggested a harmony between conditions that governed rational choice and a person's intuitive and political judgements and that it was not a neutral one. He acknowledged that Aristotle and subsequently Sidgwick used this method.

Taking a cue from Chomsky, Rawls pointed out that the aim was to formulate principles 'which make the same discriminations as the native speaker' (Rawls ibid: 47). He used the original position in two capacities—as an analytic device and as a justificatory device. As an analytical device it tried to understand the conception of justice with its formal requirements like generality, publicity, finality that apply to the principles. It tried to reduce complex social problems and the choice of principles to simple cognizable problem of individual choice. In its justificatory role, it defended the choice of the two principles through the hypothetical original position. Brian Barry (Barry 1973: 10–11) pointed out that there was no guarantee that the principles chosen in the original position were just and that it was not clear what was deducible and what was not. Goodwin (1993), Lyons (1972), Macpherson (1977), Nagel (1973) and Teitelman (1972) accused Rawls of writing a liberal individualist bias into the original position, thereby, undermining the claim that it was fair.

In his reply, Rawls clarified that he used the word individualism to mean plurality of human life and the right of each to equal liberty rather than viewing social life as a means to individual ends. Barry (1989) pointed out that Rawls' theory of justice contained two distinct (and in some respects plainly incompatible) concepts of what it was for a human practice to be just. A just practice was one which was to the advantage of all its human participants by treating all its human participants impartially. However, for a practice to be to the advantage of all its participants, it must give each of them a good reason to accept it. Rawls showed that the second of these requirements was a lot more demanding than the first. He argued that over a wide range of cases the two together were not plausibly compatible with the requirement that a just practice should treat the interests of all its participants impartially. If human agents chose clearly and freely for themselves they would insist on the best terms they could get and this would reflect the initial inequalities of power. Egoistic rational choice, even under uncertainty, would yield practices that would treat real human agents impartially, only if impartiality was directly imposed upon their agency. In addition, if impartiality was to be imposed upon their agency directly, what was the point of presenting them as egoistic choosers in the first place?

Brian Barry (1995) showed how poorly the contractual method fares, contrary to its own intentions. Where the theories were internally coherent the answers were unappealing (except for Hobbesians and the utilitarians) and where the answers were appealing, like that of Rawls' difference principle, it was inconsistent in its reasoning. Instead, Barry proposed instead impartiality, an idea that principles and rules should be capable of forming the basis of free agreement among people who held different conceptions of good, seeking agreement on reasonable terms by excluding information that might prejudice the process of deliberation. This was Rawls' aim, but he was critical of Rawls' theory on the grounds that there could be no disagreement between people faced with identical information and reasoning in an identical fashion. There was no room for actual bargaining among people who did not know what their ends were. Instead he relied on Scanlon's proposal for an alternative 'original position', one in which well-informed people in a situation of equal power tried to reach an agreement with others who were similarly motivated, on terms that could not be reasonably rejected. He instructed that one should act without regard for one's own interests, situation or relation with others in everyday life. However, he did not define reasonable, which played the role of background constraints on the type of argumentation allowed in Scanlonian original position. He clarified that reasonable did not include religious dogma (Rawls ibid: 29, 30, 122-123, 162-163), cultural communities that claimed special advantage (Rawls ibid: 8, 115), those who rejected the authority of expert opinions, arguments and evidence (Rawls ibid: 104–106), those who hold false beliefs (Rawls ibid: 208), those who lacked knowledge that other societies did things differently and that their own could feasibly be different in various ways (Rawls ibid: 107) and those who were impressed by their own experiences than that of the others (Rawls ibid: 181), thus leaving out a small circle that Barry approved. He concluded by saying that his next volume examined the appropriate role for impartiality and the principles of justice that was supplied by the theory of justice as impartiality (Rawls ibid: 257). Barry and Scanlon like Rawls, justified moral principles as an outcome of a fair agreement. According to Pateman (1979), the Rawlsian system differed from the liberal social contract theory in a fundamental and a decisive way as it did not offer a justification of political obligation in a liberal state, but like Hegel, purported to show why one would and should accept the state as rational and necessary. But Rawls' state was different from that of Hegel as it was a 'social union of unions', a result of his oscillation between extreme abstract individualism and socialized being.

Two Principles of Justice

Rawls clarified that the principles of justice were to apply to the basic structure of a society that dealt with both the economic and social system. The former shaped the aspirations and wants of the citizens, determined what they were and what they wanted to be while the latter not only specified the institutional framework for satisfying these wants and needs but also new ones for the future (Rawls 1972: 259). The role of the basic structure was to 'secure just background conditions against which the actions of individuals and associations take place. Unless this structure is appropriately regulated and corrected, the social process will cease to be just, however free and fair particular transactions may look when view by themselves' (Rawls ibid 1977: 160). The basic structure was procedurally neutral. Its institutions and policies did not exemplify any particular religious, philosophical or moral doctrines, what he termed as comprehensive conception (Rawls ibid 1988: 263). The two principles of justice that were chosen through the original position were initially stated as follows:

(1) Each person is to have an equal right to the most extensive basic liberty, compatible with a similar liberty for others.

(2) Social and economic inequalities are to be arranged so that they are both (a) reasonably expected to be to everyone's advantage and (b) attached to position and offices open to all (Rawls 1972: 60).

Wolff (1977) accused Rawls of falling into the same trap as his utilitarian opponents, namely of confusing justice with welfare and the phrases 'everyone's advantage' and 'equally open to all' as ambiguous. Rawls acknowledged that this part of the second principle could be interpreted in terms of Pareto criterion, which stated that group welfare was at an optimum when it was impossible to make any one man better off without at the same time making at least one other man worse off. In 'Distributive Justice' (1969a), Rawls pointed out the incompleteness of the Pareto criterion, not only vis-à-vis allocation of goods among individuals but also vis-à-vis the many arrangements of an institution and its basic structure. He observed that the Pareto principle could serve as a limited criterion of efficiency, but not as a criterion of justice. The first principle embodied the notion of liberty. The second part of the second principle along with the first principle guaranteed equality. The first part of the second principle embodied the idea of fraternity. The final statement of the second principle read as follows:

> Social and economic inequalities are to be arranged so that they are both (a) to the greatest benefit of the least advantaged and (b) attached to offices and positions open to all under conditions of fair equality of opportunity (Rawls ibid: 83).

Rawls suggested one measure of determining the least advantaged, namely income and wealth and not the social position, "All persons with less than median income and wealth may be taken as the least advantaged segment" (Rawls ibid: 98). Since the two principles were to be applied to the basic structure it 'is to be arranged to maximise the worth of the least advantaged of the complete scheme of equality liberty shared by all' (Rawls ibid: 205). The second principle (a) was called the difference principle or 'maximin' and the second principle (b) was the fair equality of opportunity. The difference principle, 'tells us to rank alternatives by their worst possible outcomes: we are to adopt the alternative the worst outcome of which is superior to the worst outcomes of the others' (Rawls ibid: 153).

Rawls took into cognizance Tawney's criticisms about equality of opportunity, and acknowledged that it enabled only individuals of exceptional ability to overcome the disadvantages which accrue by birth. It was of very little help to individuals of average or ordinary ability. Through fair equality of opportunity Rawls sought to mitigate the disadvantages imposed by both natural endowments and social circumstances and in the process, the notion of fairness undercuts a meritocratic society. The first principle required, 'equality in the assignment of basic liberties'. Basic liberties of a citizen were political liberty (right to vote and to be eligible for public office), freedom of speech and assembly, liberty of conscience and freedom of thought, freedom of person along with the right to hold personal property and freedom from arbitrary arrest and seizure, as defined by the rule of law. The second principle applied to the distribution of income and wealth, the design of organizations that regulated differences in authority, responsibility and chains of command (Rawls ibid: 61). The first principle was lexically prior to the second and second principle (b) was lexically prior to second principle (a). This ordering implies that a departure from the institutions of equal liberty required by the first principle could not be justified or compensated for by the greater social and economic advantages. These principles implied that the social structure was divisible into two or more distinct parts, in which the first principle applied to one and the second to the other. If the parties in the original position felt that their basic liberties could be effectively exercised, they would not exchange a lesser liberty for an improvement in economic well-being. Taking into consideration Lessnoff's (1971) suggestion that restrictions on liberty were unjust unless, either (a) they were necessary to prevent unjust inequalities or (b) they were to the advantage of everyone whose liberty was restricted, Rawls restated the priority rule of liberty. The superior position was not accorded to liberty as such but rather to the list of liberties described as basic. Rawls did not offer a general definition of liberty from which this list could be deduced. The first principle and its priority rule were finally as follows:

> Each person is to have equal right to the most extensive total system of equal basic liberties compatible with a similar system of liberty for all … . The principles of liberty can be restricted only for the sake of liberty. There are two cases (a) a less extensive liberty must strengthen the total system of liberty shared by all, and (b) a less than equal liberty must be acceptable to those citizens with the lesser liberty (Rawls 1972: 250).

Liberty and its Priority

Rawls placed liberty at the centre of his theory of justice by regarding a list of liberties as basic. He endorsed Constant's assertion of liberty of the moderns to be of greater value than the liberty of the ancients. 'While both sorts of freedom are deeply rooted in human aspirations, freedom of thought and liberty of conscience, freedom of person and the civil liberties, ought not to be sacrificed to political liberty, to the freedom to participate equally in political affairs' (Rawls ibid: 202–203). He considered this question to be a substantive political philosophy requiring a theory of rights and justice to answer it and defined liberty as therefore, secondary. Reiterating MacCallum he explained liberty with reference to three aspects: the agents who were free, the restrictions or limitations from which one was free, and their ambit of freedom. He distinguished between "a concept of justice as meaning a proper balance between competing claims from a conception of justice as a set of related principles for identifying the relevant considerations which determines this balance" (Rawls ibid: 10). On this basis he distinguished between liberty and its worth. The first principle recognized and granted equal liberty to all, compatible with the like liberty for everyone. He conceded that inequalities in wealth and power affect the worth of liberty but left the equality of liberty intact. Liberty was represented by the complete system of the liberties of equal citizenship, while the worth of liberties to persons and groups was proportional to their capacity to advance their ends within the framework the system defined. "Freedom as equal liberty is same for all ... but the worth of liberty is not the same for everyone ... . The lesser worth of liberty is however compensated, for, since the capacity of the less fortunate members of society to achieve their aims would be even less were they not to accept the existing inequalities whenever the difference principle is satisfied" (Rawls ibid: 204).

The principle of equal liberty when applied to the political procedure defined by the constitution was the principle of equal participation, which would be realized within a constitutional democracy. The representative body, which was the legislature with law-making functions, determined the basic policies and was accountable to the electorate. It would be elected for a limited term and was more than an advisory or registering body endorsing the decisions of the Executive. Elections—fair and free—would be held regularly on the basis of universal adult franchise. The principle of loyal opposition, along with freedom of speech, freedom of association and freedom of assembly would be recognized and guaranteed if democratic government was to succeed. To ensure that liberties were not formal, Rawls offered the second principle, fair value of political liberties and fair political procedures whereby citizens were roughly equal in political power. He recommended freeing the dependence of political parties of big business and monopolies through sufficient tax revenues and public finance of election costs. Plural voting, public monies and abolition of gerrymandering guaranteed participation and ensured the self-worth of a person and the worth of liberty. The principle of participation also recognized that each citizen was eligible to join political parties, run for elections and hold places of authority. The traditional devices of constitutionalism namely bicameral legislature, separation of powers, checks and balances, bill of rights with judicial review were consistent with equal political liberty provided it applied to everyone. Furthermore, in society with private ownership of the means of production, property and wealth would be distributed widely. Rawls accepted that the two principles secured the integrity of religious and moral freedom.

Equal liberty of conscience was the only principle that the person in the original position acknowledged. They cannot take chances with their liberty by permitting the dominant religious or moral doctrines to persecute or suppress others. The state cannot favour any particular religion nor could it attach penalties to any particular religious affiliation. Liberty of conscience was limited by the common interest in public order and security on the assumption that it was not superior to moral and religious interests nor did the government have any right to suppress philosophical beliefs on the pretext that it conflicted with the interests of the state. Given the principles of justice the state was viewed as an association of equal citizens. It would try to regulate individuals' pursuit of their moral and spiritual interests in accordance with the principles agreed to in the original position of equality. In this way the government acted as an agent of the public by helping them to satisfy their demands of their public conception of justice. Further, liberty of conscience would be limited only on grounds of reasonable expectations, that by not doing so, it can damage the public order which the government had to maintain. Toleration was derived from common sense and not from the practical necessities or reasons of the state. All religious views were to receive full and equal tolerance as toleration led to stability of the system.

Daniels (1975) and Hart (1975) argued that historical experience demonstrated that inequalities of wealth led to inequalities of power resulting in inequalities of liberties. Economic factors played as much an important role in constraining liberties as legal restrictions and public opinion. In response to this criticism Rawls replaced 'the most extensive total system' with 'a fully adequate scheme' taking into account the exercise of moral powers in the social circumstances what he called the 'two fundamental cases' (Rawls 1982: 41). The first fundamental case connected with the capacity for a sense of justice concerns, 'the application of the principles of justice to the basic structure of society and its social policies'. The second related to the capacity for a conception of good, 'concerns the application of the principles of deliberative reason in guiding our conduct over a complete life' (Rawls ibid: 47). Certain liberties like freedom of thought and political liberties were necessary for the exercise of sense of justice in the first case. Liberty of conscience and freedom of association would apply in case of the second. The remainder would be combined with the two cases. The amended first principle read as follows: "Each person has an equal right to a fully adequate scheme of equal basic liberties, which is compatible with a similar scheme of liberties for all" (Rawls ibid: 5).

Rawls clarified that no particular liberty had a priority. The scheme of basic liberties, which he called a family of liberties were to be equally distributed among citizens. The various liberties were adjusted to one another to ensure the availability of the most adequate scheme for the exercise of the two moral powers. The worth of the political liberties to all citizens, whatever their social or economic position must be approximately equal, or at least sufficiently equal, in the sense that everyone had a fair opportunity to hold public office and influence the outcome of political decision (Rawls ibid: 42). The constitution protected the basic liberties as well as the fair value of the political parties. It also specified a just political procedure and incorporated restrictions that protect basic liberties and secure their priority thereby safeguarding them from the vagaries of legislative policy making. The rest—non-basic rights and matters of economic policy—were left to the legislative stage. Hart (1975) and Daniels (1975) pointed out that the criterion 'most extensive scheme' was quantitative and simplistic. Rawls responded by pointing out that basic liberties shall be the same for everyone as one can obtain greater liberty for oneself only if others are granted the same greater liberty (Rawls 1982: 56). Basic liberties as a family had priority. Liberty anchored to the primary good of equal right to self-respect implied that the self esteem of an individual can be enhanced only by interacting with others as a full-fledged member of an egalitarian political society. Rawls' belief in the moral equality of persons made him view the individual who enjoyed counting blades of grass as fulfilling his nature just as Berlin accepted that there was not just one indicator of either contentment or excellence.

Berlin's defence of liberty as part of his overall scheme of pluralism was both formidable and appealing, but it gave rise to a practical problem as to how the different values could become operational when it came to pragmatic social and political policy. The question was one of choosing between values. There was a need to distinguish between privately pursued ends and publicly enforced rules. Liberalism meant leaving people free, within limits, to pursue their individual conceptions of goods, whose limits were defined by certain publicly enforced rules of right. This distinction between right and good was attempted by Rawls (Lessnoff 1999: 223). Rawls accepted plurality of ends but, unlike Berlin, considered liberty to have a lexical priority over claims of social and economic equality in well-ordered society. In Rawls' rights-based theory, the liberal state bound together people with divergent views, together with the help of shared political conceptions and public ways of reasoning, that even if they were moral they were generated by any particular partisan moral theory.

Difference Principle and Notion of Equality

Rawls argued that his difference principle, which he called democratic equality, was different from liberal equality and the system of natural liberty. The difference principle was a maximizing principle and functions within a generation and the just savings principle operated between generations. It tipped the balance in the favour of equality by removing the bias of social and natural contingencies. Inequalities arising out of natural endowments and by birth were to be compensated, for they were undeserved. It was not the same as that of redress. It transformed the aims of the basic structure so that the total scheme of institution no longer emphasized social efficiency and technocratic values. It treated natural talents of individuals as social assets whose benefits were to be shared by all individuals. Desert and merit were rejected as the basis of justice.

> The naturally advantaged are not to gain merely because they are more gifted, but only to cover the costs of training and education and for using their endowments in ways that help the less fortunate as well. No one deserves his greater natural capacity nor merit a more favourable starting place in society (Rawls 1972: 101–102).

The reasoning was that, natural distribution was neither just nor unjust. They simply represented natural facts. The two principles corrected this arbitrariness as 'no one deserves his place on the distribution of native endowments any more than one deserves one's initial starting place in society' (Rawls ibid: 104). Rawls recognized that fortune played an arbitrary role in the distribution of natural abilities. He did not obliterate natural endowments but rather gave incentives to the well-off to ensure productivity, which in turn led to the elevation of the worst off. Unlike the principle of utility that treated some individuals as means to the ends of others the difference principle treated all individuals both as means and as ends. Individual assets were, social assets, which was why he emphasized the need for reciprocal advantages and benefits, since society recognizes mutual respect between individuals.

The 'difference principle' maximized the minimum and was conceived as a basic right (Martin 1985). It was offered as an alternative to the Pareto principle, as a measure of social welfare. Rawls did not accept trade-offs between efficiency and equality. The maximin or the difference principle that he advocated did not aim at the fulfilment of needs nor did it merely guarantee that the poor will remain above the social minimum. It advocated procedural elevation of the life prospects of the least well-off. Since risk aversion was an important human motivation the maximin was a lifesaver, just in case, anyone happened to be in the worst-off category. The transfer branch of the government provided for allowances in case of unemployment and benefits to the family. Rawls did not merely advocate taxation of the incomes of the rich to subsidize directly or indirectly the incomes of the poor as done by the welfare state. Once transfers ensured elevation of the worst-off, the remainder will be regulated by the price mechanism, which when compared to central planning was efficient in determining production and consumption of goods, both scarce and abundant. The index of identifying the worse-off will be an economic criterion (Rawls 1972: 98).

The whole thrust of Rawls was on reciprocal benefits and advantages where every individual contributed to society and derived benefits in the process. The naturally advantaged gained not because they were more gifted but because they were being reimbursed the expenses incurred for their training and education, and for using their assets and skills for the benefit of the naturally disadvantaged. Incentives were given to the well off in order to secure efficiency and productivity. He considered natural endowments as the outcome of natural lottery and productive capacities as social assets. The individual was not the sole proprietor of his endowments or a privileged recipient of the advantages that it accrued. He argued, like Kant did, that individual talent and aptitudes had a social origin. However, Rawls did not obliterate unequal individual endowments. He took into account the criticisms against the liberal idea of equality of opportunity that it applied only to individuals with extraordinary abilities ignoring ordinary human beings. Through the second part of his second principle he alleviated the disadvantages by birth and social circumstances and undermined a meritocratic society. Rawls was not interested in nullifying individual, achievements, but insisted on its utilization for the benefit of the least advantaged. He was concerned with majority and minority deprivation. It was the liberalism for the disadvantaged and the underprivileged. The second principle was an acknowledgement of and a tribute to the long socialist critique of liberal equality. Significant assertions of Rawls were his opinion that 'strict equality was inefficient' and his endorsement of Tucker's opinion that 'Marxism was beyond justice'. He rejected trade-off between efficiency and equity and spoke of reciprocal benefits, as he treated productive capacities as social assets. He accepted social stratification, implicitly rejecting the argument of class divided societies. His idea combined growth with equality, which represented the post-Second World War liberal-social democracy consensus. This was a view that Anthony Crosland (1918–77) too voices as evident from the following observation:

> The achievement of greater equality without intolerable social stress and a probable curtailment of liberty depends heavily on economic growth. The better off have been able to accept with reasonable equanimity a decline in their relative standard of living because growth has enabled them (almost) to maintain the absolute standard of living despite redistribution (Plant 1984: 16).

Rawls injected into competitive and private forms of social cooperation attributes of genuine reciprocal relationships and transformed them. He ensured a system that was stable, efficient and just and one not bereft of social responsibility towards the less privileged. While Rawls attempted to construct a theory in which liberty and equality were compatible, Nozick's theory gave primacy to liberty accepting inequalities as they were. Nozick rejected Rawls' argument that the better off accepted and cooperated in the society to elevate the worst-off. He argued that people in subordinate position accepted their position as facts of their existence and willingly receive orders from those with superior talents. He opposed imposition of constraints in the name of fairness on voluntary social cooperation, for those who were already its beneficiaries benefit more. Hayek reiterated the classical liberal conviction that inequalities due to upbringing, inheritance and education as permitted by the ideal of liberty, actually benefits society as a whole. Inequality was good, in itself. It was not only inevitable but also desirable in a free society for 'spill over effects' from the existence of private wealth were significant. These private sources of wealth nourish innovation and experiment in science and arts and act as a bulwark against the expansion of the state. Dworkin distinguished between inequalities that were 'endowment sensitive' from those that were 'ambition sensitive'. The former referred to the advantages that some enjoyed as a result of arbitrary distribution of resources while the latter related to those actions of a person that made him successful. "By making this distinction, and reserving moral appraisal for the results of ambitions, he is implicitly restoring the idea of desert to distributive questions. The distinction between deserts and entitlements, which is a feature of procedural justice, is abandoned, because in Dworkin's scheme there will be no unjust entitlements" (Barry 1995: 197). This followed from his assertion that every person was entitled to 'equal concern and respect', and a denial of adequate resources to people was a violation of that right.

The foremost critics of Rawlsian egalitarianism emerged in the United States, in the mid 1960s, from amongst the liberals who styled themselves as Neo-conservatives. They observed that the United States was in the grip of implacable and intense egalitarianism and, Rawls as its representative thinker, shifted the meaning of equality to mean one of opportunity to one of outcome (Bell 1979: 5). The concept of equality was enlarged beyond its traditional scope of political rights and political power to include equity in economic power, social status and authority. The moral fervour with which equality was projected, resulted in a new despotism, which posed a singular threat to liberty (Nisbet 1974a and 1974b) and if ignored, will destroy the fabric of the liberal society (Kristol 1979). Contemporary populism, in its desire for wholesale egalitarianism insisted in the end on complete levelling. It was not for fairness but against elitism—its impulse was not justice, but re-sentiment. The populists were for power, but against authority represented in the superior competence of individuals. Since they lacked authority they want power (Bell 1973: 453).

The Neo-conservatives regarded the clamour for equity warily, since it was difficult to fulfil such a desire. Kristol, Nisbet and to some extent Frankel asserted that it was the intellectuals who cherish such an aspiration with the objective of extending their power through the state. They were skeptical of extensive governmental intervention and accepted the ethics of liberal capitalism and decision-making through the free market, buttressed by traditions, customs and historical norms. They defended the classic liberal principle of equality of opportunity and admitted that an overzealous government with the aim of promoting equity threatened merit advancement, with the aim of promoting equity. Increase in the government activity encroached on the spontaneity of the individuals and voluntary organizations. The Neo-conservatives saw the shift from equality of opportunity to equality of condition as a mood towards populist levelling, resentment against authority represented in the superior competence of the individual. As a result, excellence, professional authority and technical expertise were compromised with. They rejected Rawlsian theory for its undue stress on egalitarianism. Nisbet (1974b) compared Rawls with the eighteenth-century philosophers and in particular to Rousseau, for his emphasis on the notion of an absolute individual and the idea of an absolute moral community which were seen as complementary and compatible. The first principle that Rawls offered did not have so much liberty as equals shared in a vast homogenized structure called liberty. It was utterly outweighed in mass and use by the second principle. Rawls, like Rousseau, expressed liberty in the language of equality and made the two virtually synonymous. The fair equality of opportunity coupled with the difference principle tipped the scale in the favour of an egalitarian society. The conception of justice will be better, if Rawls abandoned his first principle. Much of the difficulty lies in the fact that he repeatedly presented liberty as an overall system in which individuals were to have 'equal shares' rather than in the nature of liberty itself. *A Theory of Justice* is 'consecrated to as radical a form of egalitarianism as might be found anywhere outside the pages of social contract' (Nisbet 1974a: 117). For Kristol, the concept of equality lacked a clear and precise meaning. It was not equality of incomes that was at stake. Rather the professional classes raised the banner of equality against the business community to gain power and status, for they regarded the bourgeois society as deficient in its conception of common good.

Bell castigated Rawls for not making it clear as to whether 'we are to accept the subjective evaluation of individuals as the moral norm, or an objective standard, and on what basis' (Bell 1973: 446). Reiterating an oft-repeated assertion, Bell observed that usually people evaluate unfairness or deprivation by comparing with their peers rather than by an absolute standard. People tolerate disparities in income and wealth provided they were justly earned. A social policy had to be such, to be able to determine as to the genuinely disadvantaged from those who out of choice like to remain disadvantaged. Any classification of the disadvantaged had to take precaution, for they might face social stigmatization because of such a classification. A principle of equality had to be necessarily universal to guarantee impartiality of treatment to persons while simultaneously minimizing administrative arbitrariness. Bell pointed out that Rawls, like Jencks, did not discuss either 'work' or 'effort' or merit, though he considered meritocracy. The fact was that there were different kinds of inequalities relating to income, wealth, status, power, opportunity (occupational and social) and education, 'There is not one scale but many, and the inequalities in on scale are not coupled completely with inequality in every other' (Bell 1973: 452). In this context, Bell formulated an alternate conception of a just meritocracy, which meant social equality and respect for each person. Each person was entitled to a basic set of services and income, which will ensure his security and dignity. Meritocracy was defined as "those who have earned status or have achieved positions of rational authority by competence... . They are men who are the best in their field, as judged by their fellows" (Bell 1973: 454).

Walzer observed, that there was no reason to assume only a single curve and that "most people (different in each case) cluster around the middle of whatever we can construct with smaller numbers at the lower and higher ends" (Walzer 1973: 399). Walzer (1983) conceived a 'post-liberal state' that accepted moral membership in a community as the greatest good and had a concern for the issue of complex equality. The underlying notion of the idea of complex equality was that each resource must be distributed according to a principle appropriate to its own sphere. The critics on the left criticized Rawls for not narrowing the gap between the advantaged and disadvantaged and in not abolishing the category of the worst-off. Macpherson (1977) pointed out that, for Rawls a classless society was 'unthinkable' and in principle 'impossible' and accused Rawls for neglecting the way exploitation works, affecting the transfer of human powers leading to inequality in a capitalist society.

Other critics objected to the fact that the well-off and the naturally gifted had to make sacrifices for the least favoured. Harsanyi (1975: 605) viewed the difference principle as a result of an artificial and forced interpretation of the Kantian injunction of 'treating one another not as means but as ends'. Schaefer (1973: 24) observed that the difference principle violated the Kantian dictum of reciprocal freedom and accused Rawls of 'treating men unequally so as to make them equal'. Sandel (1982) reiterating Nozick (1974) argued that the Kantian dictum that 'no one deserves his natural assets' did not imply that one's assets should be treated as common assets. Arrow (1973: 247–248) conceded the assumption that Rawls made, but observed that it was difficult, however, to convince students that the productivity principle was not completely self-evident. However, Rawls' critics misunderstood the clear and precise relationship that Rawls established between individual performance, not on desert but with reference to one's contributions to society viewed as a reciprocal exchange of services. His two principles of justice ensured moral equal among individuals by attenuating uncompassionate selfishness and "deprives men of threat advantages against one another" (Chapman 1975: 590). The distinctiveness of the individual was preserved and recognized within a societal context. Neither the well-off nor the worse-off were required to make undue sacrifices, which was disproportionate to the benefits they received. He synthesized liberalism with economic egalitarianism by taking into account the notions of just reward and human needs. Crick (1972: 602) concedes that 'he is profoundly wrong but almost perfectly relevant'. Rawls, like Weber, viewed society as composed of disparate income groups. He was writing at a time when even after one hundred years none of Marx's predictions about capitalism had come true. Far from collapsing, capitalism has demonstrated resilience and has survived due to its adaptability (Galbraith 1990).

The Rawlsian paradigm revived the debate on equality and inequality in the modern political theory. Equality for Rawls was an operational concept tied to his procedural theory of justice. He accepted the fact that strict equality was inefficient and that inequality was an inevitable part of society. The innovative feature of his theory was that inequality was justified if it led to the elevation of the worst-off. Rawls did not lament, like Plato and Aristotle, on inequality as the cause of instability and revolutions in a society. Nor did he, like Rousseau, consider inequality to be the source of human misery, moral degradation and corruption, neither did he, like Gandhi, accept a poor society, which was equal as compared to a rich society, based on inequalities of wealth and status. His endeavour was to justify the level of morally acceptable inequalities within advanced affluent societies with a pragmatic approach to achieve tangible, substantive and long-term equality. It was certainly not 'an exercise in guilt' (Wolin 1986: 184).

Two Conceptions of Justice and Notion of Primary Social Goods

Rawls offered two conceptions of justice—general and special. The two principles along with their priority rule constitute the special conception, while the general conception permits inequalities in any primary good, which is expressed as follows: "All social values—liberty and opportunity, income and wealth and the bases of self-respect—are to be distributed equally unless distribution of, any or all of these values is to the advantage of the least favoured (Rawls 1972: 303). In non-ideal societies, liberty did not enjoy lexical priority over other social values. Primary goods were central because they were important to an individual's overall good that was determined 'by what is for him the most rational long-term plan of life given reasonably favourable circumstances ... good is the satisfaction of rational desire' (Rawls ibid: 92–93). The primary goods—rights and liberties, powers and opportunities, income and wealth and self-respect—were distributed by the basic structure of a society. Primary goods specified the well-being and expectations of the representative person. Other primary goods were health and vigour, intelligence and imagination which were described as natural goods. Rawls distinguished between the thin theory and the full theory of good. The former was "to secure the premises about primary good required to arrive at the principles of justice" (Rawls ibid: 396). In full theory of good, the principles of justice were secured as moral concepts with which the notion of good was connected were considered. In full theory, rational plans and human good were consistent with the principles of justice. The values of personal affection and friendship, meaningful work and social cooperation, the pursuit of knowledge and the fashioning and contemplation of beautiful objects were not only a prominent part of the rational plan but these could be advanced in a manner as permitted by justice.

The notion of self-respect was crucial to the understanding of the idea of rational person. Initially, he did not include self-respect among the primary goods, but subsequently used it with great frequency identifying it as the most important category "without which nothing may seem worth doing" (Rawls ibid: 440). People increased their self-respect by what he called the Aristotelian Principle: "On other things being equal, human beings enjoy the exercise of their realized capacities (their innate or trained abilities) and this enjoyment increased the more the capacity is realized or greater its complexity" (Rawls ibid: 426). The notion of self-respect and the Aristotelian principle established the status of liberty and opportunity as primary as it implied the ability to choose.

Rawls countered the criticism that primary goods have an individualistic bias with the help of three observations: (i) Income and wealth was the legal command over the material means in general necessary to realize people's needs and interests, whether as individuals or as members of associations and the desire for such goods was not peculiar to a particular type of society. (ii) Income and wealth could be held in many forms—public and associational as well as private and individual. It was true that the theory of good used the notion of an individual's plan of life but this did not imply that such plans must be individualistic. (iii) The desire for income and wealth was distinct from the desire to be wealthy and being wealthy was not a primary good (Rawls 1975: 542).

In his Dewey lectures (1980) Rawls pointed out that the power to form a conception of good was a core aspect of moral personality and an expression of autonomous choice. He accepted that irreconcilable and deep differences of fundamental significance were a permanent condition of human life. He insisted on impartiality as no single conception of good would be accorded a privileged position suppressing coercively other conceptions. In the Tanner lectures (1982) Rawls developed the notion of the priority within an institutional structure which were "necessary for the development and the full and informed exercise of the two moral powers" (Rawls ibid: 22–23).

Institutional Framework of the Well-ordered Society

Rawls described the institutional framework that applied the principles of justice. From the original position the parties moved on to a constitutional convention to choose a constitution that would prescribe the powers of government and the basic rights of the citizen. They, then move on to the legislative stage where the justice of laws and policies were to be assessed, and then to the stage when rules were applied to particular cases by judges and administrators. The last stage was when the principles of justice were applied and such a society for Rawls was well-ordered with a political system that was a constitutional democracy, thus, implicitly rejecting the erstwhile communist societies since these lacked democratic culture and freedom.

Like Arendt, Rawls accepted the importance of constitutionalism as a method of change, as a check against absolute and unaccountable power. A constitution lends stability and durability to the polity and also provided the essential structure for realizing freedom and accepted civil disobedience to rectify possible lapses in the political system. Rawls' well-ordered society was a social union of union with final ends, which were shared because they valued common institutions and activities as good in themselves. It differed from a private society where interests were competing and not complementary. Its institutions lacked rationality except for the benefit of the individual's private pursuits and "everyone prefers the most efficient schemes that gives him the largest share of assets" (Rawls 1972: 521). The societal dimension of an individual's existence was underlined in Rawls' theory.

The economic system combined the market with state regulation. The government had four branches that regulated the free competitive economy. The allocation branch kept the price system competitive by preventing the formation of an unreasonable market power and change property rights through taxes and subsidies. The stabilization branch took care of employment opportunities. The transfer branch was responsible for maintaining a social minimum by way of unemployment and family allowances. The distribution branch preserved an approximate justice in distributive shares by means of taxation and brings about necessary adjustments in the rights of property to rectify unequal distribution rather than merely increasing the revenue. The exchange branch, supposedly the fifth one, looked after the citizens' preferences and various social interests by adhering to Wickshell's unanimity criterion. This suggested that if the public made an efficient use of social resources there ought to be some scheme for distributing extra taxes among different kinds of tax payers that was unanimously approved. Pateman (1979) observed that Rawls advocacy of workers councils would not bring economic democracy to the workplace as he viewed democracy as a political concept. Unless political obligation was conceived as a horizontal and not vertical relationship between citizens that manifested through multifarious associations it would not undercut the liberal 'umpire' state and its claim to authority.

Following the method of avoidance, Rawls remained indeterminate about the type of regime for he considered his principles as compatible even with the liberal socialist regime (Rawls 1972: 280). He thereby revived the framework of political speculation that was predominant till the nineteenth century, where the distinction between liberalism and socialism did not exist. This distinction has become redundant before the end of the twentieth century, following the demise of communism. Rawls was the first major political theorist to transcend this ideological categorization invented within the specificity of the twentieth century. He represented the post-Second World War Keynesian consensus between social democracy and liberal-democratic capitalism.

Natural Duties and Political Obligation

A legitimate and just government was one that exuded justice of political institutions and procedures and justice in its measures, a view that Rawls advanced. A principle of fairness, according to Rawls, had two parts, to demonstrate how obligations arose in the first instance, when the institutions were just and second, when one voluntarily accepted its benefits to further one's interest. The second stipulation was a kind of gratitude argument, for co-operation required some restriction of one's liberty. It was illegitimate—a form of cheating—for anyone to act as a free rider without some special justification. Nozick disagreed with this argument, for benefits, which were an accidental result of one's activities, imposed no obligation on others. Regarding the first, Rawls stated that when the constitution and its social structure were reasonably just, one was obliged to comply even with unjust laws (Rawls 1972: 351). Injustice might be tolerable if it was fairly distributed amongst all the groups and would disappear by the dynamics of the democratic process in the long run. However, this was no justification to comply with laws that denied our basic liberties (Rawls ibid: 355). Besides obligation, Rawls also stipulated natural duties and considered the most important duty to support and further just institutions. This consisted of two parts—first, was where one had to comply with and contribute one's share to just institutions when they exist, and second, to assist in the establishment of just arrangements when they did not exist. Rawls mixed moral obligation (gratitude) with consent, for the whole point behind the appeal of the principle of fairness was that obligation was generated by voluntary acceptance of certain benefits of cooperative political enterprise. Rawls builds into his theory of just government a notion of democracy. The argument of just government steered clear of some of the conceptual problems of the consent theory and the problem of those who did not agree to it because it considered a person's obligation to pursue justice as moral and unconditional, unless of course the government deviated from the course of providing justice. It also helped one to, 'distinguish between general obligation to a just regime and a modified—or annulled—obligation to particular unjust laws, and allows a theory of disobedience to be formulated without too much inconsistency' (Goodwin 1993: 312).

Civil Disobedience

Rawls accepted that even in a well-ordered society serious violations of justice occurred. He limited his enquiry to the role of civil disobedience in a democratic society since a state of near justice required a democratic regime. In such a state, it was the conflict of duties that gave rise to the problem of civil disobedience. It involved the extent to which citizens felt it was their duty to obey the laws enacted by the legislative majority, in order to defend their liberties and their duty to oppose injustice. A constitutional theory of disobedience had three aspects as follows: (i) It defined the possible reasons for dissent and distinguished it from other forms of opposition in a democratic authority. This might range from protests and demonstrations to militancy and organized resistance. (ii) The reasons for civil disobedience and the conditions under which such an action was justified in a democratic regime that was more or less just. (iii) It should explain the role of civil disobedience within a constitutional system as an appropriate mode of protest (Rawls 1972: 363–364).

Rawls considered civil disobedience as a public, non-violent and conscientious act contrary to law, usually done with the intention of bringing about a change in the policies and laws of the government. It was a political act, which was justified by the moral principles that defined a conception of civil society and public good. It was based on a political conviction as opposed to self or group interests. In the context of constitutional democracy, this involved a conception of justice which acted as a point of reference to the citizens to regulate their political affairs and interpret the constitution. It was a political act within the limits of the allegiance to the rule of law with the purpose of restoring democratic norms and processes that were ignored or overthrown. It was addressed to the majority that wielded political power. It was guided and justified by the principles of justice that regulated the constitution and its social institutions. It was a public act since it addressed to the sense of justice of the majority giving them an opportunity to reconsider the measures that were being protested against. It was a warning, which the dissenters gave for not honouring the conditions of social co-operation as they were undermined when basic liberties were persistently violated. Rawls specifically ruled out appeal to, 'principles of personal morality or to religious doctrines' although he accepts, 'these may coincide with and support one's claims' (Rawls ibid: 365).

Rawls granted to the minority the right to draw the 'attention of the majority to acknowledge their legitimate claims' (Rawls ibid: 366). He considered the possibility of injustice being meted out on a minority and in this context he mentioned religious minorities. He was not explicit as to whether the minority sought justice, recognition, status and rights as individual members for themselves, or as a group. Civil disobedience was an expression of one's conviction and was based on principles that regulated civic life and public life. It had to be non-violent, for in a situation where civil disobedience became necessary, only a law was broken but not the fidelity to the system of law. Rawls insisted that social arrangements, however, efficient can be unjust. He granted the right to disobey in case the principle of equal liberty and fair equality of opportunity were violated, and if a minority was suffering for a long time and if avenues for legal redress were not available. Like Arendt, Rawls confined acts of civil disobedience to redress political grievances but excluded social and economic ones as evident from his decision to prohibit civil disobedience if there were violations of the difference principle. Pateman (1979) considered the conception of civil disobedience to be exceedingly narrow as it would not be invoked if there was a breach of the difference principle. It overlooked the fact that different social positions would inevitably lead to the exclusion of categories of working class and women.

Rawls ruled out the possibility of anarchy as long as there was sufficient working agreement in the individuals' conception of political justice. What was required was an understanding of its meaning as embodied in the ethos of the democratic institutions. 'If legitimate civil disobedience seem to threaten civil peace the responsibility falls not so much on those who protest as upon those, whose abuse of authority and power justified such opposition' (Rawls 1969b: 255). For him, civil disobedience was distinct from conscientious refusal, which was non-compliance with a more or less direct legal injunction or administrative order. Civil disobedience unlike conscientious refusal was addressed to the sense of justice in the majority. In the latter, the conviction of the community cannot be invoked nor was it based on political principles. It might be founded on religious or other principles that were found in variance of the constitution. However, in reality, this distinction did not exist.

Rawls articulated a fully developed theory of civil disobedience within a liberal constitutional democracy. Till date, this was the most in-depth philosophical analysis on the subject so far. The liberals within the tradition who preceded him offered insights, which he incorporated in his analyses. Hobbes' arguments anticipated the recent discussions on civil disobedience, namely the need for a civil disobedient to willingly accept penalties and prove that he was breaking a law for a political reason and was otherwise an allegiant citizen, who had faith in the rule of law. Locke acknowledged the right of the people to resist an unjust government. In America, Jefferson extended the Lockean theory of consent by emphasizing the majority needs to be conscious about minority rights and opinions. He regarded the government as the main violator of individual thought and opinion, but did not rule out the possibility of an over enthusiastic press and public opinion hindering independence of mind and conscientious judgement. Tocqueville regarded unlimited power wherever lodged as a threat to justice and individual liberty and recommended disobedience when there was a transgression of those limits. Hegel allowed justified disobedience, if the state was not rational by which he meant its ethical substance. If the state failed to provide for welfare and was inadequate in serving as means to the satisfaction of the citizen then the basis of the state became insecure. He recognized the possibility of justified disobedience and acknowledged that the inequalities of civil society in his day brought into focus the validity of obligations for a large number of poor people, but did not outline the concrete measures that disobedience should take. Moreover, he did not grant this right convincing legal form (Tunick 1998: 529–530). For Green, the majority and the minority had the right of resistance provided they demonstrate that it was for common good. Each citizen had the right to judge whether a particular law conformed to common good, but had no right to break the law as long as there were legal methods for changing or abolishing the disputed law. This was because common good suffered whenever there was resistance. It was only within non-democratic systems or where the law-making authority was itself obscure that individuals had a right of resistance provided there was a guarantee that authority would qualitatively change and the general social order would remain intact with its set of rights. This distinction between democratic and non-democratic system was set aside when Green discussed slavery in the context of the American civil war. He defended the duty of the slaves to reject state laws since these denied basic rights. Even those who supported the cause of the slaves must disobey legitimately the laws upholding slavery provided they ensure that if they violated these laws there will be no anarchy and loss of general freedom. Green did not distinguish between disobedience to a particular law or policy from the issue of overthrowing government. He regarded disobedience as a revolutionary activity.

Later Writings

In *Political Liberalism* Rawls responded to his Communitarian and Republican critics by wrestling with the problem of cultural heterogeneity within liberal states. He clarified that the principles of justice were independent of comprehensive philosophical or religious doctrine. He gave us an attractive vision of a social order that every citizen found legitimate, despite immense variances in their personal values, thus, accepting the public-private divide that liberal theory upheld. Rawls formulated the political as latent in the public political cultures of a democratic society and applied the conception to the basic structure. He built upon only those ideas that were to be found within the shared political culture of a constitutional democracy—individuals as citizens limited to the political sphere—accepted pluralism as the permanent feature of modern societies. He de-linked social justice from diverse moral aspirations and the aims of individuals within the society. Moral ideals, in the sense of conceptions of justice, were one thing and justice was another. By emphasizing on the political, Rawls stated that his well-ordered society was not a community or an association. A community was governed by comprehensive religious, philosophical and moral doctrines while an association had final ends and aims. Rawls stresses on the political and the fact that society has no final ends and aims. None including a philosopher should be able to identify one form of life as best for all humankind unless he had access to the creator's intentions. The distinctiveness of human society was in its variety, diversity and unending competition of ideals and languages. Here, his ideas were akin to that of Berlin.

Rawls was more explicit by claiming that his principles of justice exemplified the content of a liberal political conception of justice and were not derived from rational choice. He specified certain basic rights, liberties and opportunities, which were prior to the claims of general good. It expressed an egalitarian form of liberalism in virtue of three elements:

(1) A guarantee of the fair value of the political liberties so that these were not purely formal.
(2) Fair equality of opportunity and
(3) Difference principle.

Rawls introduced social minimum rather than maximize the long-term expectations of the least advantaged members of society. He clarified his conception of the individual, which his critics said was ahistorical and abstract. He pointed out a person had two sides—the communicative, consensus seeking, politically active, reasonable face and the other, a private and autonomous face with his own distinctive good guided by a comprehensive morality. Such a person knew that political justice required that he should not try to build his private moral ideas into the basic institutions of his society. This was the first commandment of political liberalism. Institutions were not individuals and criteria of right and wrong that apply to the institutions were not those applicable to persons. Justice was merely one among the many virtues to which persons for different reasons aspired. It was the great and prime virtue of social institutions, and hence, of public life.

Rawls said that he was not called upon to propose some general method of resolving problems of public policy and of private conflicts of duty and that he was writing about the basic structure of institutions in a just society, not about choice of policies. The political liberal left space for the plurality of moral views which would be found in any society provided they were reasonable. With help of reason one reached an overlapping consensus regarding diverse views, and an agreement about the political conception, which was not otherwise possible, if each insisted on using their metaphysical grounds as foundations of a public agreement on justice. Public endorsement of metaphysical grounds was not possible, given the pluralist nature and the presence of incommensurable visions of human good in modern liberal societies. This meant that comprehensive doctrines were excluded from public deliberations on justice. Rawls considered these as central in the private identity of citizens, but not in the public sphere, which was the arena where political goals were articulated. However, the public-private that he upheld broke down when he considered a specific moral issue—abortion. On basis of three arguments—due respect for human life, ordered reproduction of political society including the family and equality of women as equal citizens, he supported abortion. He considered reason as an attribute of all free and autonomous citizens. Contending parties were to sort out rival claims on the basis of certain neutral values like impartiality, consistency and equal opportunity. Justice as fairness remained the main procedural value in an adversarial process where neither side debated or imposed its moral convictions on the rest of society by force.

In *The Law of Peoples: the Idea of Public Reason Revisited*, Rawls extended the argument to the global society. He tried to work out in the Law of Peoples that liberal and non-liberal people could agree upon to govern their international relations. He distinguished five types of political regime. There were liberal peoples whose governments guaranteed the familiar set of civil and political rights and the material means to exercise those rights effectively. There were decent hierarchical societies, that were neither fully liberal nor fully democratic, which protected the human rights of their people, that had a decision-making process that allowed political leaders to consult with major social groups and were externally non-aggressive. Then there were the 'outlaw states' that were either internally repressive or externally aggressive or both. The fourth category was the 'burdened societies' that lacked material resources to create the well-ordered society of the first two kinds. Finally, there were 'benevolent absolutisms' which respected the human rights of its people, but did not contain mechanisms of consultation that made the rulers accountable to the governed. Rawls devoted very little attention to this type of regime.

Rawls underlined the point that there were different kinds of non-liberal regimes, some which liberals found tolerable and others not. He paid considerable attention to decent hierarchical societies, which he described as those where a particular religious outlook was widely adhered to and was politically dominant. It was clear that he had the Islamic societies in mind. These societies were governed by what Rawls called 'a common good idea of justice', which lent legitimacy to the political regime since it was widely shared. Its members consented to follow the same international principles that citizens of liberal societies did, like freedom, protection of human rights, prohibition of war except in self-defence and assistance to peoples of burdened societies. Rawls tried to explain their acceptability among peoples with diverse political cultures with the help of the idea of an original position consisting of 'representatives' of different societies.

Rawls characterized peoples as having, in ideal theory, three basic features of decency—institutional, cultural and moral. Institutionally, each people has a 'reasonably just ... government that serves their fundamental interests'. This included protection of their territory, preservation of their political institutions, culture, independence and self-respect as a corporate body; and a guarantee of their safety, security and well-being (Rawls 1999: 23–29, 34–35). Culturally people were united by what J.S. Mill called 'common sympathies'. For Rawls, like Berlin, this meant the idea of nationality based on a 'common language and shared historical memories' (Rawls ibid: 23–25). Finally, each people had 'a moral nature', in that each was firmly attached to a moral conception of right and justice that was reasonable (Rawls ibid: 23–24, 61–68). Each, in rationally advancing their fundamental interests, proposed to abide by the fair terms of co-operation, provided other peoples did so as well. Decent people did not mean persons who were free and equal, but those under a bona-fide system of law. A law governed scheme of social cooperation differed from a 'scheme of commands imposed by force' because persons recognized, understood and acted on the law without being coerced to do so. Rawls developed the notion of decent people with the aim of developing liberal principles of global justice that were tolerant of people with different moral and political traditions. In *Political Liberalism*, Rawls had already emphasized that toleration was the key to stability of a well-ordered society.

Rawls reminded his readers that decent non-liberal peoples accepted a liberal law of peoples because they were reasonable and did not engage in aggressive wars or pursue expansionist ends or fail to respect the civic order and integrity of other peoples. Decent people accepted principles that honour human rights. Their fundamental interests—in security, independence, trade benefits—would lead them to accept and adopt the laws of peace and these, according to Rawls, were nothing less than liberal principles of global justice. Many critics chastened Rawls for giving a sympathetic description of the decent hierarchical societies, for Rawls tried to convince his readers of the need to tolerate these societies as bonafide members of the world and as consisting of people with a different political culture. Rawls was still willing to describe these societies as decent even though these societies limit the rights of other religions and also those of women, but as long as these impositions were not burdensome.

Another significant feature of Rawls' recent book was a highly watered down difference principle, the most distinctive aspect of his theoretical formulation. The procedural elevation of the least advantaged members of the society as stated in *A Theory of Justice* indeed was the result of the years of socialist critique of liberalism. Rawls stated that this principle would apply within the well-ordered society rather than across the world as a whole. In *The Law of Peoples* he made it clear that the difference principle applied only among citizens. Among peoples it will assume the idea of duty to help burdened peoples make their cultural adjustments and achieve the material threshold that leads to decency. Within liberal societies, citizens were assured their requisite primary goods that enabled them to use their freedom intelligently and effectively. If they decided to go substantially towards the principle of equality, Rawls would be happy, but he no longer thought that the long-term elevation of the worst off members was a categorical requirement of social justice.

CONCLUSION

Rawls' significant contribution was the restoration of the concept of justice at the centre of argument about politics, the place it has occupied since the time of Plato. In his definition of social justice he detached the conception from the diverse moral aspirations and aims of individuals within the society. He insisted that moral ideals constituted one sphere and, justice another, thus adhering to the pluralist faith. Furthermore, he revived the grand old style of political theorizing akin to the classical tradition.

A Theory of Justice elicited diverse response from its critics. Barry (1973) labelled it as 'Gladstonian and Spencerian'. Bell (1973) considered it as essentially incorporating a socialist ethic. Hampshire (1972) gave it the appellation of being a Christian incorporating the ideas akin to those the English socialists like Crosland and Tawney. Nisbet (1974 a&b) termed it as Rousseaun in spirit. Wolffe (1977) dismissed it as utopian. Sen (1974) and Bloom (1975) saw it as a corrective to utilitarianism. Macpherson (1973) saw it as revised liberalism. Gutman (1989) saw Rawls' liberalism as democratic socialism.

For the last three decades, the epic theory of Rawls' theoretical construct as delineated in *A Theory of Justice* dominated political theory like a colossus. No worthwhile political theorizing in the contemporary world was possible without a reference to it, a fact acknowledged by even his most ardent critic, Nozick. However, the same might not be true of his later two publications, which appeared more in the nature of clarifications rather than as fundamental contributions to basic principles. Even in the limited endeavour *Political Liberalism*, he accepted the overall parameter of a liberal framework by guaranteeing the right and choice of abortion to the individual. However, in *The Law of Peoples* this basic commitment to a minimum liberal constitutional and democratic order with the primacy of the individual was missing.

According to Rawls the idea of a world state was not feasible but he did believe that global economic cooperation would evolve its own institutions which might multiply and develop as independent institutions and have widespread influence on people's lives. He spoke of a well ordered society for two reasons: first was the belief in the ideal of a democratic society that started with Rousseau and then developed by Kant down to present day times. Second was his belief, as stated in the

Law of Peoples for human beings to think in terms of a reasonably just society (Freeman 2007: 455–56 and 461–62).

It was rather disappointing as to why Rawls chose to isolate non-liberal societies from its liberal critics at a time when the liberal idea has gained credence after the demise of authoritarianism of all shades, both right and left. Rawls himself has travelled a long distance from the universalistic yardstick that he adopted in his landmark book *A Theory of Justice,* which categorically rejected the then prevailing communist regimes, for they lacked the basic human freedoms and a democratic culture. A classic in political theory emerges by transcending the local and by focusing on the universal and perennial. Rawls' *A Theory of Justice* was a masterpiece because it contained this intrinsic quality. It transcended the theoretical as well as the practical application of capitalism and socialism and identified freedom, equity, efficiency and stability as common criteria of the well-ordered constitutional democratic society. *The Law of Peoples* lacked this vision and spirit. Had Rawls stopped with *A Theory of Justice* he would have still been assured of immortality as the high priest of liberalism in the second half of the twentieth century.

Bibliography

Ackrill, J.L. (1975): *Aristotle the Philosopher*, Oxford, Oxford University Press.

Allan, D.J. (1970): *The Philosophy of Aristotle*, Oxford, Oxford University Press.

Anderson, P. (1974): *Passages from Antiquity to Feudalism*, London, New Left.

_________ (1976): *Considerations on Western Marxism*, London, New Left.

Andrews, A. (1967): *The Greek Society*, Harmondsworth, Penguins.

Annas, J. (1977): Mill and the subjection of women, *Philosophy*, Vol. 52, pp. 174–194.

_________(1981): *An Introduction to Plato's Republic*, Oxford, Oxford University Press.

Arblaster, A. (1984): *The Rise and Decline of Western Liberalism*, Oxford, Blackwell.

Ashcraft, R. (1971): Hobbes' natural man, *Journal of Politics*, Vol. 33, pp. 1077–1091.

_________ (1975): On the problem of methodology and the nature of political theory, *Political Theory*, Vol. 3, pp. 5–25.

_________ (1980): Political theory and the problem of ideology, *Journal of Politics*, Vol. 42, pp. 687–705.

_________ (Ed.) (1991): *John Locke: Critical Assessments*, 4 Vols., London, Routledge.

Bobonich, C. (2002): *Plato's Utopia Recast: His Later Ethics and Politics*, Oxford, Oxford University Press.

Bahro, R. (1978): *The Alternative in Eastern Europe*, London, New Left.

Ball, T. (1995): *Reappraising Political Theory*, Oxford, Oxford University Press.

Bambrough, R. (1965): *New Essays on Plato and Aristotle*, Oxford, Oxford University Press.

Bambrough, R. (Ed.) (1967): *Plato, Popper and Politics,* Cambridge, Cambridge University Press.

Barker, E. (1951): *Principles of Social and Political Theory,* Oxford, Clarendon Press.

_________ (1959): *The Political Thought of Plato and Aristotle,* New York, Dover Publications.

Barker, R. (1978): *Political Ideas in Modern Britain,* London, Methuen.

Barnes, J. (Ed.) (1992): *The Cambridge Companion to Aristotle,* Cambridge, Cambridge University Press.

Barry, B. (1972): Warrender and his critics, *Hobbes and Rousseau,* M. Cranston and R.S. Peters (Eds.), New York, Anchor Books.

_________ (1989a): The strange death of political philosophy, *Democracy, Power and Justice: Essays in Political Theory,* B. Barry (Ed.), Oxford, Clarendon Press.

_________ (1989b): *Theories of Justice,* Hemel Hempstead, Harvester-Wheatsheaf.

Baumgold, D. (1988): *Hobbes' Political Theory,* Cambridge, Cambridge University Press.

Bell, D. (1960): *The End of Ideology,* New York, Free Press.

Beiser, F. (Ed.) (1991): *The Cambridge Companion to Hegel,* Cambridge, Cambridge University Press.

Bellamy, R. (Ed.) (1990): *Victorian Liberalism: Nineteenth Century Political Thought and Practice,* Cambridge, Polity Press.

_________ (1993): Introduction: The demise and rise of political theory, *Theories and Concepts of Politics: An Introduction,* R. Bellamy (Ed.), Manchester, University of Manchester Press.

Benhabib, S. (1992): *Situating the Self: Gender, Community and Postmodernism in Contemporary Ethics,* New York, Routledge.

Berlin, Sir I. (1953): *The Hedgehog and the Fox,* London, Weidenfeld and Nicolson.

_________ (1959): *John Stuart Mill and the Ends of Life,* London, Edgar G. Dunstan & Co.

_________ (1962): The age of enlightenment, *The Great Ages of Western Philosophy,* Vol. 2, Boston, Houghton Mifflin.

_________ (1964): Hobbes, Locke and Professor Macpherson, *Political Quarterly,* October–December, pp. 444–468.

_________ (1990): *The Crooked Timber of Humanity: Chapters in the History of Ideas,* London, Hogarth Press.

Blackburn, R. (Ed.) (1972): *Ideology in Social Science,* London, Fontana.

_________ (Ed.) (1978): *Revolution and Class Struggle: A Reader in Marxist Politics,* Brighton, Harvester.

Bottomore, T. (1973): *Karl Marx,* Oxford, Basil Blackwell.

_________ (1981): *Modern Interpretations of Marx,* Oxford, Oxford University Press.

Boucher, D. (1985): *Texts in Contexts,* Dordrecht, Martinus Nijhoff.

_________ and Kelly, P (Eds.), (2009): *Political Thinkers: From Socrates to the Present,* 2nd ed., Oxford, Oxford University Press.

Bourne, H.R.F. (1876): *The Life of John Locke,* 2 Vols., New York, Harper & Row.

Bowie, J. (1947): *Western Political Thought: A Historical Introduction from the Origins to Rousseau,* London, Jonathan Cape.

_________ (1951): *Hobbes and His Critics: A Study in Seventeenth Century Constitutionalism,* London, Jonathan Cape.

_________ (1954): *Politics and Opinion in the Nineteenth Century: A Historical Introduction,* London, Jonathan Cape.

Brennan, T. and Pateman, C. (1977): Mere auxiliaries to the Commonwealth: Women and the origins of liberalism, *Political Studies,* XXVII, pp. 183–200.

Brinton, C. (1933): *English Political Thought in the Nineteenth Century,* London, Allen Lane.

Bromwich, D, "Wollstonecraft as a critic of Burke", *Political Theory,* Vol. 23, No. 4, November, 1995.

Broome, J.H. (1963): *Rousseau: A Study of His Thought,* Oxford, Oxford University Press.

Brown, K.C. (Ed.) (1965): *Hobbes' Studies,* Cambridge Mass., Harvard University Press.

Buchan, M. (1999): *Women in Plato's Political Theory,* New York, Routledge.

Burnham, J. (1943): *The Machiavellians,* New York, Double Day.

Burns, J.H. (Ed.) (1991): *The Cambridge History of Political Thought,* pp. 1450–1700, Cambridge, Cambridge University Press.

Bury, J.B. (1920): *The Idea of Progress: An Inquiry into its Origin and Growth,* New York, Dover.

Carnoy, M. (1984): *State and Political Theory,* Princeton, NJ, Princeton University Press.

Carr, E.H. (1934): *Karl Marx: A Study in Fanaticism,* London, Dent.

Carver, T. (1983): *Marx and Engels: The Intellectual Relationship*, Brighton, Harvester.

_________ (Ed.) (1991): *The Cambridge Companion to Marx*, Cambridge, Cambridge University Press.

Cassirer, E. (1932): *The Philosophy of the Enlightenment*, Princeton, NJ, Princeton University Press.

_________ (1982): *Kant's Life and Thought*, J. Haden (Trans.), New Haven, Connecticut, Yale University Press.

_________ (1989): *The Question of Jean-Jacques Rousseau*, New Haven, Yale University Press.

Catlin, G. (1922): *Thomas Hobbes as Philosopher, Publicist and Man of Letters*, Oxford, Clarendon Press.

_________ (1950): *A History of Political Philosophers*, London, Allen & Unwin.

Caute, D. (1966): *The Left in Europe since 1789*, London, Collier.

Chapell, V. (Ed.) (1994): *The Cambridge Companion to Locke*, Cambridge, Cambridge University Press.

Charvet, J. (1974): *The Social Problem in the Philosophy of Rousseau*, London, Dent.

Claeys, G. (1989): *Thomas Paine: Social and Political Thought*, London, Routledge.

Cohen, G.A. (1979): *Karl Marx's Theory of History: A Defence*, Oxford, Oxford University Press.

Coker, F.W. (1938): *Readings in Political Philosophy*, New York, Macmillan.

Cole, G.D.H. (1956): *A History of Socialist Thought*, 5 Vols., London, Macmillan.

_________ (1958): *Rousseau's A Discourse on the Origin of Inequality in the Social Contract and the Discourses*, translated with an Introduction, London, Dent.

Coleman, F.M. (1977): *Hobbes and America: Exploring the Constitutional Foundations*, Toronto, University of Toronto Press.

Coleman, J. (2000): *A History of Political Thought*, Oxford, Blackwell Publishers.

Cone, C.B. (1957): *Burke and the Nature of Politics*, 2 Vols., Lexington, University of Kentucky Press.

Confucius (1979): *The Analects*, D.C. Lau (Trans.), Harmondsworth, Penguins.

Cook, I. (1998): *Reading Mill: Studies in Political Theory*, London, Macmillan.

Cott, N.F. (1987): *The Grounding of Modern Feminism*, New Haven, Yale University Press.

Cowling, M. (1963): *Mill and Liberalism*, Cambridge, Cambridge University Press.

Cranston, M. (Ed.) (1964): *Western Political Philosophers*, London, Fontana.

________ (1973): *The Mask of Politics and other Essays*, London, Allen Lane.

________ and Peters, R. (Eds.) (1972): *Hobbes and Rousseau: A Collection of Critical Essays*, New York, Anchor Books.

Crespigny, A. de and Minogue, K. (Eds.) (1975): *Contemporary Political Thinkers*, London, Methuen.

Crick, N. (1964): *In Defence of Politics*, Harmondsworth, Penguins.

Croce, B. (1969): *What is Living and What is Dead in the Philosophy of Hegel*, D. Ainslie (Trans.), New York, Russell & Russell.

Dahl, R. (1963): *Modern Political Analysis*, Englewood Cliffs, NJ, Prentice-Hall.

Daly, J. (1979): *Sir Robert Filmer and English Political Thought*, Toronto, University of Toronto Press.

Davidson, W.L. (1957): *Political Thought in England: The Utilitarians from Bentham to Mill*, Oxford, Oxford University Press.

Dent, N.J.H. (1992): *A Rousseau Dictionary*, Oxford, Blackwell,

Djilas, M. (1957): *The New Class*, London, Thames & Hudson.

Dunn, J. (Ed.) (1992): *Democracy: The Unfinished Journey 503 BC-1993 AD*, Oxford, Oxford University Press.

Durkheim, E. (1960): *Montesquieu and Rousseau*, Ann Arbor, University of Michigan Press.

Eienstein, H. (1984): *Contemporary Feminist Thought*, London, George Allen and Unwin.

Eisenstein, Z. (1984): *Feminism and Sexual Equality*, New York, Monthly Review Press.

Elshtain, J.B. (Ed.) (1982): *The Family in Political Thought*, Brighton, Harvester.

Eulau, H. (1964): *The Behavioural Persuasion in Politics*, New York, Random House.

Evans, J. (1986): *Feminism and Political Theory*, New York, Alfred A. Knopf.

________ (1995): *Feminist Theory Today: An Introduction to Second Wave Feminism*, London, Sage.

Evans, M. (Ed.) (1972): *The Woman Question*, London, Fontana.

Evans, R. (1977): *The Feminists*, London, Croom Helm.

Falco, M.J.(Ed.) (1996): *Feminist Interpretations of Mary Wollstonecraft*, Pennsylvania, Pennsylvania State University Press.

Ferrari, G.R.F. (2007): *The Cambridge Companion to Plato's Republic*, Cambridge, Cambridge University Press.

Filmer, R. (1949): *Patriarcha and Other Political Works,* P. Laslett (Ed.), Oxford, Blackwell.

Findlay, J.N. (1958): *Hegel: A Re-examination,* London, Allen & Unwin.

Fine, G. (Ed.), (1999): *Plato,* 2 Vols., Oxford, Oxford University Press.

Finley, M.I. (1963): *The Ancient Greeks,* Harmondsworth, Penguins.

Flew, A. (1971): *An Introduction of Western Philosophy: Ideas and Argument from Plato to Sartre,* Indianapolis, Bobbs and Merrill Co.

Forbes, D. (1975): Introduction to *Hegel's Lectures on the Philosophy of World,* H.B. Nisbet (Trans.), Cambridge, Cambridge University Press.

Fox-Genovese, E. (1991): *Feminism without Illusions: A Critique of Individualism,* Chapel Hill, University of North Carolina Press.

Freedman, E.B. (2007): *The Essential Feminist Reader,* New York, Modern Library.

Freedman, J. (2002); *Feminism,* New Delhi, Viva Books.

Friedrich, C.J. (1953): *The Philosophy of Hegel,* New York, Modern Library.

Gadamer, H. (1986): *The Idea of Good in Platonic-Aristotelian Philosophy,* New Haven, Yale University Press.

Gatens, M. (1991): *Feminism and Philosophy: Perspectives on Difference and Equality,* Cambridge, Polity Press.

Gauthier, D.P. (1969): *The Logic of Leviathan,* Oxford, Clarendon Press.

Gay, P. (1952): *The Dilemma of Democratic Socialism: Eduard Bernstein's Challenge to Marx,* New York, Columbia University Press.

________ (1970): *The Enlightenment: An Interpretation,* 2 Vols., London, Wildwood House.

Germino, D. (1972): *Modern Western Political Thought: Machiavelli to Marx,* Chicago, University of Chicago Press.

Gettel, R.G. (1924): *History of Political Thought,* New York, Novell & Co.

Ghoshal, U.N. (1966): *A History of Hindu Political Theories,* Calcutta, Oxford University Press.

Gilbert, A.H. (1938): *Machiavelli's Prince and its Forerunners,* Durham, NC, Duke University Press.

Gilbert, F. (1944): Machiavelli: The renaissance of the art of war, *Makers of Modern Strategy,* E.M. Earle (Ed.), Princeton, NJ, Princeton University Press.

________ (1954): The concept of nationalism in Machiavelli's Prince, *Studies in the Renaissance,* Vol. 1, pp. 38–48.

________ (1965): *Machiavelli and Guicciardini: Politics and History in Sixteenth Century Florence,* Princeton, NJ, Princeton University Press.

Glotz, G. (1930): *The Greek City and its Institutions,* New York, Alfred A. Knopf.

Goldsmith, M.M. (1966): *Hobbes' Science of Politics,* New York, Columbia University Press.

Gough, J.W. (1950): *John Locke's Political Philosophy: Eight Studies,* Oxford, Blackwell.

Gray, A. (1946): *The Socialist Tradition: Moses to Lenin,* London, Longmans Green.

Gray, J. (1983a): *Mill on Feminism,* London, Routledge.

———— (1983b): *Mill on Liberty: A Defence,* London, Routledge.

———— (1986): *Liberalism,* London, Open University Press.

Greenleaf, W.H. (1983): *The British Political Tradition,* 2 vols., London, Methuen.

Grimsley, R. (1973): *The Philosophy of Rousseau,* Oxford, Oxford University Press.

Grote, G. (1867): *Plato and the other Companions of Socrates,* London, John Murray.

Gunnell, J.G. (1979): *Political Theory: Tradition and Interpretation,* Cambridge, Winthrop.

———— (1986): *Between Philosophy and Politics: The Alienation of Political Theory,* Amherst Mass., University of Massachusetts Press.

Gutherie, W.K.C. (1975): *The Greek Philosophers: From Thales to Aristotle,* Cambridge, Cambridge University Press.

Hale, J.R. (1960): *Machiavelli and the Renaissance Italy,* New York, Macmillan.

Hall, J.C. (1973): *Rousseau: An Introduction to His Political Philosophy,* Cambridge Mass., Harvard University Press.

Hall, S. and Gieben, B. (Eds.) (1992): *Formations of Modernity,* Oxford, Polity Press.

Halliday, R.J. (1968): Some recent interpretations of John Stuart Mill, *Philosophy,* Vol. 43, pp. 1–17.

Hallowell, J.H. (1954): *The Moral Foundation of Democracy,* Chicago, University of Chicago Press.

Hampson, N. (1968): *The Enlightenment,* Harmondsworth, Penguins.

Hampton, J. (1986): *Hobbes and the Social Contract Tradition,* Cambridge, Cambridge University Press.

Harrington, M. (1989): Towards a new socialism, *Dissent,* Spring, pp. 153-163.

Hart, H.L.A. (1982): *Essays on Bentham, Jurisprudence and Political Theory,* Oxford, Oxford University Press.

Havelock, E.A. (1957): *The Liberal Temper in Greek Politics*, London, Jonathan Cape.

Hayek, F.A. (Ed.) (1951): *John Stuart Mill and Harriet Taylor: Their Correspondence*, Chicago, University of Chicago Press.

Hazard, P. (1954): *European Thought in the Eighteenth Century*, London, Hollis and Carter.

Hearnshaw, F.J.C. (Ed.) (1925): *The Social and Political Ideas of Some Great Thinkers of the Renaissance and Reformation*, London, George Harrap.

Hearnshaw, F.J.C. (1933): *Conservatism in England*, London, Macmillan.

Heilbroner, R. (1980): *Marxism: For and Against*, New York, Oxford University Press.

Held, D. (1987): *Models of Democracy*, Oxford, Polity Press.

Hill, C. (1958): *Puritanism and Revolution*, London, Fontana.

_________ (1975): *The World Turned Upside Down*, Harmondsworth, Penguins.

Himmelfarb, G. (1974): *On Liberty and Liberalism: The Case of John Stuart Mill*, New York, Alfred A. Knopf.

Hirschmann, N.J. and Stefano, C. Di. (1996): *Revisioning the Political Feminist: Reconstructions of Traditional Concepts in Western Political Theory*, Boulder, Westview Press.

Hook, S. (1933): *Towards an Understanding of Karl Marx*, New York, John Day.

_________ (1962): *From Hegel to Marx: Studies in the Intellectual Development of Karl Marx*, New York, University of Michigan Press.

Hulling, M. (1983): *Citizen Machiavelli*, Princeton, NJ, Princeton University Press.

Hunt, C. (1957): *The Theory and Practice of Communism*, London, Geoffrey Bees.

Huntington, S.P. (1957): Conservatism as an ideology, *American Political Science Review*, Vol. 51, June, pp. 453-473.

Jayaswal, K.P. (1978): *Hindu Polity: A Constitutional History of India in Hindu Time*, 4th ed., Bangalore, Bangalore Printing.

Johnson, C.L. (2002): *The Cambridge Companion to Mary Wollstonecraft*, Cambridge, Cambridge University Press,

Jones, W.T. (1975): *Masters of Political Thought: Machiavelli to Bentham*, Calcutta, Oxford University Press.

Jowett, B. (1905): *Aristotle's The Politics*, Oxford, Clarendon Press.

_________ (1953): *The Republic of Plato*, Oxford, Oxford University Press.

Kateb, G. (1979): *Political Theory: Its Nature and Uses*, New York, St. Martin's Press.

Kelley, G.A. (1969): *Idealism, Politics and History*, Cambridge, Cambridge University Press.

Kennedy, E. and Mendus, S. (1987): *Women in Western Political Philosophy*, Brighton, Harvester.

Kolakowski, L. (1972): *Positivist Philosophy: From Hume to the Vienna Circle*, Harmondsworth, Penguins.

Kramer, M.H. (2004): *John Locke and the Origins Private Property: Philosophical Explorations of Individualism, Community, and Equality*, Cambridge, Cambridge University Press.

Kramnick, I. (1990): *Republicanism and Bourgeois Radicalism: Political Ideology in Late Eighteenth Century England and America*, Ithaca, Cornell University Press.

Kraut, R. (Ed.) (1993): *The Cambridge Companion to Plato*, Cambridge, Cambridge University Press.

__________ (1997): *Plato's Republic: Critical Essays*, Lanham MD, Rowman and Littlefield.

Kristol, I. (1986): *Reflections of a Neo-conservative—Looking Back*, New York, Basic Books.

Kymlicka, W. (1990): *Contemporary Political Philosophy: An Introduction*, Oxford, Clarendon Press.

Lancaster, L.W. (1975): *Masters of Political Thought: Hegel to Dewey*, Calcutta, Oxford University Press.

Laski, H.J. (1922): *Karl Marx: An Essay*, London, Unwin Books.

Lasswell, H. (1936): *Politics: Who Gets What, When, and How*, New York, McGraw-Hill.

Leftwich, A. (Ed.) (1984): *What is Politics*! Oxford, Blackwell.

Lerner, M. (1932): *Ideas are Weapons*, New York, Macmillan.

Lessnoff, M. (1986): *Social Contract*, London, Macmillan.

Lichtheim, G. (1961): *Marxism: An Historical and Critical Study*, London, Routledge.

__________ (1971): *From Marx to Hegel and other Essays*, London, Orbach & Chambers.

MacCunn, J. (1964): *Six Radical Thinkers*, New York, Russell & Russell.

MacIntyre, A. (Ed.) (1972): *Hegel: A Collection of Critical Essays*, New York, Anchor.

__________ (1981): *After Virtue: A Study in Moral Theory*, London, Duckworth.

__________ (1990): *Three Rival Theories of Moral Enquiry: Encyclopaedia, Genealogy and Tradition*, Notre Dame, University of Notre Dame Press.

Mack, M.P. (Ed.) (1969): *The Bentham Reader*, New York, Pegasus.

Mackie, J.L. (1994): *Problems from Locke,* Oxford, Oxford University Press.

Magee, B. (1998): *The Story of Philosophy,* London, DK Ltd.

Marshall, J. (1994): *John Locke: An Historical Account of the Argument of the Two Treatises of Government,* Cambridge, Cambridge University Press.

Macpherson, C.B. (1977): *The Life and Times of Liberal Democracy,* Oxford, Oxford University Press.

Mandel, E. (1976): *Introduction to Karl Marx, The Capital,* London, Penguins.

Manfield, H.C. (1979): *Machiavelli's New Modes and Orders,* Ithaca, Cornell University Press.

Mannheim, K. (1986): *Conservatism,* London, Routledge & Kegan Paul.

Marcuse, H. (1964): *One Dimensional Man,* Boston, Beacon.

Martin, K. (1954): *French Liberal Thought in the Eighteenth Century,* New York, New York University Press.

Masters, R.D. (1968): *Political Philosophy of Rousseau,* Princeton, NJ, Princeton University Press.

Maxey, C.C. (1948): *Political Philosophies,* New York, Macmillan.

Mazlish, B. (1975): *James and John Stuart Mill,* New Brunswick, NJ, Transaction.

McCloskey, H.J. (1971): *John Stuart Mill: A Critical Study,* London, Macmillan.

McLellan, D. (1969): *The Young Hegelians and Karl Marx,* London, Macmillan.

McNeilly, N. (1968): *The Anatomy of Leviathan,* London, Macmillan.

Medvedev, R. (1971): *Let History Judge,* New York, Alfred A. Knopf.

Mehring, F. (1936): *Karl Marx, The Story of His Life,* E. Fitzgerald (Trans.), London, Allen & Unwin.

Mehta, U.S. (1992): *The Anxiety of Freedom, Imagination and Individuality in Locke's Political Thought,* Ithaca, Cornell University Press.

Miliband, R. (1977): *Marxism and Politics,* Oxford, Oxford University Press.

Miller, D. (1990): The resurgence of political theory, *Political Studies,* Vol. 38.

Miller, J.D.B. (1962): *The Nature of Politics,* Harmondsworth, Penguins.

Miller, R. (1984): *Analyzing Marx,* Princeton, NJ, Princeton University Press.

Mills, C.W. (1962): *The Marxists,* Harmondsworth, Penguins.

Moore, J.M. (1975): *Aristotle and Xenophon on Democracy and Oligarchy,* London, Dent.

Morrall, J.B. (1979): *Aristotle,* London, Hutchinson.

Mukherjee, S. and Ramaswamy, S. (2000), *A History of Socialist Thought: From the Precursors to the Present,* New Delhi, Sage.

Nelson, B.R. (2008): *Western Political Thought*, New Delhi, Pearson Longman.

Nisbet, R. (1967): *The Sociological Tradition*, London, Heinemann.

_________ (1975): *The Twilight of Authority*, New York, Basic Books.

_________ (1980): *Conservatism: Dream and Reality*, Minneapolis, University of Minnesota Press.

Oakeshott, M.J. (1946): *Introduction to Hobbes' Leviathan*, Oxford, Blackwell.

_________ (1962): *Rationalism in Politics*, London, Methuen.

O'Gorman, F. (1973): *Edmund Burke: His Political Philosophy*, London, Allen & Unwin.

Okin, S.M. (1988): *J.S. Mill's The Subjection of Women*, Indianapolis, Bobbs and Merrill Co.

_________ (1989): *Justice, Gender, and the Family*, New York, Basic Books.

Ollman, B. (1977): *Alienation: Marx's Conception of Man in Capitalist Society*, Cambridge, Cambridge University Press.

Osborn, A.M. (1940): *Rousseau and Burke*, New York, Simon & Schuster.

O'Sullivan, N. (1976): *Conservatism*, London, Dent.

Outhwaite, W. (1986): *Habermas*, Cambridge, Polity Press.

Paine, T. (1973): *The Rights of Man*, Harmondsworth, Penguins.

Pangle, T. (1988): *The Spirit of Modern Republicanism*, Chicago, University of Chicago Press.

Parekh, B. (Ed.) (1974): *Jeremy Bentham: Ten Critical Essays*, London, Croom Helm.

_________ (1982): *Contemporary Political Thinkers*, Oxford, Martin Robertson.

Parry, G. (1978): *John Locke*, London, Allen & Unwin.

Pateman, C. (1993): *The Disorder of Women*, Cambridge, Polity Press.

_________ (1994): Feminist critiques of the public/private dichotomy, *Feminism*, S.M. Okin and J. Mansbridge (Eds.), London, Routledge.

_________ and Gross, E. (Eds.) (1987): *Feminist Challenges: Social and Political Theory*, Boston, Northeastern University Press.

Pater, W. (1930): *Plato and Platonism*, London, Macmillan.

Pelczynski, Z.A. (Ed.) (1984): *State and Civil Society: Studies in Hegel's Political Philosophy*, London, Athlone Press.

Peters, R. (1956): *Hobbes*, Harmondsworth, Penguins.

Phillips, A. (1987): *Divided Loyalties: Dilemmas of Sex and Class*, London, Virago.

Plamentaz, J. (1949): *Mill's Utilitarianism*, Oxford, Oxford University Press.

Plant, R. (1983): *Hegel*, Oxford, Basil Blackwell.

_________ (1991): *Modern Political Thought*, Oxford, Blackwell.

Pocock, J.G.A. (1957): *The Ancient Constitution and the Feudal Law*, Cambridge, Cambridge University Press.

________ (1975): *Politics, Language and Time*, London, Methuen.

Polin, R. (1953): *Political Philosophy of Thomas Hobbes*, Paris, Presses Universitaires de France.

Portis, E.B. (1994): *Reconstructing the Classics: Political Theory from Plato to Marx*, New Jersey, Chatham House.

Poulantaz, N. (1973): *Political Power and Social Classes*, London, New Left.

Preus, S. (1979): Machiavelli's functional analysis of religion: Context and object, *Journal of the History of Ideas*, XL, pp. 171–190.

Raab, F. (1964): *The English Face of Machiavelli: A Changing Interpretation 1500–1700*, London, Routledge.

Ramaswamy, S. (1990): *Liberty, Equality and Social Justice: Rawls' Political Theory*, New Delhi, Ajantha Publications.

________ (2003): *Political Theory: Ideas and Concepts*, New Delhi, Macmillan.

Rauch, L. (1981): *The Political Animal: Studies in Politics from Machiavelli to Marx*, Amherst Mass., University of Massachusetts Press.

Rees, J. (1956): *Mill and His Early Critics*, London, University of Leicester Press.

________ (1958): A phase in the development of Mill's ideas on liberty, *Political Studies*, VI, pp. 33–44.

Rees, J. (1960): A re-reading of Mill on liberty, *Political Studies*, VIII, pp. 113–129.

________ (1966): Was Mill for liberty? *Political Studies*, XIV, pp. 72–77.

Regan, W.L. (1965): *Locke's Two Treatises on Civil Government*, London, Dent.

Rice, D. H. (1998): *A Companion to Plato's Republic*, Oxford, Oxford University Press.

Riley, P. (1983): *Kant's Political Philosophy*, Totowa, New Jersey, Rowman and Littlefield.

Robson, J.M. (1968): *The Improvement of Mankind: The Social and Political Thought of J.S. Mill*, Toronto, University of Toronto Press.

Rogers, G.A.J. (Ed.) (1994): *Locke's Philosophy: Content and Context*, Oxford, Clarendon Press.

________ and Ryan, A. (1988): *Perspectives on Thomas Hobbes*, Oxford, Clarendon Press.

Rorty, R. (1979): *Philosophy and the Mirror of Nature*, Princeton, NJ, Princeton University Press.

Rosen, F. (1983): *Jeremy Bentham and Representative Democracy*, Oxford, Oxford University Press.

Rosenblum, N.L. (1978): *Bentham's Theory of the State*, Cambridge Mass., Harvard University Press.

Ross, W.D. (1951): *Plato's Theory of Ideas*, Oxford, Clarendon Press.

Rossi, A.S. (Ed.) (1970): *Essays on Sex Equality*, Chicago, University of Chicago Press.

Ryan, A. (1970): *The Philosophy of John Stuart Mill*, London, Macmillan.

_________ (1973): *The New Political Economy of J.S. Mill*, London, Routledge & Kegan Paul.

_________ (1979): *The Idea of Freedom*, Oxford, Oxford University Press.

_________ (1983): Hobbes, toleration and the inner life, *The Nature of Political Theory*, D. Miller (Ed.), Oxford, Clarendon Press.

_________ (1984): *Property and Political Theory*, Oxford, Blackwell.

Ryle, G. (1966): *Plato's Progress*, Cambridge, Cambridge University Press.

Salkever, S.G. (1990): *Finding the Mean: Theory and Practice in Aristotelian Political Philosophy*, Princeton, NJ, Princeton University Press.

Santas, G. (2006): *The Blackwell Guide to Plato's Republic*, Princeton, NJ, Princeton University Press.

Schochet, G.J. (1975): *Patriarchalism in Political Thought*, Oxford, Basil Blackwell.

Scruton, R. (1980): *The Meaning of Conservatism*, London, Macmillan.

Seligar, M. (1968): *The Liberal Politics of John Locke*, London, Allen & Unwin.

Sesonske, A. (1966): *Plato's Republic: Interpretation and Criticism*, London, Belmont Wadsworth Publishing Co.

Shanley, M.L. (1989): *Feminism, Marriage and the Law in Victorian England, 1850–1895*, Princeton, NJ, Princeton University Press.

Shiva, V. (1988): *Staying Alive: Women, Ecology and Development*, London, Zed.

Shklar, J. (1969): *Men and Citizens: A Study of Rousseau's Social Theory*, London, Cambridge University Press.

_________ (1976): *Freedom and Independence: A Study of the Political Ideas of Hegel's Phenomenology of Mind*, Cambridge, Cambridge University Press.

Shorey, P. (1903): *The Unity of Plato's Thought*, Chicago, University of Chicago Press.

Siedentop, L.A. (1979): Two liberal traditions, *The Idea of Freedom*, A.J. Ryan (Ed.), Oxford, Oxford University Press.

Simmons, A. (1992): *The Lockean Theory of Rights*, Princeton, NJ, Princeton University Press.

_________(1993): *On the Edge of Anarchy: Locke, Consent and the Limits of Society*, Princeton, NJ, Princeton University Press.

Skinner, Q. (1984): The idea of negative liberty, *Philosophy in History,* R. Rorty, J.B. Schneewind and Q. Skinner (Eds.), Cambridge, Cambridge University Press.

_________ (1990): The republican idea of political liberty, *Machiavelli and Republicanism,* Cambridge, Cambridge University Press.

_________ (1998): *Liberty before Liberalism,* Cambridge, Cambridge University Press.

_________ (2002): *Vision of Politics,* 2 Vols., Cambridge, Cambridge University Press.

Skorupski, J. (1998): *The Cambridge Companion to Mill,* Cambridge, Cambridge University Press.

Sorell, T. (1986): *Hobbes,* London, Routledge.

Spellman, J. (1964): *The Political Theory of Ancient India,* Oxford, Clarendon Press.

Spellman, W.M. (1997): *John Locke,* New York, St. Martin's Press.

Steintrager, J. (1977): *Bentham,* Ithaca, Cornell University Press.

Stephen, Sir L. (1900): *The English Utilitarians,* 3 Vols., London, Duckworth.

_________ (1961): *Hobbes,* Ann Arbor, University of Michigan-Press.

Stirk, P. and Weigall, D. (1995): *An Introduction to Political Ideas,* New York, St. Martin's Press.

Strauss, L. (1964): *The City and the Man,* Chicago, Rand McNally & Co.

_________ (1968): *Liberalism: Ancient and Modern,* New York, Basic Books.

Stokes, P. (2010): *Philosophy 100 Essential Thinkers,* London, Arcturus.

Sullivan, V.B. (1996): *Machiavelli's Three Romes: Religion, Human Liberty and Politics Reformed,* Dekalb, Ill., Northern Illinois University.

Tannenbaum, D.G. and Schultz, D. (1998): *Inventors of Ideas: An Introduction to Western Political Philosophy,* New York, St. Martin's Press.

Taylor, C. (1979): *Hegel and Modern Society,* Cambridge, Cambridge University Press.

Ten, C.L. (1980): *Mill on Liberty,* Oxford, Clarendon Press.

Thomas, CD. (1927): *Chinese Political Thought,* New York. Prentice-Hall.

Tierney, Brian (Ed.) (1969): *Great Issues in Western Civilization,* New York, Random House.

Tocqueville, A. de. (1968): *Democracy in America,* 2 Vols., J.R Mayer and M. Lerner (Ed.), London, Fontana.

Tsurutani, Takesugu (1968): Machiavelli and the problem of political development, *Review of Politics,* Vol. 30, July, pp. 316–331.

Tuck, R. (1979): *Natural Rights Theories: Their Origin and Development,* Cambridge, Cambridge University Press.

Tucker, R.C. (1961): *Philosophy and Myth in Karl Marx,* Cambridge, Cambridge University Press.

Van Dyke, V. (1960): *Political Theory: A Philosophical Analysis,* Stanford, Stanford University Press.

Varma, V.P. (1974): *Studies in Hindu Political Thought and its Metaphysical Foundations,* Delhi, Motilal Banarasidas.

Viereck, P. (1956): *Conservatism: From John Adams to Churchill,* Connecticut, University of Connecticut Press.

Villari, P. (1892): *The Life and Times of Niccolo Machiavelli,* 2 vols., London, Unwin Books.

Viroli, M. (1998): *Machiavelli,* Oxford, Oxford University Press.

Vlastos, G. (Ed.) (1971): *Plato: A Collection of Critical Essays,* Notre Dame, University of Notre Dame.

———— (1973): *Platonic Studies,* Princeton, NJ, Princeton University Press.

Vogelin, E. (1975): *From Enlightenment to Revolution,* Durham, NC, Duke University Press.

———— (1978): *History of Political Ideas,* 2 vols., Columbia, University of Missouri Press.

Volpe, G. della. (1978): *Rousseau and Marx,* London, Lawrence and Wishart.

von Leyden, W. (1982): *Hobbes and Locke: The Politics of Freedom and Obligation,* London, Macmillan.

Waldron, J. (2002): *God, Locke and Equality: Christian Foundations of John Locke's Political Thought,* Cambridge, Cambridge University Press.

Wallas, G. (1908), *Human Nature in Politics,* London, Constable.

———— (1923): Jeremy Bentham, *Political Science Quarterly,* 38, March, pp. 45–56.

Watkin, J.W.N. (1973): *Hobbes' System of Ideas,* London, Hutchinson.

White, N.P. (1979): *A Companion to Plato's Republic,* Indianapolis, Heckett.

White, S.K. (1994): *Edmund Burke: Modernity, Politics and Aesthetics,* Thousand Oaks, Sage.

———— (Ed.) (1994): *The Cambridge Companion to Habermas,* Cambridge, Cambridge University Press.

Whitefield, J.M. (1947): *Machiavelli,* Oxford, Oxford University Press.

Wild, J. (1953): *Plato's Modern Enemies and the Theory of Natural Law,* Chicago, University of Chicago Press.

Wilkins, B.T. (1967): *The Problem of Burke's Political Philosophy,* Oxford, Blackwell.

Wood, N. (1967): Machiavelli's concept of virtù reconsidered, *Political Studies,* Vol. 15, June, pp. 159–172.

Yack, B. (1993): *The Problem of the Political Animal: Community, Justice and Conflict in Aristotelian Thought*, Berkeley, University of California Press.

Yolton, J. (1956): *John Locke and the Way of Ideas*, Oxford, Clarendon Press.

__________ (Ed.) (1977): *The Locke Reader*, Cambridge, Cambridge University Press.

Yovel, Y. (1980): *Kant and the Philosophy of History*, Princeton, Princeton University Press.

Zimmer, H. (1951): *Philosophies of India*, New York, Pantheon.

References

Ackerman, B. (1980): *Social Justice in the Liberal State*, New Haven, Yale University Press.

Airakainen, T. and Bertman, M.A. (Eds.) (1989): *Hobbes: War Among Nations*, Avebury, Brookfield.

Allen, J.W. (1931): Jeremy Bentham, *The Social and Political Ideas of Some Representative Thinkers of the Revolutionary Era*, F.J.C. Hearnshaw (Ed.), London, George Harrap.

_________ (1967): *A History of Political Thought in the Sixteenth Century*, London, Methuen.

Almond, G.A. (1996): Political science: The history of the discipline, *A New Handbook of Political Science*, R.E. Goodin and H.D. Klingemann (Eds.), Oxford, Oxford University Press.

Althusser, L. (1969): *For Marx*, London, Allen Lane.

Arendt, H. (1959): *The Human Condition*, Chicago, University of Chicago Press.

_________ (1973): *On Revolution*, Harmondsworfh, Penguins.

Aristotle (1962): *The Nicomachean Ethics*, W.D. Ross (Ed.), Oxford, Clarendon Press.

_________ (1979): *The Politics*, E. Barker (Trans.), Oxford, Oxford University Press.

Arrow, K. (1963): *Social Choice and Individual Values*, New Haven, Yale University Press.

_________ (1973): Some Ordinalist-Utilitarian Notes on Rawls' Theory of Justice, *Journal of Philosophy*, 70, pp. 245–263.

Ashcraft, R. (1978): Ideology and Class in Hobbes' Political Theory, *Political Theory*, 6, pp. 27–62.

Ashcraft, R. (1980): Revolutionary Politics and Locke's Two Treatises of Government, *Political Theory,* Vol. 8, pp. 429–485.

________ (1986): *Revolutionary Politics and Locke's Two Treatises of Government,* London, Allen & Unwin.

________ (1987): *Locke's Two Treatises of Government,* London, Unwin & Hyman.

Aubrey, J. (1962): *Brief Lives,* O.L. Dick (Ed.), Harmondsworth, Penguins.

Avineri, S. (1969): *Karl Marx on Colonialism and Modernization: His Despatches and other Writings on China, India, Mexico, the Middle East and North Africa,* New York, Cambridge University Press.

________ (1972): *Hegel's Theory of the State,* Cambridge, Cambridge University Press.

________ (1976): *The Social and Political Thought of Karl Marx,* New Delhi, S. Chand.

Ball, T. (1980): Utilitarianism, feminism and the franchise: James Mill and his critics, *History of Political Thought,* Vol. 1, pp. 91–115.

________ (1984): The Picaresque Prince: Reflections on Machiavelli and moral change, *Political Theory,* Vol. 12, pp. 521–536.

Barker, E. (1948): *Social Contract,* Oxford, Oxford University Press.

________ (1950): *Political Thought in England from Herbert Spencer to the Present Day,* Oxford, Oxford University Press.

________ (1964): *Greek Political Theory: Plato and His Predecessors,* New Delhi, B.I. Publications.

________ (1979): *The Politics of Aristotle,* Translated with Introduction, Notes and Appendix, London, Oxford University Press

________ (1995): *Aristotle's Politics,* Oxford, Oxford University Press.

Barker-Benfield, G.J. (1989): Mary Wollstonecraft: Eighteenth Century Commonwealth Woman, *Journal of History of Ideas,* pp. 95–108.

Barnes, J.S. (1982): *Aristotle,* Oxford, Oxford University Press.

Barry, B. (1973): *A Liberal Theory of Justice,* Oxford, Clarendon Press.

________ (1989): *Theories of Justice,* London, Harvester Wheatshef.

________ (1995): *Justice as Impartiality,* Oxford, Clarendon Press.

Barry, N.P. (1995): *Introduction to Modern Political Theory,* London, Macmillan.

Beatty, J. (1976): Plato's happy philosopher and politics, *Review of Politics,* 38, pp. 545–575.

Bell, D. (1973): *The Coming of Post-Industrial Society,* New York, Penguins.

________ (1979): 'Meritocracy and Equality', in *The New Egalitarianism,* D.F. Schaefer (Ed.), Washington, Kennikat Press.

Benn, S.I. and Peters, R.S. (1959): *Social Principles and the Democratic State*, London, Allen & Unwin.

Bentham, J. (1962): An Introduction to the Principles of Morals and Legislation, *The Works of Jeremy Bentham, (1838–1843)*, 11 Vols., J. Bowring (Ed.), New York, Russell & Russell.

________ (1965): *Anarchical Fallacies*, Baltimore, Johns Hopkins University Press.

________ (1977): *A Fragment of Government*, J.H. Bums and H.L.A. Hart (Eds.), London, Athlone Press.

________ (1983): *Constitutional Code*, 2 Vols., F. Rosen and J.H. Burns (Eds.), Oxford, Clarendon Press.

Berki, R.N. (1977): *The History of Political Thought: A Short Introduction*, London, Dent.

Berlin, Sir I. (1963): *Karl Marx: His Life and Environment*, Oxford, Oxford University Press.

________ (1969): *Four Concepts of Liberty*, Oxford, Oxford University Press.

________ (1978): *Men of Ideas*, B. Magee (Ed.), Oxford, Oxford University Press.

________ (1980): *Concepts and Categories*, London, Hogarth Press.

________ (1992): *Conversations with Isaiah Berlin* by *R. Jahanbegloo*, London, Peter Halban.

________ (1997): The Originality of Machiavelli, *The Proper Study of Mankind: An Anthology of Essays*, Isaiah Berlin, Henry Hardy and Roger Hausher (Eds.), London, Chatto and Windus, pp. 269–325.

Bernstein, E. (1961): *Evolutionary Socialism*, E.C. Harvey (Trans.), New York, Schoken Books.

Bloom, A. (1968): *The Republic of Plato*, New York, Basic Books.

________ (1975): 'Justice: Rawls versus the Tradition of Political Philosophy, *American Political Science Review*, Vol. 69, pp. 648–662.

________ (1986): Rousseau on the equality of the sexes, in: *Justice and Equality Here and Now*, Frank S. Lucash (Ed.), Ithaca, Cornell University Press.

Bluhm, W.H. (1965): *Theories of Political System: Classics of Political Thought and Modern Political Analysis*, Englewood Cliffs, NJ, Prentice-Hall.

Bondurant, J.V. (1958): *Conquest of Violence: The Gandhian Philosophy of Conflict*, Berkeley, University of California Press.

Boralevi, L.C. (1984): *Bentham and the Oppressed*, Berlin, University Press.

Bottomore, T. (Ed.) (1983): *A Dictionary of Marxist Thought*, Oxford, Blackwell.

Bramhall, J. (1658): *The Catching of the Leviathan*, London, The Silver Library.

Brecht, A. (1965): *Political Theory: The Foundations of Twentieth Century Political Thought*, Bombay, The Times of India Press.

Bromwich, D. (1998): Edmund Burke as the last defender of pre-capitalist morality, *Times Literacy Supplement*, January Vol. 16, pp. 4–5.

Bronowski, J. and Mazlish, B. (1960): *Western Intellectual Tradition*, Harmondsworth, Penguins.

Brown, I.C. (1981): Machiavelli and the new philosopher prince, *History Today*, Vol. 31, pp. 15–20.

Burckhardt, J. (1921): *The Civilization of the Renaissance in Italy*, S. Midddlemore (Trans.), London, Allen & Unwin.

Burke, E. (1774): Speech to the electors of Bristol, in *The Political Reason of Edmund Burke*, F.P. Canavan (Ed.), Durham, NC, Duke University Press.

________ (1969): *Reflections on the Revolution in France*, C.C. O'Brien (Ed.), Harmondsworth, Penguins.

Butler, M.A. (1978): Early liberal roots of feminism: John Locke and the attack on patriarchy, *American Political Science Review*, Vol. 72, pp. 135–150.

Butterfield, H. (1962): *The Statecraft of Machiavelli*, New York, Collier.

Caine, B. (1992): *Victorian Feminism*, New York, Oxford University Press.

Canavan, F.P. (1960): *The Political Reason of Edmund Burke*, Durham, NC, Duke University Press.

Carr, E.H. (1965): *What is History*? Harmondsworth, Penguins.

Carver, T. (1981): *Engels*, Oxford, Oxford University Press.

Cassirer, E. (1937): Enlightenment, *Encyclopaedia of Social Sciences*, New York, Macmillan.

________ (1945): *Rousseau Kant Goethe: Two Essays*, Princeton, NJ., Princeton University Press.

________ (1946): *The Myth of the State*, New Haven, Yale University Press.

Caute, D. (1967): *Essential Writings of Marx*, New York, Collier.

Chabod, F. (1958): *Machiavelli and the Renaissance*, D. Moore (Trans.), New York, Harper & Row.

Chapman, J.W. (1956): *Rousseau—Totalitarian or Liberal?* New York, Columbia University Press.

________ (1975): "Rawls A Theory of Justice', *American Political Science Review*, Vol. 69, pp. 588–593.

Charvet, J. (1982): *Feminism*, London, Dent.

Chilcote, R.H. (1981): *Theories of Comparative Politics: The Search for a Paradigm Reconsidered*, Boulder, Westview Press.

Clarendon, E.H. (1676): *A* brief view and survey of the dangerous and pernicious errors to Church and State, *Hobbes' Leviathan*, London, The Silver Library.

Cobban, A. (1950): *The Debate on the French Revolution*, London, Black.

_________ (1953): The decline of political theory, *Political Science Quarterly*, Vol. LXVIII, pp. 321–337.

_________ (1960a): *In Search of Humanity*, New York, Braziller.

_________ (1960b): *Edmund Burke and the Revolt against the Eighteenth Century*, London, Allen & Unwin.

_________ (1964): *Rousseau and the Modern State*, London, Unwin University Books.

Colie, R.L. (1965): The social language of John Locke: A study in the history of ideas, *Journal of British Studies*, Vol. 4, pp. 29–51.

Colletti, L. (1969): *From Rousseau to Lenin, Studies in Ideology and Society*, J. Merrington and J. White (Trans.), New Delhi, Oxford University Press.

Collini, S., Winch, D. and Burrow, J. (1983): *That Noble Science of Politics*, Cambridge, Cambridge University Press.

Conniff, J. (1977): Burke, Bristol and the concept of representation, *Western Political Quarterly*, Vol. 30, pp. 329–341.

Coole, D. (1993): *Women in Political Theory: From Ancient Misogyny to Contemporary Feminism*, New York, Harvester Wheatsheaf.

Cornford, EM. (1945): *Plato's Theory of Knowledge*, New York, Humanities Press.

Cornforth, M. (1968): *The Open Philosophy and the Open Society: A Reply to Sir Karl Popper's Refutation of Marxism*, London, Lawrence and Wishart.

Cranston, M. (1952): The politics of John Locke, *History Today*, Sept., pp. 618–622.

_________ (1957): *John Locke: A Biography*, London, Longman.

_________ (1986): *Philosophers and Pamphleteers: Political Theorists of the Enlightenment*, Oxford, Oxford University Press.

Crick, B. (1973): *Political Theory and Practice*, New York, Basic Books.

Cross, R.C. and Woozley, A.D. (1951): *Plato's Republic: A Philosophical Commentary*, Oxford, Blackwell.

Crossman, R. (1939): *Plato Today*, London, Allen & Unwin.

Curtis, M. (1961): *The Great Political Theories, 2* Vols., New York, Avon.

Dahl, R.A. (1958): Political theory today, *World Politics*, XI, October, pp. 89–102.

_________ (1986): *Democracy, Liberty and Equality*, Oslo, Norwegian University Press.

Daniels, N. (1975): *Reading Rawls*, New York, Basic Books.

DeGrazia, S. (1989): *Machiavelli in Hell*, Princeton, NJ, Princeton University Press.

Derathe, R. (1950): *Le rationalism de Jean-Jacques Rousseau*, Paris, Presses Universitaires de France.

Dickinson, H.T. (1977): *Liberty and Property: Political Ideology in the Eighteenth Century*, New York, Holmes & Meier.

Dinwiddy, J. (1975): Bentham's transition to political radicalism 1809–1810, *Journal of the History of Ideas*, Vol. XXXV, pp. 683–700.

Djilas, M. (1990): Social democracy is a worldwide movement, *Moscow News Weekly*, March 12, p. 7.

Downs, A. (1957): *An Economic Theory of Democracy*, New York, Harper & Row.

Doyle (1963): *A History of Political Thought*, London, Jonathan Cape.

Draper, H. (1977): *Karl Marx's Theory of Revolution: State and Bureaucracy*, New York, Monthly Review Press.

Dunn, J. (1968a): *The Political Thought of John Locke—An Historical Account of the Argument of the Two Treatises of Government*, Cambridge, Cambridge University Press.

________ (1968b): Justice and the Interpretation of Locke's Political Theory, *Political Studies*, Vol. 16, pp. 68–87.

________ (1979): *Western Political Theory in the Face of the Future*, Cambridge, Cambridge University Press.

________ (1984): *Locke*, Oxford, Oxford University Press.

Dunning, J.A. (1902): *History and Political Theories*, New York, Macmillan.

Durant, W. (1939): *The Story of Civilization*, 11 Vols., New York, Simon & Schuster.

________ (1953): *The Story of Philosophy*, New York, Pocket Books.

Dworkin, R. (1977): *Taking Rights Seriously*, Cambridge Mass., Harvard University Press.

Eachard, J. (1672): *Dialogues*, London, Tonnies.

Easton, D. (1953): *The Political System: An Inquiry into the State of Political Science*, New York, Wiley.

________ (1965): *A Framework of Political Analysis*, Englewood Cliffs, NJ, Prentice-Hall.

________ (1969): The new revolution in political science, *American Political Science Review*, Vol. 63, December, pp. 1051–1061.

________ (1997): The future of the post-behavioural phase in political science, *Contemporary Empirical Political Theory*, K.R. Monroe (Ed.), Berkeley, University of California Press.

Ebenstein, W. (1969): *Great Political Thinkers*, New Delhi, Oxford & IBH.

Edel, A. (1968): *Aristotle and His Philosophy*, Chapel Hill, NC, University of North Carolina Press.

Eisenstein, Z.A. (1986): *The Radical Future of Liberal Feminism*, New York, Longman.

Elliot, C. (1967): Problems of Marxist Revisionism, *Journal of the History of Ideas*, Vol. 28, pp. 71–89.

Elshtain, J.B. (1981): *Public Man, Private Woman: Women in Social and Political Thought*, Princeton, NJ, Princeton University Press.

Elster, L. (1986): *Making Sense of Marx*, Cambridge, Cambridge University Press.

Emerson, R.W. (1965): *Essays: First and Second Series*, New Delhi, Eurasia Publishing House.

Evans, J. (1986): *Feminism and Political Theory*, London and New York, Sage.

Femia, J.V. (1998): *The Machiavellian Legacy: Essays in Italian Political Thought*, Basingstoke, Macmillan.

__________ (2004): *Machiavelli Revisited*, Cardiff, University of Wales.

Fischman, D. (1991): *Political Discourse in Exile: Karl Marx and the Jewish Question*, Amherst Mass., University of Massachusetts Press.

Fite, W. (1934): *The Platonic Legend*, Oxford, Clarendon Press.

Foster, M.B. (1975): *Masters of Political Thought: Plato to Machiavelli*, Calcutta, Oxford University Press.

Franklin, J. (1978): *John Locke and the Theory of Sovereignty*, Cambridge, Cambridge University Press.

Freeman, M. (1980): *Edmund Burke and the Critique of Political Radicalism*, Oxford, Blackwell.

Freeman, S. (2007): *Rawls*, London & New York, Routledge.

Fried, A. and Sanders, R. (1964): *Socialist Thought: A Documentary History*, New York, Avon.

Friedlander, P. (1969): *Plato*, Vol. 3, H. Meyerhoff (Trans.), Princeton, NJ, Princeton University Press.

Fukuyama, F. (1992): *The End of History and the Last Man*, Harmondsworth, Penguins.

Galbraith, J.K. (1990): Communism has failed because it did not adapt, *The Times of India*, 27th February.

Gatens, M. (1991): The Oppressed State of My Sex: Wollstonecraft on Reason, Feeling and Equality *Feminist Interpretations and Political Theory*, M.L. Shanley, and C. Pateman, (Eds.), Cambridge, Polity Press.

Gellner, E. (1994): *Conditions of Liberty: Civil Society and its Rivals*, London, Hamish Hamilton.

Germino, D. (1967): *Beyond Ideology: The Revival of Political Theory*, New York, Harper & Row.

Gibbins, J. (1990): J.S. Mill, liberalism and progress, *Victorian Liberalism: Nineteenth Century Political Thought and Practice*, R. Bellamy (Ed.), Cambridge, Polity Press.

Giddens, A. (1995): *A Contemporary Critique of Historical Materialism*, London, Macmillan.

Gilbert, F. (1939): The Humanist concept of the *Prince*, *Journal of Modern History*, Vol. 11, pp. 449–483.

Glaser, D. (1995): Normative Theory, *Theory and Methods in Political Science*, D. Marsh and G. Stoker (Eds.), London, Macmillan, pp. 21–41.

Gooch, G.P. (1920): *Germany and the French Revolution*, London, Macmillan.

Goodwin, B. (1993): *Using Political Ideas*, Chichester, John Wiley & Sons.

Gouldner, A.W. (1980): *The Two Marxisms: Contradictions and Anomalies in the Development of Theory*, New York, Oxford University Press.

Gramsci, A. (1971): *Prison Notebooks*, London, Lawrence & Wishart.

Gray, J. (1989): *Liberalisms: Essays in Political Philosophy*, London, Routledge.

Grube, G.M.A. (1935): *Plato's Thought*, London, Athlone Press.

Gunnell, J.G. (1978): The myth of the tradition, *American Political Science Review*, Vol. 72, pp. 122–134.

________ (1987): Political Theory and Political Science, *The Blackwell Encyclopaedia of Political Thought*, D. Miller (Ed.), Oxford, Blackwell.

Gutman, A. (1989): *Liberal Equality*, Cambridge, Cambridge University Press.

Habermas, J. (1991): What does Socialism mean today? The revolutions of recuperation and the need for new thinking, *After the Fall: The Failure of Communism and Future of Socialism*, R. Blackburn (Ed.), London, Verso.

Hacker, A. (1954): Capital and carbuncles: The "great books" reappraised, *American Political Science Review*, Vol. 48, pp. 775–786.

________ (1961): *Political Theory: Philosophy, Ideology, Science*, New York, Macmillan.

Halevy, E. (1928): *Growth of Philosophical Radicalism*, M. Morris (Trans.), London, Faber & Faber.

Hallowell, J.H. (1960): *Main Currents in Modern Political Thought*, New York, Holt.

Hampsher-Monk, I.W. (1987): *The Political Philosophy of Edmund Burke*, London, Longman.

________ (1992): *Modern Political Thought from Hobbes to Marx*, Oxford, Basil Blackwell.

Hampshire S. (1975): 'A New Philosophy of the Just Society', *New York Review of Books*, 24th February, pp. 34–39.

Harding, N. (1981): *Lenin's Political Thought*, 2 Vols., London, Macmillan.

Harrison, R. (1983): *Bentham*, London, Routledge.

Harsanyi, J.C. (1975): Can the Maximin Principle serve as a basis for morality?, *American Political Science Review*, Vol. 69, pp. 594–606.

Hart, H.L.A. (1975): Rawls on Liberty and its Priority, in *Reading Rawls*, N. Daniels (Ed.), New York, Basic Books.

Hawkins, M. (1969): *Aristotle*, London, Athlone Press.

Hazard, P. (1952): *The European Mind*, Cleveland, Meridian.

Hearnshaw, F.J.C. (Ed.) (1931): *The Social and Political Ideas of Some Representative Thinkers of the Revolutionary Era*, London, George Harrap.

Heater, D. (1990): *Citizenship: The Civic Ideal in World History, Politics and Education*, London, Orient Longman.

Hegel, G.W.F. (1969): *Philosophy of Right*, T.M. Knox (Trans.), Oxford, Oxford University Press.

Heilbroner, R.L. (1989): No Alternative to Capitalism, *New Perspective Quarterly*, Vol. 6, Fall, pp. 4–10.

Heinaman, R. (Ed.), (1998): *Aristotle and Moral Realism*, London, VCL Press.

Held, D. (1983): The Frankfurt School, in *A Dictionary of Marxist Thought*, T. Bottomore (Ed.), Oxford, Blackwell.

_________ (1984): *Political Theory and the Modern State*, Oxford, Polity Press.

_________ (1991): *Political Theory Today*, Oxford, Polity Press.

Hempel, C.G. (1966): *Philosophy of Natural Science*, Engelwood Cliffs, NJ, Prentice-Hall.

Heywood, A. (1999): *Political Theory: An Introduction*, 2nd ed., London, Macmillan.

Hill, C. (1972): Thomas Hobbes and the Revolution in Political Thought, in *Political Theory and Ideology*, J. Shklar (Ed.), London, Macmillan, pp. 35–47.

Himmelfarb, G. (1969): Bentham scholarship and the Bentham problem, *Journal of Modern History*, Vol. 14, pp. 185–192.

_________ (1970): *Victorian Minds*, New York, Harper Touch Books.

Hobbes, T. (1991): *Leviathan*, R. Tuck (Ed.), Cambridge, Cambridge University Press.

Hobsbawn, E. (2011): *How to Change the World: Tales of Marx and Marxism*, New York and Boston, Little Brown.

Hoffman, S. (1977): *Marx and the Theory of Praxis*, London, Oxford University Press.

Hook, S. (1958): *From Hegel to Marx: Studies in the Intellectual Development of Karl Marx,* New York, Humanities Press.

Howe, I. (Ed.) (1972): *A Handbook of Socialist Thought,* New York, Pantheon.

Hume, L.J. (1981): *Bentham and Bureaucracy,* Cambridge, Cambridge University Press.

Hunt, R.N. (1975): *The Political Ideas of Marx and Engels,* London, Macmillan.

Huntington, S.P. (1993): *The Clash of Civilizations,* New York, Simon & Schuster.

Irwin, T. (1995): *Plato's Ethics,* Oxford, Oxford University Press.

Jackson, J.H. (1969): Tom Paine and the Rights of Man *Political Ideas,* D. Thompson (Ed.), Harmondsworth, Penguins.

Jaegar, W. (1923): *Aristotle: Fundamentals of the History of His Development,* Oxford, Clarendon Press.

Jaegar, W. (1945): *Paideia,* Vol. 3, G. Hinghet (Trans.), Oxford, Clarendon Press.

Joad, C.E.M. (1966): *Philosophy,* New York, Premier Books.

Johnson, P. (1988): *Intellectuals,* London, Orion.

Kant, I. (1964): *Metaphysical Principles of Virtue,* J.W. Ellington (Trans.), Indianapolis, Bobbs Merrill.

________ (1970): *Political Writings,* H. Reiss (Ed.), H.B. Nisbet (Trans.), Cambridge, Cambridge University Press.

Kaufman, W. (1965): *Hegel's Political Philosophy,* New York, Atherton.

Keane, J. (1988): *Civil Society and the State,* London, Verso.

Kendall, W. (1941): *John Locke and the Doctrine of Majority Rule,* Urbana, University of Illinois Press.

Kenny, A. (1994): *A History of Western Philosophy,* Oxford, Blackwell.

Kerber, L.K. (1980): *Women of the Republic: Intellect and Ideology in Revolutionary America,* North Carolina, Duke University.

Keynes, J.M. (1936): *The General Theory of Unemployment, Interest and Money,* London, Macmillan.

Kirk, R. (1960): *The Conservative Mind: From Burke to Eliot,* New York, Garden City.

Kitto, H.D.F. (1951): *The Greeks,* Harmondsworth, Penguins.

Klosko, G. (1986): *The Development of Plato's Political Theory,* New York, Methuen.

Kolakowski, L. (1981): *Main Currents of Marxism,* 3 Vols., Oxford, Oxford University Press.

Kramnick, I. (Ed.) (1976): *Thomas Paine's Common Sense,* Harmondsworth, Penguins.

_________ (1977): *The Age of Edmund Burke: The Conscience of an Ambivalent Conscience,* New York, Basic Books.

_________ (Ed.) (1982): *Mary Wollstonecraft's A Vindication of the Rights of Woman,* Harmondsworth, Penguins.

Kristol, I. (1979): About Equality in *The New Egalitarianism,* D.L. Schaefer (Ed.), Washington, Kennikat Press.

Kuhn, T. (1970): *The Structure of Scientific Revolutions,* Chicago, University of Chicago Press.

Lamprecht, S.P. (1918): *The Moral and Political Philosophy of John Locke,* New York, Columbia University Press.

Laski, H.J. (1920): *Political Thought from Locke to Bentham,* Oxford, Oxford University Press.

_________ (1936): *Rise of European Liberalism,* London, Unwin Books.

Lasky, M.J. (1976): *Utopia and Revolution,* London, Macmillan.

Laslett, P. (1957): Introduction, in *Philosophy, Politics and Society,* 1st series, P. Laslett and W.G. Runciman (Eds.), Oxford, Blackwell.

_________ (1960): *John Locke's Two Treatises of Government,* Cambridge, Cambridge University Press.

Lasswell, H.D. and Kaplan, A. (1952): *Power and Society: A Framework for Political Inquiry,* New Haven, Yale University Press.

Lawson, G. (1657): *Examination of the Political Part of Mr. Hobbs, His Leviathan,* London, The Silver Library.

Leach, R. (1991): *British Political Ideologies,* New York, Pantheon.

Lerner, M. (1950): *Niccolo Machiavelli's The Prince and the Discourses: An Introduction,* New York, Random House.

Lessnoff, M.H. (1971): 'John Rawls' A Theory of Justice', *Political Studies,* Vol. 19, pp. 63–80.

_________ (1999): *Political Philosophers of the Twentieth Century,* Oxford, Basil Blackwell.

Levinson, Ronald, B. (1953): *In Defense of Plato,* Cambridge Mass., Harvard University Press.

Locke, J. (1960): *Two Treatises of Civil Government,* P. Laslett (Ed.), Cambridge, Cambridge University Press.

Lyons, D. (1972): Rawls versus Utilitarianism, *The Journal of Philosophy,* Vol. 18, pp. 535–545.

Machiavelli, N. (1950): *The Prince and the Discourses,* M. Lerner (Ed.), New York, Random House.

MacIntyre, A. (1971): *A Short History of Ethics,* New York, Macmillan.

_________ (1976): *Hegel: A Collection of Critical Essays,* New York, Anchor Books.

MacIver, R.M. (1926): *The Modern State,* Oxford, Oxford University Press.

Mack, M.P. (1955): The Fabians and the Utilitarians, *Journal of the History of Ideas,* Vol. 16, pp. 76-88.

_________ (1962): *Jeremy Bentham: An Odyssey of Ideas,* New York, Columbia University Press.

Macpherson, C.B. (1968): *Introduction to Hobbes'Leviathan,* Harmondsworth, Penguins.

_________ (1973): *The Political Theory of Possessive Individualism, Hobbes to Locke,* Oxford, Clarendon Press.

_________ (1977): *Democratic Theory: Essays in Retrieval,* Oxford, Clarendon Press.

_________ (1980): *Burke,* Oxford, Oxford University Press.

MacRae, D. (1974): *Weber,* Oxford, Oxford University Press.

Magee, B. (1984): *Popper,* London, Fontana.

Marcuse, H. (1954): *Reason and Revolution: Hegel and the Rise of Social Theory,* London, Routledge & Kegan Paul.

Marion-Young, I. (1996): Political Theory: An Overview, *A New Handbook of Political Science,* R.E. Goodin and H.D. Klingemann (Eds.), Oxford, Oxford University Press.

Marshall, J. (1994): *Locke: Resistance, Revolution and Responsibility,* Cambridge, Cambridge University Press.

Marshall, P. (1992): *Demanding the Impossible: A History of Anarchism,* London.

Martin, R. (1985): *Rawls and Rights,* Kansas, University of Kansas Press.

Marx, K.H. (1975): *The Communist Manifesto,* Moscow, Progress Publishers.

_________ (1977a): *Selected Works, I,* Moscow, Progress Publishers.

_________ (1977b): *Selected Works, II,* Moscow, Progress Publishers.

_________ (1977c): *Selected Works, III,* Moscow, Progress Publishers.

Masters, R.D. (1996): *Machiavelli, Leonardo and the Science of Power,* Notre Dame and London, University of Notre Dame Press.

McIlwain, C.H. (1932): *The Growth of Political Thought in the West,* New York, Macmillan.

McIntosh, D. (1984): The modernity of Machiavelli, *Political Theory,* Vol. 12, No. 2, May, pp. 184–203.

McLellan, D. (1971): *The Thought of Karl Marx,* London, Macmillan.

_________ (1983): *Karl Marx: The First 100 Years,* London, Fontana.

Meinecke, F. (1957): *Machiavellianism: The Doctrine of Raison d'etat and its Place in History*, D. Scott (Trans.), London, Routledge & Kegan Paul.

Miliband, R. (1965): Marx and the state, *The Socialist Register*, pp. 278–296.

Mill, J.S. (1902): *Principles of Political Economy*, London, Unwin Books.

———— (1924): *Autobiography*, New York, Random House.

———— (1950): *Mill on Bentham and Coleridge*, London, Fontana.

———— (1963): *Collected Works of John Stuart Mill*, 21 vols., J.M. Robson (Ed.), Toronto, University of Toronto Press.

———— (1976): *Utilitarianism: On Liberty and Considerations on Representative Government*, London, Fontana.

———— (1985): *The Subjection of Women*, M. Warnock (Ed.), London, Dent.

Miller, D. (Ed.) (1987): *The Blackwell Encyclopaedia of Political Thought*, Oxford, Basil Blackwell.

Miller, S. (1997): Edmund Burke revisited, *Partisan Reviexy*, 4, pp. 562–571.

Minogue, K.R. (1973): *Hobbes' Leviathan*, New York, Everyman's Library.

Morrow, J. (1998): *History of Political Thought: A Thematic Introduction*, London, Macmillan.

Mulgan, R.G. (1977): *Aristotle's Political Theory: An Introduction for Students of Political Theory*, Oxford, Clarendon Press.

Nagel, T. (1973): 'Rawls on Justice', *Philosophical Review*, 82, pp. 220–234.

Nettleship, R.L. (1967): *Lectures on Plato's Republic*, London, Macmillan.

Neuman, W.L. (1900): *The Politics of Aristotle*, 4 vols., Oxford, Clarendon Press.

Nietzsche, F. (1955): *Beyond Good and Evil*, M. Cowea (Trans.), Chicago, Gateway Books.

Nisbet, R. (1969): *History of the Idea of Progress*, New York, Basic Books.

———— (1973): *The Social Philosophers*, New York, Thomas Y. Crowell Co.

———— (1974a): The Pursuit of Equality, *The Public Interest*, Vol. 35, pp. 103–120.

———— (1974b): Rousseau and Equality *Encounter*, September, pp. 44–48.

———— (1990): *The Quest for Community*, New York, Oxford University Press.

Nixon, E. (1971): *Mary Wollstonecraft: Her Life and Times*, London, J.M. Dent and Sons Ltd.

Nozick, R. (1974): *Anarchy, State and Utopia*, New York, Basic Books.

Oakeshott, M.J. (1933): *Experience and Its Modes*, Cambridge, Cambridge University Press.

_________ (1956): Political Education, in *Philosophy, Politics and Society*, 1st series, P. Laslett and W.G. Runciman (Eds.), Oxford, Blackwell.

_________ (1975): *Hobbes on Civil Association*, Oxford, Basil Blackwell.

O'Brien, C.C. (Ed.) (1968): *Burke's Reflections on the Revolution in France*, Harmondsworth, Penguins.

Okin, S.M. (1979): *Women in Western Political Thought*, Princeton, NJ, Princeton University Press.

Olschki, L. (1976): *Machiavelli the Scientist*, Berkeley, University of California Press.

Parkin, C.W. (1969): Burke and the Conservative tradition, *Political Ideas*, D. Thomson (Ed.), Harmondsworth, Penguins.

Parry, G. (1964): Individuality, politics and the critique of paternalism in John Locke, *Political Studies*, Vol. 12, No. 1, pp. 163–177

Pateman, C. (1975): Sublimation and reification: Locke, Wolin and the liberal democratic conception of the political, *Politics and Society*, Vol. 5(4), pp. 441–467.

_________ (1979): *The Problem of Political Obligation: A Critical Analysis of Liberal Theory*, New York, John Wiley and Sons.

_________ (1987): *Democracy, Feminism and Political Theory*, Oxford, Polity Press.

_________ (1988): *The Sexual Contract*, Cambridge, Polity Press.

_________ (2009): Wollstonecraft in *Political Thinkers: From Socrates to the Present*, 2nd ed., David Boucher and P. Kelly (Eds.), Oxford, Oxford University Press.

_________ and Gross, E. (Eds.) (1986): *Feminist Challenges: Social and Political Theory*, Northeastern University Press.

Pitkin, H.F. (1967): *The Concept of Representation*, Berkeley, University of California Press.

_________ (1973): The roots of conservatism: Michael Oakeshott and the denial of politics, *Dissent*, Fall, pp. 496–525.

_________ (1984): *Fortune is a Woman: Gender and Politics in the Thought of Niccolo Machiavel*, Berkeley, University of California Press.

Plamentaz, J. (1963): *Man and Society*, 2 Vols., London, Longman.

_________ (1966): *The English Utilitarians*, Oxford, Basil Blackwell.

_________ (1969): *German Marxism and Russian Communism*, London, Longman.

Plant, R. (1984): *Equality, Markets and the State*, Fabian Tract No. 494, London, Fabian Publications.

Plato (1955): *The Republic,* Harmondsworth, Penguins.

Plumb, J.H. (1967): *England in the Eighteenth Century,* Harmondsworth, Penguins.

Pocock, J.G.A. (1962): The history of political thought: A methodological enquiry, *Philosophy, Politics and Society,* 2nd series, P. Laslett and W.G. Runciman (Eds.), Oxford, Blackwell.

_________ (1971): *The Machiavellian Moment: Florentine Republic Thought and the Atlantic Republican Tradition,* Princeton, NJ, Princeton University Press.

_________ (1980): Review of political theory: tradition and interpretation, *Political Theory,* Vol. 8, pp. 563–567.

_________ (1985): *Virtue, Commerce and History,* Cambridge, Cambridge University Press.

Pollock, F. (1911): *History of the Science of Politics,* London, Methuen.

Popper, Sir K.R. (1945): *The Open Society and Its Enemies,* 2 Vols., London, Routledge & Kegan Paul.

_________ (1963): *The Poverty of Historicism,* London, Routledge & Kegan Paul.

_________ (1968): Plato in *Encyclopaedia of Social Sciences,* London, Macmillan.

_________ (1996): *The Lessons of the Century: Talks on Freedom and the Democratic State,* London, Routledge.

Proctor, C.E. (1990): *Women, Equality and the French Revolution,* New York, Basic Books.

Radhakrishnan, S. (1974): *Eastern Religions and Western Thought,* New Delhi, Oxford University Press.

Randall, J.H. (1970): *Plato: Dramatist of the Life of Reason,* Oxford, Oxford University Press.

Raphael, D.D. (1990): *Problems of Political Philosophy,* 2nd ed., London, Macmillan.

Rappard, W. (1955): *The Secret of American Prosperity,* New York, Anchor Books.

Rawlinson, H.G. (1937): *Legacy of India,* Oxford, Oxford University Press.

Rawls, J. (1969a): Distributive Justice in *Philosophy, Politics and Society,* 3rd series, P. Laslett and W.G. Runciman (Eds.), Oxford, Blackwell.

_________ (1969b): The Justification of Civil Disobedience in *Civil Disobedience in Theory and Practice,* H. Bedeau (Ed.), New York, Pegasus.

_________ (1971): *A Theory of Justice,* 2nd ed. (1972), Oxford, Oxford University Press.

Rawls, J. (1975): Fairness to Goodness, *Philosophical Review*, Vol. 84, pp. 536–584.

_________ (1977): The Basic Structure as Subject, *American Philosophical Quartely*, Vol. 14, pp. 159–165.

_________ (1980): Kantian Constructivism in Moral Theory, *The Journal of Philosophy*, Vol. 77, pp. 515–572.

_________ (1982): Basic Liberties and their Priority in *The Tanner Lectures on Human Values*, S. McMurrin (Ed.), Cambridge, Cambridge University Press.

_________ (1988): 'The Priority of Right over Good', *Philosophy and Public Affairs*, Vol. 14, pp. 223–251.

_________ (1993): *Political Liberalism*, New York, Columbia University Press.

_________ (1999): *The Law of Peoples: The Idea of Public Reason Revisited*, Cambridge, Cambridge University Press.

Reeve, C.D.C. (2004): *Plato's Republic*, Indianapolis, Indiana. Hackett Publishing Company.

Reiss, H. (Ed.), (1970): *Kant's Political Writings*, H.N. Nisbet (Trans.), London, Cambridge University Press.

Resnick, D. (1984): Locke and the rejection of the ancient constitution, *Political Theory*, Vol. 12, 1.

Riemer, N. (1962): *The Revival of Democratic Theory*, New York, Appleton-Century Crofts.

Riley, P. (1980): *Will and Legitimacy*, Cambridge Mass., Harvard University Press.

_________ (1986): *The General Will before Rousseau: The Transformation of the Divine into the Civic*, Princeton, NJ, Princeton University Press.

_________ (1987): Kant, Immanuel in *The Blackwell Encyclopaedia of Political Thought*, Oxford, Basil Blackwell.

Ring, J. (1985): *Mill's Feminism*, New York, Harvester Wheatsheaf.

Robson, J.M., Moir, M. and Moir, J. (1988): *Collected Works of J.S. Mill: XXX: Writings on India*, London, Routledge.

Rogers, G.A.J. (1990): The father of commonsense, *The Times Higher Education Supplement*, August 31, pp. 11 and 14.

Rorty, R. (1994): Strangers and Liberals, *Political Theory*, February 22, pp. 167–175.

Rosen, F. (1990): The origin of liberal Utilitarianism, in *Victorian Liberalism: Nineteenth Century Political Thought and Practice*, R. Bellamy (Ed.), Cambridge, Cambridge University Press.

Ross, W.D. (1924): *Aristotle,* London, Methuen.

Rousseau, J.J. (1911): *Emile, or On Education,* B. Foxley (Trans.), New York, Everyman's Library.

_________ (1958): *A Discourse on the Origin of Inequality in the Social Contract and Discourses,* G.D.H. Cole (Trans.), London, Dent.

Rubel, M. (1968): Karl Marx, in *Encyclopaedia of Social Sciences,* London, Macmillan.

Russell, B. (1961): *History of Western Philosophy,* London, Allen & Unwin.

Russett, B. (1993): *Grasping the Democratic Peace,* Princeton, Princeton University Press.

Ryan, A. (1965): Locke and the Dictatorship of the Bourgeoisie, *Political Studies,* Vol. 13, pp. 219–230.

_________ (1974): *J.S. Mill,* London, Routledge & Kegan Paul.

_________ (1985): 'John Rawls' in *The Return of the Grand Theory in the Human Sciences,* Q. Skinner (Ed.), Cambridge, Cambridge University Press.

Ryan, A. (1987): John Stuart Mill, in: *The Blackwell Encyclopaedia of Political Thought,* D. Miller (Ed.), Oxford, Basil Blackwell.

Sabine, G.H. (1939): What is political theory?, *Journal of Politics* Vol. 1(1), pp. 1–16.

_________ (1973): *A History of Political Theory,* 4th ed., revised by T.L. Thorson, New Delhi, Oxford and IBH, First published in 1937.

Sakharov, A. (1989): *My Country and the World,* New York, Random House.

Sandel, M. (1982): *Liberalism and the Limits of Justice,* Cambridge, Cambridge University Press.

Sarkar, J. (1973): *Shivaji and the Marathas,* Bombay, Orient Longman.

Sarton, G. (1969): *A History of Science,* Cambridge Mass., Harvard University Press.

Sartori, G. (1993): Totalitarianism, model mania and learning from error, *Journal of Theoretical Politics,* Vol. 5(1), pp. 5–22.

Saxonhouse, A. (1985): *Women in the History of Political Thought: Ancient Greece to Machiavelli,* New York, Praegar.

Scanlon, T.M. (1982): 'Contractualism and Utilitarianism' in *Utilitarianism and Beyond,* A. Sen and B. Williams (Eds.), Cambridge, Cambridge University Press.

Schaefer, D.L. (1973): 'The sense and nonsense of Justice: Rawls' A Theory of Justice', *The Political Science Reviewer,* Fall, pp. 1–26.

Schumpeter, J. (1976): *Capitalism, Socialism and Democracy,* London, Allen & Unwin.

Scruton, R. (1982): *Kant*, Oxford, Oxford University Press.

Semple, J. (1992): *Bentham's Prison: A Study of the Panopticon Penitentiary*, Oxford, Clarendon Press.

Sen, A. (1974): Rawls versus Bentham: An Axiomatic Examination of the Pure Distribution Problem *Theory and Decision*, Vol. 4, pp. 301–309.

Shanley, M.I. and Pateman, C. (1991): *Feminist Interpretation and Political Theory*, Cambridge, Polity Press.

Shklar, J.N. (1998): *Redeeming American Political Thought*, Chicago, University of Chicago Press.

Shumer, S.M. (1979): Machiavelli: Republican politics and its corruption, *Political Theory*, Vol. 7, pp. 5–34.

Sibley, M.Q. (1981): *Political Ideas and Ideologies*, New Delhi, Surjeet Publications.

Sinclair, T.A. (1951): *A History of Greek Political Thought*, London, Routledge.

Singer, P. (1980): *Marx*, Oxford, Oxford University Press.

_________ (1983): *Hegel*, Oxford, Oxford University Press.

Skinner, Q. (1966): The ideological context of Hobbes' political thought, *The Historical Journal*, IX, pp. 286–317.

_________ (1969): Meaning and understanding in the history of ideas, *History and Theory*, Vol. 8, pp. 3–53.

_________ (1981): *Machiavelli*, Oxford, Oxford University Press.

_________ (1990): *The Foundations of Modern Political Thought*, 2 Vols., Cambridge, Cambridge University Press.

Smith, S.B. (1989): *Hegel's Critique of Liberalism*, Chicago, University of Chicago Press.

Spragens, Jr., T. (1976): *Understanding Political Theory*, New York, St. Martin's Press.

Starobinski, J. (1988): *Jean-Jacques Rousseau: Transparency and Obstruction*, A. Goldhammer (Trans.), Paris, Plon.

Stefano, C.D. (1994): Masculinity as ideology in political theory: Hobbesian man considered, in *Feminism*, Vol. I, S.M. Okin and J. Mansbridge (Eds.), London, Routledge.

Stephen, Sir L. (1902): *History of English Thought in the 18th Century*, 2 vols., London, London School of Economics and Political Science.

_________ (1961): *Hobbes*, Ann Arbor, University of Michigan Press.

Strachey, R. (1978): *The Cause: A Short History of the Women's Movement in Great Britain*, London, Virago.

Strauss, L. (1936): *The Political Philosophy of Hobbes: Its Basis and Genesis*, Oxford, Clarendon Press.

Strauss, L. (1949): Political philosophy and history, *Journal of the History of Ideas,* Vol. 10, pp. 30–50.

_________ (1950): On the Spirit of Hobbes' Political Philosophy, *La Revue International de Philosophie,* IV, pp. 405–431.

_________ (1952): *Natural Right and History,* Chicago, University of Chicago Press.

_________ (1958): *Thoughts on Machiavelli,* Chicago, University of Chicago Press.

_________ (1959): *What is Political Philosophy and Other Studies?* Glencoe, The Free Press.

_________ (1962): Epilogue, in *Essays on the Scientific Study of Politics,* H. Storing (Ed.), New York, Holt.

_________ (1964): *Studies in Platonic Political Philosophy,* Chicago, University of Chicago Press.

Talmon, J.L. (1960): *The Origins of Totalitarian Democracy and Political Messianism: The Romantic Phase,* London, Seeker and Warburg.

Tarcov, N. (1984): *Locke's Education for Liberty,* Chicago, University of Chicago Press.

Tawney, R.H. (1954): *Religion and Rise of Capitalism,* Harmondsworth, Penguins.

Taylor, A.E. (1926): *Plato: The Man and His Work,* London, Methuen.

_________ (1938): The ethical doctrine of Hobbes, *Philosophy,* Vol. 13, pp. 406–424.

Teitelman, M. (1972): 'The Limits of Individualism', *The Journal of Philosophy,* Vol. 69, pp. 545–556.

Thomas, W. (1985): *Mill,* Oxford, Oxford University Press.

Tomaselli, S. (Ed.) (1993): *Mary Wollstonecraft: Political Writings,* London.

Thorson, T.L. (1963): *Plato: Totalitarian or Democrat?* New Jersey, Prentice-Hall.

Todd, J. (Ed.) (1989): *A Wollstonecraft Anthology,* Cambridge, Polity Press.

_________ (Ed.) (1993): *Mary Wollstonecraft's A Vindication of the Rights of Men and A Vindication of the Rights of Woman,* Cambridge, Polity Press.

Torrey, N.L. (1960): *Les Philosophes: The Philosophers of the Enlightenment and Modern Democracy,* New York, Capricorn.

Toynbee, A. (1934): *A Study of History,* 12 Vols., Oxford, Oxford University Press.

Tuck, R. (1989): *Hobbes,* Oxford, Oxford University Press.

_________ (1993): The Contribution of History in *A Companion to Contemporary Political Philosophy,* R.E. Goodin and P. Petitt (Eds.), Oxford, Blackwell.

Tulloch, G. (1989): *Mill and Sexual Equality,* London, Blackwell.

Tully, J. (1980): *A Discourse on Property: John Locke and His Adversaries,* Cambridge, Cambridge University Press.

_________ (1988): *Meaning and Context—Quentin Skinner and his Critics,* Cambridge, Polity Press.

_________ (1993): *An Approach to Political Philosophy: Locke in Contexts,* Cambridge, Cambridge University Press.

Tunick, M. (1998): Hegel on Justified Disobedience, *Political Theory,* Vol. 26, No. 4, pp. 514–535.

Vaughan, C.E. (1925): *Studies in the History of Political Philosophy before and After Rousseau,* Manchester, University of Manchester Press.

_________ (1962): *The Political Writings of Jean-Jacques Rousseau,* 2 Vols., New York, Wiley.

Viroli, M. (1998): *Machiavelli,* Oxford, Oxford University Press,

Vlastos, G. (1968): Justice and happiness in the Republic, *Philosophy,* Vol. 65, pp. 665–674.

Vogelin, E. (1952): *The Nejv Science of Politics,* Chicago, University of Chicago Press.

von Leyden, W. (1985): *Aristotle on Equality and Justice: His Political Argument,* London, Macmillan.

Waldron, J. (1987): *Nonsense upon Stilts: Bentham, Burke and Marx on the Rights of Man,* London, Methuen.

Walzer, M. (1973): In Defence of Equality, *Dissent,* Fall, pp. 339-407.

_________ (1983): *Spheres of Justice: A Defense of Pluralism and Equality,* New York, Basic Books.

_________ (1989): The State of Political Theory, *Dissent,* 17, Summer, p. 337.

Wardle, R.M. (1987): *Mary Wollstonecraft: A Critical Biography,* London, Richard Press.

Warrender, H. (1957): *The Political Philosophy of Hobbes: His Theory of Obligation,* Oxford, Clarendon Press.

Watkins, F.H. (1961): *The Age of Ideology—Political Thought from 1750 to the Present,* New Delhi, Prentice-Hall.

Weber, M. (1958): Politics as a vocation, in *From Max Weber,* H.H. Gerth and C.W. Mills (Eds.), New York, Oxford University Press.

Weldon, T.D. (1953): *The Vocabulary of Politics,* Harmondsworth, Penguins.

Whitehall, J. (1679): *The Leviathan Found Out,* London, The Silver Library.

Williams, B. (1980): Introduction, in *Sir Isaiah Berlin's Concepts and Categories,* London, Hogarth Press.

Williams, H. (1983): *Kant's Political Philosophy*, Oxford, Oxford University Press.

Williams, R. (1958): *Culture and Society*, Harmondsworth, Penguins.

_________ (1981): *Culture*, Fontana, Glasgow.

Williford, M. (1975): Bentham on the rights of woman, *Journal of the History of Ideas*, Vol. 38, pp. 167–176.

Wilson, E. (1941): *To The Finland Station*, London, Seeker and Warburg.

Winspear, A.D. (1940): *The Genesis of Plato's Thought*, New York, Russell.

Wolfe, B. (1969): *Marxism: One Hundred Years in the Life of a Doctrine*, New York, Avon.

Wolff, R. P. (1977): *Understanding Rawls*, Princeton, NJ, Princeton University Press.

Wolin, S. (1960): *Politics and Vision: Continuity and Innovation in Western Political Thought*, Boston, Little Brown.

_________ (1968): Political theory: Trends and goals, *International Encyclopedia of the Social Sciences*, Vol. 12, New York, Macmillan.

_________ (1969): Political theory as a vocation, *American Political Science Review*, LXII, pp. 1062–1082.

_________ (1970): *Hobbes and the Epic Tradition of Political Theory*, Los Angeles, William Andrews Clark Memorial Library of the University of California.

_________ (1977): Hannah Arendt and the ordinance of time, *Social Research*, Vol. 44, Spring, pp. 91–105.

_________ (1986): 'Contract and Birthright', *Political Theory*, Vol. 14, pp. 179–194.

_________ (1987): Democracy and the welfare state, *Political Theory*, Vol. 15, No. 4, pp. 467–500.

Wollstonecraft, M. (1970): *A Vindication of the Rights of Man*, Gainsville, Florida, Gainesville.

_________ (1985): *A Vindication of the Rights of Woman*, London, Dent.

Wood, N. (1968): Machiavelli, *Encyclopaedia of Social Sciences*, London, Macmillan.

_________ (1984): *John Locke and Agrarian Capitalism*, Berkeley, University of California Press.

Wootton, D. (Ed.) (1993): *Political Writings of John Locke*, Stanford, University of California Press.

Wykes, D. (1987): *A Preface to Orwell*, London, Lawrence and Wishart.

Zeller, E. (1955): *Outlines of the History of Greek Philosophy*, New York, Meridian.

Author Index

Subject Index